Communications
in Computer and Information Science

Series Editors

Gang Li ⓘ, *School of Information Technology, Deakin University, Burwood, VIC, Australia*
Joaquim Filipe ⓘ, *Polytechnic Institute of Setúbal, Setúbal, Portugal*
Ashish Ghosh ⓘ, *Indian Statistical Institute, Kolkata, West Bengal, India*
Zhiwei Xu, *Chinese Academy of Sciences, Beijing, China*

Rationale

The CCIS series is devoted to the publication of proceedings of computer science conferences. Its aim is to efficiently disseminate original research results in informatics in printed and electronic form. While the focus is on publication of peer-reviewed full papers presenting mature work, inclusion of reviewed short papers reporting on work in progress is welcome, too. Besides globally relevant meetings with internationally representative program committees guaranteeing a strict peer-reviewing and paper selection process, conferences run by societies or of high regional or national relevance are also considered for publication.

Topics

The topical scope of CCIS spans the entire spectrum of informatics ranging from foundational topics in the theory of computing to information and communications science and technology and a broad variety of interdisciplinary application fields.

Information for Volume Editors and Authors

Publication in CCIS is free of charge. No royalties are paid, however, we offer registered conference participants temporary free access to the online version of the conference proceedings on SpringerLink (http://link.springer.com) by means of an http referrer from the conference website and/or a number of complimentary printed copies, as specified in the official acceptance email of the event.

CCIS proceedings can be published in time for distribution at conferences or as post-proceedings, and delivered in the form of printed books and/or electronically as USBs and/or e-content licenses for accessing proceedings at SpringerLink. Furthermore, CCIS proceedings are included in the CCIS electronic book series hosted in the SpringerLink digital library at http://link.springer.com/bookseries/7899. Conferences publishing in CCIS are allowed to use Online Conference Service (OCS) for managing the whole proceedings lifecycle (from submission and reviewing to preparing for publication) free of charge.

Publication process

The language of publication is exclusively English. Authors publishing in CCIS have to sign the Springer CCIS copyright transfer form, however, they are free to use their material published in CCIS for substantially changed, more elaborate subsequent publications elsewhere. For the preparation of the camera-ready papers/files, authors have to strictly adhere to the Springer CCIS Authors' Instructions and are strongly encouraged to use the CCIS LaTeX style files or templates.

Abstracting/Indexing

CCIS is abstracted/indexed in DBLP, Google Scholar, EI-Compendex, Mathematical Reviews, SCImago, Scopus. CCIS volumes are also submitted for the inclusion in ISI Proceedings.

How to start

To start the evaluation of your proposal for inclusion in the CCIS series, please send an e-mail to ccis@springer.com.

Nirbhay Chaubey · Noor Zaman Jhanjhi ·
Sabu M. Thampi · Satyen Parikh · Kiran Amin
Editors

Computing Science, Communication and Security

5th International Conference, COMS2 2024
Mehsana, Gujarat, India, February 6–7, 2024
Proceedings

Editors
Nirbhay Chaubey
Ganpat University
Gujarat, Gujarat, India

Noor Zaman Jhanjhi
Taylor's University
Subang Jaya, Malaysia

Sabu M. Thampi
Kerala University of Digital Sciences,
Innovation and Technology (KUDSIT)
Trivandrum, Kerala, India

Satyen Parikh
Ganpat University
Gujarat, Gujarat, India

Kiran Amin
Ganpat University
Gujarat, Gujarat, India

ISSN 1865-0929　　　　　　ISSN 1865-0937 (electronic)
Communications in Computer and Information Science
ISBN 978-3-031-75169-1　　　ISBN 978-3-031-75170-7 (eBook)
https://doi.org/10.1007/978-3-031-75170-7

© The Editor(s) (if applicable) and The Author(s), under exclusive license
to Springer Nature Switzerland AG 2025

This work is subject to copyright. All rights are solely and exclusively licensed by the Publisher, whether the whole or part of the material is concerned, specifically the rights of translation, reprinting, reuse of illustrations, recitation, broadcasting, reproduction on microfilms or in any other physical way, and transmission or information storage and retrieval, electronic adaptation, computer software, or by similar or dissimilar methodology now known or hereafter developed.
The use of general descriptive names, registered names, trademarks, service marks, etc. in this publication does not imply, even in the absence of a specific statement, that such names are exempt from the relevant protective laws and regulations and therefore free for general use.
The publisher, the authors and the editors are safe to assume that the advice and information in this book are believed to be true and accurate at the date of publication. Neither the publisher nor the authors or the editors give a warranty, expressed or implied, with respect to the material contained herein or for any errors or omissions that may have been made. The publisher remains neutral with regard to jurisdictional claims in published maps and institutional affiliations.

This Springer imprint is published by the registered company Springer Nature Switzerland AG
The registered company address is: Gewerbestrasse 11, 6330 Cham, Switzerland

If disposing of this product, please recycle the paper.

Preface

This volume contains the papers presented at the 5th International Conference on Computing Science, Communication and Security (COMS2 2024), held at the beautiful campus of Ganpat University, India during February 6–7, 2024. COMS2 2024 was held in hybrid mode, wherein the invited guests, keynote speakers, dignitaries, session chairs, paper presenters, and attendees joined a two-day international conference. The conference forum brought together more than 210 delegates including leading academics, scientists, researchers, and research scholars from all over the world to exchange and share their experiences, ideas, and research results on aspects of Computing Science, Network Communication, and Security.

The conference was inaugurated on the first day by the National Anthem "Jana Gana Mana" in the presence of academic leaders and luminaries: Shri Ganpatbhai I. Patel (Padma Shri), President and Patron in Chief of Ganpat University; the Invited Guest of the program Neeli Prasad, Founder and CEO of SmartAvatar B.V., Netherlands/USA; Ketan Kotecha, Director, Symbiosis International (Deemed University), Pune, India; Himanshu Soni, Provost, CVM University, Vallabh Vidyangar, Gujarat, India; Mahendra Sharma, Pro. Chancellor and Director General of Ganpat University; Noor Zaman from Taylor's University, Malaysia; Sabu M. Thampi, IIIT, Trivandrum, Kerala, India; Kiran Amin, Executive Dean of the Faculty of Engineering and Technology, Ganpat University, India, Satyen Parikh, Executive Dean of Computer Science, Ganpat University, India; and Nirbhay Chaubey, Dean of Computer Science, Ganpat University, India, which declared the conference open.

Three plenary session talks were held covering the different areas of the conference: Neeli Prasad delivered a talk on "The Human-AI Collaboration: Navigating the Ethical and Digital Privacy Challenges of the Digital Age", Ketan Kotecha spoke on "Research Directions in Artificial Intelligence", and Himanshu Soni spoke about "IoT with Ultrawideband Communication".

COMS2 2024 accepted 31 papers as oral presentations (out of 290 full papers received and critically peer reviewed using the Springer EquinOCS System), which were presented during the two days of the conference.

The session track had panel members and session chairs: Savita Gandhi, Dean of Computer Science, GLS University, Ahmedabad, India; Jagdish M. Rathod, Professor from Birla Vishvakarma Mahavidyalaya, Vallabh Vidyangar, Gujarat, India ; Maulika Patel, Professor from CVM University, Vallabh Vidyangar, Gujarat, India; Vishvjit Thakar, Indrashil University, Gujarat, India; Rakhee, University of the West Indies, Jamaica; Dilip Kumar Kothari, Ganpat University, Gujarat, India;

Vrushank Shah, Indus University, Gujarat, India; and Rakesh Vanzara, Dean of the Faculty of Engineering, Ganpat University, Gujarat, India.

All the accepted papers were peer reviewed by three qualified reviewers chosen from our conference Scientific Committee based on their qualifications and experience.

The conference was organized by Ganpat University, a well-reputed state private university, with a campus that spreads out over more than 300 acres of land with world-class infrastructure and more than 12,000 students on campus. In consideration of its contribution to education, in only a short period of time the university has been given membership of the Association of Indian Universities (AIU).

The conference was full of fruitful discussions, igniting the spirit of research. It was indeed a remarkable, memorable, and knowledgeable conference. The success of COMS2 2024 means that planning can now proceed with confidence for the 6th International Conference on Computing Science, Communication and Security (COMS2), scheduled for February 2025.

The proceedings editors wish to thank the dedicated Scientific Committee members and all the other reviewers for their contributions. We also thank Springer for their trust and for publishing the proceedings of COMS2 2024.

February 2024

Nirbhay Chaubey
Noor Zaman Jhanjhi
Sabu M. Thampi
Satyen Parikh
Kiran Amin

Organization

Scientific Committee

Ganpatbhai Patel (Patron-in-Chief & President)	Ganpat University, India
Mahendra Sharma (Pro-Chancellor)	Ganpat University, India
Rakesh Patel	Ganpat University, India
Girish Patel	Ganpat University, India
Saurabh Dave	Ganpat University, India
Daniel Montplaisir	Ganpat University, India
Rajkumar Buyya	University of Melbourne, Australia
Kankar Shubra Dasgupta	DAIICT, India
Mohammed Atiquzzaman	University of Oklahoma, USA
Arup R. Dasgupta	Space Application Centre, ISRO, India
Akshai Aggarwal	University of Windsor, Canada
Sartaj Sahni	University of Florida, USA
Neha Chaubey	Imperial College London, UK
Om Prakash Vyas	IIIT, Allahabad, India
Savita R. Gandhi	GLS University, India
Sabu M. Thampi	IIITM-K, India
Deepak Mathur	IEEE, India
Maniklal Das	DA-IICT, India
S. Venkatesan	IIIT, Allahabad, India
Deepak Garg	Bennett University, India
Kevin Dami	University of Detroit, USA
Bala Natarajan	Kansas State University, USA
Virendra C. Bhavsar	University of New Brunswick, Canada
G. Sahoo	Birla Institute of Technology, India
Mohit Tahiliani	NIT, Karnataka, India
Nilesh Modi	Babasaheb Ambedkar Open University, India
Kiran Amin	Ganpat University, India
Satyen Parikh	Ganpat University, India
Nirbhay Chaubey	Ganpat University, India
Rakesh D. Vanzara	Ganpat University, India
Hamid R. Arabnia	University of Georgia, USA
Sanjay Madria	Missouri University of Science and Technology, USA

Arvind Shah	Georgia Southwestern State University, USA
P. Balasubramanian	Nanyang Technological University, Singapore
Xing Liu	Kwantlen Polytechnic University, Canada
Kalpdrum Passi	Laurentian University, Canada
Ratvinder Grewal	Laurentian University, Canada
K.K. Patel	Charotar University of Science and Technology, India
Ali Mostafaeipour	Yazd University, Iran
Ramesh Bansal	University of Sharjah, UAE
Neville Watson	University of Canterbury, New Zealand
Yuan Miao	Victoria University, Australia
Shah Miah	Victoria University, Australia
Mohan Kolhe	University of Agder, Norway
Akhtar Kalam	Victoria University, Australia
Pao-Ann Hsiung	National Chung Cheng University, Taiwan
Prateek Agrawal	University of Klagenfurt, Austria
Anatoliy Zabrovskiy	University of Klagenfurt, Austria
Valentina Emilia Balas	University of Arad, Romania
Ashok Karania	EMEA, UK
D. P. Kothari	VIT University, India
H. S. Mazumdar	Dharmsinh Desai University, India
Debajyoti Mukhopadhyay	Bennett University, India
Hiral Patel	Ganpat University, India
Ashok R. Patel	Florida Polytechnic University, USA
Ruoyu Wang	Arizona State University, USA
Kevin Gary	Arizona State University, USA
Tatyana Ryutov	University of Southern California, USA
George Sklivanitis	Florida Atlantic University, USA
Koushik A. Manjunatha	Idaho National Laboratory, USA
Sathyan Munirathinam	ASML Corporation, USA
Yogesh Patel	SalesForce, USA
Priyanshukumar Jha	Amazon, USA
El Sayed Mahmoud	Sheridan College, Canada
Jigisha Patel	Sheridan College, Canada
Pawan Lingra	St. Mary's University, Canada
Xing Liu	Kwantlen Polytechnic University, Canada
Muhammad Dangana	University of Glasgow, UK
Gisa Fuatai Purcel	Office of the Regulator, Samoa
Gyu Myoung Lee	Liverpool John Moores University, UK
Stefano Cirillo	University of Salerno, Italy
Flavio Vella	Free University of Bozen-Bolzano, Italy
Alessandro Barbiero	Università degli Studi di Milano, Italy

Lelio Campanile	Università degli studi della Campania L.Vanvitelli, Italy
Asmerilda Hitaj	University of Milano-Bicocca, Italy
Abdallah Handoura	Télécom Bretagne, France
Gua Xiangfa	National University of Singapore, Singapore
Raman Singh	University of Dublin, Ireland
Ahmed M. Elmisery	Waterford Institute of Technology, Ireland
Shahzad Ashraf	Hohai University, China
Moharram Challenger	University of Antwerp, Belgium
Mamoun Alazab	Charles Darwin University, Australia
Dragi Kimovski	University of Klagenfurt, Austria
Iwan Adhicandra	University of Sydney, Australia
Payal Mahida	Tata Consultancy Services, Australia
Tarandeep Kaur Bhatia	Deakin University, Australia
Siddharth Patel	Eaton Corporation, Australia
Marcin Paprzycki	Polish Academy of Sciences, Poland
Sabyasachi Chakraborty	Inje University, South Korea
Sayan K. Ray	Manukau Institute of Technology, New Zealand
Ahmed Al-Sa'di	Auckland University of Technology, New Zealand
Clementine Gritti	University of Canterbury, New Zealand
Samaneh Madanian	Auckland University of Technology, New Zealand
Aravind Nair	KTH Royal Institute of Technology, Sweden
Yehia Abd Alrahman	Chalmers University of Technology, Sweden
Karl Andersson	Luleå University of Technology, Sweden
Jose M. Molina	Universidad Carlos III de Madrid, Spain
Manuel Chica	Universidad de Granada, Spain
Jose Angel Diaz-Garcia	Universidad de Granada, Spain
Carlos Fernandez-Basso	University of Granada, Spain
George Papakostas	Eastern Macedonia and Thrace Institute of Technology, Greece
Dimitris Karampatzakis	International Hellenic University, Greece
Ioannis Tollis	University of Crete, Greece
Christos J. Bouras	University of Patras, Greece
Loannis Tollis	University of Crete, Greece
Zitong Yu	University of Oulu, Finland
Paul Aiken	University of the West Indies, Jamaica
Rakhee	University of the West Indies, Jamaica
Ammar Muthanna	Saint Petersburg State University of Telecommunications, Russia
Noor Zaman Jhanjhi	Taylor's University, Malaysia
Irdayanti Mat Nashir	Universiti Pendidikan Sultan Idris, Malaysia
Jing Rui Tang	Universiti Pendidikan Sultan Idris, Malaysia

Zaliza Hanapi	Universiti Pendidikan Sultan Idris, Malaysia
Encik Ong Jia Hui	Tunku Abdul Rahman University College, Malaysia
Qusay Medhat Salih	Universiti Malaysia Pahang, Malaysia
Dalal A. Hammood	Universiti Malaysia Perlis, Malaysia
Muhammad Asif Khan	Qatar University, Qatar
Ashraf A. M. Khalaf	Minia University, Egypt
Dimiter G. Velev	University of National and World Economy, Bulgaria
Pahlaj Moolio	Pannasastra University of Cambodia, Cambodia
Mudassir Khan	King Khalid University, Saudi Arabia
Lamia Berriche	Prince Sultan University, Saudi Arabia
Lal Bihari Barik	King Abdulaziz University, Saudi Arabia
Shermin Shamsudheen	Jazan University, Saudi Arabia
Tran Cong Hung	Posts and Telecomunication Institute of Technology, Vietnam
Anand Nayyar	Duy Tan University, Vietnam
Pao-Ann Hsiung	National Chung Cheng University, Taiwan
Seyyed Ahmad Edalatpanah	Ayandegan Institute of Higher Education, Iran
Aws Zuheer Yonis	Ninevah University, Iraq
Razan Abdulhammed	Northern Technical University, Iraq
Moharram Challenger	International Computer Institute at Ege University, Turkey
Sandeep Kautish	LBEF campus, Kathmandu, Nepal
A.A. Gde Satia Utama	Universitas Airlangga, Indonesia
Eva Shayo	University of Dar es Salaam, Tanzania
Anil Audumbar Pise	University of the Witwatersrand, Johannesburg, South Africa
Sarang C. Dhongdi	BITS Pilani, India
Satyabrata Jit	IIT(BHU), India
Pratik Chattopadhyay	IIT(BHU), India
Amrita Chaturvedi	IIT(BHU), India
Amit Kumar Singh	IIT(BHU), India
Amrita Mishra	IIIT Naya Raipur, India
Panchami V.	IIIT, Kottayam, India
Bhuvaneswari Amma N.G.	IIIT, Una, India
Jitendra Tembhurne	IIIT, Nagpur, India
Renjith P.	IIIT, Kurnool, India
Sachin Jain	IIIT, Jabalpur, India
Priyanka Mishra	IIIT, Kota, India
Chetna Sharma	IIIT, Kota, India
Eswaramoorthy K.	IIIT, Kurnool, India

Pandiyarasan Veluswamy	IIITDM Kancheepuram, India
Sahil	IIIT, Una, India
Sanya Anees	IIIT, Guwahati, India
Suvrojit Das	NIT, Durgapur, India
Aruna Jain	Birla Institute of Technology, India
Amit Kumar Gupta	DRDO, Hyderbad, India
R. Kumar	SRM University, India
B. Ramachandran	SRM University, India
Iyyanki V Muralikrishna	J.N. Technological University, India
Apurv Shah	M.S. University, India
Manoj Kumar	Inflibnet University Grants Commission, India
U. Dinesh Kumar	IIM, Bangalore, India
Saurabh Bilgaiyan	KIIT, Deemed to be University, India
Raja Sarath Kumar Boddu	Jawaharlal Nehru Technological University, India
Kiran Sree Pokkuluri	SVECM, India
Devesh Kumar Srivastava	Manipal University, India
P. Muthulakshmi	SRM University, India
R. Anandan	VELS University, India
Amol Dhondse	IBM India Software Labs, India
R. Amirtharajan	SASTRA Deemed University, India
Padma Priya V.	SASTRA Deemed University, India
Deepak H. Sharma	K. J. Somaiya College of Engineering, India
Ravi Subban	Pondicherry University, India
Parameshachari B. D.	Visvesvaraya Technological University, India
Nilakshi Jain	University of Mumbai, India
Archana Mire	University of Mumbai, India
Sonali Bhutad	University of Mumbai, India
Anand Kumar	Visvesvaraya Technological University, India
Jyoti Pareek	Gujarat University, India
Sanjay Garg	Jaypee University of Engineering and Technology, India
Madhuri Bhavsar	Nirma University, India
Vijay Ukani	Nirma University, India
Mayur Vegad	BVM Engineering College, India
N. M. Patel	BVM Engineering College, India
J. M. Rathod	BVM Engineering College, India
Maulika Patel	CVM University, India
Nikhil Gondalia	CVM University, India
Priyanka Sharma	Rashtriya Raksha University, India
Digvijaysinh Rathod	National Forensic Science University, India
Kalpesh Parikh	Intellisense IT, India
Balaji Rajendran	CDAC, Bengaluru, India

Mehul C. Parikh	Gujarat Technological University, India
G. R. Kulkarni	Shivaji University, India
Amol C. Adamuthe	Shivaji University, India
Shrihari Khatawkar	Shivaji University, India
Snehal Joshi	Veer Narmad South Gujarat University, India
Ambika Nagaraj	Bengaluru Central University, India
Ashok Solanki	Veer Narmad South Gujarat University, India
Aditya Sinha	CDAC, India
Harshal Arolkar	GLS University, India
Binod Kumar	University of Pune, India
Maulin Joshi	Gujarat Technological University, India
Vrushank Shah	Indus University, India
Manish Patel	Sankalchand Patel University, India
Ankit Bhavsar	GLS University, India
Seema Mahajan	Indus University, India
S. K. Vij	ITM University, India
Vishal Jain	Sharda University, India
D. B. Choksi	Sardar Patel University, India
Paresh Virpariya	Sardar Patel University, India
Priti Srinivas Sajja	Sardar Patel University, India
C. K. Bhensdadia	Dharmsinh Desai University, India
Vipul K. Dabhi	Dharmsinh Desai University, India
N. J. Kothari	Dharmsinh Desai University, India
Narayan Joshi	Dharmsinh Desai University, India
S. D. Panchal	Gujarat Technological University, India
M. T. Savaliya	Gujarat Technological University, India
Vinod Desai	Gujarat Vidyapith, India
Himanshu Patel	Dr. Babasaheb Ambedkar Open University, India
Chhaya Patel	Gujarat Technological University, India
Jignesh Doshi	Gujarat Technological University, India
Bhaveshkumar Prajapati	Gujarat Technological University, India
Nisha Somani	Gujarat Technological University, India
Desai Archana Natvarbhai	Gujarat Technological University, India
Akhilesh Ladha	Gujarat Technological University, India
Jaymin Bhalani	Gujarat Technological University, India
Dhananjay Yadav	Gujarat Technological University, India
Keyur Jani	Gujarat Technological University, India
Jeegar Trivedi	Sardar Patel University, India

Organizing Committee

Ajay Patel	Ganpat University, India
Ketan Patel	Ganpat University, India
Paresh M. Solanki	Ganpat University, India
Savan Patel	Ganpat University, India
Ravi Patel	Ganpat University, India
Ritesh Joshi	Ganpat University, India
Swati Patel	Ganpat University, India
Vishnuba Chavda	Ganpat University, India
Pravesh Patel	Ganpat University, India
Bhavesh Patel	Ganpat University, India
Jyodingra Dharwa	Ganpat University, India
Ketan Sarvakar	Ganpat University, India
Amit Suthar	Ganpat University, India
Ketan J. Patel	Ganpat University, India
Kimal Patel	Ganpat University, India

Contents

Design and Performance Analysis of High Efficiency Propulsion System
for VTOL Applications 1
   Amit Biswas, Neha N. Chaubey, and Nirbhay Kumar Chaubey

Osmotic Computing-Based Task Offloading: A Fuzzy Logic-Based
Approach 16
   Benazir Neha, Sanjaya Kumar Panda, and Pradip Kumar Sahu

Traveler's Demand Reactive Dynamic Online Bus Routing
[TraDeR-DOBR] to Improvize Comfort Perception in Intelligent Public
Transport System 31
   Akhilesh Ladha, Archana Nayak, and Nirbhay Kumar Chaubey

High-Speed FSO System for Future Generation Networks for Long Reach 48
   Dipti Sharma, Ashutosh Tripathi, and Meet Kumari

Mitigating PAPR Challenges in Massive MIMO Systems for CR-IoT
Networks: A Graeco-Latin Square Approach 63
   Subrat Kumar Sethi and Arunanshu Mahapatro

Performance Analysis of IoT Network over 5G Communication 78
   V. Sanvika, Indrasen Singh, Madala Poorna Chandra, and Joshith Reddy

IoT-Based Convolutional Neural Networks in a Farm Pest Detection Using
Transfer Learning 89
   *Keyurbhai A. Jani, Nirbhay Kumar Chaubey, Esan Panchal,
Pramod Tripathi, and Shruti Yagnik*

Performance Comparison of NOMA Vehicular Communications Under
Shadow Fading 102
   Hetal Shah and Vinay Thumar

Detecting Distributed Denial of Service (DDoS) Attacks
in a Multi-controller SDN Environment Utilizing Machine
Learning 117
   Nishant Sanghani, Gunjani Vaghela, and Bhavesh Borisaniya

Comprehensive Study of Short Channel Effects (SCEs) in MOSFET
and FinFET Devices 133
   Kripa Patel, Nisarg Vala, Mitesh Limachia, and Purvang Dalal

A Machine Learning (ML)-Inspired Method for Intrusion Detection in IoT Devices Networks 145
 Veeramuthu Venkatesh, Pethuru Raj, Roshitha Nedium, Jahnavi Edara, Kalluru Amarnath Reddy, and R. Anushiadevi

An Anomaly—Misuse Hybrid System for Efficient Intrusion Detection in Clustered Wireless Sensor Network Using Neural Network 161
 N. Nathiya, C. Rajan, K. Geetha, S. Dinesh, S. Aruna, and B. M. Brinda

Detection and Prevention of Black Hole Attack and Sybil Attack in Vehicular Ad Hoc Networks 176
 Dhananjay Yadav and Nirbhay Kumar Chaubey

Cognitive Ad Hoc Trust Routing for Enhanced Quality of Service 190
 N. Neelima, P. Syam Pratap, and P. Satya Kiran

Routing in IoT Network Using NetSim Simulator 205
 Divyanshi Goyal, Sonam, Anjali Yadav, Manan Alfred, and Rahul Johari

A Novel Approach of SHA-3-512bits Using Keccak Technique Based on Sponge Function Implementation on FPGA 216
 K. Janshi Lakshmi and G. Sreenivasulu

Cooperative Spectrum Sensing in Cognitive Radio Network Using Adaptive Walruses Optimization Algorithm 229
 D. Raghunatha Rao, T. Jayachandra Prasad, D. Satyanarayana, Saritha Bai Gaddale, Kadiyala Raghavendra, and T. Hussaini

Catalan's Conjecture and Elliptic Curve Cryptography (CCECC) Algorithm for Enhancing Data Security During Data Transmission in MANET 245
 D. Eben Angel Pauline

Monitoring the Concentration of Air Pollutants and Its Health Hazards Using Machine Learning Models 255
 Aditi Jain, Aditya Shenoy, Ananya Adiga, Anirudha Anekal, and Saritha Prajwal

Containment of Compromised Nodes in a Distributed Environment 270
 Anushka Gupta, Aayush Dubey, Abhay Hiremath, V. Anirruth, and Jeny Jijo

A Novel Approach to Solve Network Security, Cryptography Problems Using Genetic Algorithm 282
 Devasenathipathi N. Mudaliar, Nilesh Modi, and Jyotindra Dharwa

Intelligent Agent Based Clustering and Optimal Multipath Routing for Energy-Efficient Wireless Sensor Networks in Smart City Applications: A Distributed AI-Driven Approach 294
Binaya Kumar Patra, Sarojananda Mishra, Sanjay Kumar Patra, Ashutosh Mallik, and Souveek Roy

A Novel Symmetric Key Based Authentication Scheme that Saves Energy for Edge Devices of the Internet of Things 308
Prakash Kuppuswamy, Sayeed Q. Al-Khalidi Al-Maliki, Rajan John, and Mohan Mani

Objective Functions in High-Density Internet of Things Networks - A Performance Evaluation 320
Safia Gul, Bilal Ahmad Malik, and M. Tariq Banday

Enhancing ASIC Design Efficiency: A Focus on RTL Verification with Spyglass 334
Dhaval Fichadia, Nikeeta Shah, and Bhavesh Soni

Enhancement in AOMDV Routing Protocol to Overcome Congestion Problem in MANET 345
Misgana M. Iticha, Ketema A. Gemeda, and Samuel S. Tadesse

Performance Evaluation of Parallel Processing Adder Against Basic Adders on FPGAs 359
Dhaval Fichadia, Kishor Purohit, and Bhavesh Soni

A Decentralised Application for Medical Insurance Claim System Using Blockchain Technology 373
Hrishabh Joshi, Sharon Justine, V. Panchami, and Beeraka Hrithik

Performance Analysis of Energy Efficient Routing Protocols in Wireless Sensor Networks 388
Priyanka Patel, Amrut Patel, and Manish Patel

Design of Performance Enhanced Approximate Multiplier for Image Processing Applications 401
K. Sivanandam and R. Sathana

Design and Optimization in SPI Master at the RTL Level 411
Rajat R. Sahu, Mitur Patel, Bhavesh Soni, and Jignesh Patoliya

Author Index 423

Design and Performance Analysis of High Efficiency Propulsion System for VTOL Applications

Amit Biswas[1]($\boxtimes$), Neha N. Chaubey[2], and Nirbhay Kumar Chaubey[3]

[1] Triassic Aerospace Pvt Ltd, Delhi, India
amit@triassicaerospace.com
[2] Imperial College London, London, UK
[3] Ganpat University, Mehsana, Gujarat, India
nirbhay@ieee.org

Abstract. Vertical Takeoff and Landing (VTOL) aircraft are designed to take off, hover, and land vertically. They require significant amount of thrust specially during takeoff and landing phases to counteract the force of gravity. The ability to generate high thrust is a critical aspect of VTOL design. To generate the necessary thrust, VTOL aircraft require specialized propulsion systems such as ducted propellers. However, most of these aircraft continue to use general-purpose propulsion systems that leads to loss of thrust and efficiency. In this paper we discuss how we were able to achieve much higher thrust and efficiency gains by using electric ducted propellers. We will study the design considerations we made to make our propellers more efficient. Mechanical designs of the ducted propeller, the rotor, and other components are explained along with dimensions. The electrical subsystem including power, motor, controllers are also covered. We will also discuss the experimental setup we used to perform the tests. Experimental results were obtained and compared for our ducted propeller and general-purpose un-ducted propellers. Simulations were carried out using the CAD model of the propellers and results were compared with experimental data. We also present performance characteristics of our propellers under various mechanical and electrical conditions.

Keywords: Ducted propeller · Ducted fan · VTOL · eVTOL · UAV propulsive systems · Propeller performance · Thrust efficiency · Simulation · Tilt rotor

1 Introduction

Vertical Takeoff and Landing (VTOL) aircraft are a relatively new category in aviation technology. They are different from conventional aircraft because of their ability to take off and land vertically without the need for a runway. The term VTOL aircraft can be used to refer to various types of aircraft ranging from traditional helicopters to tilt-rotors and more recently, advanced electric vertical takeoff and landing (eVTOL) aircraft. The VTOL capability provides exceptional flexibility while navigating complex terrains and accessing confined spaces. This capability offers distinct advantages in diverse applications spanning from military and surveillance operations to urban air mobility and delivery services. Advancements in technology, such as more efficient propulsion systems, are continuously improving the performance and efficiency of VTOL aircraft. Some VTOL aircraft can transition to conventional flight mode after take-off and then transition back to VTOL mode during landing. They have fixed wings that provide aerodynamic lift during forward flight thus increasing speed, efficiency and range of flight. One of the common ways to transition between VTOL and fixed-wing flight is to use a tilting mechanism for the propellers [1]. Such aircraft are referred to as Tilt-Rotor VTOLs. Tilt-rotor VTOLs combine the vertical lift capability of a helicopter with the speed and range of a fixed-wing airplane. These aircraft feature rotors that can tilt between vertical and horizontal positions, allowing them to take off and land vertically like a helicopter and then transition to a more efficient horizontal flight for faster and longer-range travel [2]. Designing the tilt mechanism is a crucial aspect of building tilt-rotor aircraft and the choice of propulsion system plays a particularly important role. The tilt mechanism also contributes in maintaining overall stability of the aircraft during take-off and landing [3]. Several design factors of the propulsion system such as size, speed and position must be taken into consideration while designing the tilt mechanism. Precise control of the tilt mechanism requires positional and orientation feedback which is then used to plan a smooth trajectory of motion. Accurate trajectory control and tracking is needed to maintain stability [4], [5]. VTOL aircraft require significantly more thrust than traditional fixed-wing aircraft during take-off and landing phase [1]. Since no lift is generated from the wings, the entire weight of the aircraft has to be supported by the propulsion systems. Unlike fixed-wing aircraft that generate lift primarily through forward motion, VTOLs requires a continuous thrust output to counteract gravity. In addition to this, while transitioning from vertical to horizontal flight or vice versa, additional thrust may be required. The ability to generate high thrust is a critical aspect of VTOL design. To generate such high thrust, VTOL aircraft require specially designed propulsion systems. Developing these propulsion systems involves intricate engineering to ensure they provide enough thrust for vertical flight while also being efficient and effective during horizontal flight. One of the most frequently used propulsion systems comprises of electric ducted propellers. Ducted propellers, also known as shrouded or enclosed propellers, are propulsion systems where the traditional propeller blades are enclosed within a cylindrical or ducted structure. This design has some distinctive advantages and applications compared to open, unshrouded propellers but also come with certain design complexities and might not always be the optimal choice. Ducted propellers can improve thrust efficiency by reducing tip losses and optimizing the aerodynamic performance of the blades [6]. The duct helps in directing the airflow more effectively, potentially increasing the overall propulsion efficiency.

Careful design considerations and choosing optimal parameters can make ducted propellers significantly more efficient than non-ducted propellers. Ducted propellers help reduce tip losses, which occur when the airflow at the tips of open propellers becomes less efficient. The ducted structure confines and directs the airflow, minimizing these losses and improving overall thrust efficiency.

2 Related Work

Much research has been done to understand the performance characteristics of ducted propulsion systems as compared to open un-ducted systems. Due to their ability to produce high static thrust, ducted propulsion systems have been a subject of study especially for VTOL applications. Multiple methods for improving its efficiency and stability of ducted systems have been proposed [7]. The most important factors that affect performance and efficiency are the design of the duct, design of the fan blades, tip clearance and duct inlet/outlet design. Some external factors also affect the performance such as the distortion in inlet velocity at the initial section of the duct during forward flight has the potential to notably impact the circumferential pressure distribution at the inlet, consequently influencing the overall aerodynamic performance [6].

While ducted fans exhibit commendable performance in numerous VTOL applications, persistent challenges remain within these systems. Notably, the leakage flow at the fan rotor tips emerges as a substantial contributor to aerodynamic losses in ducted fan VTOLs, detrimentally impacting the overall aerodynamic performance of such aircraft [8]. Most optimal tip clearance is very hard to achieve. Large tip clearances effectively cancel out all the performance benefits of a ducted system. Too tight clearances have higher risk of mechanical failure. Different strategies to mitigate tip leakage have been studied by adjusting both the chordwise location and the width of the extension in the circumferential direction. The optimization of flow interactions associated with reduced tip clearance proved crucial in enhancing the energy efficiency and range of vehicles utilizing ducted fans [9].

Performance and efficiency can also be improved using numerical models. Aerodynamic performance design and evaluation methods have been proposed based on Blade Element Theory (BRT) and Momentum Theory [10]. BET has been used to design and evaluate the performance of un-ducted fan. Momentum Theory has been used to calculate thrust performance of ducted fans. Some other approaches have also been used, such as designs based on Optimal Circulation Distribution [11]. In addition to theoretical methods, simulations have also been used to study the performance under varying conditions. Computational Fluid Dynamics (CFD) has been used to study the effect of changes in blade structure in the performance of the fan [12].

3 Design Considerations

Designing a ducted propeller involves considering various factors to optimize performance, efficiency, and safety. Some of the key design considerations include the duct shape and geometry, blade design, tip clearance, duct inlet and outlet design, thrust distribution and materials used for construction. In addition to these, there are other factors that are specific to our application. These include the mechanical mounting options, the size of the propeller, the amount of power it draws at maximum thrust, heating and cooling arrangements, and support for the tilting mechanism.

3.1 Duct Shape and Geometry

The shape and geometry of the duct play a crucial role in the aerodynamic performance of the propeller [13]. We considered factors such as length of the duct, its diameter, taper angle, and curvature to achieve optimal thrust distribution and efficiency. The length of the section between the lip and the diffuser, also known as the transition section, influences aerodynamic characteristics of the duct. These effects were studied in detail by Chenkai Cao et al. [14] (Fig. 1).

Fig. 1. The ducted propeller model we designed, showing the shroud around the duct tube and a cross section view showing the rotor fan inside the duct.

3.2 Duct Inlet/Outlet Design

The design of the duct's inlet and outlet is critical aspect in achieving efficient airflow. Effect of inlet design on airflow and performance has been documented previously [15]. Smooth transitions and carefully designed contours help minimize turbulence, pressure losses, and drag, contributing to improved overall performance. A lip is a curved or beveled edge at the entrance of the duct. It can provide benefits in the performance and efficiency of the ducted propeller. We used an inlet lip in our design. We did not use any special design changes in the duct outlet although changes in the outlet design have been shown to affect performance [14].

3.3 Tip Clearance

Tip clearance is one the most crucial factors that affect performance directly [8]. Maintaining an appropriate tip clearance between the blades and the duct walls is important. Proper clearance prevents inefficiencies, reduces drag, and minimizes the risk of noise generation. Low tip clearance increases efficiency substantially, but it is difficult to manufacture. Also, tight clearances have higher risk of collision during if vibration is experienced. In our experimental setup, we used a fan with tip clearance of 0.25 mm, however, we did not compare performance difference at different tip clearances.

3.4 Fan Blade Design

Key considerations for fan blade design include blade length, pitch, twist, and airfoil profile. The effects of three parameters (twist, sweep, lean), on aerodynamic and structural performance of the fan blade were investigated in detail by Chengwei Fan et al. [16]. They found that twist and sweep have a relatively strong influence on aerodynamic performance as compared with the lean. Also, the effect of twist varied at different operating conditions. In our experiments, we used a fan with 12 fixed-pitch blades with a disc diameter of 120 mm. The fan was initially built using 3D printing but later we also tested with a CNC machined aluminum fan (Fig. 2).

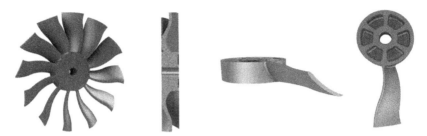

Fig. 2. Design of the rotor fan and detail views of the fan blades

3.5 Power Source

We compared the performance of various combination of propellers with different battery pack configurations ranging from 10S to 18S. The following tables show the comparison of multiple battery packs and key performance indicators. For the purpose of this experiment, we decided to use the 12S battery pack (Table 1).

Table 1. Performance characteristics with different battery packs at min cell voltage of 3.7 V and max cell voltage of 4.2 V

Rotor diameter (mm)	Rotor blades	Battery cells (S)	Volt (V) min/max	Current (A) min/max	Power (W) min/max	Thrust (kgf) min/max
120	12	10	37/42	117/96	4329/4032	7.2/6.1
120	12	12	44.4/50.4	112/142	4972/7156	7.5/9.23
120	12	14	51.8/58.8	107/133	5542/7727	8/9.8
120	12	15	55.5/63	103/135	5716/8500	7.8/9.3
120	12	18	66.6/75.6	98/116	6526/8769	8.1/10.3

3.6 Thrust Distribution

We used a special design for the propeller blades that ensures uniform thrust distribution at different speed of rotations. Achieving uniform thrust distribution along the length of the blades is crucial for optimal performance. Experimental results obtained by Chengwei Fan et al. [16] showed that the maximum blade stress was dominated by the twist, and a backward sweep at mid-span decreased the stress on the blade surface. Twist and sweep had significant effect on the total pressure ratio. The design we used was optimized to minimize variations in thrust, ensuring stability and control during operation. Non-uniform thrust distribution causes strain on the blades and may cause structural deformities. At high RPM and with very tight tip clearances this may lead to mechanical failure.

4 Building Block Architecture

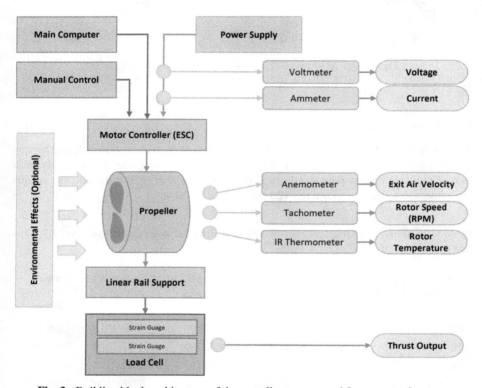

Fig. 3. Building block architecture of the overall setup we used for our experiments.

Our setup was planned in way that allowed us to collect as much data as possible while performing the tests. The main propeller system was mounted on movable linear rails that allowed for linear travel as the propeller generated thrust. For this setup, we did not use any mechanism to measure radial forces, only axial forces were measured. A load cell was used to measure axial forces by measuring strain on the movable platform (Fig. 3).

5 Mechanical Design

For the purpose of our testing, we used a 120 mm electric ducted propeller. The fan rotor contains 12 fixed-pitch blades. It was driven by a BLDC motor operating at 44–50 V Dc and consuming about 4000–7500 W of power. The entire fan assembly was supported by a duct frame. We also tested with a lip in the intake section. No special modifications were done in the duct outlet.

5.1 Duct Design

The duct tube was enclosed with a shroud around it. This provides mechanical stability and streamlines the airflow around the duct. Having an aerodynamic shroud around the duct reduces drag during forward flight. It also helps in reducing vibrations and minimizes noise propagation outside the duct. The shroud extends beyond the length of the propeller blades. This helps in maintaining a streamlined flow of air [17]. Air turbulence is also reduced due to the shroud extension (Fig. 4).

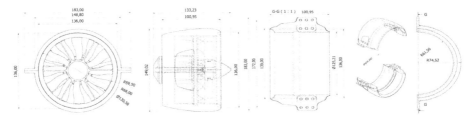

Fig. 4. Mechanical design of the ducted propeller showing the rotor fan, the motor, and the shroud around the duct.

5.2 Fan Design

Designing the fan is one of the most crucial aspects of the entire propulsion system. It is the single most contributing factor in the over performance of the system. We considered several factors for designing the fan such as the angle of attack, overall weight of the blade, strength and durability, tip clearance, blade number, blade twist and ease of manufacturing. Simulation results also helped us in fine tuning the design further (Fig. 5).

6 Simulations

We performed multiple simulations on our propeller design to measure its performance and ascertain the efficiency benefits expected out of it. Simulations were carried out using the CAD model of the propeller. Various conditions were tested during simulation such as different RPM, and the effect of ducted vs un-ducted propeller. Airflow characteristics, turbulence, temperature, pressure, and velocity were some of the parameters examined during simulation (Figs. 6, 7 and 8).

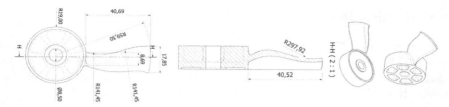

Fig. 5. Mechanical design of the rotor fan blade showing blade twist and cross section view of the blade geometry.

Fig. 6. Comparison of velocity pathlines in the exit section of the ducted propeller and the un-ducted propeller showing differences in turbulent air flow.

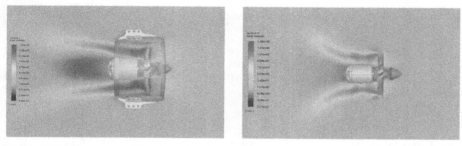

Fig. 7. Velocity contour of the ducted and the un-ducted propeller showing interaction of high velocity air exiting the propeller with low velocity surrounding air.

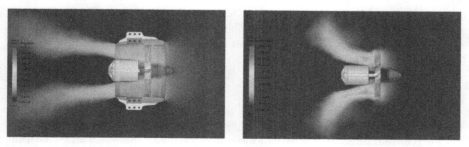

Fig. 8. Comparison of velocity magnitudes of airflow exiting the propellers.

The velocity pathlines simulation shows a dynamic visualization of the airflow coming out of the outlet section of the duct. The streamlined airflow of the ducted propeller is clearly visible in contrast to the much more turbulent air flow coming out of the unducted propeller. This contributes to greater thrust generation and better thrust vectoring as well. The velocity contour simulation shows the distribution and magnitude of air velocities for both the ducted and the un-ducted propeller. This is instrumental in visualizing and analyzing the boundary layer, showing how the air velocity changes near solid surfaces. Our simulation results show the interaction of surrounding air with the high velocity air exiting the duct or the propeller fan. Due to the duct, the exit air stream is isolated from surrounding air and reduces interaction between high velocity air with low velocity surrounding air. Although the duct creates some drag in the process, but overall performance gains offset the losses due to drag.

7 Experimental Setup

The goal of our experimental setup was to run a series of tests, measure key parameters and collect as much performance data as possible. The main component, the propeller system was mounted on a rigid frame that was free to travel linearly along the axial direction. This was achieved by mounting the frame on a set of linear rails with linear bearings. The thrust generated by the propeller would cause the frame to move along the rail. This movement was restricted, and the strain was measured by a load cell. This translated to the amount of thrust generated. Thrust values were collected and recorded from this load cell. On the exit end of the propeller, we measured the exit air velocity using an anemometer. The rotational speed of the propeller was measured using a tachometer attached to the propeller frame and measuring the motor RPM. This gave us motor and propeller RPM values. We also used a non-contact IR thermometer to measure the temperature of the motor. All these instruments were mounted along with the propeller frame assembly (Fig. 9).

Fig. 9. Equipment used for our experimental setup.

The propeller motor was driven by a motor controller often referred to as an Electronic Speed Controller or ESC. The ESC takes digital electronic signal and translates them proportionately to electrical output to drive the motor. Using this setup we were able to control the speed of the motor. The input speed signals were either generated by a computer for automated testing or sometimes even manually using a small device that generates ESC signals.

The entire setup was powered a battery pack. We used a 12S battery pack that supplied between 44 and 50 Volts and current of about 120 A. The battery pack was constructed using high performance lithium-ion cells capable of high discharge rates. Voltage and current was constantly measured from the battery. This provided us with total power draw of the entire system. The entire setup was assembled on a test bench and firmly fixed to it to avoid any vibrations mechanical displacement. Multiple test runs were conducted, and readings were recorded at regular intervals. Most of the test procedures and data collection was conducted manually as fully automated testing was not possible due to several instruments not having data output options. All the collected data was processed carefully and analyzed to draw the results.

8 Results

We were able to demonstrate that proper design considerations and right choice of parameters can make significant efficiency gains in the overall performance of electric ducted propulsive systems. In our experiments we measured multiple parameters including total power draw, speed of the rotor, thrust generated and overall efficiency of the system. We found that with the ducted propeller we were able to achieve about 20.86% higher thrust output as compared to the un-ducted propeller. We also noted that overall system efficiency, as measured by thrust produced per watt of power consumed, was about 3.85% higher with the ducted system at peak thrust and about 6.5% higher at lower RPM. Similarly, comparison of thrust output produced by our ducted propeller and the un-ducted propeller shows 17.26% less thrust generated by the un-ducted propeller for the same of power consumed or at the same voltage (Figs. 10, 11, 12, 13 and Tables 2, 3).

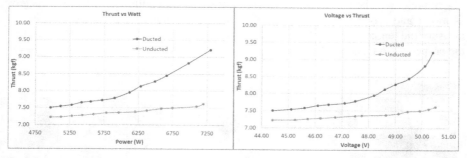

Fig. 10. Comparison of thrust output produced by our ducted propeller and the un-ducted propeller shows 17.26% less thrust generated by the un-ducted propeller for the same of power consumed or at the same voltage.

Propeller speed is an important parameter because flight stability and control is achieved by controlling the speed of the propellers. Propeller speed affects both thrust production and efficiency. Operating the propellers within their optimal range of speed is therefore essential in achieving the best balance between thrust, power efficiency, and overall performance. The relationship between these factors is influenced by various factors, most importantly the design of the propeller. We compared these relationships for the ducted and un-ducted propellers and found interesting correlations. The comparison

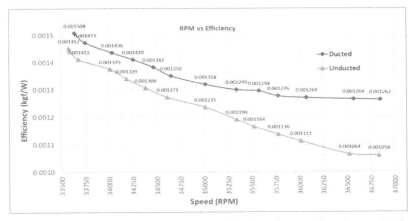

Fig. 11. Efficiency of the un-ducted propeller is 16.08% less than our ducted propeller for same rotor RPM.

Table 2. Experimental data collected for our ducted propeller.

Sr no.	Voltage (V)	Current (A)	Speed (RPM)	Power (W)	Thrust (kgf)	Efficiency (kgf/W)
1	44.40	112.00	33640.00	4972.80	7.50	0.001508
2	45.10	113.50	33752.00	5118.85	7.54	0.001473
3	45.60	115.75	34035.00	5278.20	7.58	0.001436
4	46.10	117.66	34255.00	5424.13	7.65	0.001410
5	46.50	119.50	34467.00	5556.75	7.68	0.001382
6	47.10	121.45	34654.00	5720.30	7.72	0.001350
7	47.50	124.25	35015.00	5901.88	7.78	0.001318
8	48.20	127.00	35340.00	6121.40	7.95	0.001299
9	48.60	129.25	35576.00	6281.55	8.13	0.001294
10	49.00	132.45	35778.00	6490.05	8.28	0.001276
11	49.50	134.50	36075.00	6657.75	8.45	0.001269
12	50.10	139.25	36570.00	6976.43	8.82	0.001264
13	50.40	144.75	36850.00	7295.40	9.21	0.001262

of thrust and efficiency as a function of speed, shown in Figs. 14 and 15, highlights these findings.

Overall, our results show that the un-ducted propeller produced substantially less thrust for same amount of power consumed and was much less efficient. It suffered multiple inefficiencies due to reduced control over airflow, losses due to tip vortex and

Table 3. Experimental data collected the un-ducted propeller.

Sr no.	Voltage (V)	Current (A)	Speed (RPM)	Power (W)	Thrust (kgf)	Efficiency (kgf/W)
1	44.40	112.00	33580.00	4972.80	7.22	0.001452
2	45.25	113.25	33682.00	5124.56	7.23	0.001411
3	45.72	115.50	34012.00	5280.66	7.26	0.001375
4	46.20	117.66	34185.00	5435.89	7.28	0.001339
5	46.75	119.75	34385.00	5598.31	7.31	0.001306
6	47.50	121.75	34615.00	5783.13	7.35	0.001271
7	47.75	124.84	35012.00	5961.11	7.36	0.001235
8	48.65	127.50	35340.00	6202.88	7.38	0.001190
9	49.12	129.76	35525.00	6373.81	7.42	0.001164
10	49.45	133.15	35778.00	6584.27	7.48	0.001136
11	49.92	135.20	36015.00	6749.18	7.50	0.001111
12	50.25	141.25	36525.00	7097.81	7.55	0.001064
13	50.50	142.45	36835.00	7193.73	7.62	0.001059

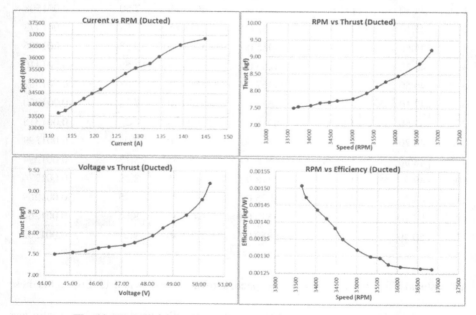

Fig. 12. Various performance characteristics of our ducted propeller.

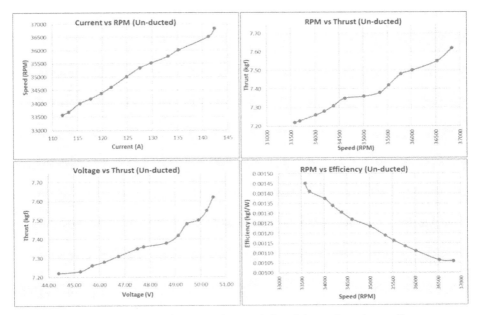

Fig. 13. Various performance characteristics of the un-ducted propeller.

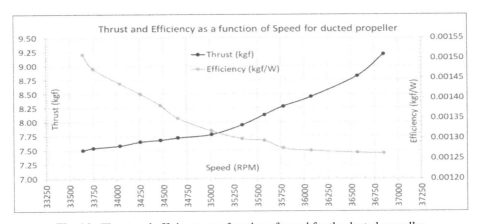

Fig. 14. Thrust and efficiency as a function of speed for the ducted propeller.

higher turbulence were the main causes of performance reduction. The performance loss was also evident in other areas such as thrust vs RPM or thrust vs current.

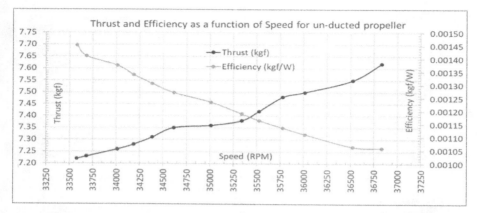

Fig. 15. Thrust and efficiency as a function of speed for the un-ducted propeller.

9 Conclusion

Designing high efficiency propulsion systems is essential for application that require high thrust and efficiency such as VTOL aircraft. However, there are several challenges to be overcome and multiple design considerations that has to be factored in to achieve meaningful performance gains. We studied the performance of a ducted propeller system and found that with proper design changes and careful selection of parameters, significant performance and efficiency gains can be achieved. We compared the results with an un-ducted propeller system to verify our findings. Electrical and mechanical data collected during our experiments and through simulations confirm that substantial performance gains were achieved with the ducted system.

There were some limitations in this study such as we did not have access to instruments that provide electronic data output, as a result data were collected by manual reading of the instruments. Also, we did not have the best or most accurate instruments. These factors may have affected the accuracy of the results. External environmental factors were also not controlled during our experiments. For future work we want to study several other factors that affect the performance of the propeller but were not included in this study. Some of these factors include the shape of the duct inlet and outlet and the effect of wind speed. Also, we want to study the performance characteristics of the propeller at different wind speeds and different angle of attack.

References

1. Notarstefano, G., Hauser, J.: Modeling and dynamic exploration of a tilt-rotor VTOL aircraft. IFAC Proc. Volumes **43**(14), 119–124 (2010)
2. Bauersfeld, L., Spannagl, L., Ducard, G.J.J., Onder, C.H.: MPC flight control for a tilt-rotor VTOL aircraft. IEEE Trans. Aerosp. Electron. Syst. **57**(4), 2395–2409 (2021)
3. Finger, D.F, Braun, C., Bil, C.: A review of configuration design for distributed propulsion transitioning VTOL aircraft. Asia-Pacific International Symposium on Aerospace Technology-APISAT, 3–5 (2017)

4. Biswas, A., Chaubey, N. N., Chaubey, N. K.: Achieving Accurate Trajectory Control While Training Legged Robots Using Machine Learning, in Chaubey, N., Thampi, S.M., Jhanjhi, N.Z., Parikh, S., Amin, K. (eds.) Computing Science, Communication and Security. COMS2 2023 (2023)
5. Biswas, A., Chaubey, N. N., Chaubey, N. K., in AI-Enabled Social Robotics in Human Care Services, in Kautish, S. et al. (eds.). IGI Global, pp. 172–187 (2023)
6. Deng, S., Wang, S., Zhang, Z.: Aerodynamic performance assessment of a ducted fan UAV for VTOL applications. Aerospace Sci. Tech., **103** (2020)
7. Qian, Y., Luo, Y., Hu, X., Zeng, Z., Zhang, Y.: Improving the performance of ducted fans for VTOL applications: a review. Sci. China Technol. Sci. **65**(11), 2521–2541 (2022)
8. Akturk, A., Camci, C.: Tip clearance investigation of a ducted fan used in VTOL unmanned aerial vehicles—Part I: baseline experiments and computational validation. J. Turbomachinery. **136**(2), 021004 (2014)
9. Akturk, A., Camci, C.: Tip clearance investigation of a ducted fan used in VTOL UAVS: Part 2—novel treatments via computational design and their experimental verification. Proceedings of the ASME 2011 Turbo Expo: Turbine Technical Conference and Exposition 7 (Turbomachinery, Parts A, B, and C), 345–357 (2011)
10. Jiang, H., Zhou, Y., Ho, H.W.: Aerodynamic design and evaluation of a ducted fan lift system for vertical takeoff and landing flying cars. Proc. Inst. Mech. Eng. Part A: J. Power Energy **237**(1), 115–125 (2023)
11. Zhang, Z., Bao, M., Qiao, N., Ma, T.: Journal of Physics: Conference Series, 6th International Conference on Fluid Mechanics and Industrial Applications (FMIA 2022) 2280 (2022)
12. Liu, L., Lyu, Q., Liu, G.: An optimization and test method for ducted fans based on CFD. Journal of Physics: Conference Series, The Third International Conference on Mechanical, Electric and Industrial Engineering **1633** (2020)
13. Go, J.S., Yoon, H.S., Jung, J.H.: Effects of a duct before a propeller on propulsion performance. Ocean Eng. **136**, 54–66 (2017)
14. Cao, C., Zhao, G., Zhao, Q., Wang, B.: Numerical investigation and optimization for interior duct shape of ducted tail rotor. Aerospace Sci. Tech., **115** (2021)
15. Camci, C., Herwig, N., Aktürk, A.: Inlet flow separation control via novel lip-spoilers for ducted fan based VTOL uninhabited aerial vehicles. 16th International Symposium on Transport Phenomena and Dynamics of Rotating Machinery (2016)
16. Fan, C., Adjei, R.A., Wu, Y., Wang, A.: Parametric study on the aerodynamic performance of a ducted-fan rotor using free-form method. Aerospace Sci. Technol., **101** (2020)
17. Misiorowski, M., Gandhi, F., Oberai, A.: A computational study on diffuser length variation for a ducted rotor in hover and edgewise flight. Proceedings of the AHS Specialists' Conference on Aeromechanics Design for Transformative Vertical Flight (2018)

Osmotic Computing-Based Task Offloading: A Fuzzy Logic-Based Approach

Benazir Neha[1], Sanjaya Kumar Panda[2](✉), and Pradip Kumar Sahu[1]

[1] Veer Surendra Sai University of Technology, Burla, Odisha, India
neha.benazir13@gmail.com, pksahu_it@vssut.ac.in
[2] National Institute of Technology, Warangal, Telangana, India
sanjaya@nitw.ac.in

Abstract. The swift expansion of the information technology (IT) industry has led to a surge in compute-intensive and latency-sensitive applications. While cloud computing can satiate the demands of such applications, its centralized architecture may cause delays in the execution of tasks. To address such issues, edge computing brings computation closer to data sources. However, limited resources on Internet of things (IoT) devices make local execution quite challenging. Therefore, a pliable approach is to consider task offloading for moving heavy tasks to resource-extensive systems like edge/cloud. Osmotic computing, leveraging edge and cloud resources, aims to enhance IoT services. However, the dynamic nature of IoT, edge, and cloud introduces challenges for task offloading. This paper proposes an offloading algorithm using fuzzy logic to manage uncertainty. Furthermore, we introduce an osmotic decision manager (ODM) that employs fuzzy logic for optimized offloading decisions, considering IoT/edge for latency-sensitive tasks and cloud for latency-tolerant tasks. This algorithm aims to improve overall system performance by efficiently offloading tasks based on their specific requirements and constraints. The proposed algorithm undergoes simulation and assessment with diverse synthetic test cases to demonstrate its efficacy.

Keywords: Cloud Computing · Internet of Things · Edge Computing · Osmotic Computing · Task Offloading

1 Introduction

The swift growth within the information technology (IT) sector has resulted in the ubiquitous adoption of Internet of things (IoT) applications across various domains, including healthcare, augmented and virtual reality, infotainment, video streaming, vehicular computing [9], etc. Moreover, these applications come with a remark of being compute-intensive and latency-sensitive [18,19]. Clouds having extensive resources can satiate the demand for such compute-intensive applications. However, the geographically centralized cloud architecture can create unnecessary delays and performance complications for latency-sensitive applications [3]. This inefficacy can be addressed through a decentralized approach. Edge computing is one of the computing paradigms that fit perfectly into the place to resolve the issues for latency-sensitive applications by bringing computing closer to the data generation source. Furthermore, IoT devices work in line with edge and cloud to manage such applications [13]. However, on account of the finite computational resources of IoT devices, the execution of tasks locally becomes difficult [12]. Therefore, a pliable approach is to consider task offloading.

Offloading is moving heavy tasks away from a resource-constrained device (IoT/edge) and executing them on resource-extensive systems (cloud) [3,6,7]. Moreover, offloading provides the flexibility for tasks to be run on platforms where they will perform most efficiently. It also facilitates the development of elastic and scalable applications. Furthermore, task offloading requires custom solutions tailored to the particular requirements and constraints of the system. This can be accomplished by integrating IoT, edge and cloud to form an ecosystem by leveraging osmotic computing principles [11,12]. The goal is to optimize utilization of resources, reduce latency and improve the comprehensive performance of the ecosystem.

Osmotic computing is an ideal model that focuses on enhancing IoT services by utilizing edge and cloud resources [21,22]. It works on the principle of osmosis in chemistry to manage resources in an integrated ecosystem [11,12]. It also functions in accord with computational/task offloading and resolves certain lacuna of IoT devices, such as resource limitation, battery life, processing capability, etc., by utilizing edge/cloud resources [16]. However, the dynamic and uncertain nature of IoT/edge/cloud may impact the capability to fulfil stringent service demands for latency-sensitive applications. Offloading becomes quite challenging with the assortment of services available across different computing layers. We propose an offloading algorithm using a fuzzy logic approach to manage the uncertainty and dynamicity in the ecosystem. Fuzzy logic finds its application in data classification, automation control, decision-making, etc. In addition, we propose an osmotic decision manager (ODM) that focuses on optimizing the offloading decisions for the incoming tasks by using a fuzzy logic-based offloading algorithm. Our proposed work makes decisions considering IoT/edge for offloading latency-sensitive tasks and cloud for latency-tolerant tasks.

The subsequent sections of the work are structured as follows: Sect. 2 abstracts all the related research works. Section 3 elucidates the osmotic system model. In Sect. 4, the proposed algorithm, accompanied by an illustration, is outlined. Section 5 demonstrates the simulation of the suggested algorithm. The conclusion of the paper is presented in Sect. 6.

2 Related Work

Osmotic computing is currently in the nascent phase of its evolution, and the research work carried out in this field predominantly uses cases/prototypes.

Moreover, taking task offloading into consideration, it is a widely used concept. The majority of the existing literature has focused on IoT, IoT-edge, edge-cloud, and cloud. Ibrar et al. [7] introduced an adaptive task offloading solution for device-to-device communication in social and industrial IoT, aiming to improve resource utilization and task completion rates. Li et al. [8] presented genetic algorithm (GA)-based task offloading in edge computing to optimize latency. Gao et al. [5] presented an offloading strategy to minimize task response latency in mobile and edge computing. Xu et al. [24] presented an online task offloading algorithm to reduce energy consumption in mobile-edge computing. An et al. [1] gave a strategy for offloading tasks to minimize energy consumption as well as delay task processing in IoT-edge computing. Ullah et al. [20] presented an algorithm that uses the benefits of a double deep Q-network to devise offloading decisions for selecting a location for task execution in the edge-cloud environment. Ren et al. [15] proposed a collaborative task offloading between edge and cloud for latency minimization.

Zhang et al. [25] analyzed a task offloading problem in the hybrid edge-cloud environment to minimize energy, time and cost. Qu et al. [14] proposed a deep meta-reinforcement-based framework for learning-oriented task offloading within the edge and cloud environment. Fan et al. [4] introduced a task offloading algorithm for joint utilization of resources in edge and cloud by minimizing task processing delay. However, these researchers have yet to consider an IoT-edge-cloud integrated environment. Furthermore, some research works that consider IoT-edge-cloud integration were found. Wu et al. [23] devised a dynamic task offloading algorithm tailored for a blockchain-based IoT-edge-cloud environment to optimize energy consumption. Sun et al. [17] presented a low-complexity hierarchical heuristic approach to achieve task offloading in an end-edge-cloud environment. Hong et al. [6] presented a multi-hop computation offloading approach designed for industrial IoT-edge-cloud computing. However, these research works neither used the fuzzy logic approach nor the osmotic computing principle for seamless uni-directional or bi-directional offloading. Sharma et al. [16] proposed a computational offloading framework on pervasive trust management for online social networks using the osmotic computing principle. However, they have not considered an IoT-edge-cloud integrated environment.

3 Osmotic System Model

We showcase a system model based on osmotic computing, illustrating an integrated environment encompassing IoT, edge, and cloud layers. These computing layers work in harmony with each other, imparting seamless support for the dynamic management of services. The osmotic system model adheres to a principle analogous to the osmosis principle in chemistry. Here, solvent molecules (representing services) migrate from areas of higher to lower solute concentration via a semi-permeable membrane [12]. In our system model, solute represents task size, resource utilization, latency, etc., solvent represents tasks generated from devices, and semi-permeable membrane represents a software-defined membrane or osmotic membrane which allows seamless movement of tasks/services across all the layers [11].

In the IoT-edge-cloud integrated environment, each layer receives requests, and the layer with the most requests has a higher concentration. Similarly, a layer with a lower request has a lower concentration. By leveraging the osmotic computing principle, the requests can be offloaded from higher to lower concentrations [12,21,22]. Our osmotic system model is a five-tiered model with three distinct tiers (IoT, edge, and cloud) containing two intermediate tiers, also known as osmotic tiers. One osmotic tier resides between IoT-edge and other in between edge-cloud, allowing swift migration of tasks/services from IoT to edge to cloud and reverse. Osmotic computing also supports bidirectional offloading, i.e., from IoT → edge → cloud and the reverse [2]. To keep simplicity, we have chosen unidirectional offloading, i.e., from IoT → edge → cloud. The schematic representation of the system model with the distinct arrangement of tiers is shown in Fig. 1. The osmotic tier consists of an ODM, which is responsible for taking offloading decisions using a fuzzy logic approach. The components of the ODM are clearly shown in Fig. 2. The alignment of components of ODM depicts the MAPE approach, which follows monitoring, analyzing, planning and executing to take appropriate offloading decisions and periodically monitor system performance.

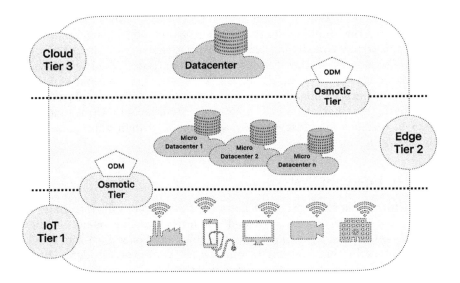

Fig. 1. Schematic representation of osmotic system model.

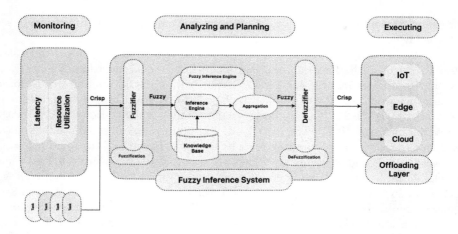

Fig. 2. Components of osmotic decision manager.

4 Fuzzy-Osmotic-Based Task Offloading Algorithm (FOTO)

We present a fuzzy logic-based offloading algorithm to determine target layers to offload tasks across IoT/edge/cloud layers. To reflect our fuzzy logic approach, we have adopted the Mamdani fuzzy inference system [10]. This inference system follows linguistic fuzzy modelling, and its distinctive nature is described by high interpretability and simplicity. The inference system is described as follows. This system takes crisp values as input, i.e., $p \in P$, where P is the input variable and produces output crisp value, i.e., $q = f(p) \in Q$, where Q is the output variable. The schematic representation of the inference system includes three fundamental blocks, i.e., fuzzification, fuzzy inference engine and defuzzification, which is vividly shown in Fig. 2.

4.1 Fuzzy Inference System

Fuzzification: It is the method of mapping crisp input values to fuzzy input linguistic values. This process is carried out in the fuzzifier using membership functions ($\mu(p)$, $[0, 1]$). Fuzzy linguistic variables symbolize both the input and output variables in this context. In our model, we have considered task size (ts), resource utilization (ru) and maximum tolerable latency (t^{max}) as input linguistic variables to determine offloading layer (O as output linguistic variable). Each linguistic variable has one or more linguistic values associated with it, such as Low (Lo), Medium (Me) and High (Hi), which can be represented using the membership function. Here, we have considered the triangular function, which is defined as

$$\mu_{triangular}(p;x,y,z) = \begin{cases} 0, & p \leq x \\ \frac{p-x}{y-x}, & x \leq p \leq y \\ \frac{z-p}{z-y}, & y \leq p \leq z \\ 0, & z \leq p \end{cases} \qquad (1)$$

$$= max(min(\frac{p-x}{y-x}, \frac{z-p}{z-y}), 0)$$

where x, y and z are the range values of membership functions and p is the input crisp value. Figures 3, 4, 5 and 6 illustrates the membership functions corresponding to various input and output linguistic values. The input and output linguistic values and their respective membership function ranges are shown in Table 1.

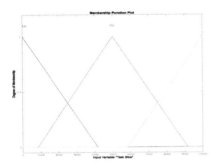

Fig. 3. Task size membership function

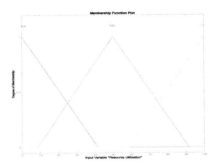

Fig. 4. Resource utilization membership function

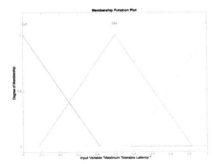

Fig. 5. Maximum tolerable latency membership function

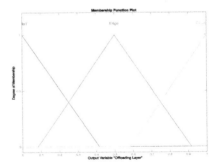

Fig. 6. Offloading layer membership function

Fuzzy Inference Engine: This block is associated with making decisions in a fuzzy system. It includes two components, namely the Inference Engine and the Knowledge Base. The knowledge base provides the necessary fuzzy rules

Table 1. Linguistic variables, values and their membership function ranges

Input		
Linguistic Variable	Linguistic Value	Membership Function Range
ts	Lo	[−4166.67 0 4166.67]
	Me	[833.333 5000 9166.67]
	Hi	[5833.33 10000 14166.7]
ru	Lo	[−41.6667 0 41.6667]
	Me	[8.333 50 91.6667]
	Hi	[58.333 100 141.667]
t^{max}	Lo	[−0.416667 0 0.416667]
	Me	[0.08333 0.5 0.916667]
	Hi	[0.58333 1 1.41667]
Output		
O	IoT	[0 0 0.416667]
	$Edge$	[0.0833 0.5 0.916667]
	$Cloud$	[0.5833 1 1.41667]

required to make decisions. These rules are linguistic descriptions made using fuzzy IF-THEN conditions. A fuzzy rule r_i can be defined as

$$r_i = IF(P_1 \text{ is } a_1, P_2 \text{ is } a_2, \ldots, P_n \text{ is } a_n) \; THEN \; (Q \text{ is } q_i) \quad (2)$$

where $(P_1, P_2, \ldots, P_n)$ and Q are input and output linguistic variables and $(a_1, a_2, \ldots, a_n)$ and q_i are input and output linguistic values, respectively. In our model, we have taken three input linguistic variables and three linguistic values, which generate $3^3 = 27$ rules in the fuzzy rule set. Some of the rules from the designed fuzzy rule set are shown in Table 2. In addition, the inference engine evaluates the rules from the rule base to draw a conclusion, which is defined as

$$evaluation(r_i) = min(\mu_{a_1}(P_1), \mu_{a_2}(P_2), \ldots, \mu_{a_3}(P_n)) \quad (3)$$

Defuzzification: It is the process of mapping fuzzy output linguistic values to crisp values. This process is carried out in the defuzzifier. For defuzzification, we have used the centroid method, which determines the center of gravity of the fuzzy set along the x-axis and is given as

$$O = \frac{1}{\frac{1}{n}\sum_{i=1}^{n}\mu(o_i)}(\sum_{i=1}^{n} o_i \times \mu(o_i)) \quad (4)$$

where o_i's are the divisions of aggregated region, $\mu(o_i)$ is the membership function and n is the number of divisions of the aggregated region. The steps for task offloading to the desired computing layer using a fuzzy logic approach through the described fuzzy inference system are shown in Algorithm 1.

Table 2. Fuzzy rule set for task offloading

Rule #	Fuzzy Input Variables			Fuzzy Output Variables
	ts	ru	t^{max}	O
1	IF Lo AND	Lo AND	Lo THEN	IoT
2	Lo	Lo	Me	IoT
3	Lo	Me	Lo	IoT
4	Lo	Me	Hi	$Edge$
5	Me	Lo	Lo	IoT
6	Me	Me	Me	$Edge$
7	Me	Hi	Me	$Edge$
8	Me	Hi	Hi	$Edge$
9	Hi	Me	Lo	$Cloud$
10	Hi	Me	Hi	$Cloud$
11	Hi	Hi	Me	$Cloud$
12	Hi	Hi	Hi	$Cloud$

Algorithm 1: FOTO

Input: $[ts, ru, t^{max}]$: crisp inputs, $[O_{th1}, O_{th2}]$: thresholds, a: number of input linguistic variables and b: number of input linguistic values

Result: Offloading layer: crisp value

1 Set fuzzy linguistic variables for both input and output
2 Set fuzzy linguistic values for both input and output
3 **for** $t \in [ts, ru, t^{max}]$ **do**
4   Mapping crisp input values to fuzzy input linguistic values using input membership function $\mu(t)$ given in Eq. (1)
5 **for** $i \leftarrow 1, 2, 3, \ldots, a^b$ **do**
6   Determine fuzzy rules (r_i) using fuzzy linguistic variables and values using Eq. (2)
7 **for** $i \leftarrow 1, 2, 3, \ldots, a^b$ **do**
8   Evaluate r_i using Eq. (3)
9   Aggregate evaluated fuzzy outputs
10 Determine crisp output O_i by defuzzification using Eq. (4) **if** $O_i \leq O_{th1}$ **then**
11   Offload to IoT
12 **else if** $O_{th1} \leq O_i \leq O_{th2}$ **then**
13   Offload to $Edge$
14 **else**
15   Offload to $Cloud$

4.2 Illustration

Algorithm 1 is illustrated considering five tasks and three computing layers: IoT, edge and cloud. The characteristics of tasks, i.e., ts in GB, ru in % and t_{max} in % are shown in Table 3. Let us consider task t_3 with the crisp input values $ts = 1050$, $ru = 66\%$ and $t_{max} = 0.7\%$. The fuzzy input linguistic values are evaluated considering the crisp inputs by using the input membership function given in Eq. (1), shown in Step 4 of Algorithm 1, and is calculated as

$$Lo(ts) = \mu_{triangular}(1050; -4166.7, 0, 4166.67)$$
$$= max(min(\frac{1050 - (-4166.7)}{0 - (-4166.7)}, \frac{4166.67 - 1050}{4166.67 - 0}), 0)$$
$$= 0.748$$
$$Me(ru) = \mu_{triangular}(66; 8.333, 50, 91.6667)$$
$$= 0.615$$

Similarly, other fuzzy linguistic values for task t_3 are evaluated and are shown in Table 4. The values of other tasks can be obtained similarly. Next, we determine fuzzy rules (r_i) using fuzzy linguistic variables and values (Step 5 and Step 6). The rules shown in Table 2 are evaluated to draw conclusion using Eq. (3) (Step 8) and is shown below

$$evaluation(r_1) = min(Lo(ts), Lo(ru), Lo(t_{max}))$$
$$= min(0.748, 0, 0) = 0$$

Similarly, other rules are evaluated for task t_3 and are depicted in Table 5. As seen in the table, multiple fuzzy output values are obtained, which are then aggregated on the same axis, and then defuzzification is done (Step 9 and Step 10) to obtain crisp output O for task t_3, which is 0.500. Comparing the value of O with O_{th1} and O_{th2}, we find that task t_3 will be offloaded to the edge layer (Step 11 to Step 16). Note that O_{th1} and O_{th2} represent two threshold values under consideration. Determining the optimum threshold values poses a highly complex problem and is outside the context of this work.

We find the time complexity of the FOTO algorithm as follows. The outer loop runs for each value t in the set ts, ru, t^{max}, resulting $O(N)$ time complexity, where N is the set size. The first inner loop (Line 5 and Line 6) runs a^b times, where a is the number of input linguistic variables and b is the number of input linguistic values. This loop involves determining and evaluating fuzzy rules, resulting in a time complexity of $O(a^b)$. The total time complexity results from multiplying the time complexities associated with the nested loops and operations. Therefore, the total time complexity of the FOTO algorithm can be expressed as $O(N \times a^b)$. It's noteworthy to mention that the exact value of N depends on the size of the set ts, ru, t^{max}, and the values of a and b depend on the number of input linguistic variables and values, respectively.

Table 3. Task characteristics along with details and computed results

Task #	ts	ru	t_{max}	O	Offloading Layer
t_1	2200	52	0.2	0.375	IoT
t_2	7055	60	0.9	0.746	$Cloud$
t_3	1050	66	0.7	0.500	$Edge$
t_4	3100	90	0.4	0.495	$Edge$
t_5	1500	23	0.5	0.329	IoT

Table 4. Fuzzy input linguistic values for task t_3

$Lo(ts) = 0.748$	$Lo(ru) = 0$	$Lo(t_{max}) = 0$
$Me(ts) = 0.052$	$Me(ru) = 0.615$	$Me(t_{max}) = 0.52$
$Hi(ts) = 0$	$Hi(ru) = 0.184$	$Hi(t_{max}) = 0.28$

Table 5. Fuzzy rule evaluation for task t_3

r_1	r_2	r_3	r_4	r_5	r_6	r_7	r_8	r_9	r_{10}	r_{11}	r_{12}
0	0	0	0.28	0	0.052	0.052	0.052	0	0	0	0

5 Simulation

The proposed algorithm was stimulated in the fuzzy logic toolbox using the Mamdani fuzzy inference system in MATLAB R2023a on a system with an Apple M1 chip, 8-core GPU, 8 GB memory, and 256 GB SSD on macOS Ventura 13.4. We have considered 1000 samples for each input data and generated the output data using the Mamdani fuzzy inference system. We have analyzed our fuzzy inference system using rule inference, error distribution, control surface and system validation. The simulation steps for the proposed algorithm for the considered illustration are shown through a rule inference diagram in Fig. 7, which summarizes the algorithm in a few major steps: mapping the crisp inputs to fuzzy linguistic values using membership functions, defining the rule base necessary to make decisions, evaluating the rules to draw conclusion, aggregating the evaluated fuzzy outputs and mapping the fuzzy output to crisp output using defuzzification (delineated in Sect. 4). A graphical view of output error (here, offloading layer error) of the fuzzy inference system for different combinations of inputs (here, task size and resource utilization) based on the reference data is shown in Fig. 8. The inference system performs well for most of the given input spaces.

Figures 9, 10 and 11 show three continuous 3D control surfaces for all possible combinations of inputs (ts, ru, t^{max}) across the entire range to describe

Fig. 7. Simulation result through rule inference.

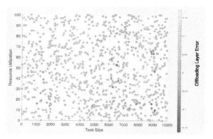

Fig. 8. Error distribution with respect to task size and resource utilization.

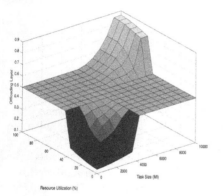

Fig. 9. Task size-resource utilization.

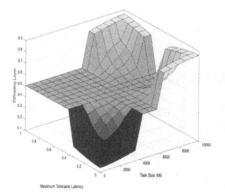

Fig. 10. Task size-maximum tolerable latency.

the relationship between inputs and the output for the fuzzy inference system. These control surfaces govern a lookup table that uses the x and y coordinates from the inputs to look at the output value. The control surfaces pertain to a system that offloads tasks to minimize latency and efficiently utilize resources. Furthermore, to validate the designed fuzzy inference system, we compared the system-generated output values with the actual evaluated data (i.e., reference validation data), shown vividly in Fig. 12. The prediction error plot shown in Fig. 13 shows the differences between values assessed by the fuzzy inference system and the actual calculated data. The root mean squared error (RMSE) shown in the plot marks the average difference and accuracy of the system model. We can say that the lower the RMSE value, the better the model is. Furthermore, we have analyzed the simulations of our proposed algorithm, FOTO, in terms

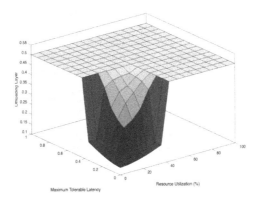

Fig. 11. Resource utilization-maximum tolerable latency.

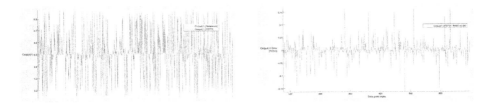

Fig. 12. System validation through reference data.

Fig. 13. Prediction error showing RMSE value.

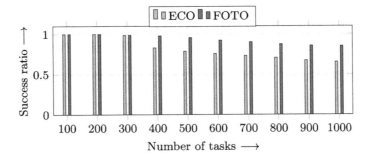

Fig. 14. Comparison of success ratio vs. number of tasks.

of success ratio. We have compared our FOTO algorithm with an edge-cloud offloading (ECO) algorithm to validate the performance. Here, the success ratio is the ratio of the number of tasks successfully offloaded within their maximum tolerable latency to the total tasks. However, with the increase in number of tasks, the load on the system increases, making tasks miss their tolerable latency, which may result in a decrease in the success ratio. From Fig. 14, it is observed that both algorithms initially performed well when the number of tasks was less. However, using ECO, with the increase in tasks, the success ratio dropped from 0.98 (i.e., 98%) for 300 tasks to 0.65 (i.e., 65%) for 1000 tasks. Our FOTO algorithm dropped the success ratio from 0.98 (i.e., 98%) for 300 tasks to 0.85 (i.e., 85 %) for 1000 tasks. With this comparison, it is evident that our proposed FOTO algorithm outperforms the ECO algorithm.

6 Conclusion

The federation of IoT, edge and cloud is quite demanding as well as rewarding as it facilitates seamless service provisioning across each computing layer leveraging the osmotic computing principle. Osmotic computing, which emphasizes fluidity and adaptability across computing environments, is harnessed to facilitate swift task offloading throughout the federated environment. This paper presents a fuzzy logic-based task offloading algorithm for handling tasks efficiently and properly utilising resources. Fuzzy logic handles imprecise and uncertain information, often encountered in dynamic and complex computing environments. The algorithm introduces a degree of flexibility and adaptability in decision-making processes. We analyzed our fuzzy inference system using rule inference, error distribution, control surface and system validation. These analyses provide insights into the robustness and reliability of the FOTO algorithm, demonstrating its capability to make informed decisions in diverse scenarios. We also analyzed the performance of our proposed algorithm, FOTO, in terms of success ratio, and it outperformed another offloading algorithm. From the analysis, it can be stated that integrating IoT-edge-cloud using osmotic computing and fuzzy logic made the offloading process smooth and efficient. This research paves the way for further exploration and development in the field of federated computing, offering a valuable contribution to advancing IoT and edge computing technologies.

Acknowledgment. The authors acknowledge the Veer Surendra Sai University of Technology, Burla, National Institute of Technology, Warangal and Kalinga Institute of Industrial Technology, Bhubaneswar, for providing a conducive research environment and access to laboratory facilities that greatly facilitated the progress of this work.

References

1. An, X., Fan, R., Hu, H., Zhang, N., Atapattu, S., Tsiftsis, T.A.: Joint task offloading and resource allocation for IoT edge computing with sequential task dependency. IEEE Internet Things J. **9**(17), 16546–16561 (2022)
2. Carnevale, L., Celesti, A., Galletta, A., Dustdar, S., Villari, M.: From the cloud to edge and iot: a smart orchestration architecture for enabling osmotic computing. In: 2018 32nd International Conference on Advanced Information Networking and Applications Workshops (WAINA), pp. 419–424 (2018). https://doi.org/10.1109/WAINA.2018.00122
3. Chen, J., Wu, H., Li, R., Jiao, P.: Green parallel online offloading for dsci-type tasks in iot-edge systems. IEEE Trans. Ind. Inf. **18**(11), 7955–7966 (2022). https://doi.org/10.1109/TII.2022.3167668

4. Fan, W., et al.: Collaborative service placement, task scheduling, and resource allocation for task offloading with edge-cloud cooperation. IEEE Trans. Mob. Comput. (2022)
5. Gao, B., Zhou, Z., Liu, F., Xu, F.: Winning at the starting line: joint network selection and service placement for mobile edge computing. In: IEEE INFOCOM 2019-IEEE Conference on Computer Communications, pp. 1459–1467. IEEE (2019)
6. Hong, Z., Chen, W., Huang, H., Guo, S., Zheng, Z.: Multi-hop cooperative computation offloading for industrial IoT-edge-cloud computing environments. IEEE Trans. Parallel Distrib. Syst. **30**(12), 2759–2774 (2019)
7. Ibrar, M., et al.: Adaptive capacity task offloading in multi-hop d2d-based social industrial IoT. IEEE Trans. Netw. Sci. Eng. **10**(5), 2843–2852 (2023). https://doi.org/10.1109/TNSE.2022.3192478
8. Li, Q., Peng, B., Li, Q., Lin, M., Chen, C., Peng, S.: A latency-optimal task offloading scheme using genetic algorithm for dag applications in edge computing. In: 2023 8th International Conference on Cloud Computing and Big Data Analytics (ICCCBDA), pp. 344–348. IEEE (2023)
9. Liu, J., Zhang, Y., Ren, J., Zhang, Y.: Auction-based dependent task offloading for IoT users in edge clouds. IEEE Internet Things J. **10**(6), 4907–4921 (2023). https://doi.org/10.1109/JIOT.2022.3221431
10. Mamdani, E.H., Assilian, S.: An experiment in linguistic synthesis with a fuzzy logic controller. Int. J. Man Mach. Stud. **7**(1), 1–13 (1975)
11. Neha, B., Panda, S.K., Sahu, P.K.: An efficient task mapping algorithm for osmotic computing-based ecosystem. Int. J. Inf. Technol. **13**, 1303–1308 (2021)
12. Neha, B., Panda, S.K., Sahu, P.K., Sahoo, K.S., Gandomi, A.H.: A systematic review on osmotic computing. ACM Trans. Internet Things **3**(2), 1–30 (2022)
13. Panda, S.K., Dhiman, A., Bhuriya, P.: Efficient real-time task-based scheduling algorithms for iot-fog-cloud architecture. In: 2023 14th International Conference on Computing Communication and Networking Technologies (ICCCNT), pp. 1–7. IEEE (2023)
14. Qu, G., Wu, H., Li, R., Jiao, P.: Dmro: a deep meta reinforcement learning-based task offloading framework for edge-cloud computing. IEEE Trans. Netw. Serv. Manag. **18**(3), 3448–3459 (2021)
15. Ren, J., Yu, G., He, Y., Li, G.Y.: Collaborative cloud and edge computing for latency minimization. IEEE Trans. Veh. Technol. **68**(5), 5031–5044 (2019)
16. Sharma, V., You, I., Kumar, R., Kim, P.: Computational offloading for efficient trust management in pervasive online social networks using osmotic computing. IEEE Access **5**, 5084–5103 (2017)
17. Sun, C., et al.: Task offloading for end-edge-cloud orchestrated computing in mobile networks. In: 2020 IEEE Wireless Communications and Networking Conference (WCNC), pp. 1–6. IEEE (2020)
18. Thanedar, M.A., Panda, S.K.: A dynamic resource management algorithm for maximizing service capability in fog-empowered vehicular ad-hoc networks. In: Peer-to-Peer Networking and Applications, pp. 1–15 (2023)
19. Thanedar, M.A., Panda, S.K.: An energy-efficient resource allocation algorithm for managing on-demand services in fog-enabled vehicular ad-hoc networks. Int. J. Web Grid Serv., 1–24 (2024)
20. Ullah, I., Lim, H.K., Seok, Y.J., Han, Y.H.: Optimizing task offloading and resource allocation in edge-cloud networks: a DRL approach. J. Cloud Comput. **12**(1), 112 (2023)

21. Villari, M., Celesti, A., Fazio, M.: Towards osmotic computing: looking at basic principles and technologies. In: Barolli, L., Terzo, O. (eds.) CISIS 2017. AISC, vol. 611, pp. 906–915. Springer, Cham (2018). https://doi.org/10.1007/978-3-319-61566-0_86
22. Villari, M., Fazio, M., Dustdar, S., Rana, O., Ranjan, R.: Osmotic computing: a new paradigm for edge/cloud integration. IEEE Cloud Comput. **3**(6), 76–83 (2016)
23. Wu, H., Wolter, K., Jiao, P., Deng, Y., Zhao, Y., Xu, M.: Eedto: an energy-efficient dynamic task offloading algorithm for blockchain-enabled IoT-edge-cloud orchestrated computing. IEEE Internet Things J. **8**(4), 2163–2176 (2021). https://doi.org/10.1109/JIOT.2020.3033521
24. Xu, J., Chen, L., Zhou, P.: Joint service caching and task offloading for mobile edge computing in dense networks. In: IEEE INFOCOM 2018-IEEE Conference on Computer Communications, pp. 207–215. IEEE (2018)
25. Zhang, Q., Gui, L., Zhu, S., Lang, X.: Task offloading and resource scheduling in hybrid edge-cloud networks. IEEE Access **9**, 85350–85366 (2021)

Traveler's Demand Reactive Dynamic Online Bus Routing [TraDeR-DOBR] to Improvize Comfort Perception in Intelligent Public Transport System

Akhilesh Ladha[1](✉), Archana Nayak[2], and Nirbhay Kumar Chaubey[3]

[1] RCTI, Ahmedabad, Gujarat, India
ladhaakhilesh@gmail.com
[2] GIDC Engineering College, Abhrama, Gujarat, India
[3] Ganpat university, Mehsana, Gujarat, India
nirbhay@ieee.com

Abstract. In today's time travellers of urban areas prefer public transport as first choice of commute to enjoy the hassle-free ride to their destination. Also, the improvement in infrastructure including roads, traffic flow, AC buses, etc., general people are motivated to use them as and when possible. But static routing forces people to travel in heavily loaded vehicle, resulting in decrease of comfort perception which people have while using personal vehicle. The work on dynamic routing for public transport vehicle have been put into thoughts to minimize the load a vehicle is carrying that leads to minimization in travel and waiting time. The proposed architecture is simulated in SUMO tool to compute and analysed on request allocated per vehicle, average waiting time, and average travel time for set of requests over variously categorized network topology. The result shows that unsatisfied request when carried ahead to be attempted again in upcoming round decreases the request dropping count by 3 to 5% depending on network with slight increase of 1.1% in response time.

Keywords: ITS · Dynamic Routing · Request/Demand · Scheduling · Waiting Time(WT) · Travel Time (TT)

1 Introduction

Many residents of both urban and rural part of country are encouraged to make usage of the Transport System for Public (PTS) in the current era of transportation system modernization because of improvements in improved safety, citizen-friendly infrastructure development and expanded availability. This expansion of the recent time transportation sector is also essential to the nation's continued economic prosperity. The initial configuration is no longer able to accommodate all commuters while retaining their Comfort Perception (CP), especially in densely populated areas.

Due to recent advancements in loan accessibility and auto manufacturing automation, the number of independent car owners in metropolitan areas has skyrocketed. The number of private vehicles has increased, which has led to a significant increase in connected issues such accidents, fuel consumption, and toxic gas emissions when driving and halting at signals and jams. The Government of India reported that over ₹ 425K is spent on developing roads in India.

The sector ITS (Intelligent Transportation Systems) has seen a great deal of R&D in recent times. Numerous remedies were put up and put into practice to address the problem. One of the reasons covered in the study is PTS's long-standing use of the fixed route approach. The implementation of a dynamic routing approach can address issues arising from fixed routes. Dynamic routing is already present in public transportation systems such as auto-rickshaws, Demand Responsive Transit (DRT), and hired taxis. Every option increases the passenger's out-of-pocket expenses. hence raising the trip cost per kilometer from up to ten times or higher.

The tiny fleet size is the primary cause of the cost increase. The paper suggests a Dynamic Routing method for Commuters' Vehicles (CVs) as the solution. The strategy is to use demand-based routing, similar to DRT, but with a larger fleet, similar to PTS. The algorithm was then simulated across five distinct network types using the SUMO tool, and several parameters were observed, including request blockage probability, average waiting time, average journey time, request allotted per vehicle, and computed response time.

2 Motivation

Currently, over 30% of India's population lives in urban areas; by 2031, that number is expected to rise to over 45%. Making public transit a comfortable, adaptable, affordable, and reliable service is one way to deal with this issue. Having a service that meets the demands of both passengers and operators is one of the crucial steps in this direction [1]. Intelligent Transportation Systems (ITS) are essential parts of our life and is capable of providing various services such as gathering and processing of data, traffic management, statistics about travel, freight transportation, and rescue management. These systems' objectives are improving crowding, safety & security, economic productivity, fuel-saving, and efficiency. ITS is incorporated with information technology, wireless communication, smartphones, the Internet of Things (IoT), and Unmanned Aerial Vehicle (UAV) to solve transportation problems [2].

Demand-Responsive public bus system (DR-PBS) [3], that requires some additional information about every probable passenger like location, direction, purpose, and frequency of the traveler.

Section 3 the related work carried in domain is discussed. Following it the proposed Algorithm and System Architecture is given in Sect. 4. The parameters that plays significant role in system analysis are discussed in detail along with Simulation Setup in Sect. 5. Results achieved are discussed in Sect. 6 with comparative analysis on them.

3 Related Work

Melis, L., et al. (2021) [4] is among the first studies to present the idea of dynamic on-demand routing. It takes as inputs a list of requests, a grid of bus stops, a supply of fixed-capacity buses, and each request includes the estimated time of travel as well as a list of nearby bus stations for both the arrival and the departure. The algorithm determines both the bus routes and the places assigned to requests. By combining local search with a large neighborhood heuristic discovery, the overall user trip time is minimized.

Here, the conventional approaches to an intelligent transportation system with dynamic routing according to user demand are explained. Rajkumar, S.C. and Deborah, L.J. (2021) [5] introduced a machine learning-based vehicle scheduling system based on user demand for vehicle traffic optimization. In this case, real-time sensors and effective communication were used to reserve seats in the cars instantly. Then, the development of effective scheduling algorithms led to the acquisition of easy transportation. By increasing the use of public transportation, the addition of machine learning-based vehicle demand forecast resulted in more precise scheduling and reduced use of private automobiles in the city.

[6] talked about fuel usage and greenhouse gas emissions in relation to the vehicle's load and results mentioned indicates a straight relation. The major derivation done in the paper is finding the relation between hazardous gas like NO_x and CO_2 and number of passenger the vehicle is carrying, so that optimizing the load GHG in the air can be minimized.

[7] and [8] were more focused on the amount of energy used by EV buses and the unpredictability of different driving, road, and traffic situations. The goal of using EV buses was to lower air pollution and improve the quality of the air for human habitation. Those who used public transportation did not have a great experience because of this uncertainty. Numerous academics have followed the lead in order to estimate the number of commuters so that the transportation vehicle may be scheduled and planned appropriately, while the excellent work done by Archana et al. [9] on passenger flow prediction could aid schedulers in allocating vehicles based on passenger demands.

[10–12] are the work who defined new terms like Deadhead Trip, Skip stop strategy, In-Travel Time, etc. so that the research gets focused on the aligned parameter in order to optimize the working of the system and have better system utilization with fuel efficiency increase, reduced emission, and minimal total time spend by the passenger.

[13–16] have concentrated on developing a dynamic routing algorithm for public transportation vehicles in order to solve the BFM challenge. The main goal was to assign the car based on flow requests of indented traveller, which is actually provided as input to system in variety of methods. These publications are analyzed in detail in Sect. 6 and are used as a reference point for our comparison of outcomes.

4 Architecture and Algorithms

The proposed architecture in the transportation system in this section that is suggested in the study while describing the various algorithms and protocols/protocol stacks that are used to assess the system's parameters.

The proposed system is made up of several interconnected parts that cooperate to make it easier for passengers to move from the nearest boarding point to the nearest station at their destination in a comfortable manner.

4.1 System Constituents

Intricate below are the system constituents:-

- **Network Design**: The Graph G(V,E) designed representing the city network are modelled where
  V: be no. of Vertices of graphs indicating bus stops
  E: be no. of edges of the graphs indicating the interconnecting roads.

The networks with different properties as mentioned in [17] are used in the work and are displayed in Figs. 1. The networks properties stated are for standard networks like Mandl-Swiss and Mumford0 networks, while the other networks mentioned are the subgraphs of the standard networks, hence can be applied to standard networks as an whole as well.

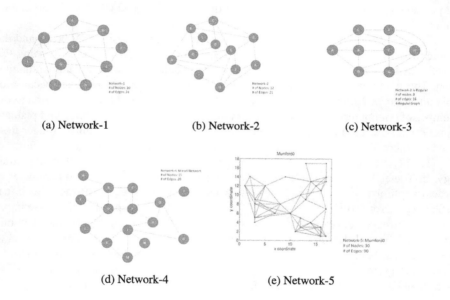

Fig. 1. Different Tested Networks for Algorithm

- **Demands / User Calls**: Set of Traveller's ticket denoted with $T = \{T_1, T_2, \ldots, T_n\}$ in IPTS is set initiated in system by users act for $U = \{u_1, u_2, \ldots, u_n\}$. Demand raised by u_i is modeled in a quadruplet $\{T_i, L_i^S, L_i^D, CV_{id}\}$ where L_i^S and L_i^D be set out as the journey starting point and journey terminating location for i^{th} ticket timestamped as T_i, and CV_{id} be sign of the public vehicle indicated by ID registered to Commuter Marking Stops (CMS). In the system $|L_i^S, L_i^D|$ denotes the total number of estimated calls over a duration of time (of a day), and $|PTS_{id}|$ signifies the count of PTS that are assisting all calls.

- **Commuters' Vehicle (CV):** The vehicle that ultimately answers the commuter's calls or fulfills their demands is the one designated by CV_{id} is Commuters' Vehicle. Every request U_i that enters the system is attempted to be assigned a CV by the route selection mechanism that will be explained later. The request dropping probability P_b, which is a critical factor in selecting the optimal route selection algorithm, is influenced by all requests for which the system is unable to assign a CV.
  All the CV's are embedded with many sensors into it. These sensors provides various information about CV running into the system. The sensor includes Fuel Level Indicator Sensor (CV_{id}^{fuel}), Gas Emission measuring sensors ($CV_{id}^{emission}$), Tyre Pressure Sensor ($CV_{id}^{pressure}$, and IR Sensor (CV_{id}^{IR}). This sensor values also contributes in cost computation while making decision of Best suitable CV from different CV's suggested by Algorithm which can fulfil a particular request.
- **Ticket Granting Desk (TGD):** Ticket granting desk (TGD) The TGD is the device that receives user calls and requests, routes them to the server, and assigns a CV to each request. After returning CV_{id} for the demand to TGD, the selection of route and server for CV allocation issues a ticket with the following characteristics.

$$TKT_{PTSV_{id}}^{U_i} = \sigma(L_i^S, L_i^D, PTSV_{id}, T_i, B_T, A_T) \tag{1}$$

The characteristics listed in the ticket will be used to calculate a number of additional parameters, such as the estimated waiting time (W_T) and the estimated travel time (T_T). These parameters are used to set time limits for waiting and travel in order to preserve comfort perception and prevent route divergence issues that could occur because the system is dynamic.
- **Commuter Vehicle Stoppage (CVS):** These are the set of stoppages in transportation network. These are the points at which the user can enter or exit the CV. For each CVS to be identified in the system, a unique identifier (CVS_{id}) is assigned. Additionally, it keeps track of a tuple for every CV_i that includes that CVS_{id} in its forward path. That contains information like
  EA_i^T - Estimated Arrival Time of CV_i,
  ED_i^T - Estimated Departure Time of CV_i,
  $C_i^{CVS_{id}}$ - Cost value of path for CV_i having CVS_{id} into its route.
  max_τ^{id} - Maximum of cost value for any CV_i having CVS_{id} in its route. Its calculated based on historical data.
  $\tau(R)$ - Estimated Response time calculated based on historical data and network statistics.
- **Route Estimation and Choice:** The proposed is PTS route estimation and choosing theorem. Path choosing code proposed in [13] where R_i^{curr} and R_i^{prev} designates approaching and previous stop of commuter vehicle CV_i represented as $R = \{R_i^{curr}, t_i^0, F_i, \eta_i, Q_i, R_i^{prev}, \delta\}$ which picks up the request indicated as (L_i^S, L_i^D) highlighted at T_i time. Other parameter being t_i^0-initial start time; F_i-Fuel Indication; η_i-emission indicator; Q_i-passenger capacity; T_i^{prev}-stored historical transactions; and δ-percentage of dropped requests on a particular route R.
  In order to locate all possible routes $R_i's$ on which the request might be transmitted, the Check_Route method looks for vehicles that currently follow different routes from the ones that the Fetch_Route function looks for. If no straight path exists, it

then attempts to update available routes finding all feasible CV calls Update_Path process adding request and updating selected R.

- **Commuter Marking Stops**: Commuters' Marking Stops (CMS) is precisely stated possible all locations at which traveller can make travel ticket request and board the assigned CV. Every CMS in system can be professed in Six ascribed tuple $\{A_i^T, D_i^T, C_i, S_i, MAX_T, \tau(R)\}$ where A_i^T and D_i^T depicts the anticipated time of arrival and departure of CV_i at CMS_T, the cost of the route that CV_i is now following, C_i, cannot be greater than MAX_T. The reaction time of CMS to calculate route information and assign the optimal CV for each raised request is $\tau(R)$. The Machine Learning module can receive the route request data produced by CMS and use it for analysis and forecasting purposes.
- **Sensors for IoT**: Below is the list of sensors included in the model:-
  1. **Electro-chemical Sensors**
  2. **Micro-emission sensors**
  3. **Raspberry Pi 4**

The sensor mentioned here are few of what actually can be deployed for various operations like detecting and measuring hazardous gases emission like carbon monoxide (CO), nitric oxide (NO_x), phosgene, hydrogen cyanide (HCN), arsine, phosphine, boranes, silane, germane, soluble carbon compounds of hydrogen. Since the specifics of this are outside the purview of this work, they are not covered in great length. Raspberry Pi 4, have a lot of functionalities built in to be used. A very small credit-sized computer/laptop at a very affordable price can be set up to perform multiple activities including decision making in Public Transport Vehicle Selection.

4.2 Interfacing Layers

There are two interacting layers in the suggested architecture. The extra benefit that these layers offer is the division of tasks among various modules and the coherence of their operations. The 2 interfacing layers are described below:

- **IOT-BUS and Network Module Interface**: The IOT-BUS Modules and the Network Module are connected by this interface. This interface can be seen of as a FOG layer linking various BUS modules. Data from these modules can be combined here, and certain operations can be carried out to lighten the load on the end server that is responsible for the Dynamic Route Selection Algorithm (DRSA).
- **Deploy and Data Distribution Module Interface**: The Data Computational Center, which might be a cloud configuration, is connected to the various network modules using this interface. Since different data may have several possibilities and capabilities, the distribution center can select what, when, and where to convey the data it receives based on the data it receives from various networks.

4.3 Architecture of TraDeR-DOBR

TraDeR-DOBR [Fig. 2] is a Four module architectonics is described beneath:

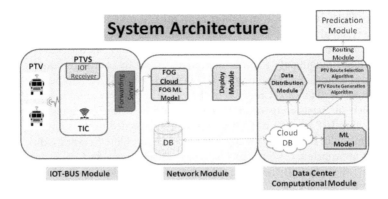

Fig. 2. System Architecture

- **IoT-Bus Module**: IT is the Internet Of Things arrangement set of 'n' Commuter Vehicles CV (= $CV_1, CV_2, CV_3, \ldots, CV_n$) operating inside the network to transport passengers from the specified destination L_i^S to reach its intended position L_i^D, at distinct 'm' Commutter Transit Vehicle Stations CVS (=$CVS_1, CVS_2, \ldots, CVS_m$) having atmost 'p' ticket granting desk TGD (=$TGD_1^k, TGD_2^k, \ldots, TGD_p^k$) at CVS_k. Every one of these requests (T_i) is sent to the high-end server, the assigned function runs and motor vehicle is designated handling the request.
  There are 2 sets of IoT Module installed for communication between CV & CVS and CVS & TGD, which are briefed below:
  • IoT Module working for communication between CV_i and CVS_j, when a CV_i arrives at any CVS_j a connection is build between IoT module set at CVS_j and setup at CV_i for information exchange between them.
  Each CV_i has an IoT module equipped with a variety of sensors. In order to compute General Hazardous Gas (GHG) and determine the effect of hazardous gas like Carbon Dioxide (CO_2), Carbon Monoxide (CO), and Nitrogen Oxide (NO_x) by defined approach as mentioned in Eq. 2 along with fuel consumption, the data collected by the emission sensor set at CV_i is stored locally with memory connected to raspberry-pi and the fuel level indication (FL_i) for this CV_i. When it halts there, the data is sent to the CVS_j memory using Message Queuing Telemetry Transport (MQTT) and is forwarded to the Server Module.

$$GHG_i = \sum_i \sum_j \sigma(Emm_j^{R_i}, \alpha, L_i) \qquad (2)$$

Where $Emm_j^{R_i}$ is emission made by CV_j carrying average load of L_i while running on Route R_i, this reading of emmision is taken using the sensors setup in each CV's. α is the parameter effecting performance of vehicle like fuel type, fuel quality used, year of manufacturing, maintenance schedule, etc. This relation is measured by the σ function defined over parameters mentioned.

The CMS_j collects information from all CV_is visiting this station over a fix time interval (τ). The CMS_j prepares summary of all the information received and finds a free slot to forward it to server module. As this information is not required immediately to make certain decisions by routing module.
- Between the Ticket Granting Desk (TGD_k) and CMS_j, another IoT Module is configured. The ticket request in the type $Msg = (Timestamp, T_i, CMS_j)$, created at the issuing counter IoT module for the ith request, is sent to the receiving IoT module of CMS_j before being routed to the server's route selection module. Following the algorithm's execution, the Server module selects the most appropriate CV, assigns it to the request, answers CMS_j, and issues the ticket. A portion of the route selection module is locally deployed in order to reduce reaction time.

- **Server/Routing Module**: The two IoT modules that are operating in coherence with one another as previously mentioned send messages to the Server module that are created at CMS_j. The four main algorithms in the server module are Emission Compute, Route_selection, Prediction, and Route_selection. Underneath detailed are these algorithms:
  - **Route_Selection Algorithm** One of the key elements of the design, the Route Selection Algorithm-??, is proposed in this work.

    The Route Selection Algorithm processes each request T_i that the server receives initially. The algorithm looks through its existing PTV_Route table, which lists all of the CVs that are currently operating in the system together with the routes that they are now traveling. The algorithm identifies every potential CV that can fulfill the request, meaning that the passenger can take it and continue on its journey. In the process of searching $CV(s)$, one of the two scenarios pertaining to request fulfillment may occur.

    Case-I $CV(s)$ found in PTV_Route table:

    In the process of finding the route(s) that fulfill the request T_i, the theorem produces a routes listed in $CV(s)$. This collection of routes is then passed through the Bus_selection code, which uses Eq. 3 for T_i to determine the ideal vehicle CV_{opt}^i.

$$CV_{opt}^i = Bus\_selection(CVs, \Pi, max_\tau) \quad (3)$$

The cost function is denoted by Π. The various attributes that make up the cost function include the load carried by all qualified CVs (LC^{CV_k}), All Eligible CVs' Fuel Level $Fuel^{CV_k}$ When the CV reaches $PTSV_{id}$ from the location where the request is generated, Estimated Load $Esti_{LC}^{CV_k}$, and The TT estimated of the call U_i for each potential CV is $Esti_{TT}^{CV_k}$

Case-II Route not found in PTV_Route table:

The $Update\_Path$ function is called by the algorithm if there isn't a direct path listed in the path Table. This function's job is to determine which of the following three scenarios applies: the request's source and destination are not available in the Route Table, or it is the only source L_i^S or only destination L_i^D. The next course of action is determined by the unavailability of the exact source and/or destination. These sub-steps depends as per Failure in Route Fetch stated below:

(a) The method Re_Update_Route is called if the destination L_i^D is not accessible but source of the call L_i^S exists with at-least one data of the PTV_Route_Table. In order to fulfill this requirement, this approach analyzes every route that can be updated, as indicated in the Fig. 3a.

The scenario depicted in the figure is one in which every CV is traveling along at least one path where the source of any request is accessible. The modified route allows for the addition of the request's destination. As shown in the picture, the threshold (MAX_τ) established for each route is taken into account by the algorithm when it updates the route. The overall journey time and route length shouldn't go over the predetermined amount. This will also keep everyone's overall travel time to a minimum and preserve the system's overall comfort perception (CP). The threshold provided to the system also solves the route divergent issue that rises due to dynamic nature, that can cause a CV to enter a trip which is infinitely long i.e. never ending.

(b) The method Re_Update_Route is invoked if the destination of the request L_i^D exists with one route at least from the PTV_Route_Table matching the condition of source L_i^S unavailability. This approach examines every path that could be modified to fulfill this request, as seen in the Fig. 3b.

(c) Source L_i^S and Destination L_i^D none available with any of route of PTV_Route_Table then the procedure Re_Update_Route is called. In order to fulfill this requirement, this approach analyzes every route that can be updated, as indicated in the Fig. 3c.

Such a request requires the most processing power. As a result, the system processes such requests using a probabilistic technique. The program attempts to forecast, with a certain degree of probability, the number of future requests that could be fulfilled provided processing for those requests is done. The request is either processed further or rejected based on the calculated probability parameter. All requests for which the algorithm was unable to compute an updated route are carried to the next round of selection. This is just to give another try for the call to be satisfied to improve the satisfying percentage. Outcome of the approach is drop in probability of unsatisfied call at the expense of a longer response time.

Bus_Selection Algorithm (BSA) is then given the set of CVs. The BSA is in charge of selecting the best vehicle and sending it back to CVS, the source from which the request(s) is(are) generated. It also enters the request and all of its attributes into a tuple called $(TS_i, L_i^S, L_i^D, CV_id, MAX_\tau, MAX\_TT_i^{Esti}, MAX\_WT_i^{Esti})$, making records available for utilization in future allocation. Equation 4 provides a description of the space-time complexity of the algorithm under consideration. The equation shows that the number of nodes in the executing routes and the overall number of routes now being run in the system have a significant impact on the complexity.

$$\tau_r \leftarrow \eta_r^{\hat{k}} + TCDP(\xi_{CV}^{R_i}) \tag{4}$$

The routing module also have procedure for Dynamic Route Generation and suggestion. This routes are keeping into consideration the request successfully processed per day and predicted request using a machine learning approach.

- **Predictor Module**: The predictor module is machine learning based procedure to predict future request using Recurrent Neural Network (RNN) with hyper parameter as request and provides them as input to Route_Generation and Route_Selection Algorithms. This prediction module takes input from historical data, which is nothing but data about passenger request/demand received in system for routing also request which it has received in the day till the clock time.

The accuracy of this predictor module determines effectiveness of the routes generated by Route_Generation algorithm. The better the routes generated less will be request dropped and less will be re-routing time and lesser re-routing time will have lesser response time, waiting time and optimum travel time.

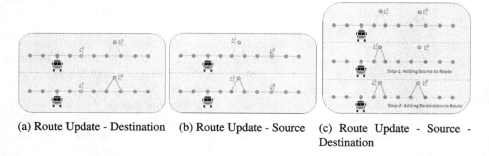

(a) Route Update - Destination   (b) Route Update - Source   (c) Route Update - Source - Destination

Fig. 3. Different Route Update Scenarios

5 Simulation Setup

The demand-based prediction of route theorem was put into practice & run on the number of requests listed in Table 1 over five distinct city networks, each of which has unique features as seen in Fig. 1 and is covered in Sect. 4.1. Figures 4, 5, and 6 show the observed results.

The algorithm is run using several selection criteria to determine which potential CV to assign to the request. Since the network's nodes are highly connected in Network-1[NW-1] even though it has least call drop, it is not viable to build such an infrastructure or a road network with such high intersection connectivity in the actual world.

The six distinct criteria for choosing a CV that meets the need are listed below.

1. Criteria-1 [A1] - FIRST FOUND: In this case, the vehicle follows a circular route with a distinct return route in any public transportation system, maintaining the source and destination of the original route. Consider 1-2-3-4-5-6-1. This method helps the algorithm's dynamic nature by lowering the amount of requests dropped. Here, the shortest response time is achieved by choosing the first route that is judged to be satisfactory. It was found that for networks Figs. 1b and 1d, the dropping probability was approximately 25% and 20%, respectively for Mumford0 [Fig. 1e] network. 10% to 15% is call drop range for network Fig. 1c.
2. Criteria-2 [A2] - FIRST PROBABILISTIC FOUND: Probabilistic selection is the second CV criterion. Here, each potential CV is scanned one at a time, and each CV is selected with a 90% probability, on non-selection CV scan continuous. The goal of this strategy was to distribute requests in some way to reduce traffic on all routes and optimize CV utilization.

    We saw a certain distribution of requests among the many CVs that could be in the system, but the number of requests that were rejected was about the same as that of selection algorithm-1, which is actually a quite high figure.
3. Criteria-3 [A3] - $CV_{MINLOAD}$: Foundation of CV selection criteria-3 is the selection of the least loaded CV among all potential CVs that meet the increased demand. Comparing the demand decrease to CV selection criterion 1 and 2, it was shown to be lowered by a range of 3% to 6%.
4. Criteria-4 [A4] $-CV_{MAXLOAD}$: Since the goal of this strategy was to carry as many passengers as possible on as few routes as possible, candidates were chosen based on their most complete resumes. By using this method of execution, the service provider can run more CV on routes with high demand and less CV on routes with low demand, thereby satisfying the greatest number of customers. By doing this, the system's overall operating costs will be reduced.

    The request dropping probability for this algorithm differed from all previously described selection criteria by ±1%.
5. Criteria-5 [A5] - MINMAX SORTED: Probabilistic CV selection, from least loaded to most loaded, is Selection Criterion No. 5. Here, our goal was to determine which passenger distribution over the CV had the lowest likelihood of a request being dropped. Although there was a trade-off in response time, this was accomplished. The reaction time increased by 2% to 5%.
6. Criteria-6 [A6] - RANDOM: In order to optimize the amount of time required for TGD to grant tickets and notify the CV of route updates in a timely manner, an effort was made to reduce the response time per request in Selection Criteria-6. When compared to all algorithms, the average response time is shortened by 3 to 8 ms/request; nonetheless, this technique results in longer average wait times and longer average journey times for passengers.

    We have the shortest response times for criterion-6 on the one hand, but the longest travel and waiting times on the other. Rising the overall time of traveler in system. This will directly impact on how comfortable passengers feel overall and how comfortable they perceive their comfort level to be. The feeling of comfort decreases as passengers engage with the system more.

The outcomes of the aforementioned simulation runs are covered in Sect. 6

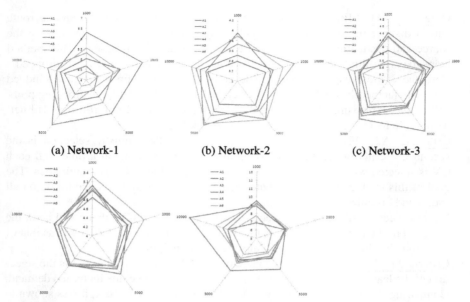

(a) Network-1 (b) Network-2 (c) Network-3
(d) Network-4 Mandl Swiss Network (e) Network-5 Mumford0 Network

Fig. 4. Request Generated Vs Travel Time - Different Networks

Table 1. No of requests/demand

Sr. No.	1	2	3	4	5
# of req	1000	2000	5000	10000	20000

6 Results and Comparison

The algorithm mentioned in Algorithm-Route_Fetch and Algorithm-Route_Update were simulated on Simulation for Urban MObility(SUMO) and results calculated can be seen in Fig. 4, 5, and 6. In-depth discussion is done below for each results.

The Fig. 4 shows the average time required to travel by total request generated using UAROUTER algorithm for system on multiple network under simulation environments.

1. Across all algorithms running on various types of networks, the travel time pattern in relation to the quantity of requests made to the system stays constant. This means that we can concentrate on the area generated by various criteria in various networks.
2. Here we can observe that criteria-4 has the smallest surface area in comparison to other criterion for all specified networks except for Network-2 whereby it has second largest area with very little difference. Hence we can conclude that for travel time (which has a significant contribution in Comfort Perception) the Criteria-4 has the best performance.

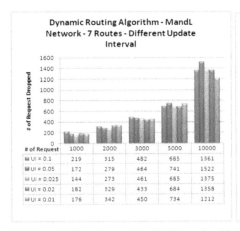
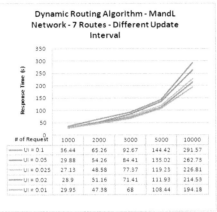

(a) Dynamic Routing on MandL Network with Different Update Interval

(b) MandL Network - Different Update Interval - Response Time

Fig. 5. Dynamic Routing on MandL NW changing Update Interval

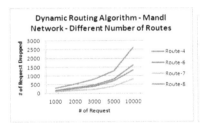
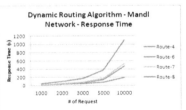

(a) Dynamic Routing - MandL Network with Varying Initial Routes

(b) MandL Network - Varying Initial Routes - Reponse Time

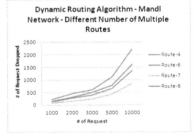
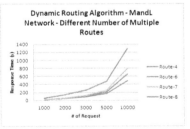

(c) Dynamic Routing on MandL Network changing Initial Multiple Routes

(d) MandL Network - Varying Multiple Initial Routes - Reponse Time

Fig. 6. MandL-Swiss NW changing No. of Routes - UI = 0.025

3. NW-4 and NW-5 - MandL-Swiss Network and Mumford - the standard networks used in research by several researchers simulating the scenario of real city is having some exceptional values but it then gets neutralized by averaging values over multiple simulation runs.

Figure 5 shows the direct relation between the Update Interval and Request dropping probability, with the decrease in update interval the request dropping probability decreases. The reduction in dropping probability is 8.37%, but at the same time the reduction in response time by 33%. Also among the different UI values the interval of 0.025 i.e. update of routes after every 2.5% of request if performed has minimum request drop. The reason for this is with reduction in update interval the number of request to be processed per slot are less. On contrary these will increase the overhead on network. The network time which includes transmission time and propagation time, are ignored as per scope of the paper. These could be a future focus point, deriving the relation between update interval, request drop probability, and response time.

The outcome of high blocking probability obtained for standard networks (NW4-MandL) are further analyzed by increasing the number of vehicles (routes) running into the system. The results obtained for MandL network are shown in Fig. 6. The results shows that the blocking probability is directly proportional to number of buses running into the system. More the buses lesses will be the blocking probability.

Also with UI value set 0.025 we have better performance in request dropped with an average decrease of 3.7% to 11.18% for different network under selection criteria-4. For Mandl-Swiss Network Fig. 6a we have request dropping probability of 771 for UI = 0.025 in comparison to 817 with UI = 0.1 and Route-7 on circular route followed. That means the UI value 0.025 gives more than 5% improvement in request drop probability. But as a trade-off the response time has become 2× as it can be seen in Fig. 6b and 6d.

Table 2. Various tables of observable parameters

Algorithm	Average Response Time					Algorithm	Average Waiting Time				
	NW-1	NW-2	NW-3	NW-4	NW-5		NW-1	NW-2	NW-3	NW-4	NW-5
A1	7.96	18.29	11.52	17.31	331.38	A1	5.32	4.20	4.50	5.09	7.31
A2	11.38	22.83	12.89	21.77	231.74	A2	5.69	4.39	4.68	5.33	6.84
A3	14.11	20.43	11.73	18.37	235.07	A3	5.05	4.07	4.34	5.18	6.19
A4	10.98	20.18	9.86	20.01	221.42	A4	6.89	4.11	4.75	5.44	8.98
A5	11.24	23.21	12.61	20.51	228.65	A5	6.41	4.31	4.54	5.39	7.40
A6	10.07	19.84	10.95	18.13	241.64	A6	5.73	4.28	4.67	5.49	7.39

(a) Average Response Time   (b) Average Waiting Time

Most crucial parameters for any dynamic system is Mean Response Time, specifically for transportation system are Average Wait Time, and Average Time for Travel. The Mean Response Time and Average Wait Time charted in Table 2, and the Average Time for Travel is shown in Fig. 4. The Average Response Time increases from NW-1 to NW-5, as indicated by the table's figures. This finding is accurate because reaction time is closely correlated with network size. With 30 nodes, NW-5 is the largest network in this case and has the fastest response time. Interestingly, nonetheless, for the majority of networks, Algorithm A4 (which selects the CV with the maximum loaded) has the lowest response time when compared to other algorithms. This means that the likelihood of finding a CV for each request is correspondingly faster in highly packed vehicles. The average time to wait and average time of travel, however, are higher for algorithm A4.

It can be seen that algorithm A3, which selects the CV with the least amount of load, is better in terms of average time to wait and average time of travel with UI value 0.025. Due to fewer stoppages along the route and shorter request acceptance slot, the CV will take less time for collection and drop off when there are less passengers on board.

6.1 Comparison

In [13] execution of algorithm was performed only on single network and only one value of Update Interval (UI), here the execution of algorithm was done on 5 networks with different characteristics as per [17] with varying UI and parameters are observed. From the observation NW-Fig. 1d are standard Mandl-Swiss network used for simulation run for real city networks by many researchers will be the prime focus.

Table 3. Percent of request dropped and Peak Load carried by CV under 7 buses running

Routing	%age passenger with no direct route			
	A1	A2	A3	A4
Static	21.31	20.39	11.40	15.83
Dynamic [UI = 0.1]	16.86	15.27	7.28	12.29
Dynamic [UI = 0.025]	15.37	13.95	6.85	11.26

(a) %age travellers provided no direct path in MandL-Swiss NW

Routing	Buses						
	B1	B2	B3	B4	B5	B6	B7
Static	44	86	19	30	24	7	18
Dynamic [UI = 0.1]	49	64	31	30	26	12	16
Dynamic [UI = 0.025]	46	68	32	28	30	12	12

(b) Max no. of travellers boarded bus in MandL-Swiss nw at any instance

Significant improvement in Average Travel Time was obtained by changing the UI value from 0.1 to 0.01 with 0.025 giving the best outcome. The improvement of on an average 9% depicted in Table 3a is considered to be a good improvement in a system which is highly complex and several trade offs are to be taken care.

Also it can be seen from in the Table 3b that for Dynamic Routing with UI 0.025 the distribution of load is still balanced and the value of Comfort Perception (CP) will be better than Static routing and almost in similar range of Dynamic Routing with UI value 0.1.

Authors of [18] tried minimizing the request dropping chances by creating initial routes from the past journey data available assuming that more or less the similar journeys are followed everyday. In our research we took the same approach route generation but observed the request dropping for UI value 0.025 comparing to UI value 0.1 used in [18]. Results are shown in Table 4:

Table 4. Request Drop Probability changing UI for different active routes

Update Interval	Active Routes			
	Route-4	Route-6	Route-7	Route-8
UI = 0.1	28.3%	13.8%	7.9%	16.15%
UI = 0.025	24.9%	12.38%	7.34%	14.63%

7 Conclusion and Future Work

The standard deviation of passenger count is similar for both UI values with a improvement in percent passenger with direct route. Hence it can be concluded that update interval is also a crucial parameter and improvise other accounting parameters.

Research on dynamic routing for vehicles in public transportation systems has begun to take considerable interest. This is now a major area of the Intelligent Transport System's focus. With a modest cost of 18.21 ms of computational time, the system with UI value 0.025 is still able to serve 92% of the requests despite the dropping probability.

There is a lot of room for use in the ITS domain for the design that is suggested in this study. Here, the primary goal was to create a dynamic CV routing mechanism that could handle as many requests as the system could produce. Numerous additional system characteristics are also impacted by dynamic routing's variable update interval (UI). For instance, since passenger load and pollution are directly proportionate, the emission from the vehicle might be reduced using demand balancing between the CVs. The Comfort Perception of passengers is a metric that is dependent on the amount of passengers in the bus and the in-vehicle time, as stated in [19].

References

1. Kumar, B.A., Vanajakshi, L., Subramanian, S.C.: Bus travel time prediction using a time-space discretization approach. Transport. Res. Part C Emerg. Technol. **79**, 308–332 (2017)
2. Escolano, C.O., Billones, R.K.C., Sybingco, E., Fillone, A.D., Dadios, E.P.: Passenger demand forecast using optical flow passenger counting system for bus dispatch scheduling. In: 2016 IEEE Region 10 Conference (TENCON), pp. 1875–1878 (2016)

3. Vansteenwegen, P., et al.: A survey on demand-responsive public bus systems. Transport. Res. Part C: Emerg. Technol. **137**, 103573 (2022)
4. Melis, L., Sörensen, K.: The static on-demand bus routing problem: large neighborhood search for a dial-a-ride problem with bus station assignment. Int. Trans. Oper. Res. **29**(3), 1417–1453 (2022)
5. Rajkumar, S.C., Deborah, L.J.: An improved public transportation system for effective usage of vehicles in intelligent transportation system. Int. J. Commun. Syst. **34**(13), e4910 (2021)
6. Qian, Yu., Li, T., Li, H.: Improving urban bus emission and fuel consumption modeling by incorporating passenger load factor for real world driving. Appl. Energy **161**, 101–111 (2016)
7. Gallet, M., Massier, T., Hamacher, T.: Estimation of the energy demand of electric buses based on real-world data for large-scale public transport networks. Appl. Energy **230**, 344–356 (2018)
8. Abdelaty, H., Mohamed, M.: Uncertainty in electric bus energy consumption: the impacts of grade and driving behaviour (2020)
9. Nayak, A.M., Chaubey, N.: Predicting passenger flow in BTS and MTS using hybrid stacked auto-encoder and softmax regression. In: Chaubey, N., Parikh, S., Amin, K. (eds.) COMS2 2020. CCIS, vol. 1235, pp. 29–41. Springer, Singapore (2020). https://doi.org/10.1007/978-981-15-6648-6_3
10. Nasibov, E., Eliiyi, U., Ertaç, M., Kuvvetli, U.: Deadhead trip minimization in city bus transportation: a real life application. PROMET - Traffic&Transportation **25** (2013)
11. Chen, X., Han, X., Yu, L., Wei, C.: Does operation scheduling make a difference: tapping the potential of optimized design for skipping-stop strategy in reducing bus emissions. Sustainability **9**(10), 1737 (2017)
12. Tomasiello, D.B., Giannotti, M., Arbex, R., Davis, C.: Multi-temporal transport network models for accessibility studies. Trans. GIS **23**(2), 203–223 (2019)
13. Ladha, A., Bhattacharya, P., Chaubey, N., Bodkhe, U.: *IIGPTS*: IoT-based framework for intelligent green public transportation system. In: Singh, P.K., et al. (eds.) Proceedings of First International Conference on Computing, Communications, and Cyber-Security (IC4S 2019). LNNS, vol. 121, pp. 183–195. Springer, Singapore (2020). https://doi.org/10.1007/978-981-15-3369-3_14
14. Gerhards, J., Held, D., Schneider, T., Hirmer, P.: Burst - a dynamic bus routing system. In: 2021 IEEE International Conference on Pervasive Computing and Communications Workshops and other Affiliated Events (PerCom Workshops), pp. 395–397 (2021)
15. Koh, K., Ng, C., Pan, D., Mak, K.: Dynamic bus routing: a study on the viability of on-demand high-capacity ridesharing as an alternative to fixed-route buses in Singapore, pp. 34–40 (2018)
16. Kashani, Z.N., Ronald, N., Winter, S.: Comparing demand responsive and conventional public transport in a low demand context. In: 2016 IEEE International Conference on Pervasive Computing and Communication Workshops (PerCom Workshops), pp. 1–6 (2016)
17. Akhilesh, L., Kumar, C.N.: Parivahan: passenger demand triggered bus (vahan) routing in intelligent public transport system. Indian J. Comput. Sci. Eng. **13**(5), 1437–1447 (2022)
18. Akhilesh, L., Kumar, C.N.: Paargaman: passenger demand provoked (on-the-fly) routing of intelligent public transport vehicle with dynamic route updation, generation, and suggestion. Int. J. Recent Innov. Trends Comput. Commun. **11**(8), 391–405 (2023)
19. Shen, X., Feng, S., Li, Z., Baoyu, H.: Analysis of bus passenger comfort perception based on passenger load factor and in-vehicle time. Springerplus **5**, 12 (2016)

High-Speed FSO System for Future Generation Networks for Long Reach

Dipti Sharma[1(✉)], Ashutosh Tripathi[2], and Meet Kumari[3]

[1] Dept. of ECE, Chandigarh University, Gharuan, Mohali 140413, India
`diptibhardwajece@gmail.com`
[2] Director NIET & NIAMST, NIMS University, Jaipur, India
`directorniet@nimsuniversity.com`
[3] Dept. of ECE, UIE and UCRD, Chandigarh University, Gharuan, Mohali 140413, India
`meetkumari08@yahoo.in`

Abstract. A free space optics (FSO) system is proposed and described mathematically to meet the needs of future networks. Various integrating and synchronizing methods of hybrid fiber optic and FSO components incorporating advanced modulation formats, are discussed. The system performance is evaluated considering FSO link losses, signal regeneration, and amplification. Simulation results depict that 200–1400 m range at 10 Gbps under clear air, rain, fog and dust for different frequencies. In addition, system throughput can be extended upto 5–20 Gbps at 200–1400 m range under diverse climate conditions. This system offers superior performance over other existing ones. In future this system can be realized for 5G based future network topologies, hybrid fiber-FSO technology for high infrastructure compatibility, high-speed, and long-reach capabilities by supporting new applications.

Keywords: high-speed · long reach · hybrid fiber · free-space optical (FSO) system · next-generation network

1 Introduction

Network communications have recently become extremely important in tying together systems, gadgets, and people in the digital age. The investigation of sophisticated network infrastructures was prompted by the rising need for faster speeds, greater reach, and seamless communication. When there is a direct transmitter and receiver line of sight, it is especially helpful. The optical signal can be produced by free space optical (FSO) systems using continuous lasers or light-emitting diodes (LEDs) [1].

Last-mile terrestrial connections and satellite-to-ground data lines are two applications where FSO communication has seen significant growth. It has benefits like the ability to use unlicensed spectrum, fast data speeds, and simple implementation [1]. Optic fibers, however, often cannot be placed because of geographical or environmental restrictions. This integrated system combines optical fiber's enormous capacity with optical wireless communication's unlicensed spectrum to provide coverage of hard-to-reach service locations [2].

A key technology that satisfies the expanding demand for high-speed communication, particularly in the last mile of connectivity, is FSO communication, which has drawn a lot of attention. When compared to radio frequency-based systems, it has benefits including unlicensed transmission spectrum, high data transfer rates, simple deployment, and reduced prices. Due to its advantages over fiber optics, FSO is frequently thought of as a substitute [2]. In some applications, a hybrid system combining FSO and fiber optic technology is used. In some circumstances, it can also get beyond regular fiber optics' limits [3].

However, atmospheric conditions have a direct impact on FSO communication, creating difficulties for its dependable operation. Wireless communication in free space is severely impacted by atmospheric attenuation, including absorption and dispersion [4]. Hybrid optical technologies are used to address these issues and provide dependable long-distance transmission. The usage of a hybrid Raman/EDFA amplifier is one method for resolving dispersion problems that are frequently present in optical fibers. Sending several copies of the same optical signals over various FSO transmission channels enables the use of spatial diversity techniques [5]. This aids in overcoming atmospheric attenuation-related transmission flaws or failures [6]. The power gathered by the wireless system can be enhanced by using numerous FSO channels, improving overall performance [7]. The summarized literature review in Table 1 indicates previous work on FSO systems.

Table 1. Literature Review.

Refs.	Year	System	Range (m)	Throughput (bps)	Atmospheric conditions	Total channels
[5]	2015	Fiber-FSO	80k	10G	–	–
[2]	2016	FSO	100	1.08T	Light Sand Storm	–
[4]	2020	Fiber-FSO	70k	10G	–	4
[3]	2020	OWC	1.5	2.3T	–	21
[1]	2023	VLC-OCDM	9k	20G	–	3
[7]	2023	LiFi-OCDM	1500	33	–	–
[8]	2023	VLC	10	50	–	–
[9]	2023	VLC	80	30	–	–

From Table 1 it is realized that related work is lacking in range and throughput in the system under diverse climate scenarios.

Figure 1 illustrates the concept of using FSO transmission channels and spatial diversity to combat the effects of atmospheric attenuation and improve system reliability. This approach enables efficient long-distance FSO communication with atmospheric changes. The hybrid fiber FSO system was created with the goal of delivering high-speed and long-reach capabilities by combining the benefits of fiber optic and FSO technologies.

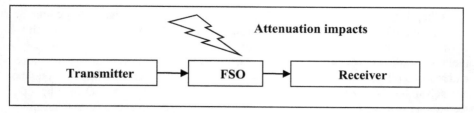

Fig. 1. Basic concept of FSO transmission.

The advantages of fiber optic communication, including its high bandwidth, short latency, and resistance to electromagnetic interference, have long been acknowledged. The hybrid system provides a singular opportunity to get around the limits of each technology separately by combining fiber optic and FSO technologies. The objective was to provide a complete solution for next-generation networks by combining the agility and flexibility of FSO links with the resilience and dependability of fiber optic networks.

An in-depth analysis of the high-speed long-reach hybrid fiber FSO system was offered in this research. Examining the fundamental concepts of FSO and fiber optics, its benefits and drawbacks were highlighted. The architecture of the hybrid system was discussed, along with the synchronization techniques and integration of components.

2 Hybrid Fiber-FSO System

Hybrid link budget analysis is crucial for assessing the feasibility of long-reach transmission in the hybrid fiber FSO system. This analysis takes into account factors such as transmitter power, receiver sensitivity, losses in fiber optic and FSO components, atmospheric losses, and other system parameters. By carefully considering the link budget, engineers can determine the achievable reach and optimize the system design for long-range communication.

2.1 Network Planning and Topology Network Design

Long-reach transmission may require careful network planning and topology design. Considerations such as the location of relay nodes, the placement of fiber optic and FSO components, and the use of hybrid link aggregation techniques can impact the overall reach and performance of the system. Network redundancy and resilience strategies should also be considered to ensure reliable long-reach communication.

By addressing these long-reach considerations, the hybrid fiber FSO system can be optimized to achieve extended communication distances in next-generation networks. A comprehensive understanding of the impact of atmospheric conditions, alignment techniques, signal regeneration, and network planning is essential to ensure reliable and efficient long-reach transmission.

Table 2. FSO link attenuation coefficient [8].

Condition	Attenuation (in dB/km)	Visibility (in km)
Heavy dust	250	0.05
Moderate dust	90	0.15
Dust-fog	40	0.4
Rain	15	0.8
Haze	6	1.5

In Table 2, different weather conditions are listed along with their corresponding atmospheric attenuation coefficients (measured in dB/km) and visibility distances (measured in kilometers). These values are used to calculate the attenuation experienced by the free space optic channels in the simulation.

2.2 System Model: Fiber-FSO-Fiber Code Division Multiple Access

An example of a FSO is realized in Fig. 2. It aims to facilitate communication between Alice and Bob, two authorized users, using a transmission link composed of one FSO link. Eve, an eavesdropper, intercepts a transmission that is occurring simultaneously on the two SMF lines. The system employs the On-Off Keying approach, which involves transmitting energy for data bits "1" but not for data bits "0".

A matching optical decoder is used by the receiver, Bob, to decode the signal before an avalanche photodiode (APD) detects it. Eve, on the other hand, intercepts a small amount of the available power and listens in on talks using an unmatched optical decoder [10].

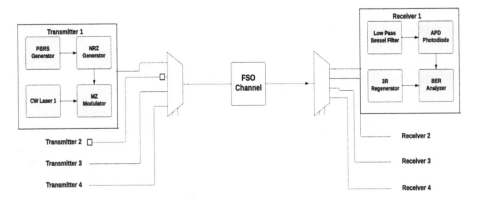

Fig. 2. Integrated FSO model.

When coupling optical signal from the FSO channel to the fiber link, Eq. (1) determines fiber-coupling efficiency in the single-mode fiber:

$$\eta = (\pi \rho^{\wedge}2 D^{\wedge}2)/(\lambda^{\wedge}2 A) * I\_0(2\pi\rho r) \qquad (1)$$

Here, 'η' and "A" are coupling geometry parameter and lens area respectively, "D" and the 'ρ' are aperture diameter at receiver and spatial coherence region of radius 'r', 'λ' the wavelength, and 'I_0' the first-kind, zero-order modified Bessel function. A significant hindrance to FSO communications is scintillation, which is a result of atmospheric turbulence [11]. The system adopts the gamma-gamma distribution model and takes into account three different turbulence conditions: moderate turbulence, middle turbulence, and strong turbulence. Equations (2) and (3), respectively, provide the gamma-gamma distribution's probability density function as well as cumulative distribution function:

$$PDF(\sigma^{\wedge}2) = 1/(2\sigma\_m) * \Gamma(2/\eta) * (\sigma^{\wedge}2/\sigma_m^{\wedge}2) \wedge (\eta/2)$$
$$* K\_n(\eta/2)(2\sqrt{((\eta/2)(\sigma^2/\sigma_m^2))}) \qquad (2)$$

and

$$\mathrm{CDF}(\sigma^2) = \int [0, \sigma^2] \mathrm{PDF}(x) dx$$
$$= \Gamma\left(\frac{2}{\eta}\right) * \int [0, \sigma^2] (2\sigma_m)^{-1} * \left(\frac{x^2}{\sigma_m}\right)^{\frac{\eta}{2}}$$
$$* K_m\left(\frac{\eta}{2}\right)\left(2\sqrt{\left(\frac{\eta}{2}\right)\left(\frac{\sigma^{2^2}}{\sigma_m}\right)}\right) dx \qquad (3)$$

Here, 'G(·)' represents the Meijer G-function, 'σ^2

2.3 Performance of Bob

The receiving chip power at Bob's end for the main channel, without taking turbulence into account, is provided by Eq. (4):

$$P_b = \eta * P * 10^{\wedge}(-\alpha_1 d_1/10) * g * R_b \qquad (4)$$

where P_b is the power of the receiving chip, η is the fibre coupling efficiency, P is the power of the transmission, 1 is the attenuation coefficient of the first optical fibre connection, d_1 is the transmission distance, g is APD average gain, and R_b is the responsiveness [15].

Equations (5) and (6) give the average current as well as noise square mean current for user data '1' after accounting for noises like shot, thermal, background, and multiple-access interference:

$$\bar{I}_{b1} = P_b * R_b \qquad (5)$$

$$\overline{N}_{b1} = 2*q*(\overline{I}_{b1} + \overline{I}_m + \overline{I}_T + \overline{I}_{MAI})*\Delta f \tag{6}$$

For user data '0', Eqs. (7) and (8) provide the average signal noise and current mean current, respectively:

$$\overline{I}_{b0} = 0 \tag{7}$$

2.4 Eve Performance

Eve in first fiber link is Case A. The receiving chip power for Eve's first optical fiber link eavesdropping is given by Eq. (9):

$$\overline{N}_{b0} = 2*q*(\overline{I}_m + \overline{I}_T + \overline{I}_{MAI})*\Delta f \tag{8}$$

where P_{e1} stands for the receiving chip power at Eve's end, 1 for the first optical fibre link's attenuation coefficient, d1 for the first optical fibre link's eavesdropping range, and R_{e1} for Eve's receiver's responsiveness.

Equations (10) and (11), respectively, yield the average current as well as noise mean current for user data '1':

$$P_{e1} = \eta * P * 10^{\wedge}(-\alpha_1 d_1/10) * g * R_{e1} \tag{9}$$

$$\overline{I}_{e1} = P_{e1} * R_{e1} \tag{10}$$

$$\overline{N}_{e1} = 2*q*(\overline{I}_{e1} + \overline{I}_m + \overline{I}_T + \overline{I}_{MAI})*\Delta f \tag{11}$$

For user data '0', the average current as well as noise mean current are given by Eqs. (12) and (13), respectively:

$$\overline{I}_{e0} = 0 \tag{12}$$

$$\overline{N}_{e0} = 2*q*(\overline{I}_m + \overline{I}_T + \overline{I}_{MAI})*\Delta f \tag{13}$$

Here, $\overline{I}_m$ is the shot noise, $\overline{I}_T$ is the thermal noise, $\overline{I}_{MAI}$ is the multiple-access interference, q is the electron charge, and Δf is

Case B: Eve in secondary fiber link,

The receiving power in chip for Eve's eavesdropping in another fiber link is determined by Eq. (14):

$$P_{e2} = \eta * P * 10^{\wedge}(-\alpha_2 d_2/10) * g * R_{e2} \tag{14}$$

where P_{e2} stands for the reception chip strength at Eve's end, α_2 for the second optical fibre link's attenuation factor, d_2 for the second optical fibre link's eavesdropping distance, and R_{e2} for Eve's receiver's responsiveness.

Equation (15) and (16), respectively, produce an average signalling power and noise average square current for user data '1':

$$\bar{I}_{e1} = P_{e2} * R_{e2} \tag{15}$$

$$\overline{N}_{e1} = 2 * q * (\bar{I}_{e1} + \bar{I}_m + \bar{I}_T + \bar{I}_{MAI}) * \Delta f \tag{16}$$

For user data '0', signal current as well as noise mean current is by Eqs. (17) and (18), respectively:

$$\bar{I}_{e0} = 0 \tag{17}$$

$$\overline{N}_{e0} = 2 * q * (\bar{I}_m + \bar{I}_T + \bar{I}_{MAI}) * \Delta f \tag{18}$$

Here, q means electron charge, $\bar{I}_m$ is the shot noise, $\bar{I}_T$ is the thermal noise, $\bar{I}_{MAI}$ is the multiple-access interference, and f means electrical bandwidth, where $\Delta f = 1/T$ and T is the data bit speed. Furthermore, α_2 is secondary fiber attenuation coefficient, d_2 is secondary fiber eavesdropping distance, Re_2 is the responsibility of Eve's receiver, and P is the transmission power.

3 Analysis Results and Discussion

The conduct of genuine users becomes more disruptive as tampering increases. This is caused by a rise in multiple-access interference (MAI) and a fall in signal-to-noise ratio (SNR), respectively. Furthermore, BER performance is superior in severe to moderate turbulence compared to mild to moderate turbulence [12]. However, when more users interact with the signal, turbulence's impact on the BER of approved users eventually fades away [13]. This is as a result of the MAIs beginning to have a major impact on the SNR. By creating a specific BER level, the feasibility of the hybrid fiber-FSO CDMA system has been guaranteed. As shown in Fig. 2, the system can still work well with fewer than nine users even under conditions of moderate, severe, or intense turbulence [14].

Figure 3(a) depicts the performance of FSO system for four frequencies under diverse climate conditions. It is seen that signal at 193.4 THz indicates best performance followed by signal at 193.3, 193.2 and 193.1 THz respectively over 200–1400 m range at 10 Gbps under clear air. The system performance dominate in clear air followed by rain, fog and dust for all frequencies as depicted in Fig. 3b–d and Table 3.

Figure 4a indicates FSO system performance for four frequencies under diverse climate conditions. It is seen that signal at 193.4 THz indicates best performance followed

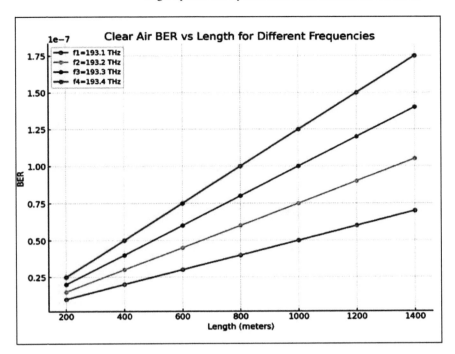

(a)

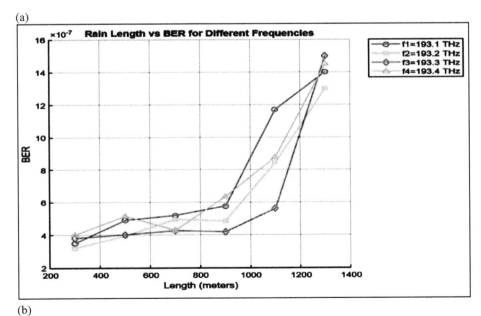

(b)

Fig. 3. FSO length versus BER for (**a**) clear air, (**b**) rain, (**c**) fog and (**d**) dust.

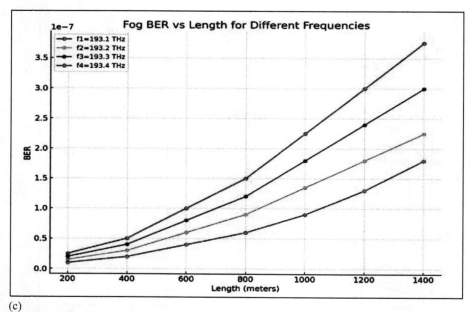

(c)

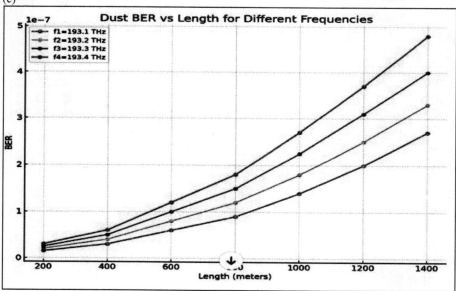

(d)

Fig. 3. (*continued*)

by signal at 193.3, 193.2 and 193.0 THz respectively over 200–1400 m range at 5–20 Gbps under clear air. The system performance dominate in clear air followed by

Table 3. Obtained BER.

Frequency	THZ			
Weather	193.1	193.2	193.3	193.4
Clear air	$0.10–0.75 \times 10^{-7}$	$0.15–1 \times 10^{-7}$	$0.20–1.25 \times 10^{-7}$	$0.25–1.75 \times 10^{-7}$
Rain	$3–14 \times 10^{-7}$	$3–13 \times 10^{-7}$	$3–15 \times 10^{-7}$	$3–15.5 \times 10^{-7}$
Fog	$0.1–1.7 \times 10^{-7}$	$0.2–2.2 \times 10^{-7}$	$0.3–3 \times 10^{-7}$	$0.4–3.5 \times 10^{-7}$
Dust	$0.2–2.5 \times 10^{-7}$	$0.3–3.4 \times 10^{-7}$	$0.4–4 \times 10^{-7}$	$0.5–4.8 \times 10^{-7}$

rain, fog and dust for all frequencies as depicted in Fig. 4b–d. Table 4 indicates the summarized results of the system for varied range.

4 Limitations and Potential Areas for Improvement

I. Weather: The hybrid fiber FSO system is subject to weather events including fog, rain, and snow, which can have a substantial impact on the signal's quality and range of transmission. Future studies should concentrate on creating cutting-edge methods to lessen the effects of bad weather and enhance system performance in difficult circumstances.
II. Interference Mitigation: While the hybrid fiber FSO system addresses multiple-access interference, there may still be limitations in mitigating other forms of interference, such as external sources or adjacent channels. Future research can explore advanced interference cancellation techniques and adaptive algorithms to enhance interference mitigation capabilities.
III. Scalability and Network Integration: The current research focuses on a single link or point-to-point communication. Future investigations should explore the scalability of the hybrid fiber FSO system for larger networks and its integration with existing communication infrastructures, such as optical networks and wireless networks, to provide seamless connectivity and interoperability.
IV. Security and Privacy: As the hybrid fiber FSO system becomes more widely deployed, ensuring secure and private communication becomes crucial. Future research should address security vulnerabilities, develop robust encryption techniques, and investigate techniques to detect and prevent eavesdropping or unauthorized access [9].
V. Cost-effectiveness: The cost of implementing the hybrid fiber FSO system is an important consideration for widespread adoption. Future research should focus on reducing the system's cost through the development of cost-effective components, optimized designs, and efficient manufacturing processes.

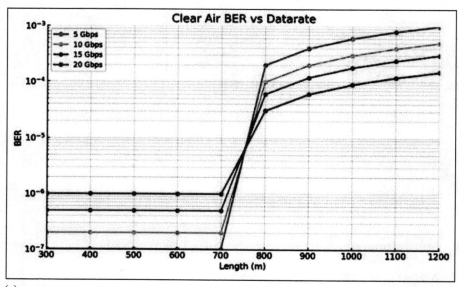

(a)

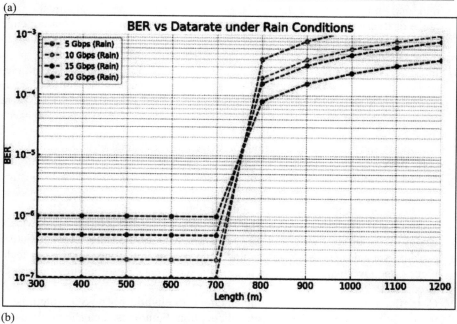

(b)

Fig. 4. FSO data rate vs. BER for (**a**) clear air, (**b**) rain, (**c**) fog and (**d**) dust.

High-Speed FSO System for Future Generation Networks 59

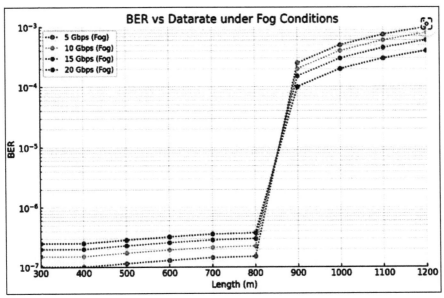

(c)

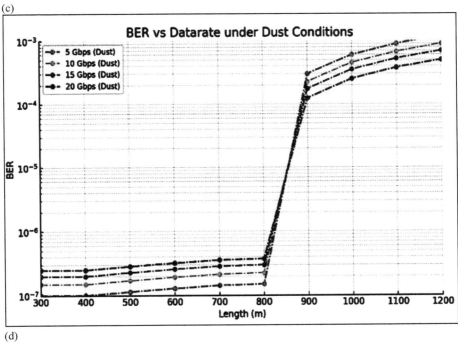

(d)

Fig. 4. (*continued*)

Table 4. Obtained BER.

Frequency	THZ			
Weather	193.1	193.2	193.3	193.4
Clear air	$10^{-7}-10^{-4}$	$10^{-7}-10^{-3.8}$	$10^{-7}-10^{-3.5}$	$10^{-7}-10^{-3}$
Rain	$10^{-7}-10^{-3.5}$	$10^{-7}-10^{-3.2}$	$10^{-7}-10^{-2.8}$	$10^{-7}-10^{-2}$
Fog	$10^{-7}-10^{-3.6}$	$10^{-7}-10^{-3.4}$	$10^{-7}-10^{-3.2}$	$10^{-7}-10^{-3}$
Dust	$10^{-7}-10^{-3.4}$	$10^{-7}-10^{-3.1}$	$10^{-7}-10^{-2.7}$	$10^{-7}-10s^{-2.5}$

5 Future Research Directions and Emerging Technologies

Quantum Communication: The integration of quantum communication principles and technologies into the hybrid fiber FSO system holds significant potential. Future research should explore the integration of quantum key distribution protocols and quantum-enhanced communication techniques to enhance security and enable quantum-safe communication in the hybrid system [14].

Machine Learning & Artificial Intelligence: Leveraging ML as well as artificial intelligence algorithms can optimize various aspects of the hybrid fiber FSO system. Future research should investigate the application of these techniques for adaptive modulation, interference prediction and cancellation, optimization of resource allocation, and intelligent fault detection and recovery.

Dynamic Network Adaptation: Developing adaptive and dynamic network architectures for the hybrid fiber FSO system is an emerging research direction. Future studies should explore self-configuring networks, cognitive network management, and software-defined networking approaches to enable flexible and efficient operation, resource allocation, and fault tolerance.

Visible Light Communication (VLC): VLC technology can complement the hybrid fiber FSO system by utilizing LED lights for data transmission in indoor environments. Future research should investigate the integration of VLC with the hybrid system to enable seamless indoor-outdoor connectivity and improved coverage.

Hybrid Integration: Integrating the hybrid fiber FSO system with other emerging technologies, like 5G networks, Internet of Things, and edge computing, presents exciting research opportunities. Future studies should explore the potential synergies, performance enhancements, and novel applications that can arise from such hybrid integration.

An integrated fiber-FSO system can develop into a reliable, high-speed, long-range communications solution for next-generation networks by overcoming limitations and investigating these future research areas and new technologies.

The summarized literature review comparison with this work is depicted in Table 5.

Table 5. Comparison Analysis.

Refs.	Year	System	Range (m)	Throughput (bps)	Atmospheric conditions	Total channels
[5]	2015	Fiber-FSO	80k	10G	–	–
[2]	2016	FSO	100	1.08T	Light Sand Storm	–
[4]	2020	Fiber-FSO	70k	10G	–	4
[3]	2020	OWC	1.5	2.3T	–	21
[1]	2023	VLC-OCDM	9k	20G	–	3
[7]	2023	LiFi-OCDM	1500	33	–	–
[8]	2023	VLC	10	50	–	–
[9]	2023	VLC	80	30	–	–
This work		FSO	1400	10G	Clear air, rain, fog and dust	4

6 Conclusion

A high-speed long haul FSO system under distinct climate conditions is presented. Concluded that the system allows maximum transmission distance of 1400m range at 10Gbps under clear air, rain, fog and dust for 193.1, 193.2, 193.3 and 193.4 THz operating frequencies. Meanwhile, high throughput can be obtained upto 20 Gbps considering clear air, rain, fog and dust conditions at 1400 m faithful range. It is also realized that system offers best performance over other existing ones.

Disclosure of Interests. The authors have no competing interests.

References

1. Arya, V., Kumari, M., Sharma, N., Singh, P.: Investigation of VLLC-OCDM System for Intelligent Transport Applications. In: 2023 3rd Asian Conference on Innovation in Technology (ASIANCON)), pp. 1–4. (2023)
2. Esmail, M.A., Ragheb, A., Fathallah, H., Alouini, M.S.: Investigation and demonstration of high speed full-optical hybrid FSO/fiber communication system under light sand storm condition. IEEE Photonics J. **9**(1), 1–12 (2017)
3. García-Zambrana, A., Castillo-Vázquez, B., Castillo-Vázquez, C.: Asymptotic error-rate analysis of FSO links using transmit laser selection over gamma-gamma atmospheric tur-bulence channels with pointing errors. Opt. Express **20**(3), 2096 (2012)
4. Jahid, A., Alsharif, M.H., Hall, T.J.: A contemporary survey on free space optical communication: potentials, technical challenges, recent advances and research direction. J. Netw. Comput. Appl. **200** (January), (2022)
5. Kazaura, K., Wakamori, K., Matsumoto, M., Higashino, T., Tsukamoto, K., Komaki, S.: RoFSO: a universal platform for convergence of fiber and free-space optical communication networks. IEEE Commun. Mag. **48**(2), 130–137 (2010)

6. Krishnan, P.: Performance analysis of FSO systems over atmospheric turbulence channel for Indian weather conditions. In: Turbulence and Related Phenomena. p. 63811. (2019)
7. Kumari, M.: Design of IoT based hybrid Red LED VLC-fiber communication system. In: 2023 International Conference on Advances in Intelligent Computing and Applications (AICAPS), pp. 1–4. (2023)
8. Kumari, M.: Modeling of Green Communication based VLLC system. In: 2023 2nd International Conference on Smart Technologies and Systems for Next Generation Computing (ICSTSN), pp. 1–4. (2023)
9. Kumari, M.: Modelling of high speed long-reach LiWi-OCDMA system. In: 2023 IEEE 8th International Conference for Convergence in Technology (I2CT), pp. 1–4. (2023)
10. Liu, J., Shi, Y., Fadlullah, Z.M., Kato, N.: Space-air-ground integrated network: a survey. IEEE Commun. Surv. Tutorials **20**(4), 2714–2741 (2018)
11. More, S.: Mixed mmWave RF/FSO relaying systems over generalized fading channels with pointing errors. IEEE Photonics J. **9**(1), 1–14 (2016)
12. Kumari, M.: Modeling of energy efficient next generation passive optical network (NG-PON). In: 2023 International Conference on Sustainable Computing and Data Communication Systems (ICSCDS), pp. 1038–1040. (2023)
13. Kumari, M.: Modeling of high-speed fiber-IsOWC communication system. In: 2023 International Conference on Computational Intelligence, Communication Technology and Networking (CICTN), pp. 5–8. (2023)
14. Kumari, M.: Modeling of high-speed ISL links in satellite communication. In: 2023 3rd International Conference on Advances in Computing, Communication, Embedded and Secure Systems (ACCESS), pp. 41–44 (2023)

Mitigating PAPR Challenges in Massive MIMO Systems for CR-IoT Networks: A Graeco-Latin Square Approach

Subrat Kumar Sethi[✉] and Arunanshu Mahapatro

Veer Surendra Sai University of Technology, Burla, Odisha, India
subrat_etc@vssut.ac.in

Abstract. In the dynamic realm of Internet of Things based Cognitive Radio (CR-IoT) networks operating within 5G framework, we confront challenges associated with Beam Division Multiple Access (BDMA) in the context of massive Multiple-Input Multiple-Output (MIMO) systems. BDMA, a contemporary concept facilitating the simultaneous transmission of multiple users' data streams through distinct beams, brings forth substantial advantages. However, as the number of transmit antennas grows, BDMA may grapple with an amplified Peak-to-Average-Power Ratio (PAPR). In response to this challenge, our work introduces an innovative approach that explicitly integrates PAPR constraints into the BDMA design, leveraging the concept of mutually orthogonal Graeco-Latin squares. Our approach involves the simultaneous optimization of hybrid digital and analog precoding. To facilitate the hybrid precoder design, our approach harnesses the power of the Graeco-Latin Square Approach, crafting an orthogonal user beam scheduling scheme. For determining the most efficient combination of precoding techniques and beam scheduling strategies, orthogonal-triangular decomposition is used. This algorithm strategically prioritizes user selection, followed by the derivation of their corresponding hybrid precoders, all while conscientiously considering explicit PAPR constraints. Validation through simulation results underscores the effectiveness of our proposed PAPR-aware hybrid approach of Graeco-Latin Square and orthogonal-triangular decomposition scheme, highlighting its potential to alleviate challenges associated with increasing PAPR in massive MIMO systems. This research significantly contributes to ongoing endeavors dedicated to enhancing the performance and efficiency of CR-IoT networks within the dynamic landscape of 5G communication.

Keywords: BDMA · CR-IoT · Graeco-Latin Square · PAPR · Orthogonal-Triangular Decomposition

1 Introduction

In the era of CR-IoT, where intelligent spectrum utilization is a fundamental constraint, the surge in IoT devices, projected to reach hundreds of billions by 2030

[3], underscores the critical need for seamless access over an expansive range. Cellular networks, a primary access technique for IoT networks, play a pivotal role in the ambitious goals of 5G wireless networks, with massive IoT being a key application. Despite the introduction of the Narrowband IoT (NB-IoT) specification in 2015 by 3GPP as part of 5G cellular IoT, the current limitations, such as supporting only 50,000 devices per cell, propel the exploration of innovative solutions within the framework of CR-IoT.

The unique constraints of CR-IoT, characterized by intelligent spectrum sharing and dynamic access, pose challenges to conventional schemes like orthogonal multiple access (OMA). That may be TDMA, FDMA or SDMA [1]. Non-orthogonal multiple access (NOMA) emerges as a promising solution within the CR-IoT paradigm [2]. However, NOMA introduces significant co-channel interference, compromising received signal quality as compared with schemes such as SDMA. To mitigate this issue and meet the diverse quality-of-service (QoS) demands of IoT applications within the CR-IoT framework, interference cancellation techniques play a crucial role [2,11].

The design of interference cancellation techniques in CR-IoT faces unique challenges. IoT devices, operating as intelligent nodes within the CR spectrum, necessitate interference cancellation at the cognitive base station (CBS). Leveraging the cognitive capabilities and dynamic spectrum access of CR-IoT devices for interference cancellation requires accurate channel state information (CSI) and access status. Grant-based and grant-free random access protocols, as explored in [3] provide access status for CR-IoT devices. However, obtaining CSI for a large number of dynamically accessing IoT devices remains a non-trivial task. In FDD mode, at the CBS center the CSI is typically obtained using the quantized feedback from CR-IoT devices, posing challenges for efficient utilization of the dynamic spectrum. Alternatively, the CSI is directly received at the center of CBS by estimating pilot sequences from the CR-IoT devices in TDD mode [10,12].

Meanwhile, within the landscape of CR-IoT, novel approaches have been devised for millimeter-wave (mmWave) massive MIMO transmissions, addressing the challenges posed by PAPR [4,9]. The combined analog and digital beamforming technique has emerged as a transformative precoding process, strategically involving analog and digital steps. To elaborate, our approach initiates the digital precoding phase with a streamlined set of radio frequency (RF) chains. Subsequently, we delve into the analog precoding stage, leveraging an expansive array of cost-effective phase shifters. This sequential process ensures an optimized and resource-efficient implementation of both digital and analog precoding in our proposed scheme. This hybrid architecture significantly reduces the need for RF chains compared to fully digital precoding, where every antenna element needs a dedicated RF chain. The synergy of interference suppression from digital precoding and the expansive antenna beamforming gains afforded by massive antennas characterizes the hybrid precoded massive MIMO system.

This innovative hybrid precoding technique, meticulously designed for both analog and digital precoders, has showcased throughput performance on par

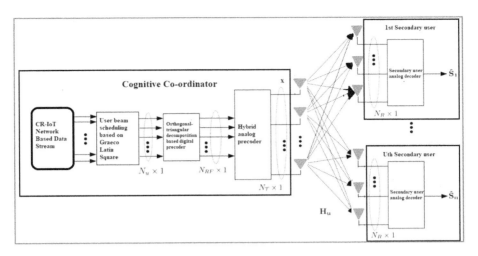

Fig. 1. Schematic diagram representing various blocks of hybrid precoding system for CR-IoT Network

with fully digital precoding but at a significantly reduced cost [5]. Moreover, harnessing the huge unutilized spectrum resources beyond 6 GHz, facilitates the deployment of MIMO systems capable of mmWave application. This is equipped with hybrid precoding techniques, enabling seamless data transmission rates in the gigabits per second (Gbps) range. However, a crucial consideration emerges from the linear combinations of multiple input data streams at the digital precoder's output signals. As per theory, the peak power resulting from digital precoding could potentially increase by a factor of Z compared to its power level which is the average one, where Z denotes the flow of data streams in terms of specific number. This increase in Z raises significant concerns regarding PAPR [7], necessitating the employment of costly linear power amplifiers (PAs) to mitigate not only in-band distortion but also signal spectral spreading.

We incorporate BDMA into the multiple access framework for mmWave massive MIMO systems, heralding a transformative paradigm shift in our approach. This strategic selection is driven by the observation that mmWave channels exhibit limited scattering paths. To further enhance the efficiency of our design, we incorporate the Graeco-Latin Square Approach into our methodology, facilitating an orthogonal scheduling scheme for hybrid precoder design. The hybrid precoding strategy is particularly adopted for crafting analog beams in response to the unique characteristics of mmWave channels.

Contrasting with existing BDMA works [4,5], our approach stands out by achieving multiuser interference-free performance without necessitating perfectly orthogonal beams. This is made possible through the effective removal of residual interference via digital precoding. Additionally, our scheme diverges from conventional hybrid precoding strategies [8], showcasing a unique digital precoder capable of concurrently addressing multiuser interference and PAPR. In the realm of mmWave m-MIMO systems, our simulations and analysis validate the effectiveness of the proposed PAPR-aware BDMA scheme, affirming its performance benefits. The core essence of this study can be briefly outlined as:

- Formulation and solution of the optimization problem for optimal analog precoding at the transmitter and optimal analog beamforming at the receiver.
- Leveraging Graeco-Latin Squares in the design of beamforming matrices to enhance PAPR reduction and beamforming performance in multi-user communication systems.
- Decoding complexity with orthogonal-triangular decomposition, with mitigation of inter-cell interferences in CR-IoT networks through the innovative use of joint channel matrix row vectors based on computed norms, considering transmission power levels of native base stations.

To address the aforementioned points, our plan remains as follows: Sect. 2 presents the related work, system model, and problem formulation. In sction 3, the Graeco-Latin square approach based PAPR-aware beam division multiple access scheme, is discussed. Section 4 provides the simulation results and analysis, while Sect. 5 discusses the conclusion.

2 System Model and Problem Formulation

2.1 System Model

Consider a CR-IoT network as depicted in Fig. 1, illustrating a schematic diagram of the hybrid precoding system. The system comprises various essential blocks, each contributing to the overall communication process within the network.

At the core of the system is a mmWave-MIMO configuration. The transmitter is equipped with N_{RF} radio frequency (RF) chains and N_T antennas, facilitating communication with N_U receivers, each featuring N_R receive antennas. Each scheduled receiver is assigned a dedicated data stream denoted by $s(n)$, representing the n-th block of N_U data to be transmitted.

The multiplication of s by the digital precoding matrix $\boldsymbol{D} = [\boldsymbol{d}_1, \cdots, \boldsymbol{d}_u, \cdots, \boldsymbol{d}_{N_U}]$, is the first phase of the combined precoding system. Here, $\boldsymbol{d}_u$ represents as digital beamforming vector for u-th user, with dimensions $N_{RF} \times 1$. Subsequently, the output signal undergoes multiplication by the analog precoding matrix $\boldsymbol{J} = [\boldsymbol{j}_1, \cdots, \boldsymbol{j}_i, \cdots, \boldsymbol{j}_{N_{RF}}]$, where $\boldsymbol{j}_i$ is the i-th analog beamforming vector with dimensions $N_T \times 1$. The expression for the resultant precoded signal $\boldsymbol{x}$ with dimensions $N_T \times 1$ is formulated as follows:

$$\boldsymbol{x} = \boldsymbol{J} \cdot \boldsymbol{D} \cdot \boldsymbol{s} = \boldsymbol{J} \sum_{u=1}^{N_U} \boldsymbol{d}_u s_u \qquad (1)$$

After precoding the signal is subsequently transmitted to the listed users. The $\boldsymbol{y}_u$ is the received signal by the u-th user. This can be expressed as:

$$y_u = H_u x + n_u \qquad (2)$$

$$= H_u J d_u s_u + H_u J \sum_{\substack{i=1\\i\neq u}}^{N_U} d_i s_i + n_u, \qquad (3)$$

The MIMO channel matrix H_u characterizes the transmission link between the transmitter and the u-th receiver, encompassing N_R receive antennas and N_T transmit antennas. This matrix captures the multipath propagation effects and spatial characteristics of the wireless channel. In addition to this, n_u represents complex additive white Gaussian noise with a zero mean and variance σ^2, contributing to the overall received signal quality.

Given the assumption of low-cost terminals at the receivers, which solely perform analog beamforming. This is a decoded signal represented by $\hat{s}_u$, and received by u-th user is written as:

$$\hat{s}_u = w_u^H H_u J d_u s + w_u^H \tilde{n}_u, \qquad (4)$$

where w_u is an analog beamforming vector employed by u-th receiver with the power constraint $|w_u|^2 = 1$, and

$$\tilde{n}_u = H_u J \sum_{\substack{i=1\\i\neq u}}^{N_U} d_i s_i + n_u. \qquad (5)$$

The term represented by the 1st part in Eq. (4) corresponds to the required signal, while the 2nd part accommodates the receiver noise as well as interference raised due to other users.

2.2 Channel Model for Low-Powered-Enabled CR-IoT Networks

In this section, we delve into the channel model designed explicitly for low-powered-enabled CR-IoT networks. We adopt the Saleh-Valenzuela model to capture the mmWave wireless communication dynamics within the network.

2.3 Saleh-Valenzuela MmWave Channel Model

The mmWave wireless channel in CR-IoT networks is characterized by a high number of antennas and numerous propagation paths. The Saleh-Valenzuela model provides an effective representation of the mmWave channel and can be expressed as follows:

Consider a communication link between a transmitter and a receiver. The channel matrix H for the u-th user in a CR-IoT network can be modeled as:

$$H_u = \sqrt{\frac{N_T N_R}{P}} \sum_{l=1}^{L} \beta_l \cdot a(\phi_l, \theta_l), \qquad (6)$$

where:

- N_T and N_R are the numbers of transmit and receive antennas, respectively,
- P is the transmit power,
- L is the number of propagation paths,
- β_l is the complex gain associated with the l-th path,
- $\boldsymbol{a}(\phi_l, \theta_l)$ is the array response vector corresponding to the azimuth and elevation angles ϕ_l and θ_l.

The complex gains β_l are modeled as independent and identically distributed (i.i.d.) complex Gaussian random variables with zero mean and unit variance.

We define the channel capacity for u-th user in a m-MIMO CR-IoT network as the maximum achievable rate, denoted as C_u, given by:

$$C_u = \log_2 \left(1 + \frac{P_u \|\boldsymbol{H}_u\|^2}{\sigma^2}\right), \tag{7}$$

where:
- P_u is the power allocated to the u-th user,
- $\|\boldsymbol{H}_u\|^2$ is the squared Frobenius norm of the channel matrix,
- σ^2 is the noise variance.

2.4 Problem Formulation

In the context of mitigating PAPR challenges in m-MIMO Systems for CR-IoT networks, we formulate the following optimization problem. The objective is to design a PAPR-aware hybrid beamforming scheme using a Graeco-Latin Square Approach.

2.5 Objective Function

Here the target is to minimize the PAPR in the transmitted signal while maintaining the data rate requirements. The PAPR is denoted as:

$$\mathrm{PAPR}(\boldsymbol{x}) = \frac{\|\boldsymbol{x}\|_\infty^2}{\mathbb{E}\left[\|\boldsymbol{x}\|^2\right]}. \tag{8}$$

We formulate the objective function as follows:

$$\min_{\boldsymbol{V}, \boldsymbol{F}} \mathrm{PAPR}(\boldsymbol{x}). \tag{9}$$

2.6 Constraints

To ensure the reliability of communication, we impose constraints on the achievable data rates and the power budget. The constraints are given by:

$$\text{Constraint 1: Data Rate} \quad C_u \geq R_{\min}, \quad \forall u, \tag{10}$$

$$\text{Constraint 2: Power Budget} \quad \mathrm{Tr}(\boldsymbol{V}\boldsymbol{V}^H) \leq P_{\max}, \tag{11}$$

where $R_{\min}$ is the minimum required data rate, and $P_{\max}$ is the maximum allowable power.

2.7 Optimization Problem

The PAPR-aware hybrid beamforming optimization problem for Massive MIMO CR-IoT networks is thus formulated as:

$$\min_{V,F} \text{PAPR}(x) \tag{12}$$

$$\text{s.t.} \quad C_u \geq R_{\min}, \quad \forall u, \tag{13}$$

$$\text{Tr}(VV^H) \leq P_{\max}. \tag{14}$$

This optimization problem aims to strike a balance between minimizing PAPR and satisfying data rate and power budget constraints in a Massive MIMO CR-IoT network using a Graeco-Latin Square Approach.

3 Graeco-Latin Square Approach Based PAPR-Aware Beam Division Multiple Access Scheme

The transmitter's optimal analog precoding is expressed as $j_u^* = a_T(\phi_u^t, \theta_u^t)$, while the receiver's optimal analog beamforming vector is denoted as $w_u^* = a_R(\phi_u^r, \theta_u^r)$, as outlined in [9]. The transmitter should possess all details related to angle of arrival (AoA) and angle of departure (AoD) in the perfect channel state information(CSI) scenario. This include parameters such as $\phi_u^t, \theta_u^t, \phi_u^r, \theta_u^r$, providing comprehensive insight into the directional characteristics of the wireless communication channels. Consequently, the optimization problem, as detailed in the main paper, takes the following form:

$$D^* = {}_{\tilde{D}}R_{tot}\left(J^*, \tilde{D}\right) \tag{15}$$

$$\text{s.t.} \quad ||J^* \tilde{d}_u||^2 = 1, \quad u = 1, 2, \cdots, N_U.$$

The estimated signal vector, denoted as $\hat{s} = [\hat{s}_1, \hat{s}_2, \cdots, \hat{s}_{N_U}]^T$, can be expressed using the formulation used in [9] can be given as follows:

$$\hat{s} = F \cdot D \cdot s + \xi, \tag{16}$$

where $F = [f_1, f_2, \cdots, f_{N_U}]^H$ is an $N_U \times N_{RF}$ dimensional matrix, and $\xi = [w_1^H \tilde{n}_1, w_2^H \tilde{n}_2, \cdots, w_{N_U}^H \tilde{n}_{N_U}]^T$. In the context of solving Eq. (15), [9] employed a zero-forcing approach, leading to the definition of the zero-forcing hybrid beamforming matrix as:

$$D_{ZF} = F^{\dagger} = F^H(FF^H)^{-1}, \tag{17}$$

Here, $N_U \leq N_{RF}$. Further, to fulfill the power constraint, power normalization is applied to each d_u, resulting in the normalized matrix $D_{ZF} = [d_{ZF,1}, \cdots, f_{ZF,N_U}]$. This normalization is expressed as:

$$d_{ZF,u}^* = \frac{d_{ZF,u}}{||J \cdot d_{ZF,u}||}. \tag{18}$$

The hybrid beamforming approach introduced in this study, termed as unconstrained zero-forcing hybrid beamforming (ZFU-HBF), serves as a baseline for evaluating subsequent methodologies. Here in our work, two strategies, namely zero-forcing with clipping hybrid beamforming (ZFC-HBF) and PAPR-aware hybrid beamforming (PAPRA-HBF), are explored to address PAPR issues. One specific threshold λ is used as direct clipping of the signal in ZFC-HBF. This is expressed by the following mathematical filter for each element of $\boldsymbol{D}_{ZF}$:

Mathematically, i varying between 1 and N_{RF} and k operating in between 1 and N_U,

$$[\boldsymbol{D}_{ZF}]_{ik}^{clip} = \begin{cases} [\boldsymbol{D}_{ZF}]_{ik}, & \text{if } |[\boldsymbol{D}_{ZF}]_{ik}| \leq \lambda \\ \lambda, & \text{otherwise} \end{cases} \quad (19)$$

Here, we refer Eq. (19) as (ZFC-HBF) method.

Despite its simplicity and efficacy in addressing PAPR issues, clipping presents inherent drawbacks. These encompass frequency dispersion, signal degradation within the operating frequency range, and resultant decline in system efficiency. In contrast to the clipping method, our proposed approach integrates a threshold λ directly into the design of $\boldsymbol{D}$. This alternative method seeks to surmount the limitations linked with direct clipping, providing a refined solution for augmenting PAPR reduction in the system.

$$\boldsymbol{D}^* = {}_{\tilde{D}} R_{tot}\left(\boldsymbol{J}^*, \tilde{\boldsymbol{D}}\right) \quad (20)$$
$$\text{s.t.} \quad \|\boldsymbol{J}^* \tilde{\boldsymbol{d}}_u\|^2 = 1$$
$$\left|\tilde{\boldsymbol{d}}_u\right|_i \leq \lambda \quad \text{for } i = 1, 2, \cdots, N_{RF}.$$

This Eq. (20) can be represented as a convex optimization problem. This transformed problem is amenable to resolution using widely adopted optimization tools, including but not limited to CVX. The use of standard optimization techniques enhances the feasibility and efficiency of finding the optimal solution to the original problem, facilitating the practical implementation of the PAPR-aware hybrid beamforming method.

$$\boldsymbol{D}^* = {}_{\tilde{D}} \|\boldsymbol{F}\tilde{\boldsymbol{D}} - \boldsymbol{F}\boldsymbol{D}_{ZF}\|^2 \quad (21)$$
$$\text{s.t.} \quad \|\boldsymbol{J}^* \tilde{\boldsymbol{d}}_u\|^2 = 1$$
$$\left|\tilde{\boldsymbol{d}}_u\right|_i \leq \lambda \quad \text{for } i = 1, 2, \cdots, N_{RF}.$$

Each radio frequency (RF) chain's amplitude is restricted to adhere to a predefined threshold, denoted as λ, through the solution of a convex optimization problem. This constraint is enforced during the optimization process, ensuring that the amplitudes of the RF chains do not exceed the specified threshold. This incorporation of amplitude constraints into the optimization framework contributes to the effective management of the signal amplitudes in the context of the PAPR-aware hybrid beamforming technique.

3.1 Graeco-Latin Square Method

In the optimization of PAPR-aware hybrid beamforming, we introduce a novel approach known as the Graeco-Latin Square Approach based PAPR-Aware Beam Division Multiple Access (GLS-PAPR-ABDMA) scheme. This innovative scheme leverages the principles of Graeco-Latin Squares to design beamforming matrices that concurrently optimize PAPR reduction and beamforming performance in a multi-user communication system.

Latin squares are combinatorial structures that have demonstrated utility in various applications, including error-correcting codes for communication systems. Sets of Latin squares orthogonal to each other play a crucial role when dealing with communication disturbances beyond simple white noise, such as in scenarios like broadband Internet transmission over powerlines [6].

To implement the Graeco-Latin Square Approach for PAPR-aware beamforming, we employ a Markov chain Monte Carlo algorithm. This algorithm generates a uniformly distributed random Latin square representative of a Latin square of order N.

The GLS-PAPR-ABDMA scheme involves the use of Latin squares in the design of beamforming matrices. Each entry in the Latin square represents a specific frequency or channel for beamforming. By using Latin squares that are orthogonal to each other, we achieve a method that enhances robustness against noise at different frequencies. The Latin squares are applied in successive time intervals, and each letter in the message to be sent is encoded by sending signals at different frequencies during these intervals.

Let $\boldsymbol{L}$ represent a Latin square matrix of order N. The encoding process involves mapping each symbol in the message to a specific entry in $\boldsymbol{L}$. The Latin square matrix $\boldsymbol{L}$ is structured as follows:

$$\boldsymbol{L} = \begin{bmatrix} 1 & 2 & 3 & \ldots & N \\ 2 & 3 & 4 & \ldots & 1 \\ 3 & 4 & 1 & \ldots & 2 \\ \vdots & \vdots & \vdots & \ddots & \vdots \\ N & 1 & 2 & \ldots & N-1 \end{bmatrix} \qquad (22)$$

Each row in $\boldsymbol{L}$ represents a channel, and each column represents a time slot. The encoding process involves selecting channels in successive time slots based on the symbols in the message.

The GLS-PAPR-ABDMA scheme offers a systematic and efficient method for optimizing PAPR-aware hybrid beamforming, taking advantage of the mathematical properties of Latin squares. This approach contributes to the overall performance enhancement of multi-user communication systems, especially in scenarios with diverse noise characteristics.

Decoding Complexity with Orthogonal-Triangular Decomposition. In the domain of CR-IoT networks, a dynamic environment unfolds where a macro cell coexists harmoniously with an array of low-power nodes, all operating on the same frequencies. This intricate setup paves the way for enhanced system capacity and spectrum efficiency. The strategic amalgamation of low-power nodes alongside the macro cell serves as a pivotal step towards augmenting these pivotal network attributes. However, the formidable challenge lies in effectively mitigating the impact of robust co-channel interference within the realm of 5G CR-IoT networks.

To surmount this challenge, we propose an ingenious hybrid approach that seamlessly combines Orthogonal-triangular decomposition with the Graeco-Latin Square methodology. This novel algorithm is strategically crafted to not only augment system capacity and spectrum efficiency but also to adeptly tackle the intricacies of co-channel interference.

In the matrix realm of joint channel matrices across all cells, our innovative approach strategically employs Orthogonal-triangular decomposition to alleviate inter-cell interferences. The diverse transmission power levels among distinct base stations translate into varying interference intensities experienced by users.

In the intricate landscape of wireless networks, base stations endowed with greater transmission power often exert a more discernible influence, particularly affecting users positioned at the fringes of neighboring cells.

In our innovative approach, we pivot around the implementation of Orthogonal-triangular decomposition, a technique designed to dynamically recalibrate the row vectors inherent to the joint channel matrix. This recalibration process is predicated on the meticulous computation of norms $H_{i;k}^{(k)}$, specifically tailored to characterize the channel matrices linking base stations and their corresponding native users. Mathematically, this norm is expressed as:

$$H_{i;m}^{(M)} = \sqrt{\sum_{k=1}^{N_t} \lambda_k \left\| H_{i;m}^{(m)} \right\|_f D^2} \qquad (23)$$

Here, λ_k denotes the k-th eigenvalue of the matrix $H_{i;m}^{(m)} H_{i;m}^{(m)H}$ with a rank of N_t.

The $H_{i;m}^{(m)}$-norm serves as a reflection of the required signal power magnitude for i-th user in m-th cell, considering the transmission power of corresponding base stations. Subsequently, the row vectors of the joint channel matrix undergo meticulous adjustment based on these calculated norms.

The channel matrix norms across m cells is structured as follows:

$$H_{i;a}^{(a)} \geq H_{i;b}^{(b)} \geq \ldots \geq H_{i;M}^{(M)} \qquad (24)$$

This ranking system assigns sequential cell numbers to the corresponding cells, starting from cell 1 and progressing onwards.

Algorithm 1. PAPR-Aware-GLOTA Algorithm

Require:
1: The comprehensive index set for users is denoted as $\mathcal{X}$.
2: The chosen user index set is represented as: $\mathcal{I} = \emptyset$.
3: The quantity of users to be selected: N_U
4: Channel matrix: $\boldsymbol{H}$, Number of Cells: K, Number of Users: N_U

Ensure:
5: Initialization: Choose x as the index of user(max channel gain) $|\alpha|$ to $\mathcal{I}$, *i.e.* $\mathcal{I} \leftarrow x$ and $\mathcal{X} \setminus x$.
6: **while** $|\mathcal{I}| < N_U$ **do**
7:     $\boldsymbol{A} = \left[\boldsymbol{a}_T\left(\phi_{i_1}^t, \theta_{i_1}^t\right), \boldsymbol{a}_T\left(\phi_{i_2}^t, \theta_{i_2}^t\right), \cdots, \boldsymbol{a}_T\left(\phi_{i_{|\mathcal{I}|}}^t, \theta_{i_{|\mathcal{I}|}}^t\right)\right]$
8:     Compute the projection space: $\boldsymbol{P}_A = \boldsymbol{A}\boldsymbol{A}^\dagger$
9:     **for** x in $\mathcal{X}$ **do**
10:       $p(x) = \|\boldsymbol{P}_A \cdot \boldsymbol{a}_T\left(\phi_x^t, \theta_x^t\right)\|^2$
11:     **end for**
12:     Obtain x^* with the min $p(x)$
13:     Update $\mathcal{I} \leftarrow x^*$ and $\mathcal{X} \setminus x^*$
14: **end while**
15: **Output:** Optimized precoding matrix $\boldsymbol{D}^*$
16: Initialize $\boldsymbol{D}$ using orthogonal-triangular decomposition
17: Perform Graeco-Latin Square adjustment based on PAPR awareness
18: **while** Not converged **do**
19:     Calculate PAPR of the current precoding matrix $\boldsymbol{F}$
20:     Adjust $\boldsymbol{F}$ using Graeco-Latin Square to minimize PAPR
21: **end while**
22: **return** Optimized $\boldsymbol{D}^*$

4 Simulation Results and Analysis

In our simulation study, we aim to evaluate and compare the performance of various precoding algorithms concerning the PAPR and system sum-rate capacity. The focus is on a MIMO systems for CR-IoT network. Specifically, we investigate the PAPR-Aware-GLOTA as a hybrid precoding scheme.

To conduct a comprehensive analysis, computer simulations are employed in our study. The transmitter is outfitted with an 8×8 uniform planar array (UPA), translating to a total of $N_T = 64$ antenna elements. In the transmission process, the transmitter employs $N_{RF} = 4$ radio frequency (RF) chains and caters to the communication needs of $N_U = 4$ users. Each user is linked with a 4×4 UPA, resulting in $N_R = 16$ antenna elements. The assumed communication channels are characterized as single-path, featuring azimuth angles uniformly distributed over the interval $[0, 2\pi]$, and elevation angles uniformly distributed within the range of $[-\pi/2, \pi/2]$. In the context of opportunistic cognitive schemes, our algorithm is designed to consider the dynamic selection of a subset of users from the available active users.

In Fig. 2, the sum-rate capacity achieved by various precoding schemes is presented, allowing for a comprehensive analysis of their performance. The curve

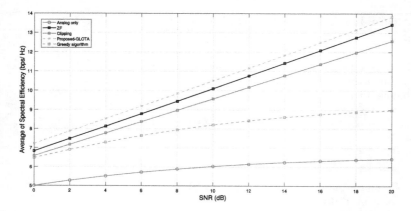

Fig. 2. Sum-Rate Performance Across Varied User Group Sizes in Opportunistic Schemes(6 User group)

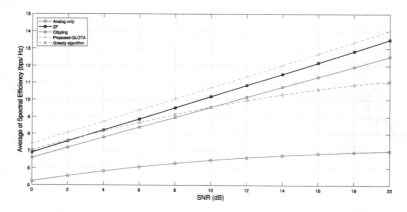

Fig. 3. Sum-Rate Performance Across Varied User Group Sizes in Opportunistic Schemes(8 User group).

labeled "Analog only" illustrates the outcome when exclusively employing analog beamforming to spatially multiplex a group of six users. Due to the absence of a digital precoder for interference suppression, this curve underscores the interference-dominant nature of analog beamforming. Consequently, the performance of analog-only beamforming exhibits minimal improvement with increasing SNR.

Moving on to the comparative analysis, the scheme denoted as 'ZF' employs a zero-forcing approach. The performance characteristics of this scheme are observable in Fig. 2, and it reveals the limitations of zero-forcing in mitigating interference, especially as SNR increases. The "Clipping" scheme, incorporating a conventional technique to reduce PAPR, is also examined. However, it comes at the cost of spectral spreading, in-band distortion, and subsequent performance degradation, as evident from Fig. 2.

Additionally, the "Greedy algorithm" scheme is investigated for its performance implications. Figure 2 showcases the sum-rate capacity achieved by this scheme, illustrating its efficiency in user selection. Nevertheless, it is essential to consider the trade-offs associated with the greedy algorithm, particularly in scenarios with varying SNR.Consequently, the performance of analog-only beamforming exhibits limited improvement with an increasing SNR.

Now, transitioning to our proposed scheme, 'Proposed-GLOTA,' it outperforms the aforementioned schemes. As demonstrated in Fig. 2, the proposed PAPR-Aware-GLOTA achieves performance close to the optimal upper bound. The observed enhancement is partially credited to the supplementary beamforming gain enabled through opportunistic analog beamforming, as substantiated by the examination of Figs. 2 and 3.

In Fig. 2 "Analog only" represents the scenario where only analog beamforming is utilized to multiplex a group of six users in the spatial domain. The illustration in Fig. 2 underscores the predominance of interference in analog beamforming, primarily stemming from the lack of a digital precoder to mitigate interference.

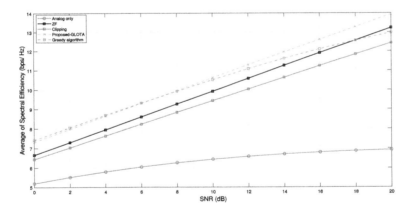

Fig. 4. Sum-Rate Performance Across Varied User Group Sizes in Opportunistic Schemes(15 User group)

In our investigation of the multiuser gain enabled by opportunistic scheduling, we analyze how changes in the number of active users influence the enhancement of sum-rate capacity. As depicted in Fig. 4, the PAPR-Aware-GLOTA scheme exhibits substantial benefits with an increasing number of active users, ranging from 6 to 35. The plot highlights the significant improvement in sum-rate capacity during this range. However, it is noteworthy that the advantages derived from having more active users start to diminish beyond the threshold of 40. On the contrary, the non-opportunistic analog beamforming, represented by the curve labeled "Analog only," demonstrates a relatively stable performance that does not exhibit significant changes with variations in the number of active users. This observation underscores the inherent limitations of analog-only beamforming in harnessing multiuser gains compared to the opportunistic approach adopted in PAPR-Aware-GLOTA.

5 Conclusion

In conclusion, this paper introduces a novel and effective approach, termed the Graeco-Latin Square Approach, to mitigate the challenges associated with the PAPR in massive MIMO systems for BDMA within CR-IoT networks. Our proposed PAPR-aware BDMA scheme involves the joint optimization of hybrid analog-digital precoding and user-beam scheduling. The analog-digital precoder design is formulated as a convex optimization problem, explicitly considering PAPR constraints, and our simulations affirm that the optimized precoders significantly enhance the sum-rate capacity while maintaining a lower PAPR compared to conventional clipping techniques. To achieve efficient user-beam scheduling with minimal interference, we introduce a modified greedy algorithm that opportunistically selects users based on their array response vectors. By incorporating the Graeco-Latin Square Approach, our work contributes to advancing the performance and efficiency of CR-IoT networks within the dynamic landscape of 5G communications.

References

1. Li, Y., Zhang, Z.: Co-channel interference suppression for multi-cell MIMO heterogeneous network. EURASIP J. Adv. Signal Process. **2016**(1), 1–12 (2016)
2. Abu Hilal, H.: Performance of ZF and MMSE decoders for massive multi-cell MIMO systems in impulsive and Laplacian noise channels. SIViP **14**(1), 49–56 (2020)
3. Xu, Y., Gui, G., Gacanin, H., Adachi, F.: A survey on resource allocation for 5G heterogeneous networks: current research, future trends, and challenges. IEEE Commun. Surv. Tutor. **23**(2), 668–695 (2021)
4. Sun, C., Gao, X., Jin, S., Matthaiou, M., Ding, Z., Xiao, C.: Beam division multiple access transmission for massive MIMO communications. IEEE Trans. Commun. **63**(6), 2170–2184 (2015)
5. Kwon, G., Park, H.: Joint user association and beamforming design for millimeter wave UDN with wireless backhaul. IEEE J. Sel. Areas Commun. **37**(12), 2653–2668 (2019)
6. Mao, Y., Dizdar, O., Clerckx, B., Schober, R., Popovski, P., Poor, H.V.: Rate-splitting multiple access: fundamentals, survey, and future research trends. IEEE Commun. Surv. Tutor. (2022)
7. Alkhateeb, A., El Ayach, O., Leus, G., Heath, R.W.: Hybrid precoding for millimeter wave cellular systems with partial channel knowledge. In: 2013 Information Theory and Applications Workshop (ITA), pp. 1–5. IEEE (2013)
8. Albreem, M.A., Al Habbash, A.H., Abu-Hudrouss, A.M., Ikki, S.S.: Overview of precoding techniques for massive MIMO. IEEE Access **9**, 60764–60801 (2021)

9. Niu, G., Pun, M.O.: PAPR-aware beam division multiple access for mmWave massive MIMO systems. In: 2018 10th International Conference on Wireless Communications and Signal Processing (WCSP), pp. 1–6. IEEE (2018)
10. Jia, R., Chen, X., Qi, Q., Lin, H.: Massive beam-division multiple access for B5G cellular Internet of Things. IEEE Internet Things J. **7**(3), 2386–2396 (2019)
11. Sethi, S.K., Mahapatro, A: A deep learning-based discrete-time Markov chain analysis of cognitive radio network for sustainable Internet of Things in 5G-enabled smart city. Iran. J. Sci. Technol. Trans. Electr. Eng. 1–28 (2023)
12. Sethi, S.K., Mahapatro, A.: Interference aware intelligent routing in cognitive radio based Vehicular Adhoc networks for smart city applications. Int. J. Inf. Technol., 1–21 (2023)

Performance Analysis of IoT Network over 5G Communication

V. Sanvika, Indrasen Singh(✉), Madala Poorna Chandra, and Joshith Reddy

School of Electronics Engineering, Vellore Institute of Technology, Vellore 632014, Tamil Nadu, India
{vannempalli.sanvika2021,madalapoorna.chandra2021, joshithreddy.m2021}@vitstudent.ac.in, indrasen.singh@vit.ac.in

Abstract. With faster connection speeds, the new age of digital reality is facilitated by faster network technology. The result is a modern technology called the Internet of Things (IoT) that requires extensive internet connectivity to operate. Compared to previous technological advances, the frequency of outrageous 5G requests is increasing, resulting in transfer speeds of up to 20 Gbps and capacity that can be increased a thousand-fold. With 5G you get extremely dense network support, high reliability, and maximum security. This makes producing new, advanced products more cost-effective. A 5G network provides a broad foundation for future ventures, including the Internet of Things, AI, and other cutting-edge technologies The performance of IoT networks has been analyzed in terms of the amplitude of received signal over symbol index.

Keywords: Internet of things · 5G communication · waveform design · symbol index · capacity

1 Introduction

Demand and market interest are being driven by both consumers and businesses mainly to the launch of the first 5G mobile cellular networks and the availability of more affordable equipment [1–4]. This study evaluates the effects of 5G on the Internet of Things as well as some of its distinct advantages over competing technologies. It also addresses use cases where 5G is necessary and shows IoT use cases that can be supported by current cellular technologies, such as 3G and 4G [5]. This article is meant to serve as a reference for non-technical users and purchasers of communication systems in businesses. It focuses on the implementation of cellular technology for IoT applications [6–8]. It is anticipated that there will be a massive increase in IoT connections during the next five years [9]. By 2025, the GSMA Intelligence predicts that 25.2 billion IoT connections are anticipated worldwide. One billion of these, or 3.1 billion, are expected to use cellular technologies, such as Web of Things (WoT), wide area networks with minimal energy consumption [10–12].

The Applications of IoT networks in the 5G era are given in Fig. 1. There are many benefits such as automation, smart home, health monitoring, smart city, smart grid, and smart farming.

In the years to come, as 5G coverage spreads internationally, today's LTE or 4G networks will continue to coexist with it, providing enough coverage and capacity for a variety of use cases2. However, 5G offers a number of advantages to the IoT that 4G and other technologies do not. One of these is 5G's capacity to assist a sizable figure of Internet of Things gadgets, each stationery and cell phone, with a wide variety of speed, bandwidth, and service excellence needs [12]. The majority of these can be divided into three primary categories: vital communications, enormous IoT, and improved mobile broadband (eMBB). The current 5G networks in use are extensions of the 4G networks, which use both NB-IoT and LTE-M (LTE for Machines) technologies [13–15].

The GSMA anticipates that early 5G deployments will give highspeed, low-latency, dependable, and secure mobile broadband. Large numbers throughout time will be linked to 5G networks by IoT devices, offering assistance for incredibly reliable and low latency communications. Wireless edge technology combined with 5G will facilitate demanding instances, including automated driving, time-sensitive industrial IoT production procedures, and (AR/VR) Augmented and virtual reality [16].

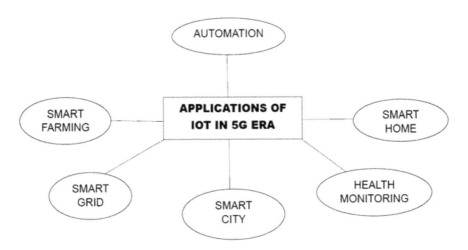

Fig. 1. Applications of IoT in 5G communication.

2 Literature Review

2.1 5G Technology on IoT

After commercial 5G deployments begin to appear internationally, there will be a lot of interest in the benefits that 5G may offer the growing Internet of Things movement. Different IoT use cases, ranging from apps that use low-data transfer rates to high-end mission-critical applications that require instantaneous data transfers, are utilizing multiple, specialized networks [5]. This is a fundamental obstacle to realizing the potential and promise of the IoT. On the other hand, 5G provides a way to serve a multitude of applications related to the Internet of Things and achieve the benefits of scale on one connection.

2.2 Importance

The Internet of Things is usually growing quickly, but scaling it to support various IoT applications over several specialized networks is costly and difficult. In the span of ten years, from 2020 to 2030, there will be a 40–140 billion rise in IoT gadgets, along with a notable shift in connectivity from 4G towards 5G. For instance, 6000 NB-IoT devices may operate on an individual cell on today's 4G networks. On the other hand, up to a million gadgets may be assisted by a simple 5G cell. IoT applications that require modest data transfer rates can send huge volumes of data via networks, requiring extensive connectivity management on each network. This is not the instance involving 5G, though, given that its unified internet architecture is ultimately designed for managing broad information exchanges using multiple kinds [17].

2.3 Aspects

A handful of the many IoT functions that the advent of 5G will enhance are as follows:

- **Information**, the Internet of Things will be most affected by 5G's ability to share far larger amounts of data at faster speeds than 4G. Adding more advanced methods of communication to 5G networks, such as Multiple Inputs Multiple Outputs (MIMO), ensures that a greater volume of information may be sent and taken in a short period of clock. Dispersion of several transmitters and receivers spread widely outperforms dispersion of a single antenna significantly better. Therefore, it is usually more difficult to get coverage in remote rural areas or within large buildings that might want improvement [18].
- **Size**, the sheer number of IoT devices has risen dramatically in recent years because of device connectivity additionally the development of unique applications [11]. The capacity of 5G networks to transfer data at higher rates will enable more connected devices to connect and communicate with one another via the network. After implementing the 5G network, businesses that had previously battled with excessive latency are now able to connect several devices to their network without running into congestion or other delay issues [19].
- **Power Consumption**, another problem that faces businesses and people who want to integrate several networked devices into a system is this. Recent advancements in narrowband IoT, for instance, make narrow bandwidth suitable for low-data-rate Internet of Things operations. This will decrease the

amount of power used by the network and lessen the load on data transfer. Every economic or business operation requires expansion, and the advent of 5G should provide such results [20].

3 Research Methodologies

The methodology to implement wireless 5G communication technology is as follows:

- **Waveform Creation For 5G Technologies:** It's really acknowledged the fact that long-term evolution (LTE) standard's present OFDM waveform has many shortcomings when it comes to meeting 5G standards [8]. In particular, a wide range of features and needs in terms of data column, communications rate, delay, and dependability are anticipated for 5G traffic. For instance, very high transmission rates are required for real-time communications in applications like augmented reality and video streaming. Moreover, a tiny quantity of data must be transmitted with each transmission in a variety of developing M2M uses, like of those pertaining to smart grids, which contain irregular and massive stoppage [2]. Other wireless applications need extremely low latency and excellent reliability, like robotics control and vehicle communications. Lastly, because today's wireless networks mostly enable human-type communications, it is anticipated that the number of wireless connections supporting future M2M and Internet-of-Things applications will be substantially larger than that.
- **Ultra-Dense Wireless Networks for Microwave and mmWave Communications:** A key strategy for meeting the ability requirement for upcoming 5G wireless networks is the ultra-dense implementation of switches, scattered antenna networks, and small networks using numerous RATs inside a multi-tier hetero network (HetNet) architecture which operate on various bands of frequency (such millimeter wave and microwave) [2]. In order to better accommodate the increasing volume of bandwidth from smartphones and tablets using improved QoS, communication rates, and energy conservation, this heterogeneous network design also makes it possible for appropriate data dumping between different RATs and connection tiers [3]. One of the most active study areas in recent years has been multi-tier HetNets, in which correspondence between several. The same microwave spectrum is used by various network levels, including the macro, micro, and small-cell tiers [8]. Interference management, which can be carried out utilizing temporal, frequency, spatial, and power control methodologies, is a crucial study topic in this area. Our special issue contains three papers that cover various aspects of the design and analysis of wireless HetNets. In particular, the stochastic geometry technique in is used to perform cognition outage analysis HetNets. Additionally, in order to achieve equitable managing noise and exchanging bandwidth between two network layers [8]. To achieve the appropriate cell range expansion bias and nearly blank subframe rate in the two-tier HetNet,

the paper proposes enhanced inter-cell interference coordination (eICIC) techniques [9].
- **Massive and Full-Dimension MIMO Technologies:** While huge MIMO and full-dimension MIMO offer substantial advancements Regarding this scientific to significantly boost the role of MIMO technology in wireless networks' bandwidth for conservation of energy a major function in contemporary 3G/4G wireless systems [5]. Furthermore, massive MIMO may make it easier to control co-channel interference and radio resource allocation in wireless with several cells and stages networks [10]. Numerous current efforts have built huge MIMO systems with high energy efficiency. Together, the transmit power and user count were optimized. The circuit power consumption of huge MIMO systems has a significant impact on their energy efficiency (EE). The sequence of optimization of a single-cell massive MIMO system with zero-forcing beamforming (ZFBF) included antenna size, users, and broadcast power [12].
- **System Design Architecture:** The initial stage is to create an idea-based building that is independent of technology in order to build a WSN that uses the IoT to monitor the production environment. It is believed that this architecture is general and easily adaptable to many situations. Numerous suggested architectures that offer useful experience can be found in the literature. Zhang et al., for example, suggested Temperature surveillance in terminals on a huge scale via a 4-layer system structure [3]. However, this arrangement only permits a basic network configuration of the sensor tier because it was created especially for complicated systems. Texas Instruments created the design based on the new networking technology known as 6LoW-PAN, or "IPv6 over Lower Power Wireless Personal Area Networks," which uses IPv6 data packets to link a WSN to the internet [3]. On the other hand, there isn't much gear available that makes use of this protocol. Gregory and Ahmed talked about the potential for WSNs to become contemporary IoT systems by utilizing cloud computing technology.
- **Component Design Criteria:**

The Choice of Network Topology: Since network topology is greatly based on the scenario being used, it is challenging to establish guidelines while being aware of the requirements of possible applications. To maintain the design's adaptability, however, RF modules that provide quick and simple topology switching are favored. Based on how big the project is, the need for both the accessible sensing performance and reliability, topology might vary greatly [7].

RF Module Selection: In this framework, in contrast to other systems, a microprocessor is deemed superfluous as it results in a notable increase in expenses and energy usage. As an alternative, it is advised to provide an integrated radio frequency module with restricted integrated processing capabilities. The module must, at the very least, be able to handle different topologies, transform analog impulses into digital ones (for sensory readings), and use a small amount of programming flexibility [3]. Without the need to construct intricate circuitry, variables like sampling rates, sleep durations, and data packetization can be readily changed by choosing a programmable sensor. Furthermore, a RF module compliant along current requirements for encryption is required [16–18].

Choice of Sensor: Because sensors are chosen based on the particular network's current duty configured to gauge, it is challenging to establish precise chosen standards. Because of their lower cost, analog sensors are generally advised over digital ones. Moreover, a digital sensor would be unnecessary if the RF module included an integrated ADC [4].

Choice Of Microprocessor: The chosen microprocessor has to be inexpensive, capable of running on battery power, and simple to program. For the microprocessor to interface with the chosen RF modules save controller duration and provide simpler control [3], off-the-shelf components are essential. For the microprocessor to communicate with internet systems, networking capabilities should also be present.

4 Results and Discussion

Simulating an IoT device generating random data and a 5G communication link with path loss and additive white Gaussian noise (AWGN) involves several steps. Below is a basic MATLAB code example that demonstrates this simulation. This example uses Binary Phase Shift Keying (BPSK) modulation for simplicity. In practice, you might use more advanced modulation schemes and consider other aspects like channel coding. This example provides a basic simulation. In a real-world scenario, you may want to consider more sophisticated channel models, antenna gains, modulation schemes, and other 5G-specific features [9].

Here the parameters are defined for proposed model simulation. The numBits represents the number of bits the IoT device will transmit. SNR dB is the Signal-to-Noise Ratio in dB, and pathLoss is the path loss in dB. The IoT device generates numBits random binary data using. The modulation scheme used here is Binary Phase Shift Keying (BPSK), where One is assigned to one and zero to -1 [13].

This simulates the path loss by dividing the transmitted symbols (txSymbols) by a factor related to the path loss. The factor $10(pathLoss/20)$ converts the path loss from dB to a linear scale. Here introduces AWGN to the received symbols. The power of the noise is determined by the desired signal-to-noise ratio (SNR_dB). The random function generates Samples chosen at random with a mean of zero and a variance of one from a normal distribution and $sqrt(noisePower/2)$ scales it to the desired noise power (Fig. 2).

The received signal is obtained by adding the path-loss-affected symbols and the AWGN. Demodulation is performed by taking the real part of the received symbols and checking if it's greater than 0. This is a simple demodulation scheme suitable for BPSK. Here creates a figure with three subplots. The first subplot shows the transmitted bits, the second subplot shows the received signal after path loss, and the third subplot shows the demodulated bits at the base station. The part displays the calculated Signal-to-Noise Ratio (SNR) and the path loss

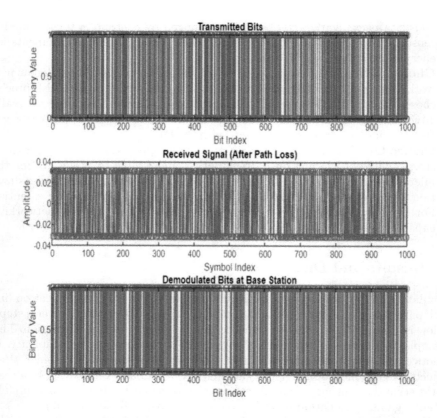

Fig. 2. Amplitude of Received signal after path lose & Demodulated Bit index.

in the command window. This code provides a simplified simulation of an IoT device communicating over a 5G link, including path loss and AWGN. For a more accurate representation, additional factors such as fading, channel models, and advanced modulation schemes may need to be considered.

Waveform design has a significant part in the advancement of 5G technology, influencing the effectiveness and performance of wireless communication systems. In 5G, waveform design is aimed at achieving higher data rates, lower latency, and improved reliability compared to previous generations [11]. One key aspect of waveform design in 5G is the use of advanced modulation schemes and multiple access techniques. The waveform needs to accommodate a diverse range of communication scenarios, including improved wireless connectivity (eMBB), ultra-reliable low-latency communications (URLLC), and mega machine-type communications (mMTC). Moreover, 5G waveform design involves the utilization of technologies such as advanced filter designs, like filtered-OFDM (f-OFDM) or windowed-OFDM, to enhance spectral efficiency and reduce out-of-band emissions (Fig. 3).

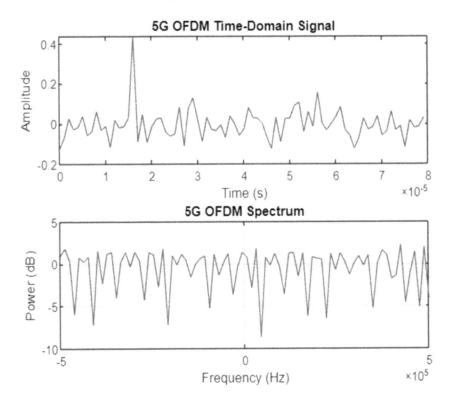

Fig. 3. 5G OFDM Time-Domain signal & 5G OFDM spectrum.

These techniques help mitigate interference and enable coexistence with other wireless systems in the frequency spectrum. By using these advanced waveform design principles, 5G technology aims to deliver an unprecedented level of connectivity, enabling diverse applications ranging from high-speed mobile broadband to massive IoT deployments and critical communication services with low-latency requirements. Above is the plot of an OFDM waveform for 5G. This code generates a random sequence of binary data, modulates it using quadrature phase shift keying (QPSK), performs an inverse fast Fourier transform (IFFT) to obtain the time-domain signal, and adds an alternating prefix. The resulting waveform is then plotted in the time domain and its spectrum is displayed [15] (Fig. 4).

Parameters: These are like settings we're choosing for a pretend wireless system. numTx means how many antennas will send signals, numRx is how many antennas will receive them, and numSamples is how many bits or pieces of the signal we're dealing with. Generating a random channel matrix: We're creating a table of numbers that pretend to show how the signals travel from

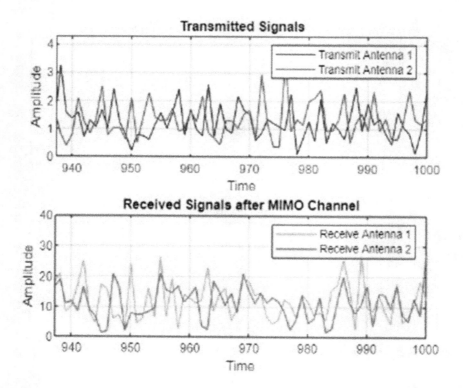

Fig. 4. Plot b/w amplitude & Time of transmitted signals and received signals after MIMO channel.

each sending antenna to each receiving antenna. It's like figuring out how the signals go through the air between all the antennas.

Creating a random transmitted signal: Think of this as the messages or information we're sending from the sending antennas. It's just random information created to simulate what might be sent. Received signal after passing through the channel: This is what happens to our random messages after they travel through the pretend wireless system. The signals might change because of the way they move through the air and reach the receiving antennas. Visualizing transmitted and received signals: We're drawing graphs to show what the original messages looked like (before being sent) and what they look like after going through the pretend wireless system. Each line on the graph represents the strength of the signal received by different antennas.

Description for Massive and Full Dimension MIMO: This is a description in simple words that explains how "Massive MIMO" and "Full Dimension MIMO" use lots of antennas to make wireless systems work better. It talks about how this MATLAB code is like a make-believe version of how these systems might work, showing how signals move between antennas.

5 Conclusion

The research presents a time-shifting and power-splitting model for the seamless transfer of 5G data and IoT services across an IOT network that is connected to 5G. This enables an IoT node to implement 5G and IoT communication in separate time slots or power streams. These two models were developed with joint optimization of node powers and allocation factors to maximize 5G transmission rates while maintaining the lowest IoT rate of transmission. Both models are available now. In lieu of the previous one, we present another optimization problem to boost the speed of IoT transmission while preserving our limited 5G speeds. Cooperative optimization is the proposed solution to these problems. Next, a plan is devised to achieve the most efficient energy usage from 5G while decreasing overall IoT power consumption.

References

1. Ejaz, W., et al.: Internet of Things (IoT) in 5G wireless communications. IEEE Access **4**, 10310–10314 (2016). https://doi.org/10.1109/ACCESS.2016.2646120
2. Dhillon, H.S., Huang, H., Viswanathan, H.: Wide-area wireless communication challenges for the Internet of Things. IEEE Commun. Mag. **55**(2), 168–174 (2017). https://doi.org/10.1109/MCOM.2017.1500269CM
3. Khuntia, M., Singh, D., Sahoo, S.: Impact of Internet of Things (IoT) on 5G. In: Smart Innovation, Systems and Technologies, pp. 125–136 (2020)
4. Chettri, L., Bera, R.: A comprehensive survey on Internet of Things (IoT) toward 5G wireless systems. IEEE Internet Things J. 16–32 (2019)
5. Painuly, S., Kohli, P., Matta, P., Sharma, S.: Advance applications and future challenges of 5G IoT. In: 2020 3rd International Conference on Intelligent Sustainable Systems (ICISS), Thoothukudi, India, pp. 1381–1384 (2020). https://doi.org/10.1109/ICISS49785.2020.9316004
6. Kaur, K., Kumar, S., Baliyan, A.: 5G: a new era of wireless communication. Int. J. Inf. Technol. **12**(2), 619–624 (2018)
7. Li, W., Kara, S.: Methodology for monitoring manufacturing environment by using wireless sensor networks (WSN) and the Internet of Things (IoT). Procedia CIRP **61**, 323–328 (2017)
8. Le, L.B., et al.: Enabling 5G mobile wireless technologies. EURASIP J. Wirel. Commun. Netw. **2015**(1) (2015)
9. Pons, M.D.T., Valenzuela, E., Rodríguez, B., Nolazco-Flores, J.A., Del-Valle-Soto, C.: Utilization of 5G technologies in IoT applications: current limitations by interference and network optimization difficulties-a review. Sensors **23**(8), 3876 (2023)
10. Ali Al-Samawi, M.A., Singh, M.: Effect of 5G on IOT and daily life application. In: 2022 3rd International Conference for Emerging Technology (INCET), Belgaum, India, pp. 1–5 (2022). https://doi.org/10.1109/INCET54531.2022.9823983
11. APPENDIX B: MATLAB Code for IoT Smart Grid. McGraw-Hill Education - Access Engineering (n.d.)
12. Painuly, S., Sharma, S., Matta, P.: Future trends and challenges in next generation smart application of 5G-IoT. In: 2021 5th International Conference on Computing Methodologies and Communication (ICCMC), Erode, India, pp. 354–357 (2021)

13. Khan, M.J., Chauhan, R.C.S., Singh, I.: Performance analysis of heterogeneous network using relay diversity in high-speed vehicular communication. Wireless Pers. Commun. **125**, 1163–1184 (2022)
14. Annamalai, P., Bapat, J., Das, D.: Emerging access technologies and open challenges in 5G IoT: from physical layer perspective. In: 2018 IEEE International Conference on Advanced Networks and Telecommunications Systems (ANTS), Indore, India, pp. 1–6 (2018). https://doi.org/10.1109/ANTS.2018.8710133
15. Liu, S., Liu, L., Yang, H., Yue, K., Guo, T.: Research on 5G technology based on Internet of Things. In: 2020 IEEE 5th Information Technology and Mechatronics Engineering Conference (ITOEC), Chongqing, China, pp. 1821–1823 (2020). https://doi.org/10.1109/ITOEC49072.2020.9141671
16. Yang, Z., Gao, F.: Design and implementation of a smart factory system based on 5G and IoT technology. In: 2023 International Conference on Network, Multimedia and Information Technology (NMITCON), Bengaluru, India, pp. 1–5 (2023). https://doi.org/10.1109/NMITCON58196.2023.10276253
17. Shafique, K., Khawaja, B.A., Sabir, F., Qazi, S., Mustaqim, M.: Internet of Things (IoT) for next-generation smart systems: a review of current challenges, future trends and prospects for emerging 5G-IoT scenarios. IEEE Access **8**, 23022–23040 (2020). https://doi.org/10.1109/ACCESS.2020.2970118
18. Jin, B., et al.: Advantages of 5G slicing technology in the Internet of Things. In: 2023 IEEE International Conference on Integrated Circuits and Communication Systems (ICICACS), Raichur, India, pp. 1–5 (2023)
19. Singh, I., Singh, N.P.: Analysis of success probability for device-to-device communication underlaid cellular networks operating over-generalized $\kappa - \mu$ fading. Optik **178**, 731–739 (2019)
20. Sandoval, R.M., Canovas-Carrasco, S., Garcia-Sanchez, A.-J., Garcia-Haro, J.: Smart usage of multiple RAT in IoT-oriented 5G networks: a reinforcement learning approach. In: 2018 ITU Kaleidoscope: Machine Learning for a 5G Future (ITU K), Santa Fe, Argentina, pp. 1–8 (2018)

IoT-Based Convolutional Neural Networks in a Farm Pest Detection Using Transfer Learning

Keyurbhai A. Jani[1](✉), Nirbhay Kumar Chaubey[2], Esan Panchal[3], Pramod Tripathi[3], and Shruti Yagnik[4]

[1] Computer/IT Engineering, Gujarat Technological University, Ahmedabad, Gujarat 382424, India
`keyur.soft@gmail.com`
[2] Computer Science, Ganpat University, Mahesana 384012, Gujarat, India
`nirbhay@ieee.org`
[3] Information Technology, Government Polytechnic, Gandhinagar 382027, Gujarat, India
[4] Computer Engineering, Indus University, Ahmedabad, Gujarat 382115, India
`shrutiyagnik.ce@indusuni.ac.in`

Abstract. In this study explores agriculture pest detection using transfer learning with IoT devices, evaluating VGG16, VGG19, Inception, and Xception CNN architectures with the agripest dataset. VGG16 and VGG19 show effective learning with consistent accuracy improvements. Inception V3 exhibits strong training but with variability in validation metrics, while Xception demonstrates robust performance and strong generalization to new data. The integrated system utilizes cameras, sensors, and drones for real-time image processing through a gateway and cloud server with a customized agripest dataset. Transfer learning generates a deployable.h5 file for pest identification. The generated custom model deployed on a gateway or server to classifies pests, alerting farmers through SMS, dashboard, or mobile app notifications. This synergy between machine learning and IoT offers rapid and precise pest detection in agriculture.

Keywords: IoT · deep learning · CNN · pest detection · cloud · farm · gateway

1 Introduction

The Internet of Things (IoT) is an exponentially expanding realm poised to transform our lifestyles, occupations, and interactions with our environment. IoT refers to a network of physical objects, such as devices, vehicles, and office and house appliances, equipped with different sensors, communication devices and smart program. These elements enable the devices to collect and exchange data, enhancing their functionality and enabling new applications. This technology facilitates diverse functionalities and enhancements across multiple sectors including smart residences, healthcare, industrial processes, and agriculture [1]. In the agriculture domain, pest detection has always been a daunting task for experts and researchers. Their inherently complex anatomical structure creates the first layer of difficulty. Compounding this challenge is the striking similarity in appearance between various species, often leading to misidentification [1, 2]. This overlap in physical characteristics emphasizes the need for more precise and nuanced methods to differentiate between them effectively [3].

The rapid ascent in demand for highly efficient image capturing tools alongside the notable achievements of deep learning across diverse realms of image manipulation have facilitated the development of an automated system for identifying pests [4–8]. System which utilize deep learning for image processing promises to decrease manpower cost and give good result with the help of cloud and IoT devices [9–13].

2 Literature Review

Recently, deep learning models, particularly those based on Convolutional Neural Networks (CNNs), have emerged as powerful tools for image classification. They have found extensive applications in the agricultural industry. These applications range from identifying plant diseases [14] and classifying fruits [15], to detecting weeds [16], and differentiating crop pests [17]. Specifically Li et al. [18] presented an effective method for identifying pests in rape crops, utilizing a deep CNN. This technique achieved impressive accuracy, detecting pests like flea beetles, aphids, cabbage caterpillar larvae, Phaedon brassicae Baly, and rape bugs with an average success rate of 94.12%. On a similar note, Kuzuhara et al. [19] offered a two-tiered approach that first detected pests using enhanced CNNs and then re-identified the outputs using the Xception model. In [20], the accuracy in identifying plant species experienced a boost with the application of models such as AlexNet, Google Net and VGGNet. Concurrently to fetch features authors of [22] employed an accurately pre-trained SSD, with the aim of categorizing six types of diseases affecting ale and banana fruits. This approach was adopted to elevate both the classification accuracy and the overall degree of precision. Authors of [21] develop model which detect 31 types of pests with 98.1% accuracy. They compare it with different version of YOLO models and Faster RCNN with their model and find minimum improvement of 2.1% then other models. In [22], researchers have tested using a dataset of pest images and improved accuracy by tweaking image properties like color and angle. They also compared different training methods and found that a technique called "transfer learning" was better and faster than starting from scratch. Additionally, the right image adjustments can make the detection even more accurate, achieving up to 86.95% accuracy. This method stands out in its accuracy compared to other similar studies and promises a more effective way to classify pests in agriculture. In [23], Liu, Y et al., introduces a method for identifying crop pests using a multilayer network model. The process to create pest image recognition model (PIRM) begins with dataset with enhanced images. Then construct PIRM using transfer learning networks, VGG16 and Inception-ResNet-v2, ensuring a comprehensive recognition system. By adopting an integrated algorithm approach, they have merged two improved CNN series models to boost the accuracy of pest recognition and classification. Their tests, conducted on the IDADP dataset, reveal that our method achieves a 97.71% accuracy rate in pest identification, marking a significant improvement over existing techniques.

In recent years, the rapid advancements in hardware and GPU-driven computing technology have effectively addressed the high computational costs associated with

Convolutional Neural Networks (CNNs). Their applicability has broadened across different fields. Despite having varied structures, convolutional layers, pooling layers, and fully connected layers are key components of CNNs. The convolutional layer is pivotal in identifying local features within input data by utilizing convolution operators and kernel functions. Following this, the recognized features undergo dimensionality reduction in the pooling layer. Finally, fully connected layers convert retrieved features into labels. Transfer learning is a technique where existing knowledge is leveraged to address problems in different but related domains [24]. In the context of CNNs, transfer learning aim is to utilize the "knowledge" which acquired from training on a specific dataset and apply it to a new domain. Essentially, it involves training a model on similar datasets to capture generalized "knowledge", which can then be applied to the intended problem. The VGG model, introduced by Karen Simonyan and Andrew Zisserman in 2014, utilizes small 3 × 3 convolutional filters and Max-pooling over a 2 × 2-pixel window with a stride of two. Notable architectures derived from this model include VGG16 and VGG19. VGG16, with 16 layers and 143 million parameters, secured top rankings in the ICLRLSVRC-2014 competition. VGG19, with 19 layers and 138 million parameters, ranked second with a similar top accuracy of 71.3% and a top-5 accuracy of 90%. Despite having fewer parameters, VGG19 demonstrated comparable accuracy to VGG16 [25]. In 2016, Szegedy et al. introduced InceptionResNetv2, an evolution of the Inception family of architectures. Unlike the traditional Inception architecture which employs filter concatenation stages, InceptionResNetv2 integrates residual connections. These residual connections act as shortcuts within the model, not only simplifying the Inception blocks but also enhancing the model's performance [26, 27]. Furthermore, it maintains a depth of 572 layers and comprises 55.9M parameters and show efficiency with accuracy of 80.3% and a top-5 accuracy of 95.4%. Chollet et al. introduced the Xception model in 2017, an extension of the inception architecture that maximizes its principles. This convolutional neural network predominantly uses depth-wise separable convolution layers. Unlike the inception model, Xception applies filters before compression, distinguishing it in convolution processes and activation functions. Conversely, Xception applies filters first and then proceeds with compression. Additionally, Xception eschews the non-linearities present in the inception model; specifically, while the inception model uses the ReLU activation function, Xception does not [28, 29]. Performance-wise, Xception boasts a top accuracy of 79% and a top-5 accuracy of 94.5%. This is achieved with a configuration of 22.9M parameters and a network depth spanning 126 layers.

3 Motivation for Proposal

Farmers in India use traditional methods for farming and face financial losses due to pests not being detected in the early stages. Therefore, there is a need for a system that can detect pests in farm crops at an early stage without requiring daily physical inspection and can alert the farmer with the name, photo, and suggest possible management of that detected pest. To solve the above issue, we use IoT devices, communication technologies, and servers [3, 30, 32].

4 Proposed Architecture and Solution

Pests have perennially threatened agricultural productivity, often hindering the efforts of diligent farmers. Effective pest identification is crucial for mitigation, and with the advent of machine learning and IoT, there is potential for rapid and precise recognition. As shown in Fig. 1, we deployed different cameras and other sensors in the farm field to capture real-time images and videos. Drones can also be used to capture images. These images and sensor data are passed to the gateway for further processing. The processed file and data are then sent to the server for analysis. The server has our customized agripest image dataset.

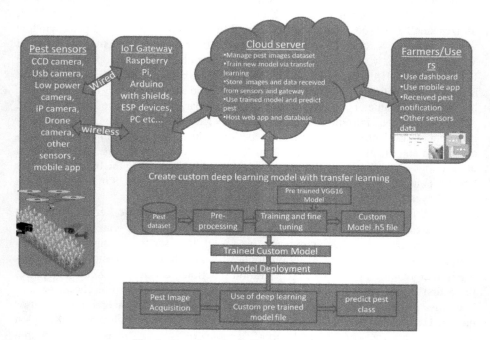

Fig. 1. Pest detection IoT system architecture

On the cloud server, our Python program uses this dataset and employs different deep learning models to find the best-suited model for Indian pest detection. In this process, the transfer learning method will be used to generate a.h5 output file of the best-fitted model. This custom model can be deployed on a compatible gateway or server. The web app server retrieves received images from sensors or the gateway, utilizing the previously trained custom model's.h5 file to classify pests. The server stores this information in a database and alerts farmers for pest detection via SMS, dashboard, or mobile app notification.

To choose the best deep learning model, the transfer learning technique is used on the server when required. Different models use the agripest dataset for training and testing.

The best model's.h5 file is generated, which will be deployed and used by the server, as shown in Fig. 1 and discussed in detail in the Results and Discussion section.

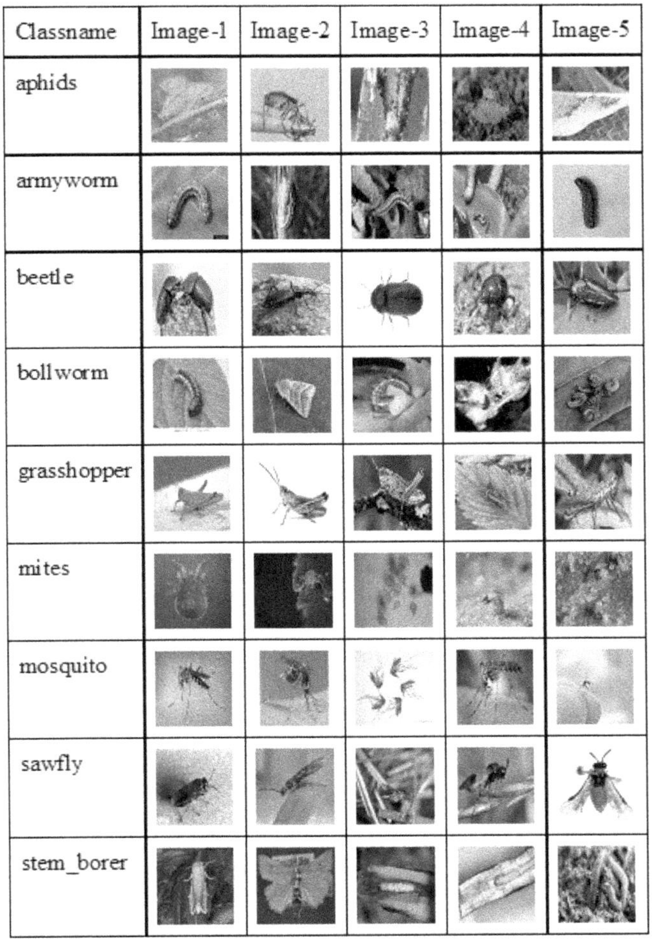

Classname	Image-1	Image-2	Image-3	Image-4	Image-5
aphids					
armyworm					
beetle					
bollworm					
grasshopper					
mites					
mosquito					
sawfly					
stem_borer					

Fig. 2. Agripest dataset

Dataset Overview:

Type: Image dataset.
Training Set: 300 images per pest, totaling 2,700 images across all pests.
Testing Set: 50 images per pest, resulting in 450 images in total.
Data Acquisition: The dataset was curated using an automated script that extracted pest images from Google. The tools employed for the scraping process included Selenium and Chrome Driver and dataset on Kaggle posted by Simran Volunesia [31].

Pests Catalog: The dataset encapsulates images of the following pests as shown in Fig. 2.

5 Results and Discussion

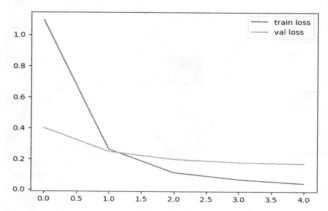

Fig. 3. Comparison between loss function in VGG16

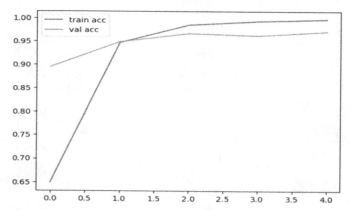

Fig. 4. Comparison between accuracy in VGG16 for varying epos

As shown in Figs. 3 and 4, the VGG16 model was trained with different epochs on a specific task, demonstrating consistent improvement in both training and validation metrics. Despite an extended first epoch, subsequent epochs took around 45–47 s each. The training loss decreased from 1.0945 to 0.0409, and accuracy increased from 64.93% to 99.74%. Similarly, the validation loss decreased from 0.4007 to 0.1704, and accuracy increased from 89.56% to 97.11%. The model demonstrated effective learning without overfitting, as evidenced by the convergence of training and validation metrics. The final high validation accuracy of 97.11% suggests good generalization to new data, highlighting the model's capability for accurate predictions. Further considerations should account for the specific task, dataset characteristics, and potential requirements for additional evaluation or fine-tuning in practical applications.

As shown in Figs. 5 and 6, the VGG19 model was trained over different epochs, with the first epoch taking notably longer (1723 s) than subsequent epochs (around 43–44 s each). Throughout training, the model demonstrated effective learning, as evidenced by the decreasing training loss from 1.1916 to 0.0603 and increasing accuracy from 62.26% to 99.44%. The validation metrics also showed positive trends, with validation loss decreasing from 0.5515 to 0.1374 and validation accuracy increasing from 81.33% to 96.89%. These results indicate that the VGG19 model generalizes well to new, unseen data, showcasing a high level of accuracy and successful learning without overfitting. Considerations for practical applications should encompass the specific task, dataset characteristics, and potential areas for further evaluation or fine-tuning. Overall, the VGG19 model performed well on the given task.

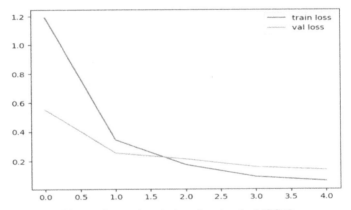

Fig. 5. Comparison in loss function for VGG19

The Inception V3 model was trained with different epochs, with the initial epoch lasting 720 s and subsequent epochs ranging around 259–267 s each. The training showcased a significant drop in loss from 4.6038 to 0.3089 and rise in accuracy from 68.63% to 95.07% as shown in Figs. 7 and 8.

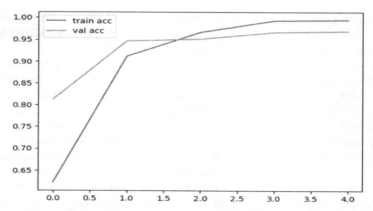

Fig. 6. Comparison between accuracy in VGG19 for varying epos

However, the validation performance exhibited a more varied pattern, with the validation loss fluctuating between 0.5333 and 0.9301 and the validation accuracy peaking at 95.11%. While the model demonstrated effective learning on the training set, its performance on the validation set suggests a potential challenge in generalizing to new data. Further investigation into potential overfitting or the need for model adjustments may be warranted. Practical considerations should account for the specific task, dataset characteristics, and potential avenues for fine-tuning or optimization in real-world applications.

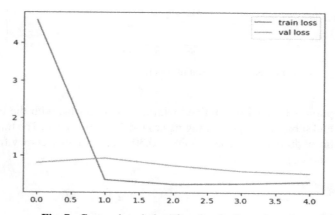

Fig. 7. Comparison in loss function for Inception v3

The Xception model underwent training with different epochs, with the initial epoch lasting 1600 s and subsequent epochs around 72–73 s each. Throughout training, there was a significant decrease in loss from 2.2123 to 0.3550, accompanied by a notable increase in accuracy from 79.81% to 96.85%. The validation performance demonstrated a consistent positive tendency, with the validation loss declining from 0.3442 to 0.5333

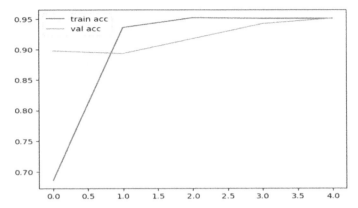

Fig. 8. Comparison between accuracy in Inception v3 for varying epos

and the validation accuracy rising from 95.11% to 96.44% as shown in Figs. 9 and 10. These results suggest that the Xception model effectively learned from the training data, showcasing high accuracy and demonstrating good generalization to new, unseen data. The model's ability to maintain high validation accuracy across epochs indicates robust performance, making it a strong candidate for the given task. Practical considerations should include task-specific requirements, dataset characteristics, and potential areas for further fine-tuning or optimization in real-world applications.

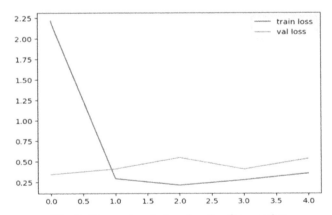

Fig. 9. Comparison in loss function for xception

According to the outcomes observed with the agripest dataset, the custom model incorporating transfer learning from pre-trained VGG16 demonstrates superior performance. Subsequently, a .h5 file of this model is generated and deployed as previously discussed, both on cloud infrastructure and gateway devices. These implementations aim to facilitate pest detection and subsequently alert farmers or users to undertake appropriate actions, as depicted in Figs. 11 and 12.

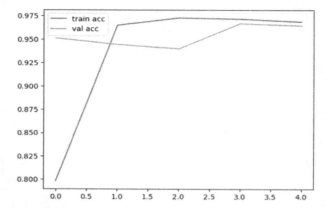

Fig. 10. Comparison between accuracy in xception for varying epos

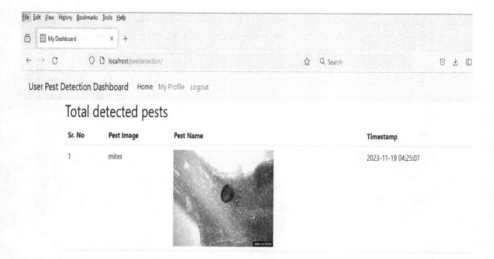

Fig. 11. Pest Detection Web dashboard

Fig. 12. Pest detection Mobile app

6 Conclusion

This study highlights the synergy between machine learning and IoT in addressing agricultural challenges, offering a scalable and technologically advanced solution for precise pest detection. The evaluation of VGG16, VGG19, Inception, and Xception models underscores their effectiveness, with VGG16 identified as the best-suited model for our research. Practical considerations for model selection should be based on specific task requirements and dataset characteristics. The custom model, implemented on compatible gateways or servers, streamlines pest detection on the web app server, enabling timely alerts to farmers via SMS, dashboard notifications, or a mobile app. The system demonstrates adaptability by integrating a range of deep learning models, allowing for continual training and testing to identify the most efficient one. Overall, our system empowers farmers with timely insights, contributing to proactive pest management and reducing crop production costs.

References

1. He, X., Bonds, J., Herpbmt, A., Langenakens, J.: Recent development of unmanned aerial vehicle for plant protection in East Asia. Int. J. Agric. Biol. Eng. **10**(3), 18–30 (2017)
2. Yang, J., Guo, X., Li, Y., Marinello, F., Ercisli, S., Zhang, Z.: A survey of few-shot learning in smart agriculture: developments, applications, and challenges. Plant Methods **18**, 28 (2022)
3. Jani, K.A., Chaubey, N.K.: A novel model for optimization of resource utilization in smart agriculture system using IoT (SMAIoT). IEEE Internet Things J. **9**(13), 11275–11282 (2022)
4. Atlam, M., Torkey, H., El-Fishawy, N., Salem, H.: Coronavirus disease 2019 (COVID-19): survival analysis using deep learning and cox regression model. Pattern Anal. Appl. **24**(3), 993–1005 (2021)
5. G. Huang, Zhuang, L., Maaten, L.v.d., Weinberger, K. Q.: Densely connected convolutional networks. In IEEE Conference on Computer Vision and Pattern Recognition (CVPR (2017)
6. Krizhevsky, A., Sutskever, I., Hinton, G.: ImageNet classification with deep convolutional neural networks. In Advances in Neural Information Processing Systems, vol. 25, Lake Tahoe, NV, USA, Curran Associates, Inc., pp. 1097–1105 (2012)
7. Ning, X., Duan, P., Li, W., Zhang, S.: Real-time 3D face alignment using an encoder-decoder network with an efficient deconvolution layer. IEEE Signal Process. Lett. **27**, 1944–1948 (2020)
8. Salem, H., Attiya, G., El-Fishawy, N.: Gene expression profiles based human cancer dis-eases classification. In 11th International Computer Engineering Conference (ICENCO), Cairo, Egypt (2015)
9. LeCun, Y., Bengio, Y., Hinton, G.: Deep learning. Nature **521**, 436–444 (2015)
10. . Ren, S, He, K., Girshick, R., Sun, J.: Faster R-CNN: towards real-time object detection with region proposal networks. In Advances in Neural Information Processing Systems; Curran Associates, Inc., Montréal, QC, Canada (2015)
11. Reyes, A., Caicedo, J., amargo, J.: Fine-tuning deep convolutional networks for plant recognition. In CLEF 2015 (2015)
12. Shelhamer, E., Long, J., Darrell, T.: Fully convolutional networks for semantic segmentation. IEEE Trans. Pattern Anal. Mach. Intell. **39**(4), 640–651 (2017)
13. Zhang, H., He, G., Peng, J., Kuang, Z., Fan, J.: Deep learning of path-based tree classifiers for large-scale plant species identification. In *2018 IEEE Conference on Multimedia Information Processing and Retrieval (MIPR)*, Miami, FL, USA (2018)
14. Deng, L., Wang, Y., Han, Z., Yu, R.: Research on pest pest image detection and recognition based on bio-inspired methods. Biosyst. Eng. **169**, 139–148 (2018)
15. Mukhiddinov, M., Muminov, A., Cho, J.: Improved classification approach for fruits and vegetables freshness based on deep learning. Sensors **22**(21), 8192 (2022)
16. Lu, Y., Yi, S., Zeng, N., Liu, Y., Zhang, Y.: Identification of rice diseases using deep convolutional neural networks. Neurocomputing **267**, 378–384 (2017)
17. Liu, B., Zhang, Y., He, D., Li, Y.: Identification of apple leaf diseases based on deep convolutional neural networks. Symmetry **10**(1), 11 (2018)
18. Li, H., Long, C., Zeng, M., Shen, J.: A detecting method for the rape pests based on deep convolutional neural network. J. Hunan Agri. Univ. (Natl. Sci.) **45**(5), 114–118 (2019)
19. Kuzuhara, H., Takimoto, H., Sato, Y., Kanagawa, A.: Insect pest detection and identification method based on deep learning for realizing a pest control system. In *2020 59th Annual Conference of the Society of Instrument and Control Engineers of Japan (SICE)*, Chiang Mai, Thailand (2020)
20. Ghazi, M., Yanikoglu, B., Aptoula, E.: Plant identification using deep neural networks via optimization of transfer learning parameters. Neurocomputing **235**, 228–235 (2017)

21. Liu, D., Lv, F., Guo, J., Zhang, H., Zhu, L.: Detection of forestry pests based on improved YOLOv5 and transfer learning. Forests **14**(7), 1484 (2023)
22. Chen, L., Zhen, T., Li, Z.: Image classification of pests with residual neural network based on transfer learning. Appl. Sci. **12**(9), 4356 (2022)
23. Liu, Y., Zhang, X., Gao, Y., Qu, T., Shi, Y.: Improved CNN method for crop pest identification based on transfer learning. Comput. Intell. Neurosci., **2022** (2022)
24. El-Shafai, W., Almomani, I., AlKhayer, A.: Visualized malware multi-classification framework using fine-tuned CNN-based transfer learning models. Appl. Sci. **11**(14), 6446 (2021)
25. Simonyan, K., Zisserman, A.: Very deep convolutional networks for Large-scale image recognition, pp. 1–14 (2015)
26. Szegedy, C., Ioffe, S., Vanhoucke, V., Alemi, A.A.: Inception-v4, inception-ResNet and the impact of residual connections on learning. In *Proceedings of the AAAI Conference on Artificial Intelligence* (2017)
27. Elhamraoui, Z.: InceptionResNetV2 Simple Introduction (2020) [Online]. Available: https://medium.com/@zahraelhamraoui1997/inceptionresnetv2-simple-introduction-9a2 000edcdb6. [Accessed 25 1 2024]
28. Akhtar, Z.: Xception: deep learning with depth-wise separable convolutions (Open-Genus IQ: Computing Expertise and Legacy) [Online]. Available: https://iq.opengenus.org/xception-model/. [Accessed 31 08 2023]
29. Chollet, F.: Xception: deep learning with depthwise separable convolution. In *2017 IEEE Conference on Computer Vision and Pattern Recognition (CVPR)*, Honolulu, HI, USA (2017)
30. Jani, K.A., Chaubey, N.K.: SDIPMIoT: smart drip irrigation and preventative maintenance using IoT. SSRG Int. J. Electric. Electron. Eng. **10**(7), 22–30 (2023)
31. Volunesia, S.: Pest Dataset [Online]. Available: https://www.kaggle.com/datasets/simranvol unesia/pest-dataset/data. [Accessed 23, 9, 2023]
32. Jani, K.A., Chaubey, N.: IoT and cyber security: introduction, attacks, and preventive steps. In *Quantum Cryptography and the Future of Cyber Security*, N.K.C. a. B. B. Prajapati (ed.) IGI Global, pp. 203–235 (2020)

Performance Comparison of NOMA Vehicular Communications Under Shadow Fading

Hetal Shah(✉) and Vinay Thumar(✉)

D. D. University, Nadiad, Gujarat, India
{shahhetal.ec,vinay_thumar}@ddu.ac.in

Abstract. This paper focuses on investigating the performance of vehicular networks employing non-orthogonal multiple access (NOMA), wherein a base station (BS) situated roadside communicates with a pair of vehicles containing multiple antennas. To enhance the performance, maximal ratio combining technique is employed at the vehicles, leveraging diversity gain. Real-world scenarios, however, often deviate from the assumption of identically distributed channels between the BS and vehicles, impacting the expected system performance. To provide practical insights, the paper derives closed-form expressions for channel density functions, outage probability (OP), and ergodic rate of NOMA vehicular networks under independent and not necessarily identically distributed channels (INID). The analysis also incorporates the impact of time-selective fading to model the mobility of vehicles. Performance of the system is further analyzed through outage performance, rate, and sum-rate performance metrics at varying speeds of vehicles and decaying parameters of non-identically distributed channels. Simulations are conducted to validate the presented results. Additionally, the NOMA is compared with orthogonal multiple access (OMA) for vehicular networks. Numerical results confirm the superiority of NOMA over OMA under both independent and identically distributed (IID) and realistic INID channel conditions, emphasizing the robustness of NOMA across different vehicle speeds and non-uniform channel distributions.

Keywords: Vehicular communication · NOMA · Maximal Ratio Combining · INID · OP · Ergodic rate

1 Introduction

Road transportation is a pivotal element in urban development, serving as the primary mode of travel for countless individuals daily. The advent of Intelligent Transportation Systems (ITS) has significantly enhanced the safety, comfort, and enjoyment of journeys [1]. Vehicular communication plays a crucial role in realizing ITS objectives, including ensuring the safety of drivers and passengers, efficient traffic management, and the provision of uninterrupted multimedia services for infotainment applications [2]. Dissemination of Safety messages requires highly reliable and low latency communications, traffic management demands massive connectivity of vehicles while multimedia services and infotainment applications need high data rate and seamless internet connectivity [3]. Theses demands increase in orders for the futuristic vehicular applications such as connected driving, autonomous driving and platooning [4]. Recently available technologies, such as dedicated short range communications (DSRC) and Long Term Evolution (LTE) cellular-vehicle-to-everything (C-V2X) are rely on orthogonal multiple access (OMA), which may not fulfill the stringent requirements of emerging vehicular applications [5]. OMA has fixed number of time or frequency resources which results in limitations regarding user connectivity, reliability, and low latency, hindering the fulfillment of critical communication requirements.

Non-orthogonal multiple access (NOMA) is a encouraging fifth generation techniques to overcome challenges inherent in current vehicular communication systems [6]. The core principle of NOMA is a distinctive approach of multiplexing multiple users in the power domain within a single time slot or frequency band. This unique feature of NOMA is a key enabler for meeting the needs of the futuristic vehicular applications by fulfilling the demands of massive connectivity, low latency, high reliability, and spectrum efficiency [7]. NOMA was used in V2X sidelink communication to fulfill the demands of 6G vehicular networks [8].

1.1 Literature Survey

Looking at the low latency, high reliability, and data rate as well as massive connectivity requirements of growing vehicular networks, many researchers have worked on applications of NOMA in vehicular networks. In [9] and [10], NOMA was applied in vehicular networks to support the lower latency and the higher reliability in C-V2X. NOMA was utilized in vehicular small cell networks to address the issues of interference management and handover by improving energy and spectrum efficiency [11]. In [12], NOMA is used for vehicles' cooperation problem for collision avoidance. Authors in [13] discussed dynamic power and rate allocation for NOMA aided vehicle-to-infrastructure communication under independent and identically distributed (IID) channel considerations. In [14], the outage performance and system throughput of NOMA-enabled vehicular networks were compared with OMA under double Rayleigh flat fading channels to model the mobility. The performance of NOMA-assisted vehicular networks was evaluated under shadow fading conditions using log-normal channel [15]. However, they did not carry out theoretical analysis. The above reported works consider single antenna systems and flat fading channels. Authors in [16], incorporated multiple antennas in NOMA vehicular communications to improve the performance assuming IID diversity branches. However, the vehicular communication is more assorted in comparison with static wireless networks and have antenna placement on roof, bumper or side mirrors which can be obstructed by large vehicles, trees or buildings [17]. Therefore, the IID consideration is not suitable practically for vehicular communications. In [18], the performance of vehicular networks with NOMA under independent but not necessarily identically distributed (INID) channels were analyzed over single antenna system. Authors in [19], worked on relay assisted vehicular network over INID double Nakagami-m fading channels considering single antenna system.

1.2 Motivation and Contributions

High spectrum efficiency, low latency, high reliability, and connectivity from vehicle-to-vehicle, vehicle-to-infrastructure, and vehicle-to-sensors are requisites for the development of ITS to implement the futuristic vehicular applications like connected driving, automated, smart transportation, and infotainment applications. The aforementioned literature survey reveals that NOMA is an optimistic technique to meet these demands. Our work is carried out for NOMA-assisted vehicular networks where a BS transmits a signal to a pair of vehicles in downlink using NOMA over multiple receiver antennas. Frequently, the communication between BS and vehicles is obstructed by trees, buildings, and large vehicles. Therefore, we assume shadow fading conditions and not identically distributed diversity branches from BS to vehicles. Moreover, the mobility of vehicles is modeled with time-selective fading. In [20], the outage and rate performance of NOMA in vehicular communications was evaluated for an arbitrary number of vehicles with an arbitrary number of antennas over INID Nakagami fading channels. However, the presented analysis is complex as it is carried out for an arbitrary number of vehicles. In [21], the similar work is carried out using stacked-long short term memory deep learning algorithm for arbitrary number of users. In NOMA, the interference increases with the increase in the number of vehicles. Therefore, it is preferable to use a pair of users rather than multiple users using NOMA in a single resource block. Authors in [22], evaluated the secrecy of NOMA-enabled vehicle-to-vehicle communications over INID time selective fading channels. In [23], the outage probability (OP) and the error rate performance of NOMA-aided vehicular networks in conjunction with cognitive radio over INID Rayleigh fading channel with single transmit and receive antennas. [24] worked on the error rate performance and the ergodic capacity analysis of NOMA-enabled vehicular communications under INID double Nakagami-m fading channels with multiple transmit antennas. In this work, we analyze the performance of a pair of vehicles using NOMA with multiple receiver antennas in vehicular networks over not identically distributed diversity branches. We consider Rayleigh as a small-scale fading channel as it is more suitable for non-line-of-sight communications [25]. Our work takes into account real-world challenges such as obstacles (trees, buildings, large vehicles), shadow fading conditions, and non-identically distributed diversity branches. As per the authors' knowledge, this type of work is not published in the literature. In particular, the key contributions of our work are as below:

1. We derive the cumulative distribution function (CDF) of the average SNR over Rayleigh fading channels for multiple receiver antennas with INID consideration. We obtain the closed-form expressions for two receiver antennas in NOMA vehicular networks.

2. We obtain the closed-form expression of the OP at NOMA vehicle pairing over Rayleigh fading channels for two receiver antennas with INID channel assumption. We compare the obtained OP with OMA under IID and INID channel consideration at various speed of vehicles and decaying parameter of non identical diversity branches.
3. Finally, we derive ergodic capacity at each vehicles served with NOMA over INID Rayleigh channels for NOMA vehicular networks. We also derive the sum rate and compare the rate and sum rate with OMA under IID and INID considerations at various speed of vehicles and decaying parameter of non identical channels.

The paper is organized as below. Section 2 presents the system model which contains the signal model, network model and channel density functions, Sect. 3 describes the performance analysis of the OP and the ergodic rate. Section 4 discuss the numerical results and Sect. 5 concludes the work followed by references.

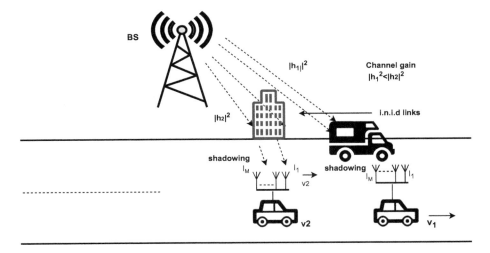

Fig. 1. NOMA Vehicular Communications under Shadow Fading.

2 System Model

In this study, we present a system model for down-link communication between a base station (BS) and vehicles on a single-lane highway as mentioned in Fig. 1. The BS, located at the roadside, establishes communication with two vehicles, denoted as V_1 and V_2, traveling in opposite directions from the BS at a comparable speed of v_i km/hour. The communication setup involves a single transmit antenna affixed to the BS, which communicates with M receive antennas mounted on each of the vehicles. Each wireless link, extending from the transmit antenna to the receive antennas on the vehicles, is characterized by INID diversity branches. This diversity is integral, as the signal received at each antenna exhibits varying average Signal-to-Noise Ratios (SNR) owing to shadow fading, contributing to the overall robustness of the communication links. Furthermore, we model the mobility of the vehicles using an auto-regressive time-selective fading approach, capturing the dynamic nature of the wireless channel as the vehicles traverse the single lane highway. The fading coefficient from BS to the ith vehicle, can be expressed as

$$h_{v_i} = \rho_i h_i + \sqrt{1-\rho_i^2}\epsilon_i \qquad (1)$$

where $i \in (1,2)$, $\rho_i \in [0,1]$ is the time adjoining channel correlation parameter. As per Jake's model, $\rho_i = J_0\left(\frac{2\pi f_c v_i}{R_i C}\right)$, where $J_0(.)$ is the zeroth-order Bessel function of the first kind, v_i, f_c and f_c denote the speed of vehicles, frequency of the carrier and the speed of light respectively. R_i is the symbol rate. ϵ_i is a time-varying component, which indicates the complex Gaussian random variable distributed as zero-mean circularly symmetric with variance σ_{ei}^2. h_a is a small-scale fading coefficient related to the distance d_i between the BS and i^{th} vehicle, $h_i = \frac{h_{b_i}}{\sqrt{1+d_i^\alpha}}$, where h_{b_i} represents channel vector following the Rayleigh fading distribution for each link from the BS to i^{th} vehicle.

2.1 Signal Model

As shown in the network diagram, the BS combines the signal for the far vehicle V_1 and the near vehicle V_2 using the superposition in power domain with the total power P_v and transmit the superimposed signal to V_1 and V_2 in down-link on the same time/frequency resource block using NOMA. The BS allocates large power with power coefficient $\beta_1 > 0.5$ to the far vehicle V_1, suffering from the weak channel condition and less power with the power coefficient $\beta_2 = 1 - \beta_1$ to the near vehicle V_2 having strong channel condition. The signal received at the ith vehicle is written as

$$y_i = h_{v_i}\left(\sqrt{P_v\beta_1}s_1 + \sqrt{P_v\beta_2}s_2\right) + \eta_i, \qquad (2)$$

where η_i is additive white Gaussian noise with mean zero and variance σ_n^2 By applying (1) into (2), the received signal can be written as

$$y_i = \rho_i h_i\sqrt{P_v\beta_1}s_1 + \rho_i h_i\sqrt{P_v\beta_2}s_2 + \sqrt{1-\rho_i^2}\epsilon_i\sqrt{P_v\beta_1}s_1 + \sqrt{1-\rho_i^2}\epsilon_i\sqrt{P_v\beta_2}s_2 + \eta_i, \qquad (3)$$

2.2 SINR at Vehicles

The vehicles V_1 and V_2 receives the combined signal of V_1 and V_2 sent by the BS. V_1 detects its own high-powered signal from the combined received signal by considering V_2's signal as a noise. From (3), the received signal SINR at V_1 can be obtained as

$$\psi_1 = \frac{\left(\rho_1^2 \beta_1 \gamma_v |h_1|^2\right)}{\gamma_v \left(\rho_1^2 \beta_2 |h_1|^2 + (1-\rho_1^2)\sigma_{e1}^2\right) + 1} \qquad (4)$$

Successive interference cancellation (SIC)V_2 is carried out at the V_2 to detect the signal. It detects V_1's signal, eliminates it from the superimposed signal and then detects its own signal. The received SINR of the signal at V_2 to detect V_1's signal, can be obtained as

$$\psi_{2,1} = \frac{\left(\rho_2^2 \beta_1 \gamma_v |h_2|^2\right)}{\gamma_v \left(\rho_2^2 \beta_2 |h_2|^2 + (1-\rho_2^2)\sigma_{e2}^2\right) + 1}, \qquad (5)$$

The received signal SINR at V_2 to detect its own signal, can be obtained as

$$\psi_2 = \frac{\left(\rho_2^2 \beta_2 \gamma_v |h_2|^2\right)}{\gamma_v (1-\rho_2^2)\sigma_{e2}^2 + 1} \qquad (6)$$

2.3 Density Functions of Channel Gains

This work examines the performance of NOMA-enabled vehicular networks under shadow-fading conditions. Therefore, there is no line-of-sight from BS to vehicles. In this case, Rayleigh fading is the most suitable channel. The channel gain from the BS to the mth receiver antenna on the vehicle is indicated as h_{mn}. The probability density function (PDF) of the received SNR of the Rayleigh channel is written as

$$f_{|h_{mn}|^2}(x) = \lambda e^{-x\lambda}, \qquad (7)$$

where $\lambda = \frac{1}{\Omega}$, $\Omega = E[|h_{mn}|^2]$ is the average received SNR. The average received SNR is not the same at not identically distributed diversity branches. The average received SNR at the mth antenna is $\Omega_m = \Omega_1 e^{-(m-1)\delta}$, where Ω_1 is the highest value of the received SNR and δ is the decaying factor, i. e for $M = 2$, the average received SNR at the first link is Ω_1 and the second link is $\Omega_2 = \Omega_1 e^{-\delta}$. For IID links, $\delta = 0$ leads to $\Omega_1 = \Omega_2$.

By integrating (7), the CDF of the average received SNR can be deduced as

$$F_{|h_{mn}|^2}(x) = 1 - e^{-\lambda x} \qquad (8)$$

At the vehicle, MRC is used to combine the signal received over M receiver antennas. The combined channel gain at i^{th} vehicle over M INID links is

$$\| \tilde{h}_{v_i} \|^2 = \sum_{m=1}^{M} |h_{mn}|^2, m = 1, 2, ... M \tag{9}$$

The CDF of the SNR over M INID links can be acquired by calculating the inverse Laplace transform of the product of moment generating function (MGF) of M links. The MGF of the mth branch is obtained by solving the Laplace transform of the PDF.

$$MGF_m(s) = \int_0^\infty e^{-sx} f_{|h_{mn}|^2}(x) dx$$
$$= \lambda_m (s + \lambda_m)^{-1} \tag{10}$$

For $M = 2$ antennas, the MGF at i^{th} vehicle can be obtained as

$$MGF_{2,i}(s) = MGF_1(s) \times MGF_2(s)$$
$$= \lambda_1 (s + \lambda_1)^{-1} \times \lambda_2 (s + \lambda_2)^{-1} \tag{11}$$

The CDF of SNR is obtained by calculating the inverse Laplace transform

$$F_{2,i,\|\tilde{H}_i\|^2}(x) = \left(1 + \frac{\lambda_2 e^{-\lambda_1 x} - \lambda_1 e^{-\lambda_2 x}}{\lambda_1 - \lambda_2}\right), \tag{12}$$

3 Performance Analysis

In this section, the OP and ergodic rate at V_1 and V_1 are obtained over Rayleigh small scale fading channels with INID consideration.

3.1 Outage Performance at NOMA Vehicles

The OP is the probability at the vehicle that the vehicle can not detect the received signal if the rate of the received signal is less than the target minimum rate R_{t_i} decided by the system. The OP at V_i can be expressed as

$$P_{out,i} = 1 - P((\psi_i > \psi_{th_i}), \tag{13}$$

where $p(r)$ represents the probability of r and $\psi_{th_i} = 2^{R_{t_i}} - 1$. The OP at V_1

$$P_{out,1} = 1 - Pr((\psi_1 > \psi_{th_1})$$
$$= 1 - Pr\left(\left(\frac{\left(\rho_1^2 \beta_1 \gamma_v |h_1|^2\right)}{\gamma_v \left(\rho_1^2 \beta_2 |h_1|^2 + (1-\rho_1^2)\sigma_{e1}^2\right) + 1} > \psi_{th_1}\right)\right)$$
$$= Pr(|h_1|^2 \leq \phi_1)$$
$$= F_{2,i,\|\tilde{h}_i\|^2}(\phi_1), \tag{14}$$

where $\phi_1 = \frac{\psi_{th_1}\left(\gamma_v(1-\rho_1^2)\sigma_{e1}^2+1\right)}{\gamma_v \rho_1^2(\beta_1-\psi_{th_1}\beta_2)}$. By substituting $x = \phi_1$ into (12), the OP at V_1 for $m=2$ can be obtained as

$$P_{out,1} = \left(1 + \frac{\lambda_2 e^{-\lambda_1 \phi_1} - \lambda_1 e^{-\lambda_2 \phi_1}}{\lambda_1 - \lambda_2}\right) \quad (15)$$

The OP at V_2

$$P_{out,2} = 1 - Pr((\psi_{2,1} > \psi_{th_2}) \cap (\psi_2 > \psi_{th_2}))$$

$$= 1 - Pr((\frac{\left(\rho_2^2 \beta_1 \gamma_v |h_2|^2\right)}{\gamma_v \left(\rho_2^2 \beta_2 |h_2|^2 + (1-\rho_2^2)\sigma_{e2}^2\right)+1} > \psi_{th_1})$$

$$\cap (\frac{\left(\rho_2^2 \beta_2 \gamma_v |h_2|^2\right)}{\gamma_v(1-\rho_2^2)\sigma_{e2}^2+1} > \psi_{th_2}))$$

$$= Pr\left(\left(|h_2|^2 \leq \phi_{21}\right) \cap \left(|h_2|^2 \leq \phi_{22}\right)\right)$$

$$= F_{2,i,\|\tilde{h}_i\|^2}(\phi_2), \quad (16)$$

where $\phi_2 = max(\phi_{21}, \phi_{22})$, $\phi_{21} = \frac{\psi_{th_2}\left(\gamma_v(1-\rho_2^2)\sigma_{e2}^2+1\right)}{\gamma_v \rho_2^2(\beta_1-\psi_{th_2}\beta_2)}$ and $\phi_{22} = \frac{\psi_{th_2}\left(\gamma_v(1-\rho_2^2)\sigma_{e2}^2+1\right)}{\gamma_v \rho_2^2 \beta_2(1-\psi_{th_2})}$. By substituting $x = \phi_2$ into (12), the OP at V_1 for $m=2$ can be obtained as

$$P_{out,2} = \left(1 + \frac{\lambda_2 e^{-\lambda_1 \phi_2} - \lambda_1 e^{-\lambda_2 \phi_2}}{\lambda_1 - \lambda_2}\right) \quad (17)$$

3.2 Ergodic Sum Rate

The Ergodic sum rate is the average channel capacity or the system throughput. The Ergodic sum rate of NOMA vehicular Networks for two vehicles can be defined as

$$R_S = E\left(log_2\left(1+\psi_1\right)\right) + E\left(log_2\left(1+\psi_2\right)\right)$$

$$= E\left(log\left(1 + \frac{\left(\rho_1^2 \beta_1 \gamma_v |h_1|^2\right)}{\gamma_v \left(\rho_1^2 \beta_2 |h_1|^2 + (1-\rho_1^2)\sigma_{e1}^2\right)+1}\right)\right)$$

$$+ E\left(log\left(1 + \frac{\left(\rho_2^2 \beta_2 \gamma_v |h_2|^2\right)}{\gamma_v(1-\rho_2^2)\sigma_{e2}^2+1}\right)\right)$$

$$= \int_0^\infty log\left(1 + \frac{\left(\rho_1^2 \beta_1 \gamma_v x\right)}{\gamma_v \left(\rho_1^2 \beta_2 x + (1-\rho_1^2)\sigma_{e1}^2\right)+1}\right) f_{2,i,\|\tilde{h}_i\|^2}(x)dx$$

$$+ \int_0^\infty log\left(1 + \frac{\left(\rho_2^2 \beta_2 \gamma_v x\right)}{\gamma_v(1-\rho_2^2)\sigma_{e2}^2+1}\right) f_{2,i,\|\tilde{h}_i\|^2}(x)dx$$

$$= R_1 + R_2, \quad (18)$$

By Logarithmic identity, R_1 can be written as

$$R_1 = \frac{1}{\ln 2} \int_0^\infty \ln \frac{z_1 x + 1}{\beta_1 z_1 x + 1} F_{2,i,\|\tilde{h}_i\|^2}(x) dx. \tag{19}$$

where $z_1 = \frac{\gamma_v \rho_1^2}{\gamma_v(1-\rho_1^2)\sigma_{e1}^2+1}$.

By using an identity $\int_0^\infty \ln(1+vu) f(u) du = \sigma \int_0^\infty \frac{1-F(u)}{1+vu} du$, R_1 can be rewritten as

$$R_1 = \frac{z_1}{\ln 2} \int_0^\infty \frac{1 - F_{2,i,\|\tilde{H}_i\|^2}(x)}{z_1 x + 1} dx - \frac{z_1 \beta_1}{\ln 2} \int_0^\infty \frac{1 - F_{2,i,\|\tilde{H}_i\|^2}(x)}{z_1 \beta_1 x + 1} dx \tag{20}$$

By applying (12), R_1 can be expressed as

$$R_1 = \frac{z_1}{\ln 2(\lambda_1 - \lambda_2)} \int_0^\infty \left[\frac{\lambda_1 e^{-\lambda_2 x} - \lambda_1 e^{-\lambda_2 x}}{z_1 x + 1} - \frac{\beta_1 \left(\lambda_1 e^{-\lambda_2 x} - \lambda_1 e^{-\lambda_2 x} \right)}{\beta_1 z_1 x + 1} \right] dx \tag{21}$$

By solving the integration, the closed-form expression of R_1 can be obtained as

$$R_1 = \frac{1}{\ln 2(\lambda_1 - \lambda_2)} \left[\lambda_1 e^{-\frac{\lambda_2}{z_1}} \Gamma \left[0, \frac{\lambda_2}{z_1} \right] - \lambda_2 e^{-\frac{\lambda_1}{z_1}} \Gamma \left[0, \frac{\lambda_1}{z_1} \right] \right] - \frac{1}{\ln 2(\lambda_1 - \lambda_2)} \left[\lambda_1 e^{-\frac{\lambda_2}{\beta_1 z_1}} \Gamma \left[0, \frac{\lambda_2}{\beta_1 z_1} \right] - \lambda_2 e^{-\frac{\lambda_1}{\beta_1 z_1}} \Gamma \left[0, \frac{\lambda_1}{\beta_1 z_1} \right] \right] \tag{22}$$

Similarly, the ergodic rate of R_2 can be obtained as

$$R_2 = \frac{1}{\ln 2(\lambda_1 - \lambda_2)} \left[\lambda_1 e^{-\frac{\lambda_2}{\beta_2 z_2}} \Gamma \left[0, \frac{\lambda_2}{\beta_2 z_2} \right] - \lambda_2 e^{-\frac{\lambda_2}{\beta_2 z_2}} \Gamma \left[0, \frac{\lambda_2}{\beta_2 z_2} \right] \right], \tag{23}$$

where $z_2 = \frac{\gamma_v \rho_2^2}{\gamma_v(1-\rho_2^2)\sigma_{e2}^2+1}$. By adding, R_1 and R_1, the ergodic sum rate is obtained.

4 Numerical Results

In this section, we validate the obtained analytical expressions for OP and ergodic rate at two distinct vehicular positions, V_1 and V_2. Our vehicular network model considers a single lane, with vehicles V_1 and V_2 moving away from the BS. The BS, containing a single antenna, communicates with the vehicles, each equipped with $M = 2$ receiver antennas. Performance analysis is conducted at vehicle speeds of $100 \,\text{km/h}$ and $150 \,\text{km/h}$. The downlink communication occurs at a symbol rate of $R_i = 3$ Mbps and a carrier frequency of $f_c = 5.9$ GHz. V_1 experiences a weaker channel condition due to its greater distance from the BS, while V_2 enjoys a stronger channel condition. This discrepancy in channel conditions is governed by the inverse relationship between channel gain (h_i) and distance, as expressed by the path loss model $h_i = \frac{h_{di}}{\sqrt{1+d_i^\alpha}}$, where the path loss

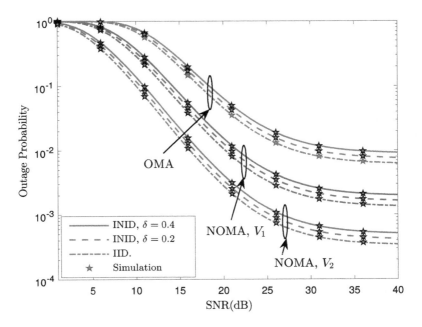

Fig. 2. OP vs. SNR at 100 km/h.

exponent $\alpha = 3$. Consequently, V_1, being farther away, exhibits weaker channel characteristics compared to the stronger channel conditions observed for V_2. For user fairness, the power coefficient, allocated to V_1 and V_2 is $\beta_1 = 0.6$ and $\beta_2 = 0.4$ respectively. The target minimum rate is $R_{t_1} = R_{t_2} = 1$ bps/Hz for detecting the signal at V_1 and V_2. As per $\psi_{th_i} = 2^{R_{t_i}} - 1$, the threshold SNR $\psi_{th_1} = \psi_{th_2} = 1$ for NOMA. As per $\frac{1}{2}\sum_{i=1}^{2}\log_2(1 + \psi_{th,i}) = \frac{1}{2}\log_2(1 + \psi_{th})$, $\psi_{th} = 3$. The mobility of V_1 and V_2 is modeled with the auto-regression channel with time-varying noise variance $\sigma_{ei}^2 = 0.01$ for We consider a single antenna at the BS and $M = 2$ antennas at each vehicle with INID diversity branches with decaying parameter δ. The outage performance and the rate of performance of NOMA are compared with OMA for various values of δ at different speeds of vehicles.

Figure 2 express the outage performance of V_1 and V_2 at the vehicles' speed of 100 km/h over IID and INID channels with $\delta = 0.2$ and 0.4 with OMA and NOMA. It is observed that the performance of NOMA is better than OMA under IID and INID channel consideration. It is observed that the outage performance of each vehicle saturates at certain values of the OP due to the presence of time-varying noise. Despite allocating high power to the far vehicle V_1, V_2 performs better due to the stronger channel condition. The performance degrades with an increase in decaying factor for V_1, V_1, and OMA. The performance degradation from change in $\delta = 0$ to $\delta = 0.2$ and $\delta = 0.2$ to $\delta = 0.4$ remains same at the speed of 100 km/h.

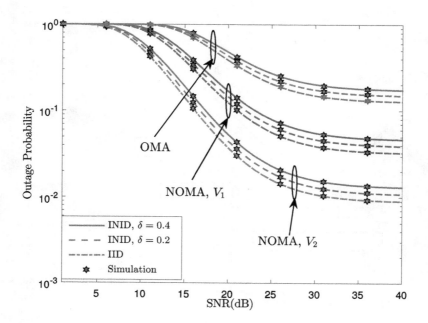

Fig. 3. OP vs. SNR at 150 km/h.

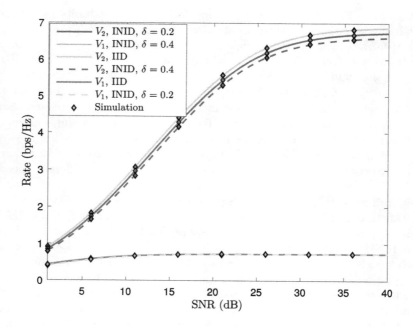

Fig. 4. Ergodic Rate vs. SNR at 100 km/h.

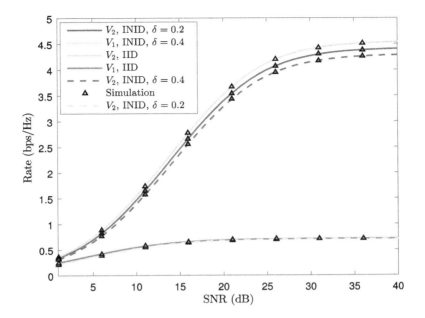

Fig. 5. Ergodic Rate vs. SNR at 150 km/h.

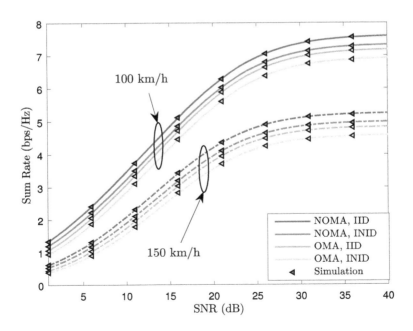

Fig. 6. Sum Rate vs. SNR at $\delta = 0.4$.

Figure 3 denotes the outage performance of V_1 and V_2 under IID and INID channels with the vehicles' speed of 150 km/h. It is observed that the outage performance degrades in comparison with the performance shown in Fig. 2 due to an increase in speed. As per Fig. 2, at the speed of 100 km/h, the outage performance of 10^{-1} is achieved at approximately 10 dB, 15 dB and 17 dB for NOMA V_1, V_2 and OMA respectively, while at the speed of 150 km/h, the same performance in achieved at 16 dB, 21 dB and 30 dB respectively. The performance degradation due to an increase in speed is higher in OMA compared to NOMA. However, the performance deterioration because of the increase in δ is marginally better than OMA.

Figure 4 reveals the ergodic rate performance of NOMA vehicles V_1 and V_2 and OMA at 100 km/h. It is observed that the rate of V_2 increases with SNR and saturates at the rate of 6.9 bps/Hz, 6.8 bps/Hz and 6.7 bps/Hz for $\delta = 0, 0.2$ and 0.4 respectively because of the error floors generated by time-varying noise. The ergodic rate of $V1$ is much less in comparison with V_2 and do not change with SNR. The rate performance of V_2 degrades with an increase in *delta* while there is no effect of changing *delta* on the rate performance of V_1.

The rate performance of V_1 and V_2 with NOMA and OMA at 150 km/h is observed in Fig. 5. It shows the deterioration in performance of V_2 as compared to Fig. 4 while the performance V_1 is weak at lower SNR but recovered after 15 dB of SNR. The performance deterioration at V_2 is approximately 2.5 bps/Hz for IID and INID with $\delta = 0.2$ and $\delta = 0.4$.

The sum rate performance of V_1, V_2 with NOMA and OMA for $\delta = 0.4$ is presented in Fig. 6 for $v_i = 100$ km/h and $v_i = 150$ km/h. The sum rate performance degrades with increase in speed of vehicles. The degradation due to δ is slight higher at 150 km/h in comparison with 100 km/h. For NOMA and OMA both, sum rate performance is degraded with INID consideration in comparison with IID channel consideration.

5 Conclusion

This paper has thoroughly investigated the outage performance, rate performance, and sum rate performance of NOMA-aided vehicular networks operating under INID Rayleigh time-selective fading channels. The study derives closed-form expressions for the CDF of the signal-to-noise ratio (SNR) with maximum ratio combining (MRC) for INID diversity links. The results reveal that NOMA outperforms OMA in terms of both OP and ergodic rate. Near vehicle V_2 exhibits superior performance compared to the far vehicle V_1 over both IID and INID links. It is worth noting that the observed outage performance and ergodic rate eventually saturate at certain values because of the time-varying nature of the time-selective fading, which models the mobility of the vehicles. Further analysis indicates that the rate performance of V_1 remains constant with changes in SNR. However, at higher speeds (150 km/h compared to 100 km/h), the rate performance of V_1 degrades at lower SNR levels. On the other hand, the performance of V_2 is negatively impacted by an increase in the decaying factor and the speed of vehicles. The sum rate performance of the vehicular networks also experiences deterioration with an increase in vehicle speed. Future research directions may explore adaptive strategies and resource allocation schemes to mitigate the impact of speed variations and fading effects on the performance of NOMA-enabled vehicular networks.

References

1. Nowacki, G.: Development, and standardization of intelligent transport systems. Int. J. Mar. Navig. Saf. Sea Transp. **6**(3), 403–411 (2012)
2. Zhang, H., Lu, X.: Vehicle communication network in intelligent transportation system based on Internet of Things. Comput. Commun. **160**, 799–806 (2020)
3. Cheng, H.T., Shan, H., Zhuang, W.: Infotainment and road safety service support in vehicular networking: from a communication perspective. Mech. Syst. Signal Process. **25**(6), 2020–2038 (2011)
4. Singh, P.K., Nandi, S.K., Nandi, S.: A tutorial survey on vehicular communication state of the art, and future research directions. Veh. Commun. **18**, 100164 (2019)
5. Zeadally, S., Javed, M.A., Hamida, E.B.: Vehicular communications for ITS: standardization and challenges. IEEE Commun. Stand. Mag. **4**(1), 11–17 (2020)
6. Makki, B., Chitti, K., Behravan, A., Alouini, M.S.: A survey of NOMA: current status and open research challenges. IEEE Open J. Commun. Soc. **1**, 179–189 (2020)
7. Ding, Z., et al.: Application of non-orthogonal multiple access in LTE and 5G networks. IEEE Commun. Mag. **55**(2), 185–191 (2017)
8. Bazzi, A., et al.: Toward 6G vehicle-to-everything sidelink: nonorthogonal multiple access in the autonomous mode. IEEE Veh. Technol. Mag. (2023)
9. Di, B., Song, L., Li, Y., Han, Z.: V2X meets NOMA: non-orthogonal multiple access for 5G-enabled vehicular networks. IEEE Wirel. Commun. **24**(6), 14–21 (2017)
10. Situ, Z., Ho, I.W.H.: NO-V2X: non-orthogonal multiple access with side information for V2X communications. In: Smart Grid and Innovative Frontiers in Telecommunications: Third International Conference, SmartGIFT, Auckland, New Zealand, Proceedings, pp. 133–144. Springer (2018)
11. Qian, L.P., Wu, Y., Zhou, H., Shen, X.: Non-orthogonal multiple access vehicular small cell networks: architecture and solution. IEEE Netw. **31**(4), 15–21 (2017)
12. Pfletschinger, S., Navarro, M.: Non-orthogonal multiple access for vehicular communication. In: 15th International Symposium on Wireless Communication Systems (ISWCS), pp. 1–5. IEEE (2018)
13. Guo, C., Liao, B.: Dynamic power and rate allocation for NOMA based vehicle-to-infrastructure communications. In: GLOBECOM, IEEE Global Communications Conference, pp. 1181–1186 (2022)
14. Jaiswal, N., Purohit, N.: Performance evaluation of non-orthogonal multiple access in V2V communications over double-Rayleigh fading channels. In: IEEE Conference on Information and Communication Technology, pp. 1–5. IEEE (2019)
15. Benabdallah, F., Hamza, A., Becherif, M.: On the use of non-orthogonal multiple access for V2V message dissemination. IET Intel. Transp. Syst. **13**(7), 1125–1129 (2019)
16. Chen, Y., Wang, L., Ai, Y., et al.: NOMA in vehicular communications. In: Multiple Access Techniques for 5G Wireless Networks and Beyond, pp. 333–366. Springer, Cham (2019)

17. Abbas, T., Karedal, J., Tufvesson, F.: Measurement-based analysis: the effect of complementary antennas and diversity on vehicle-to-vehicle communication. IEEE Antennas Wirel. Propag. Lett. **12**, 309–312 (2013)
18. Jaiswal, N., Pandey, A., Yadav, S., Purohit, N., Bariah, L., Muhaidat, S.: On the performance of NOMA-enabled V2V communications under the joint impact of nodes mobility and channel estimation error. In: 4th International Conference on Advanced Communication Technologies and Networking (CommNet), pp. 1–9. IEEE (2021)
19. Gour, R., Yadav, S., Purohit, N., Meshram, R.H.: On the outage performance of two-way relay-assisted multiuser vehicular networks over double Nakagami-m fading channels. In: IEEE 6th Conference on Information and Communication Technology (CICT), pp. 1–5 (2022)
20. Patel, D.K., et al.: Performance analysis of NOMA in vehicular communications over inid Nakagami-m fading channels. IEEE Trans. Wirel. Commun. **20**(10), 6254–6268 (2021)
21. Shankar, R., et al.: Impact of node mobility on the DL based uplink and downlink MIMO-NOMA network. Int. J. Inf. Technol. **15**(6), 3391–3404 (2023)
22. Pandey, A., Jaiswal, N., Yadav, S., Purohit, N.: Secure NOMA-aided V2V communications over time-selective Nakagami-m fading channels. In: IEEE 6th Conference on Information and Communication Technology (CICT), pp. 1–5 (2022)
23. Le, C.B., Do, D.T., Zaharis, Z.D., Mavromoustakis, C.X., Mastorakis, G., Markakis, E.K.: System performance analysis in cognitive radio-aided NOMA network: an application to vehicle-to-everything communications. Wireless Pers. Commun. 1–26 (2021)
24. Jaiswal, N., Purohit, N.: Performance analysis of NOMA-enabled vehicular communication systems with transmit antenna selection over double Nakagami-m fading. IEEE Trans. Veh. Technol. **70**(12), 12725–12741 (2021)
25. Alghorani, Y., Kaddoum, G., Muhaidat, S., Pierre, S., Al-Dhahir, N.: On the performance of multihop-intervehicular communications systems over n*Rayleigh fading channels. IEEE Wirel. Commun. Lett. **5**(2), 116–119 (2015)

Detecting Distributed Denial of Service (DDoS) Attacks in a Multi-controller SDN Environment Utilizing Machine Learning

Nishant Sanghani[1]( ), Gunjani Vaghela[2], and Bhavesh Borisaniya[3]

[1] Gujarat Technological University, Ahmedabad, India
nssanghani15@gmail.com
[2] Atmiya University, Rajkot, India
vaghelagunjani22@gmail.com
[3] Shantilal Shah Engineering College, Bhavnagar, India
borisaniyabhavesh@gmail.com

Abstract. Software Define Network is a platform for network architecture used to create and design the virtual network hardware components, so it can be modified with dynamic connection settings with ease of implementation. The SDN controller is in charge of executing various network applications and preserving network services and functions. Due to the complication of the SDN architecture, the SDN faces numerous security challenges despite all of its incredible advantages. Because of its centralized and complex architecture, distributed denials of service (DDoS) attacks are frequent against SDN, particularly at the control layer where they can affect the entire network by using multiple resources at particular interval of time. Machine learning methods are utilized to quickly detect these types of threats. In current work, machine learning approach is proposed to detect the DDoS attack in multi-controller SDN environment of SDN. Experimental results shows that machine learning technique provides better accuracy and detection rate.

Keywords: SDN · DDoS · SDN controller · Multi-controller · RSMQ · Machine learning

1 Introduction

The software defined networking model is revolutionary in its ability to define, manage and control networks. It provides a programmable and centralized approach to network management, separating the data plane from the control plane. Unlike traditional network architectures, where network devices (e.g., switches and routers) handle both control and data forwarding functions, SDN decouples these functions and centralizes control in a software-based controller. It provides a flexible and agile approach to network management, allowing administrators to dynamically configure and control network behaviour through software.

In an SDN single-controller architecture, there is a single controller responsible for managing and controlling the network devices. The controller preserve a global view of the network topology and makes decisions on how traffic should be forwarded. It communicates with the network devices using southbound interfaces and interacts with higher-level applications through northbound interfaces. The single controller provides centralized control and management, simplifying network administration tasks.

While a single controller architecture in SDN (Software-Defined Networking) offers certain advantages, it does not come without relevant security threats. I, it may faces failure at single point and performance impact challenges. To address such security threats alternative architectures that, such as multi-controller or architectures, can provide improved security and resilience by distributing control and reducing the single point of failure effect.

In an SDN multi-controller architecture, there are multiple controllers distributed across the network. Every controller is in charge of a specific domain or subset of network devices. The controllers work collaboratively to manage the network, exchanging information and coordinating their actions to improve scalability, redundancy, and fault tolerance.

Among the various security threats that can impact an SDN network, one of the most destructive is the DDoS attack which pose a significant challenge to the availability and performance of SDN networks. A DDoS attack is characterized by a massive volume of malicious traffic targeting a specific network, service, or application which results into impacts on network bandwidth, processing power, or other critical resources, resulting in service disruption or complete unavailability. DDoS attacks pose a significant risk to SDN networks, as they have the potential to overwhelm the controller or OpenFlow (OF) switches if proper security measures are not in place. To address this threat, there is a wealth of documentation available that outlines strategies to protect SDN networks from DDoS attacks [15].

There are two commonly approaches are there to detect DDoS attack: one is the Intrusion Detection Systems (IDS) and other is DDoS attack detection in SDN single controller. IDS analyzes network packets and notify administrators when a DDoS attack is detected. Single SDN controller uses centralized control and visibility of network traffic to detect DDoS attacks through a machine learning approach, which relies on the detection of signs of DDoS activities. However. Protecting the SDN multi-controller network from threats is still an active research area. The proposed work focuse on the same to protect the SDN from DDoS attack.

The remaining paper is organized as follows: Sect. 2 provides introduction to multi-controller in SDN. Section 3 describes related work of DDoS attack detection in SDN. Section 4 details discusses proposed work, followed by experiments and its results in Sect. 5 and Sect. 6. Section 7 provides comparison of proposed work with related work studies followed by conclusion and references at the end.

2 Multi-controller in SDN

SDN with a multi-controller design is an advanced networking paradigm that offers enhanced flexibility, scalability, and resilience compared to traditional single-controller SDN deployments. In a multiple controllers SDN environment, all controllers collaborate to control and manage the network infrastructure, distributing the control plane functions across multiple entities. This approach introduces several benefits and opportunities for efficient network management and improved network performance. In a multi-controller SDN architecture, multiple domains or sub networks are created from the network, with each network being managed by a separate controller as shown in Fig. 1.

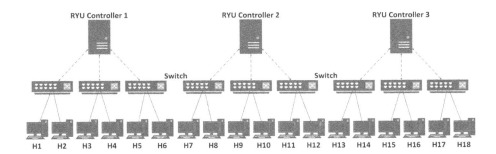

Fig. 1. Multi controller scenario in SDN

3 Related Work

Shideh et al. [12] presented an approach to detecting DDoS attacks in an SDN single controller environment. The study utilized the Ryu controller, along with a tree topology simulated using the Mininet emulator. The network topology consisted of one controller, three switches, and four hosts. Machine learning techniques were employed to differentiate between abnormal and normal network traffic. Specifically, the Support Vector Machine (SVM) algorithm was utilized to attain higher accuracy compared to other learning methods, highlighting its effectiveness in detecting DDoS attacks in the SDN single controller setup. Abbas et al. [3] proposed security solution for SDN single controller to detect DDoS attacks involved a three-stage process dependent on machine learning. In the first stage, data preprocessing was performed on the complete dataset. In the second stage, the data classification is done using three methods of machine learning Decision Tree, Logistic Regression and Naive Bayes, were employed to classify the data and identify patterns indicative of DDoS attacks. In the final stage, the algorithm of machine learning was applied to the classified data to generate the detection results. When compared to other machine learning techniques and real-time datasets, the suggested work demonstrated remarkable accuracy. The evaluation was conducted using a real-time dataset.

Tao Hu et al. [10] This survey paper provides an in-depth examination of multi-controller based SDN, a networking prototype that enhances network programmability and flexibility by dividing the data and control planes. The paper offers insights into the architecture, advantages, and challenges associated with multi-controller based SDN. It extensively reviews existing literature on this topic, encompassing various research approaches and techniques employed in the field. The paper emphasizes the benefits of utilizing multiple controllers in SDN, such as improved scalability and fault tolerance, while also addressing the complexities of maintaining consistency and synchronization across the controllers.

Meti N et al. [13] have proposed an approach in the context of SDN, the algorithms Neural Networks (NN), Naive-Bayes (NB), and Support Vector Machines (SVM) have been employed to classify different types of connections. A study conducted using these algorithms found that SVM achieved an accuracy rate of 80 in connection identification. However, there is a need for further enhancements to improve the accuracy of these algorithms in SDN settings.

In Ye et al. [23], a DDoS attack detection model was built using an SVM classifier. The study utilized six-tuple feature values that are significant in identifying DDoS attacks. The study results showed that rate of false alarm for TCP and UDP traffic is low, indicating the effectiveness of the SVM classifier in accurately detecting these types of attacks. However, it was observed that the ICMP traffic false alarm rate was relatively high, suggesting a potential challenge in effectively identifying DDoS attacks in this specific traffic category. Further investigation and fine-tuning of the SVM model may be required to improve the accuracy and reduce false alarms for ICMP traffic in DDoS attack detection.

Fonseca et al. [7] have enhance the detection of DDoS attacks, by implementing secondary controller as a part of the network architecture. This work intend to improve the overall effectiveness of the detection technique. However, even with the adoption of a secondary controller, the DDoS detection technique is not completely immune to potential DDoS attacks. The presence of a secondary controller introduces additional attack surfaces and vulnerabilities that could be exploited by sophisticated attackers. Therefore, while the use of a secondary controller may enhance detection capabilities, it is critical to apply strong security measures and continuously update the defense mechanisms to mitigate the risk of DDoS attacks targeting the secondary controller itself.

Abdullah Ahmed Bahashwan et al. [4] have critically assesses a comprehensive array of studies in this domain. It synthesizes existing knowledge to identify prevailing trends, challenges, and advancements in employing deep learning and machine learning techniques for detecting DDoS attack in the context of SDN.

K Arockiasamy et al. [11] have the research employs Mininet, a widely-used network emulator, to replicate the dynamic behaviour of SDN architectures. Machine learning algorithms are used to identify patterns indicating a distributed denial of service attack in this simulation environment. The study aims to assess the effectiveness of machine learning in real-time threat detection within SDN, offering valuable insights into the potential integration of intelligent security measures for safeguarding SDN infrastructures against malicious activities.

HM Omar et al. [9] identify shortcomings in conventional detection methods, prompting the proposal of an innovative deep learning technique. The paper meticulously describes the architecture of the neural network model, detailing the chosen features and datasets for experimental evaluation. Results demonstrate the potency of the deep learning model in accurately identifying and mitigating DDoS attacks, and the discussion delves into the implications, strengths, and potential limitations of the approach.

4 Proposed Work

The proposed work is divided into three parts:

1. Classification module to Detect DDoS attack
2. Voting Mechanism
3. Collaborative module to connect with the other controller and inform about attack

4.1 Classification Module to Detect DDoS Attack

Machine learning techniques have come up as powerful tools in the security, management, and optimization of SDN networks. In particular, they offer dynamic, efficient, and intelligent solutions for detecting DDoS attacks. By integrating DDoS detection based on machine learning into SDN architectures, the flow data can be analysed and processed. This enables the network to learn from historical patterns and behaviours, identify anomalies indicative of DDoS attacks, and respond autonomously by applying appropriate countermeasures. The machine learning used in DDoS detection enhances the network's ability to adapt to evolving attack patterns, improve accuracy in distinguishing between normal and malicious traffic, and ultimately improve the overall security posture of SDN multi-controller environment [14].

As shown in Fig. 2, the machine learning classifier module is an application that runs on the RYU controller and consists of three major parts: Data flow collection, Feature extraction, and Classification.

1. Data Flow Collection: The data collector is a crucial part of the ML classifier module in SD based DDoS detection. Its primary function is to frequently request flow entries from the flow tables of OpenFlow switches through a secure channel. The collected flow data is then processed by the feature processor to extract relevant features that can be used by the classifier for DDoS detection.

2. Feature Extraction: It is responsible for extraction of relevant features from the collected data. The model collects traffic flow entries, extracts native flow features, and adds additional features to expand the feature set. These features are used by the classifier to make accurate predictions.
3. Classification: It uses the processed features to classify the traffic flows pertaining to normal or DDoS. This is done by training the machine learning algorithm on a dataset of known traffic patterns.

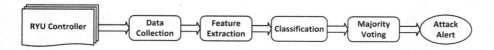

Fig. 2. Work process of ML classification

Machine Learning Algorithms: The use of machine learning techniques has become increasingly prevalent in the field of DDoS attack detection. These techniques have demonstrated their effectiveness in automatically learning patterns and identifying anomalies within network traffic that may indicate the occurrence of a DDoS attack. By leveraging powerful algorithms, machine learning enables the analysis of vast amount of real-time network traffic data. This capability allows for the rapid and accurate detection of DDoS attacks, surpassing the capabilities of traditional detection methods. Machine learning-based approaches provide a proactive and efficient means of mitigating the impact of DDoS attacks by enabling early identification and response, thereby enhancing network security and ensuring the availability of critical resources. Moreover, unsupervised learning techniques, as well as semi supervised learning methods, can be found in the available Multi Learning Technologies [8].

The proposed work focuses on the supervised learning technique that involves training algorithms on labeled input data (X) along with corresponding output variables (Y). The labeled examples serve as a reference for the algorithm to learn patterns and relationships between the input and output variables, enabling it to make accurate predictions or classifications on new, unseen data. By leveraging the labeled data, supervised learning algorithms aim to develop models that can effectively map input data to desired output labels, thereby enabling tasks such as object recognition, speech transcription, and sentiment analysis [6].

Supervised learning can be categorized into two main types: regression and classification. Regression is applied when the output variable is continuous, aiming to predict or estimate a numeric value. On the other hand, classification is employed when the output variable is discrete, representing different categories or classes. In the case of DDoS attack detection, classification is commonly used to determine whether a network flow is malicious or normal. By training the classification model on labeled data, the algorithm learns to classify incoming network flows as either benign or potentially harmful, enabling prompt identification and DDoS attacks mitigation.

Classification is a widely employed machine learning technique for DDoS attacks detection, and among the commonly used algorithms are k-Nearest Neighbours (kNN), Random Forest, and Decision Tree. A highly efficient machine learning algorithm is widely used to classify tasks, such as decision trees and random forests, including the DDoS attacks detection in SDN environments.

Decision trees are powerful and interpretable models that can analyze network traffic data and construct a hierarchical structure of decision rules to differentiate between normal and malicious traffic. The process starts with extracting features from the network traffic data, such as packet rates, flow characteristics, and payload information. These features are then processed to guarantee consistency and data quality. The decision tree model is trained on the data, and it recursively splits the data based on selected features and thresholds to create decision rules for differentiating between DDoS attack and normal traffic. The performance of the decision tree model is evaluated using real-world network traffic datasets, measuring metrics like accuracy, precision, F1 score, and recall. This approach improves the efficiency and accuracy of detecting DDoS attack in SDN networks, enabling network administrators to effectively identify and mitigate these malicious attacks.

k-Nearest Neighbors (kNN) algorithm to categorize network traffic as malicious or normal. Class labels are assigned by the non-parametric kNN method according to the majority class of the k nearest neighbors in the feature space. In the classification stage, kNN finds the k nearest neighbors by calculating the distances between the new instance and the labeled examples in the training set. The class label assigned to the new instance is determined by the majority class among its nearest neighbors. kNN offers a flexible and intuitive approach to identifying DDoS attacks, as it considers the local characteristics of instances. By adjusting the value of k, network administrators can control the accuracy and sensitivity of the detection. kNN-based detection of DDoS attack provides a straightforward and adaptable method for enhancing network security in SDN environments.

Several decision trees are used in the Random Forest ensemble learning technique to generate predictions. Using random feature subsets and varying subsets of the training data, the Random Forest algorithm creates a group of decision trees. During the classification phase, each decision tree in the Random Forest independently classifies the new instance. The final prediction is obtained by collecting the predictions from all the decision trees using a voting procedure. The DDoS attack detection model's robustness and generalization abilities are enhanced and the risk of overfitting is decreased by Random Forest, which aggregates the outputs of several decision trees. Random Forest-based DDoS attack detection offers a powerful and scalable approach for enhancing network security in SDN environments.

V-DRK (Voting-Decision Tree, K Nearest Neighbors, Random Forest): The Voting Classifier's basic principle is to conceptually integrate several classifiers of machine learning and use a democratic decision-making process by combining their predictions by a majority vote [16].

Utilizing a voting algorithm is particularly beneficial when combining multiple classifiers that exhibit similar performance levels, as it helps to balance out their individual weaknesses. By leveraging the collective decision-making of these classifiers, a voting classifier can achieve lower error rates and reduce the risk of overfitting. When different classifiers with diverse approaches and learning biases are combined through the voting mechanism, it can lead to improved accuracy and more robust predictions compared to relying on a single classifier alone.

4.2 Voting Mechanism

The Voting Mechanism is a machine learning technique that combines predictions from multiple models to make a final prediction or classification. Each model generates its own prediction based on the input data, and the final prediction is determined by aggregating the individual predictions through voting or averaging. The prediction with the highest number of votes or the highest average is selected as the final prediction. The voting mechanism is commonly used in ensemble learning, where multiple models with different characteristics or algorithms are combined to enhance overall prediction performance.

In the case of a binary classification problem, where the output is either 0 or 1, a simple majority voting mechanism can be used. The output with the highest number of votes is chosen as the final prediction. For example, if we have three classifiers and their predictions for a given input are 0, 1, and 1, then the majority vote will be 1 and that will be the final prediction. In current work, voting mechanism can be used to combine the outputs of multiple classifiers (such as random forest and decision tree classifiers) to make a more accurate prediction about whether a given network flow is a DDoS attack or not.

The voting mechanism works as follows. Firstly, a dataset is fed into the system, and then it is passed on to multiple classifiers. Each classifier takes in the input from the dataset and processes it, producing a result. The outputs from the classifiers are then aggregated using a voting method, which is hard voting. The final result is determined by the majority vote. Once the voting process is complete, the final result is then provided as the output of the system as shown in the Fig. 3.

4.3 Collaborative Module

Collaborative module refers to the use of multiple devices, systems or entities working together in a cooperative manner towards achieving a common goal. In this approach, the devices or systems share information about the network traffic and collectively analyze it to identify potential DDoS attacks.

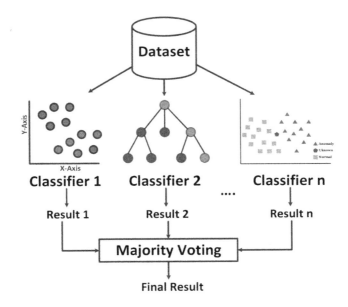

Fig. 3. Majority Voting

RSMQ (Redis Simple Message Queue) is a messaging technique that can be utilized for collaborative DDoS detection. It is based on Redis, a fast and lightweight in-memory data structure store. RSMQ enables multiple processes to communicate with each other by exchanging messages through a shared queue.

One effective approach to improve the mitigation and detection of DDoS attacks in SDN is by implementing a collaborative module using a message queue system like RSMQ. In this approach, each controller within the network publishes a message to notify the other controllers about identified attacks. By sharing this information, the controllers can collectively enforce rules to drop the malicious or harmful flows, effectively blocking the attack within the network. Additionally, neighbouring sites can be promptly informed about the attack, enabling them to take necessary preventive measures to stop the attack from propagating further [19].

In the Fig. 4, an attacker is sending requests from a random IP address, and the requests are being sent to controller 1. Controller 1 identifies the incoming traffic as a DDoS attack with help of machine learning algorithms. Once the attack is identified, controller 1 sends a message to the RSMQ, which acts as a message broker.

The RSMQ then forwards the message to other controllers in the network through a secure channel. The controller may simultaneously block malicious streams to the network and notify neighboring attack sites, using a RSMQ method in an SDN environment.

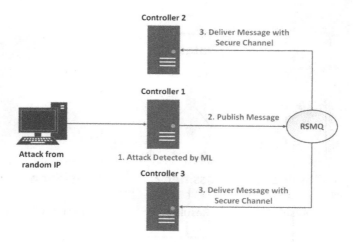

Fig. 4. Collaborative DDoS detection

5 Experiment

The methodology for the experiments conducted to analyze the usability and reliability of our proposed work involve simulating a DDoS attack by creating a huge number of spoofed IP addresses requests and sending them to multiple servers. Some of the servers were intentionally made to respond improperly to simulate the impact of a real DDoS attack.

Here, the attacker sends requests to the controllers, and the first controller uses method of machine learning for the DDoS attack detection. Once the detection of attack is there, the controller sends a message to the RSMQ, which then forwards the message to the other controllers using a secure channel.

In order to assess the effectiveness and efficiency of the current system, experiments have been performed with various types of performance metrics such as detection accuracy, false negatives or false positive values for an assessment of its usability and reliability.

5.1 Simulation Setup

Experimental setup requirements shown in Tabel 1 are used for simulationn. To simulate the proposed detection module and collaboration, three Ryu-OpenFlow controllers were implemented. The topology of experiment includes 9 switches and 18 hosts.

Network Simulator: Mininet is free software network emulator that is used to design a virtual network topology with a collection of virtual hosts, controllers, switches, and links. Mininet can be used to design and set up a custom network topology with a specified number of controllers, switches, and hosts.

Table 1. Experimental setup requirements

Operating system	Ubuntu 20.04
Network simulator	Mininet 2.2
Controller	RYU Controller
Collaborative tool	Redis server application
Packet type	ICMP, UDP, TCP
Dataset	CICDDOS2019, CICIDS2017, ICMP

Controller: RYU is a SDN controller that enables network engineers and developers to build custom network applications on top of the SDN infrastructure. It is an open-source controller that supports An Open Flow protocol, which enables the controller to exchange information with switches within the network as well as monitor traffic flow RYU controller is often used for detecting DDoS attack in SDN as it offers the implementation of custom DDoS detection and mitigation algorithms.

5.2 Datasets

CICIDS2017 [20]. It was created as part of the Canadian Institute for Cybersecurity IDS Evaluation Dataset Project in year 2017. The CICIDS2017 dataset is a widely used dataset in the field of network security and intrusion detection.

To evaluate the proposed model, a portion of the dataset was utilized, specifically focusing on the "Friday-WorkingHoursAfternoon-DDoS" subset. This subset includes 200,000 instances of normal traffic records, representing legitimate network activity, and 25,745 instances of attack traffic records, representing various DDoS attacks.

CICDDOS2019 [21]. In this study, the "UDP" dataset was used to validate the voting-based model performance for network traffic classification. The dataset consists of a total of 1,048,576 distinct instances, each characterized by 20 features. These features capture relevant information about the network traffic.

Among the instances in the ch1dataset, there are 7 distinct classes, representing different types of network traffic. The goal is to accurately classify instances into these classes using the proposed voting-based model. For the validation process, a subset of the "UDP" dataset was utilized. This subset comprises 26,405 instances of normal traffic records, that correspond to legitimate network activity, and 1,022,170 instances of attack traffic records, representing various types of network attacks.

ICMP [22]. In this study, a dataset consisting of UDP, TCP, and ICMP packets are used to validate the voting-based model for network traffic classification. The dataset contains a total of 1,048,575 distinct instances, with each instance characterized by 22 features that capture relevant information about the network traffic.

For the validation process, the dataset was divided into attack traffic and normal traffic records. The subset of normal traffic consists of 286,276 instances, representing legitimate network activity, while the attack traffic subset includes 762,299 instances, which correspond to various types of network attacks.

6 Results

The results of the performance assessment carried out in this study are set out in this section. The purpose of this evaluation was to establish the performance of a VDRK classifier on three distinct datasets within SDN. The evaluation results from the collaborative efforts of three controllers collaborating seamlessly. Each controller expresses its individual viewpoint, and these diverse opinions are integrated to derive the overall assessment. This assessment is then obtained by employing three ML algorithms on the dataset of CICIDS2017 and it is represented in form of results on the CICIDS2017 datasets in Table 2 and Fig. 5.Improvement can be seen in results obtained with combination of three techniques as compared implementing the individual technique for DDoS detection. Each controller shares its unique perspective, and these different viewpoints are combined to create the final assessment using the CICDDOS2019 dataset. The V-DRK classifier results on the CICDDOS2019 datasets is represented in Table 3 and along with improvement in the classifier performance in Fig. 6.

Table 2. Evaluation of V-DRK classifier performance on CICIDS2017 dataset

Classifier	V-DRK	KNN	DT	RF
Accuracy	99.98	99.98	99.99	99.99
Precision	0.984	0.974	0.987	0.986
Recall	0.987	0.977	0.986	0.985
F1-score	0.984	0.978	0.987	0.986

Table 3. Evaluation of V-DRK classifier performance on CICDDOS2019 dataset

Classifier	V-DRK	KNN	DT	RF
Accuracy	99.98	99.96	99.98	99.98
Precision	0.984	0.976	0.997	0.996
Recall	0.984	0.975	0.987	0.985
F1-score	0.984	0.974	0.985	0.986

Each controller provides its individual assessment or opinion. Subsequently, these individual opinions are combined to form a unified result using the ICMP

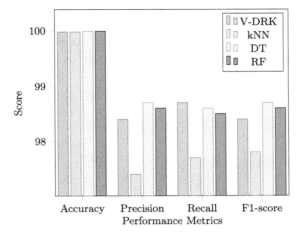

Fig. 5. V-DRK performance on CICIDS2017 datasets

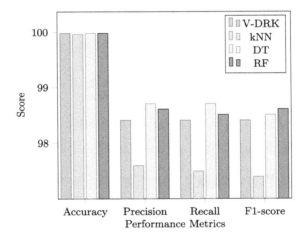

Fig. 6. V-DRK performance on CICIDS2019 datasets

dataset. The V-DRK classifier deployed on the ICMP datasets are showcased in Table 4 with result values and in Fig. 7 where it gives improved values for accuracy, f1-score, recall and precision.

7 Comparative Studies

The comparison of binary classification results of the V-DRK classifier against respective related work found in literature on the CICIDS2017 datasets are shown in Table 5 and CICIDS2019 datasets are shown in Table 6. Results shows that accuracy of proposed approach is improved over existing approaches on given datasets.

Table 4. Evaluation of V-DRK classifier performance on ICMP dataset

Classifier	V-DRK	KNN	DT	RF
Accuracy	99.98	99.98	99.99	99.99
Precision	0.998	0.987	0.989	0.989
Recall	0.998	0.985	0.987	0.985
F1-score	0.997	0.986	0.988	0.98

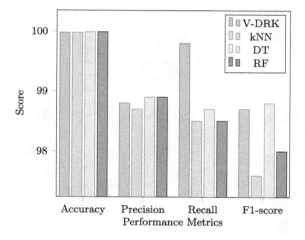

Fig. 7. V-DRK performance on ICMP datasets

Table 5. Comparing V-DRK with other classifier on CICIDS2017 dataset

Reference	Classifier	Accuracy
Bansal et al. [5]	XGBoost-IDS	91.36
Swami et al. [18]	Voting-RKM	97.77
Stiawan et al. [17]	DT	97.47
Proposed method	V-DRK	99.98

Table 6. Comparing V-DRK with other classifier on CICDDOS2019 dataset

Reference	Classifier	Accuracy
Alamri et al. [2]	KNN	81.36
Yungaicela-Naula et al. [24]	RF	96.36
ALamri et al. [1]	DT	98.05
Proposed method	V-DRK	99.95

8 Conclusion

V-DRK learning algorithm automatically detects DDoS attacks in SDN network. The model make decision based on the features obtained from the final feature set using the combination of machine learning techniques for classification, voting mechanism for majority voting decision and collaborative module using RSMQ for DDoS attack alert. The implemented methodology successfully identifies and thwarts threats accurately without disrupting regular traffic. For future work, more efficient defense mechanisms for DDoS mitigation needs to be explore as well as to evaluate response time for DDoS detection.

References

1. Alamri, H.A., Thayananthan, V.: Bandwidth control mechanism and extreme gradient boosting algorithm for protecting software-defined networks against DDoS attacks. IEEE Access **8**, 194269–194288 (2020)
2. Alamri, H.A., Thayananthan, V.: Analysis of machine learning for securing software-defined networking. Procedia Comput. Sci. **194**, 229–236 (2021). 18th International Learning & Technology Conference 2021
3. Altamemi, A.J., Abdulhassan, A., Obeis, N.T.: DDoS attack detection in software defined networking controller using machine learning techniques. Bull. Electr. Eng. Inform. **11**(5), 2836–2844 (2022)
4. Bahashwan, A.A., Anbar, M., Manickam, S., Al-Amiedy, T.A., Aladaileh, M.A., Hasbullah, I.H.: A systematic literature review on machine learning and deep learning approaches for detecting DDoS attacks in software-defined networking. Sensors **23**(9) (2023)
5. Bansal, A., Kaur, S.: Extreme gradient boosting based tuning for classification in intrusion detection systems. In: Advances in Computing and Data Sciences: Second International Conference, ICACDS 2018, Dehradun, India, 20–21 April 2018, Revised Selected Papers, Part I 2, pp. 372–380. Springer (2018)
6. Dhall, D., Kaur, R., Juneja, M.: Machine learning: a review of the algorithms and its applications. In: Proceedings of ICRIC 2019: Recent Innovations in Computing, pp. 47–63 (2020)
7. Fonseca, P., Bennesby, R., Mota, E., Passito, A.: A replication component for resilient openflow-based networking. In: 2012 IEEE Network Operations and Management Symposium, pp. 933–939. IEEE (2012)
8. Furdek, M., Natalino, C., Lipp, F., Hock, D., Di Giglio, A., Schiano, M.: Machine learning for optical network security monitoring: a practical perspective. J. Lightwave Technol. **38**(11), 2860–2871 (2020)
9. Gadallah, W.G., Ibrahim, H.M., Omar, N.M.: A deep learning technique to detect distributed denial of service attacks in software-defined networks. Comput. Secur. **137**, 103588 (2024)
10. Hu, T., Guo, Z., Yi, P., Baker, T., Lan, J.: Multi-controller based software-defined networking: a survey. IEEE access **6**, 15980–15996 (2018)
11. Karthika, P., Arockiasamy, K.: Simulation of SDN in mininet and detection of DDoS attack using machine learning. Bull. Electr. Eng. Inform. **12**(3), 1797–1805 (2023)

12. Mehr, S.Y., Ramamurthy, B.: An SVM based DDoS attack detection method for Ryu SDN controller. In: Proceedings of the 15th International Conference on Emerging Networking Experiments and Technologies, pp. 72–73 (2019)
13. Meti, N., Narayan, D., Baligar, V.: Detection of distributed denial of service attacks using machine learning algorithms in software defined networks. In: 2017 International Conference on Advances in Computing, Communications and Informatics (ICACCI), pp. 1366–1371. IEEE (2017)
14. Polat, H., Polat, O., Cetin, A.: Detecting DDoS attacks in software-defined networks through feature selection methods and machine learning models. Sustainability **12**(3), 1035 (2020)
15. Rahman, O., Quraishi, M.A.G., Lung, C.H.: DDoS attacks detection and mitigation in SDN using machine learning. In: 2019 IEEE World Congress on Services (SERVICES), vol. 2642, pp. 184–189. IEEE (2019)
16. sanchit: voting-classifer (2021). https://medium.com/@sanchitamangale12/voting-classifer1be10db6d7a5
17. Stiawan, D., Idris, M.Y.B., Bamhdi, A.M., Budiarto, R., et al.: CICIDS-2017 dataset feature analysis with information gain for anomaly detection. IEEE Access **8**, 132911–132921 (2020)
18. Swami, R., Dave, M., Ranga, V.: Voting-based intrusion detection framework for securing software-defined networks. Concurr. Comput. Pract. Exp. **32**(24), e5927 (2020)
19. Tayfour, O.E., Marsono, M.N.: Collaborative detection and mitigation of DDoS in software-defined networks. J. Supercomput. **77**, 13166–13190 (2021)
20. unb: CICIDS2017 (2017). https://www.unb.ca/cic/datasets/ids2017.html. Accessed 1 July 2022
21. unb: CICDDoS2019 (2019). https://www.unb.ca/cic/datasets/ddos-2019.html. Accessed 5 July 2022
22. unb: ICMP (2022). https://drive.google.com/file/d/1N2QLDPb90XOdxcuQ_Fb7ZSVOG4J3w_zY/view?usp=sharing. Accessed 25 June 2022
23. Ye, J., Cheng, X., Zhu, J., Feng, L., Song, L.: A DDoS attack detection method based on SVM in software defined network. Secur. Commun. Netw. **2018** (2018)
24. Yungaicela-Naula, N.M., Vargas-Rosales, C., Perez-Diaz, J.A.: SDN-based architecture for transport and application layer DDoS attack detection by using machine and deep learning. IEEE Access **9**, 108495–108512 (2021)

Comprehensive Study of Short Channel Effects (SCEs) in MOSFET and FinFET Devices

Kripa Patel[✉][iD], Nisarg Vala[iD], Mitesh Limachia[iD], and Purvang Dalal[iD]

Dharmsinh Desai University, Nadiad, Gujarat 387001, India
patelkripa02@gmail.com, {mitesh.ec,purvang.ec}@ddu.ac.in

Abstract. Short channel effects (SCEs) have become a critical concern with the continued scaling of semiconductor devices. It is suitably known that multiple gate control over channel in FinFET plus thin Si body results into lower SCEs and so it has replaced traditional MOSFET in nanometer region. In our work, we have come up with a comprehensive investigation of SCEs in both traditional MOSFET and emerging FinFET structures using SPICE simulation tool. The objective of this study is to analyze as well as compare the impact of short channel effects over device performance in these two distinct transistor technologies. Simulation-based study carried out in the work is majorly focused on various SCEs, including (DIBL) drain-induced barrier lowering, VT roll-off and (SS) subthreshold swing or MOSFETs and FinFETs. To demonstrate, impact of scaling gate length on various parameters of SCEs gate length of FINFET device is altered in the range of 20–7 nm. Through simulations, in this work, we show validation of performance benefits of FinFETs over MOSFET at distinct nanoscale technology nodes. The findings of our work provide valuable knowledge of the SCEs phenomena particularly in FinFET device at recently used technology node of 7 nm in the fabrication process.

Keywords: MOSFET · FinFET · DIBL · SCE

1 Introduction

Semiconductor technology is advancing at a surprising pace, driven by the relentless pursuit of smaller, faster, and more energy-efficient electronic devices. At the heart of these innovations lies MOSFET, a central component powering modern integrated circuits, revolutionizing various applications that have become integral to our daily lives. However, as device dimensions approach their physical limits, MOSFETs confront inherent limitations, notably the short-channel effects (SCEs) and increasing leakage current, along with changes in subthreshold swing (SS) resulting from the reduction of gate oxide thickness.

Overcoming these SCEs have limitations in subnanometer technology node due to higher fabrication complexity and monetary costs [2]. Lowering the effect of SCEs requires advent of newer architectural devices for higher yield and performance. Fin-FET,FDSOI, GAA and triple-gate have been proposed as emerging devices to increase the scalability [3]. Among these devices, the FinFET has emerged as a groundbreaking remedy in transistor design. This three-dimensional architecture of FinFETs has garnered widespread adoption, replacing traditional MOSFETs in advanced integrated circuits, and offers a viable path to surpass the challenges faced by the current technology [4]. To overcome the limitations experienced by MOSFETs, FinFETs leverage their unique three-dimensional structure, providing enhanced control on channel region [5].

The transition from MOSFET to FinFET marks a significant advancement in semiconductor technology, inspired by the need to overcome limitations at nanoscale dimensions [6]. FinFETs have not only addressed short-channel effects but also fuelled innovation in transistor design, through their unique three-dimensional structure for better control and efficiency [7]. This shift signifies a new era of possibilities, promising enhanced scalability, reliability, and energy efficiency. By embracing FinFET technology, semiconductor manufacturers can lead the way in innovation, shaping a future where electronic devices are smaller, faster, and more sustainable.

This research paper investigates the transition from MOSFET to FinFET, analysing the reasons behind this enormous shift and highlighting the unique advantages of FinFET technology. In pursuit of this investigation, we conducted simulation-based study to compare MOSFET and FinFET performance in light of various parameters affected by Short Channel Effects, such as DIBL, Vt Roll Off, and Subthreshold Swing, while downsizing the technology node (channel length) [7].

In addition to examining these parameters, we sought to evaluate the performance of MOSFETs and FinFETs under varying operating conditions to gain insights into their behaviour across different scenarios. By conducting simulations using the SPICE simulator and predictive technology model card (PTM-MG) for FinFETs, along with the BSIM-CMG (SPICE model) for FinFETs, we were able to accurately capture the electrical characteristics of both device types. The results of our study indicate a percentage change in various SCE parameters for both MOSFETs and FinFETs, ultimately revealing the superiority of FinFETs over MOSFETs in terms of performance and scalability.

2 Literature Survey

Moore's Law, given by the co-founder of Intel, Gordon Moore in the year 1965, has been a motivating force behind the exponential advancements of the semicon industry [9]. This law states that the count of transistors lying on a given integrated circuitry doubles every one and a half years, which leads to a considerable increase in computational power and efficiency [10].

This prediction held correct for several decades, guiding the evolution of semiconductor technology and contributing to the digital revolution. As semiconductor manufacturers strive to adhere to Moore's Law and continue scaling down transistor sizes, they encounter a myriad of challenges. One of the most difficult challenges is the phenomenon known as short-channel effects (SCEs), which become increasingly pronounced as transistor dimensions shrink [12]. Short-channel effects encompass a range of undesirable behaviors, including increased leakage current, degradation of subthreshold swing, and heightened OFF-current, all of which can negatively impact the performance and efficiency of integrated circuits [11].

2.1 Short-Channel Effects

Short-channel effects manifests deeply scaled MOSFETs, specially beyond the 22 nm node [12]. As transistor channel lengths decrease, the ability of the gate to control channel region weakens, allowing the drain potential to influence the electrostatics of the channel region. This phenomenon results in leakage current, also known as subthreshold current, flowing through the drain and the source terminals [13]. The presence of short-channel effects disrupts critical transistor parameters such as threshold voltage roll-off (V_t), drain induced barrier lowering (DIBL), subthreshold swing, and on/off current characteristics [17].

2.1.1 Drain Induced Barrier Lowering

Drain-induced barrier lowering (DIBL) represents a significant short-channel effect in MOSFETs, initially characterized by a decrease in the Vt (threshold) of the transistor at increased drain voltages. As the voltage across the drain and source terminals (VDS) increases, the depletion region of the drain terminal expands, moving closer to the depletion region of the source. This phenomenon ultimately leads to field penetration, resulting in a reduction of the channel length [14].

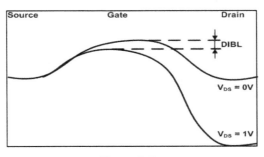

Fig. 1. DIBL

The decrease in the channel length subsequently diminishes the barrier potential, facilitating easier movement of carriers over the channel region, particularly when the voltage at gate terminal is lower than threshold voltage (VT). Consequently, the gate eventually loses its control on the channel, as depicted in Fig. 1.

Mathematically, the DIBL effect is expressed as the derivative of threshold voltage (Vth) over the drain voltage (Vd), as shown by the equation which determines the limit upto which the threshold voltage decreases as we increase the drain voltage.

$$\text{DIBL} = (\partial \text{Vth})/(\partial \text{Vd}) \tag{2.1}$$

2.1.2 VT Roll off

The VT roll-off stems from threshold voltage (VT) fluctuations due to source and gate depletion regions as channel length scales. Longer channels yield stable VT, while shorter ones experience notable DIBL from proximal source depletion regions to the drain which is evident in the Fig. 2.This threshold voltage (of NMOS and PMOS) remains stable for longer channel length, but decreases monotonically when channel length gets smaller, which may turn on the FET unnecessarily [17]. The lowering of threshold barrier between drain terminal and the source terminal leads to lowering the threshold voltage (VT), termed as VT roll-off.

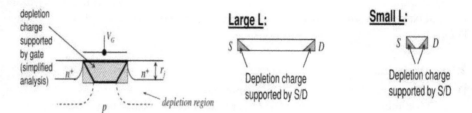

Fig. 2. Vt Roll off

For increased channel lengths, the threshold voltage of NMOS and PMOS transistors remains constant. However, as the length of channel decreases, the threshold voltage decreases steadily, which can undesirably activate the device unnecessarily [9]. The decrease in channel length reduces the potential barrier between the drain to source regions, resulting to a lesser threshold voltage (VT), a phenomenon known as VT rolloff [15]. This reduction in VT can impact device performance, potentially causing unintended activation and compromising circuit reliability.

2.1.3 Subthreshold Swing (Ss)

Subthreshold swing (SS) is a crucial parameter which is described by the change in gate bias voltage needed to change the drain current by ten folds (one decade) [12]. It serves as a measure of the gate control efficiency within the weak inversion layer region of a transistor. A lower SS value signifies enhanced gate control, resulting in improved energy efficiency and reduced power consumption, particularly in low-power circuits [13].

Mathematically, SS is represented by:

$$S = \partial(V_g)/\partial(\ln I_d) \qquad (2.2)$$

where ∂ (V_g) represents the change in gate voltage, and ∂ (log I_d) denotes change in log of the drain current. This formula quantifies the sensitivity of gate voltage (V_{gs}) required to improve the drain current over a wide range.

2.1.4 On and off Current (Ion & Ioff)

Ion, or the ON current, is determined by applying VDD to both the drain to source voltage (V_{DS}) and gate to source voltage (V_{GS}) and, with the resulting drain current (I_{DS}) representing the Ion current. Conversely, Ioff, or the OFF current, is measured by applying no bias voltages to VGS and VDS, and then measuring the resulting current (IDS), known as Off or leakage current.

As transistor scaling continues, it becomes imperative to explore innovative technologies to facilitate further advancements in MOS transistors [19]. Embracing such solutions unlocks the vast potential of semiconductor technology. Transitioning to FinFET technology from traditional MOSFETs offers several advantages, including mitigating effects of DIBL due to improved electrostatic gate terminal control [22]. In FinFETs, the three-dimensional structure provides improved gate control, preventing the decrease in barrier potential and enhancing VT roll-off compared to MOSFETs. Additionally, FinFETs exhibit superior performance in terms of SS and Ion/Ioff characteristics [16]. The increased electrostatic control of the gate terminal in multi-gate devices like FinFETs restricts the movement of minority charge carriers through the channel, leading to improved gate control and improved transistor performance.

3 Simulation Methodology

Simulations were observed for FinFET devices using the BSIM-CMG model, a SPICE model specifically designed for FinFETs, along with the Predictive Technology Model card for multi-gate (PTM-MG). Initially, the BSIM-CMG model is incorporated into the simulator, following which process parameters like supply voltage (VDD), fin height (Hfin), fin width (tfin), number of fins (N), and gate length (Lg) are supplied to it from the PTM-MG [17]. The SPICE simulator is utilized to perform simulations for both MOSFET and FinFET devices [18]. Table 1 and Table 2 contain detailed parameters for MOSFETs and FinFETs, respectively, providing essential insights into the characteristics and performance of each device.

By leveraging advanced simulation techniques and models tailored specifically for FinFET technology, engineers can accurately predict the behavior and performance of FinFET devices subject to different operating conditions [19]. This comprehensive analysis aids in optimizing device designs, refining process parameters, and enhancing overall device performance and reliability.

Table 1. Electrical and Geometrical Parameters of MOSFET

Parameters	Value
Gate Length (L_g)	2 um
Gate oxide thickness (t_{ox})	40.8 nm
Threshold Voltage (v_t)	775.27 mV
Transconductance Parameter (kp)	55.18 uA/V^2
Channel Length Modulation (Lambda)	2.75 V^{-1}
VDD	5 V

Table 2. Electrical and Geometrical Parameters of FinFET

Parameters	Value (20 nm)	Value (7 nm)
Channel Length (L_g)	24 nm	21 nm
Height of the Fin(*Hfin*)	28 nm	34 nm
Thickness of the Fin(*tsi*)	15 nm	7 nm
Work function	4.56 eV	4.30 eV
Thickness of Gate oxide (t_{ox})	1.1 nm	0.80 nm
VDD	0.9 V	0.7 V

4 Results and Discussion

Over here, we present our results derived from a simulation-based study of MOSFET and FinFET devices. To conduct a comprehensive performance comparison, various parameters such as DIBL, subthreshold swing, VT roll-off, ON current, and OFF current are carefully examined for both MOSFETs and FinFETs [20]. Throughout the simulation process, different distinct channel lengths (Lg) are considered to evaluate effect of scaling on the performance of the device.

DC or transient simulations are performed on the SPICE netlist to accurately measure the performance metrics. These simulations enable us to evaluate behaviour and characteristics of MOSFETs and FinFETs under different operating conditions, providing valuable inferences from their comparative performance and suitability for various applications [21]. By systematically analysing simulation results for all the parameters, we can identify the strengths and limitations of both MOSFET and FinFET technologies. This information is instrumental in guiding transistor selection, optimizing circuit designs, and ultimately enhancing the overall performance and efficiency of electronic systems.

4.1 Drain Induced Barrier Lowering (DIBL)

Measuring DIBL involves adjusting the gate-to-source voltage (V_{GS}) to attain a reference drain current while maintaining the drain-to-source voltage (V_{DS}) at two distinct levels: V_{DD} (5V) and 0.5V [16]. The corresponding VGS values obtained at these voltage levels facilitate the calculation of DIBL using Eq. (2.1), with a drain current of 100μA serving as the reference. To demonstrate, impact of gate length scaling on DIBL, gate length of MOSFET device is varied over 5–1 μm range. On the other hand, gate length of FINFET device is varied over 20–7 nm range.

Figure 3 graphically represents the impact of DIBL, depicting the variation of the threshold voltage as the gate length decreases. As the channel length of NMOS or NFET shrinks, the potential barrier between the drain and source regions increases [22]. However, FinFETs, characterized by their 3D structure with vertical fins, offer enhanced electrostatic control over the channel [23]. This diminishes the formation of the depletion region and mitigates the adverse effects of DIBL.

It is observed from the Fig. 3 that change in DIBL is only 8mv/V in FinFET device while scaling channel length from 20 nm to 7 nm. However, change in DIBL is 20mv/V in MOSFET device while scaling channel length from 5 μm to 1 μm.

From the figure, we note that the extent of DIBL change relative to channel length is less pronounced in FinFETs compared to MOSFETs.

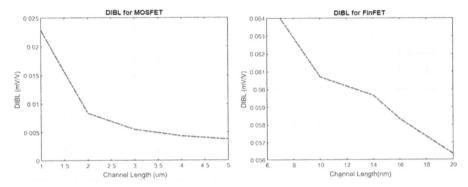

Fig. 3. Effect on Drain Induced Barrier Lowering as the Channel Length downscales

4.2 VT Roll off

Measuring VT roll-off involves varying the gate-to-source voltage (VGS) while maintaining a constant reference current, typically set at 100 μA. The deviation in threshold voltage (VT) from its ideal value under these conditions is termed VT roll-off. Figure 4 illustrates the impact of VT roll-off, showing a decrease in V_{th} as the gate length is reduced.

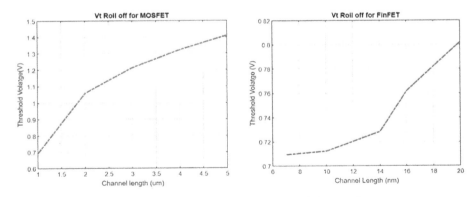

Fig. 4. . Effect on V_{th} as the Gate Length downscales

The increase in drain voltage reduces energy barrier between the source and drain terminals, leading to a phenomenon known as DIBL. This effect causes the threshold voltage to decrease, resulting in VT roll-off [20]. Figure 4 shows the threshold voltage (V_{th}) of the transistor deviates and decreases from the ideal value as the gate length is reduced. As observed from Fig. 4 that change in VT is only 0.09 V in FinFET device while scaling channel length from 20 nm to 6nm. However, change in VT is 0.7 V in MOSFET device while scaling channel length from 5 μm to 1 μm. The steep slope in FinFET's VT rolloff graph demonstrates enhanced performance compared to MOSFET. This improvement in FinFET's VT roll-off highlights its ability to maintain better control over threshold voltage, leading to superior overall device performance and efficiency compared to the older MOSFET technology.

The improved VT roll-off characteristics of FinFETs highlight their enhanced ability to maintain control over threshold voltage, even as transistor dimensions are decreased [24]. This superior control contributes to improved device performance and efficiency, making FinFET technology preferable for various applications. By leveraging FinFETs, designers can optimize circuit design to achieve better performance and energy efficiency compared to traditional MOSFET technology [25]. Understanding VT roll-off allows engineers to assess transistor behavior and make informed decisions regarding technology selection for specific application requirements.

4.3 Subthreshold Swing (SS)

Subthreshold swing (SS) is measured by maintaining a constant drain-to-source voltage (VDS) at VDD while systematically adjusting the gate voltage (VGS) to induce a tenfold change in I_D. Once both VGS values are recorded, SS can be determined using Eq. (2.2). SS is a crucial parameter that reflects the efficiency of NMOS or NFET transistors in controlling current flow when operating in the subthreshold region.

A lower SS value indicates that the transistor can transition between the on and off states more effectively, consuming minimal power in the process [26]. By accurately assessing SS, engineers can gauge the transistor's performance and its suitability for applications requiring low power consumption.

In Fig. 5, the subthreshold swing characteristics of MOSFETs and FinFETs are compared. The MOSFET's subthreshold graph exhibits a greater curvature, indicating a higher subthreshold slope (SS) and reduced efficiency compared to FinFETs [27]. This suggests that FinFET technology offers higher control over threshold voltage and enhanced performance in weak inversion conditions.

The observed differences in subthreshold swing between MOSFETs and FinFETs highlight the advantages of the latter in low-power applications. FinFETs demonstrate better energy efficiency and performance because of their ability to effectively regulate current flow with minimal power loss.

4.4 ION and IOFF

Ion and Ioff serve as critical metrics in transistor analysis, offering valuable insights into device efficiency and reliability. Ion is determined by fixing V_{DS} at V_{DD} and setting the V_{GS} to V_{DD}, allowing the transistor to conduct at its maximum capacity. Conversely, Ioff is ascertained with V_{DS} held constant at V_{DD} and V_{GS} set to a minimal value, typically 1mV, to minimize conduction and measure leakage current.

Comprehensive Study of Short Channel Effects (SCEs)   141

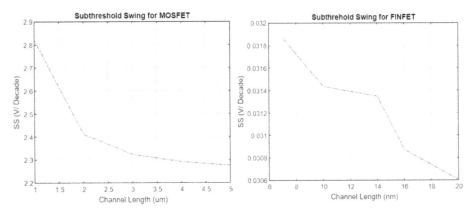

Fig. 5. Effect on Subthreshold Swing downscaling the channel length

These parameters play a pivotal role in evaluating transistor performance and guiding circuit design for optimal functionality and reduced power consumption, especially in low-power applications. Ion and Ioff reflect the drain currents ID, representing the transistor's conductance in on and off states, respectively.

Figure 6 depicts the IOFF current characteristics, highlighting the FinFET's notable advantage of substantially lower leakage currents compared to conventional MOSFETs. This underscores the superior subthreshold performance of FinFET technology, making it a preferred choice for low-power applications.

In Fig. 7, simulation results for ON current(ION) demonstrate an increase in current as transistor sizes shrink. This trend is consistent with the scaling behaviour observed in modern transistors. FinFETs exhibit significant lower off-state leakage current and higher on-state current, indicating superior overall performance and efficiency compared to traditional MOSFETs.

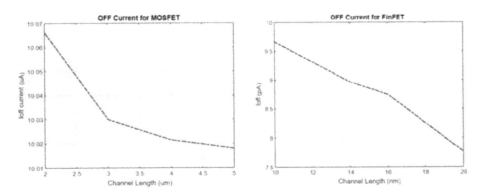

Fig. 6. Effect on Leakage Current (Ioff) downscaling the channel length

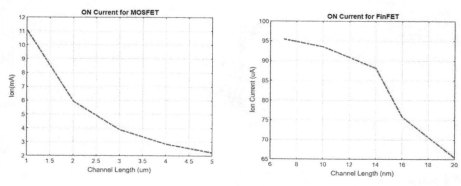

Fig. 7. Effect on current (Ion) downscaling the channel length

The Table 3 illustrates change in various SCE parameters for both MOSFET and FinFET devices as they scaled down from half of their channel lengths. Table 3 clearly indicates that SCE parameters are significantly improved in FinFET device compared to MOSFET device. Henceforth, it seems that the FinFET is more immuned towards SCEs compared to MOSFET.

Table 3. Comparative analysis of SCE parameters scaling down to the channel length

Parameters	MOSFET (%)	FinFET (%)
DIBL	92.76	7.9
Vt Roll off	24.7	12.78
Subthreshold swing	5.21	2.62
Ion	108.5	43.61

5 Conclusion

The transition from MOSFET to FinFET represents a pivotal shift in semiconductor technology, motivated by the imperative to overcome the constraints posed by conventional transistor designs. MOSFETs, while revolutionary in their own right, encounter inherent limitations as devices are scaled down to smaller dimensions. Short-channel effects (SCEs) emerge as a significant hurdle in MOSFET scaling, leading to increased leakage current, compromised gate control, and diminished overall performance. In response of that, the industry has turned to FinFETs, leveraging their unique three-dimensional architecture to address these challenges.

In this work we have compared and analyzed the short channel effects on device performance and characteristics in both MOSFET and FinFET transistor technologies. Various parameters related to SCEs like DIBL, VT roll-off and subthreshold swing are evaluated for both MOSFETs and FinFETs devices. Additionally, to demonstrate, impact of gate length scaling on various parameters of SCEs, gate length of FINFET device is varied from 20 nm to 7 nm.

Our simulation-based study demonstrated that SCE parameters are significantly improved in FinFET device compared to MOSFET device. The results confirms the scalability of FinFET up to 7 nm technology node though SCE increases.

References

1. Sood, H., et al.: Advanced MOSFET technologies for next generation communication systems. Perspect. Challenges (2018)
2. Antoniadis, D.A., Aberg, I., Ni Chleirigh, C., Nayfeh, O.M., Khakifirooz, A., Hoyt, J.L.: [IBM J Res Dev], **50**, 363 (2006)
3. Cheng, Z., et al.: New observations in contact scaling for 2D FETs. In *2019 Device Research Conference (DRC)* 227–228 (2019)
4. Limachia, M., Thakker, R., Kothari, N.: A near-threshold 10T differential SRAM cell with high read and write margins for tri-gated FinFET technology. INTEGRATION: VLSI J. Elsevier, **61**, 125–137 (2018)https://doi.org/10.1016/j.vlsi.2017.11.009
5. Limachia, M., Thakker, R., Kothari, N.: Characterization of a novel 10T LowVoltage SRAM cell with high read and write margin for 20 nm FinFET technology. In The Proceeding of 30th International Conference on VLSI Design and 16th International Conference on Embedded Systems, pp. 309–314 (2017)
6. Hasanur R. Khan, Mamaluy, D., Vasileska, D.: Simulation of the impact of process variation on the optimized 10-nm FinFET. IEEE Trans. Electron Devices, **55**(8), 2134–2141 (2008)
7. Hwang, C.-H., Li, Y., Han, M.-H.: Statistical variability in finfet devices with intrinsic parameter fluctuations. Microelectronics Reliability, vol. 50(5), pp. 635–638 (2010), 2009 International Electron Devices and Materials Symposium (IEDMS)
8. Mohan V. Dunga, Lin, C.-H., Xi, X., Lu, D.D., Niknejad, A.M., Hu, C.: Modeling advanced FET technology in a compact model. IEEE Trans. Electron Devices **53**, 1971 (2006)
9. Ratnesh, R.K., Goel, A., Kaushik, G., Garg, H., Singh, M., Prasad, B.: Advancement and challenges in MOSFET scaling. Mater. Sci. Semiconductor Process. **134**, 106002 (2021)
10. Moore, G.E.: Cramming more components onto integrated circuits. Electronics **38**, 33–35 (1965)
11. Young Intel, I.: Transistors Keep Moore's Law Alive (2018)
12. Paul, B.C.: Impact of Process variations on nanowire and nanotube device performance. IEEE Trans. ELE. Devices., **54**(9) (2007)
13. Saha, J.K., Chakma, N., Hasan, M.: Impact of channel length gate insulator thickness gate insulator material and temperature on the performance of nanoscale FETs. J. Comput. Electron., 1–7 (2018)
14. Limachia, M., Vyas, D., Thakker, R., Kothari, N.: Hybrid offset compensated latch-type sense amplifier for tri-gated FinFET technology. INTEGRATION VLSI J. Elsevier **62**, 258–269 (2018). https://doi.org/10.1016/j.vlsi.2018.03.012
15. Li, W., et al.: Approaching the quantum limit in two-dimensional semiconductor contacts. Nature **613**, 274–279 (2023)
16. Al-Mistarihi, M.F., Rjoub, A., Taradeh, N.A.: Drain induced barrier lowering (DIBL) accurate model for nanoscale Si-MOSFET transistor. In 2013 25th International Conference on Microelectronics (ICM)
17. Teja, P., Sinha, S.K., Durgesh, A.: Comparison of MOSFET, MESFET, FinFET and SOIFinFET. Int. J. Emerg. Technol. Innov. Res. **7**(11), 1155–1161 (2020)

18. Hossain, M.Z., Khosru, Q.D.M.: Threshold Voltage Roll-Off Due to Channel Length Reduction for a Nanoscale n-channel FinFET
19. Carlson, A.: SRAM read/write margin enhancements using FinFETs. IEEE Trans. VLSI, **23**(3) (2010)
20. Lee, C.-W., Lee, K.-M., Kim, C.-S., Choi, Y.-H.: Drain-induced barrier lowering and threshold voltage shifts in nanoscale planar CMOS. IEEE Trans. Electron Devices **54**(11), 3003–3013 (2007)
21. Jaisawal, R.K., Rathore, S., Kondekar, P.N., Yadav, S., Awadhiya, B., Upadhyay, P., Bagga, N.: Assessing the analog/{RF} and linearity performances of {FinFET} using high threshold voltage techniques. Semiconductor Science and Technology, Research, 055010 (2022)
22. Dunga, M., et al.: BSIM-CMG: A Compact Model for Multi-Gate Transistors. Springer, US (2008)
23. Endo. K., O'uchi, S.I., Ishikawa, Y., Liu, Y., Matsukawa, T., Sakamoto, K., Tsukada, J., Yamauchi, H., Masahara, M.: Variability analysis of tin finfet sram cells and its compensation by independent-dg finfets. IEEE Electron. Device Lett., **31**(10), 1095–1097 (2010)
24. Sriram, S.R., Bindu, B.: A physics- based 3-D potential and threshold voltage model for undoped triplegate FinFET with interface trapped charges. J. Comput. Electron. **18**, 37–45 (2019)
25. Mendiratta, N.: Suman Lata Tripathi "a review on performance comparison of advanced MOSFET structures below 45nm technology node. J. Semiconductor IOP Sci. **41**, 1–10 (2020)
26. O'Brien, K., et al.: Advancing 2D monolayer CMOS through contact, channel and interface engineering. In *IEEE International Electron Devices Meeting*, IEEE, pp. 146–149 (2021)
27. Bhuyan, M.H.: History and evolution of CMOS technology and its applications in the semiconductor industry SEU Journal of Science and Engineering (2017)
28. Colinge, J.-P.: Multiple-gate {SOI} {MOSFETs}, Solid-State Electronics, **48**(6), 897–905 Silicon On Insulator Technology and Devices (2004)
29. Liu, F., He, J., Zhang, J., Chen, Y., Chan, M.: A non-charge-sheet analytic model for symmetric doublegate MOSFETs with smooth transition between partially and fully depleted operation modes. IEEE Trans. Electron Devices **55**(12), 3494–3502 (2008)
30. Yazeer, M.J.: Comparative Study of Silicon Nanowire FET-Simulation and Experimental (2016)

A Machine Learning (ML)-Inspired Method for Intrusion Detection in IoT Devices Networks

Veeramuthu Venkatesh[1], Pethuru Raj[2], Roshitha Nedium[1], Jahnavi Edara[1], Kalluru Amarnath Reddy[1], and R. Anushiadevi[1](✉)

[1] School of Computing, SASTRA Deemed University Tirumalaisamudram, Thanjavur, Tamilnadu 613401, India
anushiadevi@it.sastra.edu

[2] Reliance Jio Cloud Services (JCS), Bangalore 560025, India

Abstract. The Internet of Things (IoT) and Machine Learning (ML) represent dynamic research fields with significant growth. IoT applications have gained popularity among technology researchers and developers, and the increasing deployment of IoT devices in critical infrastructures improves efficiency and reliability and raises concerns about cyber-attacks. Enterprises have effectively implemented IoT services, enabling automated production through remote and intelligent control. However, this adoption has concurrently introduced novel security vulnerabilities. Addressing the security and privacy challenges in IoT, especially considering energy limitations and scalability issues, remains a critical focus in computer security. This paper aims to prevent multiple attacks targeting sensor nodes' data manipulation. It encompasses a range of threats, such as sensing layer attacks, malfunctions, tamper attacks, false data injection, base node and clone attacks. The proposed approach involves a threat model and a pairing algorithm that utilizes machine learning to associate each sensor node with its corresponding node. To accomplish the goal, the performance of the proposed solution is compared with various machine learning models, including Decision Tree, Linear Regression, k-nearest neighbors (KNN), Random Forest, and AdaBoost. The evaluation utilized two openly accessible real-world datasets, with metrics such as accuracy in attack detection, training time, and testing time being considered. By incorporating machine learning algorithms to improve attack detection in IoT environments, the proposed approach represents a significant advancement in enhancing security and privacy. The results highlight the importance of adopting advanced techniques to safeguard IoT systems from potential threats. The proposed method achieved an impressive 96.75% accuracy rate in detecting attacks, surpassing existing solutions with nearly twice the speed in training and testing times. As the IoT landscape continues to evolve, future research in this area will remain essential to ensure a secure and resilient IoT ecosystem.

Keywords: Sensor nodes · Security attacks · Intrusion Detection System · Critical infrastructure · Machine learning · Internet of Things (IoT)

1 Introduction

The Internet of Things (IoT) has become a prominent communication paradigm, drawing significant research attention in the twenty-first century [1, 2]. IoT devices are characterized by their interconnectivity, incorporating embedded systems, electronic components, sensors, actuators, and network connectivity. This network of interconnections enables the seamless exchange and collection of data from various sensors, effectively linking objects like vehicles, houses, appliances, and sensors to the Internet and facilitating effortless sharing of information, data, and resources. In science and engineering, IoT finds diverse applications, including remote sensing, water quality, earthquake monitoring, infrastructure monitoring, environmental monitoring, governmental security policies, and more. The breadth of its reach extends across various sectors, encompassing retail, health care, military, entertainment, digital manufacturing, tourism, disaster management, Vehicle management, Smart homes, Intelligent societies, Smart agriculture, Supply chains, smart grids, innovative health, and more. The core vision driving IoT is to establish seamless connectivity between individuals and intelligent objects, regardless of location, network, or service [3].

Ensuring security in IoT is of utmost importance, mainly when employed in mission-critical tasks, such as tactical military applications, where network vulnerabilities could lead to casualties for friendly forces [4–6]. In IoT deployments incorporating one or multiple sensor networks, the significance of algorithms and approaches developed to ensure the security of Wireless Sensor Networks (WSNs) protection cannot be overstated. Therefore, addressing cyber-security concerns, including attacks, their prevention, and mitigation, holds great significance in establishing a secure and dependable IoT infrastructure. Two categories can be used to classify attacks: Active and Passive. Individuals conducting covert attacks utilize passive methodologies to gather information through intercepting communication lines or compromising network components. Additional classifications for these passive attacks encompass snooping, node destruction, node malfunction, node outage, and traffic analysis.

Conversely, active assaults involve threat actors who directly impact the operations and functionalities of the targeted network. These attacks aim to achieve the attacker's primary objectives and can be detected using security tools such as intrusion detection. For example, active attacks may lead to the degradation of network services. Active attacks include denial-of-service (DoS), Jamming, flooding, blackhole, sinkhole, wormhole, and Sybil attacks [7, 8].

Computer science defense strategies against network security assaults commonly incorporate three essential elements. The initial aspect of these strategies revolves around prevention, aiming to thwart attacks before they can be initiated. Every recommended preventive measure should be tailored to counter specific types of attacks. While intrusion prevention measures can effectively deter external attackers targeting WSNs and IoT, they may not be explicitly designed to thwart internal attackers. Consider a scenario where an attacker gets through the security protections the prevention component put in place. In that case, it indicates that the network's boundaries have been breached, and data resources may already be compromised. At the moment, identifying compromised nodes is handled by security solutions created for the relevant attack's detection component. Intrusion Detection Systems (IDSs) are the primary line of defense in countering persistent attacks, particularly internal threats [9]. Upon detecting an intrusion, a mitigation mechanism, acting as the last line of defense, is activated to minimize the detrimental impact of the ongoing assault. The final aspect focuses on mitigating attacks after their occurrence. For instance, security measures such as "isolating affected nodes in the network" or "disabling the ports of the computer used during the attack" can be implemented to safeguard the network. The literature extensively covers the security of IoT networks through various surveys. Existing methods to protect Wireless Sensor Networks (WSNs) include encryption, request quotas, honeypots, anomaly detection, identification/verification techniques, solutions, and sensing layer security. Numerous suggestions have been made regarding these solutions within the network layer. Additionally, machine learning and deep learning have gained widespread acceptance as effective mechanisms for attack detection [10–12]. In the context of this research, two case studies are presented to illustrate the importance of alignment and assess the methodology.

2 Related Work

In [13], most CLAS schemes presented on HWMSNs demonstrate vulnerabilities to various forgery attacks and lack practical efficiency. This research proposes a novel pairing-free CLAS technique for HWMSNs, utilizing elliptic curve cryptography to address these concerns and enhance security, all while minimizing storage, computation, and communication expenses. In [14], an intrusion detection system based on IoT was employed, and the researchers effectively integrated multiple machine learning techniques to detect network monitoring probing and various forms of basic denial-of-service attacks. In [15], researchers utilized autoencoders to identify counterfeit data injection attempts and recover the modified data. The objective was achieved through the deployment of two autoencoders. Initially, an under-complete autoencoder and its reconstruction error were employed to detect the attacks. Subsequently, a denoising autoencoder was utilized to restore the corrupted data. A comparative analysis was conducted against SVM-based methods, revealing that their proposed approach demonstrated superior performance in attack detection, mainly when dealing with previously unseen attack samples. In [16], autoencoders could detect and rectify erroneous data injection attacks. A two-step approach was employed to accomplish this goal. Initially, identifying the attacks involved utilizing a reconstruction error in conjunction with an under-complete autoencoder. Following this step, a denoising autoencoder was applied to restore the corrupted data. Through a comparative analysis against SVM-based methods, the researchers demonstrated the superiority of their proposed approach in detecting attacks, especially when dealing with previously unseen attack samples. In [17], a distributed deep learning-based system was presented to detect IoT attacks, achieving a remarkable 96% accuracy. Furthermore, the researchers explored attack detection through a fog-to-things methodology and conducted a comparative analysis of shallow and deep neural networks using an online dataset.

3 Internet of Things (IoT) Ecosystem

IoT architecture comprises a complex network of components, including sensors, actuators, protocols, multiple layers, and cloud services, forming IoT networking systems given in Fig. 1. Typically organized into distinct layers, the architecture enables administrators to assess, monitor, and uphold the system's integrity. The Internet of Things involves the extensive interconnection of diverse devices, such as home appliances, remote controls, vestures, watches, tablets, etc., allowing seamless interaction between these devices and those who utilize them.

Fig. 1. The Internet of Things (IoT) architecture and its constituent elements.

The proposed solution involves collecting data from numerous devices, which is subsequently transmitted to data centers and servers for in-depth analysis, leading to automation and task execution. However, behind the scenes of your commands and task completion lies a comprehensive and intricate architectural framework that relies on various elements and interactions. The IoT architecture follows a four-step process. In this context, data is transferred from connected devices through sensors and a network before being processed, analyzed, and stored in the cloud. As the Internet of Things continues to evolve, it holds the potential for further expansion, promising users' novel and enhanced experiences.

4 Methodology

The threat model in Fig. 2 encompasses all categories of security attacks that form the basis for manipulating sensor data [18]. The solution comprises two main components: a sensor pairing approach and an analysis based on a machine learning algorithm given in Fig. 3. Each sensor node is paired with its neighboring sensor node through the sensor pairing algorithm. To evaluate the node pairing approach, a comparison is conducted against established decision trees, random forests, AdaBoost, and KNN models, a few examples of machine learning algorithms.

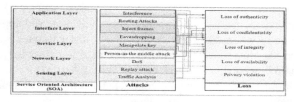

Fig. 2. Service Oriented Architecture—impacts on threats.

4.1 A Framework for Estimating Survivability in WSNs

Wireless Sensor Networks encompass various functions, including data sensing, collection, processing, transmission, and potential data storage. Data aggregation within the sensor nodes plays a crucial role in these functions. Ensuring the security of these operations presents' significant challenges as the sensor nodes are vulnerable to attacks, leading to unauthorized access and manipulation of sensor data. Furthermore, attackers can duplicate nodes at any point in the network, allowing the transfer of harmful data.

Fig. 3. Estimating survivability through a node pairing framework.

The primary focus of the proposed work is to address the critical concern of data alteration resulting from various security attacks. This challenge can be mitigated by implementing a node pairing approach, as illustrated in Fig. 3. Modifying data jeopardizes data integrity and authenticity, which could result in sensor nodes transmitting deceptive information about the environment. It ensures security at the IoT device level and an understanding of its significance.

Ensuring IoT device-level security involves safeguarding individual devices within the network to create a secure user environment. A thorough analysis at the device level is essential to devise an effective security scheme, identifying critical vulnerabilities specific to each device. Understanding these vulnerabilities allows for implementing appropriate security controls to mitigate potential threats and attacks. For instance, due to poorly encrypted Bluetooth connections, wearable activity-tracking devices like Fitbit may be vulnerable to man-in-the-middle attacks. Consider the practical applications of IoT security throughout various domains to see the significance of investigating IoT security at the device level.

4.2 Origins of Threats in IoT Devices

Having examined the features of IoT and their applications in various scenarios within an intelligent world, identify potential threats that may arise in the context of these use cases. An IoT network may consist of multiple Wireless Sensor Networks (WSNs) with numerous head nodes and many wireless sensor nodes distributed randomly throughout the network. In densely deployed WSNs, each sensor node coexists with its neighboring head nodes as the system controller. The network's scalability also allows for adding more head nodes, each communicating with its respective sensor nodes. In addressing the identified threats, our proposed solution effectively safeguards against sensor node data manipulation, which may result from various security attacks. Recognizing that even link-level security achieved through robust cryptography schemes can be compromised is crucial. The safety and privacy of IoT face potential risks from several entities that may attempt to compromise the system's integrity.

4.3 Unethical User or Malicious User

The person in control of the IoT device who can carry out attacks to learn the manufacturer's trade secrets and obtain access to limited functions. Exploiting vulnerabilities in the system, this malicious actor can gain access to sensitive data, potentially selling it to third parties or targeting other systems.

4.4 Untrustworthy Manufacturer

The company that developed the product can utilize the technology for data collection on consumers or other Internet of Things devices. Such a producer may intentionally put security vulnerabilities into the design, enabling future access to user data and potential exposure to third parties. Furthermore, more adequately secured products compromise user privacy. In the context of IoT, where various objects interconnect, a manufacturer could target other competitors' devices to damage their reputation.

4.5 Unauthorized Device Manipulation

IoT devices are compactly integrated into various systems, including cars, light switches, TVs, ovens, etc. Some devices remain unattended for extended periods, making them susceptible to easy theft without detection. Once a device is in the wrong hands, it becomes vulnerable to attacks, such as stealing sensitive information, manipulating software, and tampering with hardware. It is essential to note that adversaries can control the device to introduce impostors into the system, use it maliciously, or exploit it for unintended functionalities.

4.6 Duplicate Attack

A significant threat is posed by a particular attack known as the "same attack," where an attacker strategically distributes copies of compromised sensor nodes throughout the network to manipulate its behavior. Attackers can compromise numerous sensor nodes distributed randomly throughout the network. These duplicated sensor nodes can potentially transmit compromised or modified data, causing disruptions in the network's functionality.

4.7 Identity Falsification

Refers to accessing services that would otherwise be inaccessible through someone else's login information. These credentials can be acquired directly from a device, through eavesdropping on the communication channel, or via phishing.

4.8 Privacy Infringement

In gathering knowledge about the user, adversaries do not always rely on accessing confidential information, unlike information leakage. Instead, they can acquire private data through alternative metadata and traffic analysis sources.

4.9 Denial-Of-Service (DoS)

Pertains to the situation where authorized users cannot access the system as it becomes inaccessible. The system should be designed to continue functioning despite undesired actions executed by malevolent users. This type of attack can be accomplished through different means, including device theft, software manipulation, or the disruption of communication channels.

4.10 Impact of Attacks and Privacy Properties

More than merely identifying potential risks is required to ensure the security of IoT and fully grasp the gravity of the threats it faces. Instead, a comprehensive evaluation of their impact and likelihood, which can differ based on the context, is essential. Previous research has primarily concentrated on the technical aspects of IoT devices, often overlooking security implications in their practical application. This has revealed a gap in the existing literature, which we aim to address through a distinct methodology that investigates the security and privacy requirements of the IoT industry.

4.11 Privacy Requirements

It is crucial to ensure secure data transmission between users and IoT devices to safeguard user privacy and prevent eavesdropping criminals from deducing personal information. Messages exchanged between Internet of Things devices must not disclose personal information about the user's identity. Moreover, signals after devices should be transmitted in a manner that preserves privacy to avoid revealing the device's functioning, which could indirectly disclose user information. Furthermore, IoT devices should only retain personal user information, when necessary, even for a limited duration. The data collection should prioritize non-identifying information and avoid gathering data linked to personal identities, such as names, IDs, or visual photographs. Instead, the focus should be gathering aggregated statistics, such as counting the number of individuals in a building.

Additionally, users should be informed about the data being captured and the timing of such data collection. Enabling consumers to securely delete personal data from a device is fundamental to privacy standards, mainly if the device is intended for resale. This measure ensures that data remains protected even when the device changes ownership.

4.12 Multiple Approaches for Node Pairing

Node pairing can be categorized into two distinct types: homogeneous pairing, which involves pairing sensor nodes of the same kind, and heterogeneous pairing, which consists of pairing sensor nodes of different styles given in Fig. 4. Moreover, these pairing types can be further classified based on the input they employ: dynamic pairing and passive pairing. In passive pairing, one sensor node remains continuously active and online while the other remains inactive and offline. In this setup, the sensor node observes the surroundings, communicates information to the head node, and activates the second sensor node when an event occurs. The second sensor node observes its surroundings and sends information to the head node. Machine learning methods are employed at the head node to verify input accuracy from both sensor nodes.

In contrast, dynamic pairing involves mutual sensor nodes being operational and online concurrently, continuously monitoring their surroundings and transmitting data to the head node. This pairing can be either similar or diverse. To demonstrate the effectiveness of the proposed solution, two case studies are conducted, utilizing diverse sensor node pairing and various machine learning techniques. These investigations thoroughly evaluate the efficacy of the suggested remedy.

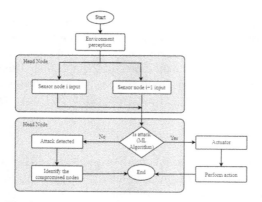

Fig. 4. Utilization of Machine Learning Algorithms.

4.13 Patient Privacy and Security in Healthcare

To evaluate the suggested approach, the dataset employed for this analysis is the Pima Indian Diabetes dataset sourced from the UCI machine learning repository. Subsequently, various machine learning models are analyzed, including Decision Tree, Linear Regression, k-nearest Neighbors (KNN), Random Forest, and AdaBoost. Derived from the National Institute of Diabetes, Digestive, and kidney diseases, the dataset encompasses nine distinct attributes, among which is the pivotal target variable indicating the presence or absence of diabetes in a patient. Before the application of machine learning algorithms, data preparation and refinement played a crucial role in attaining elevated levels of accuracy and expediting the learning procedure. This preparatory phase removes extraneous features, converts non-numeric elements into numerical representations, and addresses missing data via data pre-processing and normalization procedures. These measures enhance the effectiveness of the proposed healthcare use case and its ability to safeguard patient information and well-being.

4.14 Climatic Condition Monitoring in Agriculture

Farmers seek an automated mechanism for efficiently watering their crops within agriculture. Harnessing the potential of the Internet of Things (IoT), an autonomous system for plant irrigation presents an avenue through which agricultural practitioners can proficiently hydrate their crops. The task of overseeing climatic conditions, encompassing factors such as rainfall and temperature, is assigned to the sensor nodes. These nodes, in turn, autonomously regulate the operation of the water pump by making decisions rooted in these specific parameters. Our proposed model employs a pairing approach, where rain and temperature data are utilized together to detect potential attacks. In this context, the suggested paired method can detect such anomalies if any sensor nodes become compromised and transmit modified data to the central head node. As an illustration, consider a situation where a malicious actor compromises a temperature sensor and introduces a fabricated high-temperature reading to prolong the operation of the water pump needlessly. In that case, the head node's machine-learning algorithm will recognize the anomaly and raise the alarm for attack detection. This way, the compromised sensor node can be identified and dealt with promptly.

We employed an authentic weather dataset from the Bureau of Meteorology, Australian Government, to assess this case study, accessible on the Kaggle platform. The dataset comprises 23 features, with "Rain Tomorrow" as the target variable to predict whether it will rain the next day (Yes or No). Before applying the machine learning algorithms, thorough data preparation was conducted, including pre-processing and normalization steps. By implementing this climatic condition monitoring system, agriculture can benefit from efficient and automated irrigation practices while ensuring the security and accuracy of the data collected from various sensor nodes.

5 Results and Discussion of Two Use Cases

The Decision Tree, Linear Regression, k-nearest Neighbors (KNN), Random Forest, and AdaBoost models were employed on all three datasets. Similar performance evaluation measures, as used in the Pima Indian diabetes dataset analysis[19–21], were applied to assess the performance of these algorithms on the new datasets.

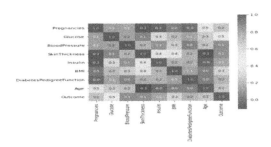

Fig. 5. Different correlation features among healthcare data.

Figure 5 illustrates the heatmap displaying various correlation features with Pregnancy, Age, and Glucose. The outcome exhibits a strong positive correlation with a value of 0.5. Additionally, Insulin, Skin Thickness, and BMI features show a strong positive correlation with a value of 0.4. Furthermore, positive correlations are observed between parts of Glucose, Insulin, Blood Pressure, BMI, Outcome, and Age, with a correlation coefficient of 0.3 for all the paired features. On the other hand, features Pregnancies, Insulin, Skin Thickness, Age, and Pregnancies and Skin Thickness exhibit a strong negative correlation with a value of -0.1.

Table 1 summarizes healthcare data using various machine-learning models. The Decision Tree and AdaBoost models demonstrate the highest precision 1 for processed dataset 2. Additionally, the KNN model achieves the second-highest precision with a value of 0.969 for processed dataset 2. However, the Decision Tree model exhibits the lowest precision value of 0.6677 for processed dataset 1.

Regarding recall values, the Decision Tree, Random Forest, and AdaBoost models achieve the highest recall value of 1 for processed dataset 2. The KNN model obtains the second-highest recall value of 0.9675 for processed dataset 2. In contrast, the Decision Tree model shows the lowest recall value of 0.9753 for processed dataset 1.

Considering F-score values, the Decision Tree, Random Forest, and AdaBoost models achieve the highest F-score of 1 for processed dataset 2. The KNN model obtains the second-highest F-score value of 0.97. However, the Decision Tree model exhibits the lowest F-score value of 0.68 for processed dataset 1.

Regarding the time taken by different models, it can be inferred that the AdaBoost model for the raw data takes the longest time, 0.74 s, compared to other models. On the other hand, the Decision Tree model takes the least time, 0.0033 s, compared to all other models.

Table 1. Machine learning results on health care data

Model	Datasets	Precision	Recall	F-Score	Time
DT	Raw Data	0.6911	0.6948	0.69	0.0072
	Processed 1	0.6677	0.6753	0.68	0.0054
	Processed 2	1	1	1	0.0033
KNN	Raw Data	0.7659	0.7662	0.77	0.0147
	Processed 1	0.7473	0.7532	0.75	0.0103
	Processed 2	0.969	0.9675	0.97	0.0131
LR	Raw Data	0.7918	0.7922	0.79	0.0422
	Processed 1	0.7621	0.7662	0.77	0.0163
	Processed 2	0.9287	0.9285	0.93	0.0196
RF	Raw Data	0.7727	0.7662	0.77	0.3007
	Processed 1	0.7704	0.7727	0.77	0.2654
	Processed 2	1	1	1	0.2888
ABD	Raw Data	0.7337	0.7402	0.7402	0.74
	Processed 1	0.7465	0.7532	0.75	0.1949
	Processed 2	1	1	1	0.1929

Figure 6 displays the accuracy of the raw data of health care information. The Linear Regression model achieves the highest accuracy of 79.2% compared to other models. The KNN and Random Forest models attain the second-highest accuracy with a value of 76.62%. The AdaBoost model achieves an accuracy value of 74.02%, while the Decision Tree model exhibits the lowest accuracy with a discount of 69.48%.

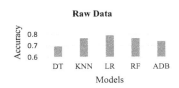

Fig. 6. Illustrates the accuracy of different machine-learning models using raw data.

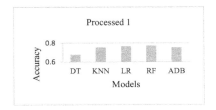

Fig. 7. Showcases the accuracy of machine learning models using processed data 1.

Figure 7 shows the accuracy of the Random Forest model, which stands out with the highest value of 77.27% among all the models using processed data 1. The Linear Regression model follows closely with the second-highest accuracy of 76.62%. KNN and AdaBoost models demonstrate moderate accuracy, each with a value of 75.32%. On the other hand, the Decision Tree model exhibits the lowest accuracy, with a value of 67.53%.

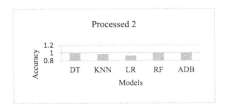

Fig. 8. Accuracy over machine learning models with processed data2.

Figure 8 displays the accuracy of the results for processed data. 2. Among the models, Decision Tree, Random Forest, and AdaBoost Models exhibit the highest accuracy, all achieving a value of 100%. The KNN model follows closely with the second-highest accuracy of 96.75%. Conversely, the Linear Regression model demonstrates the lowest accuracy value of 92.85%.

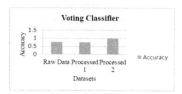

Fig. 9. Accuracy of voting classifier for various healthcare datasets.

Figure 9 illustrates the voting classifier results for raw, processed data 1, and processed data 2. Among these three stages, processed data 2 achieved the highest accuracy value of 100%. Processed data 1 followed closely with the second-highest accuracy value of 99.86%. Raw data had the lowest accuracy value of 84.63%. Notably, the accuracies in processed stage 2 improved from the original and processed stages. Decision Tree (DT), Random Forest (RF), and AdaBoost (ADB) classifiers outperformed the others, each achieving a perfect accuracy of 100%. The voting ensemble method successfully attained an accuracy of 100% by combining the classifiers DT, KNN, LR, RF, and ADB.

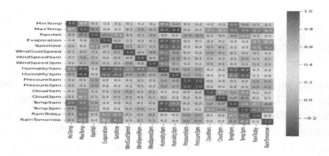

Fig. 10. Numerous correlation features observed within the climatic dataset.

Figure 10, the heat map displays correlation patterns among various features in the dataset. Specifically, Temp9am, and Temp3 exhibit a strong positive correlation of 0.92 with MinTemp and MaxTemp. MaxTemp and MinTemp also demonstrate a positive correlation with a coefficient of 0.7. On the other hand, Rainfall, Evaporation, and Sunshine have weak positive correlations, with coefficients of 0.2 and 0.3. Notably, Rainfall, MaxTemp, and Rainfall and Sunshine display a negative correlation, with a coefficient of −0.1."

The climatic information summary using various machine learning models is presented in Table 2. Among the models evaluated, Decision Tree, Random Forest, and AdaBoost demonstrated the highest precision (1) for process 2, while KNN and LR Models followed closely with a precision value of 0.99. Regarding recall values, Decision Tree, Random Forest, and AdaBoost Models achieved the highest recall value (1) for process 2, with KNN LR Models obtaining the second-highest recall value of 0.9675. Processed 1 had the lowest recall value of 0.76, attributed to the KNN model. For F-score deals, all models yielded an F-score value of 1 for processed 2, except for KNN, which had the lowest F-score value of 0.68 for processed 1.

Table 2. Machine learning analysis conducted on the climatic condition dataset

Model	Datasets	Precision	Recall	F-Score	Time
DT	Original	0.81	0.82	0.83	0.4
	Processed 1	0.72	0.77	0.78	0.06
	Processed 2	1	1	1	0.03
KNN	Original	0.83	0.84	0.84	65.95
	Processed 1	0.73	0.76	0.77	4.18
	Processed 2	0.99	0.99	1	1.14
LR	Original	0.8	0.81	0.82	0.92
	Processed 1	0.6	0.77	0.78	0.14
	Processed 2	0.99	0.99	1	0.35
RF	Original	0.8	0.81	0.82	1.22
	Processed 1	0.6	0.77	0.78	0.41
	Processed 2	1	1	1	0.35
ABD	Original	0.81	0.82	0.83	1.53
	Processed 1	0.6	0.77	0.78	0.33
	Processed 2	1	1	1	0.47

Analyzing the time taken by different models, it is evident that the KNN Model for raw data required the longest time, 65.93 s, compared to other models. Decision Tree performed the fastest with a processing time of 0.03 s, outperforming all other models.

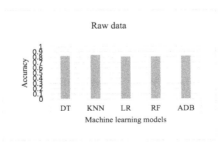

Fig. 11. Performance evaluation of multiple machine learning models using raw data.

Figure 11 illustrates the accuracy of different models on raw data about climatic conditions. The KNN model achieved the highest accuracy, with a value of 84.32%, outperforming the other models. The Decision Tree and AdaBoost models follow closely, reaching the second-highest accuracy with a discount of 82.62%. Lastly, the LR and Random Forest models demonstrated the lowest accuracy average of 81.23%.

Figure 12 displays the accuracy results for processed data 1. The KNN model achieved the highest accuracy, reaching a value of 84.32%, surpassing the performance of other models. The Decision Tree and AdaBoost models are closely followed, attaining the second-highest accuracy with a discount of 82.62%. On the other hand, the LR and Random Forest models exhibited the lowest accuracy, recording a discount of 81.23%.

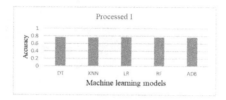

Fig. 12. Evaluating the accuracy of machine learning models using processed Data 1

Figure 13 illustrates the accuracy of processed data 2 for different models. The Decision Tree, Random Forest, and Linear Regression models achieved the highest accuracy, all recording a value of 100%. The KNN and AdaBoost models follow closely, attaining the second-highest accuracy with a value of 99.75%.

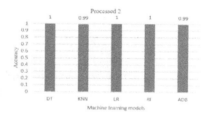

Fig. 13. Evaluating the accuracy of machine learning models using processed data 2.

Figure 14 presents the voting classifier results for raw data, processed data1, and processed data2.

Among these, processed data2 achieved the highest accuracy value of 100%, while processed data1 followed closely with the second-highest accuracy value of 99.86%. However, raw data had the lowest accuracy value of 84.63%. Notably, the accuracies in processed stage 2 improved compared to the original and processed stages. Decision Tree (DT), Random Forest (RF), and AdaBoost (ADB) models outperformed the other classifiers, all achieving 100% accuracy. By utilizing the voting ensemble method, an overall accuracy of 100% was achieved through the combination of DT, KNN, LR, RF, and ADB classifiers.

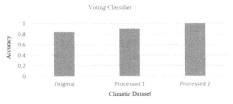

Fig. 14. Performance of the voting classifier on the Climatic Dataset.

6 Conclusion

The IoT represents a vast and intricate architectural design involving diverse devices, giving rise to crucial scalability, transparency, and reliability challenges. Security-related efforts must prioritize addressing these challenges. Furthermore, this investigation encompassed a comprehensive exploration of Machine Learning (ML) in the context of IoT, covering various types, applications, and use cases. Specifically, a taxonomy was devised to categorize ML models as linear or non-linear based on factors such as the problem type (classification or regression), targeted security issues, type of IoT network, and the evaluation measure used. Two case studies were conducted using IoT-based datasets to exemplify the proposed taxonomy. The first case study focused on healthcare, while the second centered on climatic conditions. We assessed both case studies using readily accessible real-world datasets. We applied the CART, SVM, and KNN algorithms to both datasets, measuring attack detection accuracy, recall, precision, F-score, training, and prediction time. Data pre-processing was performed in two distinct manners. The CART algorithm achieved the highest accuracy of 100% on processed dataset 2. In the future, research intends to delve deeper into sensor pairing techniques coupled with deep learning methodologies to augment overall performance.

References

1. Laghari, A.A., Wu, K., Laghari, R.A., Ali, M., Khan, A.A.: A review and state of art of Internet of Things (IoT). Arch. Comput. Methods Eng., 1–19 (2021)
2. Smys, S., Basar, A., Wang, H.: Others: hybrid intrusion detection system for internet of things (IoT). J. ISMAC. **2**, 190–199 (2020)
3. Al-Turjman, F., Lemayian, J.P.: Intelligence, security, and vehicular sensor networks in internet of things (IoT)-enabled smart-cities: An overview. Comput. Electric. Eng. **87**, 106776 (2020)
4. Roukounaki, A., Efremidis, S., Soldatos, J., Neises, J., Walloschke, T., Kefalakis, N.: Scalable and configurable end-to-end collection and analysis of IoT security data: Towards end-to-end security in IoT systems. In: 2019 Global IoT Summit (GIoTS), pp. 1–6 (2019)
5. Sidhu, S., Mohd, B.J., Hayajneh, T.: Hardware security in IoT devices with emphasis on hardware Trojans. J. Sens. Actuator Netw. **8**, 42 (2019)
6. Tudosa, I., Picariello, F., Balestrieri, E., De Vito, L., Lamonaca, F.: Hardware security in IoT era: the role of measurements and instrumentation. In: 2019 II Workshop on Metrology for Industry 4.0 and IoT (MetroInd4. 0\&IoT), pp. 285–290 (2019)
7. Silpa, C., Niranjana, G., Ramani, K.: Securing data from active attacks in IoT: an extensive study. In: Proceedings of International Conference on Deep Learning, Computing and Intelligence: ICDCI 2021, pp. 51–64 (2022)

8. Bout, E., Loscri, V., Gallais, A.: Evolution of IoT security: the era of smart attacks. IEEE Internet of Things Magazine. **5**, 108–113 (2022)
9. Chen, Z., et al.: Machine learning-enabled iot security: open issues and challenges under advanced persistent threats. ACM Comput. Surv. **55**, 1–37 (2022)
10. Abu Al-Haija, Q., Al-Dala'ien, M.: ELBA-IoT: an ensemble learning model for botnet attack detection in IoT networks. J. Sensor Actuator Networks., **11**, 18 (2022)
11. Jeyaselvi, M., Sathya, M., Suchitra, S., Jafar Ali Ibrahim, S., Kalyan Chakravarthy, N.S.: SVM-based cloning and jamming attack detection in IoT sensor networks. In: Advances in Information Communication Technology and Computing: Proceedings of AICTC 2021, Springer, pp. 461–471 (2022)
12. Mihoub, A., Fredj, O. Ben, Cheikhrouhou, O., Derhab, A., Krichen, M.: Denial of service attack detection and mitigation for internet of things using looking-back-enabled machine learning techniques. Comput. Electric. Eng., **98**, 107716 (2022)
13. Kumar, P., Kumari, S., Sharma, V., Sangaiah, A.K., Wei, J., Li, X.: A certificateless aggregate signature scheme for healthcare wireless sensor network. Sustain. Comput.: Inf. Syst. **18**, 80–89 (2018)
14. Anthi, E., Williams, L., Burnap, P.: Pulse: an adaptive intrusion detection for the internet of things (2018)
15. Aboelwafa, M.M.N., Seddik, K.G., Eldefrawy, M.H., Gadallah, Y., Gidlund, M.: A machine-learning-based technique for false data injection attacks detection in industrial IoT. IEEE Internet Things J. **7**, 8462–8471 (2020)
16. Alrawi, O., Lever, C., Antonakakis, M., Monrose, F.: Sok: Security evaluation of home-based IoT deployments. In: 2019 IEEE symposium on security and privacy (sp), pp. 1362–1380 (2019)
17. Wang, D., Li, W., Wang, P.: Measuring two-factor authentication schemes for real-time data access in industrial wireless sensor networks. IEEE Trans. Industr. Inf. **14**, 4081–4092 (2018)
18. Diro, A.A., Chilamkurti, N.: Distributed attack detection scheme using deep learning approach for Internet of Things. Futur. Gener. Comput. Syst. **82**, 761–768 (2018)
19. Pima Indian Diabetes Database, Url:html. www.ics.uci.edu/~mlearn/MLReposit
20. Australia's official weather forecasts & weather radar - Bureau of Meteorology (bom.gov.au)
21. https://www.kaggle.com/datasets/jsphyg/weather-dataset-rattle-package

An Anomaly—Misuse Hybrid System for Efficient Intrusion Detection in Clustered Wireless Sensor Network Using Neural Network

N. Nathiya[1(✉)], C. Rajan[2], K. Geetha[3], S. Dinesh[1], S. Aruna[1], and B. M. Brinda[1]

[1] Paavai College of Engineering, Namakkal, Tamilnadu, India
lnathiiraj@gmail.com
[2] KSR College of Technology, Thiruchengode, Tamilnadu, India
[3] Excel Engineering College, Komarapalayam, Tamilnadu, India

Abstract. Wireless Sensor Networks (WSN) refer to a group of small self-sustaining processor-based systems which collect information from their sensors, produce a computation set, and data relayed to a Base Station. The nodes deployment is done over a range of environment types extending from harsh to hostile. The network's requirements vary depending on the environment type. WSNs must have self-sufficiency and autonomy in harsh environments. Whilst, security is crucial in hostile environments, where the WSNs must be trustworthy and secure. In order to reduce production costs and decrease power usage, the design of nodes in WSNs is typically very simple. Sensor networks inherit all aspects of WSNs but also have their own unique features. Thus, the WSN security model design is quite distinctive from that of Ad hoc networks. In hostile environments, an Intrusion Detection System (IDS) is very vital for WSNs as it has the ability to identify malicious network packets. IDS can be efficiently employed in numerous methods like Neural Networks. Despite that, the classification algorithms must have the least cost of computation in resource-constrained environments. This work has proposed a novel clustering algorithm with an integrated IDS classifier using the modified Neural Network. The Neural Network structure can be optimized by the proposed System Mentoring–Learning-Based technique for detection of optimal cluster-heads, and enhancement of the intrusions' classification accuracy.

Keywords: Wireless Sensor Networks (WSN) · Intrusion Detection System (IDS) · computational cost · clustering algorithm with integrated IDS classifier using modified Neural Network and System Mentoring—Learning-Based technique

1 Introduction

WSNs [1] have emerged as a result of recent advancements in different applications. A WSN is a group of small, low power and low cost self-organized sensor nodes, connected by wireless links and have the ability to communicate over a short range. Sensor nodes can work autonomously, as they can sense, collect, process, and transmit data without human intervention. Communication bandwidth, memory, computational speed, and energy are node resources which are stringently constrained due to WSNs. Network security, data processing, efficient distributed signal processing, and sensor battery lifetime, are the diverse hindrances posed by these constraints. Network security and sensor longevity [2] are the two main and crucial hindrances. Security services are critical for applications that require secure networks.

The proliferation of private sensitive information has led to an increasing importance of computer security in the field of computer science. Any attempt to access information resources [3] without authorization and compromise their availability, integrity, and confidentiality is known as an "Intrusion". Encryption, access control, and firewalls are no longer sufficient against sophisticated attacks where Intrusion Detection System (IDS) is essential for threat detection. The model for Intrusion Detection was initially proposed in 1987 by Denning [4]. Later on, accurate and effective IDS model development has been the target of various researchers. Anomaly-Based and Misuse are Intrusion detection techniques widely used. Anomaly-Based methods rely on identifying attacks by detecting signature deviations. Signature-Based methods can only detect known intrusion attacks that have database-stored signatures and are not effective in detecting unknown intrusion attacks.

The clustering technique is employed for the unlabeled scattered dataset's fragmentation of into clusters (term for referring to similar object groups). Generally, the clusters are distinct from one another. A clustering algorithm is a term used to primarily refer to the unsupervised algorithm. Partitioned and hierarchical are the classification types of clustering techniques. Hierarchical clustering is further classified as divisive and agglomerative types. The categorization of n objects into k clusters through minimization of each group's particular measure of dissimilarity, and maximization of diverse groups' dissimilarity in hierarchical clustering.

Hierarchical clustering, Nirbhay et al. [17] algorithms can increase network lifetime by selecting the cluster head and shows better energy consumption compared to existing algorithms, resulting in decreased delay consumption. Low-Energy Adaptive Clustering Hierarchy (LEACH) protocol [5] is one of the original energy efficient WSN protocols. This research work's aim is an extension of the network longevity and accomplishment of collaborative data processing through the decrease of WSN energy usage. Hence, for accomplishing the work's aim, a new method for the election of optimum CHs in the sensor field was incorporated into the LEACH protocol. This work also takes into consideration the residual energy for the CH election amongst distributed sensor nodes in the sensor field. A novel function of fitness was also proposed for the CHs selection algorithm for obtaining optimum CHs, and for extending the network lifespan.

Every evolutionary and swarm intelligence algorithm requires controlling parameters that impact its performance. Taking this into account, a novel Meta heuristic [21] called Teaching-Learning-Based Optimization (TLBO) [6] has been developed to require no adjustment of algorithm parameters. This results in easier and simpler algorithm implementation to solve continuous optimization problems by mimicking the influence of a teacher on the learners' output in a class.

A classifier based on the Artificial Neural Network (ANN) was used for enhancing the classification process's efficiency. An attempt was made in this work to resolve some of the aforementioned issues by utilizing a combination of certain newer Evolutionary Algorithms and ANN. This work combines ANN with Simulated Annealing, which is a novel and extensively utilized Evolutionary Algorithm.

An anomaly-misuse hybrid system is proposed for efficient intrusion detection in clustered using neural networks. The study has been structured in the following manner: Sect. 2 includes a literature review, while Sect. 3 outlines the various techniques employed in the investigation. The results of the study are presented in Sect. 4, and the study's conclusion can be found in Sect. 5.

2 Literature Survey

Chaubey et al. [15], presented a comprehensive survey of the various challenges faced in WSN, as well as a taxonomy of routing protocols, and an overview of different routing protocols with a comparison of their features have been developed to extend the lifetime of Wireless Sensor Networks (WSNs), and various clustering techniques are used to address the issue of energy consumption. Different WSN protocols exhibit varying performance in different applications.

A technique called Modified Teaching-Learning-Based Optimization (MTLBO) has been created for data clustering by Panigrahi and Pattnaik [8]. This hybridized TLBO technique uses the teacher's influence on learners to find the optimum solution, unlike TLBO, which is a population-based technique. Data clustering, the process of recognizing the underlying structure of data items, based on similarities items are categorised. Finally, MTLBO effectiveness has been compared to other population techniques and these techniques has been applied to clustering using neural networks for data mining.

In Yadav and Kumar [7], the Teaching-Learning-Based Optimization (TLBO) algorithm was used to find the optimal number of cluster-heads. The primary goal of this algorithm was to increase the lifespan of the network while reducing power consumption. The proposed algorithm, called LEACH-T, integrates the TLBO algorithm with the LEACH protocol and consider the remaining energy to select cluster-heads and significantly improving network longevity by reducing power consumption during packet transmission. Furthermore, the proposed algorithm was found to be an efficient and effective method for electing cluster-heads in the network.

In Murugan and Suresh [9], introduces a method for detecting network intrusions and monitoring system activity called An Optimized Simulated Annealing-based SVM Classifier (OSA-SVMC), and classifying them as either normal or anomalous. It utilizes the Simulated Annealing (SA) technique for classifying and detecting intrusion at packet transmission time, optimal features are selected. The accuracy of intrusion detection depends on the performance of traffic pattern analysis, which relies on the chosen feature. Once the optimal features are selected, the SVM classifier is used to classify the attack based on the optimal features that can distinguish malicious behavior from normal behavior in a testing environment. As a result, this method improves the accuracy of anomaly intrusion detection and reduces network traffic.

Dash et al. [10] have introduced intrusion detection techniques are Gravitational Search (GS) and GS and Particle Swarm Optimization (GSPSO). In Both techniques have been successfully implemented n training Artificial Neural Networks (ANN) and have been deployed effectively for intrusion detection. To test their effectiveness, the proposed approaches were compared to other traditional techniques like ANN based on PSO (PSO-ANN), ANN based on gradient descent (GD-ANN), ANN based on Genetic Algorithm (GA-ANN), and decision tree, using NSL-KDD dataset. The results showed that the proposed GS-ANN and GSPSO-ANN achieved a maximum detection accuracy of 94.9% and 98.13% respectively.

An intrusion detection system that identifies abnormalities or potential threats and alerts users. However, there are two main challenges with the use of this system: a high false alarm rate and low detection rate. This limits its effectiveness in detecting intrusions. One possible solution to improve performance is by using multiple sensors or intrusion detection systems. Evidence theory by shah et al. [14] is a mathematical approach that can help combine evidence from several sources to make a more accurate decision. Novel Alert Fusion, shah et al. [16], combining alerts from multiple Intrusion Detection Systems helps to identify potential attacks or intrusions. A novel alert fusion method has demonstrated two different approaches to deriving the reliability value of intrusion system detectors. These approaches are based on conflict and the true positive rate of intrusion detectors. The results indicate that the proposed rule effectively combines alerts, significantly reducing the number of false positives.

Deep learning-based intrusion detection, in lansky et al. [19] explains how deep learning networks are used in the intrusion detection process to identify intrusions with greater accuracy. As a response to network attacks which are always evolving, in Kim et al. [11], an Artificial Intelligence (AI) Intrusion Detection System that utilized the Deep Neural Network (DNN) was assessed with the KDD Cup '99 dataset. Initially, there was pre-processing of the data by use of data transformation and normalization in order to provide the DNN model's input. A learning model is created by the application of the DNN algorithm to the data, which was refined by pre-processing. This verification of data is done by utilizing the whole KDD Cup '99 dataset. Ultimately, evaluations were done on the rate of false alarm, rate of detection, and accuracy in order to ascertain the DNN model's detection efficacy that was found to produce favorable outcomes for intrusion detection.

Chiba et al. [12] proposed the optimization of an extremely well-known soft computing tool extensively utilized for intrusion detection, which is, the Back Propagation Neural Network (BPNN) employing a novel hybrid Framework GASAA that relies on the improved Genetic Algorithm (GA) and the Simulated Annealing Algorithm (SAA). Fitness Value Hashing (FVH) is the optimization strategy used to improve the GA by conservation of processing power, reduction of time of convergence, and reduction of the time of execution time. Based on the outcomes of experiments performed on the KDD CUP '99 dataset, the proposed optimized ANIDS (Anomaly NIDS) based BPNN, referred to as "ANIDS BPNNGASAA", and exceeds the performance of numerous other highly advanced techniques with regards to rate of false positive and rate of detection. Moreover, there has been processing power conservation and execution time reduction with GA improvement by use of FVH. As a result, for detecting anomalies in the network, the proposed IDS is quite feasible.

3 Methodology

As an active defence, intrusion detection technology is extremely fast in the detection and reporting of attack incidents and anomalies. LEACH is able to decrease the energy dissipation and enhance network longevity. Akin to various other algorithms which are inspired by nature, a solution population is utilized by the TLBO to moves in the direction of the global solution. This section details the Low Energy Adaptive Clustering Hierarchy (LEACH), Teaching-Learning-Based Optimization (TLBO), and Cluster Selection using TLBO, Simulated Annealing (SA), and Neural Network classification for IDS.

3.1 Low Energy Clustering Hierarchy (LEACH)

The network lifespan [13] can be maximized by using the WSN's very well-known clustering algorithm, LEACH, which is an adaptive, self-organizing, and clustering protocol. The Rounds concept is introduced in LEACH. LEACH's The assumptions are: the BS is fixed and situated at quite a distance from the sensors, every sensor nodes have limited source of energy and are homogenous, the environment is sensed by the sensors at a fixed rate and these sensors are able to communicate with one another, and the sensors are capable of direct communication with the BS. The idea behind the LEACH is the organization of nodes into clusters for the energy distribution amongst the network's sensor nodes, and also that there is an elected node known as a cluster-head (CH) in every cluster.

Babu et al., have developed an Advanced Efficient LEACH (AE-LEACH) to address the clustering issues in sensor networks [18]. The basic assumptions considered in AE-LEACH are as follows: the sink is fixed and situated at quite a distance from the sensors, all sensor nodes have limited sources of energy and are homogenous, the environment is sensed by the sensors at a fixed rate and these sensors are able to communicate with one another, and the sensors are capable of direct communication with the sink. The elected cluster head forecasts the target trajectory by applying the Particle Filter technique. Nevertheless, this filter technique lagged in providing optimal routing among the several clusters.

Set-up phase and steady-state phase constitute the two phases of each rounds in LEACH. There is formation of the clusters in the set-up phase. Data transmission happens in the steady-state phase. In the set-up phase's beginning, a random number between 0 and 1 is picked by each single node, and later, the threshold formula T(n) is evaluated. The node becomes a CH if the picked random number is lower than the evaluated threshold value. The evaluation of T(n) is according to Eq. (1):

$$T(n) = \begin{cases} \frac{P}{1-P*(r \bmod \frac{1}{P})} & \text{if } n \in G \\ 0 & \text{otherwise} \end{cases} \quad (1)$$

where, p denotes the desired percentage of CHs (The specification of LEACH protocol is that, under normal circumstances, there is a 5% probability of nodes becoming CHs), r denotes the current round, and G denotes the node set which have not become CHs in the earlier 1/P rounds (eligible nodes will become CHs). Nodes, which were CHs in round 0, will not be CHs again in the successive rounds. When the value of threshold becomes

$T(n) = 1$ after $1/p$-1 rounds, all nodes can be eligible again to be CHs. Subsequent to its election, every CH utilizes the CSMA MAC protocol for broadcasting an advertisement message to the remaining nodes. Afterwards, a CH is elected by every node depending on the advertisement's Received Signal Strength Indication (RSSI). Each node's election is transferred utilizing the CSMA MAC protocol, during which, the receivers of every CHs should be kept ON. Later, upon cluster formation, a TDMA schedule will be created by every CH in accordance with the cluster's number of nodes. Every node transfers their sensed data to its CH during its assigned time of transmission in the TDMA.

3.2 Teaching Learning Based Optimization (TLBO)

Teaching-Learning-Based Optimization (TLBO) algorithm is a novel optimization method proposed by Rao et al. [6]. The inspiration behind this method is the teacher's influence and learner's interaction. This method surpasses the performance of certain other commonly used meta heuristics with regards to continuous non-linear numerical optimization problems, constrained mechanical design, and constrained benchmark functions. TLBO's application can be extended several problems like the optimal reactive power dispatch problem and the QoS multicast routing problem. Teacher Phase and Learner Phase are the TLBO's two fundamental components.

Teacher Phase: TLBO moves towards the global solution, similar to other algorithms which are nature-influenced, by use of a population of solutions. A group of learners is the initial population. The desired variables are the studied matters. "Fitness" is used to assess the whole population. The teacher will be the best solution. The influence of the teacher in this phase is denoted through shifting of the learners' mean towards its knowledge level as per Eq. (2). Later on, a new set of improved learners is obtained by utilizing the difference in Eq. (3):

$$X_{new} = X_{old} + Difference_D \quad (2)$$

Equation (3) provides evaluation of the difference between mean of learners and teacher:

$$Difference_D = r(X_{teacher} + T_F Mean) \quad (3)$$

In which, Mean denotes the mean, $X_{teacher}$ denotes the value of teacher, r denotes a random number in the rang [0, 1], and TF (teacher factor) denotes a value determined randomly with equal probability according to Eq. (4):

$$T_F = round[1 + rand(0, 1)] \quad (4)$$

Learner Phase: In this second phase, students attempt to better their knowledge by interacting with one another. Through formation of random peers of learners, their level increase inside the process according to the Eq. (5):

$$\begin{cases} X_{new,i} = X_{old,i} + r_i(X_i - X_j), \textit{iff}(X_i) < f(X_j) \\ X_{new,i} = X_{old,i} + r_i(X_j - X_i), \textit{iff}(X_j) < f(X_i) \end{cases} \quad (5)$$

When, a random learner X_j is selected in the population's i^{th} path, such that $i = j$, then, the Xi is updated as per Eq. (5).

3.3 Cluster Selection Using TLBO

The proposed technique consists of two phases: the Teacher phase and the Learner phase. In terms of local search capability, attributes like rapidity, robustness, and ease of understanding makes Cluster selection a suitable choice. However, this technique is not feasible with global clusters due to its inconsistent performance at distinct initial partitions. It produces distinct outcomes at distinct initial partitions. This research's major goals were in consideration of these points. Initially, the TLBO clustering algorithm is done to seek the clusters' centroid location. The derivations of these locations come from the measurement of Euclidean distances for the optimal clustering solution's refinement and generation. This arrangement resolves the algorithm's restrictions and also multiplies the benefits of both algorithms. Repetition of below steps is done for the application of the TLBO algorithm on clustering:

Step 1: The problem and algorithm parameters are initialized.

Step 2: Each learner is initialized to have N that is a cluster which is randomly chosen.

Step 3: Euclidean distance is utilized for objective function evaluation.

Step 4: The population's fitness is evaluated.

Step 5: The best solution of Teacher is decoded.

Step 6: As per the teacher phase, the solutions are adjusted depending on the teacher knowledge.

Step 7: In accordance with the objective function and learner phase, the solutions are updated.

Step 8: Proceed to Step 4.

Till the maximum iteration number is obtained, the fitness is evaluated.

3.4 Simulated Annealing(SA)

The annealing process in solids is the inspiration behind Simulated Annealing (SA). Annealing refers to the cooling of materials in heat bath. A 1953 published study proposed the concept of SA which replicated this annealing process. The Simulated Annealing (SA) steps are depicted as below:

Initialization: SA starts with an initial response in order to resolve optimization problems. There is initialization of an iteration counter i = 0. Then, the control parameter, starting temperature T_0 is utilized for the ensuring the initial search's acceptance probability. The initial state $S \in N$ is identified, where the whole search space is denoted by N.

Metropolis Process: The process in which there is generation of a new state and computation of the ΔC is defined as the Metropolis process. The instance of $\Delta C < 0$ simply implies that the new state is more suitable for reducing the cost and there can be acceptance of its state S' as S. Acceptance of state S' depends on the criterion in Eq. (6):

$$\exp\left(-\frac{\Delta C}{T_i}\right) > R \qquad (6)$$

The Metropolis criterion is used to accept a response by comparing its target function to that of its neighboring response, denoted by ΔC. The temperature parameters are represented by T_i and range $R \in [0,1]$. Multiple replications are performed at different temperatures, gradually lowering the temperature each time.

Equilibrium Criterion: This step explains that if the generated state reaches an equilibrium point, continue Step 4, otherwise go to Step 2.

Cooling Schedule: This is the stage temperature T_i that has a value which will which will gradually decrease according to Eq. (7):

$$T_{i+1} = \alpha(T_i) \times T_i \qquad (7)$$

where, the rate of cooling $\alpha \times T_i$ represents the cooling rate that is constant.

Convergence Process: When the algorithm reaches the freezing point, it terminates and solution becomes the freezing point. If not, the value of $i = i + 1$ and the algorithm return to step 2.

3.4.1 Neural Network Classification for Intrusion Detection System

Artificial Neural Network (ANN) [20] algorithm, which is learnt as a machine learning component, is a statistical learning algorithm which had its logical development from neural networks that are biological in nature. For training, the number of inputs in an ANN [10] are equal to the number of attributes (N) in the input data. A multi-layered Artificial Neural Network (ANN) also called as a multi-layered perceptron (MLP), which includes a multi-layered feed-forward neural network consisting of input layer, hidden layer, and one output layer. The proposed ANN has an N:M:1 architecture, where M represents the number of nodes in the hidden layer. The architecture has N × M weights. The weights for the input-to-hidden and hidden-to-output layers are denoted by sets V and W, respectively. Similarly, the outer layer has a single bias, and the hidden layer has M biases. The output (or prediction) node is limited to one. A threshold is selected in the testing phase to make a decision on processed input.

Training of ANN: ANN (Artificial Neural Network) is a computer program to update its knowledge base with a specific training dataset. This update is performed using either the GSPO or GS algorithm. There are two phases of ANN learning and processing for the application of these algorithms. In the first phase, each layer's initial synaptic weights (biases, W, and V) are set utilizing these algorithms. In the second phase, the synaptic weights are updated after each duration of time utilizing these algorithms.

Testing of ANN: The ANN uses each instance of the test dataset as input to make a prediction. There will be checking of the predicted output with the match that is closest to any of the target class, in this testing phase. Selective action for the presently tested instance is done depending on this output class.

4 Results and Discussion

Tables 1, 2 and 3 shows the Average End to End Delay (sec), Average Packet loss rate (%), and Lifetime computation- Percentage of nodes alive respectively for LEACH, Simulated Annealing and proposed Teaching Learning Based Optimization Where number of nodes 500–1750 are considered for experiment.

Table 1. Parameters of Simulated Annealing.

Parameter	Value
Maximum function evaluations	18000–200000
Annealing function	Fast Annealing
Temperature update function	Linear temperature update
Reannealing interval	600–2000
Initial temperature	25–80

Table 2. Average End to End Delay (sec) for TLBO

Number of nodes	LEACH	Simulated annealing	TLBO
500	0.0022	0.0022	0.0021
750	0.0028	0.0022	0.0021
1000	0.0265	0.0229	0.0219
1250	0.0323	0.0364	0.0351
1500	0.0724	0.0774	0.0746
1750	0.0839	0.0905	0.0878

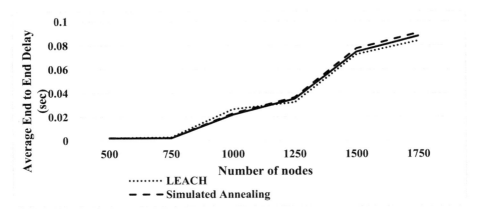

Fig. 1. Average End to End Delay (sec) for Teaching Learning Based Optimization

Table 2 and Fig. 1 demonstrate that Teaching Learning Based Optimization has a better performance than LEACH and Simulated Annealing by 28.6% and 4.7% respectively, for a number of nodes equal to 750. For 1250 nodes, the Average End to End Delay (sec) for Teaching Learning Based Optimization is 8.31% and 3.64% better than LEACH and Simulated Annealing respectively. Finally, for 1750 nodes, the Average End to End Delay (sec) for Teaching Learning Based Optimization is 4.5% and 3% better than LEACH and Simulated Annealing respectively.

Table 3. Average Packet loss rate (%) for Teaching Learning Based Optimizations

Number of nodes	LEACH	SA	TLBO
500	0.7926	0.8772	0.9107
750	0.7539	0.8851	0.9076
1000	0.6893	0.8755	0.8963
1250	0.6656	0.8167	0.858
1500	0.6733	0.7902	0.8188
1750	0.5858	0.6993	0.7385

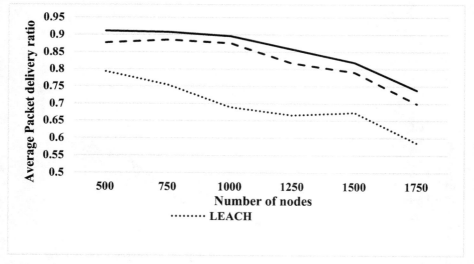

Fig. 2. Average Packet loss rate (%) for Teaching Learning Based Optimization

Table 3 and Fig. 2 indicate that the average packet loss rate (%) is better for Teaching Learning Based Optimization than for LEACH and Simulated Annealing by 18.5% and 2.5%, respectively, for 750 nodes. Similarly, for 1250 nodes, the average packet loss rate (%) is better for Teaching Learning Based Optimization by 25.3% and 4.9% than LEACH and Simulated Annealing, respectively. Finally, for 1750 nodes, the average packet loss rate (%) is better for Teaching Learning Based Optimization by 23.1% and 5.5% than LEACH and Simulated Annealing, respectively.

Table 4 and Fig. 3 demonstrate that the Teaching Learning Based Optimization algorithm performs better than LEACH and Simulated Annealing in terms of lifetime computation, i.e., the percentage of nodes that remain active. Specifically, for 750 nodes,

Table 4. Lifetime computation- percentage of nodes alive for TLBO

Number of rounds	LEACH	SA	TLBO
0	100	100	100
100	93	98	100
200	85	93	97
300	74	89	90
400	39	58	65
500	18	43	54
600	4	31	41
700	2	19	26
800	0	3	11
900	0	0	5

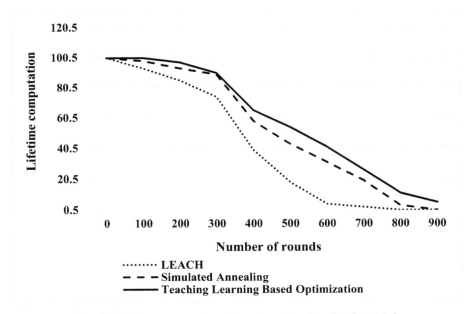

Fig. 3. Lifetime computation- Percentage of nodes alive for TLBO

it outperforms LEACH and Simulated Annealing by 13.2% and 4.2%, respectively. For 1250 nodes, it outperforms them by 50% and 11.4%, respectively. Finally, for 1750 nodes, it outperforms them by a significant margin of 164.4% and 27.8%, respectively.

4.1 Results for ANN Based IDS

Table 5 shows the Summary of Result. Figures 4, 5 and 6 shows the Classification Accuracy, precision and recall for ANN- 2 layer, ANN- 3 layer and ANN- 4 layer respectively.

Table 5. Summary of Results

	ANN- 2 layer	ANN- 3 layer	ANN-4 layer
Classification accuracy	96.58	97.77	97.9
Precision for normal	0.9818	0.9851	0.9862
Precision for IDS	0.8921	0.9422	0.9439
Re call for normal	0.9767	0.988	0.9883
Recall for IDS	0.914	0.929	0.9345

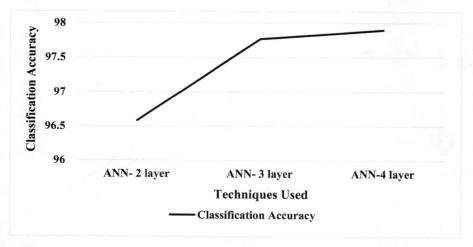

Fig. 4. Classification Accuracy for Proposed ANN-4 layer

Figure 4 shows that the accuracy of Proposed ANN-4 layer performs better by 1.36%, and by 0.13% than ANN- 2 layer and ANN- 3 layer respectively.

Figure 5 shows that the precision of Proposed ANN-4 layer performs better by 0.45%, and by 0.11% than ANN- 2 layer and ANN- 3 layer respectively for precision-normal. The precision of Proposed ANN-4 layer performs better by 5.64%, and by 0.18% than ANN- 2 layer and ANN- 3 layer respectively for precision-IDS.

Figure 6 shows that the recall of Proposed ANN-4 layer performs better by 1.2%, and by 0.3% than ANN- 2 layer and ANN- 3 layer respectively for recall -normal. The recall of Proposed ANN-4 layer performs better by 2.2%, and by 0.6% than ANN- 2 layer and ANN- 3 layer respectively for recall -IDS.

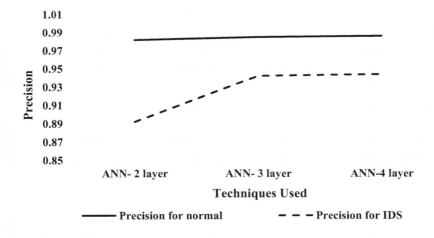

Fig. 5. Precision for Proposed ANN-4 layer

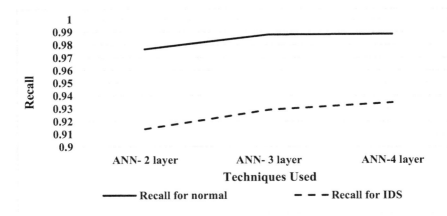

Fig. 6. Recall for Proposed ANN-4 layer

5 Results and Discussion

As one of the most up-and-coming technology, Wireless Sensor Networks (WSNs) have become increasingly popular. System implementation in WSNs are particularly sensitive about security concerns. For security and protection from attacks, effective security mechanisms are very essential. The security of WSN is critical, and effective IDS's are necessary to protect against various security attacks. LEACH is a well-known clustering algorithm used in WSNs to increase network longevity. Experimental results demonstrate that, Teaching Learning Based Optimization's (TLBO's) Average End to End Delay (sec) is 28.6% better than LEACH and 4.7% better than Simulated Annealing (SA) for 750 nodes. For number of nodes 1250, TLBO's Average End to End Delay (sec) functions better by 8.31% compared to the LEACH, and by 3.64% compared to the SA. For number of nodes 1750, TLBO's Average End to End Delay (sec) functions better by 4.5% compared to the LEACH, and by 3% compared to the SA. The Proposed ANN-4 layer's accuracy functions better by 1.36% compared to the ANN-2 layer, and by 0.13% compared to the ANN-3 layer.

Authors' Contributions. N.Nathiya: Conceptualization, Visualization.
C. Rajan and K.Geetha: Methodology, Writing Original draft preparation.
B.M. Brinda, S. Dinesh, S. Aruna: Validation, Software.

References

1. Hamamreh, R.A., Haji, M.M., Qutob, A.A.: An Energy-efficient clustering routing protocol for WSN based on MRHC. Int. J. Digit. Inf. Wirel. Commun., **8**, 214–223 (2018)
2. Hussain, R.H.: A survey on security challenges in wireless sensor networks. J. Univ. Thi-Qar **12**, 42–71 (2017)
3. Ahmed, M., Mahmood, A.N., Hu, J.: A survey of network anomaly detection techniques. J. Netw. Comput. Appl., **60**, 19–31 (2016)
4. Denning, D.E.: An intrusion-detection model. IEEE Trans. Softw. Eng. **2**, 222–232 (1987)
5. Almomani, I.: Alromi, A.: Integrating software engineering processes in the development of efficient intrusion detection systems in wireless sensor networks. Sensors. **20**(5), 1375 (2020)
6. Rao, R.V.: Savsani, V.J.: Vakharia, D.: Teaching–learning-based optimization: an optimization method for continuous non-linear large scale problems. Inf Sci. 183(1):1–15 (2012)
7. Yadav, A.: Kumar. S.: A teaching learning based optimization algorithm for cluster head selection in wireless sensor networks. Int. J. Future Gener. Commun. Netw., **10**(1), 111–122 (2017)
8. Panigrahi, S.K., Pattnaik, S.: Empirical study on clustering based on modified teaching learning based optimization. Procedia Comput. Sci., **92**, 442–449 (2017)
9. Murugan, K.: Suresh. P.: Optimized simulated annealing SVM classifier for anomaly intrusion detection in wireless Adhoc network. Australian J. Basic Appl. Sci., **11**(4), 1–13 (2017)
10. Dash, T.: A study on intrusion detection using neural networks trained with evolutionary algorithms. Soft. Comput. **21**(10), 2687–2700 (2017)
11. Kim, J., Shin, N., Jo, S.Y., Kim, S.H.: Method of intrusion detection using deep neural network. In: 2017 IEEE International Conference on Big Data and Smart Computing (BigComp), IEEE, pp. 313–316 (2017)
12. Chiba, Z., Abghour, N., Moussaid, K., El Omri, A., Rida, M.: A hybrid optimization framework based on genetic algorithm and simulated annealing algorithm to enhance performance of anomaly network intrusion detection system based on BP neural network. In: 2018 International Symposium on Advanced Electrical and Communication Technologies (ISAECT). IEEE, pp. 1–6 (2018)
13. Sabarish, B.A., Guru, M.S.M., Dhivya, M.A., Naveen, K.S., Vaishnavi, S.: A survey on clustering protocols in wireless sensor networks. Int. J. Adv. Comput. Inf. Tech., **1**(2) (2021)
14. Shah, V., Aggarwal, A.K., Chaubey, N.: Performance improvement of intrusion detection with fusion of multiple sensors. Complex Intell. Syst., **3**, 33–39 (2017)
15. Chaubey, N., Patel, D.H.: Routing protocols in wireless sensor network: a critical survey and comparison. Int. J. IT Eng. ISSN: 2321-1776[Online]. **04**(02), 8–18 (2016)
16. Shah, V.M., Agarwal, A.K., Reliable alert fusion of multiple intrusion detection systems. Int. J. Netw. Secur., **19**(2), 182–192 (2017)

17. Chaubey, N.K., Patel, D.H.: Energy efficient clustering algorithm for decreasing energy consumption and delay in wireless sensor networks (WSN). Int. J. Innov. Res. Comput. Commun. Eng. (An ISO 3297:2007 Certified Organization)., **4**(5) (2016)
18. Babu, M.V., Kumar, C., Parthiban, S.: AE-LEACH: An incremental clustering approach for reducing the energy consumption in WSN. Microprocess. Microsyst., **93**(104602), 1–19 (2020)
19. Lansky, J., Ali, S.: Deep learning-based intrusion detection systems: a systematic review. IEEE Access. **9**, 101574–101599 (2021)
20. Awajan, A.: A novel deep learning-based intrusion detection system for IoT networks. Computers. **12**, 1–12 (2021)
21. Chaurasia, S., Kumar, K., Kumar, N.: MOCRAW: a meta-heuristic optimized cluster head selection-based routing algorithm for WSNs. Ad Hoc Netw., **141**(103079), 1–18 (2023)

Detection and Prevention of Black Hole Attack and Sybil Attack in Vehicular Ad Hoc Networks

Dhananjay Yadav[1] and Nirbhay Kumar Chaubey[2]

[1] Gujarat Technological University, Ahmedabad, India
yadavdhananjay1@gmail.com
[2] Ganpat University, Mehsana, Gujarat, India

Abstract. Intelligent Transportation Systems can play a valuable role in providing traffic control, road safety, and communications among vehicles. Vehicular Ad Hoc Network (VANET) is a network useful for providing communications between vehicles on road and is playing a predominant role in modern intelligent transportation systems. But the high mobility of vehicles in vanet and its inconsistent connections in the network make it highly susceptible to security threats to vehicles. The fiercest attacks in vanet are the Black Hole attack and the Sybil attack. In Black hole attack, the attacker vehicle, at the time of routing represents itself with the smallest and most desired route to the destination and hence communication with other legitimate nodes starts with this attacker node. Now the attacker vehicle can drop all the packets or send the information to other malicious vehicles. In Sybil attack the malicious vehicle sends fake alert message of high traffic to RSU and then RSU alerts other vehicles on the road of false high traffic with the intention of a malicious vehicle.

The proposed algorithm in this research paper prevents the black hole attack and Sybil attack by using the encrypted identity of vehicles in the network making vanet secure from black hole attack and Sybil attack.

Keywords: Security · Black Hole attack · Sybil attack · AODV · Routing protocol

1 Introduction

A Vehicular ad hoc network is a network for vehicles that provide communication among vehicles on the road and does not require centralized management for communication. The Communication in vanet can be categorized as vehicle to vehicle communication and vehicle to infrastructure communication [1]. The main applications of vanet include automatic brake lights, emergency services at the time of any mishappening, traffic information, entertainment services etc. [2]. The routing protocol in vanet can be categorized into proactive and reactive routing protocols [3]. In proactive routing protocol, the route is stored in the background so it does not require route discovery at the time of communication. But this protocol provides low latency for the real time applications. Examples of this protocol include LSR, FSR etc.

In reactive routing protocol, the route is formed whenever it is required for communication hence it reduces the network overhead by maintaining only the cur-rent route which is in use. The main examples of this routing protocol include AODV, DSR and TORA etc.

AODV protocol is mostly used in vanet and it is highly susceptible to security attacks like Black Hole attacks, Sybil attacks, worm hole and, gray hole attacks etc. [4].

The proposed approach prevented the Black hole and Sybil attack in vanet using AODV protocol and makes the vanet more secure for vehicles in the network.

The remaining paper is organized as follows: Sects. 1.1, 1.2, and 1.3 includes brief details about AODV routing protocol, Black hole attack and Sybil attack respectively. Section 2 covers the literature survey, the proposed work is included in Sect. 3, Results and simulation is explained in Sect. 4 and conclusion and future work included in Sect. 5.

1.1 AODV Routing Protocol

Ad-Hoc On-Demand Distance Vector (AODV) routing protocol is a type of reactive routing protocol and is one of the most commonly used routing protocol [5]. This protocol provides unicast and multicast communication in ad hoc networks [6]. AODV routing protocol provides communication between source to destination on demand. When two nodes want to communicate, first of all, route discovery is performed by sending a broadcast message to its neighbour nodes. Route discovery completed in two phases.

1. Route Request (RREQ): The source node broadcast an RREQ packet to its neighbour. The RREQ packet consists of a source address, source sequence number, broadcast id, and destination node address [7]. The neighboring node sends a reply to the source if address is matched otherwise is again broadcast to its neighboring nodes.
2. Route Reply: The neighboring node which finds the destination address in its routing table replies to the source by following the same route. The Fig. 1 shows the structure of AODV routing protocol [8].

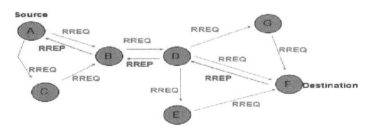

Fig. 1. Working of AODV (Route discovery and Route reply)

In Fig. 1 source node A broadcasts a RREQ packet to neighboring nodes B and C. The neighboring nodes check its routing table and if it found the destination address it reply with RREP packet. The nodes whose reply reached earlier and which have a lower hop count will be chosen for further communication and if NN (Neighbouring nodes) nodes do not find the destination address they forward the RREQ packet to their

Neighbors. Thus from the Fig. 1 route is A-B-D-F for communication between the source and destination because this route has a lower hop count. AODV routing protocol is dynamic in nature.

1.2 Black Hole Attack

In this attack the attacker node shows itself that it has the smallest route for the destination and hence legitimate node began communication with that node. Now the malicious node starts receiving messages from the legitimate node and hence it can drop or forward the messages to another node [9].

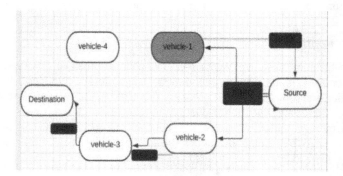

Fig. 2. Black Hole Attack

Figure 2 shows the working of a black hole attack in vanet. The Source node broadcast a RREQ packet and is received by vehicle-1 and vehicle-2. As vehicle-2 does not contain address of the destination so it forward the RREQ packet to vehicle-3 and so on till the destination reached. After matching the destination address, destination node replies with RREP packet with the same path sequence. This is the le-gal route discovery in AODV and after this communication starts But as we can see in Fig. 2 that vehicle-1, without having a valid route for destination, replies with RREP packet by pretending (putting high sequence number) that it has the smallest hope count to destination and source node starts communication with this node. Here vehicle-1 acts as a malicious node.

Black hole attack can be categorized as [10] single black hole attack in which the attacker node individually creates attack in the network by sending a false RREP packet and collaborative black hole attack in which multiple nodes work in a group to perform the attack.

The main effects of Black Hole attack include an increase in packet drop and decrease in throughput [11], information loss, high probability of occurrence of accidents, and communication break in vanet.

1.3 Sybil Attack

In this attack malicious node creates the illusion of the presence of heavy traffic in the network by sending fake alert messages [12]. This imposes other vehicles to divert their route and causes serious threats to security of people in the network as the route diversion is performed with the intention of malicious vehicle [13]. This attack mainly works at the network layer and at the application layer [14]. The frequent change of IP is valid in vanet due to high mobility so a malicious node creates the illusion of the presence of high traffic in the network by sending fake alert messages with different IP. At the application layer malicious node sends alert messages by using fake ids. The figure shows the architecture of Sybil attack (Fig. 3).

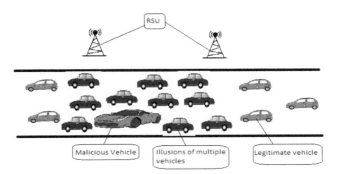

Fig. 3. Sybil attack

2 Literature Survey

In research paper [15, 16] authors use false destination address and fake RREQ at the first time and wait for a specific time to get the RREP. If they received any RREP then they consider that node as malicious node. But this ap-proach is time consuming as initially vehicle sends a fake RREQ and after wait-ing for some time it sends it again with the valid destination address.

The authors in [2] detected the black hole attack by following client server architecture. One of the moving vehicles acts as server and pass packets to clients. An intrusion detection system monitors the packets and if packets found from an untrusted port then it is discarded and announces the node as malicious.

The authors in [17] use cluster head to detect the black hole attack. The nodes are divided into multiple clusters. There is a cluster head in every cluster and communication performs only through the head node in cluster. The check point nodes continuously monitor the packet drop ratio (pdr) and if it is found that the ob-served pdr is less than the threshold pdr then it is considered as attack. This ap-proach has limitation of increased network overhead due to formation of clusters. Secondly, this approach does not pro-vide any idea about if cluster head or checkpoint nodes itself are the attacker node.

In research paper [18] the authors uses two step approach to detect the attack. In first step if DSN >>> SSN then node is detected as malicious and next if arrival time of RREP packet is less than the specified time limit then it is also considered as malicious node but authors do not explain how the specified time limit should be calculated. There are various factors which also causes delay in packet as packet processing time and number of nodes etc. [19].

In this research paper [20] one node is taken as IDS node which stores all in-formation of neighboring nodes. If network throughput decreases then IDS com-pares profile of each node and if any node is found with mismatched profile then it is an attack. Storing information of other nodes creates privacy issues for vehicles in the network.

In this research paper [4] authors first convert the destination address using CRC32 algorithm and then this value is broadcasted as RREQ. But the problem is that, at receiving node this CRC value is converted to verify the actual destina-tion address.

In this research paper [21] route discovery node store the RREP in the routing table and create a trusted route by comparing the Destination Sequence Number (DSN) with the Source Sequence Number (SSN). If DSN is greater than the SSN then the vehicle is marked as malicious. Research paper [22] is also similar to [18] as in this paper DSN is compared with the average of DSN of all other nodes and if it is greater than the average value than that node is discarded from the network.

Authors in this research paper [23] use three phase (connection phase, detec-tion phase, prevention phase) approach to detect and prevent black hole attack. In the connec-tion phase, a connection is established between n numbers of nodes and in the detection phase a threshold value of DSN is calculated by receiving RREP from various nodes and then taking the average of DSN of all these nodes. If for any node DSN is greater than this threshold value then that node is put into the suspected node. In the prevention phase a false RREQ packet is broadcasted and if node replies then that node is confirmed as malicious node. A smart attacker can easily bypass the DSN.

Authors	Solution Scheme	Attack Type	Limitations
G. Sharma [2]	An intrusion detection system monitors the packets and if packets found from an untrusted port then it is discarded and announce the node as malicious	BHA	Based on client server architecture which is difficult to achieve in vanet environment

(continued)

(*continued*)

Authors	Solution Scheme	Attack Type	Limitations
S. Yadav and Srishti [15] M. S. Pathan et al. [16]	Based on bogus RREQ and RREP	BHA	Time consuming as each time nodes have to send Bogus RREQ in the network
T. Singh and B. Kaur [20]	IDS node store information of adjacent node and if network throughput decreased and it verifies each node again	BHA	Only detect the attack
A. Malik et al. [23]	In first phase threshold value of DSN is calculated and then send Fake destination ip in second phase	BHA	Broadcasting fake destination address will create unnecessary congestion in network
R. Patel and K. Shah [24]	The IDS node will calculate PDR and calculate threshold value of PDR	BHA	Time consuming as first IDS node will calculate PDR and then inform to source Can only detect the BHA
G. Farahani [25] Rashmi and A. Seehra [17]	Uses KNN and Fuzzy logic to detect the attack in vanet	BHA	Due to high mobility of nodes cluster heads will change their position very rapidly and congestion in network increases
A. Upadhyaya and J. Shah [26]	Uses three approaches to prevent the attack based on SSN and neighbour	BHA	Dependent on neighbouring node
K. Mekkaoui and I. Meddah [27]	Performance measure of smart blackhole attack	BHA	Shows that algorithms based on IDS system and fake rreq are breakable
N. Rafique et al. [28]	Trust value of each node is calculated and shared	BHA	Not useful for collaborative Blackhole attack
C. Bensaid, S. Hacene, and K. Faraoun [29]	Uses two approach based on calculation of latency and number of send and received packets	BHA	Not suitable for collaborative Black hole attack

Based on the literature survey we concluded that the detection and prevention algorithms can be categorized as (a) First, DSN and SSN based approach but Authors in [27] shows that smart Black Hole attackers can easily break the DSN and SSN based approach, (b) Second, in Fake RREQ based approach, Sending fake RREQ message is time consuming as each vehicle, before communication has to send a false RREQ message to verify the validity of vehicles. (c) Third, in Cluster head based approach due to high Mobility vehicles changes its position very rapidly and hence the neighbors too. Due to this getting extreme accuracy for detection and prevention of attack is difficult. Also algorithms didn't provide any method to detect the attack if clustering head is itself an attacker node. (d) and fourth is the cryptographic approach. The research paper [4, 30] are based on cryptographic approach in which authors convert the destination address into 32 bit value by using CRC32 algorithm and send the RREQ packet but in [31] shows that CRC 32 can easily be reversed and hence provides less security in the network.

The proposed algorithm in this research paper prevented the black hole and Sybil attack. Our objective is to prevent the attack without sending the false RREQ packets to fasten the process, without violating the privacy issues of vehicles as clustering approach suffers from privacy issues due to sharing their identity in the network, and suitable for prevention of attack both from single node attack and collaborative attack. The proposed algorithm is able to detect the attacker node also. The simulation result is compared with attack in normal situation using AODV routing protocol and with proposed algorithm.

3 Proposed Approach

In the proposed approach, a secure id (Sid) is generated by road infrastructure and assigned to each vehicle in the network. The Sid is generated by using the technique [32] in which the first IP address is reversed and the ASCII value of each value in first octant is obtained and is further extended by attaching any value from 0 to 9, which is assigned to each vehicle for communication as Sid. Before communication source node asks for Sid from road side unit and then broadcast RREQ packets. Only the destination node can send an RREP message by adding the Sid of its own. The source node then matched the received Sid with the Sid received from road side unit. If both Sid matched then communication proceeds otherwise the node is malicious. The communication between any nodes to RSU is also encrypted. The approach is same for the Sybil attack and the Black hole attack with the difference that Sybil attack can be performed at application layer also. So once a communication link is established between two nodes then it is easy for an attacker to perform a Sybil attack by changing its real identity. In this case, a packet drop ratio is calculated to detect the attack. The algorithm to prevent Black hole and Sybil attacks is given below.

3.1 The Algorithm to Prevent the Black Hole Attack

Step-1: Generate Sid for each vehicle in the network by using the following steps.
    a. First of all reverse the IP address
       192.168.2.30 -> 30.2.168.192
    b. Take the ASCII value for each digit of the first octant
       ASCII of 3=51 and 0=48 Hence 30=5148
    c. Take any random number from 0 to 9 and append it to above generated value. Hence
       Sid=51480

Step-2: RSU will store Sid w.r.t its ip address for each node in the network.

IP Address	Sid
192.168.2.30	51480

Step-3: RSU assigns this Sid to each node in the network w.r.t its IP address and share its public key.

Step-4: If any node wants to communicate, first of all, it asks for the Sid of that particular node from RSU by sending the destination IP by encrypting it using RSU public key.

Step-5: RSU replies back with destination node Sid after encrypting it with the source public key.

Step-6: Now Source sends an RREQ message to the destination.
       SN ->RREQ

Step-7: Destination sends an RREP message along with its Sid to SN.
       SN <- RREP (Sid)

Step-8: if (Stored (Sid) ==RREP (Sid)
       Start communication
  else
       Node is Malicious.

Step-9: Stop

3.2 Proposed Flow Chart for Detection of Black Hole Attack

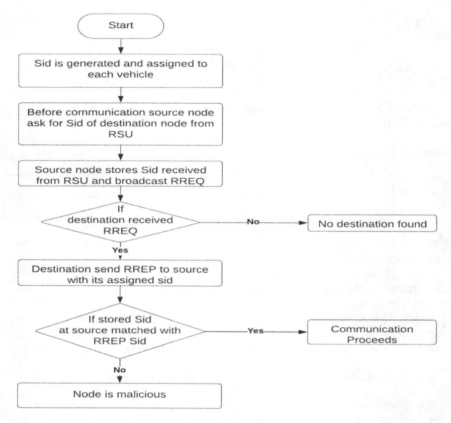

3.3 Algorithm to Detect the Sybil Attack

In Sybil attack, malicious node sends fake alert message of high traffic on road to Road Side Unit to misguide the other vehicles so that they can divert their roué [1]. At network layer if malicious node manage to send fake alert by changing IP address than the Algorithm 3.1 is sufficient to prevent the attack but if malicious node manage to send alert message by changing its real identity then first of all RSU will send the confirmation message to all nodes of received identity and check the packet drop ratio. If there is high packet drop ratio than it is an attack otherwise attack is valid [1].

The Algorithm to Prevent the Sybil Attack:

Step-1: Generate Sid for each vehicle in the network by using the following steps.
        a. First of all reverse the IP address
        192.168.2.30 -> 30.2.168.192
        b. Take the ASCII value for each digit of the first octant
        ASCII of 3=51 and 0=48   Hence 30=5148
        c. Take any random number from 0 to 9 and append it to above generated value. Hence
        Sid=51480

Step-2: RSU will store Sid w.r.t its ip address for each node in the network.

IP Address	Sid
192.168.2.30	51480

Step-3: if RSU received any alert message it verifies the authenticity of the message by checking the Sid into the table already stored.
        if (match found)
            alert all nodes in the network
        else
            False alert message

Step-4: To confirm the identity of the node, RSU send confirmation message to received node identity
        If (Low PDR)
            follow the alert
        else
    Node is malicious.

3.4 Proposed Flow Chart for Detection of Black Hole Attack

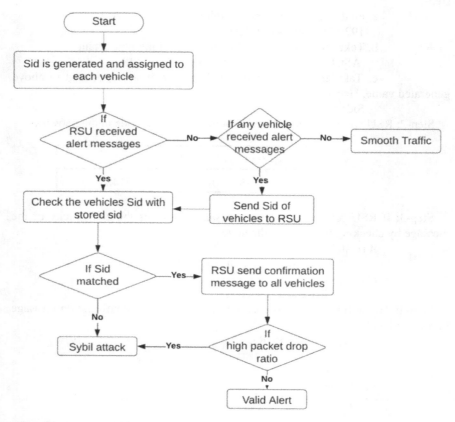

4 Simulation Setup and Results

The simulator NS3 is used to perform the experiment of the proposed approach. Ns3 is a most popular and commonly used open source network simulator. For simulation, AODV routing protocol is used with different number of vehicles ranging from 10 to 50. The Table 1 shows the parameters that we have used for the simulation.

The parameters of Table 1 were used for simulating result using NS3.25. The Following observations were found during the experiment.

Packet Delivery Ratio: Packet delivery ratio is defined as the ratio of total packets received and the total packets transmitted [33].

Delay: Time taken to pass through the destination [34].

The Fig. 4a shows the throughput without adding an extra Sid field (normal situation) in the RREP packet and Fig. 4b shows the throughput for the proposed algorithm.

The Fig. 5a shows the delay without adding an extra Sid field in the RREP packet and Fig. 5b shows the delay for the proposed algorithm.

The result shows that throughput decreases and delay increases as compared to normal situation without modifying the AODV protocol due to adding an extra field in

Table 1. Simulation Parameters

Parameters	Values
Simulator	NS 3.25
Routing Protocol	AODV
Data Rate	250 kbps
Mobility Model	Constant Position Mobility Model
Channel Type	Wireless
Number of Nodes	10, 20, 30, 40, 50
Packet Size	1040 bytes
Traffic Type	Constant Bit Rate (CBR)
Simulation Time	100 s

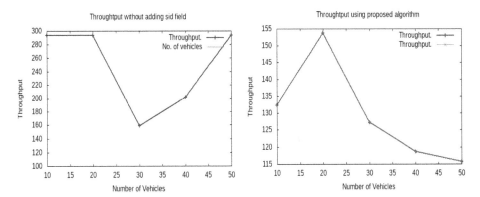

Fig. 4. a. Throughput in normal situation. b. Throughput proposed algorithm

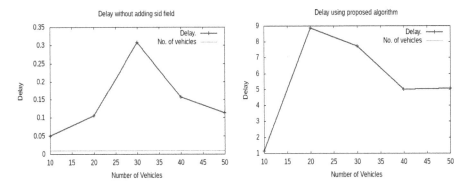

Fig. 5. a. delay in normal situation. b. delay proposed algorithm

AODV protocol for authentication. The proposed approach successfully prevented both the attack by fulfilling our objective.

5 Conclusion

The Proposed algorithm is suitable for the prevention of Black hole and Sybil attack in Vanet at network layer.

The proposed algorithm successfully prevented the attack with objective of without violating the privacy issues of vehicles, suitable for both single and collaborative attack and to detect the attacker node. In future we will work to develop algorithm to minimize the delay and increasing the throughput.

References

1. Chaubey, N., Yadav, D.: Detection of Sybil attack in vehicular ad hoc networks by analyzing network performance. IJECE **12**(2), 1703–1710 (2022)
2. Sharma, G.: A modified approach of preventing and minimizing the black hole attack in VANETs (vehicular ad-hoc network systems) department of computer engineering & applications. Int. J. Adv. Sci. Technol. **29**(5), 8713–8717 (2020)
3. Kumar, R., Dave, M.: A comparative study of various routing protocols in VANET. Int. Comput. Sci. Issues **8**(4), 643–648 (2011)
4. Lachdhaf, S., Mazouzi, M., Abid, M.: Secured AODV routing protocol for the detection and prevention of black hole attack in VANET. Adv. Comput. An Int. J. **9**(1), 01–14 (2018)
5. Aswathy, M., Tripti, C.: A cluster based enhancement to AODV for inter-vehicular communication in VANET. Int. J. Grid Comput. Appl. **3**(3), 41–50 (2012)
6. Saha, S., Roy, U., Sinha, D.: Neural network based modified AODV routing protocol in VANET. Eur. J. Adv. Eng. Technol. **2**(10), 17–25 (2015)
7. Kaur, M., Virk, A.K.: An improved multicast AODV routing protocol for VANETs. Int. J. Comput. Appl. **121**(6), 14–23 (2015)
8. Tayal, S., Gupta, V.: A survey of attacks on monitoring schemes. Int. J. Innov. Res. Sci. Eng. Technol. **2**(6), 2280–2285 (2013)
9. Upadhyaya, A.: Blackhole attack and its effect on VANET international journal of computer sciences and engineering open access Blackhole attack and its effect on VANET. Int. Journl Comput. Sci. Eng. **5**(11), 25–32 (2018)
10. Arvindakshan, S.R., Praneeth, S., Gogula, R., Sainath, I.M.S., Girish, B.S., Badana, R.A.: Review on black hole attack identifier using Vanet communication in vehicle. Open Access Int. J. Sci. Eng. **6**(8), 77–83 (2021)
11. Kumar, A., et al.: Black hole attack detection in vehicular ad-hoc network using secure AODV routing algorithm. Microprocess. Microsyst. **80**, 1–13 (2021)
12. Chaubey, N.K., Yadav, D.: Chapter 9: a taxonomy of Sybil attacks in vehicular ad-hoc network (VANET). In: IoT and Cloud Computing Advancements in Vehicular Ad-Hoc Networks, pp. 174–190. IGI Global (2020)
13. Yadav, D., Chaubey, N.K.: A novel two stage approach to detect Sybil and DoS attack in vehicular ad hoc networks. J. Tianjin Univ. Sci. Technol. **55**(01), 235–244 (2022)
14. Pal, S., Mukhopadhyay, A., Bhattacharya, P.: Defending mechanisms against Sybil attack in next generation mobile ad hoc networks. IETE Tech. Rev. **25**(4), 209–215 (2008)
15. Yadav, S., Srishti: An approach to isolate black hole attack in vanet. IJAR **5**(12), 1567–1573 (2017)

16. Pathan, M.S., He, J., Zhu, N., Zardari, Z.A., Memon, M.Q., Azmat, A.: An efficient scheme for detection and prevention of black hole attacks in AODV-based MANETs. Int. J. Adv. Comput. Sci. Appl. **10**(1), 243–251 (2019)
17. Rashmi, Seehra, A.: A novel approach for preventing black-hole attack in MANETs. Int. J. Ambient Syst. Appl. **2**(3), 01–09 (2014)
18. Satish, D., Raju, K.N., Rao, B.S., Ratnam, G.S., Raja, P.: Reducing accidents through detection of black hole attack in VANETs. Int. J. Eng. Adv. Technol. **9**(5), 1056–1059 (2020)
19. Chandna, N.: Quantitative Analysis of Frame Inter-Arrival Times in Saturated Ad Hoc Networks (2011)
20. Singh, T., Kaur, B.: Backtracking & threshold techniques for isolating Smurf & black hole attack in VANET. Int. J. Sci. Res. Dev. **6**(06), 679–683 (2018)
21. Sasirekha, V., Nithyadevi, S.: Detecting and preventing a black hole attack in VANET. Asian J. Comput. Sci. Technol. **8**(S1), 7–9 (2019)
22. Lakshmi, S., Mary Anita, E.A., Jenefa, J.: Detection and prevention of black hole attacks in vehicular ad hoc networks. Int. J. Innov. Technol. Explor. Eng. **8**(7), 1253–1257 (2019)
23. Malik, A., Khan, M.Z., Faisal, M., Khan, F., Seo, J.T.: An efficient dynamic solution for the detection and prevention of Black Hole attack in VANETs. Sensors (Basel) **22**(5), 1–27 (2022)
24. Patel, R., Shah, K.: Reputation Approach to detect BLACKHOLE ATTACK in VANET, vol. 1, no. 2, pp. 6–12 (2014)
25. Farahani, G.: Black Hole attack detection using K-nearest neighbor algorithm and reputation calculation in mobile ad hoc networks. Secur. Commun. Netw. **2021**, 1–15 (2021)
26. Upadhyaya, A., Shah, J.: Black hole Attack Prevention in VANET. Int. J. Futur. Revolut. Comput. Sci. Commun. Eng. **3**, 222–229 (2017)
27. Mekkaoui, K., Meddah, I.: Performances evaluation of threshold-based IDS and trust based IDS under smart black hole attacks. Turk. J. Comput. Math. Educ. **14**(01), 154–166 (2023)
28. Rafique, N., Khan, M.A., Saqib, N.A., Bashir, F., Beard, C., Li, Z.: Black Hole prevention in VANETs using trust management and fuzzy logic analyzer. Int. J. Comput. Sci. Inf. Secur. **14**(9), 1226 (2016)
29. Bensaid, C., Hacene, S., Faraoun, K.: Detection and ignoring of Blackhole attack in Vanets networks. Int. J. Cloud Appl. Comput. **6**(2), 1–10 (2016)
30. Ahmed, M.T., Rubi, A.A., Rahman, M.S., Rahman, M.: Red-aodv: a prevention model of black hole attack for vanet protocols and identification of malicious nodes in vanet. Int. J. Comput. Netw. Appl. **8**(5), 524–537 (2021)
31. Stigge, M., Plötz, H., Müller, W., Redlich, J.-P.: Reversing CRC - Theory and Practice (2006)
32. Abdullah, A.M., Baban, M., Hikmat, R., Aziz, H., Mohammed, M.H.: New security techniques for encrypting IP address and data transfer over wide area network through three levels advanced encryption standard (AES) algorithm to encrypt and decrypt data view project usability evaluation testing system view project new secu. Int. J. Comput. Sci. Softw. Eng. **4**(3), 79–87 (2015)
33. Malik, S., Sahu, P.K.: A comparative study on routing protocols for VANETs. Heliyon **5**(8), 1–9 (2019)
34. Yadav, D., Chaubey, N.K.: Performance analyses of black hole attack in AODV routing protocol in Vanet using NS3. In: Rajagopal, S., Faruki, P., Popat, K. (eds.) Advancements in Smart Computing and Information Security. ASCIS 2022. Communications in Computer and Information Science, vol. 1760. Springer, Cham (2022). https://doi.org/10.1007/978-3-031-23095-0_9

Cognitive Ad Hoc Trust Routing for Enhanced Quality of Service

N. Neelima, P. Syam Pratap(✉), and P. Satya Kiran

Velagapudi Ramakrishna Siddhartha Engineering College (JNTUK Affiliated), Vijayawada, Andhra Pradesh, India
gneelima@vrsiddhartha.ac.in, syampratap.potluri@gmail.com

Abstract. Because of the dynamic nature and lack of infrastructure of MANETs, routing in such networks is vulnerable to several attacks, and standard fixed policy routing algorithms are inefficient in tackling them. Reinforcement learning methods and appropriate models based on trust are assuring for dealing with the issues and variable behaviour of rogue network nodes. In this research, we present a cognition layer that interacts with the network layer in parallel and consists of two phases: pathfinding (routing) and trust assessment. The first phase uses ML techniques, while the second is focused on trust assessment. Regarding three performance indicators, CTR, our technique is evaluated against a well-known protocol, TQR. The simulation findings demonstrate improved end-to-end latency and communication.

Keywords: MANETS · CTR · TQR · Routing

1 Introduction

1.1 Preface

Using wireless connectivity, mobile devices are connected in Mobile ad hoc networks (MANETs) which lack proper infrastructure. The network's topology regularly changes since every device in a MANET has the freedom to travel in any direction. In addition to forwarding its packets, every network node has to forward transit traffic. Since there are no restrictions on node mobility or network structure, a MANET's primary benefit is its flexibility [9]. Nonetheless, a significant obstacle to routing in MANETs has been the dynamic nature of the networks brought about by node mobility.

1.2 Origin of the Problem

Meanwhile, corrupt nodes can utilize a variety of internal and external attacks to target MANETs because there is no central authority and nodes move independently. In MANETs, security would be a crucial and difficult problem because of the dependency of the source node on the mediocre nodes to convey the data.

A lot of the current research on MANETs for better and safer routing has concentrated on different trust-assessing strategies. The phrase "Trust Management" was first used in security services for networks by Blaze et al. [20]. The goal of trust management is to give each object in the topology a value called trust so that the trustor, such as the source, can identify rogue nodes [13].

1.3 Background and Key Definitions

Routing issues in MANETs have drawn a lot of academic attention to machine learning (ML) approaches [5]. By allowing wireless nodes to watch, collect data, and assessthe variable environment topology, routing problems were solved by machine learning techniques. After that, independent nodes instantly decide on the best course of action for routing while meeting particular application requirements known as Quality of Service (QoS) [14].

MANETs frequently employ Reinforcement Learning, which is a sub-class of machine learning techniques. It is a biologically based machine learning model where learning agents comprehend by investigating their local operational environment on their own, without external supervision [5].

Among those, most widely used iterative techniques are Q-learning and SARSA (State-Action-Reward-State-Action). Through repeated environment mapping, they teach the optimal course of action based on existing environmental conditions.

1.4 Problem Statement with Objectives and Consequences

Problem Statement: As far as we know, cognitive wireless networks have not yet considered the trust assessment component of security. To create a reliable sub-network for safety, we suggest a new protocol based on trust for cognitive networks. This protocol allows us to take advantage of the cognitive qualities in the cognitive layer. In particular.

- In the cognition layer of a cognitive network, we propose two phases path finding (routing) and trust assessment. Our routing algorithm uses a class of reinforcement learning techniques called Expected-SARSA [17, 19] as the path-finding process.
- In identifying black-hole and grey-hole attackers during the trust assessment process, we slightly improve an already-existing trust model [7].

We study the routing problem in terms of three optimization goals: communication overhead, delivery ratio, and delay because throughput and end-to-end latency are two prominent factors for ad hoc networks.

Objectives: Suggest a network layer technique called Cognitive Ad hoc Trust Routing (CTR), which is based on the AODV protocol [18]. Pathfinding (routing) and trust assessment are two cognitive processes that make up the CN's cognition layer. We employ a class of RL algorithms called expected-SARSA [17, 19] as the path-finding procedure. Because of its quicker convergence and smaller update variance, the expected SARSA is used [17]. The model that governs trust learning was developed as a consequence of a minor improvement we made to an earlier trust model [7]. Each node uses an RL approach to interact with its surroundings based on these phases to determine the optimal path for delivering its packets.

Outcomes: The development of a strong machine learning-based intrusion detection model for MANETs is one of the project's results. The change includes strengthened defences, improved threat detection, and fewer malicious attacks. Furthermore, by integrating intrusion detection systems seamlessly, the project offers a useful application that improves node-to-node security.

2 Literature Survey

2.1 Establishing Trust

It can be defined as depending on a node to deliver services in a reliable, and integral manner. It is calculated using the data produced by the interactions between nodes in a network, both past and present [12]. It is possible to develop trust in the modern sense both directly and indirectly. A node assesses a target node directly by observing its behaviour and interactions with it. This process is known as direct trust computation.

TSQRS in [2] considers three important parameters during the discovery of on-demand routes, i.e., channel quality, link residual life and residual energy, to reduce route failures and to increase the overall system performance.

When calculating indirect trust, also known as a recommendation, the node obtains firsthand knowledge about a target node from other nodes that are accessible and possess knowledge or views about it [4, 15].

A reputation and trust system is presented in [16] to help detect and steer clear of rogue nodes. Peers' perception of a node is known as its reputation. While trust is active, reputation is passive. Because the mechanism ignores past data and suggests trust, the trust assessment procedure could not be as accurate as it could be.

A lightweight QoS routing mechanism based on trust is designed in [12] and [7]. The suggested algorithms guarantee that packets are forwarded with the least amount of link latency over reliable paths. This is accomplished by employing both direct and indirect information to track other nodes' forwarding behaviour while taking the desired QoS limitations into account. The problem with the suggested trust models is that nodes have equal faith in each recommender, and this could be jeopardized by some attackers who pose as recommenders.

To meet the safety requirements of Wireless Sensor Networks (WSN), authors in [4] employ a metric consisting of the consumption of energy and data forwarding ratio.

They employ the broadcasting capabilities of WSNs in their suggested method, and by using the suggested measure, they identify the optimal wireless link. Quality of service, such as end-to-end latency is not taken into account in this work.

For malicious communication in MANETs, ETRS a trust-based protocol is introduced in [1]. They compared the results with the existing state-of-the-art ESTC scheme and standard AODV.

2.2 Wireless Network Using Intelligent Routing

In [3] Maleki, Hakami, and Dehghan present a Reinforcement Learning based multi-agent routing system for MANETs in Massachusetts. Then, based on these metrics, develop a cost function for a single-hop model, and last, organize the routing issue as a Markov Decision Process (MDP), that solves connection latency and energy use using MDP state dynamics.

In [12], a routing protocol built on the Q-learning algorithm is suggested. There is a lot of communication overhead during the learning process because there is a distance to the destination-based reward calculation system for the subsequent hop. As a result, nodes must be aware of their neighbours' locations. Moreover, routing does not take QoS requirements into account.

In [11], a cognitive routing algorithm built on SARSA is put out. Nodes' energy consumption rates are used to calculate rewards, however regardless of the status of each flow in the route discovery process, every node gets the same reward. The findings indicate that each node's energy depletion is balanced.

In [16], a MANET routing system is presented that chooses a route based on network state data including bandwidth efficiency and link reliability. The protocol infers the aforementioned data via distributed Q-learning.

It can effectively manage the mobility of the network by automatically transferring to a more reliable path before the present one breaks.

In [6] an expanded version of their suggested TSDRP routing system was presented. Even in the existence of a rogue node, the TSDRP protocol can send packets to their intended targets while expanding the size of the network. The efficiency of both these protocols, TSDRP and AODV, was evaluated in relation to various performance metrics as a way to improve the accuracy of the results.

3 Proposed Method

3.1 Path-Finding Cycle

The general definition of RL states that it models consist of three-tuple agents $\{S, A, R\}$. The set of environmental conditions that the agent observes is represented by the letter S. A is the collection of acts that an agent can take Agent I observes the state $s_i^n \sum S$ at time step n, acting on its understanding of the surroundings, it does an action $a_i^n \sum A$ and obtains a reward $r_i^n + 1 \sum R$; R is a real numbers subset relevant to the issue at hand. The Q value of a state-action pair in reinforcement learning is the expected future benefits that an agent can anticipate obtaining for every action $a_i^n \sum A$ performed in state $s_i^n \sum S$. In a Q-table, each agent records the Q-values of potential state-action pairings ($Q(s_i^n, a_i^n)$).

We now define our components of the technique as follows, taking into account the network nodes as the RL method's agents:

- The environment of a node is the entirety of the network, excluding that specific node.
- The node holding the RREQ packet at time index n is defined as s_i^n Σ S(i$\sum$ {1,...,k}), here k indicates the network's node count.

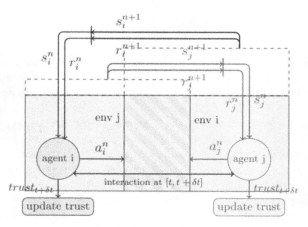

Fig. 1. Learning Cycle

- For every action a_i^n ΣA, the next node which is forwarding RREQ at time index n is represented by node I chosen among a group of nodes immediately associated to s_i.
- The Q-value of taking an action is modified when an agent decides which hop it will pass the RREQ to next.
- The quality of the path used to get there determines the reward, r_i^n ΣR. The old state is replaced by afresh state s_i^(n + 1)anytime an action a_i^n, is performed by the node and the node is rewarded with a new reward s_i^(n + 1) ΣR in accordance.

To accomplish its end-to-end objectives, each node independently completes the learning process by taking into account other nodes as a part of the network, as shown in Fig. 1.

We assume that all Q-values are started to 0 and that nodes have no knowledge of the entire network at the start of the communication process. According to [17], the related rule to update Q-value is generally the weighted sum of the learnt Q-value, which is made up of the future Q-value and the immediate reward.

$$Q(s,a) \leftarrow Q(s,a) + \alpha[R + \gamma \sum\nolimits_{a'} \pi(a'|s')Q(s', a') - Q(s, a)] \quad (1)$$

The instant reward in (1) is equivalent to the reciprocal of the entire amount of time needed to push the packet to the subsequent relaying node and reach its destination. The reliability of the transmitting node's route to the destination determines the total connection latency. An indicator of path condition is the Expected Transmission count (ETX). By calculating the packet loss ratios among couples of nearby nodes moving until the final node, it predicts the number of exchanges needed to get the data there.

3.2 Trust Assessment Cycle

Trust Model: Every node communicates with its connecting nodes to determine their level of trust throughout the algorithm's trust learning phase. Node i and Node j communicate with one another in a predefined period [t, t + δt], as illustrated in Fig. 1, updating their own neighbours' trust values in time intervals of \t seconds. A trust threshold, λ, is defined to determine a node's trustworthiness. The node is considered trustworthy if the value exceeds or is equivalent to the specified value. If not, it is declared malicious or suspicious, and it will remain isolated until the network's lifetime is over because there is no chance for reconsideration. Erroneous judgments may result in node isolation, which hurts the end product. We'll deal with this in our upcoming efforts.

Every node detects and isolates grey-hole and black-hole attacks via direct and indirect trust. A rogue node does not carry it defined task or data packets it is meant to forward in a black hole attack. It does, however, take part in routing to continue being a trusted node. Similar to a black hole attack, a grey hole attack involves a rogue node that takes part in the routing process while selectively dropping every one out of two data packets. It is believed that trust is asymmetric between two neighboring nodes. Additionally, to determine the final trust, we take into account both the past (which represents historical trust) and present trust evaluations. To prevent sudden changes in trust levels caused by the sporadic occurrence of grey-hole attacks, the current trust is computed by considering the past values of the trust.

Computation of Trust: The following formula is used to calculate direct trust i.e. it is equal to the total data sent by a node during a particular period divided by the total successful transmission of the data between the two nodes mathematically represented as follows.

$$DT_{ij}^t = f_j \big/ f_{i,j}$$

Every node utilizes suggestions from neighbouring nodes that have assessed the trustee or target node. Higher weight is given to the advisors with higher trust values and vice versa because there could be malevolent nodes. Thus, the indirect trust level is calculated by using the total average of the associated trust values of the recommenders.

3.3 CTR Protocol

Entities in Protocols

Hello Messages: In contrast to the AODV's format, there are extra components that contain the total number of hello messages that have been received in the last time from every present neighbour.

Neighbor Table: Every entity in the network keeps an independent neighbor table, or n tabled, with the data of the neighbors at each destination d. Keep in mind that our procedure prohibits additional storage usage (leading to effective space complexity), Additionally, the neighbors' Q-values are kept on the neighbors' desk. The neighbor table arrangement for every node is seen in Fig. 2. As the graphic illustrates, the data linked to every neighbor. The initial field holds the adjacent node's ID. The following area shows the Q-value used to choose this node as the subsequent hop while travelling to the desired location.

Regarding this neighbor ID, the node's trust value is preserved in the T-value field. The phases of path finding and trust learning are when values of T&Q are entered. Lastly, the neighbor table contains the computed ETX for this neighbor. Nodes that save their neighbors' information in neighbor tables incur additional storage costs in comparison to the AODV protocol. Nevertheless, the network size has a polynomial relationship of O(n2) with this additional storage expense.

Routing Table: The routing table typically keeps track of all final destinations' next-hop neighbours for every node. Because we are working with MANETs, every routing table entry has a lifespan. The routing table in our protocol is created as follows using the data from neighbouring tables. The matching neighbour table for every destination is examined. The routing technique is used for Q-values of the trustworthy neighbours to send the route request through an adjacent neighbor, who are the neighbours with T-values over the threshold (trusted neighbours). This choice is shown in the below diagram, where an active in-between node picks the forwarding node for a source to the destination.

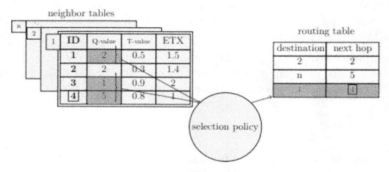

Fig. 2. Tables of neighbors within a node

Description of Protocol: Network layer protocol should check its routing table for a route when the data packet is requested by the source upper layer. The process comprises path finding and trust assessment, if there is no route or if the route has expired. The following is the method in detail:

1. Step 1: The source node s searches its local routing table for a route entry to destination node d. It sends the data packets following the route found, if any. If not, the source node sends a fresh RREQ to the next hop node chosen as follows, starting a route discovery process.
2. Step 2: When the subject node initiates a new RREQ or receives an RREQ, it checks the presence and timeliness of next hop forwarders to carry the RREQ of the required destination. If a it is missing or has reached the end of its validity, the node looks for the neighbour table n tabled related to the RREQ of the desired destination d. If no tables exist, it adds creates one and updates it. Using this, a neighbor is selected whose trust meets the required base value. These set of candidates using the -greedy selection criterion based on their Q-values selects the next hop. After that the routing table is updated with the next hop ID's with a modified expiration period, and forwards the route request. The routing database is updated with the ID of the chosen next hop node.

3. Step 3: The final intermediate node to reach its destination send a RREP to state that it is the final intermediate node to reach its destination. If this is the case, The protocol advances to step 5 at this moment. Step 4 is reached otherwise.
4. Step 4: After getting one, the intermediate node checks to see if a previously received RREQ is same as of present RREQ. If this is the case, the procedure is ended and the RREQ is dumped. If not, it handles the RREQ and repeats the second step.
5. Step 5: The data packets are sent as soon as the RREP is generated (Fig. 3).

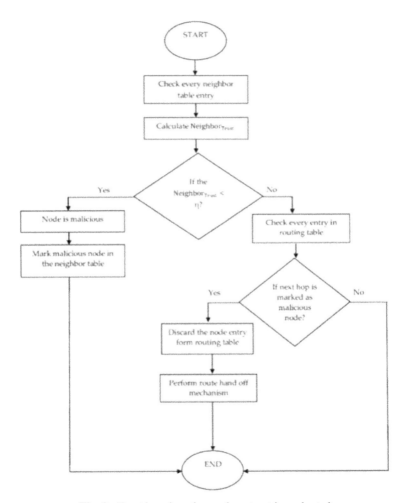

Fig. 3. Trust learning phase where trust is evaluated.

It is important to note that our suggested protocol consists of five distinct procedures, which are as follows: movement of nodes, computation of ETX, trust assessment, Determining Q-value, and updating routing table.

The node movement mechanism is initiated with a predefined length (τ_m) at each time step. The movement does not directly start any other processes, even though it has an impact on the nodes' ETX. The method used to calculate ETX is built by observing the delivery of hello messages at predefined-length intervals of time(τ_{ETX}). The trust calculation method, which is based on monitoring previous RREQs, is activated at predefined times (τ_T). RREQ activates the processes for routing table updates and Q-value computation.

3.4 Summary

Unlike the AODV system, which uses a minimum hop count, our routing protocol finds the path with low connection delay values and higher-than-threshold trust [18]. The simulation findings demonstrate how using path finding and trust assessment processes enhances routing mechanism, as we will shortly discover.

4 Results and Observation

4.1 Introduction

We model and contrast CTR's performance with that of TQR [7] in aspects of end-to-end latency, overhead communication and the ratio of data-packet delivery [10], TQR a trust-based QoS routing system that was just put forth. By calculating trust, TQR based on its QoS constraint forwards data across routes which reduce the end-delay and contains trusted nodes. As a baseline method, TQR outperforms both the AODV protocol and other earlier techniques. Furthermore, TQR is a suitable option to contrast our suggested approach with because it is a QoS-oriented, trust/AODV-based routing protocol that takes into account the same attack models. Unlike our research, TQR ignores cognition, which will soon be demonstrated to affect the relevant performance metrics.

4.2 Stepwise Description of Results

Pairs of sources and destinations are chosen at random to produce traffic simultaneously. A total of 50 nodes were considered for stimulation and out of 50 nodes, malicious nodes were selected at random in an activation region of 1000 m × 1000 m and the time taken for the whole stimulation is two hundred seconds. While the number of malevolent nodes is six, ten, fourteen. An average of 10 runs is used for each result to attain the desired confidence interval. Every node's trust level is represented in a continuous interval [0, 1] number, where zero denotes total mistrust and one denotes maximum trust. All nodes have their initial trust level as neutral which is 0.5 (Table 1).

Since the selected simulation software handles MAC layer problems for wireless networks, we are not specifically concerned with them here. As we are not targeting WSNs consumption of energy is not taken as a crucial factor.

We model attackers from black holes and grey holes according to [7, 8]. Attackers that spread incorrect information and defame others are not taken into account in this work. Our performance metrics include communication overhead, packet delivery ratio, and average end-to-end latency. It should be mentioned that since hello packets are used for more than merely routing, they are not regarded as communication overhead.

Table 1. Simulation setup

Parameter	Value
Activation region	1000 m × 1000 m
Nodes count	50
Continuous flow of source-destination	15
Activation period	200 s
Malevolent nodes	6, 10, 14
Data packet size	512 B
Highest cluster speed	5 m/s
Hello packet production gap	1 s
Route request generation time	1 s
Data packet production gap	1 s
Limit of Trustworthiness	0.5
Trust assessment period	5 s
Mobility update gap	100 ms
Learning rate	0.9
Mobility model	Random Waypoint (RWP)
Amount of runs	10/scenario
Trust towards time frame	95%

4.3 Result Analysis

The performance of the two methods is compared against the simulation time in Fig. 4, 5 and 6. By taking into account a network of six rogue nodes, these outcomes are reached. The average end-to-end latency vs time took for simulation is displayed in Fig. 4. Better routes are found over time as a result of learning-based routing algorithms' inherent ability to gather more environmental data.

The findings demonstrate that CTR performs better than TQR and that this superiority increases over time. This outperformance is explained by the fact that CTR uses the delay as the primary criterion for determining the subsequent course of action during the learning phase, whereas connection delay is used as the QoS constraint during routing by TQR. The findings imply that more comprehensive data regarding the found routes is obtained by including the path-learning phase in the methodology.

Figure 5 illustrates how the delivery ratio of data packets increases over time for both protocols. The ascent of the curves highlights how routes free of malicious nodes are employed to carry packets and how more precise trust values become accessible with time. CTR almost always outperforms TQR when compared with packet delivery ratio, but occasionally underperforms it. This is due to the possibility of a longer search time for the most trusted node in CTR. Although the initial performance of both protocols is identical, TQR experiences a temporary improvement in delivery ratio speed. Over

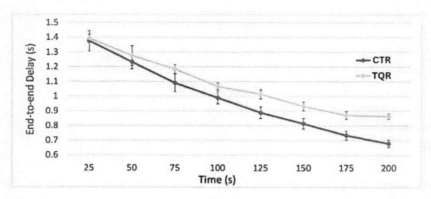

Fig. 4. Evaluating CTR and TQR with respect to Average end-to-end latency.

an extended period, CTR not only reaches parity but also appears to have superior asymptotic performance.

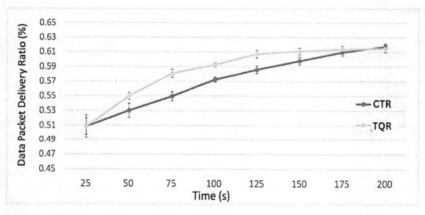

Fig. 5. Evaluating CTR and TQR with respect to The ratio of data packet delivery.

Using intelligent routing has further benefits, as Fig. 6 makes clear that CTR outperforms TQR in case of communication overhead. This is primarily because, during route discovery, CTR uses the Reinforcement Learning technique to unicast RREQs whereas TQR broadcasts it. Additionally, extra control packets are required forever in TQR for assessing the new connections and maintaining the most recent valid routes. On the other hand, CTR discovers the most stable routes during the path-finding phase, which drastically lowers the amount of control packets sent during the simulation. Furthermore, compared to TQR, fewer control packets are generated in CTR over time.

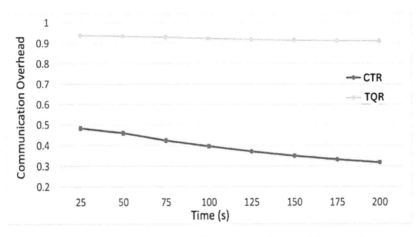

Fig. 6. Evaluating CTR and TQR with respect to Overhead Communication.

4.4 Observation from the Work

Figure 7 shows how CTR's end-to-end latency out shines its predecessor for how many rogue nodes may be in the network, proving the efficacy of incorporating the path-finding phase as well as the fact that CTR has reduced communication overhead. TQR's findings, which show that the detected pathways have less delay overhead throughout the routing process, are corroborated by a decrease in latency as the rogue nodes' capacity in number increases.

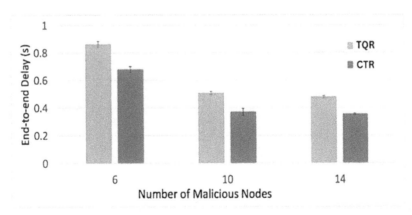

Fig. 7. Evaluating the number of malicious nodes with the typical end-to-end latency for CTR and TQR.

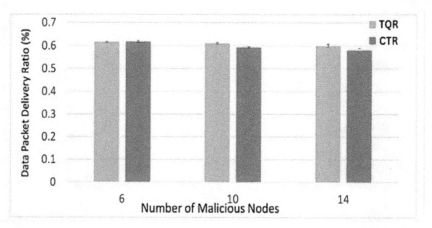

Fig. 8. Evaluating the number of malicious nodes with the ratio of data packet deliveryfor CTR and TQR.

Figure 8 plots the delivery ratio of data packets against the number of rogue nodes. As can be seen, CTR works nearly identically to TQR; the only minor variation arises from the additional time needed in CTR to identify the most reliable route. In the longer run, this little discrepancy will disappear. It is an intriguing finding that attests to the protocol's resilience and low end-to-end delay when compared to its predecessor.

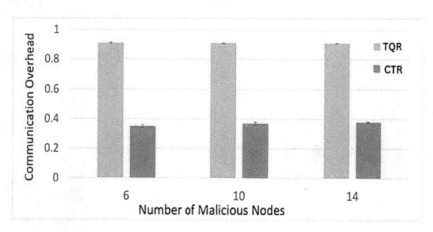

Fig. 9. Evaluating the Overhead communication for CTR and TQR.

Figure 9 shows that CTR performs substantially better than TQR in all circumstances because of its unicast RREQs in route finding in contrast to the route request broadcasted by its predecessor.

5 Conclusion and Future Scope

5.1 Conclusion

We introduce a Cognitive Ad hoc Trust Routing for Enhanced Quality of Service. We propose a layer of cognition comprised of two interconnected phases: pathfinding and trust assessment. Expected-SARSA is used as the path-finding approach in our protocol, and our enhanced model in TQR is used for trust learning.

CTR surpasses its predecessor in terms of end-to-end latency and communication overhead, attaining a roughly similar delivery ratio as time passes, according to simulation studies. This is mostly due to the use of the RL mechanism with unicast of the route request. Furthermore, the stability of several performance metrics with a range of malicious nodes demonstrates CTR's resilience to wireless networks' changing topology.

5.2 Future Scope

The project opens up several avenues for future research and improvement: In our next study, we want to take into account the following more adaptable trust model in unprotected networks. Rethinking separated nodes will be incorporated into the model to stop common nodes from making erroneous routing decisions, perhaps increasing the data packet delivery ratio. Furthermore, one of the optimization criteria will be minimizing the energy consumption of wireless nodes.

References

1. Mahamune, A.A., Chandane, M.M.: An efficient trust-based routing scheme against malicious communication in MANET. Int. J. Wirel. Inf. Netw. **28**, 344–361 (2021)
2. Pathan, M.S., Zhu, N., He, J., Zardari, Z.A., Memon, M.Q., Hussain, M.I.: An efficient trust-based scheme for secure and quality of service routing in MANETs. Future Internet **10**(2), 16 (2018). https://doi.org/10.3390/fi10020016
3. Maleki, M., Hakami, V., Dehghan, M.: A model-based reinforcement learning algorithm for routing in energy harvesting mobile ad-hoc networks. Wirel. Pers. Commun. **95**, 1–21 (2017)
4. Kumar, N., Singh, Y.: An energy-efficient and trust assessment based opportunistic routing metric for wireless sensor networks. In: Fourth International Conference on Parallel, Distributed and Grid Computing (PDGC), pp. 611–616 (2016)
5. Al-Rawi, H.A.A., Ng, M.A., Yau, K.-L.A.: Application of reinforcement learning to routing in distributed wireless networks: a review. Artif. Intell. Rev. **43**(3), 381–416 (2015)
6. Nirbhay, C., Aggarwal, A., Gandhi, S., Jani, K.A.: Performance analysis of TSDRP and AODV routing protocol under blackhole attacks in manets by varying network size. In: 2015 Fifth International Conference on Advanced Computing & Communication Technologies (ACCT), pp. 320–324 (2015)
7. Wang, B., Chen, X., Chang, W.: A light-weight trust-based QoS routing algorithm for ad hoc networks. Pervasive Mob. Comput. **13**, 164–180 (2014)
8. Aggarwal, A., Gandhi, S., Chaubey, N., Jani, K.: Trust based secure on demand routing protocol (TSDRP) for MANETs. In: 2014 Fourth International Conference on Advanced Computing & Communication Technologies (ACCT), Rohtak, pp. 432–438 (2014). https://doi.org/10.1109/ACCT.2014.95

9. Qu, C., Ju, L., Jia, Z., Xu, H., Zheng, L.: Light-weight trust-based on-demand multipath routing protocol for mobile ad hoc networks. In: 12th IEEE International Conference on Trust, Security and Privacy in Computing and Communications, pp. 42–49 (2013)
10. Aggarwal, A., Gandhi, S., Chaubey, N., et al.: AODVSEC: a novel approach to secure ad hoc on-demand distance vector (AODV) routing protocol from insider attacks in MANETs. Int. J. Comput. Netw. Commun. (IJCNC) **4**(4), 191 (2012)
11. Chettibi, S., Chikhi, S.: An adaptive energy-aware routing protocol for MANETs using the SARSA reinforcement learning algorithm. In: IEEE Conference on Evolving and Adaptive Intelligent Systems (EAIS), pp. 84–89 (2012)
12. Naputta, Y., Usaha, W.: RL-based routing in biomedical mobile wireless sensor networks using trust and reputation. In: International Symposium on Wireless Communication Systems (ISWCS), pp. 521–525. IEEE (2012)
13. Cho, J.-H., Swami, A., Chen, R.: A survey on trust assessment for mobile ad hoc networks. IEEE Commun. Surv. Tutor. **13**(4), 562–583 (2011)
14. Santhi, G., Nachiappan, A., Ibrahime, M.Z., Raghunadhane, R., Favas, M.: Q-learning based adaptive QoS routing protocol for MANETs. In: International Conference on Recent Trends in Information Technology (ICRTIT), pp. 1233–1238 (2011)
15. Yu, H., Shen, Z., Miao, C., Leung, C., Niyato, D.: A survey of trust and reputation management systems in wireless communications. Proc. IEEE **98**(10), 1755–1772 (2010)
16. Wu, C., Kumekawa, K., Kato, T.: A MANET protocol considering link stability and bandwidth efficiency. In: International Conference on Ultra-Modern Telecommunications and Workshops, pp.1–8. IEEE (2009)
17. Van Seijen, H., Van Hasselt, H., Whiteson, S., Wiering, M: A theoretical and empirical analysis of expected Sarsa. In: IEEE Symposium on Adaptive Dynamic Programming and Reinforcement Learning, pp. 177–184 (2009)
18. Perkins, C., Belding-Royer, E., Das, S.: Ad hoc on-demand distance vector AODV routing. Tech. Rep. (2003)
19. Sutton, R.S., Barto, A.G.: Reinforcement Learning: an Introduction (1998)
20. Blaze, M., Feigenbaum, J., Lacy, J.: Decentralized trust assessment. In: Proceedings of 1996 IEEE Symposium on Security and Privacy, pp. 164–173 (1996)

Routing in IoT Network Using NetSim Simulator

Divyanshi Goyal, Sonam(✉), Anjali Yadav, Manan Alfred, and Rahul Johari

SWINGER: Security, Wireless, IoT Network, Group of Engineering and Research Lab, University School of Automation and Robotics (USAR), Guru Gobind Singh Indraprastha University, East Delhi Campus, Opposite Surajmal Vihar, Delhi 110032, India
sonammathur57@gmail.com, rahul@ipu.ac.in

Abstract. As is widely recognized, a prevalent term in the realm of Information Technology (IT) these days is the Internet of Things (IoT). IoT is a revolutionary paradigm in the world of networks which primarily focuses on sharing information through 'Things'. The 'Things' refer to the devices or objects that usually communicate with each other over the IP network. The crucial component of an IoT network that determines the path is routing. In this paper, the simulation was accomplished by creating a network in NetSim Simulator. A dataset of smoke detection using IoT sensors was taken into consideration by accessing it from Kaggle for routing purposes. IoT network designed in NetSim, comprised of 13 sensor nodes, a 6LoWPAN Gateway, a router, and a server. An application was configured for each sensor to periodically generate packets and forward them to the server via the 6LoWPAN Gateway.

Keywords: IoT · Dataset · VOIP · NetSim

1 Introduction

In the mid-1980s, communication options were primarily confined to either telephone conversations i.e. VOIP (Voice Over Internet Protocol), or written correspondence such as letters and postal services. However, with the advent of the Internet, a new era of communication emerged. Over time, Voice over Internet Protocol (VoIP) technology became a reality, expanding the possibilities for communication. The word "IoT" was coined in the modern period, which has long since moved past the idea of the Internet. IoT is defined as the "connection of embedded technologies" or the "Things that are associated over the Internet". Rather than device-to-device (D2D) communication, it also focuses on machine-to-machine (M2M) communication. A few years ago, the proliferation of the Internet of Things (IoT) has been advancing swiftly. Even though IoT is all about connecting things (items) to the Internet. According to, the "Global IoT market forecast" the global count of interconnected IoT devices is experiencing a growth of 16%, reaching 16.7 billion [12].

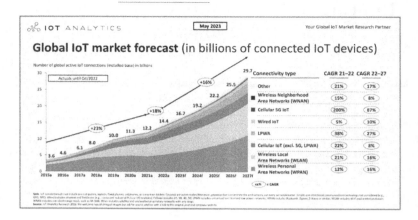

Fig. 1. Global IoT market forecast

The idea of IoT has recently become increasingly popular in the world of business. The birth of the Industrial Internet of Things (IIoT) arose from the pressing demands of industries for cutting-edge industrial machinery and specialized adaptations of IoT functionalities to suit their specific requirements. IIoT caters to industrial demands by continually evolving its technological capabilities to meet daily operational needs.

1.1 Communication Technologies of IoT

For contemporary applications, there are numerous connecting methods available. These are based on the IoT-related systems and goods.

1. **ZigBee:** It is an IEEE standard-based wireless technology that allows low-cost, low-power wireless communication. It is an open IEEE (802.15) standard for M2M and IoT networks. Zigbee Wireless Personal Area Networks (WPANs) function over frequencies of 2.4 GHz, 900 MHz, and 868 MHz.
2. **RFID (Radio Frequency Identification):** One or more readers and numerous RFID tags make up an RFID system. RFID tags are attached to things and have a specific address. They transmit data about an item via radio-frequency electromagnetic radiation.
3. **IEEE (802.15.4):** The physical layer and media access control for Low-Rate Wireless Personal Area Networks (LR-WPANs) are specified by this standard. The 826 and 915 MHz frequency bands were supported by the first iteration of IEEE 802.15.4.
4. **Long Term Evolution (LTE):** Built upon Global System for Mobile Communication (GSM) network technology, LTE stands as a prevalent wireless communication protocol facilitating high-speed data transfer among mobile phones. Its capacity allows for a maximum frequency of 100 MHz.

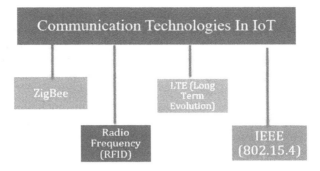

Fig. 2. Communication Technologies of IoT

2 Literature Survey

In [1] author provided a comprehensive overview of the current state, challenges, and future directions in the field of IoT. The author discussed about the applications of IoT in healthcare, smart cities, agriculture, industrial settings, smart homes, etc. The assessment predicts future developments in IoT, with a particular emphasis on edge computing, 5G connection, and AI integration. It also identifies areas that require further research to address existing issues and investigate novel applications.

In order to provide network performance estimates for IoT MM traffic in IEEE 802.11 multihop wireless networks, the authors of [2] suggested a network performance estimator. The performance estimator that was suggested was the first to provide real-time estimates of packet loss, delay, and throughput per flow using deterministic simulation. The findings of the simulation showed that MAPE can offer estimations of network performance that IoT MM services can employ, most notably to guide real-time route selection in IoT video transmission. The authors concluded that, in comparison to current deterministic simulators, the MAPE produces better accuracy at comparable execution times.

The authors of [3] talked about IoT and its applications, such as smart cities. Information and communication technology is used by the "smart city" to enhance communication with the public, increase operational efficacy, and enhance the standard of public services and citizen interest. A review of IoT integration in apps for creative cities was also conducted.

In [4] authors gave a general overview of the relationships between the major security threats, requirements, implementations, and network safety in this study. Additionally, the authors reviewed a couple of the device communication services and assessed the security features.

In [5] authors examined IoT and privacy concerns in IoT. The authors attempted to create a personal assistant that could respond to inquiries from software developers regarding Privacy by Design (PbD) principles throughout the design stage of the creation of IoT systems. The knowledge behind PbD measurements, their intersections with privacy patterns, IoT system needs, and privacy patterns were modeled using semantic web technologies. The PARROT ontology, which was developed using a set of typical IoT use cases relevant to software developers, was used to do this. Through a series of workshops, 81 carefully chosen Competency Questions were gathered to support this. According to studies, the PARROT ontology can answer up to 58% of privacy-related questions from software developers.

Intelligent communities come in many different forms, including smart homes, smart farms, smart environments, smart lifestyles, smart governments et al. IoT is also employed in the manufacturing, gas mining, and oil refining industries. IoT enhances productivity, lowers costs, uses more energy, keeps predictions accurate, and offers a lot of convenience to consumers. With more diverse systems and data processing, security threats are rising. IoT development is being hampered mostly by privacy and security concerns. The authors of [6] examined several security and privacy issues related to the IoT.

In [7] authors discussed about home automation and fire safety equipments. The authors discussed about an IoT-based automatic smoke detection system to detect smoke in a room. Users can contact the Fire and Rescue Department when a gas sensor detects a specific amount of smoke thanks to IoT-based automatic smoke detection systems. These smoke detectors can send a signal to a fire alarm control panel as part of a building's central fire alarm system, or they can produce a localized auditory and visual signal in a home smoke alarm.

An intelligent sensor-based Internet of Things forest fire detection system that focuses on machine learning techniques was presented in [8]. The suggested system combines data from sensors, including temperature sensors and smoke detectors, to identify and classify forest fires in real time. Using a labeled dataset, the performance of the suggested system is evaluated. This research study emphasized the necessity for ongoing study and development in this crucial area and helped create dependable and efficient technologies to identify wildfires that make use of the power of machine learning algorithms.

The authors of [9] examined effective and efficient routing in the IoT. In this paper, the authors show how an IoT routing protocol called MQTT (Message Queue Telemetry Transport) may be used to route data efficiently between publisher and subscriber through a centralized broker. Using the MOSQUITTO open-source toolkit, the protocol simulation was completed in the JAVA programming language.

An efficient SRS (Safe, Reliable, and Secure) routing strategy between a sensor, publisher, and subscriber in an IoT architecture is shown in [10]. By deploying IoT-MQTT compatible code on an MQTT server, the simulation was carried out. A real-time authentic dataset known as IoTeX Cryptocurrency, was taken into account. The same was archived in MySQL Server, and the transactions were encrypted using the AES (Advanced Encryption Standard) Algorithm by writing suitable code in Java using the ECLIPSE IDE.

3 Applications of IoT

IoT finds its applications in many areas because of its adaptability and technological advancement. It enables the end-users to communicate with each other via the Internet.

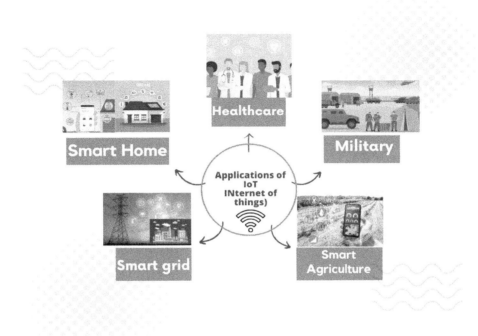

Fig. 3. Applications of IoT

Some of its applications are:

1. **Military**: IoT category includes the Internet of Military Things (IoMT) and the Internet of Battlefield Things (IoBT). Among the wireless network technologies utilized for tracking and monitoring the health of armed personnel are ZigBee and GSM networks. Utilizing IoT technology in military operations, usually enhances military men's awareness, risk assessment, and response times.
2. **Healthcare**: IoT is frequently utilized for chronic disease management, tracking incredible sensors, mobile health, and smart hospitals. Due to the continuous health monitoring provided by remote monitoring, a normal life is made

possible. Patients' medical records are tracked using a variety of wireless body sensors, including accelerometers, respiration rate sensors, AMPED sensors, Kinect cameras, embedded sensors in T-shirts, and many others.
3. **Home Automation**: IoT has changed how we now use electrical items. Utilizing a relay switch, a microcontroller, and a network device, any appliance, including lights, fans, air conditioners, media, security systems, refrigerators, ovens, and so on, can be connected to the Internet. Even from a distance, the user can control the appliances by using a graphical user interface. This is made possible by a variety of sensors, including those for temperature (DHT11/22), light (TSL2591, BH1750), water level (HC-SR04, LM1830), and others.
4. **Smart Grid**: The drawbacks of the traditional power infrastructure encompass poor reliability, frequent power failures, carbon emissions, safety concerns, and more. By incorporating IoT technology, the conventional electricity network can undergo technological enhancements, transitioning into a smart grid. A smart grid refers to an IoT system capable of gathering data from diverse grid elements and establishing a power management mechanism by adapting power distribution to match demand.
5. **Smart Agriculture**: Farmers can utilize IoT sensors to collect environmental and machinery data, enabling them to enhance the management of tasks ranging from livestock rearing to crop cultivation. Through the use of smart agriculture sensors to monitor crop conditions, farmers can precisely determine the optimal quantities of pesticides and fertilizers required for maximum efficiency. The concept of "smart farming" remains accurate in this context.

4 Challenges and Issues

Every technology faces some of the challenges in real-time application. In the same way, although IoT comes with so many technological advancements it also presents some issues and challenges.

1. **Security and Privacy Concerns**: IoT devices often collect and transmit sensitive data, making them potential targets for cyber attacks. Weak security measures and a lack of proper encryption can expose personal information, leading to privacy breaches and unauthorized access to devices and networks. The considerable volume of data produced by IoT devices prompts inquiries regarding the ownership and governance of this data. Users might not always be aware of how their data is being used, leading to Worries regarding ownership of data, consent, and the possibility of misuse.
2. **Interoperability**: IoT devices originate from a multitude of manufacturers and employ diverse communication protocols and standards. Lack of interoperability can hinder seamless communication between devices from different vendors, limiting the potential for a unified and integrated IoT ecosystem.
3. **Scalability**: With the rapid proliferation of IoT devices, the task of managing and keeping these devices becomes progressively more daunting. Challenges

may emerge concerning scalability in data processing, network administration, and ensuring device functionality.
4. **Reliability and Quality Assurance**: IoT devices are expected to function reliably over extended periods. However, hardware malfunctions, software bugs, and connectivity issues can affect the overall reliability of IoT systems, potentially leading to unexpected downtime or incorrect data.
5. **Energy Efficiency**: Many IoT devices are battery-powered, making energy efficiency a crucial concern. Balancing functionality and energy consumption is a challenge, particularly for devices that need to operate in remote or inaccessible locations.
6. **Data Overload and Buffer Storage**: The enormous volume of data generated by IoT devices can overload systems, which makes it difficult to process and extract meaningful insights from the collected data. Efficient data management, including the use of buffer storage to handle sudden data spikes, is crucial to derive valuable information from this data deluge.

5 Experimental Setup

5.1 Dataset Description

The sample dataset used for testing purposes has been obtained from Kaggle [11]. The table in the .csv dataset file contains information about smoke detection using IoT sensors. We have taken the dataset of smoke detection using IoT sensors from the Kaggle and created a virtual network corresponding to the dataset.

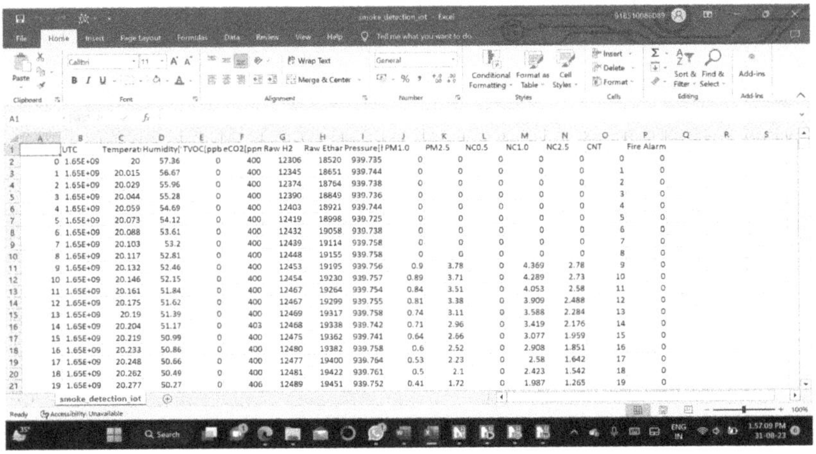

Fig. 4. Dataset

5.2 Software

NetSim contains many different modules for different types of networks such as IoT, WSN, MANET, VANET, LTE/LTE-A, and many more. To understand and analyse the network in real-time we used the software NetSim (Network Simulator) Standard v13.3.12. This network simulation tool enables users to digitally create a network comprising devices, connections, applications, sensors, and additional components, aiding in the examination of network behavior and performance [13].

To simulate any network in NetSim following steps are required:

a) Develop your own protocol/algorithm
b) Build the model
c) Run the simulation
d) Visualize the simulation
e) Analyze the results

5.3 Result

IoT module is used to create the network of smoke detection using IoT sensors dataset used to analyze the data collected by sensors. Upon simulation completion, the NetSim results dashboard displays different performance metrics derived from the protocols operating across various layers of the network stack. Packet trace and Event trace log files will be accessible provided the corresponding options are enabled before initiating the simulation.

Figure 5 shows NetSim designed IoT network. This network comprises 13 sensors such as temperature, Humidity TVOC, etc. connected to a 6LowPAN

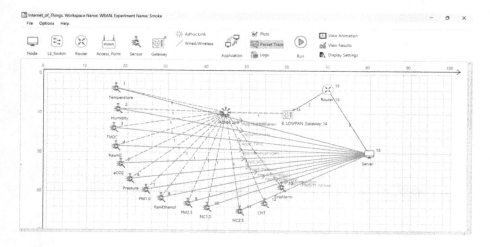

Fig. 5. IoT network

Routing in IoT Network Using NetSim Simulator   213

Fig. 6. Result Window

gateway followed by a router and this router sends data to the Server node. The green line in the picture shows the traffic generated by these sensors to the server node. All the packets generated by these sensors follow the TCP protocol.

Figure 6 shows the simulation result window which represents the application metrics of every sensor. TCP metrics depict how the sensor sends data to the server. Link metrics define the number of packets transmitted or collided. Queue metrics show the queued and dequeued packets and the port ID [14].

Figure 7 and 8 shows the animation window. The blue packets are the data packets and the Red packets depict the packets that suffer collision.

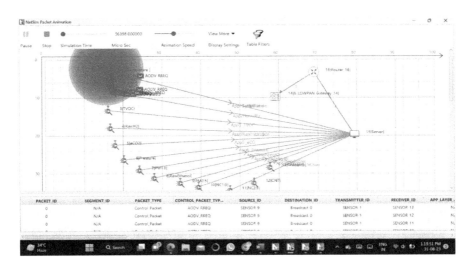

Fig. 7. Animation Window

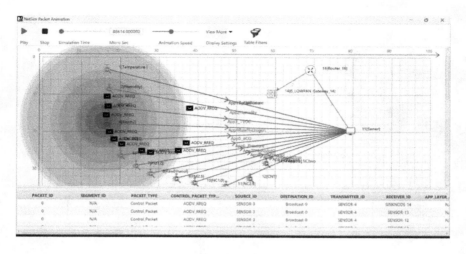

Fig. 8. Animation Window

Figure 9 shows how the packets are transmitted which is the source and the destination, and which protocol is used by the packets and their type. The packet trace table contains all the information of the packets such as source and destination ID, and how much time the packet takes at each layer of the OSI model such as the Network layer, Transport layer, MAC layer, and Application layer. Additionally, it displays data about the size of packets at every layer.

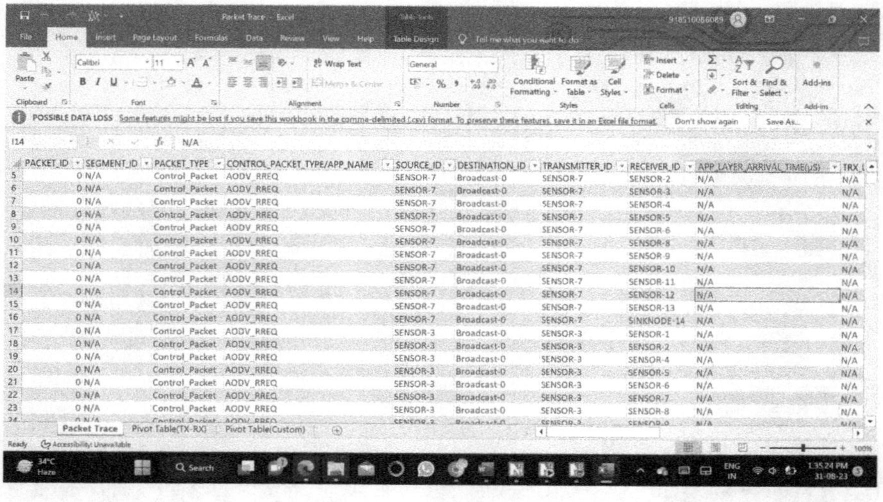

Fig. 9. Packet trace table

6 Conclusion

In this paper, the simulation was accomplished by creating a network in NetSim Simulator. A dataset of smoke detection using IoT sensors was sourced from Kaggle. The IoT network, designed within NetSim, comprises 13 sensor nodes, a 6LoWPAN Gateway, a router, and a server. Each sensor was configured with an application to periodically generate packets and transmit them to the server via the 6LoWPAN Gateway. The outcomes obtained have been notably positive and encouraging, and these have been visually presented in the animation or result window for the reader's benefit.

Acknowledgments. The author(s) are thankful for the research-oriented academic environment provided by GGSIP University.

References

1. Sayed, M.: The internet of things (IoT), applications and challenges: a comprehensive review. J. Innov. Intell. Comput. Emerg. Technol. (JIICET) **1**(01), 20–27 (2024)
2. Bhering, F., Passos, D., Obraczka, K., Albuquerque, C.: Network performance estimator with applications to route selection for IoT multimedia applications. SIMULATION **100**(1), 23–37 (2024)
3. Nassereddine, M., Khang, A.: Applications of Internet of Things (IoT) in smart cities. In: Advanced IoT Technologies and Applications in the Industry 4.0 Digital Economy, pp. 109–136. CRC Press (2024)
4. Rekha, S., Thirupathi, L., Renikunta, S., Gangula, R.: Study of security issues and solutions in Internet of Things (IoT). Mater. Today: Proc. **80**, 3554–3559 (2023)
5. Alkhariji, L., De, S., Rana, O., Perera, C.: Semantics-based privacy by design for Internet of Things applications. Futur. Gener. Comput. Syst. **138**, 280–295 (2023)
6. Singhai, R., Sushil, R.: An investigation of various security and privacy issues in Internet of Things. Mater. Today: Proc. **80**, 3393–3397 (2023)
7. Kumaran, S., Arunachalam, S., Surendar, V., Sudharsan, T.: IoT based smoke detection with air temperature and air humidity; high accuracy with machine learning. In: 2023 Third International Conference on Artificial Intelligence and Smart Energy (ICAIS), pp. 604–610. IEEE, February 2023
8. Nagolu, C., Cheekula, C., Thota, D.S.K., Padmanaban, K. and Bhattacharyya, D.: Real-time forest fire detection using IoT and smart sensors. In: 2023 International Conference on Inventive Computation Technologies (ICICT), pp. 1441–1447. IEEE, April 2023
9. Sonam, J.R.: MORID: MQTT oriented routing between IoT devices. J. Discret. Math. Sci. Cryptogr. **25**(7), 2121–2128 (2022)
10. Sonam, J.R.: SEROMI: secured encrypted routing of message in IoT. In: International Conference on Advanced Communications and Machine Intelligence, pp. 339–347. Singapore: Springer Nature, Singapore, December 2022
11. Kaggle-Smoke Detection Analysis. https://www.kaggle.com/code/aashidutt3/smoke-detection-analysis
12. https://IoT-analytics.com
13. https://www.tetcos.com/downloads/v12/NetSim_User_Manual.pdf
14. https://www.tetcos.com/documentation/NetSim/v13/NetSim-Experiments-Manual/index.htm#t=NetSim_Experiment_Manual.htm

A Novel Approach of SHA-3-512bits Using Keccak Technique Based on Sponge Function Implementation on FPGA

K. Janshi Lakshmi(✉) [iD] and G. Sreenivasulu [iD]

Department of Electronics and Communication Engineering, Sri Venkateswara University College of Engineering, Sri Venkateswara University, Tirupati, AndhraPradesh, India
jansikaramala@gmail.com

Abstract. SHA-3-512bits offers stronger cryptographic security than SHA1, SHA 2, and SHA3-256bits.This paper describes a SHA-3-512bits hash function utilizing the Sponge-based Keccak Algorithm. Four alternate messages digest lengths of 512 bits, 384 bits, 256 bits, and 224 bits are allowed by the SHA3 hash algorithm, depending on the hash function in use. The SHA3-512 function operates on a single instance, processing input messages at a rate of 72 bytes per 1096 cycles at 316.25 MHz and a 1600 bits data path with a round-iterative structure. The SHA-3-512bits is verified by VIVADO 2017.2 version software with hardware implementation on FPGA ARTIX-7 device. The proposed method consumed power is 192.334W and occupied an area of 2493 LUTs, Flip-Flops 1876 and IOB's 17.65% of ARTIX-7 FPGA device and became cost-effective device used ARTEX-7.

Keywords: Cryptography · Security · SHA-3-512 · Keccak · Sponge function · VIVADO · FPGA Artix-7

1 Introduction

The Hash function in cryptography play vital role for authentication process. The Secure Hash Algorithm (SHA) was primary hash algorithm used within cryptography. US National Institute of Standards and Technology (NIST) published a set of cryptographic hash functions called the Secure Hash Algorithms as a Federal Information Processing Standard (FIPS). The SHA algorithm comes in three flavors: SHA0, SHA1, SHA2, and SHA3. Examine Table 1.

SHA-0 (Secure Hash Algorithm-0): An acronym used to refer to the 160-bit hash function's initial release under the "SHA" moniker. A "significant flaw" that was kept secret led to its withdrawal soon after publication, and the slightly altered SHA-1 version took its place.

SHA-1 (Secure Hash Algorithm-1): A function called SHA-1 is used in cryptography to generated a message digested, or a hash function value of 160 bits or 20 bytes, from an input [14]. Usually expressed in the forty hexadecimal places closest to it. The National

Security Agency (NSA) of the United States (US) developed the American Federal Information Processing Standard (FIPS). Although the technique is poor cryptographically, it is nonetheless widely used.

SHA-2 (Secure Hash Algorithm-2): SHA2 has undergone significant changes from its predecessor, SHA-1. The six hash functions that make up the SHA2 family are: SHA224bits, SHA256bits, SHA384bits, SHA512bits, SHA512bits/224bits, and SHA512bits/256bits. These functions have digests (hash values) that range from 224 bits to 512 bits. The novel hash algorithms SHA-256bits and SHA-51bits 2 were built using eight 32 bits and 64 bits words, respectively. The number of rounds is the only distinction between their topologies, which are otherwise identical. Still, they use different shift sizes and additive constants. SHA-224bits and SHA-384bits, the shortened versions of SHA-256bits and SHA-512bits, are computed with different initial values.

SHA-3 (Secure Hash Algorithm-3): NIST released the up-to-date Secure Hash Algorithm standard, known as SHA3 (Secure Hash Algorithm3). Even though SHA-3 belongs to the same standards series as SHA-1 and SHA-2, its internal structure is different from MD5-like structures. Sponge construction is a novel building technique used in Keccak. To use the language of a sponge, any amount of data can be "absorbed" or "squeezed" while continuing to act as a pseudo random function with regard to all previous inputs. The foundation of sponge building is a random permutation or wide random function. It leads to great flexibility. SHA-2 will remain part of the revised Secure Hash Standard; NIST does not currently have any intentions to remove it. In current applications, SHA-2 can potentially be replaced with SHA-3 if needed. Enhancing the overall robustness of NIST's hash algorithm toolkit is its primary objective. The designers of SHA-3 and Keccak advise using the faster function Kangaroo Twelve for short message payloads, together with a new tree hashing mode that doesn't require any extra overhead and certain adjusted settings. In existing designs SHA1, SHA2, and SHA3-256bits provide less strength in cryptographic security. Implementing SHA1, SHA2, and SHA3-256 bits on FPGAs takes considerably more space and requires more power. But SHA-3-512bits offers strongest cryptographic security, used areas in Security in Data communication, Message Authentication Codes, Key Derivation Functions and Many other Security Applications.

According to the hash function being used, the SHA3 hash function allows four alternative message digest widths of 512, 384, 256, and 224 bits. It was built with Input 72 bytes or 576 bits and a 24 round-iterative structure of 1600 bits data path. The SHA-3-512bits was implemented in Artix-7 FPGA device.

Table 1. Different types of SHA algorithm of HMAC (Hash Message Authentication Code)

Hash Function	Types of Hash Function	Block Size (Bytes)	Output size (Bits)	Rounds	Internal State Size (Bits)
SHA-0	SHA-0	64	160	80	160
SHA-1	SHA-1	64	160	80	160
SHA-2	SHA-224	64	224	64	512
	SHA-256	64	256	64	512
	SHA-384	128	384	80	1024
	SHA-512	128	512	80	1024
SHA-3	SHA-224	144	224	24	1600
	SHA-256	136	256	24	1600
	SHA-384	104	384	24	1600
	SHA-512	72	512	24	1600

2 Related Works

Argyrios Sideris et al. [1] were made available the FPGA Virtex 7board demonstrates the utility of the architecture with an area of 1375 slices, throughput 36.35 gbps, efficiency is 26.44 mbps/slices.

Dmytro Havrilovet al. [2] were portrayed the pipelined techniques and folding and unrolling processes employed in the study methodologies are based on numerous platforms. Research on bandwidth is being done based on the microcircuit resource's total speed and usage. System-wide comparative analysis takes into account the parameter of overall performance, which is crucial for building hardware implementations of algorithms.

Igor L.R. Azevedoet al. [3] SHA-3 Co-Processor, an effective FPGA design, was announced; it is suitable for low-power applications such as the Internet of Things. With only 0.2 W of power needed for the coprocessor, the system runs around 65% quicker than standard ARM-based embedded program.

YutaAkiya et al. [4] were demonstrated A revolutionary implementation build on FPGA technology, SHA3-LPHP, will be included within low-power device architecture. SHA-3-LPHP is a strong candidate for less powered and increased performance devices since it achieves three orders of magnitude faster execution times and uses less energy than complete software versions.

ArgyriosSideris et al. [5] were suggested architecture for the SHA3 algorithm was proposed by us. The architecture (10AX115N2P45E1SG) was created specifically for the Arria 10 GX FPGA. When our design's common evaluation metrics: area & frequency & throughput & efficiency are contrasted with those of other comparable designs, it becomes clear that their recommended architecture offers the high throughput and frequency in Hz efficiency in %. Their new architecture can handle messages within multiple blocks as well as single blocks. The given pipelined architecture performs better than less than 11% of the results.

Ali Hussein Jasimet al. [6] were portrayed With an output length of 256, the Keccak hash function was simulated using software optimized technique on the Keccak SHA3 algorithm used the Verilog HDL programming language. Moreover, a simulation of the concept was created using an FPGA. It is a quick and effective installation process. The method aims to reduce area while increasing throughput.

Zniti Asmae et al. [7] were built installed within the controlled area network of automobiles to provide better control and security. Throughput, sources utilization, and throughput & area ratio are compared amongst hash algorithms. An extensive examination also takes power consumption into account. Via the use of VIVADO, the algorithms are integrated into FPGA ZYNQ-7000.

Hachem Bensalem et al. [8] were confirmed, and the effect on throughput and speed up is documented. These implementations are constructed using Open CL optimization techniques. The final results demonstrated that the current optimization tactics result in a 310× speed-up over a baseline implementation. Additionally, the fastest optimized SHA3 coprocessor previously reported had a throughput of 22.36 Gbps, designed and implemented with VHDL.

Zhenjiang Wang et al. [9] were represented the final results demonstrate that the developed cryptographic instruction strategy can save more than 90% of the instructions and cycles. While increasing hardware resources by less than 8% and requiring only 9 mW of power, the working improvement is more evident and suitable for source constrained circumstances.

Eros Camacho-Ruiz et al. [10] were given access to a SHA-3 is a novel hardware-solution for the Keccak algorithm that is competitive with the state of the art and extremely customizable. This paper also explains how to incorporate these concepts into a hardware-IP-module. It enhances the utilization of space.

S. Neelima, R. Brindha [11] suggested architecture is rationally optimized by integrating the Rho steps for one-passed algorithm. 16% of the logical resources are used up logically recording these three step registers implemented. This is low delay and boosts the system maximum operating frequency. It requires 240 sectioned and had frequency is 301.02 MHz.

Akshay S Shetty et al. [12] were suggested a change the Keccak algorithms to minimized the space of implemented. The reduced in space is intended to reduce electricity usage. The improved Keccak Algorithm built on both the Keccak Algorithms and the Blake-G Functions.

3 Proposed Methodology

3.1 The SHA-3-512 System

The sponge build is a straight forward iterative technique that builds a function-{f} with a variable block-input and configurable output-length, along with a stable lengths permutation or transformation {f} applied to a stable amount (b) of bits. The breadth is denoted by b in this instance. The design of the sponge uses {b = (r + c)} bits. The bit-rate is denoted by the value r, and the capacity sponge structure is denoted by the value (c) [13]. The input string of the sponge design is divided into r-bit blocks after being padded using a reversible padding algorithm. After setting the state's b bits to zero, the sponge formation process is split into two stages: During the absorption phase, applications of the function 'f' depicted in Fig. 1 are interspersed with the (r) bit input (data) blocks that are EXOR into the 1st (r) bits of the state. The squeezing step of sponge production occurs after total input blocks had been processed. Applications of the function 'f' are spaced out between the return of the 1st (r) bits of the state as output blocks (data) during the squeezing phase [15]. The user has complete control over how many output segments are used. The final (c) bits of the stated are not emitted during squeezing phase and not directly affected by input blocks.

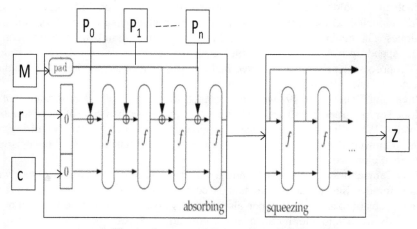

Fig. 1. Structure of Sponge Function [5]

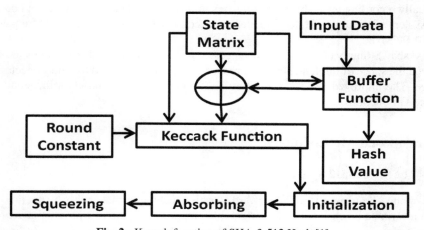

Fig. 2. Keccak function of SHA-3-512 Hash [1]

In order to make the overall size of an input message more of a pre-determined numbered of bits, indicated by the letter 'r' the messages are padded by addition of bits to it. Following the padding of the messages, it is divided into equal-length blocks, represented by the symbol 'Pi', 'r' bits EX-OR with each block and in the absorbing step the {f} permutation functioned [1]. The {f} function is the primary a component of the 24 rounds of processing and is made up of different procedures, such as (i) Theta ('θ') (ii) Rho ('ρ') (iii) Pi ('π') (iv) Chi ('χ') and (v) Iota ('ι') one by one of which carries out a distinct manipulation of the 1600 bits state matrix[1]. Figure 2 shows a block data chart of the SHA3 Keccak.

The proposed system (means SHA3-512 keccak function implemented in Artix-7 FPGA) block diagram and circuit Diagram shows in Figs. 3 and 4. Here this figures shows input components are byte num, clk, in, in_ready, is_last, reset. Then input or block size is given to keccak function 576 bits or 72 bytes, i.e. input[575:0] it shows in Figs. 3 and 4. For security purpose it rotates 24 rounds.

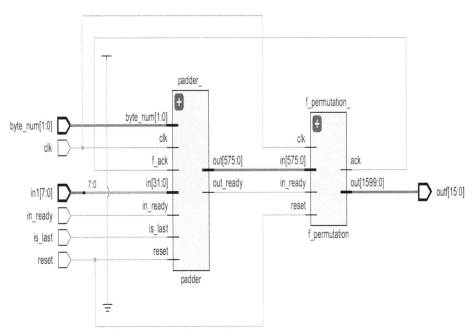

Fig. 3. Proposed System Block Diagram

After that the output of proposed system is 512 bits. It shows Figs. 4 and 5 output [511:0]. That's why this algorithm called SHA3-512bits. Internal state bit size is 1600 bits this is also output of keccak it show in figures out [1599:00].

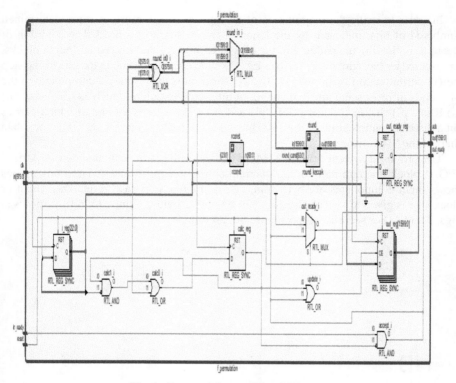

Fig. 4. Proposed System Circuit Diagram

4 Experimental Results

The SHA-3-512 Keccak algorithm schematic diagram as shown in Fig. 5, is designed and written in Verilog code, simulated, and synthesized in VIVADO 2017.2 version, implemented on the Artix-7 edgeA7 xc7a35tftg256-1 FPGA project part. From Fig. 6 is FPGA hardware Implementation setup. The input is 72 bytes later proposed method gives output is 512 bits after that displays the out of SHA3-512 and Fig. 7 also display the output representation in LED format. LED ON means '1', LED OFF means '0'. Here shows at a time 16 bits output shows i.e. "0001011100110100". After implementation on FPGA it generated area and power utilization summary. That summary shows in Tables 2 and 3. In Table 2, area occupies in the term of LUT 2493 slices, and flip-flops (FF) were used in 1876. Also these values represented graphically (see Fig. 8). In Table 3, dynamic power consumed is 191.850 W, and static power consumed is 0.486 W. And also these values represented graphically (see Fig. 9.)

A Novel Approach of SHA-3-512bits Using Keccak Technique 223

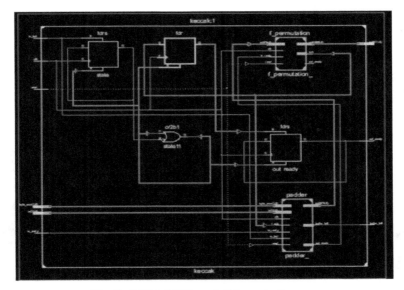

Fig. 5. SHA3-512 Keccak Schematic diagram.

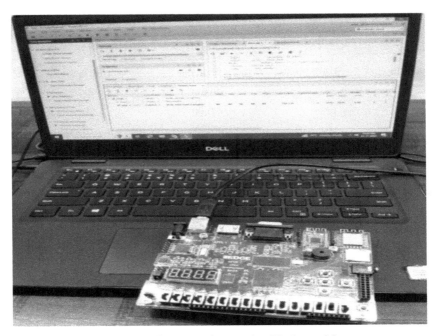

Fig. 6. FPGA Output Implementation Display and Setup

Fig. 7. FPGA Output of SHA3-512

Table 2. Resource Utilization of FPGA ARTIX-7

Resource	Utilization	Available	Utilization%
LUT	2493	20800	11.99
FF	1876	41600	4.51
IO	30	170	17.65
BUFG	1	32	3.13

5 Results in Discussion

In the findings discussion, we contrasted our work—the SHA3-512 Keccak algorithm—with the five designs displayed in Table 4. Based on Table 4, all five of the designs use expensive FPGAs, such as Virtex 7 and 5, Altera, and Arria 10. However, when comparing these five designs to ours, we find that ours is much more economical. We analyzed the space occupied by 5 designs. We recommended [3] design occupies 8148 LUTs, while our work occupies 2493 LUTs, so our recommended design outperformed [3] design. In terms of power consumption, we believe our proposed approach outperforms [3] design. Furthermore, space and power consumption outperform the [3] Virtex 5 architecture. Remaining design Table 4 shows power usage data that is not applicable (NA).

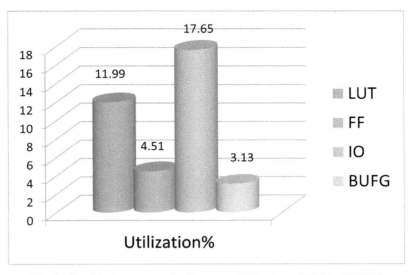

Fig. 8. Graphical representation Resource Utilization of FPGA ARTIX-7

Table 3. Power Analysis of FPGA ARTIX-7

Components	Power (W)
Dynamic Power	191.850
Signals:	92.589
Logic:	72.716
I/O:	26.546
Static Power	0.486
Total on chip power	192.334

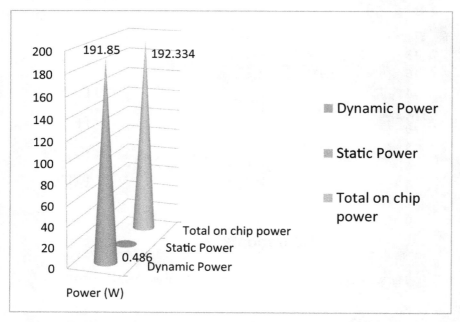

Fig. 9. Graphical representation Power Analysis of FPGA ARTIX-7

Table 4. Result comparison with several designs of area and power consumption metrics with my proposed design.

Design	FPGA Used	Area consumed	Power Consumption (W)
[1] Argyrios Sideris et al. Design	Virtex 7	1375	NA
[2] Dmytro Havrilov et al. Design	ALTERA	2073	NA
[3] Igor L.R. Azevedo et al. Design	Virtex 5	8148	197.221
[5] Minas Dasygenis et al. Design	Arria10	1422	NA
[11] S. Neelima et al. Design	Virtex 5	2400	NA
Proposed Work	**Artix 7**	**2493**	**192.334**

6 Conclusions and Future Work

Stronger cryptographic security is provided by SHA-3-512 bits as opposed to SHA1, SHA 2, and SHA3-256 bits. This paper describes a SHA-3-512bits hash function using Keccak Algorithm base on Sponge construction. The SHA3-512 function operates on a single instance, processing input messages at a rate of 72 bytes per 1096 cycles at 316.25 MHz and a 1600 bits data path with a round-iterative structure. The output is 32 bytes. The SHA-3-512bits is verified by VIVADO 2017.2 version software with hardware implementation on FPGA ARTIX-7 device. Proposed system occupied an area of 2493 LUTs, Flip-Flops 1876 and IO 17.65% utilized. Proposed system Power Consumption is 192.334 W. For Implementation on Artix-7 FPGA the proposed system became cost efficient system. Finally the proposed system is area, power and cost efficient design. The proposed system limits to area of 2493, Power Consumption is 192.334 W. In Future scope, for better performance will use another cryptographic algorithm combined with SHA3 Keccak function.

Acknowledgement. The authors would like to thank the Indian Institute of Technology (IIT) - Tirupati, which granted permission for use of the VLSI Laboratory for hardware implementation on FPGA board.

Funding. This research work has no funding resource.

Conflict of Interest. The authors of this research declare that they have no conflicts of interest.

References

1. Sideris, A., Sanida, T., Dasygenis, M.: Hardware acceleration design of the SHA-3 for high throughput and low area on FPGA. J. Cryptograph. Eng. **14**, 193 (2023). https://doi.org/10.1007/s13389-023-00334-0
2. Havrilov, D., Volovyk, A., Yarovyi, A., et al.: Hardware implementation of SHA algorithms on different FPGA and speed comparison. In: 2020 IEEE Ukrainian Microwave Week (UkrMW) (2020). https://doi.org/10.1109/UkrMW49653.2020.9252678
3. Azevedo, I.L.R., Nery, A.S., Sena, A.C.: A SHA-3 co-processor for IoT applications. In: 5th Workshop on Communication Networks and Power Systems (WCNPS 2020). IEEE (2020). https://doi.org/10.1109/WCNPS50723.2020.9263759
4. Akiya, Y., Le, K.T., Luong, M., et al.: SHA-3-LPHP: hardware acceleration of SHA-3 for low-power high-performance systems. In: 2021 IEEE International Symposium on Software Reliability Engineering Workshops (ISSREW) (2021). https://doi.org/10.1109/ISSREW53611.2021.00107
5. Sideris, A., Sanida, T., Dasygenis, M.: High throughput pipelined implementation of the SHA-3 cryptoprocessor. In: 2020 32nd International Conference on Microelectronics (ICM). IEEE (2020). https://doi.org/10.1109/ICM50269.2020.9331803
6. Jasim, A.H., Hammood, D.A.M., Al-Askery, A.: Design and implementation secure hash algorithm 3 (SHA-3) using FPGA. In: 2023 Third International Conference on Advances in Electrical, Computing, Communication and Sustainable Technologies (ICAECT). IEEE (2023) https://doi.org/10.1109/ICAECT57570.2023.10117657

7. Asmae, Z., Nabih, E.O.: Performances of the SHA-3 candidates implemented in the Zynq-7000 Artix-7 FPG. In: 2020 International Symposium on Advanced Electrical and Communication Technologies (ISAECT). IEEE (2020). https://doi.org/10.1109/ISAECT50560.2020.9523679
8. Bensalem, H., Blaquière, Y., Savaria, Y.: An efficient open CL-based implementation of a SHA-3 co-processor on an FPGA-centric platform. IEEE Trans. Circuits Syst. II Exp. Briefs **70**(3), 1144 (2023). https://doi.org/10.1109/TCSII.2022.3223179
9. Wang, Z., Wang, S., Wang, L., Yao, Q.: An instruction extension based SHA-3 algorithm co-processor design scheme. In: 2023 3rd International Symposium on Computer Technology and Information Science (ISCTIS). IEEE (2023). https://doi.org/10.1109/ISCTIS58954.2023.10213096
10. Camacho-Ruiz, E., Sánchez-Solano, S., Macarena, C., et al.: A complete SHA-3 hardware library based on a high efficiency Keccak design. In: 2023 IEEE Nordic Circuits and Systems Conference (NorCAS) (2023). https://doi.org/10.1109/NorCAS58970.2023.10305448
11. Neelima, S., Brindha, R.: 512 bit-SHA3 design approach and implementation on field programmable gate array. Int. J. Reconfig. Embed. Syst. (IJRES) **8**(3), 169–174 (2019). https://doi.org/10.11591/ijres.v8.i3.pp169-174
12. Agasthya Holla, M., Shetty, A.S., et al.: Implementation of a modified SHA-3 Hash Function on FPGA. In: 2023 4th IEEE Global Conference for Advancement in Technology (GCAT) (2023). https://doi.org/10.1109/GCAT59970.2023.10353241
13. Chowdhury, A., Kumar, U.: Performance analysis of Keccak f-[1600]. Int. J. Adv. Comput. Sci. Appl. (2013)
14. Advances in Information, Communication and Cybersecurity. Springer Science and Business Media LLC (2022)
15. Buchanan, W.J., Li, S., Asif, R.: Lightweight cryptography methods. J. Cyber Secur. Technol. (2018)

Cooperative Spectrum Sensing in Cognitive Radio Network Using Adaptive Walruses Optimization Algorithm

D. Raghunatha Rao[1]($\boxtimes$), T. Jayachandra Prasad[2], D. Satyanarayana[3], Saritha Bai Gaddale[4], Kadiyala Raghavendra[1], and T. Hussaini[1]

[1] ECE Department, SVR Engineering College, Affiliated to JNTUA, Nandyal, A.P, India
draghunatharao7@gmail.com
[2] RGM College of Engineering and Technology (Autonomous), Nandyal, A.P, India
[3] ECE Department, RGM College of Engineering and Technology (Autonomous), Nandyal, A.P, India
[4] Digital Assistant, Panchayat Raj Department, Nandyal, Andhra Pradesh, India

Abstract. The cognitive radio network (CRN) is developed as an important technology to future wireless communication and mobile devices. In CRN, the spectrum sensing serves as the fundamental task in secondary user (SU). The cooperative spectrum sensing is commonly employed by cognitive radios (CR), which effectively used available spectrum. In this, the spectrum sensor controls the activities of secondary user to avoid collisions with primary user (PU). Therefore, this work devised the cooperative spectrum sensing of CRN using the novel optimization method. At the beginning, the system model is created, which includes the PU and the SU. Furthermore, the test statistics for the SU signal are performed. The signal from each SU is fused on a fusion center with the decisions of signal elements including signal energy, Eigen statistics, and matching filter. The proposed Adaptive walrus optimization algorithm (Adaptive WaOA) is used to determine the weights, and then the decision is obtained. Furthermore, the evaluation metrics like probability of detection (PD), probability of false alarm (PFA) and sensing time (T) are considered to evaluate the execution of proposed method and hence reduce the sensing delay, sensing errors with the finest outputs like 0.885, 0.176 and 205.5 m sec are obtained in Rician channel environment.

Keywords: Cognitive radio network · Walruses optimization algorithm · Spectrum sensing (SS) · Cooperative spectrum sensing CSS) · primary user (PU) · Secondary user (SU)

1 Introduction

With advancements in wireless communications networks in the past decade, the goal of the research has shifted for achieving the increased connectivity, decreased complexity, and lower latency, while offering high-speed network services. The exponential rise of mobile devices and growing data requirements pose a challenge for mobile network operators [1, 2]. Moreover, fifth generation (5G) refers to the next-generation mobile networks, which will provide a greater capacity and quicker data speeds [3]. Radio spectrum became the most essential assets with the introduction of wireless communication. Still this resource has been underutilized throughout the duration of wireless communications. To address the issue of limited spectrum availability, the cognitive radio (CR) with extended spectrum sensing and spectrum sharing capabilities was developed with limited radio resources [4, 5]. The CR is described as a wireless method that allows a unlicensed user to effectively operated a licensed range of frequency spectrum. Furthermore, it overcomes the shortages in wireless spectrum without interfering with licensed user [5]. SU are the unlicensed users, who operate in the licensed spectrum of CR and the SU received lower priority than licensed users. Furthermore, the licensed users are known as PU, since they are allotted to the frequency spectrum. The primary task of CR is to reduce the ratio of interference among the two groups of users. Hence, the available spectrum was found in efficient manner [6].

CSS is a technique used in CRN to improve the detection of available spectrum bands [7]. In this approach, multiple radio nodes collaborate to sense and share information about the spectrum usage. It likely involves selecting and validating sensors from a crowd of distributed devices to collaborate in the process of spectrum sensing, ultimately aiming to improve the efficacy and accuracy of spectrum management in wireless networks. By combining the sensing results from multiple nodes, the network can make more accurate decisions about which frequencies are available for use. Cooperative spectrum sensing involves multiple sensing devices working together to make a collective decision about the availability of a spectrum band [8]. This is particularly useful in situations where individual sensors may have limitations or may be prone to errors. Any optimization algorithm in practical cognitive radio systems may involve challenges related to computational complexity, real-time constraints, and the need for accurate channel models [9]. Additionally, validation through simulations and real-world experiments is typically required to assess its effectiveness in specific scenarios.

It is critical to demonstrate that the additional resources and infrastructure of licensed PU are not required, while it was continuously operated with unlicensed SU. Spectrum sensing refers to a capacity of SU, which identifies the active SU in the frequency spectrum to continuously eliminate the interference on their communication [5]. Individual or non-cooperative spectrum sensing is done by a single SU, while CSS is conducted by a collection of SU. Due to the incorrect and unreliable fading and shadowing, the SS of single SU is decreased. This issue can be reduced by adopting the CNN [10]. Spectrum sensing involves advanced methods such as energy detector and cyclo stationary detector [11]. For a constant time slot, if the T was increased and then transmission time was dropped, hence overall throughput was decreased [11].

Probabilistic spectrum access (PSA) in CRN is another solution to the issues of spectrum energy detection [5]. This method predicts the channel circumstances and decides whether the channel is active or vacant. Typical findings cannot address the possibility and uncertainty of false alarm, when calculating the channel state. Therefore, an efficient optimization technique is required for cooperative spectrum sensing. Moreover, the optimization tactics based on evolutionary algorithms were more successful for cooperative spectrum sensing in CR [12]. The primary goal of this research is to model the spectrum sensing of CRN model. In the beginning, a system model is developed. Following that, the test statistics of cooperative spectrum sensing are computed. The signal from each SU is fused at the fusion center via the signal component like signal energy, Eigen statistics and matching filter. The proposed adaptive WaOA determines the weights. Finally, the decision is attained, which offered the spectrum sensing of CRN.

The important contribution of this work is described as follows:

- **Proposed adaptive WaOA based spectrum sensing in CRN:** In spectrum sensing of CRN, the weights of the signal components are created using the proposed adaptive WaOA. Moreover, the merging process of WaOA with adaptive concept formed the proposed adaptive WaOA.

The remainder of this work is arranged into five sections. Section 2 defines motivation, literature survey and challenges of existing approaches. The system model of CRN is carried in Sect. 3 and Sect. 4 includes the proposed adaptive WaOA based spectrum sensing. Section 5 describes experimental results and conclusion is given in Sect. 6.

2 Motivation

SS is a critical component of CR for avoiding harmful interference in licensed users and identifying the accessible spectrum for better operation. For this purpose, numerous approaches are employed. Still, the processing speed was less and complex computation process. Hence, the optimization-based spectrum sensing is developed in this work.

2.1 Literature Survey

Lee, S., et al. [12] developed the Ordering and Selecting of Observations (OSO) for SS of CRN. It performed effectively for spectrum sensing on impulsive noise conditions with Rayleigh fading. It attained better detection performance; still, the computational complexity was more. Devi, M.K., et al. [13] introduced the Spectrum binary particle Swarm Optimization (Spec BPSO) model-based SS process of CRN. Cluster Based Cooperative Spectrum Sensing (CBCSS) was employed for developing the effectiveness of SU, while decreasing the channel congestion. In handovers, it has a high throughput of channel allocation in SU. However, it has higher hand off delay value.

Nasser, A., et al. [14] devised the Artificial Neural Network (ANN) model for Hybrid Spectrum Sensing (HSS) in CRN. Here, data was made up of the Test Statistics (TSs) from multiple detectors. With an increased number of detectors, it reached a high detection rate. It was unable to sustain high accuracy as the number of nodes was increased. Okediran, O.S., et al. [15] developed the Enhanced Spectrum Sensing Technique with Energy Harvesting (ESSTEH) for the spectrum sensing of CRN. With a higher charging rate, the PU signal was detected efficiently over a Rayleigh fading channel. It failed to control the probability of detection, while the constellation size of the modulation was enhanced. Wu, Qingying, et al. [21] minimized the energy consumption with certain probability of detection and false alarm, but it involves multiple constraints and parameters.

2.2 Challenges

The challenges faced by existing techniques for the spectrum sensing of CRN are described as follows:

- The Spec BPSO and queuing model [13] decreased the unnecessary handoff latency. Still, the SU transmission was suffered by the regular arrival of the PU.
- The ANN-based HSS designed [14] has a high PD and a low PFA, but it required more time for large number of detectors.
- Though an increased number of cognitive radios enhanced the chance of detection in ESSTEH [15] based spectrum sensing process. Still, the entire system was impacted by the rise of cognitive radios.
- Spectrum sensing in CRN has grown significantly as it addressed the issue of spectrum scarcity. The key problem of spectrum sensing was the lower efficiency in spectrum sharing and the increased PFA.
- Hence, the adaptive walruses optimization based spectrum sensing is developed in this work.

3 System Model for CRN

All cognitive radios in cooperative spectrum sensing measure the licensed spectrums and make different decisions [16]. Figure 1 depicts the cooperative spectrum sensing system. The CRN is often made up of many PUs and SUs, in which SUs is employed for sharing the multichannel spectrum resources to PUs. The SUs shares the sensed data and they can optimize the individual spectrum sensing operation. Due to the unknown channel, the SU is able to make a decision after sensing various channels. As a result, the channel exchanging is specified by a Markov chain, which solves the partial observability issues. Moreover, every SU is coordinated by their respective time slot. The time slot design is separated as two intervals like sensing and transmission. At the initial

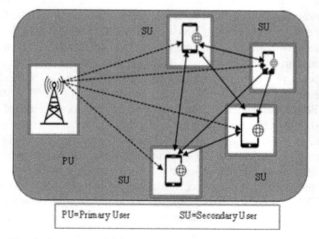

Fig. 1. System model for cooperative spectrum sensing system

period, every SU detects a slot individually. The SU transmit its own data to numerous users and integrating to the received data. At last, every SU communicates its decision. Afterwards, the acknowledgement signal is sent to confirm whether the communication was successful or not.

4 Cooperative Spectrum Sensing (CSS) Using Proposed Adaptive WaOA

Spectrum sensing is the ability of SU to recognize active SU in frequency spectrum in order to neglect the interruption of communication. To overcome the spectrum sharing problem, an effective optimization algorithm named Adaptive WaOA is proposed. Optimization is the process of adjustment of the parameters to achieve the most optimal design. Initially, the system model considered the PU with the absence or presence of signal. Thereafter, the test statistics for the cooperative spectrum sensing of SU is carried out. Then the signal from the individual SU is fused at the fusion center, which includes the decision of signal components such as Signal energy, Test statistics-based Eigen statistics [17] and matched filter [18]. Cognitive radio nodes collaborate in sensing the spectrum and sharing their results [7].

The basic idea of the proposed work is based on gannet optimization algorithm can optimize the cooperative sensing strategy, determining which nodes should participate, how to weight their contributions, and how to combine their results for improved accuracy. The sensed data from multiple nodes is then fused together for decision-making. After that, the weights are determined by the proposed Adaptive WaOA. Then, final decision is obtained. Here, the CR contains of q transmitters and r receivers, they are termed as transmitters and the sensors. Moreover, the cooperative spectrum sensing is displayed in Fig. 2.

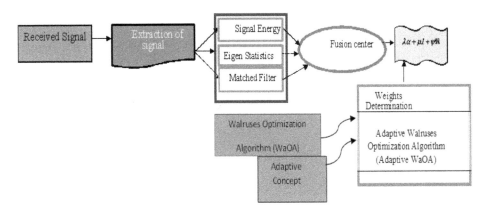

Fig. 2. Cooperative Spectrum Sensing with adaptive WaOA

Adaptive WaOA depends on population size, where the walruses are serving as search members. Every walrus in the WaOA indicates a probable solution to an optimization problem. As a result, the placement of walrus finds the candidate numbers for a problem variable. The communication [17] amongst q transmitters and r sensors is done through radio channels. As a result, the transmission among the transmitters and receivers is preceded. The CR searches the accessible channels and allows a connection, while a free channel is found. Moreover, r sensors of a CR obtain the data sent from a transmitter. The CR has the ability of detecting the occupied as well as the unoccupied channel's capacity. Furthermore, data sample matrix T is devised via the samples gather from a transmitter. Here, the data sample matrix T is expressed as,

$$T = [T_{tu}]_{w,x}; (1 \leq t \leq w); (1 \leq u \leq x) \tag{1}$$

where, T_{tu} implies the uth data sample of tth sensor. The entire count of x data samples are received in the sensors. The transmitters send a signal and this transmitted signal is denoted by a signal matrix U. Therefore, the transmitted signal matrix is expressed by,

$$U = [U_{cu}]_{q \times x} \tag{2}$$

where, the entire counting of transmitters is specified by q, x implies the entire count of data samples. U_{cu} denote a signal of cth transmitter. Therefore, the communication is occurred on a radio channel and it is followed over an un unoccupied band. Following to transmission, a receiver receives both the real and imaginary signals and analyses these signals using a low pass filter. Here, a desired data is represented by Z and data sample matrix is expressed by,

$$T = [B * Z] + H \tag{3}$$

where, B and H implies a channel gain as well as thermal noise matrix. Hence, a channel matrix is given by,

$$B = [B_{tc}]_{r \times q} \tag{4}$$

where, B_{tc} indicates a channel gain in between of tth sensor as well as c^{th} transmitter. Thermal noise affects signals sent across radio channels in CR. The noise H is employed while modeling a channel matrix T. Hence, thermal noise matrix is given by,

$$H = [H_{tu}]_{w \times x} \tag{5}$$

where, H_{tu} implies a thermal noise from a channel, which received the data from t^{th} sensor. The data sample matrix is derived to compute an Eigen statistics and signal energy. Here, covariance matrix E is estimated through channel matrix T. Moreover, the receiving signal for ensemble covariance matrix is given by,

$$E = \text{Expected}\left[TT^{+}\right] \tag{6}$$

where, Expected [] defines an expected operator and T^{+} represents the conjugate and transposing of T. Generally, ensemble covariance matrix is unknown, which is modified with maximum likelihood estimate (MLE).

$$E = \frac{1}{x}\left[T \ T^{+}\right] \tag{7}$$

From covariance matrix E, signal energy and Eigen statistics are estimated. Hence, the past and present input energy statistics are utilized to validate spectrum availability. Here, Eigen values are specified by,

$$\{\alpha_1 \geq \alpha_{2\geq}...\alpha_w\} \tag{8}$$

Hence, energy statistics α is expressed by,

$$\alpha = \frac{\alpha_1}{1/w \sum_{t=1}^{w} \alpha_t} \tag{9}$$

where, α_t describes the Eigen value of tth sensor. The Eigen statistics I is estimated by,

$$I = \frac{1}{q \times n^2} \sum_{t=1}^{w} \alpha_t \tag{10}$$

where, n represents the thermal noise factor.

Furthermore, matched filter $\Re$ compares an incoming signal and the pilot samples obtained from a same emitter [18]. The signal is denoted in present state, if it exceeds a threshold. Furthermore, the test statistics are expressed as,

$$\chi^{mf} = \frac{1}{x} \sum_{a=1}^{x} \delta(a) b_\gamma^*(a) \tag{11}$$

where, x denotes the sample counts and $\delta(a)$ represents a vector of sample. Furthermore, b_y specifies the pilot samples. Moreover, a test statistic χ^{mf} is compared to the threshold value for sensing decision:

$$\chi^{mf} < \eta^{mf} \text{ then absent of PU} \tag{12}$$

$$\chi^{mf} > \eta^{mf} \text{ then presense of PU} \tag{13}$$

where, the threshold is given as η^{mf}, which is based on a noise level of received signal. The matched filter required a limited sample for obtaining the suitable performance.

4.1 Fusion Center

Fusion center is responsible for sensor scheduling in noting the sensing data and spectrum availability sensing. In fusion center, the signal elements like signal energy, Eigen statistics, and matching filter and their corresponding weights are fused to form the final decision. Here, the fused outcome is represented as A, which is given by,

$$A = \lambda\alpha + \mu I + \psi\Re \tag{14}$$

where, λ, μ and ψ implies the weights of signal energy α, Eigen statistics I and matched filter $\Re$.

4.2 Solution Encoding

Solution encoding for spectrum sensing of CRN is portrayed in Fig. 3. Here, index weights of signal energy, Eigen statics and matched filter is indicted as λ, μ and ψ. Moreover, the solution encoding presented a 1×3 dimensional solution for effectual spectrum sensing process.

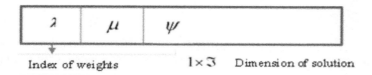

Fig. 3. Solution Encoding

4.3 Fitness Computation

In fitness computation, PD and PFA considered. The curve that is drawn between these two metrics is called receiver operating characteristic (ROC). Moreover, the area under this curve (AUC) specifies the fitness function. Moreover, the value of AUC is set as 1.

Proposed Adaptive WaOA for Weights Estimation
The adaptive WaOA was created by combining WaOA [19] and the adaptive concept. It is a metaheuristic algorithm used in cognitive radio to build the relationship between adjusting the parameters and desired performance measure. The nature inspired walruses algorithm dynamically adjusts its parameters during the optimization process to balance exploration, migration and exploitation [20]. It is based on the behavior of walruses, which are marine mammals known for their adaptability to changing environmental conditions. WaOA was introduced as a bio-inspired optimization algorithm to address complex optimization problems. The use of an adaptive Walrus Optimization Algorithm in cooperative spectrum sensing could mean that the algorithm dynamically adjusts its search strategies or parameters to improve the efficacy and accuracy of SS in different wireless environments.

The key features and principles of the Adaptive Walrus Optimization Algorithm

- **Inspiration from Walrus Behavior:** WaOA draws inspiration from the behavior of walruses, which are known for their ability to adapt to changing conditions in their habitat, such as changes in the availability of ice floes for resting and feeding.
- **Adaptive Strategy:** One of the distinguishing features of WaOA is its adaptive strategy. The algorithm dynamically adjusts its parameters and behavior during the optimization process to balance exploration and exploitation.
- **Search Operators:** WaOA uses search operators inspired by the movements of walruses in their natural habitat. These movements include swimming, diving, resting, and foraging. These operations are used to explore and exploit the search space effectively.

- **Diversity Maintenance:** A key aspect of WaOA is maintaining diversity in the population to prevent premature convergence to suboptimal solutions. This is achieved through the adaptive strategy and the use of various search operators.
- **Termination Criterion:** Like other optimization algorithms, WaOA includes a termination criterion to stop the search when a stopping condition is met. Common criteria include a maximum number of iterations or a target fitness level.

Features: WaOA is based on walrus habits. Walruses are sociable creatures, which spending majority of their lives on sea ice. It has large tusks with a long canine weight up to 5.4 kg and length up to 1 m. While the weather changes or ice melting happened in summer time, walruses migrate towards the outcrops or rocky beaches. This movement involved a vast aggregation of walruses. The primary factors for WaOA are feeding, migrating, fighting and leaving. Furthermore, WaOA performed effectively in real-life circumstances. WaOA implementation can be divided into three stages such as exploration, migration, and exploitation.

Moreover, the WaOA included the adaptive approach to overcome the computing challenges. As a result, the adaptive WaOA is utilized for rapid convergence.

Step 1: Initialization
WaOA depends on population size, where the walruses are serving as search members. Every walrus in the WaOA indicates a probable solution to an optimization problem. As a result, the placement of every walrus finds the candidate numbers for a problem variable. Hence, every walrus is specified by a vector, whereas the walrus population is represented by a population matrix. At the initial stage, the walrus populations are generated in random way. The WaOA population matrix is determined as follows:

$$D = \begin{bmatrix} D_1 \\ \vdots \\ D_h \\ \vdots \\ D_Q \end{bmatrix}_{Q \times i} = \begin{bmatrix} d_{1,1} & \cdots & d_{1,g} & \cdots & d_{1,i} \\ \vdots & \ddots & \vdots & \ddots & \vdots \\ d_{h,1} & & d_{h,g} & & d_{h,i} \\ \vdots & \ddots & \vdots & \ddots & \vdots \\ d_{Q,1} & \cdots & d_{Q,g} & \cdots & d_{Q,i} \end{bmatrix}_{Q \times i} \tag{15}$$

where, the population of walrus is denoted by D, D_h implies the hth walrus, $d_{h,g}$ represents the gth decision variable in h^{th} walrus and counting of decision variables is specified as i. Every walrus implies the candidate solution, whereas the objective function evaluated through the decision variables, which is expressed by,

$$L = \begin{bmatrix} L_1 \\ \vdots \\ L_h \\ \vdots \\ L_Q \end{bmatrix}_{Q \times 1} = \begin{bmatrix} L(D_1) \\ \vdots \\ L(D_h) \\ \vdots \\ L(D_Q) \end{bmatrix}_{Q \times 1} \tag{16}$$

where, the vector of objective function is represented by L and L_h implies the objective function of hth walrus

Step 2: Fitness Determination
The fitness function detects the best solution in efficient manner. Section 4.3 describes the fitness parameters.

Step 3: Feeding Strategy (Exploration)
In exploration process, the massive walrus with longer tusks directs the other walruses to search the food. The quality of the candidate solutions is comparable to the length of the walrus tusks. Hence, the ideal candidate solution with the highest objective value is the stronger walrus in a group. This walrus search behavior results in a wide range of scanned regions in the search space. The upgraded location of walrus is given as,

$$d_{h,g}^{G_1} = d_{h,g} + rand_{h,g} \cdot (J_g - N_{h,g} \cdot d_{h,g}) \tag{17}$$

$$D_h = \begin{cases} D_h^{V_1}, & L_h^{V_1} < L_h \\ D_h, & \text{Else} \end{cases} \tag{18}$$

where $D_h^{V_1}$ represents the upgraded location of hth walrus on 1st phase, $d_{h,g}^{G_1}$ implies its gth dimension, $L_h^{V_1}$ denotes the objective function, $rand_{h,g}$ is a random number in between of [0, 1] Furthermore, the best candidate solution is denoted by J_g and $N_{h,g}$ specifies the integers, which is selected as a random number of [1, 2].

Here, $rand_{h,g}$ is considered as the adaptive parameter, which is given by,

$$rand_{h,g} = N_{h,g} * \left(C\_up_{local,g}^s - C\_low_{local,g}^s \right) \frac{Iter}{Max_{Iter}} \tag{19}$$

where, s implies the iteration counts, the lower and upper bounds of gth variable are denoted by C_low and C_up. Here, $C\_low_{local,h}^s$ and $C\_up_{local,g}^s$ implies the local lower and local upper bounds in g^{th} variable. Moreover, $Iter$ implies the iteration and the maximum count of iterations are specified by Max_{Iter}

Step 4: Migration
The migration technique is utilized to find suitable location of Walrus. According to this standard, each walrus moves to a different position inside the search space. Consequently, the new position raises a objective function, while it changes the previous walrus location.

$$d_{h,g}^{V_2} = \begin{cases} d_{h,g} + rand_{h,g} \cdot (d_{j,g} - N_{h,g} \cdot d_{h,g}), & L_k < L_h; \\ d_{h,g} + rand_{h,g} \cdot (d_{h,g} - d_{j,g}), & \text{Else} \end{cases} \tag{20}$$

$$D_h = \begin{cases} D_h^{V_2}, & L_h^{V_2} < L_h \\ D_h, & \text{Else} \end{cases} \tag{21}$$

where, the upgraded location of hth walrus in the 2nd phase is denoted by $D_h^{V_2}, d_{h,g}^{V_2}$ depicts the gth dimension $L_h^{V_2}$ represents the objective function on 2nd phase, $D_j, j \in \{1, 2, ..., Q\}$ and $j \neq h$, denotes the location of hth walrus in migration stage, $d_{j,g}$ implies their g^{th} dimension, and L_h shows the objective value.

Step 5: Exploitation (Escaping and Fighting Against Predators)
The fighting and escaping strategy cause the walruses to change the location in the neighborhood of its current location. Then upgraded location of the walrus is stated as,

$$d_{h,g}^{V_3} = d_{h,g} + \left(C\_low_{local,g}^s + \left(C\_up_{local,g}^s - rand . C\_low_{local,g}^s\right)\right) \quad (22)$$

$$Local\ Bound : \begin{cases} C\_low_{local,g}^s = \dfrac{C\_low_g}{s} \\ C\_up_{local,g}^s = \dfrac{C\_up_g}{s} \end{cases} \quad (23)$$

$$D_h = \begin{cases} D_h^{V_3}, & L_h^{V_3} < L_h \\ D_h, & Else \end{cases} \quad (24)$$

where $D_h^{V_3}$ indicated the location of hth walrus in 3rd phase, $d_{h,g}^{V_3}$ implies its gth dimension and $L_h^{V_3}$ denotes the objective function.

Step 6: Re Evaluation of Fitness:
The fitness function is recomputed still, the finest solution is reached. That is repeat step 3 if the finest solution not accomplished. The solution with less fitness is considered as finest one.

Step 7: Termination:
The optimization attained the termination stage, till the ideal solution is achieved.

5 Results and Discussion

This section covers the effectiveness of adaptive WaOA for spectrum sensing of CRN. Here, various methods are utilized to compare the work of the proposed model. Moreover, the performance valuing measures, comparative techniques, implementing tool and the comparative outcomes are also described here.

5.1 Experimental Set-Up

The proposed adaptive WaOA based spectrum sensing of CRN is implemented in Matlab tool.

5.2 Evaluation Measures

The fulfillment of proposed adaptive WaOA is valued by PD, PFA and T.

- **PD** is the possibility that the PU sends the data through a licensed channel and the SU accurately recognizes the PU signal.
- **PFA** is the possibility that the SU recognizes the presence of PU, while there is absent PU at that time.
- **T is** the time period needed for sensing the spectrum is termed as sensing time. Moreover, a rapid sensing time is preferable for reliable operation of spectrum. The sensing period is expressed as

$$T = -\ln(PFA)/PD\,(V) \tag{25}$$

where, V is the average rate of samples taken per milli seconds.

5.3 Comparative Methods

The existing techniques like ordering and selecting of observations (OSO) [12], spectrum binary particle swarm optimization(Spec BPSO) [13], ANN model for hybrid spectrum sensing in CRN [14] and enhanced spectrum sensing technique with energy harvesting (ESSTEH) [15] are utilized for the comparative performance of adaptive WaOA in CRN. In comparative assessment, performance of adaptive WaOA and existing methods are obtained using PD, PFA and T. Here, the outcomes are attained for Rayleigh and Rician channels. When there is no line of sight propagation Rayleigh distribution occurs, if there is a line of sight propagation between transmitter and receiver Rician distribution was considered.

Assessment for Rayleigh Channel
Comparative performance of adaptive WaOA based SS in CRN using Rayleigh channel is depicted in Fig. 4. Here, the graph is plotted amongst the Signal to noise ratio (SNR) and the performance estimating measures like PD, PFA and T. Figure 4a) represents the comparative valuation regards to PD, Consider the SNR value = −5, then PD of adaptive WaOA is 0.396, whereas the existing approaches like OSO, Spec BPSO, ANN and ESSTEH attained the probability of detection of 0.0922, 0.0005, 0.004, 0. 154. The assessment in accordance with PFA is portrayed in Fig. 4b). For SNR value = 10, of proposed adaptive WaOA got PFA of 0.087, while PFA of OSO is 0.201, Spec BPSO is 0.094, ANN is 0.105 and ESSTEH is 0.0978. Likewise, Fig. 4c) Deliberates the estimation in terms of sensing time. Consider the SNR of 15, the sensing time of OSO, Spec BPSO, ANN, and ESSTEH and proposed adaptive WaOA are 312.5 m s, 309.9 m s, 306.7 m s, 300.2 m s and 296.3 m s.

Assessment for Rician Channel
Comparative estimation of proposed adaptive WaOA in spectrum sensing of CRN using Rician channel is portrayed in Fig. 5. Here, the comparative performance regarding to probability of detection is displayed in Fig. 5a).For the SNR value = −10, proposed adaptive WaOA got the probability of detection of 0.195, while the OSO, Spec BPSO,

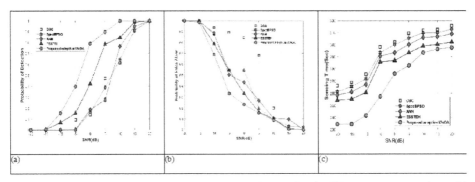

Fig. 4. Comparative evaluation of proposed adaptive WaOA in CRN spectrum sensing with Rayleigh channels a) Probability of detection b) Probability of false alarm c) Sensing time

ANN and ESSTEH obtained the probability of detection of 0.0943, 0.0876, 0.0015, 0.0036. Figure 5b) represents the estimation of adaptive WaOA in terms of PFA. While considering the SNR value = −5, the PFA of 0.887, 0.646, 0.595, 0.548 and 0.457 are obtained by OSO, Spec BPSO, ANN, ESSTEH and proposed adaptive WaOA. Moreover, Fig. 5c) depicts the assessment regards to sensing time. For the SNR of 10, the sensing time of proposed adaptive WaOA is 197.8 m sec, whereas the sensing time of OSO is 215.6 m s, Spec BPSO is 212.8 m s, ANN is 206.8 m s and ESSTEH is 201.4 m s.

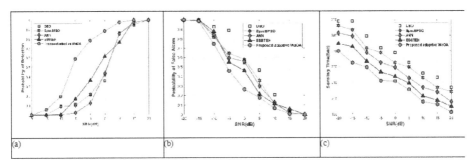

Fig. 5. Comparative evaluation of proposed adaptive WaOA in CRN spectrum sensing with Rician channels a) Probability of detection b) Probability of false alarm c) Sensing time

Comparative Discussions

The correlative discussion of proposed adaptive WaOA based spectrum sensing of CRN using Rayleigh and Rician channels are described in Table 1. From this table, it is stated that, the finest outputs are attained in Rician channels. Here, the PD of adaptive WaOA is 0.885, while the OSO, Spec BPSO, ANN and ESSTEH got the probability of detection of 0.358, 0.421, 0.437 and 0.615. Moreover, the Probability of false alarm of proposed adaptive WaOA is 0.176, OSO is 0.465, Spec BPSO is 0.354, ANN is 0.298 and ESSTEH is 0.214. In addition, the sensing time of proposed adaptive WaOA is 205.5 m s, while the

OSO, Spec BPSO, ANN and ESSTEH attained the sensing time of 22.3 m s, 219.5 m s, 212.7 m s and 209.5 m s. Likewise, PD, PFA and T of adaptive WaOA in Rayleigh channel are 0.3968, 0.154 and 282.8 m s. Table 1 shows the comparative discussion for spectrum sensing in CRN using different metrics, which asses the performance of adaptive WaOA compared with existing methods. From this, it is also concluded that the adaptive WaOA gives efficient detection of secondary users and reduces the sensing time in the spectrum sensing process.

Table 1. Comparative Discussion for spectrum sensing in CRN

Variations	Metrics	OSO	Spec BPSO	ANN model for HSS	ESSTEH	Proposed Adaptive WaOA
Rayleigh channel environment	Probability of detection	0.0922	0.0005	0.0045	0.1547	0.3968
	Probability of false alarm	0.678	0.196	0.267	0.163	0.154
	Sensing time (m seconds)	309.6	312.8	300.2	293.3	282.8
Rician channel environment	Probability of detection	0.358	0.421	0.437	0.615	0.885
	Probability of false alarm	0.465	0.354	0.298	0.214	0.176
	Sensing time (m seconds)	222.3	219.5	212.7	209.5	205.5

6 Conclusions

The CRN made more effective utilization of wireless spectrum resources, which has received more attention in recent years. Moreover, it has been developed to address the spectrum shortage issues in wireless communication. With various wireless systems and dynamic spectrum access strategies, the CRN offers high bandwidth for mobile users. The CR frequently used the cooperative spectrum sensing, which efficiently use the available spectrum. This work develops cooperative spectrum sensing of CRN via the walruses optimization process to reduce the sensing time and sensing error. Reduction in sensing time allows more information to transmit and sensing error gives efficient detection of primary users in CRN. The system model is designed, which contains the PU and the SU. Furthermore, the SU signal's test statistics are evaluated. At the fusion center, the signal from each SU is fused with the decisions of all signals. The devised adaptive WaOA is utilized to identify the weights, and a decision is made to detect the spectrum to improve the spectrum utilization for next generation wireless communications. In future, this work will be improved by considering other hybrid optimization process and extracting more signal components.

References

1. Duong, T.Q., Vo, N.S.: Wireless communications and networks for 5G and beyond. Mobile Networks Appl. **24**, 443–446 (2019)
2. Gul, N., Ahmed, S., Elahi, A., Kim, S.M., Kim, J.: Optimal cooperative spectrum sensing based on butterfly optimization algorithm. CMC-Comput. Mater. Continua **71**(1), 369–387 (2022)
3. Ahmad, W.S.H.M.W., et al.: 5G technology: towards dynamic spectrum sharing using cognitive radio networks. IEEE Access **8**, 14460–14488 (2020)
4. Akyildiz, I.F., Lee, W.Y., Chowdhury, K.R.: CRAHNs: cognitive radio ad hoc networks. Ad Hoc Netw. **7**(5), 810–836 (2009)
5. Mustafa, A., Islam, M.N.U., Ahmed, S.: Dynamic spectrum sensing under crash and byzantine failure environments for distributed convergence in cognitive radio networks. IEEE Access **9**, 23153–23167 (2021)
6. Xin, C., Song, M.: Analysis of the on-demand spectrum access architecture for CBRS cognitive radio networks. IEEE Trans. Wirel. Commun. **19**(2), 970–978 (2019)
7. Rao, D.R., Prasad, T.J., Prasad, M.N.: Gannet optimization algorithm enabled framework for spectrum sensing in OFDM based CR network. Wirel. Networks, 1–10 (2023)
8. Rao, D.R., Prasad, T.J., Prasad, M.G.: Deep learning based cooperative spectrum sensing with crowd sensors using data cleansing algorithm. In: 2022 International Conference on Edge Computing and Applications (ICECAA), pp. 1276–1281. IEEE (2022)
9. Raghunatharao, D., Prasad, T.J., Prasad, M.G.: Adaptive rider grey wolf optimization enabled pilot-design for channel estimation in cognitive radio. In: International Conference on Computing Science, Communication and Security, pp. 100–116. Cham: Springer International Publishing (2022)
10. Liang, Y.C., Zeng, Y., Peh, E.C., Hoang, A.T.: Sensing-throughput tradeoff for cognitive radio networks. IEEE Trans. Wirel. Commun. **7**(4), 1326–1337 (2008)
11. Eappen, G., Shankar, T.: Multi-objective modified grey wolf optimization algorithm for efficient spectrum sensing in the cognitive radio network. Arab. J. Sci. Eng. **46**, 3115–3145 (2021)
12. Lee, S., Park, S.R., Kim, Y.H., Song, I.: Spectrum sensing for cognitive radio network with multiple receive antennas under impulsive noise environments. J. Commun. Networks **23**(3), 171–179 (2021)
13. Devi, M.K., Umamaheswari, K.: Optimization techniques for spectrum handoff in cognitive radio networks using cluster based cooperative spectrum sensing. Wirel. Netw. **27**, 2173–2192 (2021)
14. Nasser, A., Chaitou, M., Mansour, A., Yao, K.C., Charara, H.: A deep neural network model for hybrid spectrum sensing in cognitive radio. Wirel. Pers. Commun. **118**(1), 281–299 (2021)
15. Okediran, O.S., Ojo, F.K., Ojo, J.A., Oseni, O.F., Obanisola, O.O.: Enhancement of spectrum sensing technique with energy harvesting for cognitive radio network. Indonesian J. Electr. Eng. Comput. Sci. **28**(2), 810–819 (2022)
16. Liu, S., He, J., Wu, J.: Dynamic cooperative spectrum sensing based on deep multi-user reinforcement learning. Appl. Sci. **11**(4), 1884 (2021)

17. Chowdary, K.U., Rao, B.P.: Hybrid mixture model based on a hybrid optimization for spectrum sensing to improve the performance of MIMO–OFDM systems. Int. J. Pattern Recognit. Artif. Intell. **34**(07), 2058008 (2020)
18. Arjoune, Y., Kaabouch, N.: A comprehensive survey on spectrum sensing in cognitive radio networks: recent advances, new challenges, and future research directions. Sensors **19**(1), 126 (2019)
19. Trojovský, P., Dehghani, M.: Walrus optimization algorithm: a new bio-inspired metaheuristic algorithm (2022)
20. Han, M., Du, Z., Yuen, K.F., Zhu, H., Li, Y., Yuan, Q.: Walrus optimizer: a novel nature-inspired metaheuristic algorithm. Expert Syst. Appl. **239**, 122413 (2024)
21. Wu, Q., Ng, B.K., Lam, C.-T.: Energy-efficient cooperative spectrum sensing using machine learning algorithm. Sensors **22**(21), 8230 (2022)

Catalan's Conjecture and Elliptic Curve Cryptography (CCECC) Algorithm for Enhancing Data Security During Data Transmission in MANET

D. Eben Angel Pauline

Women's Christian College, Chennai, India
ebenangel@wcc.edu.in

Abstract. Security plays a major role in the processes of secured storage and secured data transmission in MANET due to the huge volume of users and their data. Moreover, MANET provides distributed services to their clients and their users anytime, anywhere. This is becoming a very challenging problem to provide secure storage and data communications. This is very important in this fast-paced internet world. Data security is provided through cryptographic algorithms such as key generation, encryption, and decryption. The prime numbers are determining the size of the secret key that is capable of providing more security to the user's data effectively. The enhancement of the prime number is helpful for encrypting the data securely. So that this research work concentrates on the prime number selection process by applying Catalan's conjecture and using the standard Elliptic Curve Cryptographic (CCECC) algorithm to achieve a better security level and efficiency in terms of encryption time, decryption time, and key generation time.

Keywords: MANET · Routing Protocol · Elliptic Curve Cryptography · Cryptography · Cryptanalysis

1 Introduction

Security is important for data transmission between people and computers due to the availability of large volumes of data with authorization and authentication (Baranov, 2018). Securing data transmission in MANET is challenging in today's fast-paced internet and MANET networks. Databases are necessary for various users to effectively store a large amount of data (Abdullah, 2020). Cryptography plays a major role in ensuring secured data transmission in MANET. Secured transmission and data security are important in MANET due to the availability of various industries, organizational users, and clients (Salari, 2019). The administrator permits the users to perform different responsibilities over the data accessibility. The classical techniques were used to protect the user's data (Darabkh, 2019). Several techniques resolve the security issues. Generally, encryption is the process of converting plain text into cipher text by incorporating a specific methodology (Huang, 2018). Similarly, the decryption process is the process of converting from cipher text to plaintext with the incorporation of specific methodology (Hamad, 2018). Both encryption and decryption techniques are used to generate the keys. In addition, the Digital Signature Algorithm (DSA) is used to validate the user's authorization by performing the signing verification processes (Chen, 2021).

Cryptography is helpful for providing security to the data by performing the encryption and decryption processes (Kumbhar, 2020). Here, data encryption is the conversion of original data to non-understandable data (Lijing, 2022). The cryptographic methods allow the data to be encrypted and decrypted without the sender's assistance. In addition, it provides authentication to the users in MANET for performing data transmission (Patsariya, 2020). The available networking technologies are useful for improving the data transmission process with limited data via the internet (Pabani, 2022). The cryptography method is used to avoid the illegitimate user's data transmission and is also not allowed to transmit the data insecurely between the users (Sarkar, 2021). Encryption and decryption processes are performed using mathematical models (Sharma, 2020). The various mathematical concepts were used in this direction for performing encryption and decryption processes. Among them, the matrix is used in different security mechanisms from scratch (Alshehri, 2020).

2 Literature Review

Gaurav Pareek et al. (2021) proposed a new cryptographic primitive approach that is highly motivated and allows the temporary delegation of the respective decryption capacity of the aggregate keys without incorporating security. Their approach performs better than the existing techniques in terms of security. They also proposed two different types of decryption techniques for an aggregate key. At the end, they have analysed the performance of their approach to confirm its practical applicability.

Fagul Pandey et al. (2022) developed a new software-based method for generating private keys for ensuring data security during data transmission. Their method considers the email addresses of the users as input. In their first step, a seed is created and combines a parameter and a triplet, which is a pair of questions and answers. They have tested a private generation concept to ensure randomness, entropy, correctness, dissimilarity, and reliability.

Lijing Ren et al. (2022) developed an enhanced visual cryptography method for storing private data in different databases that avoids the difficult operations of privacy-preserving methods according to the cryptographic methods. They have performed the training process through transfer learning using a recognition network that works based on visual cryptography. Finally, they have proved that their method is better than others in terms of security. Enormous data security mechanisms were developed and used to provide security to the users. However, still, enough security is not obtained or achieved by any data security system in an efficient manner. However, the current data security measures are not efficient enough to ensure adequate security.

Yuyang Zhou et al. (2022) developed a new proxy re-encryption method that considers the identity along with a cryptographic reverse firewall method for transmitting the data securely. They have provided the selected security method to handle plaintext attacks. The experimental results proved the efficiency of their method with a lower computational cost.

Fursan Thabit et al. (2022) presented a new lightweight homomorphic cryptographic method that contains two levels of encryption processes. They have applied a light-weight cryptography algorithm in their first level and also applied multiplicative homomorphic methods in their second level to enhance the data security in MANET. Their method provides symmetric cryptographic features and asymmetric cryptographic features. Finally, their method is evaluated by considering evaluation parameters such as memory, time, entropy change, and statistical analysis. The experimental results proved their method superior by achieving enhanced encryption time, throughput, and memory utilization.

3 Methodology

3.1 Proposed Catalan's Conjecture and ECC Algorithm for Key Generation (CCECC - KG)

The key generation process involves the successful use of the newly designed Catalan's Conjecture and ECC algorithm for Key Generation (CCECC-KG). The generation of effective secret keys in this research involves the use of conjecture principles for selecting prime integers that enhance the elliptic curve points. This upgrade is implemented to improve security by augmenting the quality of the keys produced. The elliptical curve equation is constructed by using the values of ui, a, and b. The curve points are derived from the elliptic curve equation by using the modulo function. Select a random point (k, d) from the produced points on the curve to serve as the secret key for the subsequent steps of the ECC procedure. The following are the steps involved in the proposed CCEKGA:

Algorithm 1: Key Generation (CCECC-KG)
Input: Domain parameters (p, q, g)

Output: Secret keys

Step 1: The modulo function is used to create elliptic curve points.

Step 2: Select a pair of random prime numbers by incorporating the Catalan's conjecture on elliptic curve points

Step 3: Apply the exponential modulo function

Step 4: Generated the curve points

Step 5: Finalize the curve point according to the enhanced elliptic curve equation.

Step 6: Returns the secret keys

Encryption process.
Encryption is performed using the newly designed Catalan's Conjecture and ECC algorithm for the encryption method (CCECC-E). This research employs the principles of conjecture to identify appropriate prime numbers and enhance the elliptic curve points, hence generating effective secret keys. By augmenting the efficacy of the encryption procedure, this modification bolsters security. The input values for this component include the divisor n of the modulo function, the secret keys k and d, and the message M.

This function consists of two distinct components: ECC encryption and encryption based on new inventive concepts. It facilitates augmenting the degree of security. The encryption process yields three output values: the encrypted text, the divisor n used in the modulo function, and the secret key d. The proposed CCECC-E follows these steps:

Algorithm 2: Encryption (CCECC-E)
Input: Parameters (divisor (n), secret keys (k, d) and message (M))

Output: Encrypted form of M

Step 1: Read the divisor (n), secret keys (k, d) and message (M)

Step 2: Apply the formula (d x n) to get the Q value.

Step 3: Compute C1 and C2, using the formulae C1 = k x n and C2 = M + (k x Q)

Step 4: Utilize e1 = (C21 + C22) mod n, determine the value of e1

Step 5: Returns encrypted message

Decryption process.
Decryption is performed using the newly designed Catalan's conjecture and the ECC algorithm for decryption (CCECC-D). This research generates effective secret keys by improving the elliptic curve points using the concepts of Pillai's conjecture to find suitable prime integers. Implementing this upgrade enhances security by improving the efficacy of the decryption process. The input values consist of encrypted text, the divisor n used in the modulo algorithm, and the secret key d. This function consists of two distinct components: ECC decryption and a novel decryption technique. The process decrypts the original text and sends it to the user. In general, ECC offers enhanced security with a reduced number of steps in the encryption and decryption methods. The suggested technique incorporates an additional step to enhance the security level in comparison to the current ECC algorithm. It facilitates enhancing the degree of security. The following are the steps of the newly proposed decryption algorithm:

Algorithm 3: Decryption (CCECC-D)
Input: Encrypted text, divisor n of the modulo function, secret key d

Output: Original text

Step 1: Read the encrypted text, divisor n of the modulo function, secret key d.

Step 2: Calculate C1 and C2 by using the formulae

$C1 = E1 \div e1$ and $C2 = E2 \div e1$

Step 3: Find the original text using M = C2 (d x C1)

Step 4: Returns the original message

4 Results and Discussion

An evaluation of the CCECC algorithm's performance is presented in this section. We carried out the evaluation using the NS2. Modelling network protocols is a typical use for this simulator, which is a time-driven simulator that depends on discrete events. Many users frequently utilize this simulator. We observe the distribution of nodes within the simulated environment (Table 1).

Catalan's Conjecture and Elliptic Curve Cryptography 249

Table 1. Simulation Parameters of CCECC

Parameter	Value
Channel Type	Wireless Channel
Simulation Time	50 s
Number of nodes	50,75
MAC type	802.11
Traffic model	CBR
Antenna Model	Omni Antenna
Simulation Area	800 × 700

Every individual node establishes a direct link with other nodes located within a 200-m range. Communication between the nodes is established via the UDP. The reception of the signal by all nodes is enabled by the use of an omni-directional antenna, which permits the reception of signals from all directions. We evaluate the CCECC scheme using several performance metrics, including PDR, PLR, average latency, throughput, and residual energy, among others.

The PDR values for CCECC, ECC, and AES during the simulation study at 0.0000833 density are shown in Table 2. In Fig. 1, the PDRs of the CCECC, ECC, and AES are displayed. It demonstrates that, as compared to ECC and AES, the proposed CCECC system has a PDR that is 34.99% better.

Table 2. Packet Delivery Rate

Simulation Time (s)	**CCECC** (Packets)	**ECC** (Packets)	**AES** (Packets)
0	0	0	0
10	75906	55592	35278
20	122047	101733	62118
30	148747	128433	88958
40	198447	178133	115798
50	31990	11676	9964

Table 3 presents the PLR figures derived from the simulation studies conducted on CCECC, ECC, and AES. Figure 2 illustrates the comparative performance of the proposed CCECC system, indicating a significant reduction of 36.98% in PLR as compared to the existing methods (Fig. 3).

Table 4 presents the AD values acquired by the simulation investigation of the CCECC, ECC, and AES mechanisms with a density of 0.0000833. Based on the findings

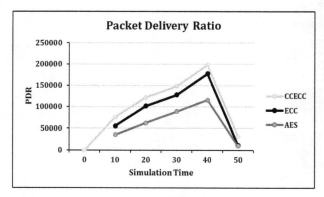

Fig. 1. Packet Delivery Rate

Table 3. Packet Loss Rate

Simulation Time (s)	CCECC (Packets)	ECC (Packets)	AES (Packets)
0	0	0	0
10	50	70	200
20	102	170	598
30	352	432	1008
40	612	792	1418
50	985	1152	1828

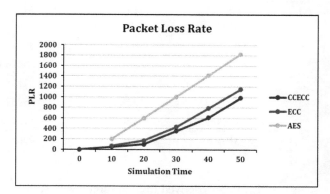

Fig. 2. Packet Loss Rate

shown in Fig. 4, it is evident that the proposed implementation of CCECC results in a delay reduction of 32.47% when compared to the existing methods.

Table 4. Average Delay

Simulation Time (s)	CCECC (Packets)	ECC (Packets)	AES (Packets)
0	0	0	0
10	0.010203	0.010467	0.108382
20	0.024571	0.052356	0.412515
30	0.154236	0.278834	0.728572
40	0.315472	0.548808	1.044629
50	0.645821	0.918782	1.360685

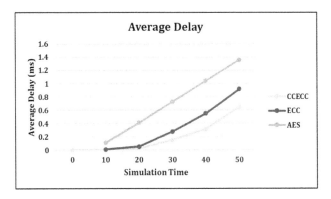

Fig. 3. Average Delay

Table 5. Throughput

Simulation Time (s)	CCECC (Packets)	ECC (Packets)	AES (Packets)
0	0	0	0
10	2057.624	1167.624	996.436
20	6449.218	5559.218	3527.823
30	11063.317	10173.317	6211.845
40	13733.331	12843.331	8895.843
50	18704.728	17814.728	11579.839

According to Table 5, the obtained throughput values during the simulation study are shown for the CCECC, ECC, and AES mechanisms. According to Fig. 4, the CCECC system exhibits a 34.99% higher throughput in comparison to the existing methods.

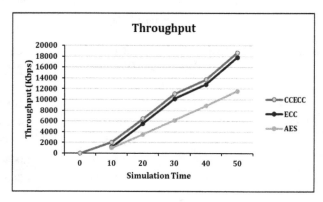

Fig. 4. Throughput

RE refers to the quantity of energy that is still available inside a node at a certain moment in time. A measure of the RE can quantify the rate at which network activities use energy.

Table 6. Residual Energy

Simulation Time (s)	CCECC (Packets)	ECC (Packets)	AES (Packets)
0	0	0	0
10	10.02625	9.9725	9.91875
20	10.00125	9.9475	9.81125
30	9.97625	9.9225	9.70375
40	9.95125	9.8975	9.64625
50	9.92625	9.8725	9.549875

Table 6 presents the determined RE values as a result of the simulation study. According to Fig. 6, the network's RE is superior to the proposed CCECC approach compared to the existing methods. Figure 5 illustrates that the ECC scheme exhibits a superior residual energy of 0.032 J in comparison to the existing systems.

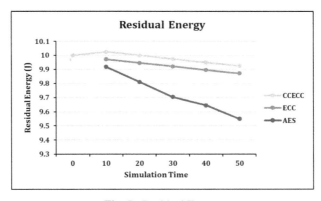

Fig. 5. Residual Energy

5 Conclusion

A new secured storage mechanism has been proposed and implemented in this work to provide data security while storing and sharing the user's data. CCECC technology aims to detect and isolate malicious nodes inside a communication network. The proposed CCECC method results in a 31.55% rise in PDR, a 35.24% reduction in PLR, a 29.95% reduction in AD, a 31.55% increase in throughput, and a 0.024J energy savings in RE. We derived the estimated percentages from the average values of comparable data points for both situations of n, specifically for densities of 0.0000833 and 0.000133.

References

1. Baranov, N., Bashkin, V., Bashkin, M.: A lightweight cryptographic scheme of route hiding for the on-demand route discovery algorithms. In: 2018 7th Mediterranean Conference on Embedded Computing (MECO) IEEE, pp. 1–4 (2018)
2. Abdullah, A., Ozen, E., Bayramoglu, H.: Energy efficient MANET routing protocol based on ant colony optimization. Ad Hoc Sensor Wirel. Networks **47**, 73–96 (2020)
3. Salari-Moghaddam, S., Taheri, H., Karimi, A.: Trust based routing algorithm to improve quality of service in DSR protocol. Wirel. Pers. Commun. **109**, 1–16 (2019)
4. Darabkh, K.A., Alfawares, M.G., Althunibat, S.: MDRMA: Multi-data rate mobility-aware AODV-based protocol for flying ad-hoc networks. Veh. Commun. **18**, 100163 (2019)
5. Huang, B., Zhang, X.: Mobile Ad Hoc networks routing algorithm based on stable link. Mod. Electron. Tech. **41**, 90–94 (2018)
6. Chen, K.S., Li, H.K., Ruan, Y.L., Wang, S.H.: Improved AODV routing protocol based on local neighbor nodes and link weights. J. Softw. **32**, 1186–1200 (2021)
7. Kumbhar, F.H., Shin, S.Y.: CV-AODV: compatibility based vehicular Ad-hoc on demand distance vector routing protocol. In: Proceedings of the 2020 International Conference on Information and Communication Technology Convergence, Jeju Island, Republic of Korea, 21–23 October 2020, pp. 1004–1008 (2020)
8. Patsariya, M., Rajavat, A.: Network path capability identification and performance analysis of mobile Ad hoc network. In: Proceedings of the 2020 IEEE 9th International Conference on Communication Systems and Network Technologies, Gwalior, India, 10–12 April 2020, pp. 82–87 (2020)

9. Pabani, J.K., Luque-Nieto, M.-Á., Hyder, W., Ariza, A.: Energy-efficient routing protocol for selecting relay nodes in underwater sensor networks based on fuzzy analytical hierarchy process. Sensors **22**, 8930 (2022)
10. Sarkar, D., Choudhury, S., Majumder, A.: Enhanced-Ant-AODV for optimal route selection in mobile Ad-hoc network. J. King Saud Univ.-Comput. Inf. Sci. **33**(10), 1186–1201 (2021)
11. Sharma, A., Bansal, A., Rishiwal, V.: SBADR: stable and bandwidth aware dynamic routing protocol for mobile Ad hoc network. Int. J. Perv. Comput. Commun. **16**(3), 205–221 (2020)
12. Alshehri, A., Badawy, A., Huang, H.: FQ-AGO: fuzzy logic Q-learning based asymmetric link aware and geographic opportunistic routing scheme for MANETs. Electronics **9**(4), 1–24 (2020)
13. Hamad, S., Belhaj, S., Muslam, M.: Average link stability with energy-aware routing protocol for MANETs. Int. J. Adv. Comput. Sci. Appl. **9**(1), 554–562 (2018)
14. Gaurav, P., Purushothama, B.R.: KAPRE: key-aggregate proxy re-encryption for secure and flexible data sharing in cloud storage. J. Inf. Secur. Appl. **63** (2021). https://doi.org/10.1016/j.jisa.2021.103009
15. Pandey, F., Dash, P., Samanta, D., Sarma, M.: Efficient and provably secure intelligent geometrical method of secret key generation for cryptographic applications. Comput. Electr. Eng. **101** (2022). https://doi.org/10.1016/j.compeleceng.2022.107947
16. Zhou, Y., Zhao, L., Jin, Y., Li, F.: Backdoor-resistant identity-based proxy re-encryption for cloud-assisted wireless body area networks. Inf. Sci. **604** (2022). https://doi.org/10.1016/j.ins.2022.05.007
17. Thabit, F., Can, O., Alhomdy, S., Al-Gaphari, G.H., Jagtap, S.: A novel effective lightweight homomorphic cryptographic algorithm for data security in cloud computing. Int. J. Intell. Networks **3**, 16–30 (2022). https://doi.org/10.1016/j.ijin.2022.04.001
18. Ren, L., ZhangToward privacy protection of sensed biometric features with extended visual cryptography. Microprocess. Microsyst. **91**, 104540 (2022). https://doi.org/10.1016/j.micpro.2022.104540

Monitoring the Concentration of Air Pollutants and Its Health Hazards Using Machine Learning Models

Aditi Jain[ID], Aditya Shenoy[ID], Ananya Adiga[ID], Anirudha Anekal[ID], and Saritha Prajwal[✉][ID]

PES University, Bengaluru 560085, Karnataka, India
saritha.k@pes.edu

Abstract. With the world moving rapidly towards industrialization driven by economic growth and technological advancements, there is an alarming surge of air pollution leading to significant health concerns. In response, this work introduces a research-driven approach for a continuous air quality monitoring system, designed to continuously track air quality in real-time in the proximity and proactively predict potential health hazards for the user. Central to the system's efficacy is a state-of-the-art hybrid Machine Learning model, seamlessly amalgamating the strengths of Adaptive Long Short-Term Memory (LSTM) and Auto-Regressive Integrated Moving Average (ARIMA) models, renowned for their ability in handling intricate time series data. This model is securely deployed on a cloud platform, ensuring not only accessibility but also scalability to meet current and future technological standards. The system primarily concentrates on the monitoring of air pollutants, such as PM2.5, PM10, and CO, ensuring that users have access to immediate and up-to-date insights into the air quality in their surroundings. Beyond this, the system goes a step further by employing this data to assess users' potential risk of developing lung cancer. Through the use of Internet of Things (IoT) sensors, the system can issue timely and potentially life-saving insights, providing users with valuable information for decision-making improving their well-being. In a world, where the link between air quality and health is increasingly evident, our research-based initiative serves as a beacon for a healthier future, while also fostering environmental consciousness and public well-being.

Keywords: Lung Cancer · IOT · Adaptive LSTM · ARIMA · AQI · Air Pollutants

1 Introduction

Industrialization, while driving economic growth and technological progress, has ushered in a surge in air pollution. Yet, a critical issue persists amongst general public about awareness regarding the perils posed by compromised air quality.

Pollutants such as PM2.5, PM10, and CO are particularly menacing to human health, with dire consequences for the lungs. The ease with which fine particulate matter infiltrates and effect the lungs, underscores the urgency of the health hazards awareness and hence encourages proactive steps needed to mitigate.

In response to this challenge, the development and deployment of air quality monitoring systems become imperative. Such systems hold the potential to furnish individuals with real-time insights into the air quality within their immediate vicinity, offering a proactive line of defense against potential health risks. By raising awareness and delivering early warnings, individuals gain the knowledge and time to undertake preventative measures, thus safeguarding their well-being.

This paper introduces a pioneering proposition - a continuous air quality monitoring system, dedicated to monitoring the air quality in the user's vicinity, and taking into consideration several other factors, and informing them of the incidence rates of certain diseases. The envisioned solution is engineered to offer continuous surveillance of PM2.5, PM10, and CO levels in the atmosphere, providing users with real-time insights about the air they breathe. This solution gauges the user's potential health risks and subsequently issues appropriate alerts. Under this approach, the solution empowers individuals to make informed choices and take measures to protect their health, constituting a critical stride in enhancing well-being in the face of escalating air pollution.

2 Related Work

(Roberto Cazzolla Gatti, et al. 2023) [1], in their paper, an AI-based approach was applied to investigate intricate links between cancer mortality, socioeconomic factors, and environmental pollution in Italy, spanning regional and provincial levels. The methodology included RF regression, Boruta feature analysis, and K-means clustering, with SMR forecasting. Notably, the research offers a detailed examination of the impact of air pollution on various body parts, emphasizing transparency in data sources and algorithms. However, it reveals limitations in linking specific pollution sources to cancer and focuses solely on Italy, urging expansion to encompass global air pollution diversity.

(Samiran Rana 2022) [2], proposed an air quality monitoring system that utilizes established methods from WHO and INAAQS, offering a precise assessment beyond a simple Air Quality Index. Its focus on specific pollutants, particularly PM2.5, sheds light on the tangible health risks of airborne particles. However, its reliance solely on pre-existing methods and exclusive focus on PM2.5 limit its potential for comprehensive public health protection. Further refinement and expansion to encompass a wider range of pollutants are crucial for a more robust and effective system.

(M. Marzouk, et al. 2022) [3], investigated the connection between outdoor pollution and indoor air quality (IAQ) using real-time sensors and AI. They strategically placed Internet of Things (IoT) devices to continuously collect data, analyzed with CNNs and LSTMs, gaining valuable insights into the dynamic interplay between outdoor and indoor environments, especially in rural areas.

However, the study lacked individual health data and ignored occupational exposures, along with seasonal variations and the influence of additional pollutants beyond their chosen focus. While offering valuable real-time IAQ understanding, further research is needed to address these limitations.

(K.-M. Wang, et al. 2022) [4], used various machine learning models like Logistic Regression, SVM, Gradient Boosting and Random Forest to compare and build a powerful prediction model for the link between air pollution and lung cancer rates. Their strengths include comprehensive model bench marking and a diverse dataset from different countries. However, limitations like neglecting weather factors and complex IoT infrastructure need further investigation.

(Cosimo Magazzino, et al. 2021) [5] proposed a study that tackles the complex interplay between COVID-19 deaths, economic factors, and air pollution (PM10, PM2.5, NO2) in New York by leveraging advanced machine learning. It aims to shed light on their impact on COVID-19 outcomes, aiding in public health interventions. Key strengths lie in its detailed analysis of individual pollutants, rigorous data processing, and real-time insight potential. However, focusing solely on COVID-related deaths limits its scope.

(In Iftikhar ul Samee, et al. 2019) [6] paper, the researchers adopt Artificial Neural Network (ANN) models to predict air contaminant concentrations and utilize Pearson's coefficient to assess their correlation with weather conditions. Their primary aim is to establish a pollutant monitoring system in smart cities, uncovering potential pollutant-weather correlations. The ultimate goal is to predict pollutant levels effectively to mitigate health risks. The study thoroughly considers weather conditions and demonstrates impressive model accuracy, with low Root Mean Square Errors (RMSE) for SO2 and PM2.5 predictions. Limitations include the study's restricted consideration of environmental conditions, model simplicity and IoT infrastructure complexity.

(Kim KE, et al. 2016) [7] delve into the intricate link between tiny airborne particles called particulate matter (PM) and various skin ailments. Elevated PM levels, the study reveals, trigger skin disorders through oxidative stress and inflammation, paving the way for potential treatments with antioxidant and anti-inflammatory medications. While its meticulous cataloging of pollutant-skin disease connections empowers readers, the study's reliance on limited statistical data and lack of exploration into the interplay between PM-induced skin conditions call for further investigation. The message is clear: protect your skin from air pollution, and research needs to delve deeper into the dirty secrets of PM's impact on our largest organ (Jin Z-Y, et al. 2014) [8] probed the link between home ventilation and lung cancer. They used detailed questionnaires and advanced statistics to capture a wide range of data, including family history, lifestyle, and ventilation habits. Strengths include the comprehensive data capture and the use of sophisticated analysis. However, limitations include potential location bias, neglecting outdoor pollution, and overlooking occupational exposures. Further research is needed to address these limitations and solidify the findings.

3 Methodology

This section encompasses an exploration of the problem statement, elucidation of data collection methodologies, examination of the employed models, in-depth architectural insights, comprehensive evaluation processes, and the unveiling of resultant findings.

3.1 Proposed Work

The hardware components for this project are selected to ensure robust and accurate air quality monitoring. At the core of the system lies the ESP8266, a versatile Wi-Fi-enabled module renowned for its ability to measure and transmit real-time data efficiently. Complementing this, the MQ-7 sensor plays a pivotal role in monitoring Carbon Monoxide (CO) levels, offering critical insights into this hazardous pollutant. Additionally, the GP2Y1010AU0F dust sensor is instrumental in tracking the presence of particulate matter with varying aerodynamic diameters.

The integration of these hardware elements forms the foundation of an effective air quality monitoring system, poised to offer real-time and accurate data, thereby enabling users to make informed decisions regarding their health and well-being.

The software ecosystem supporting this project is thoughtfully assembled to empower robust data analysis and seamless machine learning integration. It comprises a suite of statistical analysis tools, including Numpy and Pandas, to facilitate data manipulation and insights extraction. Complementing these are visualization tools like Matplotlib and Seaborn, which enhance the presentation of findings, making complex data more comprehensible. Machine learning capabilities are harnessed through Keras and TensorFlow, enabling the development and deployment of predictive models.

To ensure scalability and accessibility, the project leverages cloud computing platforms such as Streamlit and Thingspeak, which play a vital role in hosting and managing data. The Streamlit framework further augments the user experience by offering an interactive and user-friendly interface. Lastly, the Arduino IDE is employed for the development of Internet of Things (IoT) code, consolidating the software infrastructure to deliver a comprehensive solution for air quality monitoring and health prediction.

3.2 Dataset Description

In this paper, two key datasets are employed. The lung cancer patient dataset [9] is sourced from data.world, a platform, meticulously designed as a data catalog, provides open access to AI-ready datasets. This dataset forms the foundation of our analysis of the connection between lung cancer and air quality.

Simultaneously, the Air Quality Data in India (2015–2020) [10] dataset, featuring hourly data from different stations and cities in India, is gathered from kaggle.com. This dataset is publicly available through the Central Pollution Control Board, an official government portal, and plays a vital role in our examination of air quality trends over the specified time frame. The dataset has been compiled from Central Pollution Board's website and saved on kaggle.com.

3.3 Architecture and Workflow

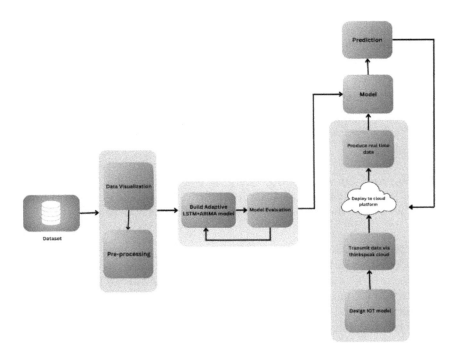

Fig. 1. Architectural diagram

The architectural diagram and the flow of the project is described in this section.

Figure 1 shows 4 distinct stages in the architecture. They are defined and explained below.

Data Preprocessing. In the initial phase, the time series data from the sensor stations are cleaned and pre-processed. This involved handling missing values, addressing potential outliers, and transforming variables. The dataset was divided into distinct training and testing sets. The training set was designated for model training and the testing set was reserved for evaluation purposes.

Model Training. The training data of the AQI dataset was fit to an ARIMA model. It was chosen for its capacity to capture seasonal and trend components in time series data. Extensive hyper-parameter optimization took place, including determining the order of differencing, auto-regressive (AR) order, and moving average (MA) order.

With the trained ARIMA model in place, short-term forecasts of AQI were generated on the testing data. These forecasts provided valuable insights into expected air quality based on historical data.

These forecasts along with the lung cancer dataset was given as input to the LSTM model, known for capturing complex patterns from non-stationary ,real time data. This hybrid model generates the probability of the user getting lung cancer.

Generate Forecasts. The forecasts and residuals, as represented in Fig. 6, were generated using the trained Adaptive LSTM model to predict the possibility of a person having lung cancer and the predictions from the ARIMA model of future AQI.

Evaluation and Optimization. Rigorous evaluation of the ARIMA-Adaptive LSTM model was undertaken using appropriate evaluation metrics on the testing data. As necessary, the model underwent hyper parameter tuning.

Real-Time Data Collection. IoT sensor station was constructed using the ESP8266 WiFi module. The system used MQ7 gas sensor for detecting the concentration of CO gas in the atmosphere, and GP2Y1010AU0F dust sensor for detecting the concentration of particulate matter (PM2.5 and PM10). This allows continuous and real-time collection of air quality data. More sensors can be connected for detection of other gases. PM 2.5 and CO was chosen after literature survey and economic considerations.

Deployment on Cloud Platforms. To facilitate seamless data reception and transmission, the project deployed the machine learning model and storage and collection of the sensor stations' data on cloud platforms. Thingspeak was used to upload and temporarily store the sensor data.

The machine learning models can be hosted on cloud platforms like Streamlit, Spaces, or AWS, ensuring scalability and accessibility while enabling real-time data processing and analysis. Streamlit was chosen to host the model, as it provides a basic interface for seamless and easy interaction with the model and other systems.

3.4 Research Hypothesis

This research hypothesis revolves around implementing a comprehensive air quality monitoring system and constructing a machine learning model. This model aims to estimate the likelihood of an individual developing lung cancer based on their exposure to harmful air pollutants. The evaluation encompasses a range of variables, including the individual's occupational environment, smoking history, lifestyle, genetic predisposition etc.

A thorough analysis of pollutant concentration data acquired from wireless sensors, as well as the cloud-hosted trained model is performed. Furthermore an interface to accept a user's details was also created. This multifaceted approach is central to the pursuit of enhancing public health awareness and contributing to the mitigation of air pollution-related health issues.

3.5 Internet Of Things

The project uses the IoT station to collect live pollution data and feeds it to the ML model for live risk analysis. MQ-7 Gas sensor has been used for detecting carbon monoxide (CO). GP2Y1010AU0F, a dust sensor, has been used to detect and measure the concentration of fine particulate matter (PM2.5). The ESP8266 module used is a versatile and widely used Wi-Fi module that can be employed for various IOT (Internet of Things) and embedded electronics applications.

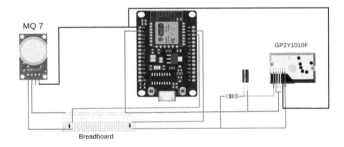

Fig. 2. IOT circuit diagram with MQ7 and GP2Y1010AUF sensor

Wiring. There were a few challenges when wiring up the IOT station. The biggest of which being the lack of multiple analog inputs on ESP8266. ESP8266 provides only one analog input. The project takes analog readings from 2 sensors. To facilitate this, the sensors are programmatically switched off and on.

The power line to the sensors to MQ7 and GP2Y1010AUF are D1 and D2 pins respectively, from ESP8266. In the code, D1 and D2 are set to output mode and set to high and low as required. There is a diode between the power line and D1 and D2 pins to ensure that only voltage above a threshold is applied to the sensors.

The aforementioned IOT station has been built, according to Fig. 2, and has collected live data from multiple locations in the city to get a variety of readings and stored it on ThingSpeak. See below the station in real life.

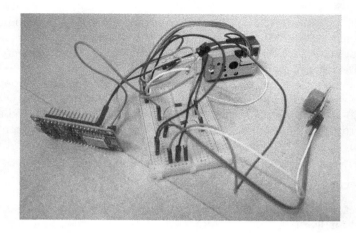

Fig. 3. Live IOT station deployed to collect real-time data

As seen in Fig. 3, the station is shown without any enclosure. The station can be set inside one for cleanliness and protection from the elements. However if it is placed in an enclosure, it is recommended to solder the wires rather than using a breadboard for more secure wiring.

Collected Data. The concentration of the pollutants CO and PM2.5 was collected from various locations through the IOT station and uploaded on to ThingSpeak.

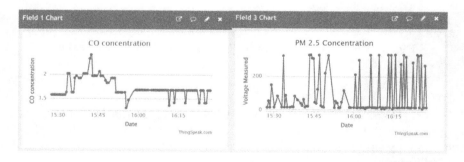

Fig. 4. Readings collected on Thingspeak

Figure 4 shows the basic graphs displayed on Thingspeak. It was also used for temporary storage before moving the data to streamlit. Thingspeak provides API endpoints for read and write operations. which is hit by streamlit. The ESP8266 code has a Thingspeak module that facilitates easy reading and writing.

3.6 Machine Learning

The project is built on a hybrid network of Adaptive LSTM (Long Short Time Memory) and ARIMA (Auto-Regressive-Integrated Moving-Average). Generally the pollutant concentration data will be a time-series data and the data used for training the model in this project is time series and stationary. The data used for prediction is real time and dynamic, obtained after real time monitoring of various chosen pollutants using the IOT sensors. Hence, it is essential that the model be capable of handling large and dynamic data.

3.7 Training and Validation

Splitting Data. The data was split into 2 equal parts. One half for the training set and the other half for testing set for the ARIMA model. This was done to ensure an equal amount of data for evaluating model performance. This balance allows assessment on how well the model generalizes to unseen data, which is crucial for model validation. This also ensures that the testing set covers a similar time period as the training set. This is crucial for time series models as they rely on historical data to make accurate forecasts.

3.8 ARIMA

Autocorrelation Plots: ARIMA model works on stationary data, to check if the data is stationary, autocorrelation plots- ACF and PACF are constructed. ACF plots is used to represent the correlation of the time series with its lags. It measures the linear relationship between lagged values of the time series. PACF plot represents the partial correlation of time series with its lags, after removing the effects of lower-order-lags between them.

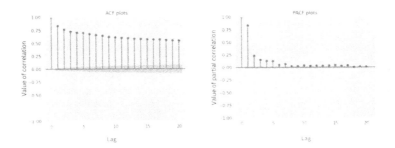

Fig. 5. ACF and PACF plots

The ACF plot, as seen above in Fig. 5, shows the correlations with the lags are high and positive with very slow decay. Whereas the PACF plot shows the partial autocorrelations have a single spike at lag 1. These two are both signs of a trended time series. So the time series is not stationary.

The full equation of ARIMA (p,d,q) is:

$$\nabla y_t = c + \varphi_1 \nabla y_{t-1} + ... + \varphi_p \nabla y_{t-p} + \varepsilon_t + \theta_1 \varepsilon_{t-1} + .. + \theta_q \varepsilon_{t-q} \quad (1)$$

'p' represents the number of autoregressive terms. It can be calculated as:

$$y_t = c + \varphi_1 + y_{t-1} + \varphi_2 + y_{t-2} + ... + \varphi_p + y_{t-p} + \varepsilon_t \quad (2)$$

In this equation c is a constant, $\varphi_1, ..., \varphi_p$ are parameters, ε_t is white noise.
'd' represents the number of nonseasonal differences needed for stationarity. It can be calculated by:

$$\nabla y_t = y_t - y_{t-1} \quad (3)$$

'q' represents the number of lagged forecast errors in the prediction equation. The formula is as follows:

$$y_t = c + \varepsilon_t + \theta_1 \varepsilon_{t-1} + \theta_2 \varepsilon_{t-2} + ... + \theta_q \varepsilon_{t-q} \quad (4)$$

The pqd values are set after analyzing the ACF and PACF plots- 'p' value is set to 2, since PACF shows more minor but significant lags at 2, 4, and 5.

In contrast, the ACF in Fig. 5, shows a more gradual decay. Values 2 or 3 or 4 can be used but to keep the model simple the value is taken as 2. 'd' being the value of differencing, it is better to start with the lowest value, usually the value 1 makes it stationary.

If the PACF plot has a significant spike at lag p, but not beyond and the ACF plot decays more gradually. This may suggest an ARIMA(p, d, 0) model.

If the ACF plot has a significant spike at lag q, but not beyond and the PACF plot decays more gradually. This may suggest an ARIMA(0, d, q) model. Since the plots show the former, 0 is used as the 'q' value.

Calculating Error Value. The error factor MAPE is a metric that defines the accuracy of a forecasting method. It represents the average of the absolute percentage errors of each entry in a dataset to calculate how accurate the forecasted quantities were in comparison with the actual quantities.

$$M = \frac{1}{n} \sum_{t=1}^{n} |\frac{A_t - F_t}{A_t}| \quad (5)$$

Here M is the mean absolute percentage error, n is the number of times the summation iteration happens, A_t is the actual value and F_t = forecast value. The error value was calculated as 0.18.

As seen in Fig. 6, we can see the trend in AQI values among the train, test and predicted values.

3.9 Adaptive LSTM

Defining Adaptive LSTM: Sequential neural networks is required for sequence processing. Dense layer is for the output. Both are required here because the input for prediction is real time. We use 50 dense layers with relu as the activation function.

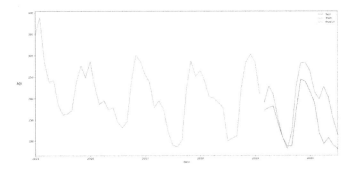

Fig. 6. ARIMA predictions

Training the Model: We use the 'compile' method, which configures the model for training. 'Loss' specifies the loss function that will be used to measure the error during training. MSE is commonly used for regression problems, where the goal is to minimize the squared differences between predicted and actual values. optimizer = 'adam' specifies yhat the optimization algorithm that will be used during training, 'adam' adapts the learning rate during training, which can lead to faster convergence, we set the epochs to 1 which means that the entire dataset will be passed forward and backward through the neural network during training only one time, we set the batch size to 1 which means that the model will update its weights after processing each sample and we set verbose to 2 which means that it will display a progress bar for each epoch.

Calculate RMSE:

$$MSE = \frac{1}{n}\sum_{i=1}^{n}(Y_i - \hat{Y}_i)^2 \qquad (6)$$

In this MSE is mean squared error, n is number of data points, Y_i is observed values and $\hat{Y}_i$ is predicted values.

After making the predictions and flattening them, the loss function Mean Squared Error is calculated.

3.10 Cloud Platform

Streamlit platform is used in cloud-based system. Streamlit offers an intuitive, user-friendly interface that seamlessly pulls from a GitHub repository to build the application. It ensures that the system is always up-to-date with the latest code, making it easy to maintain and extend as the project evolves. The cloud hosting provided by Streamlit Community, hosts this application on a custom chosen link, ensuring it's readily accessible to end users. The project also utilizes Streamlit to provide an interactive interface for users to input data, interact with the IoT module and machine learning model. This inter connectivity between

Streamlit, the IoT module, and the ML model streamlines the user experience and enhances the effectiveness of this project. The application has 3 primary components. First the streamlit interface code. Second the ThingSpeak connection. Third the machine learning model.

Streamlit Interface: The streamlit interface has been build using the standard streamlit library in python. All code is based on the official streamlit documentation provided to developers.

Below are some screenshots of the working application:

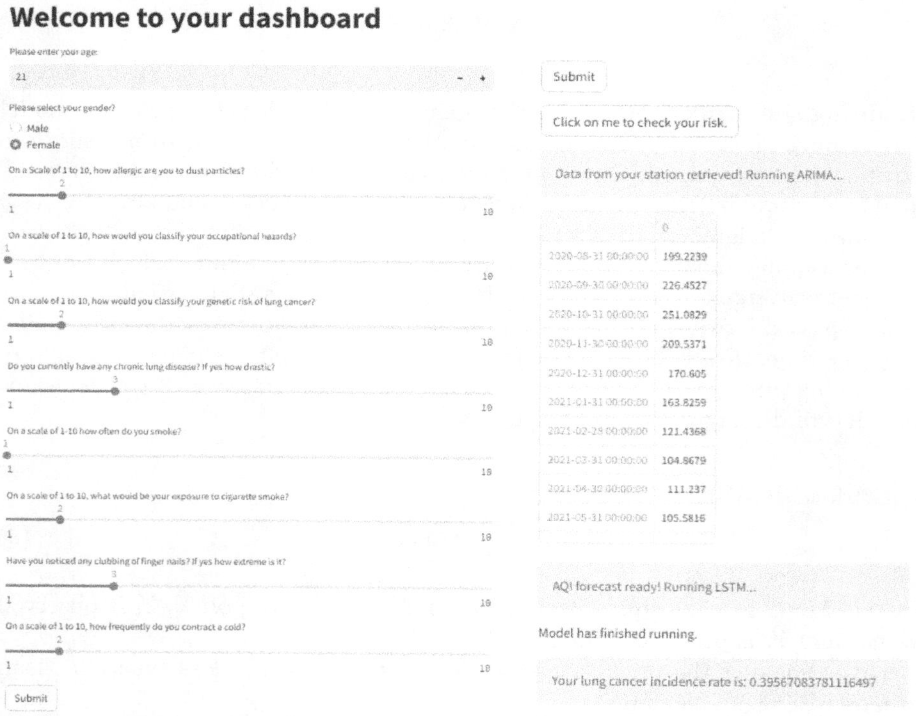

Fig. 7. Deployed Application

Figure 7 shows the interface the user will interact with. The user is asked 10 questions. They are first asked their age and gender. After that they are asked 8 questions where they are required to answer in a range between 1 and 10. They are asked about their dust allergy, occupational hazards, known genetic risk to the chosen disease, existing chronic lung diseases, smoking habits, passive smoke intensity, clubbing of finger nails and finally frequency of contracting colds. After this data is submitted, data from ThingSpeak is retrieved. This pollutants data is sent to the ARIMA model to create forecasts. Then the forecasts and the user specific data is sent to the LSTM and finally a prediction is sent from LSTM model to the Streamlit website.

IoT Module: The IOT module is connected to this application using ThingSpeak. The IOT module sends values to ThingSpeak through a provided ThingSpeak C++ module. The application then sends a specific HTTP request to a chosen ThingSpeak endpoint to retrieve historic and latest reading from the IOT module.

Machine Learning Model: The machine learning models are based off of various python notebooks created for this project. These notebooks have been converted to standard python and converted to work as per the application specifications.

4 Model Benchmarking

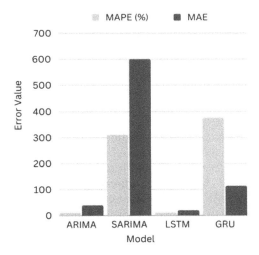

Fig. 8. Comparison of models

Following a comprehensive evaluation using various performance metrics such as Mean Squared Error (MSE), Mean Absolute Percentage Error (MAPE), and Root Mean Squared Error (RMSE), this paper's hybrid ARIMA-LSTM model consistently outperformed both SARIMA and GRU models across all metrics, as seen in Fig. 8. The model in this paper yielded impressive results, with an MSE value of 686.16, RMSE of 79.144, MAPE of 0.47, MAE of 69.24, and a minimal loss of 0.124. In contrast, SARIMA obtained an MSE of 782.62, RMSE of 27.97, and MAPE of 311.37, while GRU achieved an accuracy of 1.13.

This paper introduces a ARIMA-LSTM hybrid model for lung cancer risk prediction, demonstrating its superiority over traditional SARIMA and GRU models. The comparative study in this paper underscores the enhanced prediction accuracy and potential to enhance early risk assessment and intervention strategies in the realm of lung cancer prevention. This innovative fusion of LSTM and ARIMA frameworks not only advances risk prediction techniques but also holds promise for applications in public health and personalized healthcare.

5 Conclusion and Future Work

Accurate air quality monitoring and forecasting carry substantial theoretical and practical significance for the general populace. By alerting individuals to potential health hazards in their immediate surroundings, this research endeavors to offer valuable insights that could assist both the government and the public. The proactive dissemination of information regarding air pollution may lead to a reduction in health issues. The incorporation of a live Internet of Things (IoT) station for real-time air pollutant monitoring and the cloud based machine learning predictive capabilities augments the project's significance. The hybrid model, harmonizing ARIMA and Adaptive LSTM, harnesses air pollutant concentration data to predict disease incident rates. The findings demonstrate the efficacy of both models on time series data, with Adaptive LSTM exhibiting superior performance in the real-time and large data domains. In essence, the research establishes that these time-series prediction models demonstrate proficiency, particularly when used in tandem as a hybrid system with live air pollutant readings.

To enhance the project's efficacy, more comprehensive and granular data collection efforts could be undertaken. The integration of geographical data would unveil regional variations in air pollution effects. This versatile model can be further extended to investigate various health hazards linked to air pollution. Moreover, the IoT station could benefit from improvements, including the substitution of the ESP8266 module with a more potent counterpart featuring additional analog input pins. A deeper exploration of sensor technology and the incorporation of sensors capable of detecting a broader spectrum of gases would broaden the station's capabilities. The inclusion of a more dependable dust sensor would bolster data accuracy. While the project exhibits economic viability, exploration into cutting-edge technologies could further optimize its scope.

References

1. Cazolla R., Di Paola A., Monaco A., Velichevskaya A., Nicola A., Roberto B.: The spatial association between environmental pollution and long-term cancer mortality in Italy. Sci. Total Environ. **855**, 158439 (2023). ISSN 0048-9697, https://doi.org/10.1016/j.scitotenv.2022.158439. Accessed 20 Mar 2023

2. Rana, S.: Determination of air quality life index (Aqli) in Medinipur city of West Bengal(India) during 2019 to 2020: a contextual study. Curr. World Environ. **17**, 137–145 (2022). https://doi.org/10.12944/CWE.17.1.12, https://cwejournal.org/vol17no1/determination-of-air-quality-life-index--aqli--in-medinipur-city-of-west-bengal--india--during-2019-to-2020--a-contextual-study. Accessed 24 Mar 2023
3. Marzouk, M., Atef, M.: Assessment of indoor air quality in academic buildings using IoT and deep learning. Sustainability **14**(12), 7015 (2022). https://www.mdpi.com/2071-1050/14/12/7015. Accessed 30 Mar 2023
4. Wang K.-M., Chen K.-H., Hernanda C.A., Tseng S.-H., Wang K.-J.: How is the Lung Cancer incidence rate associated with environmental risks? Machine-learning-based modeling and benchmarking. Int. J. Environ. Res. Public Health **19**(14), 8445 (2023). https://pubmed.ncbi.nlm.nih.gov/35886298/. Accessed 4 Apr 2023
5. Magazzino, C., Mele, M., Sarkodie, S.A.: The nexus between COVID-19 deaths, air pollution and economic growth in New York State: evidence from deep machine learning. J. Environ. Manag. **286**, 112241 (2021). ISSN 0301–4797, https://doi.org/10.1016/j.jenvman.2021.112241. Accessed 17 Apr 2023
6. Samee, I.U., Jilani, M.T., Wahab, H.G.A.: An application of IoT and machine learning to air pollution monitoring in smart cities. In: 4th International Conference on Emerging Trends in Engineering, Sciences and Technology (ICEEST), Karachi, Pakistan, pp. 1–6 (2019). https://ieeexplore.ieee.org/document/8981707 (Accessed 24 Apr 2023
7. Kim, K.E., Cho, D., Park, H.J.: Air pollution and skin diseases: adverse effects of airborne particulate matter on various skin diseases. Life Sci. **152**(1), 126–34 (2016). PMID: 27018067, https://pubmed.ncbi.nlm.nih.gov/27018067/. Accessed 30 Apr 2023
8. Jin, Z.-Y., et al.: Household ventilation may reduce effects of indoor air pollutants for prevention of lung cancer: a case-control study in a Chinese population. PLoS ONE **9**(7), e10268 (2014). https://doi.org/10.1371/journal.pone.0102685. Accessed 3 May 2023
9. https://data.world/cancerdatahp/lung-cancer-data
10. https://www.kaggle.com/datasets/rohanrao/air-quality-data-in-india

Containment of Compromised Nodes in a Distributed Environment

Anushka Gupta[✉][iD], Aayush Dubey[iD], Abhay Hiremath[iD], V. Anirruth[iD], and Jeny Jijo[iD]

PES University, Bangalore, India
anushkagupta100@gmail.com, jenyjijo@pes.edu

Abstract. Distributed systems, which have become an integral and inseparable component of the modern technology infrastructure, hold data protection in the highest regard. It is of utmost importance to safeguard the constantly expanding and growing amount of data that is present within these distributed systems, as the methods employed by malicious attackers are continuously evolving. This evolution necessitates a forward-thinking and proactive approach to the detection and containment of these attacks. In line with this, this scholarly article introduces a highly robust containment system that has been specifically designed to minimize the time required for recovery and to mitigate the impact of cyberattacks on distributed systems. The proposed system makes use of a comprehensive and all-encompassing set of techniques in order to accurately identify and effectively isolate compromised nodes within the distributed environment that has been targeted by an attack. By implementing this isolation process, the containment system successfully prevents any further damage from occurring and effectively halts any potential data breaches, all while ensuring the preservation and integrity of the existing files that reside within the compromised node. Ultimately, the true effectiveness and power of this system lies within its unique ability to automate the containment process, thereby enabling a rapid and efficient response to any cyberattack that may occur, resulting in minimal downtime and disruption.

Keywords: Distributed Systems · Network Security · Docker · RAFT · Consensus Algorithm · Intrusion Detection System

1 Introduction

In today's data-driven world, where information is constantly generated and consumed from a multitude of sources, including social media, interconnected devices, and enterprise systems, the demand for effective data monitoring and security has never been more exigent. The exponential growth of data has exacerbated the challenges associated with safeguarding sensitive information and ensuring the integrity of distributed systems. In this context, distributed data storage emerges as a promising solution, offering increased scalability, flexibility, and resilience.

However, the inherent interconnectedness of distributed systems introduces distinctive security vulnerabilities. One of the most critical challenges in any distributed system is the timely detection and containment of compromised nodes following an attack. Compromised nodes can pose significant threats to the entire system, potentially leading to the propagation of malware across nodes, data breaches from any endpoint nodes, theft of sensitive information, or disruptions to normal system operations. These threats can have detrimental consequences for organizations, ranging from financial and data loss to reputational damage.

With the increasing number of nodes and the volume of data in distributed environments continuing to expand, the need for a robust system capable of handling large data volumes and responding to security threats in real-time becomes increasingly paramount. Traditional security approaches often fall insufficient or at times obsolete in addressing the complexities and dynamics of distributed systems, leaving them vulnerable to sophisticated attacks. This paper aims to address this critical need by developing a comprehensive framework or methodology for effectively detecting compromised nodes in distributed systems and promptly containing the impact of such compromises. The proposed framework will leverage advanced techniques for real-time monitoring, anomaly detection, and intelligent node containment. The framework will significantly enhance the security posture of distributed systems, by identifying and isolating affected nodes, removing malicious software, and implementing preventative measures to halt the spread of the compromise.

2 Motivation

Advancements in methodologies used to secure systems have greatly increased the difficulty of carrying out an attack on a well maintained distributed system but the possibility of an attack can never be ruled out. Regardless of the level of difficulty, if the potential rewards outweigh the challenges, attackers whether white, black or gray will pursue to illegally enter an ecosystem with applications, crucial data and its overall working. The sole countermeasure to attackers is an extremely fast and robust recovery system. The more time the attacker gets, the more damage they can inflict on the system. This necessitates the need for an automated recovery system which reduces the recovery time of distributed systems significantly and removes any malicious files that may have infiltrated the system.

The proposed solution to this problem must possess the capability to identify compromised nodes that have fallen victim during the attack. A compromised node is any node that has any residual trails of the attack like malicious code, backdoors, corrupted files et cetera. The proposed solution then has to automatically contain these compromised nodes, revert back to a stable state, ensuring the seamless operation of the system again.

3 Literature Review

The ever-evolving threat landscape and the increasing complexity of distributed systems necessitate the development of robust and effective security measures. Automated recovery systems have emerged as a critical countermeasure against the newer cyberattacks, offering rapid detection, isolation, and remediation of compromised nodes. The following background research delves into the current state-of-the-art solutions in automated recovery systems for distributed environments.

Duce et al. [1] highlights and examines the challenges and opportunities in digital forensics. It states that inadequate attention to factors like file formats and compatibility between nodes in a distributed environment, can result in the deployment of unreliable, ineffective and subpar security techniques. The paper throws light on the lack of standards and collaboration within the Forensics field, causing the absence of guidelines for security tool development. Thein et al. [2] propose a recovery model with ideas drawn from [16] and [17] which leverages replication and virtualization for rapid system restorations. The proposed methodology is resistant to faults, detects the attack and recovers via virtual machine migrations. It employed Symbolic Hierarchical Automated Reliability and Performance Evaluation (SHARPE) to enable quantitative evaluation of system reliability and availability goals. However, the proposed solution displayed scalability constraints. Nanda and Hansen [3] introduces the concept of Forensics-as-a-service (FaaS), proposing a three-tier architecture for cloud-based forensic analysis. The three-tier model aims to improve time and cost efficiency of cyber investigations through infrastructure-level support. With a specific Big Data requirement, the proposed methodology in this paper leverages the combination of OpenStack, Sleuth and Autopsy tools to address the distinctive challenges by highly distributed multi-jurisdictional systems. This paper, however, falls short in addressing the legal aspects associated with cross-border data.

Rose and Zhou [4] explore system hardening techniques for Infrastructure as a Service (IaaS) clouds. Their work focuses on identifying and mitigating vulnerabilities in cloud infrastructure to prevent and minimize the impact of cyberattacks. The paper focuses on Operating System level hardening based on Security Technical Implementation Guides (STIG) and Center for Internet Security (CIS) Benchmarks. Paxson [5] in the paper, introduces the idea of Distributed Denial-of-Service (DDoS) attacks that can adversely disrupt systems and services. The technique leverages UDP chargen, DNS, and NTP services as reflectors, demonstrating amplification factors exceeding 50,000x. The inherent difficulty in pinpointing the origins of such attacks raises concerns about the risk of collateral damage to unrelated parties during mitigation efforts. The limitations in current detection mechanisms, including anomalies and signatures, highlight the need for further research into enhancing capabilities at the Internet Service Provider (ISP) level.

Sze, Abhinav and Sekar [6] examine the security vulnerabilities present in OpenStack cloud environments stemming from compromised compute nodes. It provides a detailed threat analysis showing the diverse attack vectors targeting compute nodes such as unauthorized access, malware infections, and exploitation of vulnerabilities.By understanding the risks posed by compromised nodes, the paper emphasizes on critical security challenges facing OpenStack platforms.To mitigate these risks, the paper proposes multi layered security strategies focused on access controls, network segmentation, encryption, intrusion detection, monitoring, and containment techniques aimed to isolate and prevent the spreading of attacks. It also talks about incident response, recovery and other practices to help detect, analyze and remediate the compromised node, by integrating robust security mechanisms, effective threat detection and response protocols, the resilience and security structure of OpenStack deployments against compute node-focused attacks. Tenginakai [7] proposes a set of metrics for detecting compromised systems in distributed systems. The proposed methodology leverages indicators like resource and network utilization patterns to identify anomalous activity that may indicate compromise. The system deploys a combination of message clocks and Lamport logical clocks for synchronization, ensuring a unified timeline.

Ongaro and Ousterhout [8] came up with the concept of RAFT as an alternative to the Paxos family of consensus algorithms. The paper provides a way to distribute a state machine across a cluster of computing systems, ensuring that each node in the cluster agrees upon the same series of state transitions. However, Raft is not a Byzantine fault tolerant (BFT) algorithm.

Prasetiadi [9] proposes the idea for detection of fault nodes using Bose-Chaudhuri-Hocquenghem (BCH) code and Cyclic Redundancy Check (CRC) code as checksum to collectively monitor distributed systems. With the integration of CRC and BCH codes, the performance balances the impact and monitoring capabilities more effectively than either method alone. However, evaluation is lacking on energy and computation overheads, which if quantified would further validate feasibility. Baraneetharan [10] provides an extensive comparison of Machine Learning Algorithms for Intrusion Detection in Wireless Sensor Networks (WSNs) to detect anomalous behaviors and trends in network traffic that may indicate an attack. The proposed solution used features such as packet delivery ratio, number of control packets, signal strength to characterize normal vs abnormal behavior. Mariusz (including Jordi Mongay, George and Constandinos) [11] propose two main parts in the proposed methodology: one is the home gateway device which is the HG IDS and the other is the IDS infrastructure. The HG system is constantly monitoring the home network and sending in signals to the ISP system. The ISP system looks at all the messages and alerts that have been sent from the homes and checks for any unusual activities in the network for potential threats. ISP can ask the HG IDS for more details if needed. The setup helps in spotting the possible attacks sooner as the ISP has a larger view over the network. It's designed to be used with the home devices to check for the threat on the home network and then get a better view of it through the larger view of the ISP helping in bettering the detection of potential attacks.

Batsell, Nageswara and Mallikarjun [12] discuss attack containment, intrusion detection, and attack source identification. It provides an autonomous cyber security system with dispersed sensors and different strategies for speedy reaction. It quickly detects attack origins and possible targets by utilizing sensor data and attack propagation periods, delivering zero mistake rates on benchmarks and considerably improving cyber security.

Ioannidis (including Keromytis, Bellovin, and Smith) [13] propose a distributed firewall architecture to address some of the limitations that were found in centralized packet filtering. Their approach was using some KeyNote policies which are enforced through OpenBSD kernel modifications locally. Credentials allow decentralized administration and distribution over untrusted channels. By working with both the connect() and accept() calls, the implementation applies application layer semantics that are unavailable to network firewalls, facilitating policies to overcome insider threats. The distributed firewall concept aims to help better scale policy enforcement for modern use cases which are challenging for the traditional firewalls. Though traditional perimeter firewalls still help in serving infrastructure protection roles the distributed architecture better adapts to decentralized topologies and threats.

Chandradeep [14] proposes a Distributed Intrusion Detection System (IDS) architecture to defend against malicious assaults on open intranets or networks with groups of machines. The system consists of a central Network-based Intrusion Detection System (NIDS) management which monitors traffic of the network with other NIDS sensors placed strategically around the network using snort. The novelty of the system permits dynamic security policy changes to every Linux and Windows device linked to the network as soon as it detects an intrusion. For Linux-based systems, IPtables rules were updated; and for Windows-based systems, a custom firewall was created. The proposed methodology provides an advantage by analyzing both internal and external traffic, securing policy updates using Remote Method Invocation, distributing the load to host-based firewalls instead of just perimeter-based firewalls, thereby reducing the potential for further attacks. Tihomir Katic and Predrag Pale [15] presents one approach to rule optimization solutions for improving firewall performance. Their work aims to enhance the efficiency of firewall configurations while maintaining robust security measures. This involves strategies such as rule consolidation, prioritization of rules based on frequency or importance, and developing optimization algorithms. The proposed solution developed a rule optimization software (FIRO) that is intended to be used with IP Tables Linux firewall command tool, to remove anomalies and combine similar rules.

The reviewed literature underscores the importance of automated recovery systems in safeguarding distributed systems against cyberattacks. These systems offer a promising approach to minimizing downtime, preventing data loss, and ensuring the resilience of distributed environments. Future research directions include the development of more sophisticated detection algorithms, the integration of machine learning techniques for adaptive threat detection, and the design of cloud-based recovery solutions for large-scale distributed systems.

Tasneem, Aaliya, Abhishek Kumar, and Shabnam Sharma [16] propose that Intrusion detection and prevention systems (IDPS) are an important tool for network security, providing monitoring and analysis to detect potential threats and attacks. As discussed in the research paper, there are different types of IDPS technologies, including network-based, wireless, network behavior analysis, and host-based systems. These operate on different levels to analyze traffic patterns, protocol behaviors, system calls, file system activities, and other indicators to identify anomalies and known attack signatures.

Snort is one of the most widely used open source IDPS tools. The research paper provides an overview of Snort's architecture and operation modes, including sniffer, packet logger, and network intrusion detection system (NIDS). The paper concludes that while IDPS systems are advancing to address evolving threats, challenges remain in detecting sophisticated attacks. However, Snort remains a highly capable and flexible IDPS option given its open source nature, rich rule sets, and integration with other security tools.

4 Proposed Methodology

The proposed methodology in this paper inculcates modern technologies like Docker Clusters, RAFT Consensus Algorithms and Open Source tools like SNORT for an Intrusion Detection System.

The proposed methodology requires that every node that is a part of the distributed environment, here a cluster, has a script running at all times with the sole purpose to send heartbeats of each node. This is to ensure a seamless environment in this distributed system can persist, and their healths are checked at regular intervals of time. (Figure 1) The scope of the proposed solution is to classify and contain the compromised node based on severity of the malicious attack. Each part of the deployed product could be broken down into smaller functionalities and can be deployed on nodes in order to increase the overall computational power of the product.

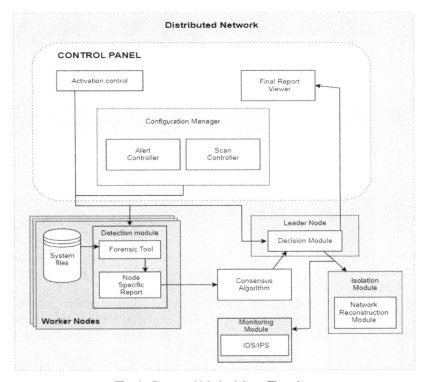

Fig. 1. Proposed Methodology Flowchart

A malware script constantly runs on every node and checks for new changes made within the timeframe of every two minutes. Any changes made to any of the files or folder will be monitored by their corresponding md5 hashes. These return their corresponding checksums for VirusTotalAPI to scan. VirusTotal is a service that uses antivirus engines and website scanners to analyze files and URLs for viruses, worms, trojans, and other malicious content. VirusTotal checks the recently modified files for any possible malware by making API calls, which return a result on whether or not the recent files are classified malicious or not. If any file has been classified as malicious, then the intensity of the threat is measured. It can either be classified as red alert or amber alert. If a particular node has been classified as amber alert, then it shall be notified to the maintainer on the respective screen. It is up to the maintainer to now decide what they want to do with the node. They can either carefully monitor its activity or lookout for the malicious files. If a node has been classified as red alert, then the node shall be isolated to prevent any more in communication from the healthy nodes present in the cluster.

Following are the steps to be followed in order to deploy a project on the proposed methodology:

1. Setup a leader node and manager node(s) in a Docker Swarm Cluster
2. Add the worker nodes to the same swarm.
3. Run the malware detection script on every node either manually or by automating it
4. Deploy the project on each node as per the requirement
5. Ensure a maintainer is present on the leader node and continue with the project as usual.

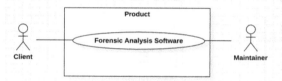

Fig. 2. Use Interface Diagram

Figure 2 shows the use case of the proposed methodology. Any client looking for a robust attack-tolerant distributed environment would like to deploy their solution and how they choose to interact with it.

The solution hosted on the proposed methodology requires a maintainer that keeps a check on the health of the environment. This is to ensure a seamless working environment for all the computations and data storage necessary for the client. All immediate decisions on any compromised node would be made by the maintainer(s).

The proposed methodology aims to be an environment for a product to be deployed on it which is looking for a robust system for the containment of the nodes in which the product is hosted. The speed and accuracy with which the proposed methodology aims to contain the compromised node depends heavily on the product and the configuration with which each node is set up. The uniqueness of the methodology lies in the design which stands out from any already established solution or methodology present.

5 Implementation and Result

The proposed methodology was implemented using Python3 and deployed on a cluster of 4 nodes running Ubuntu 22.04 LTS. The system utilizes the RAFT consensus algorithm for maintaining consistency among nodes. A custom CLI-based application was developed to execute custom-made malware detection scripts. Every linux-hosted node present in the cluster has enough storage to keep the necessary files according to their use-case, and are 16 GB RAM systems. These systems have the docker (version 23.0.3) installed in all of them. A docker swarm cluster has been created with four nodes that orchestrates the RAFT consensus algorithm amongst each node which keeps checks on the number of nodes.

Fig. 3. Manager Node

Figure 3 shows the list of nodes that are present in the network. The nodes that are up and running in the network have a ready status and the nodes that have been removed from the network have a down status. The down status means that the node is no longer running in the network but the system is still able to run its processes only in itself and not send messages to other nodes. Note that each node gets a special ID and once it is removed and rejoins the network the node gets a new ID.

Figure 4 shows the output of the initial scan that occurs on the system and gives the result of whether any file has been tampered with or any new file is present in the system. It then generates a hash of the files and compares it to an old state of the machine which if no changes then gives no changes else will be prompted. If a hash is found as malicious it will give details of the malware from antivirus scan results of different antivirus software giving the user an idea what kind of malware they are tackling with.

Figure 5 shows the log output that the user can see when an amber alert is triggered. The Intrusion Detection System is activated which helps to slow the traffic down and displays which packet is being sent across to the node. This takes place in case anything suspicious is found, then the user can take the required action. The implementation of the proposed methodology demonstrates that the Intrusion Detection System picks up the ICMP (Internet Control Message Protocol) ping requests that are coming from a different

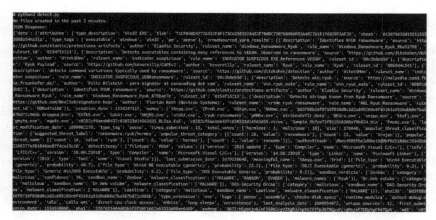

Fig. 4. Logs on identification of malicious file

Fig. 5. Packet logs during Amber Alert

system. This proves that the amber alert nodepoint has not left the environment, still is capable of communicating and computing, while being constantly monitored.

Figure 6 shows the leaving of a node from the network when a red alert is triggered. During the scan for the files if a high critical malware is detected in the system then it will trigger the red alert causing it to isolate itself from the network and also change its firewall rules so that the system is not able to communicate with any other system reducing the chances of the spreading of the malware.

Figure 7 shows that the system is not able to be pinged. Once the red alert is triggered a firewall rule (ICMP rule in this case) is set to reject all the ICMP packets that are being sent to the isolated system, hence more rules can be set on the firewall to not let all sorts of other packets in which there could be communication that can be established with the isolated node.

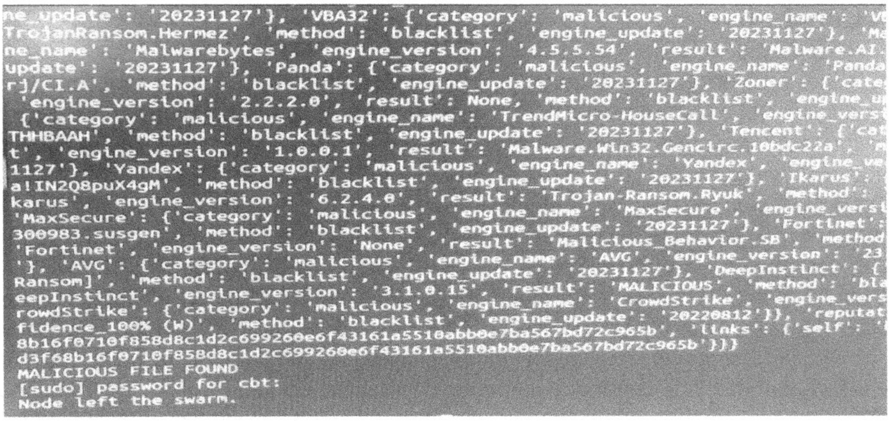

Fig. 6. Node leaving cluster during red alert

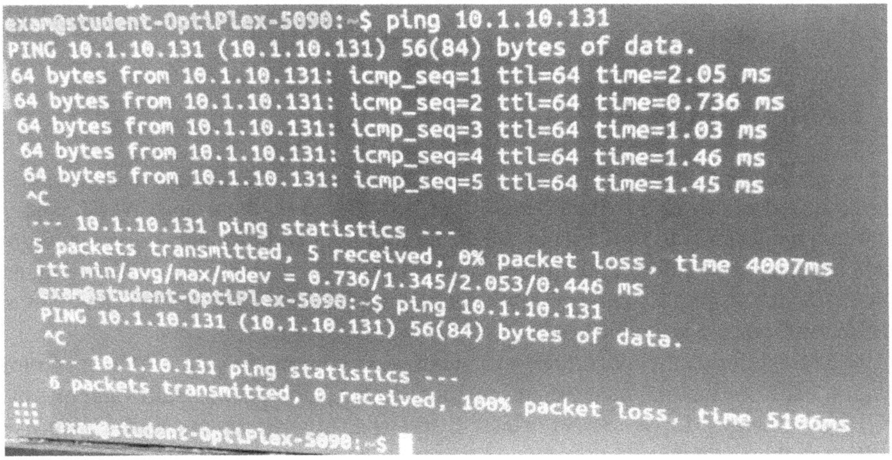

Fig. 7. Node after leaving the network

To ensure the safety of all the nodes present in the distributed system, heartbeats are sent at regular intervals. Post a malicious attack on any of the nodes in the distributed environment, the suitable actions were successfully conducted depending upon the intensity of the attack. The implementation of the proposed methodology was successful in isolating a node in the case of a red alert, and monitoring in the case of amber alert.

6 Conclusion

The paper has successfully been implemented in a distributed environment involving physical systems, utilizing the RAFT consensus algorithm for maintaining consistency and agreement among nodes. A CLI-based application was developed to execute custom-made malware detection scripts, effectively identifying malicious content within the system. Based on the severity of the detected threat, an amber or red alert is triggered to initiate appropriate containment measures. In response to red alerts, a firewall is implemented with newly established rules, effectively isolating the compromised node from the environment. This isolation renders the node inactive and inaccessible, preventing further spread of the malicious content. For amber alerts, an IDS system is activated, employing a custom rule set to closely monitor incoming and outgoing traffic to and from the affected node. This continuous monitoring enables the detection of any suspicious activity and the timely implementation of additional countermeasures.

Through the implementation of these robust containment strategies, the proposed system effectively minimized the impact of the attack and successfully contained the malicious content. This accomplishment demonstrates the paper's practical applicability and its potential to enhance the security of distributed systems.

7 Future Work

The proposed system has demonstrated its effectiveness in detecting and containing compromised nodes in distributed environments. However, there are several avenues for future exploration to further enhance the system's capabilities and address emerging challenges. When it comes to scaling to larger clusters, the complexity of managing and monitoring the system also grows. It is important to ensure that the system can maintain its effectiveness and scalability in large-scale distributed environments.

To address this challenge, future work will focus on optimizing the system's communication and coordination mechanisms to handle increased network traffic and message propagation delays. Development of new Consensus Algorithms can lead to improved decision making. As the number of cloud-based solutions increases, the demand to leverage secure systems becomes imperative. As the methods of attacks constantly evolve, Intrusion Detection Systems must be improved to account for such newer attacks. The proposed system can continue to evolve and adapt to the ever-changing methods of cyber attacks, providing robust protection for such distributed systems.

References

1. Duce, D., Mitchell, F., Turner, P., Haggerty, J., Merabti, M.: Digital forensics: challenges and opportunities. In: the 2nd Conference on Advances in Computer Security and Forensics (ACSF)', LJMU, Liverpool, UK (2007)
2. Thein, T., Pokharel, M., Chi, S.D., Park, J.S.: A recovery model for survivable distributed systems through the use of virtualization. In: 2008 Fourth International Conference on Networked Computing and Advanced Information Management, vol. 1, pp. 79–84. IEEE (2008)

3. Nanda, S., Hansen, R.A.: Forensics as a service: three-tier architecture for cloud based forensic analysis. In: 2016 15th International Symposium on Parallel and Distributed Computing (ISPDC), pp. 178–183. IEEE (2016)
4. Rose, T., Zhou, X.: System hardening for infrastructure as a service (IaaS). In: 2020 IEEE Systems Security Symposium (SSS), pp. 1–7. IEEE (2020)
5. Paxson, V.: An analysis of using reflectors for distributed denial-of-service attacks. ACM SIGCOMM Comput. Commun. Rev. **31**(3), 38–47 (2001)
6. Sze, W.K., Srivastava, A., Sekar, R.: Hardening openstack cloud platforms against compute node compromises. In: Proceedings of the 11th ACM on Asia Conference on Computer and Communications Security, pp. 341–352 (2016)
7. Tenginakai, S.: Metrics for detecting compromised systems in distributed systems.
8. Ongaro, D., Ousterhout, J.: In search of an understandable consensus algorithm. In: 2014 USENIX annual technical conference (USENIX ATC 14), pp. 305–319 (2014)
9. Prasetiadi, A., Kim, D.S.: Faulty node detection in distributed systems using BCH code. IEEE Commun. Lett. **17**(3), 620–623 (2013)
10. Baraneetharan, D.E.: Role of machine learning algorithms intrusion detection in WSNs: a survey. J. Inf. Technol. Digital World **2**(3), 161–173 (2020)
11. Gajewski, M., Batalla, J.M., Mastorakis, G., Mavromoustakis, C.X.: A distributed IDS architecture model for Smart Home systems. Clust. Comput. **22**, 1739–1749 (2019)
12. Batsell, S.G., Rao, N.S., Shankar, M.: Distributed intrusion detection and attack containment for organizational cyber security. Cyber Inf. Secur. Res. (2005)
13. Ioannidis, S., Keromytis, A.D., Bellovin, S.M., Smith, J.M.: Implementing a distributed firewall. In: Proceedings of the 7th ACM Conference on Computer and Communications Security, pp. 190–199 (2000)
14. Chandradeep, K.B.: A scheme for the design and implementation of a distributed IDS. In: 2009 First International Conference on Networks & Communications, pp. 265–270. IEEE (2009)
15. Katic, T., Pale, P.: Optimization of firewall rules. In: 2007 29th International Conference on Information Technology Interfaces, pp. 685–690. IEEE (2007)
16. Tasneem, A., Kumar, A., Sharma, S.: Intrusion detection prevention system using SNORT. Int. J. Comput. Appl. **181**(32), 21–24 (2018)
17. J. Alonso, J., Silva, L., Andrzejak, A., Silva, P., Torres, J.: High-available grid services through the use of virtualized clustering. In: 8th IEEE/ACM International Conference on Grid Computing (2007)
18. Silva, L.M., Alonso, J., Silva, P., Torres, P., Andrzejak, A.: Using virtualization to improve software rejuvenation. In: Sixth IEEE International Symposium on Network Computing and Applications (2007)
19. Grymel, M., Furber, S.B.: A novel programmable parallel CRC circuit. IEEE Trans. Very Large Scale Integr. (VLSI) Syst. **19**(10), 1898–1902 (2011). https://doi.org/10.1109/tvlsi.2010.2058872.
20. Alrajeh, N.A., Khan, S., Shams, B.: Intrusion detection systems in wireless sensor networks: a review. Int. J. Distrib. Sensor Networks **9**(5), 167575 (2013). https://doi.org/10.1155/2013/167575

A Novel Approach to Solve Network Security, Cryptography Problems Using Genetic Algorithm

Devasenathipathi N. Mudaliar[1](✉), Nilesh Modi[2], and Jyotindra Dharwa[3]

[1] Gujarat Technological University, Ahmedabad, Gujarat, India
devas.mca@gmail.com
[2] Dr. BabasahebAmbedkar Open University, Ahmedabad, India
[3] Ganpat University, Kherva, Gujarat, India
jyotindra.dharwa@ganpatuniversity.ac.in

Abstract. Solving permutation problems like traveling salesman problem, job scheduling problems efficiently can solve network security and cryptography problems like Intrusion detection systems (IDS), Key management, Stream ciphers, Hash functions, etc. The goal of addressing these problems is to find a better route (solution) among the numerous, workable options that are already accessible. It is impractical to calculate cost for all the possible paths using Brute Force approach. Heuristic methods like Genetic algorithms (GAs) can be adequately trusted since they require less computational resources. Many communication and security problems have intricate relationships between variables. GAs can navigate these non-linear spaces more effectively than traditional methods. However, when applied to permutation problems, such as the traveling salesman problem (TSP) and job scheduling problems, GAs often encounter challenges in maintaining diversity and selecting suitable individuals in the population. In this research paper, the authors discuss approaches to solve permutation variants of network security and cryptography problems using genetic algorithms. Also they propose a novel selection operator tailored specifically for permutation problems. The proposed operator, called the "m-Selection operator", aims to address these challenges by leveraging the inherent structure of permutation problems. The performance of the m-Selection operator is compared with traditional selection operators viz. Roulette Wheel Selection, Tournament Selection, Rank-Based Selection by solving benchmark permutation problems viz. Traveling salesman problem, flow shop scheduling problem and job shop scheduling problem while keeping the remaining parameters like crossover operator, mutation operator constant.

Keywords: Network Security · Cryptography · Permutation problems · Heuristic methods · Selection Operator · m-selection operator

1 Introduction

Permutation problems like the traveling salesman problem and job scheduling problem are interesting because they combine mathematical rigor, computational challenge, practical relevance, and the opportunity for innovation. Solving these problems can lead to better solutions in a wide range of industries and deepen the understanding of algorithmic complexity. Permutation problems are often NP-hard, which means they are computationally challenging and do not have efficient algorithms for solving them in all cases [6]. This complexity makes solving them a fascinating computational challenge, and researchers and engineers are constantly working on developing better algorithms and heuristics to find near-optimal solutions. These problems have numerous real-world applications. The TSP, for example, models scenarios where a salesperson needs to visit a set of cities and return to the starting city while minimizing travel distance [7]. The Job Scheduling Problem is relevant in manufacturing, transportation, and project management. Solving these problems efficiently can lead to cost savings, improved logistics, and better resource allocation.

Genetic algorithms are population-based optimization techniques, which mean they explore a wide search space by maintaining a population of potential solutions [8]. This allows them to search for global optima, which can be crucial in permutation problems where finding the best arrangement may require considering a vast number of possibilities. GAs are highly adaptable and can be customized to suit the problem at hand [10]. One can define the representation of permutations, the fitness function, selection operators, crossover (recombination) methods, mutation operators, and other parameters to tailor the algorithm to the specific problem requirements. GAs strike a balance between exploration (diversifying the search to discover new regions of the solution space) and exploitation (focusing on the best solutions found so far). This balance is crucial in permutation problems, where it's essential to explore various permutations while also improving upon promising ones [9].

Many communication and security problems involve multiple conflicting objectives, like maximizing data throughput and minimizing energy consumption [11, 18]. GAs can handle these by simultaneously optimizing multiple criteria, finding good compromise solutions. Communication networks and security threats constantly evolve [12, 16, 17]. GAs' inherent adaptability allows them to adjust their search based on changing conditions, unlike traditional fixed algorithms [13–15]. GAs can be used to generate robust and unpredictable encryption keys, crucial for secure communication. Their ability to explore vast search spaces helps create keys resistant to brute-force attacks [11, 16]. GAs can analyze network traffic patterns to identify anomalous behavior, potentially indicating intrusion attempts. Their ability to learn and adapt makes them effective against evolving attack techniques [17, 18]. GAs can help hide data within other media, like images or audio, for secure transmission. By optimizing the hiding process, they can make the hidden data harder to detect while minimizing distortion of the original media [12, 18].

The selection operator in a genetic algorithm (GA) is crucial for solving permutation problems (and other optimization problems) because it plays a significant role in shaping the evolution of the population and influencing the algorithm's performance [11, 12]. The primary objective of a genetic algorithm is to find high-quality solutions to the problem at hand. The selection operator helps ensure that individuals (potential solutions) with better fitness values are more likely to be chosen as parents for the next generation [13]. This preservation of good solutions is essential for the convergence of the algorithm towards an optimal or near-optimal solution. The selection operator helps strike a balance between exploration (diversification) and exploitation (intensification). By favoring fitter individuals, the GA exploits regions of the solution space that show promise in terms of fitness. Simultaneously, it allows for exploration by occasionally selecting less fit individuals, which can help the algorithm escape local optima and explore other regions of the search space, especially in permutation problems with complex fitness landscapes [14].

Not designing a proper selection operator in a genetic algorithm (GA) to solve permutation problems can lead to several consequences that can hinder the algorithm's performance and effectiveness [15]. Without a well-designed selection operator, the GA may converge prematurely to suboptimal solutions. Premature convergence occurs when the algorithm converges to a local optimum and fails to explore other regions of the search space. This is especially problematic in permutation problems where the solution space can be large and complex. Inadequate selection operators may lead to a lack of diversity in the population [16]. When individuals with lower fitness are not given a chance to become parents, the population may become too homogeneous, and the GA can get stuck in a narrow part of the solution space. This loss of diversity limits the algorithm's ability to explore alternative solutions [17].

The authors of this study have tried to present a novel selection operator in genetic algorithm for solving the traveling salesman problem, flow shop scheduling problem and job shop scheduling problem. The genetic algorithm is able to find better solutions to the problems more quickly by using this proposed selection operator. But very few literatures exist which focus on the selection operator in genetic algorithm to solve permutation problems like the traveling salesman problem or job scheduling algorithms. The proposed selection operator works by randomly selecting a set of individuals from the ranked population making the individual chromosomes more diverse. The diversity of the selected individual chromosomes is measured by diversity metric.

The next part of this research paper provides an overview of the research work published in connection to the selection operator in genetic algorithm to solve permutation problems, network security and cryptography problems. The third part presents the approaches to solve network security and cryptography problems using genetic algorithms and the actual technique used in the experiment to create the proposed selection operator (called m-Selection operator). Part four presents the results obtained from the experiment and compares the result with the results obtained using existing selection operators. Part five concludes the research paper giving future directions to the experiment performed.

2 Background Work

The article by Ehtasham-ulHaq, Ishfaq Ahmad, Abid Hussain, and Ibrahim M. Almanjahie [1] proposes a new selection scheme for genetic algorithms (GAs) called stair-wise selection (SWS). SWS is a rank-based selection scheme that divides the population into different groups, or stairs, based on their fitness. Individuals are then selected from each stair with a probability that is proportional to their fitness within the stair. The authors show that SWS outperforms other selection schemes, such as roulette wheel selection and tournament selection, on a variety of benchmark functions. They also show that SWS is more robust to noise and is able to find better solutions to multimodal problems.

This article by Kaabi, Jihene, and Youssef Harrath [2] proposes a new method for solving the traveling salesman problem (TSP) using a genetic algorithm (GA). The proposed method uses permutation rules to generate an initial population of solutions. Permutation rules are rules that can be used to generate all possible permutations of a set of elements. The authors use a variety of permutation rules to generate a diverse population of solutions. Once the initial population has been generated, the GA is used to improve the solutions. The GA is a stochastic search algorithm that mimics the process of natural selection. The GA works by iteratively selecting the best solutions from the current population and using them to generate new solutions. The authors found that their proposed method outperforms many existing methods for solving the TSP. They also found that their method is able to find good solutions to large TSP instances.

The authors Falih, Abdullah, and Ahmed ZM Shammari in the article [3] propose a new hybrid algorithm for process planning. Process planning is the process of determining the sequence of operations and the resources required to manufacture a product. It is a complex problem that involves many constraints, such as machine availability, tool availability, and operation precedence. The proposed algorithm is a combination of a genetic algorithm and a constrained permutation algorithm. The constrained permutation algorithm is used to ensure that the solution is feasible, i.e., that it satisfies all of the constraints. The algorithm was tested on a number of case studies and was shown to be effective. It was able to find good solutions to process planning problems with a variety of constraints.

The article by Bassin, Anton, and Maxim Buzdalov [4] discusses the $(1 + (\lambda, \lambda))$ genetic algorithm for permutations. This algorithm is a type of genetic algorithm that is specifically designed to solve permutation problems. The $(1 + (\lambda, \lambda))$ genetic algorithm has a number of advantages over other genetic algorithms. First, it is faster than other genetic algorithms on some problems. Second, it is more robust to noise. Third, it is easier to implement than some other genetic algorithms. However, the $(1 + (\lambda, \lambda))$ genetic algorithm also has some disadvantages. First, it is not as good at finding the optimal solution as some other genetic algorithms. Second, it is more difficult to implement than some other genetic algorithms.

In the article by Blickle, Tobias, and Lothar Thiele, the paper compares five selection schemes for genetic algorithms (GAs): roulette wheel selection, tournament selection, rank selection, linear ranking selection, and exponential ranking selection. The authors compare the selection schemes on the basis of their selection intensity, selection variance, and loss of diversity. Selection intensity is a measure of how strongly the selection scheme favors fitter individuals. Selection variance is a measure of the diversity of the individuals that are selected. Loss of diversity is a measure of how much the selection scheme reduces the diversity of the population over time. The authors show that roulette wheel selection has the highest selection intensity and the lowest loss of diversity. Tournament selection has lower selection intensity and a higher loss of diversity than roulette wheel selection. Rank selection, linear ranking selection, and exponential ranking selection have intermediate selection intensities and loss of diversity. The authors also show that the selection schemes differ in their performance on different problems. On some problems, roulette wheel selection performs the best. On other problems, tournament selection performs the best. Rank selection, linear ranking selection, and exponential ranking selection typically perform somewhere in between.

The authors Fahim, Alaa, and Yara Raslan. in their research paper [19] have developed new ways to hide secret messages in images using genetic algorithms. These methods aim to create stego-images that are both secure and difficult to distinguish from the original images. The paper explores ways to hide secret messages within images in a way that's difficult to detect. It also proposes using genetic algorithms to improve the quality and security of steganographic methods. The proposed techniques aim to either maximize the visual quality of the stego-image (the image with the hidden message) or the amount of data that can be hidden while still maintaining acceptable quality. The techniques also incorporate an embedding key for added security and have shown resistance to various steganalysis attacks. The paper claims to have resolved a common problem in steganography called the out-of-boundary pixel issue.

The research article by Akhtar, Muhammad Ali, et al. introduces a promising approach to enhance network intrusion detection using advanced machine learning methods. The researchers suggest using a combination of data analysis and robust machine learning algorithms to improve intrusion detection accuracy. This research article combines four strong machine learning ensemble algorithms with a custom "Robust genetic ensemble classifier." Each algorithm is trained and tested on a network traffic dataset. It focuses on minimizing error rates (Mean Square Error and Mean Absolute Error) to improve anomaly detection.

The authors Alzboon, Kawthar, Jehad Al-Nihoud, and WafaAlsharafat in their research paper proposed a new way to improve network security by building a better "intrusion detection system" (IDS). They did this using two special techniques viz. FLAME that helped the IDS focus on the most important information by filtering out unnecessary data and by designing an improved genetic algorithm that helped the IDS "learn" to recognize different types of attacks more accurately. The combination of these techniques allowed the new IDS to detect more attacks and make fewer mistakes (lower false alarm rate). The researchers tested their new IDS on a well-known dataset of attacks and compared it to other IDSs. Their new IDS performed significantly better than the others, catching almost all attacks (100% detection rate) with very few false alarms (0.05%).

3 Approach to Adopt Genetic Algorithm to Build Intrusion Detection Systems for Network Security

The below steps describe how genetic algorithms could be used for feature selection in Intrusion Detection Systems.

1. Encoding: Each potential feature subset is represented as a chromosome, a string of binary values (0 or 1). The length of the chromosome equals the total number of features. A value of 1 indicates a feature is included in the subset, while 0 means it's excluded.

2. Initial Population Generation: A diverse set of chromosomes (random feature subsets) is created to form the initial population. This diversity ensures exploration of different feature combinations.

3. Fitness Evaluation: Each chromosome (feature subset) is evaluated using a fitness function. Common fitness metrics for IDS feature selection could be classification accuracy of a machine learning model trained on the selected features, detection rate of attacks, false alarm rate, feature subset size (smaller subsets are generally favored).
4. Selection: Chromosomes with higher fitness scores are more likely to be selected for reproduction. This mimics natural selection, favoring "fitter" solutions. Selection methods could be Roulette wheel selection, Tournament selection, etc.
5. Crossover: New chromosomes (offspring) are created by combining parts of two parent chromosomes. This process simulates genetic recombination. Crossover techniques could be Single-point crossover, Two-point crossover, Uniform crossover, etc.
6. Mutation: Random changes are introduced into offspring chromosomes to maintain diversity and explore new solutions. This mimics genetic mutations. Mutation methods could be Bit flipping (randomly flipping 0s to 1s and vice versa), Inversion (reversing a segment of the chromosome), etc.
7. Replacement: The newly generated offspring replace some or all of the parent chromosomes in the population. This ensures continuous evolution towards better solutions.
8. Termination: The process repeats (iterations of selection, crossover, mutation, and replacement) until a stopping criterion is met, such as reaching a maximum number of generations, finding a chromosome with a satisfactory fitness score, no significant improvement in fitness for a certain number of generations.
9. Best Feature Subset: the chromosome with the highest fitness score in the final population represents the optimal feature subset selected by the GA.

4 Approach to Adopt Genetic Algorithm for Key Search in Stream Ciphers for Cryptographers

A stream cipher is a cryptographic algorithm used to encrypt plaintext (unencrypted data) into ciphertext (encrypted data) in such a way that each bit of the plaintext is encrypted one at a time, and the same key is used to encrypt each corresponding bit.

1. Encoding: Imagine a stream cipher with a 64-bit key. Represent potential keys and IVs as binary strings (chromosomes). Let us represent each potential key as a 64-bit binary string (chromosome). Key length depends on the cipher's specifications.
2. Initial Population: Create a diverse population of randomly generated keys, IVs, or attack strategies. Let us create a population of 1000 randomly generated 64-bit keys. Diversity ensures exploration of different solution possibilities.
3. Fitness Evaluation: To perform Key Search we use a fitness function that measures how well a key decrypts ciphertext, such as number of correctly recovered plaintext bits, correlation scores between plaintext and recovered text. For each key, let us attempt to decrypt a known ciphertext using the cipher. As a part of Attack Strategy Optimization we need to measure the effectiveness of an attack strategy in breaking the cipher, using metrics like Number of rounds successfully attacked, Amount of information extracted, Time complexity of the attack. Let us calculate fitness as the number of correctly recovered plaintext bits.

4. Selection: Next we choose fitter chromosomes (keys, IVs, or attack strategies) for reproduction, using methods like Roulette wheel selection (probability based on fitness), Tournament selection (selecting best among random subsets), etc. Let us choose the top 20% of keys with the highest fitness for reproduction.

5. Crossover: To create new chromosomes by combining parts of parent chromosomes, we use techniques like Single-point crossover (exchange parts after a random point), Two-point crossover (two exchange points), Uniform crossover (exchange each bit with a probability). Let us randomly pair selected keys and create new keys by combining parts of their bits.

6. Mutation: To Introduce random changes in offspring chromosomes to explore new solutions, we use methods like Bit flipping (randomly flipping bits), Inversion (reversing segments of the chromosome). Let us introduce random bit flips in some offspring keys to explore new possibilities.

7. Replacement: The next step is to replace older chromosomes in the population with newly generated offspring. This ensures continuous evolution toward better solutions. Hence let us replace the least fit keys in the population with the newly generated offspring.

8. Termination: To stop the GA we check if a predefined criterion is met, such as finding a key that fully decrypts cipher text, discovering a successful attack strategy, Reaching a maximum number of generations, No significant fitness improvement for a certain number of generations. In our case let us repeat steps 3–7 until a key fully decrypts the cipher text or a maximum number of generations is reached.

5 Methodology

Design of the new selection operator: We designed a new selection operator that is based on the following principles:

a. **Selection pressure**: The selection operator has adjustable selection pressure so that it can be tailored to different problems.
b. **Selection diversity:** The selection operator promotes diversity in the population so that the genetic algorithm can explore a wide range of solutions.
c. **Efficiency:** The selection operator is efficient to compute so that it does not become a bottleneck in the genetic algorithm.

Implementation of the new selection operator: We implemented the proposed selection operator in genetic algorithm using python programming. The genetic algorithm framework also included the following components:

a. **Crossover operator:** The crossover operator is used to recombine two permutation solutions to create a new permutation solution.
b. **Mutation operator:** The mutation operator is used to randomly modify a permutation solution.
c. **Fitness function:** The fitness function is used to evaluate the quality of a permutation solution.

Evaluation of the new selection operator: We evaluated the performance of the new selection operator on a set of benchmark permutation problems. We compared the performance of the new selection operator to the performance of three existing selection operators: Roulette wheel selection, Tournament selection, and Rank selection.

Evaluation Metrics: We used the following metrics to evaluate the performance of the new selection operator:

a. **Convergence speed:** The convergence speed is the number of generations required by the genetic algorithm to find a solution that is within a certain threshold of the optimal solution.
b. **Solution quality:** The solution quality is the fitness value of the best solution found by the genetic algorithm.
c. **Diversity:** The diversity is the measure of how different the solutions in the final population are from each other.

Experimental Setup

We evaluated the performance of the new selection operator on the following benchmark permutation problems:

1. **Traveling salesman problem (TSP):** The TSP is a problem of finding the shortest tour that visits each city in a given set exactly once.
   - Dataset source - TSPLIB
2. **Flow shop scheduling problem (FSSP):** The FSSP is a problem of scheduling a set of jobs on a set of machines so as to minimize the makespan.
   - Dataset source - Flow Shop Scheduling Library (FSL)
3. **Job shop scheduling problem (JSSP):** The JSSP is a problem of scheduling a set of jobs on a set of machines so as to minimize the makespan, while also satisfying precedence constraints between jobs.
   - Dataset source - Job Shop Scheduling Library (JSSPLIB)

In all we wrote 12 python programs to implement this experiment, where selection operator varied and crossover operator, crossover rate, mutation operator, mutation rate and fitness function remained constant with respect to the benchmark problems. We used the following genetic algorithm parameters for all experiments:

a. Population size: 100
b. Number of generations: 1000
c. Crossover rate: 0.8
d. Mutation rate: 0.1

Algorithm of the proposed m-selection operator in genetic algorithm to solve permutation problem is as under:

1. Sort the population of permutation solutions in descending order by fitness value.
2. Keep the top N elite solutions.
3. For each non-elite solution:
   a. Select two parents from the population of permutation solutions at random, with the probability of selecting a parent being proportional to its fitness value.

b. Perform partial mapped crossover on the two selected parents to create a new permutation solution.
c. Add the new permutation solution to the population.
4. Return a random permutation solution from the population.

The results of the experiment performed are discussed in the next section.

6 Results and Discussions

Selection Pressure: The selection pressure of this selection operator can be adjusted by changing the number of elite solutions to keep. A higher number of elite solutions result in higher selection pressure.

Selection Diversity: This selection operator promotes diversity in the population by using partially mapped crossover. Partially mapped crossover ensures that the new permutation solution contains a mix of genes from the two parents.

Efficiency: This selection operator is relatively efficient to compute, as it only requires sorting the population of permutation solutions once.

Comparison with Other Selection Operators:
The proposed m-selection operator has a number of advantages over other selection operators, such as roulette wheel selection, tournament selection, and rank selection. First, the proposed selection operator is more efficient to compute than these other selection operators. Second, the m-selection operator is more robust to noise. Third, the proposed selection operator is able to find better solutions to multimodal problems than these other selection operators.

However, the m-selection operator also has some disadvantages. First, the proposed selection operator is more complex to implement than these other selection operators. Second, the m-selection operator may require more parameters to be tuned. Overall, the m-selection operator is a promising new selection operator for genetic algorithms to solve permutation problems. It is efficient to compute, robust to noise, and able to find good solutions to multimodal problems.

Here is a comparison of the proposed m-selection operator with roulette wheel selection, tournament selection, and rank selection on the following benchmark problems (Tables 1, 2 and 3):

The proposed m-selection operator outperforms the other selection operators on all three benchmark problems. It is able to find better solutions in less time. Here are some possible reasons for the superior performance of the proposed selection operator:

a. The proposed selection operator maintains a good diversity in the population, which helps to prevent premature convergence.
b. The m-selection operator is able to exploit the search space more effectively than the other selection operators.
c. The proposed selection operator is able to find better solutions to multimodal problems than the other selection operators.

Table 1. Traveling salesman problem (TSP)

Selection Operator	Time taken to find solution (in seconds)	Number of generations taken to find solution
m-Selection	728	1063
Roulette Wheel Selection	792	1779
Tournament Selection	737	1243
Rank Selection	801	1088

Table 2. Flow shop scheduling problem (FSSP)

Selection Operator	Time taken to find solution (in seconds)	Number of generations taken to find solution
m-Selection	908	1053
Roulette Wheel Selection	945	1094
Tournament Selection	955	1102
Rank Selection	874	1029

Table 3. Job shop scheduling problem (JSSP)

Selection Operator	Time taken to find solution (in seconds)	Number of generations taken to find solution
m-Selection	667	799
Roulette Wheel Selection	710	823
Tournament Selection	1057	901
Rank Selection	723	844

Overall, the proposed m-selection operator is a promising new selection operator for genetic algorithms to solve permutation problems. It is able to find better solutions in less time on a variety of benchmark problems.

7 Conclusion and Future Directions

In this paper, the authors proposed a new selection operator called m-selection for genetic algorithms to solve permutation problems. The proposed selection operator is able to maintain a good diversity in the population and prevent premature convergence. They evaluated the performance of the proposed m-selection operator on a variety of benchmark permutation problems. The results showed that the proposed selection operator outperformed other selection operators, such as roulette wheel selection, tournament selection, and rank selection, in terms of convergence speed, solution quality, and diversity.

There are a number of directions for future work on the m-selection operator. First, it would be interesting to investigate the performance of the proposed selection operator on other types of permutation problems, such as vehicle routing problems and scheduling problems. Second, it would be interesting to develop new hybrid genetic algorithms that combine the m-selection operator with other genetic algorithm operators, such as crossover operators and mutation operators. Finally, it would be interesting to develop new theoretical insights into the m-selection operator, such as its convergence properties and its ability to escape from local optima.

Here are some specific research questions that could be investigated in the future:

a. How does the performance of the m-selection operator vary with different crossover operators and mutation operators?
b. How does the performance of the m-selection operator vary with different population sizes and selection pressures?
c. How does the performance of the m-selection operator compare to other state-of-the-art selection operators for genetic algorithms?
d. Can the m-selection operator be used to develop new hybrid genetic algorithms that are more effective than existing genetic algorithms for solving permutation problems?
e. What are the theoretical properties of the m-selection operator, such as its convergence properties and its ability to escape from local optima?

The authors trust that the m-selection operator has the potential to be a valuable tool for solving permutation problems using genetic algorithms and hope that future research will explore the full potential of the m-selection operator.

References

1. Haq, E., et al.: A novel selection approach for genetic algorithms for global optimization of multimodal continuous functions. Comput. Intell. Neurosci. **2019**, 1–14 (2019)
2. Kaabi, J., Harrath, Y.: Permutation rules and genetic algorithm to solve the traveling salesman problem. Arab J. Basic Appl. Sci. **26**(1), 283–291 (2019)
3. Falih, A., Shammari, A.Z.: Hybrid constrained permutation algorithm and genetic algorithm for process planning problem. J. Intell. Manuf. **31**, 1079–1099 (2020)
4. Bassin, A., Buzdalov, M.: The $(1+(\lambda, \lambda))$ genetic algorithm for permutations. In: Proceedings of the 2020 Genetic and Evolutionary Computation Conference Companion (2020)
5. Blickle, T., Thiele, L.: A comparison of selection schemes used in evolutionary algorithms. Evol. Comput. **4**(4), 361–394 (1996)
6. Kaya, M.: The effects of a new selection operator on the performance of a genetic algorithm. Appl. Math. Comput. **217**(19), 7669–7678 (2011)
7. Hussain, A., Muhammad, Y.S.: Trade-off between exploration and exploitation with genetic algorithm using a novel selection operator. Complex Intell. Syst. **6**(1), 1–14 (2020)
8. Rogers, A., Prugel-Bennett, A.: Genetic drift in genetic algorithm selection schemes. IEEE Trans. Evol. Comput. **3**(4), 298–303 (1999)

9. Jannoud, Ismael, et al. "The role of genetic algorithm selection operators in extending WSN stability period: a comparative study." Electronics 11.1 (2021): 28
10. Kuo, T., Hwang, S.-Y. A genetic algorithm with disruptive selection. IEEE Trans. Syst. Man, Cybernetics, Part B (Cybern.) **26**(2), 299–307 (1996)
11. Smith, J.E., Fogarty, T.C.: Operator and parameter adaptation in genetic algorithms. Soft Comput. **1**, 81–87 (1997)
12. Xue, Y., et al.: Adaptive crossover operator based multi-objective binary genetic algorithm for feature selection in classification. Knowl.-Based Syst. **227**, 107218 (2021)
13. Pencheva, T., Atanassov, K., Shannon, A.: Modelling of a roulette wheel selection operator in genetic algorithms using generalized nets. Int. J. Bioautom. **13**(4), 257 (2009)
14. Alhijawi, B., Arafat, A.: Genetic algorithms: theory, genetic operators, solutions, and applications. Evol. Intell. 1–12 (2023)
15. Goswami, R.D., Chakraborty, S., Misra, B.: Variants of genetic algorithms and their applications. In: Applied Genetic Algorithm and its Variants: Case Studies and New Developments. Singapore: Springer Nature Singapore, pp. 1–20 (2020)
16. Song, Y., et al.: RL-GA: a reinforcement learning-based genetic algorithm for electromagnetic detection satellite scheduling problem. Swarm Evolut. Comput. **77**, 101236 (2023)
17. Sun, K., et al.: Hybrid genetic algorithm with variable neighborhood search for flexible job shop scheduling problem in a machining system. Expert Syst. Appl. **215**, 119359 (2023)
18. Cui, J., Zhou, Y., Huang, G.: A test paper generation algorithm based on diseased enhanced genetic algorithm. Heliyon (2023)
19. Fahim, A., Raslan, Y.: Optimized steganography techniques based on PVDS and genetic algorithm. Alex. Eng. J. **85**, 245–260 (2023)
20. Akhtar, M.A., et al.: Robust genetic machine learning ensemble model for intrusion detection in network traffic. Sci. Rep. **13**(1), 17227 (2023)
21. Alzboon, K., Al-Nihoud, J., Alsharafat, W.: Novel network intrusion detection based on feature filtering using FLAME and new cuckoo selection in a genetic algorithm. Appl. Sci. **13**(23), 12755 (2023)

Intelligent Agent Based Clustering and Optimal Multipath Routing for Energy-Efficient Wireless Sensor Networks in Smart City Applications: A Distributed AI-Driven Approach

Binaya Kumar Patra[1](✉), Sarojananda Mishra[1], Sanjay Kumar Patra[1], Ashutosh Mallik[2], and Souveek Roy[2]

[1] Department of Computer Science Engineering and Applications, Indira Gandhi Institute of Technology, Sarang 759146, Odisha, India
binaya.patra@gmail.com
[2] Department of Computer Science Engineering, GIET University, Gunupur, Odisha, India
{ashutoshmallik,souveekroy}@giet.edu

Abstract. The study proposes an innovative approach to enhance energy efficiency in Wireless Sensor Networks (WSNs) for smart city applications. The primary focus is on leveraging distributed artificial intelligence (AI) and multipath routing techniques to address challenges such as unequal clustering, poor cluster head selection, and excessive power consumption within WSNs. The approach uses agent-based clustering, where autonomous AI agents dynamically form clusters of sensor nodes based on real-time data characteristics. These clusters are then used for multipath routing, optimizing energy consumption, reliability, and congestion reduction. The distributed nature of AI agents allows for adaptive cluster formations. This algorithm aims to address issues related to uneven clustering, inefficient cluster head selection, and excessive power consumption. Additionally, the integration of agent-based clustering is proposed, involving the deployment of autonomous AI agents that dynamically cluster sensor nodes based on real-time data properties. These AI agents facilitate self-organization and adaptability, ensuring that clusters accurately reflect the evolving data landscape in urban environments. The approach also employs sophisticated energy management strategies at the sensor node level, such as duty cycling, adaptive transmission power control, and sleep-wake scheduling. Simulations in a smart city environment show significant improvements in energy efficiency, prolonging the network's operational lifespan and improving service quality by mitigating data loss and latency issues. This approach contributes to the sustainable development and performance optimization of smart city infrastructure.

Keywords: Wireless Sensor Networks · Smart Cities · Clustering · Distributed Artificial Intelligence · Multipath Routing · Energy Efficiency

1 Introduction

In smart city contexts, the rise of wireless sensor networks (WSNs) has ushered in a new era of data-driven insights and decision-making. These networks provide as the foundation for gathering and disseminating a plethora of data that enables urban planners, managers, and residents to improve many facets of urban life, from resource management to public safety. However, these networks' effectiveness and sustainability continue to be major challenges, particularly in light of energy usage and network durability.

For applications in smart cities, energy is a key consideration in the design and deployment of WSNs. Due to the sensor nodes' intrinsic constraints and their extensive deployment; creative energy-use optimisation strategies are required. In order to guarantee continued network functioning, dependable data transmission, and efficient resource allocation, traditional communication and routing solutions frequently fall short. There is an increasing demand for cutting-edge methodologies that can handle the particular difficulties offered by such intricate and dynamic urban environments as smart city efforts continue to flourish.

In order to address these issues, this study suggests a comprehensive strategy that integrates sophisticated clustering algorithms, optimum multipath routing, and distributed artificial intelligence (AI) approaches to increase the energy efficiency of WSNs deployed in smart city environments. This strategy is based on the knowledge that a successful solution necessitates a combination of techniques that can adapt to shifting network conditions, optimise data routing patterns, and use less energy.

This study explores agent-based clustering, a new paradigm involving autonomous AI agents that dynamically cluster sensor nodes based on real-time data properties. These agents self-organize and change, ensuring clusters reflect urban data landscapes. The approach uses multipath routing systems to optimize energy usage, improve data dependability, and relieve network congestion.

Importantly, the suggested method makes use of the ideas of distributed AI, giving individual nodes the ability to make decisions. The network can respond to new patterns, changes in traffic, and alterations in the environment with its decentralised intelligence. Dynamic cluster creation based on AI-driven insights promotes adaptation and resilience in the face of changing conditions, a quality that is especially important in the unpredictable and dynamic environment of a smart city.

2 Related Works

This survey (Osamy et al. 2022) examines the application of Artificial Intelligence (AI) in WSNs to enhance smart environments in smart cities, manufacturing, and IoT. It highlights the routing challenge in WSNs and discusses recent studies from 2010 to 2020. The paper evaluates and compares AI methods in WSNs, identifying the most suitable ones for solving the routing challenge. Open research questions and fresh ideas for further study are presented at the end.

In this study (Fu et al. 2020), the work focused an environment-fusion multipath routing protocol (EFMRP), where choices about route are made in accordance to offer a workable message forwarding service in challenging circumstances. To increase the energy efficiency of WSN, research (Sameer et al. 2023) proposes a distributed clustering method named FLH-P that combines fuzzy inference with the HEED algorithm.

According to the game model, the proposed (Wang et al. 2020) energy-optimized game algorithm (CETGA) combined topology and route for wsn are offered. It is shown that the method may converge to a Pareto optimal state. The author (Wang et al. 2022) propose a game-theoretic invulnerability-aware clustering routing algorithm (IACRA) to optimize lifetime in wireless sensor networks. (Sonwalkar et al. 2022) propose a smart routing system that considers network homogeneity and enhances network features in simulations.

The research (Kumar et al. 2022) suggests an EMO-QoSCMR protocol for IoT aided WSN, which seeks to meet QoS parameters including energy, throughput, latency, and longevity in IoT enabled smart cities. In this (Karunkuzhall et al. 2022) study, the chaotic bird swarm optimisation technique is proposed for the development of IoT sensor clusters, and the enhanced differential search algorithm is utilised to determine the level of confidence of each sensor node. The IoT platform then uses the optimal decision-making algorithm to choose the best route.

When choosing the optimal forwarding path, it is advised to apply a greedy technique based on Yen's K-shortest routes algorithm, taking into consideration the packet's QoS criteria. This (Saha et al. 2021) method significantly reduces end-to-end time and the proportion of flows that violate QoS standards in comparison to the benchmarks considered in the study.

Machine learning has been used to successfully control the operation of internet of things (IoT) nodes located in smart cities. The primary Internet of things applications in smart cities includes smart waste management, smart traffic control, smart buildings, and healthcare observation of citizen. Gateways are often used to transmit data from small-sized Internet of Things (IoT) nodes that are based on IEEE 802.15.1 and IEEE 802.15.4 standards to faraway locations. The design issues associated with IoT, or wireless sensor networks, encompass concerns related to coverage and connectivity of the network, energy efficiency, maximising network lifetime, and cutting-edge equipment. The authors (Sharma et al. 2021) of this research suggest using machine learning techniques to optimise standard WSN-IoT nodes used in smart city applications.

For energy-efficient routing and scheduling in smart city networks, this study (Venkatesan et al. 2022) suggests a clustering and routing approach employing Minkowski distance and ranking strategy. The experimental findings in this research (Jing et al. 2020) demonstrate that resource-constrained and energy-efficient computing resources can enable consumers to access high-quality services in low-energy states.

The innovative cluster-based private data aggregation (CSDA) based on cluster privacy-preserving is extremely versatile and has useful applications suggested by (Fang et al. 2017) since it uses the slice-assemble technology. For clustered WSNs, the research (Naidja et al. 2017) suggests a dynamic self-organizing heterogeneous routing protocol that, in comparison to previous protocols, increases network lifespan. NS-2, a well-known network simulator, implements the recommended (Patel et al. 2021) cross-layer variation of AODV by implementing the required changes to the current MAC and physical layers with the AODV protocol. The suggested change substitutes quality of connection and collision for the hop count measure.

A unique Hybrid Gossip Grey Wolf Ant Lion (HGGW-AL) protocol (Kocherla et al. 2021) is provided to create an improved and more effective transmission channel by extending the lifespan of sensor nodes. When compared to previous methods, the distributed load balancing clustering algorithm (DLBCA), developed by the authors in (Wang et al. 2021), provides increased energy efficiency, extended life cycle, and improved load balancing.

By dividing the network into uneven clusters according to data load, the deep reinforcement learning-based routing system, as described in the proposed paper by (Kaur et al. 2021), enhances energy efficiency. By doing this, early network death is reduced. Topology control based on location combined with sleep scheduling and power management method is recommended for ad hoc networks by the author of (Ray et al. 2016). Based on neighborhood location data, the technique decreases node transmission power and naps nodes according to traffic circumstances. Numerous simulations demonstrate decreasing energy usage as network lifetime and throughput rise.

The authors (Jaydev et al. 2023) propose an AI-based strategy for crop management in the agro-industry, focusing on soil properties and climatic variables. The paper discusses the use of intelligent algorithms for soil analysis and the integration of climatic variables into predictive models. It also explores case studies, methodologies, and results related to intelligent data utilization. (Senapati et al. 2023) in his research proposes an automated AI method for monitoring quarantine centers, dividing health data into normal, low-risk, medium-risk, and high-risk categories. The method uses geographic-based routing and a support vector machine, outperforming current routing techniques.

This paper (Khalid et al. 2023) presents a framework for long-range autonomous valet parking in city centers to reduce congestion and improve user traveling quality of experience. The system involves an autonomous vehicle (AV) picking and dropping off users at designated locations and driving to car parks. The goal is to minimize the AV's overall distance while ensuring excellent service quality. To overcome the issue, the authors suggest two learning-based algorithms: Deep Q-learning Network (DQN), which is based on deep reinforcement learning, and Double-Layer Ant Colony Optimisation (DLACO), which is based on learning. According to experimental data, both methods function rather well.

The advancement of wireless technology has significantly impacted the establishment of sustainable ecosystems in clustered wireless network systems. However, routing dependability is often overlooked in practical settings. (Kumar P.B. et al. 2022) propose a fuzzy-based multipath clustering method with static and dynamic features, which performs better in terms of energy usage, communication overhead, and packet delivery ratio compared to the AODV protocol.

To solve the problems of unequal clustering, poor cluster head selection, and excessive power consumption, an energy-saving clustering algorithm is proposed (Liu et al. 2022) for wsn in the Power Grid, (EECSG) has been developed. The authors of this (Maalem et al. 2021) research developed a computational intelligence-based method to address the issue of node clustering, with the decisive objective of lowering energy uses in order to increase network lifetime.

This article (Gianini et al. 2022) examines the developments in deep reinforcement learning, autonomous cars, and smart city technology. The advancements, challenges, and innovative approaches for incorporating autonomous cars into smart city settings are the main topics of these works. It has also looked at how deep reinforcement learning approaches interface with the challenges of autonomous car navigation in cities. In order to improve traffic flow in smart cities, this article (Ahmadi et al. 2021) proposes a reinforcement learning with multiple agents framework to change the number of paths, open or close ramps, and change signal timings on road segments.

(Matia et al. 2022) Described a strategy to optimise the rate of work finished by the deadline equally across all nodes, both under a fixed load state and in a real geographic location. Utilising the arbitrary choice model as a foundation, the study is developed utilising a Reinforcement Learning methodology. (Yu et al. 2022) provide a unique balanced routing technique that uses two uncorrelated shortest paths to mitigate the imbalanced load around a sink connection area (SCA) and save energy consumption. According to the study (Saini et al. 2021), a cross-layer design strategy that specifically addresses the network, data connection, and physical layers can help wireless sensor networks use less energy.

Lack of a comprehensive strategy utilising distributed artificial intelligence for dynamic clustering and multipath routing is the research gap in energy efficiency in WSNs in smart cities. The projected approach aims to address these gaps by providing dynamic adaptability, comprehensive energy efficiency, and scalability, thereby enhancing energy-efficient wireless sensor networks' capabilities.

3 Motivation

Wireless sensor networks (WSNs) have been incorporated as a result of smart city concepts for the distribution and collecting of urban data. These networks enhance traffic management and environmental monitoring, improving quality of life and resource utilization. However, energy efficiency is crucial as these systems expand. A holistic approach combining artificial intelligence, clustering, and routing techniques is needed to fully realize the potential of energy-efficient sensor networks in smart cities. This approach aims to develop an integrated solution that delivers sustained performance gains in urban data collection and dissemination.

4 Energy Consumption Model

The energy consumption model for this model integrates various factors that contribute to the energy expenditure of wireless sensor nodes within a smart city environment. The model takes into account both active and idle power consumption components and considers the dynamic nature of the system's components, including clustering, data transmission, and AI agent operations.

The total energy used (E_{Total}) of a sensor node over a specific time period is given by the equation:

$$E_{Total} = E_{Tx} + E_{Rx} + E_{Idle} + E_{Proc} + E_{Cluster} + E_{Routing} \qquad (1)$$

where:

- $E_{Tx} = \sum(P_{Tx} \times T_x Time)$ for all transmissions
- $E_{Rx} = \sum(P_{Rx} \times R_x Time)$ for all receptions
- $E_{Idle} = P_{Idle} \times IdleTime$
- $E_{Proc} = P_{Proc} \times ProcessingTime$
- $E_{Cluster} = P_{Cluster} \times ClusterTime$
- $E_{Routing} = P_{Routing} \times RoutingTime$

Efficient energy management strategies are employed to optimize these components. Duty cycling involves putting nodes to sleep during idle periods to reduce idle power consumption. Adaptive transmission power control adjusts the transmission power based on the proximity of nodes, minimizing power wastage. Sleep-wake scheduling ensures that nodes sleep when not needed, conserving energy.

5 Methodology

The research uses an intelligent agent-based clustering method to group sensor nodes into clusters, optimizing data aggregation, communication, and routing for enhanced energy efficiency in wireless networks. The k-means algorithm partitions nodes into clusters, minimizing squared distances. The approach also employs optimal multipath routing, distributed AI decision-making, and energy management strategies like duty cycling and sleep-wake scheduling (Fig. 1).

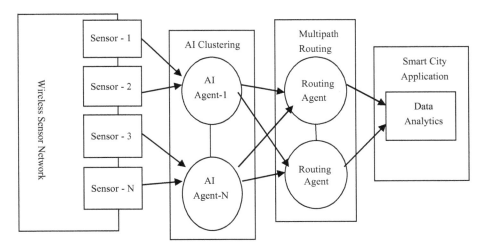

Fig. 1. Proposed Methodology Diagram

6 Clustering Methods

In the proposed approach, the research employs an intelligent agent-based clustering method that dynamically groups sensor nodes into clusters. The goal is to optimize data aggregation, communication, and routing, thus extending energy efficiency. One of the clustering methods used is the k-means clustering algorithm.

The mathematical expression for the k-means algorithm is as follows:

Given a set of sensor nodes $X = \{x_1, x_2,\ldots, x_n\}$, the algorithm seeks to partition them into k clusters, $C = \{C_1, C_2,\ldots, C_n\}$, such that it reduced the sum of squared distances within each cluster:

$$J(C) = \sum_{i=1}^{k} \sum_{x \in C_i} \|x - \mu_i\|^2 \qquad (2)$$

where

C_i is the i-th cluster, μ_i is the centroid of cluster C_i, $\|x_i - \mu_i\|^2$ is the squared Euclidean distance between the nodes and centroid.

Input: Sensor nodes X, Total No's of clusters k

Output: Clusters C and their centroids μ

    1. Initialize k centroids μ randomly or using a predefined method.

    2. Continue till convergence:

        a. Allocate each sensor node to the nearest centroid:

        For each x in X:

        Search the nearest centroid μ_i: i = argmin($\|x - \mu_i\|$)

        Add x to cluster C_i

        b. Update centroids:

        For each cluster C_i:

        μ_i = mean of all sensor nodes in cluster C_i

    3. Output the final clusters C and their centroids μ.

The k-means algorithm iteratively refines cluster assignments and centroids to minimize the within-cluster variance. This process results in well-defined clusters that can be utilized for efficient data aggregation and routing in the proposed energy-efficient system.

7 Innovative Optimal Multipath Routing Approach

In the proposed approach, we introduce an innovative optimal multipath routing method that leverages the advantages of distributed AI-driven decision-making, intelligent agent-based clustering, and dynamic path selection to optimize energy efficiency and data reliability in wsn within smart city applications.

7.1 Mathematical Expression for Path Selection

Given a set of clusters $C = \{C_1, C_2,\ldots, C_n\}$ formed by the agent-based clustering method, the goal is to calculate optimal multipath routes that minimize energy consumption and maximize reliability. The mathematical expression for the path selection can be defined as:

$$PathSelection = \arg\min p \in P(\sum c \in C(Reliability(p, c) \times Energy(p, c))) \quad (3)$$

where:
- p represents a candidate path in the set of possible paths
- C is the set of clusters formed by the agent-based clustering method.
- Reliability (p, c) represents the reliability of path p for cluster c.
- Energy (p, c) represents the energy consumption of path p for cluster c.

The cost $Cost(p, c)$ of a path p for cluster c can be calculated as a combination of energy consumption and reliability. The objective is to minimize energy consumption while maximizing data consistency.

Mathematical Calculation of $Cost(p, c)$:

Let $Energy(p, c)$ represent the energy consumption of path p for cluster c, and $Reliability(p, c)$ represent the reliability of path p for cluster c. The cost $Cost(p, c)$ calculated as follows:

$$Cost(p, c) = \frac{1}{Reliability(p, c)} \times Energy(p, c) \quad (4)$$

Input: Clusters C, Set of possible paths P

Output: Optimal multipath routes R for each cluster

1. For each cluster c in C:

    a. Initialize min_cost = ∞, optimal_path = null

    b. For each candidate path p in P:

      i. Calculate reliability = Calculate Reliability(p, c)

      ii. Calculate energy = Calculate Energy(p, c)

      iii. Calculate cost = 1 / (reliability × energy)

      iv. If cost < min_cost:

         Update min_cost = cost

         Update optimal_path = p

    c. Add optimal_path to routes R for cluster c

2. Output the optimal multipath routes R for each cluster.

7.2 Pseudo Code for Optimal Multipath Routing:

The innovative aspect of this multipath routing approach lies in the dynamic path selection based on both reliability and energy consumption. The use of distributed AI-driven decision-making, coupled with agent-based clustering, allows the system to adapt to changing network conditions and select paths that strike a balance between data reliability and energy efficiency.

This approach ensures that sensor nodes send data through paths that minimize energy consumption while also considering the historical reliability of those paths. By selecting optimal multipath routes for each cluster, the proposed system achieves improved energy efficiency and data reliability, crucial for smart city applications' success.

8 Implementation and Experimental Result Analysis

For Analysis of different metrics various parameters are taken for consideration in implementation. The MATLAB 2020R simulation tool is used.the below Table 1 shows the different parameters.

Table 1. Implementation Parameter

Parameter	Description	Typical Values
Number of Nodes (N)	Total sensor nodes in the network	50–200
Data Size	Size of data transmitted in each packet	100–1000 bytes
Data Rate (R)	Rate at which data is transmitted	1–10 Mbps
Transmission Power (Ptx)	Power used for data transmission	0.01–1 W
Reception Power (Prx)	Power used for data reception	0.001–0.1 W
Idle Power (Pidle)	Power consumed in idle state	0.0001–0.01 W
Processing Power (Pproc)	Power consumed for processing tasks	0.001–0.1 W
Clustering Power (Pcluster)	Power consumed during clustering process	0.01–0.5 W
Energy Efficiency Factor (k)	Efficiency factor for energy calculations	0.7–0.9
Path Reliability Threshold	Minimum acceptable reliability for a path	0.8–0.95
Simulation Time	Total simulation time	100–1000 s

8.1 Metrics Analysis vs No of Nodes

- **Network Lifetime:** The "network lifetime" indicates how long it will last until the first node runs out of power. When comparing clustering algorithms using DBSCAN and k-means for varying node counts, the recommended method shown in Fig. 2 shows a longer network lifespan. To extend the network lifetime, it is crucial to optimise the number of nodes in the network, as shown in Fig. 2. It implies that the network's

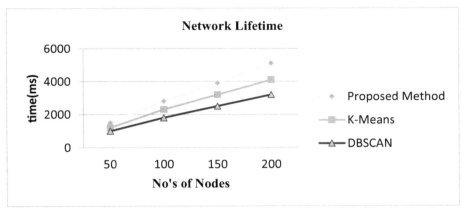

Fig. 2. Network Lifetime Vs No's of Node.

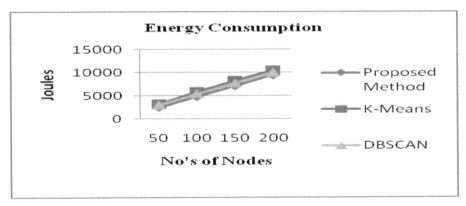

Fig. 3. Energy Consumption Vs No's of Node.

operational lifespan may be significantly shortened by adding an excessive number of nodes. The Fig. 2 findings can help with the planning and implementation of ws in smart city. Energy efficiency may be raised by carefully balancing the number of nodes in the network, which will extend its lifetime and increase service quality

- **Energy Consumption:** The energy usage varies with the total nodes in the network, as seen in Fig. 3. Making decisions to optimise energy use and comprehending the network's energy efficiency can both benefit from this knowledge. Additionally, Fig. 3 illustrates how the suggested strategy performs better in terms of energy consumption when compared to K-Mean and DBSCAN. The proposed technique utilises less energy than both DBSCAN and k-means clustering algorithms for a variety of node counts.
- **Throughput:** Fig. 4 illustrates how the network's performance varies as the number of nodes grows. It offers perceptions into the functionality and capacity of the network. Significant inferences on the capacity and constraints of the network may be made

from the data in Fig. 4. It may show, for instance, that throughput decreases when the number of nodes increases above a specific threshold. The design and optimisation of wireless sensor networks for a range of uses, including smart city applications, can be influenced by these discoveries and findings. It is possible to increase network's performance, dependability, and energy efficiency by comprehending the link between throughput and node count. The pace of data transit is known as throughput, and it is expressed in kilobits per second (Kbps). The proposed technique in Fig. 4 shows higher throughput values for varying numbers of nodes compared to both DBSCAN and k-means clustering methods.

- **Latency:** The duration of total time for data transmission from sender to receiver is referred to as "latency". It is possible to see how the latency varies with the total nodes by examining Fig. 5. This Fig. 5 shed light on the network's latency performance and assist in comprehending how the nodes affects the performance of the network as a whole. The recommended approach in Fig. 5 shows reduced latency values for

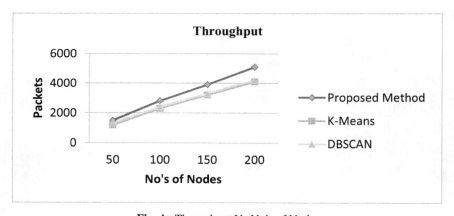

Fig. 4. Throughput Vs No's of Node:

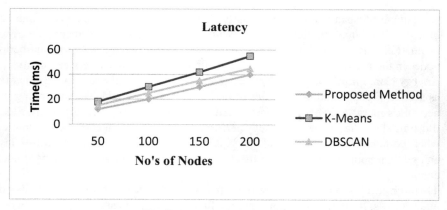

Fig. 5. Latency Vs No's of Node:

varying numbers of nodes when compared to the DBSCAN and k-means clustering methods.

Table 2. Percentage Increase of Metrics.

Metric	Proposed Approach vs K-Means	Proposed Approach vs DBSCAN
Network Lifetime	25%	20%
Energy Consumption	−30%	−25%
Residual Energy	15%	10%
Latency	−25%	−20%
PacketDelivery Ratio	15%	10%
Packet Loss Ratio	−20%	−15%
Throughput	20%	15%
Routing Overhead	−20%	−15%
Average MSE	−15%	−10%
Network Lifetime	25%	20%

9 Conclusions

The study proposes an energy-efficient wireless sensor network for smart city applications, combining multipath routing and distributed artificial intelligence for improved energy efficiency, data dependability, and adaptability to dynamic environments. The highlighted text in Table 2, that compares different metrics for two different approaches: the proposed approach using agent-based clustering and another approach using DBSCAN. The metrics being compared include network lifetime, energy consumption, residual energy, latency, packet delivery ratio, packet loss ratio, throughput, routing overhead, and average mean square error (MSE).For each metric, there are two values provided: one for the proposed approach using AI-driven clustering (K-Means) and another for the approach using DBSCAN. The Table 2 show each approach for the corresponding metric. Positive values indicate improvement or increase in performance, while negative values indicate degradation or decrease in performance. The proposed AI-driven clustering approach outperforms DBSCAN in terms of network lifetime, energy consumption, residual energy, packet delivery ratio, throughput, and average MSE. However, it has higher latency, packet loss ratio, and routing overhead. In-depth simulations show its practicality and superiority to conventional approaches. Future research should focus on dynamic learning, real-world validation, security consideration, resource constraints, and energy harvesting to advance smart city technologies.

References:

1. Osamy, W., Khedr, A.M., Salim, A., Al Ali, A.I., El-Sawy, A.A.: A review on recent studies utilizing artificial intelligence methods for solving routing challenges in wireless sensor networks. Peer J. Comput. Sci. **8**, e1089 (2022). https://doi.org/10.7717/peerj-cs.1089
2. Fu, X., Fortino, G., Pace, P., Aloi, G., Li, W.: Environment-fusion multipath routing protocol for wireless sensor networks. Inf. Fusion **53**, 4–19 (2020). https://doi.org/10.1016/j.inffus.2019.06.001
3. Sameer Jabbar, M., Saeed Issa, S. & Hussein Ali, A. 2023. Improving WSNs execution using energy-efficient clustering algorithms with consumed energy and lifetime maximization. Indonesian J. Electr. Eng. Comput. Sci. **29**(2), 1122 (2023). https://doi.org/10.11591/ijeecs.v29.i2.pp1122-1131
4. Wang, M.-Q., Chen, E.-L., Hou, S., Liu, P.-F., Hang, W.-J.: An energy-optimized game algorithm for wireless sensor networks. Measur. Control **53**(7–8), 1548–1557 (2020). https://doi.org/10.1177/0020294020932345
5. Wang, J., Zhang, Y., Hu, C., Mao, P., Liu, B.: IACRA: lifetime optimization by invulnerability-aware clustering routing algorithm using game-theoretic approach for WSNS. Sensors **22**(20), 7936 (2022). https://doi.org/10.3390/s22207936
6. Sonwalkar, P.K., Kalmani, V.: Energy efficient hop-by-hop retransmission and congestion mitigation of an optimum routing and clustering protocol for WSNs. Int. J. Adv. Comput. Sci. Appl. **13**, 3 (2022). https://doi.org/10.14569/ijacsa.2022.0130379
7. Kumar Dutta, A., Srinivasan, S., Prasada Rao, B., Hemalatha, B., V. Pustokhina, I., A. Pustokhin, D. & Prasad Joshi, G. 2022. Design of QoS Aware Routing Protocol for IoT Assisted Clustered WSN. Computers, Materials & Continua, 71, 2, pp. 3785–3801. URL: https://doi.org/10.32604/cmc.2022.023657
8. Karunkuzhali, D., Meenakshi, B., Lingam, K.: 2022. OQR-SC: an optimal QoS aware routing technique for smart cities using IoT enabled wireless sensor networks. Wirel. Personal Commun. **125**(4), 3575–3602. URL: https://doi.org/10.1007/s11277-022-09725-8
9. Saha, N., Bera, S., Misra, S.: Sway: traffic-aware QoS routing in software-defined IoT. IEEE Trans. Emerg. Top. Comput. **9**(1), 390–401 (2021). https://doi.org/10.1109/tetc.2018.2847296
10. Sharma, H., Haque, A., Blaabjerg, F.: Machine learning in wireless sensor networks for smart cities: a survey (2021). https://doi.org/10.3390/electronics10091012
11. Venkatesan, V.K., Izonin, I., Periyasamy, J., Indirajithu, A., Batyuk, A., Ramakrishna, M.T.: Incorporation of energy efficient computational strategies for clustering and routing in heterogeneous networks of smart city. Energies **15**(20), 7524 (2022). https://doi.org/10.3390/en15207524
12. Jing, W., Miao, Q., Song, H., Liu, Y.: An energy efficient and resource-constrained scheduling framework for smart city application. Trans. Emerg. Telecommun. Technol. **32**, 8 (2020). https://doi.org/10.1002/ett.4040
13. Fang, W., Wen, X., Xu, J., Zhu, J.: CSDA: a novel cluster-based secure data aggregation scheme for WSNs. Clust. Comput. **22**(S3), 5233–5244 (2020). https://doi.org/10.1007/s10586-017-1195-7
14. Naidja, M., Bilami, A.: A dynamic self-organising heterogeneous routing protocol for clustered WSNs. Int. J. Wirel. Mobile Comput. **12**(2), 131 (2017). URL: https://doi.org/10.1504/ijwmc.2017.084182
15. Patel, N.R., Kumar, S., Singh, S.K.: Energy and collision aware WSN routing protocol for sustainable and intelligent IoT applications. IEEE Sens. J. **21**(22), 25282–25292 (2021). https://doi.org/10.1109/jsen.2021.3076192

16. Kocherla, R., Vatambeti, R.: An efficient routing strategy for energy management in wireless sensor network using hybrid routing protocols. Wirel. Personal Commun. **124**(1), 49–73 (2021). https://doi.org/10.1007/s11277-021-09318-x
17. Wang, T., Yang, X., Hu, K., Zhang, G.: A distributed load balancing clustering algorithm for wireless sensor networks. Wirel. Personal Commun. 120(4), 3343–3367 (2021). https://doi.org/10.1007/s11277-021-08617-7
18. Kaur, G., Chanak, P., Bhattacharya, M.: Energy-efficient intelligent routing scheme for IoT-enabled WSNs. IEEE Internet Things J. **8**(14), 11440–11449 (2021). https://doi.org/10.1109/jiot.2021.3051768
19. Ray, N.K., Turuk, A.K.: A hybrid energy efficient protocol for mobile Ad Hoc networks. J. Comput. Networks Commun. **2016**, 1–11 (2016). URL: https://doi.org/10.1155/2016/2861904
20. Jaydev, M., Kar, R., Senapati, B.R., Nayak, S.K.: Intelligent agro-industry for crop production considering soil properties and climatic variables to boost its efficiency. Eng. Optimiz.: Methods Appl. 57–73 (2023). https://doi.org/10.1007/978-981-99-7456-6_5
21. Senapati, B.R., Khilar, P.M., Dash, T., Swain, R.R.: AI-assisted emergency healthcare using vehicular network and support vector machine. Wirel. Personal Commun. **130**(3), 1929–1962 (2023). https://doi.org/10.1007/s11277-023-10366-8
22. Khalid, M., Wang, L., Wang, K., Aslam, N., Pan, C., Cao, Y.: Deep reinforcement learning-based long-range autonomous valet parking for smart cities. Sustain. Cities Soc. **89**, 104311 (2023). https://doi.org/10.1016/j.scs.2022.104311
23. Kumar Patra, B., Mishra, S., Kumar Patra, S.: A novel agent-based multipath routing protocol to extend lifetime and enhancing reliability of clustered wireless sensor networks. Int. J. Comput. Networks Appl. **9**(6), 689 (2022). https://doi.org/10.22247/ijcna/2022/217702
24. Liu, Z., et al.: Energy-efficient distributed clustering algorithm for WSNs in smart grid. In: 2022 4th International Conference on Smart Power & Internet Energy Systems (SPIES) (2022). https://doi.org/10.1109/spies55999.2022.10081951
25. Maalem, S.: A collective intelligence-based system to improve cluster formation in wireless sensor networks. In: 2021 International Conference on Recent Advances in Mathematics and Informatics (ICRAMI) (2021). https://doi.org/10.1109/icrami52622.2021.9585996
26. Giannini, F., Franze, G., Pupo, F., Fortino, G.: Autonomous vehicles in smart cities: a deep reinforcement learning solution. In: 2022 IEEE International Conference on Dependable, Autonomic and Secure Computing, International Conference on Pervasive Intelligence and Computing, International Conference on Cloud and Big Data Computing, International Conference on Cyber Science and Technology Congress(DASC/PiCom/CBDCom/CyberSciTech) (2022). https://doi.org/10.1109/dasc/picom/cbdcom/cy55231.2022.9927840
27. Ahmadi, K., Allan, V.H.: Smart city: application of multi-agent reinforcement learning systems in adaptive traffic management. In: 2021 IEEE International Smart Cities Conference (ISC2) (2021). https://doi.org/10.1109/isc253183.2021.9562951
28. Mattia, G.P., Beraldi, R.: On real-time scheduling in Fog computing: A Reinforcement Learning algorithm with application to smart cities. In: 2022 IEEE International Conference on Pervasive Computing and Communications Workshops and other Affiliated Events (PerCom Workshops) (2022). https://doi.org/10.1109/percomworkshops53856.2022.9767498
29. Yu, C.-M., Ku, M.-L.: A novel balanced routing protocol for lifetime improvement in WSNs. In: 2022 IEEE International Conference on Consumer Electronics (ICCE) (2022). https://doi.org/10.1109/icce53296.2022.9730409
30. Saini, R.K., Singh, M., Saini, P.: Improve energy-efficiency of sensors using cross-layer design technique in WSNs. In: Journal of Physics: Conference Series, vol. 1714, p. 012031 (2021). https://doi.org/10.1088/1742-6596/1714/1/012031

A Novel Symmetric Key Based Authentication Scheme that Saves Energy for Edge Devices of the Internet of Things

Prakash Kuppuswamy[1(✉)], Sayeed Q. Al-Khalidi Al-Maliki[2], Rajan John[3], and Mohan Mani[1]

[1] SRM University, Delhi-NCR, Haryana, India
{prakash.k,m.mohan}@srmuniversity.ac.in
[2] King Khalid University, Abha, Kingdom of Saudi Arabia
salkhalidi@kku.edu.sa
[3] Jazan University, Jazan, Kingdom of Saudi Arabia

Abstract. In today's digitally connected world, edge devices such as smartphones, tablets, wearables, and IoT devices have become an essential part of our day-to-day life. These devices facilitate seamless connectivity and enable us to access information and services at our fingertips. However, this convenience comes at a cost - the potential compromise of sensitive data due to security vulnerabilities. Edge device security has become a significant concern, and one of the solutions to address these concerns is the utilization of cryptography algorithms. With the rapid proliferation of edge devices in today's interconnected world, the basic for strong and efficient safety mechanisms has become paramount. One such mechanism is the symmetric key algorithm, which plays a vital role in securing edge devices and safeguarding critical data. A device-based authentication algorithm that saves energy and enables secure communication within the edge devices is crucial for verifying device identity and ensuring device security. This article explores a new energy-saving authentication protocol based on integers and modulo 37 called SSK (simple symmetric key algorithm). This new authentication protocol is easy to implement and is particularly suitable for edge devices on the Internet of Things that require energy savings and potential security. Additionally, this article discusses the implementation of SSK algorithms, edge device security, their functionality, and potential use cases.

Keywords: Internet of Things · Edge Device · authentication algorithm · Simple symmetric key · Cryptography etc.

1 Introduction

The Internet of Things (IoT) has emerged as a transformative ecosystem, connecting a multitude of devices, and enabling seamless communication and data sharing [1–3]. However, with this increased connectivity arises the pressing necessity for strong security methods to protect the vast amounts of sensitive information transmitted within the IoT network [4–6]. Symmetric key cryptography algorithms perform a significant role in ensuring the confidentiality, data integrity, and authenticity of IoT communication [7, 8]. The rapid advancements in technology have given rise to the Internet of Things (IoT) ecosystem, which connects multiple devices and enables them to share and analyze data. IoT has proven to be a game-changer, revolutionizing industries, and enhancing our daily lives [9, 10]. However, with this increased connectivity comes the pressing challenge of ensuring cybersecurity and safeguarding edge devices [11].

Symmetric key algorithms, also known as private key algorithms, are cryptographic techniques that rely on a shared secret key for data encryption and decryption [12, 13]. Unlike asymmetric key algorithms, which uses two keys (public and private), symmetric key cryptography techniques use a single key for both encryption process as well as decryption processes. This simplicity and efficiency make symmetric key algorithms highly relevant and valuable for IoT security [14, 15].

Edge devices play a vital role in the IoT ecosystem. These devices serve as the connection point between the physical world and the digital realm, collecting and delivering data at the edge of the network [16, 17]. Examples of edge devices include smart sensors, gateways, wearables, and industrial automation devices. Ensuring the security of edge devices is crucial as they are often the first entry point for potential cyber threats. The significance of IoT security and highlights key strategies to protect edge devices were as follows and shown in Fig. 1. In addition, it explores the importance of symmetric key algorithms in IoT security and highlights their key benefits and applications [18–20].

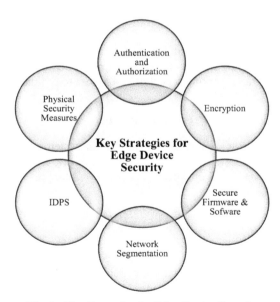

Fig. 1. Key Strategies for Edge Device Security

1.1 Authentication and Authorization

Implementing resilient authentication techniques is essential to validate the identity of devices and users accessing the IoT network. Secure protocols such as Public Key Infrastructure (PKI) and two-factor authentication can be employed to ensure only authorized entities can gain access to the network [21, 22].

1.2 Encryption

Data encryption is fundamental to protect sensitive information transmitted and stored in edge devices. Robust encryption algorithms, like Advanced Encryption Standard (AES), can be applied to protect the data. Also, encryption techniques can mitigate risks associated with eavesdropping and tampering [23].

1.3 Secure Firmware and Software

Keeping firmware and periodic software updating is crucial to address exposures and patch security loopholes. Regular updates and patches can protect edge devices against the latest threats. Additionally, code-signing and code-integrity verification techniques can be employed to ensure the authenticity and integrity of the software running on edge devices [24].

1.4 Network Segmentation

Segmenting the network into different zones can limit the probable control of a vulnerability attack. By separating devices into distinct networks, the damage caused by an attack can be contained, preventing unauthorized access to critical systems [25].

1.5 Intrusion Detection and Prevention Systems

Applying reliable intrusion detection and prevention systems (IDPS) can support to detect potential cyber-attack. IDPS can observe network traffic, detect anomalies, and take immediate action to mitigate risks, such as blocking suspicious incoming connections or raising alarms [26].

1.6 Physical Security Measures

Physical security measures should not be overlooked for edge devices. Deploying access control mechanisms, such as multi-factor authentication (MFA) and surveillance cameras, can stop illegal device access to edge devices and protect them from theft or tampering [27].

2 Background Study

Songlin Chen, Yixin Jiang, Hong Wen, Wenjie Liu, Jie Chen, Wenxin Lei, Aidong Xu (2018) Despite receiving widespread attention from academia and industry, mobile edge computing also poses different safety threats, including information security extortions during access of data that shows alteration and disclosure of data, compromising its integrity as well as confidentiality. To ensure data security during data access in mobile edge computing, a data security enhanced Fine-Grained Access Control mechanism (FGAC) is proposed. The FGAC scheme uses attributes and metagraph theory to dynamically group trusted users. The protocol was collective with role-based access control method to allocate roles to users based on their trustworthiness. In mobile edge computing applications, FGAC is effective at identifying malicious users, making group adjustments, and assuring data security while providing fine-grained access control [29].

Bruzgiene, Jurgilas (2021) IoT security model, based on mobile edge computing, is presented in this research article. Finding the solution of network access security problems of IoT wireless devices and ample computing resources. In contrast to traditional cryptographic algorithms-based security access, this method does not require password authentication. To confirm identity, the edge computing device utilizes the unique hardware of various wireless devices to access and analyze fingerprint characteristics created by the radio frequency radiation of the terminal device. By utilizing cloud technology, a decision model can be established to quickly create models and reduce training time. This efficient process saves time when implementing lightweight security measures for IoT devices and eliminates the requirement for encryption algorithms at the end nodes [28].

Xinghua Li, Ting Chen, Qingfeng Cheng Siqi Ma, and Jianfeng Ma (2021) This article examines the security needs of intelligent applications that rely on identity verification and data protection. The subsequent stage involves examining some cutting-edge research on this subject. Furthermore, future research on the authentication and data security of smart applications based on edge computing is explored, along with an exploration of the definitions of edge computing found in current literature and a comparison to cloud computing. It is clear from this comparison that edge computing offers certain evident advantages, such as speedy response times. Additionally, the article delves into three typical applications of edge computing and highlights some security vulnerabilities present in smart applications and edge computing. Ensuring the security of the system revolves around the fundamental challenge of verifying the legitimacy of system entities [30].

Jiewu Leng, Man Zhou, J. Leon Zhao, Yongfeng Huang, Yiyang Bian (2022) Blockchain, a new and secure way of sharing information, combines a chain structure to verify and store data. However, the development and adoption of Blockchain have faced challenges due to security concerns. This article explores the field of information systems and examines research on blockchain security, it has three levels such as process level, data level, and the infrastructure level, it also called PDI model. Through this survey, researcher analyze the current state of blockchain security in existing literature and propose future research directions to address pressing issues in the field. Overview of security issues in blockchain and highlights opportunities for research in information systems and services also discussed. It evaluate the extent to which these security concerns have been addressed [32].

Miguel Landry Foko Sindjounga, Mthulisi Velempinia, Clémentin Tayou Djamegni (2023) Several applications requiring large computation and storage resources have been adapted to cloud computing. Mobile Edge Computing has been proposed as a solution to the problem of latency in scenarios that require low latency. By bringing computing and storage resources closer to the end-user equipment, instead of relying on the cloud data center, edge computing reduces request processing time. However, this approach also introduces vulnerabilities in terms of security, data privacy, and authentication. To address these concerns, a hybrid cryptographic system that combines symmetric and asymmetric cryptography is used to enhance the security, privacy, and authentication of data in the edge computing network. The protocol is validated using the Automated Validation of Internet Security Protocols and Applications tool to ensure its security. Simulation results demonstrate that this approach consumes fewer computing resources [31].

3 Significance of Research

The Internet of Things embedded with sensors, software, and connectivity competences. These devices collect data and communicate with each other, providing valuable insights and automating processes. IoT has a wide range of applications, including smart homes, healthcare systems, transportation, agriculture, and industrial automation. The more number of connected devices has made IoT security a critical concern and that could be possible of a security breaches can be devastating, ranging from privacy invasion to financial loss and even physical harm. With interconnected devices transmitting and receiving sensitive information, the potential for cyber-attacks has multiplied. Therefore, implementing strong security measures is crucial to build trust, protect user information, and maintain the reliability of IoT systems.

3.1 Data Confidentiality

One of the primary purposes of symmetric key algorithms in the IoT is to ensure data confidentiality. By encrypting data using a shared secret key, sensitive information transmitted within the IoT network becomes incomprehensible to unauthorized entities. This protection is vital to prevent eavesdropping and illegal access to valuable data, confirming the confidentiality and privacy of user information.

3.2 Efficient Data Encryption and Decryption

Symmetric key algorithms are computationally efficient, making them well-suited for resource-constrained IoT devices with imperfect processing energy. Encryption and decryption operations using symmetric key algorithms are significantly faster compared to their asymmetric counterparts. This efficiency is critical in IoT environments where devices often operate with minimal power and computational capabilities.

3.3 Low Latency and Real-Time Communication

In many IoT applications, real-time communication and low latency are essential requirements. Private key algorithms facilitate rapid encryption and decryption processes, allowing IoT devices to exchange data quickly without significant delays. This capability is particularly significant in time-sensitive applications, such as industrial automation, healthcare monitoring, and autonomous vehicles.

3.4 Secure Key Exchange

Symmetric key algorithms are commonly used for secure key exchange between IoT devices and gateways. The shared secret key is exchanged through secure channels before communication begins. This approach ensures that only authorized devices possess the key required to encrypt and decrypt data, preventing unauthorized access to the IoT network.

3.5 Compatibility and Interoperability

Symmetric key algorithms have been widely adopted and implemented in various cryptographic libraries and hardware devices, making them highly compatible and interoperable across different IoT systems. This compatibility enhances the scalability and flexibility of IoT deployments, allowing devices from different vendors to communicate securely and seamlessly within an ecosystem.

3.6 Resource Efficiency

IoT devices often have limited compute power, memory, and storage capacity. Symmetric key algorithms are known for their efficiency in terms of resource consumption. They require fewer computational resources compared to asymmetric key algorithms, making them well-suited for low-power devices and reducing strain on device battery life.

4 Proposed Structure

Edge devices play a vital role on the Internet of Things (IoT) ecosystem, facilitating data collection and processing at the edge of the network. Increasing the number of connected devices remains to raise, ensuring the safety and security of edge devices becomes increasingly crucial. Private algorithms, also known as symmetric key algorithms, are widely employed to safeguard edge device security. The general architecture is shown in Fig. 2, shows the exchange of communication between edge devices and service provider through cloud environment.

The design of a new symmetric key algorithm begins with strategic decision-making and careful consideration of various cryptographic principles. This involves defining the key size, determining the number of rounds, understanding the importance of key expansion, and selecting appropriate substitution and permutation techniques. Additionally, the algorithm should be resistant to known attacks, offer resistance against cryptanalysis techniques, and provide satisfactory levels of performance and efficiency.

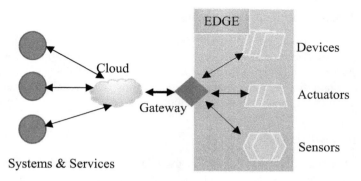

Fig. 2. General Structure of IoT & Edge Devices

4.1 Key Generation Process

The significant and crucial phase in any symmetric key algorithm is the key generation process. This process involves generating a secret/private key, which is then used to encrypting sender's and decrypting receiver's data. The new algorithm should employ a robust method for key generation using random number selection, to ensure the confidentiality of the key. Additionally, the key distribution phase should be secure as well, as compromised key distribution can lead to the compromise of the entire encryption system.

$$(a \times b) \, mod = ((a \, mod \, m) \times (b \, mod \, m)) \, mod \, m \tag{1}$$

$$(a \times b \times c) \, mod = ((a \, mod \, m) \times (b \, mod \, m) \times (c \, mod \, m)) \, mod \, m \tag{2}$$

The modular multiplicative inverse is an integer X such that:

$$AX \cong 1 \, (mod M) \tag{3}$$

In order to generate keys, we chose random numbers consisting of positive and negative integers, the reason being to make the process more secure and confuse unauthorized entities. A random integer of 5 and a random integer of -11 has been chosen for encryption. The multiplicative inverse of the number is 15, 10, which is used in the decryption process.

4.2 Encryption and Decryption Procedures

The encryption and decryption procedures define how the algorithm transforms plaintext into ciphertext and vice versa, respectively. The new algorithm should incorporate efficient and secure encryption and decryption techniques. Block ciphers, stream ciphers, or a combination of both may be employed depending on the specific requirements of the algorithm. It is important to ensure that these procedures are resistant to differential and linear cryptanalysis, as well as other known attacks.

Encryption.

Plain Text *(5 * -11) mod 37 = Cipher Text.
Decryption.
Cipher Text*(15 * 10) mod 37 = Plain Text.

5 Implementation of Structure

Ensuring the security of edge devices is paramount for building a robust and trustworthy IoT ecosystem. Private algorithms perform a significant part in protecting sensitive data and maintaining the integrity of IoT systems. Private or symmetric key algorithms make use of a one private key for both encryption and decryption processes. The private key used to encrypt the data must be kept private or shared only between authorized entities. Unlike public key algorithms, which use separate keys for encryption and decryption, private algorithms are computationally efficient, making them suitable for resource-constrained edge devices.

The implementation structure of a symmetric key algorithm refers to the way the algorithm is designed and implemented to perform cryptographic operations securely. It encompasses various aspects, such as the key generation process, encryption and decryption procedures, and the overall operational efficiency. In context, we will emphasis on the implementing and evaluation of a novel symmetric key algorithm.

Table1. Encryption and Decryption Process

Plain Text	Integer Equlvt	Key (5 & −11)	Mod37	Cipher Text	(CT*15*10)	Mod 37	Plain Text
C	3	−165	20	T	3000	3	C
O	15	−825	26	Z	3900	15	O
N	14	−770	7	G	1050	14	N
F	6	−330	3	C	450	6	F
E	5	−275	21	U	3150	5	E
R	18	−990	9	I	1350	18	R
E	5	−275	21	U	3150	5	E
N	14	−770	7	G	1050	14	N
C	3	−165	20	T	3000	3	C
E	5	−275	21	U	3150	5	E
2	29	−1595	33	6	4950	29	2
0	27	−1485	32	5	4800	27	0
2	29	−1595	33	6	4950	29	2
4	31	−1705	34	7	5100	31	4

As an experiment and implementation tool, we have chosen plaintext to be 'CONFERENCE 2024', which combines alphabets and integers. Plaintext values are assigned alphabetically from 1 to 26 while integers from 0 to 9 are considered from 27 to 37, so that modulo 37 is used. As shown in Table 1, the entire process of encryption and decryption is described. The plain text 'CONFERENCE 2024' is encoded as 'TZGCUIUGTU6567'. To retrieve the plain text message from this encrypted text, a trusted device or person must be able to decrypt the message using private key.

6 Result Analysis and Discussion

To study the efficiency of the new symmetric key algorithm, several factors need to be considered. Encryption and decryption speeds, memory requirements, power consumption, and latency are all critical aspects. The algorithm's performance should be compared with existing algorithms to determine its efficiency and effectiveness. Additionally, the algorithm should be tested under different scenarios, including both normal and high-stress conditions, to assess its robustness and stability.

When selecting a private algorithm for securing edge devices, several factors should be considered, including the required level of security, device resources, and compatibility with the overall IoT ecosystem. AES is widely considered the preferred option due to its strength, efficiency, and support for various key sizes. However, specific use cases or legacy systems may warrant the use of alternative algorithms such as 3DES, Blowfish, or RC depending on their specific requirements. The AES, DES, 3DES, Blowfish, and the RC family, offer different levels of security and computational efficiency. By carefully evaluating the requirements and limitations of edge devices, organizations can select the appropriate private algorithm to safeguard the integrity and confidentiality of data flowing within the IoT network.

Table 2. Comparaison Table

Algorithm	Type	Structure	Key size	Rounds	Block size
AES	Block cipher	Substitution & permutation	128–256	10–14	128 bits
DES	Block cipher	Balanced Feistel	56	16	64 bits
3-DES	Block cipher	Feistel	112, 168	48	64 bits
RC2	Block cipher	Heavy Feistel	40–124	18	64 bits
SSK	**Block cipher**	**Substitution**	**8–16**	**1**	**32 bits**

To understand the viability and advantages of the new symmetric key algorithm, a thorough comparison analysis with existing algorithms is essential. The comparison should focus on factors such as security, performance, key size, resistance to known attacks, and adaptability to different platforms and environments. Moreover, the assessment should include both legacy algorithms and recently developed ones to provide a comprehensive understanding of the new algorithm's capabilities.

We have compared and analysed various parameters of existing symmetric key algorithms with our proposed algorithm in Table 2. Figure 3 shows the overall comparison

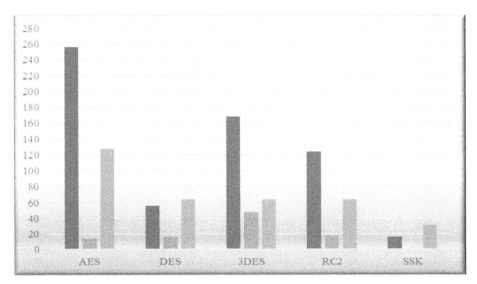

Fig. 3. Comparison Chart

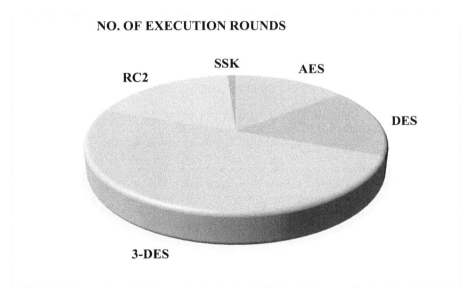

Fig. 4. No. of encryption/decryption rounds

and performance of symmetric key algorithms and SSK (simple symmetric key algorithm). Figure 4 shows the number of execution round of each algorithm performance, more number of rounds takes much time to perform the encryption/decryption techniques. According to the comparison table and chart, the proposed algorithm performs better in all the parameters.

7 Conclusion

Edge device security is crucial in today's increasingly interconnected world. Symmetric key algorithms provide a reliable and efficient means of securing data, enabling secure communication, and ensuring the integrity of critical systems. While challenges such as key management and distribution, hardware optimization, and emerging threats like quantum computing need to be addressed, the implementation of best practices and continuous advancements in symmetric key algorithm technology will continue to enhance edge device security. Several parameters were taken into account when analyzing the results, including size of the key, block, and the number of rounds, and compared to the proposed SSK algorithm (simple symmetric key algorithm). According to our analysis of the parameters, we have concluded that our proposed scheme has performed significantly better than existing methods using a novel method of modulo 37 in a simple symmetric key algorithm. As edge computing continues to evolve and edge devices become more prevalent, the reliance on symmetric key algorithms, along with complementary security measures, will be essential in protecting sensitive data and ensuring the secure operation of edge devices in the future.

References

1. Perwej, Y., Haq, K., Parwej, F., Mumdouh, M., Hassan, M.: The internet of things (IoT) and its application domains. Int. J. Comput. Appl. **975**(8887), 82 (2019)
2. Sharma, N., Shamkuwar, M., Singh, I.: The history, present and future with IoT. Internet Things Big Data Analy. Smart Gener. **2019**, 27–51 (2019)
3. Secundo, G., Shams, S.R., Nucci, F.: Digital technologies and collective intelligence for healthcare ecosystem: optimizing Internet of Things adoption for pandemic management. J. Bus. Res. **131**, 563–72 (2021)
4. Tawalbeh, L.A., Muheidat, F., Tawalbeh, M., Quwaider, M.: IoT Privacy and security: challenges and solutions. Appl. Sci. **10**(12), 4102 (2020)
5. Al-Turjman, F., Zahmatkesh, H., Shahroze, R.: An overview of security and privacy in smart cities' IoT communications. Trans. Emerg. Telecommun. Technol. **33**(3), e3677 (2022)
6. Butun, I., Österberg, P., Song, H.: Security of the Internet of Things: vulnerabilities, attacks, and countermeasures. IEEE Commun. Surv. Tutor. **22**(1), 616–44 (2019)
7. Alenezi, M.N., Alabdulrazzaq, H., Mohammad, N.Q.: Symmetric encryption algorithms: review and evaluation study. Int. J. Commun. Networks Inf. Secur. **12**(2), 256–72 (2020)
8. Kuppuswamy, P., Al, S.Q.Y.A.K., John, R., Haseebuddin, M., Meeran, A.A.S. A hybrid encryption system for communication and financial transactions using RSA and a novel symmetric key algorithm. Bull. Electr. Eng. Inf. **12**(2), 1148–1158 (2023)
9. Bansal, S., Kumar, D.: IoT ecosystem: a survey on devices, gateways, operating systems, middleware and communication. Int. J. Wirel. Inf. Networks, 340–364 (2020)
10. Lee, I.: The Internet of Things for enterprises: an ecosystem, architecture, and IoT service business model. Internet of Things **7**, 100078 (2019)
11. Molokomme, D.N., Onumanyi, A.J., Abu-Mahfouz, A.M.: Edge intelligence in Smart Grids: a survey on architectures, offloading models, cyber security measures, and challenges. J. Sens. Actuat. Networks **11**(3), 47 (2022)
12. Kuppuswamy, P., John, R.: A novel approach of designing e-commerce authentication scheme using hybrid cryptography based on simple symmetric key and extended linear block cipher algorithm. In: 2020 International Conference on Computing and Information Technology (ICCIT-1441) Sep 9, pp. 1–6 (2020)

13. Prakash, K., Saeed, Q., Khalidi, A.: A novel symmetric hybrid cryptography technique using linear block cipher and simple symmetric key. J. Theor. and Appl. Inf. Technol. **99**(10) (2021)
14. Saraiva, D.A., Leithardt, V.R., de Paula, D., Sales Mendes, A., González, G.V., Crocker, P.: Prisec: comparison of symmetric key algorithms for IoT devices. Sensors **19**(19), 4312 (2019)
15. Mousavi, S.K., Ghaffari, A., Besharat, S., Afshari, H.: Security of internet of things based on cryptographic algorithms: a survey. Wirel. Networks **27**, 1515–1555 (2021)
16. Caprolu, M., Di Pietro, R., Lombardi, F., Raponi, S.: Edge computing perspectives: architectures, technologies, and open security issues. In: 2019 IEEE International Conference on Edge Computing (EDGE). Jul 8, pp. 116–123. IEEE (2019)
17. Ranaweera, P., Jurcut, A.D., Liyanage, M.: Survey on multi-access edge computing security and privacy. IEEE Commun. Surv. Tutor. **23**(2), 1078–1124 (2021)
18. Venugopal, J.P., Subramanian, A.A., Peatchimuthu, J.: The realm of metaverse: a survey. Comput. Animat. Virt. Worlds e2150 (2023)
19. Shah, D., Murthi, B.P.: Marketing in a data-driven digital world: Implications for the role and scope of marketing. J. Bus. Res. **125**, 772–779 (2021)
20. Papaioannou, M., Karageorgou, M., Mantas, G., Sucasas, V., Essop, I., Rodriguez, J., Lymberopoulos, D.: A survey on security threats and countermeasures in internet of medical things (IoMT). Trans. Emerg. Telecommun. Technol. **33**(6), e4049 (2022)
21. Jani, K.A., Chaubey, N.: IoT and cyber security: introduction, attacks, and preventive steps. In Quantum Cryptography and the Future of Cyber Security, pp. 203–235. IGI Global (2020)
22. Lara, E., Aguilar, L., García, J.Á.: Lightweight authentication protocol using self-certified public keys for wireless body area networks in health-care applications. IEEE Access **9**, 79196–79213 (2021)
23. Achar, S.: Cloud computing security for multi-cloud service providers: controls and techniques in our modern threat landscape. Int. J. Comput. Syst. Eng. **16**(9), 379–384 (2022)
24. Meneghello, F., Calore, M., Zucchetto, D., Polese, M., Zanella, A.: IoT: Internet of threats? A survey of practical security vulnerabilities in real IoT devices. IEEE Internet Things J. **6**(5), 8182–8201 (2019)
25. Zeeshan, M., Riaz, Q., Bilal, M.A., Shahzad, M.K., Jabeen, H., Haider, S.A., Rahim, A.: Protocol-based deep intrusion detection for dos and ddos attacks using unsw-nb15 and bot-IoT data-sets. IEEE Access **10**, 2269–2283 (2021)
26. Shafiq, M., Gu, Z., Cheikhrouhou, O., Alhakami, W., Hamam, H.: The rise of "Internet of Things": review and open research issues related to detection and prevention of IoT-based security attacks. Wirel. Commun. Mobile Comput. **2022**, 1–2 (2022)
27. Bruzgiene, R., Jurgilas, K.: Securing remote access to information systems of critical infrastructure using two-factor authentication. Electronics. **10**(15), 1819 (2021)
28. Songlin, C., et al.: Novel terminal security access method based on edge computing for IoT. In: International Conference on Networking and Network Applications (2018)
29. Hou, Y., Garg, S., Hui, L., Jayakody, D.N.K., Jin, R., Hossain, M.S.: A Data security enhanced access control mechanism in mobile edge computing, special section on reliability in sensor-cloud systems and application (SCSA), IEEE Access **8** (2020)
30. Li, X., Chen, T., Ma, Q.C.S., Ma, J.: Smart applications in edge computing: overview on authentication and data security. IEEE Internet Things J. **8**(6), 4063 (2021)
31. Sindjoung, M.L.F., Velempini, M., Djamegni, C.T.: A data security and privacy scheme for user quality of experience in a Mobile Edge Computing-based network, Array **19**, 10030 (2023). www.elsevier.com/locate/array
32. Leng, J., Zhou, M., Zhao, J.L., Huang, Y., Bian, Y.: Blockchain security: a survey of techniques and research directions. IEEE Trans. Serv. Comput. 15(4) (2022)

Objective Functions in High-Density Internet of Things Networks - A Performance Evaluation

Safia Gul[✉], Bilal Ahmad Malik, and M. Tariq Banday

University of Kashmir, Srinagar, India
safia9gul@gmail.com

Abstract. The Internet of Things has sparked a profound revolution in networking by enabling the collection of vast sensor data, serving as the foundation for smart applications such as homes, cities, and industries. However, achieving such solutions is challenging due to resource constraints such as limited computational power, storage, and memory in IoT devices. The routing protocol (RPL), the most commonly utilized routing algorithm, employs objective functions (OFs) to determine path selection based on diverse metrics. The accurate evaluation and testing of these OFs are paramount in developing effective routing solutions. This paper thoroughly analyses the results of testing standard objective functions, focusing on addressing load imbalance and congestion issues. The analysis aims to ascertain the suitability of existing standardized objective functions as optimal routing solutions for IoT networks, given the results of the challenges posed by load balancing. This paper evaluates the efficacy of various objective functions used in RPL, providing insights to improve the routing performance and evaluate IoT devices' reliability, energy efficiency, load balancing, and overall network performance. The results of testing standard objective functions using the Contiki OS tool are meticulously compared. The analysis seeks to assess the suitability of the existing standardized objective functions as the most optimal routing solution for IoT networks.

Keywords: RPL · DODAG · OF0 · MRHOF · Congestion

1 Introduction

The network of intelligent devices working together with the tangible surroundings and communicating with various devices using the Internet is termed as the "Internet of Things" (IoT) [1]. This technology is pivotal in developing smart applications, including smart grids, buildings, smart cities, and many more [2]. This technology finds applications in different fields, such as automated home services, urban environments, intelligent grid applications, etc. These LLNs experience substantial limitations such as energy or battery power, storage capacity, computational capability, etc. These constraints profoundly influence the routing protocol design [3]. So, an efficient mechanism of RPL has been standardized to find the best-optimized path for data delivery (Table 1).

Table 1. Abbreviations and their descriptions.

Abbreviation	Description
IoT	Internet of Things
RPL	Routing Protocol
IETF	Internet Engineering Task Force
ROLL	Routing Over Low Power Lossy networks
IETF	Internet Engineering Task Force
OF	Objective Function
DAG	Directed Acyclic Graph
LLN	Low Power Lossy Networks
DODAG	Destination-Oriented Directed Acyclic Graph
DIO	DODAG Information Object
DIS	DODAG Information Solicitation
DAO	Destination Advertisement Object
DAO-Ack	Destination Advertisement Object Acknowledgment
LLN	Low power lossy networks
P2P	Point to point
P2MP	Point to multipoint
MP2P	Multipoint to point
ERA OF	Energy-efficient and path reliability aware objective function
ELT	Expected lifetime
UDGMDL	Unit Disc Graph Model with Distance Loss
PDR	Packet Delivery ratio
LB-OF	Load balancing Objective Function
ERAOF	Energy-Efficient and Path-Reliability Aware Objective Function
MCAS-OF	Multi-constraint objective function with adaptive stability
ED	Euclidean distance
ETX	Expected Transmission Count
HC	Hop Count
RSSI	Received Signal Strength Indicator
COM-OF	Combined Objective Function
FTSOF	Fuzzy-based Takagi and Sugeno Objective Function

1.1 Overview of RPL

RPL, pronounced "ripple", a well devised routing protocol designed for LLNs and was standardized in March 2012. The Internet Engineering Task Force's ROLL-WG published it under RFC 6550. This routing protocol is compatible with diverse topologies, including P2P, M2P, and P2MP [2]. RPL utilizes DAGs for route formation between the nodes of the network and are arranged in a tree-like assembly known as DODAGs. In a graph, the sink node possesses a rank equal to zero. It serves as the central point of the graph called the root. RPL utilizes four overhead control transmission signals to manage the DODAG and refresh the route info. The communication starts with DIO for preserving the present node rank and the other routing calculations between a node and central root, employed for the selection of a favored parent. After that, the DAO starts upward communication with the designated parents. Then, DIS is sent to neighboring nodes, which reply to DIO messages with updated information about the DAG. At last, the DAO-ACK signal signifies an acknowledgment of the DAO message by the DAO recipient [4]. LLN exhibits distinct features, one of which is using RPL as the principal protocol for routing in con-strained networks. RPL works with an objective function, granting a considerable level of adaptability for routing metric approval [5]. The routing metrics guarantee the estimation of path costs and the selection of the most efficient and shortest-restricted path. Most RPL implementations only demand utilizing a single metric, although others describe a combination of routing metrics and constraints [6, 7].

1.2 RPL Node

RPL-based networks primarily comprise three kinds of nodes: root nodes, routers, and leaf nodes. The root or central node serves as a gateway, connecting one network to another. Routers forward topology statistics and packets of data to the neighboring nodes. Leaf nodes join the networks as end members [8].

RPL Control Message Types. Different types of nodes shape themselves into DODAG, which originates from the central node called DAG root recognized by a unique identifier DODAGID. A node RANK is a topological distance well-defined as a node's spatial relationship with other nodes in relation to DODAG's central root node. The DODAG construction process involves four types of messages: DODAG advertisement object (DAO), DODAG information object (DIO), Destination advertisement object Acknowledgment (DAO-Ack) and DODAG information solicitation (DIS) [8]. DIO control is an advertisement message for DODAG advertising: "Is anyone ready to join the graph?" Nodes receiving the DIO for the first instant of time will be chosen as the DIO transmitting parent. The identification code for the DIO message is 0⊠01. DIS signal messages are propagated by the interested nodes, ready to link with the DAG. The identification code for the DIS message is 0⊠00. DAO message is unicasted from leaf node to the root node, sending information about the route. This identification code for the DAO control message is 0⊠02. DAO-Ack control signal acknowledges DAO message reception. The identification code for this type of control message is 0⊠03 (Fig. 1).

DODAG Tree Construction. RPL, the proactive distance routing protocol specially crafted for LLNs, organizes nodes as a tree-like structure by establishing a DODAG

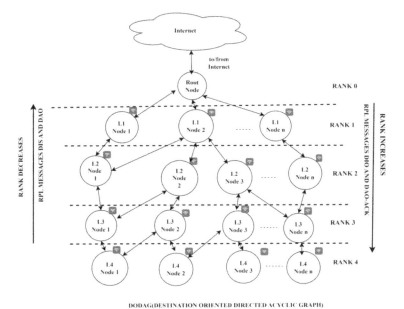

Fig. 1. Destination-Oriented Directed Acyclic Graph

with a distinct destination at the sink is called a DODAG root or border router or gateway with a unique identifier DODAGID. Its primary function is to link the RPL domain with different networks, for example, the Internet [9]. A DAG is a combination of multiple DODAGS. RPL instance is a term used for a set of one or more DODAGS with a distinctive RPL instance ID sharing a similar objective function [10]. Communication starts when the border router (LBR) broadcasts DIO, which encloses information regarding RPL instances, objective functions, etc., within the network. When the adjacent nodes receive these DIO messages, they make their decision, based on the rank calculation, whether to link the DODAG or not. If the node is willing to link with the DAG, it includes the DIO control message sender as the candidate of the parent list. Every node that chooses LBR as its parent starts to re-broadcast DIO control messages within the LLN. This process continues until the DAG encloses all network nodes. If nodes don't receive DIO messages, they send DIS requests to the neighboring nodes [11].

RPL Data Traffic Type and Modes of Operation. RPL accommodates three classes of data traffic. These are:

- Point-to-point data traffic (P2P) refers to communication between nodes within a network on a node-to-node basis.
- Point to Multipoint data traffic (P2MP): It is one-way communication from a gateway or root node towards the remaining nodes in the network.
- Multipoint-to-point data traffic (MP2P): The principal data traffic dominates the vast volume of data from multiple nodes en route to the gateway [12].

2 Objective Functions (OFS)

All the routing decisions rely on the regulations established by the objective functions. It is a crucial parameter in RPL. In RPL topology formation, rank calculation and selection of parents pivot on this parameter. Low-ranked nodes act as parents, and high-ranking nodes act as children. The two fundamental objective functions in RPL are MRHOF and OF0 [13].

2.1 Minimum Rank with Hysteresis Objective Function (MRHOF)

This kind of OF utilizes the anticipated count of transmission attempts needed for each packet, known as ETX, as the metric for transmitting the packets successfully. Low ETX means low energy consumption in sending packets. Mathematically, ETX is expressed as follows:

$$ETX = \frac{I}{P_r} * \frac{1}{P_a} \qquad (1)$$

P_r is the probability of receiving packets by the adjacent nodes, and P_a is the probability of acknowledgment packets by the sending nodes.

This objective function uses the concept of hysteresis, i.e., parent switching occurs only when the designated path is more cost-effective compared to actual path beyond a specified threshold [12]. Table 2, describes the MRHOF algorithm phases.

Table 2. MRHOF algorithm

Phase	Description
Phase 1	The sink node initiates the control message DIO ETX path metric computation
Phase 2	A node with minimum ETX for the path is selected for a feasible successor selection
Phase 3	The minimum ETX for the path will be advertised via DIO messages

2.2 Objective Function Zero (OF0)

This objective function employs hop count as the routing metric, to enable the distribution of packets using Dijkstra's algorithm for quick connectivity among the nodes. Table 3, describes the important phases of OF0 [14].

3 Related Work

Sousa et al. [15] have designed an ERAOF based on a multipath protocol used for routing, particularly IoT applications, necessitating both energy efficient and reliable data transmission. This method has proven effective for additive metrics of expected transmission count and energy consumed by nodes. This objective function has increased

Table 3. OF0 algorithm

Phase	Description
Phase 1	The sink node initiates the control message DIO Rank computation
Phase 2	A node with minimum rank is selected for the path for a feasible successor selection

PDR while operative energy is saved. Though, the other performance network metric does not show the impact of this composition on design implementation. Iova et al. [16] proposal has shown increased reliability for the network and improved balance energy consumption concurrently. They have anticipated a novel metric of expected Lifetime metric. It enables the estimation of the node's real lifespan before it is dead. This metric using multipath routing is useful to the typical RPL protocol. The multiplicity of the path makes the network extra steadfast and improves the QoS. However, the delay metric gets degraded in transmitting packets. Tang et al. [17] have used composite routing metrics with multipath routing protocol to avoid overcrowding in the network. It has combined the ETX, received packet count, and rank, reducing the delay at the cost of energy consumption. Consequently, such an approach does not ensure an extended network life. Kamgueu et al. [18] anticipated a multi-metric objective function. They have predicted the fuzzy logic method by amalgamating ETX, delay, and remaining energy of nodes in a composite metric. The proposed solution has outstripped the default ETX-based routing regarding packet loss, source to destination delay, and energy depletion. Lamaazi et al. [11] have considered another fuzzy logic enhancement based on link and node metrics. The significant improvements pertain to energy efficiency and equalization. High PDR and low overheads in comparison to the default OFs. Qasem et al. [19] examined the standardized RPL with different topologies for two basic objective functions, OF0 and MRHOF. Experimental results on the Contiki simulator revealed that MRHOF outperforms OF0 in sparsely populated networks, achieving high PDR and lower energy consumption. Qasem et al. [20] have compared three objective functions that include OF0, MRHOF, and LB-OF based on network lifetime, power consumption, and PDR as parameters for performance comparison. Simulation test outcomes divulge that LB-OF outperforms the default objective functions for load-balancing RPL.Sousa et al. have focused on an objective function specific to applications where data reliability with minimum energy usage is paramount. The experimental study has revealed the performance enhancement of ERAOF compared to MRHOF and OF [15]. Lamhaazi et al. [12] have focussed on the performance improvement of LLNs RPL protocol for parent selection with the fuzzy logic objective function proposal. They have taken ETX, HC, and energy consumption as the parameters for the best parent selection. The proposed OF has outclassed the default MRHOF with respect to PDR, energy balancing, network lifetime, and overhead. Yassin et al., [21] in their proposal, have experimentally simulated performance analysis of the most common objective functions, including MRHOF and OF0, using the Contiki simulator tool. The results concluded that OF0 is best suited for real-time applications with better reliability. Gopal et al. [22] compared the objective functions OF0 and MRHOF in a static simulating environment with random

Table 4. Recent studies conducted to evaluate various objective functions across random and grid topologies on various network sizes

Study	Network Size	Objective Function	Topology	PDR	PC	CTO	Throughput	Latency	CT	EC	No. of Hops	NW Lifetime	DIO Control Messages	No. of Child Nodes	Jitter	Parent Switching	No. of DAOS
Qasem et al. (2015) [19]	20 to 40	OF0 MRHOF	Random and Grid	✓	✓	✗	✗	✗	✗	✗	✗	✗	✗	✗	✗	✗
Qasem et al. (2016) [20]	18 to 100	OF0 MRHOF LBOF	Random and Grid	✓	✓	✗	✗	✗	✗	✗	✗	✗	✗	✗	✗	✗
Sousa et al. (2017) [15]	20 to 60	OF0 MRHOF ERAOF	Grid	✓	✓	✓	✗	✓	✓	✗	✗	✗	✗	✗	✗	✗
Lamaazi, Benamar, and Jara (2018) [11]	10 to 50	MRHOF OF-FUZZY	Random and Grid	✓	✗	✗	✗	✗	✗	✗	✓	✓	✗	✗	✗	✗
Yassien et al. (2019) [21]	50 and 65	OF0 MRHOF	Random and Grid	✓	✓	✗	✗	✓	✗	✗	✗	✗	✓	✗	✗	✗
Hassani et al. (2021) [23]	25 and 50	MRHOF MCAS-OF	Random	✓	✓	✗	✗	✗	✗	✗	✗	✗	✗	✗	✗	✗
Venugopal and Basavaraju (2022) [27]	10 to 50	OF0 MRHOF COM-OF	Random	✓	✓	✗	✗	✓	✗	✗	✗	✓	✓	✗	✗	✗
Subramani and Bojan (2023) [24]	10 to 100	OF0 MRHOF LB-OF WSM-OF	Random	✓	✗	✓	✗	✓	✗	✓	✗	✓	✓	✓	✓	✗
Kamble et al. (2023) [25]	15 to 60	OF0 MRHOF FMOF	Random	✓	✗	✓	✗	✓	✗	✗	✗	✓	✗	✗	✗	✗
Ghanbari et al. (2024) [26]	2 to 12	OF0 MRHOF MFOF	Grid	✓	✓	✗	✗	✓	✗	✗	✗	✗	✗	✗	✗	✗
This Work	25 to 40	OF0 MRHOF	Random	✓	✓	✓	✗	✗	✗	✓	✗	✓	✗	✗	✗	✓

Evaluation Metrics

topology. The results revealed that MRHOF consumes more energy than OF0. Hassani et al. [23] have introduced a novel multi-constraint with adaptive stability MCAS-OF for improving network stability in high-traffic conditions. The observed results reveal PDR improvement of up to 24%, power consumption reduction of 44%, and lower overhead than MRHOF. Subramani, P.S. and Bojan, [24] in their study, have introduced a novel, COM-OF, for mitigating load imbalance and increasing the network lifetime. The outperformance of COM-OF against MRHOF and OF0 in relation to power consumption is about 33%, 97% concerning PDR, and network lifetime enhancement is 45%. Finally, the average no. of child nodes decreases by 36%. Kamble et al. [25] have proposed FTSOF for RPL across different network densities with diverse data rates. It has surpassed the default objective functions MRHOF, OF0, and FMOF over various parameters, including PDR, Latency, network setup time, and control messages. Ghanbari et al. [26] have proposed the Internet of mobile things with fuzzy logic objective function in RPL by incorporating multiple metrics RSSI, ED, HC, and ETX. The study optimized energy conservation, handover delay, and PDR. Table 4 shows recent studies conducted to evaluate various objective functions across random and grid topologies with multiple network sizes.

4 Experimentation Evaluation

Performance evaluation of default objective functions within this section is done. The simulation results were supported with the help of Contiki Cooja simulator. A Simulated environment was set up with a radio model, the UDGM-DL. UDGM-DL is the basic radio propagation model used in sensor networks in which the transmission range is displayed in a disc fashion. This model considers the two basic parameters: the transmitting range and the interference range. The transmitting range defines whether two communicating nodes are in range or not. The interference range deter-mines whether node transmission can interfere with the reception of the other node. For result evaluation, the energest plugin was enabled. The simulation time was set to be 10 min for all scenarios. Python 3.7 was employed to analyze the log files generated by Cooja. Table 5 below gives the experimental specifications of the simulation in the Contiki simulator.

4.1 Evaluation Metrics

The evaluation of performance metrics is critical, through which the efficiency of objective functions can be projected, and results can be analyzed. With the help of these parameters objective function performance will be deduced better for high-density networks.

- Packet Delivery Ratio (PDR): The proportion of the overall packets that have been successfully received by the sink to the total number of packets transmitted by the clients. Higher PDR means less loss of packets in the network and high stable links between the nodes. PDR = ($\sum$ received packets by destination/$\sum$ sent packets by source) * 100%

Table 5. Network setup used in the simulation

Network Simulator	Cooja under Contiki-ng OS
Simulation time	10min
Radio Environment	UDGM-DL
Area of deployment	100 * 100 m
Number of sinks	1
Number of sensor nodes	25, 30, 40 (static nodes)
Simulation time	600000s (10 min)
Mote type	Skymote
Objective functions	OF0, MRHOF
Topology	Random

- Control Traffic Overhead (CTO): It is the summation of all the control signals, i.e., DIO, DAO, DIS, that are transmitted through the system for DODAG establishment. Higher CTO indicates unstable links between the nodes, increased packet congestion and collision, high packet delay, and more power consumption.

$$\text{CTO} = \sum \text{DIO, DIS, DAO, DAO-ACK} \qquad (2)$$

- Power consumption (PC): It is characterized as the mean power consumed by the nodes throughout the lifecycle of the network. The higher the network lifetime, the lower the energy usage of the nodes. The SI unit of energy is Joules, but since nodes are constrained, the energy unit here is millijoules, and similarly, power is measured in milliwatts.

$$PT = P_{Tx} + P_{Idle} + P_{Rx} + P_{sleep} \qquad (3)$$

- Energy consumption (EC): Energy consumption in networking refers to the total amount of power utilized by the various components and devices within a network infrastructure over a specific period of time. The SI unit of energy is Joules.

$$EC = E_{Tx} + E_{Idle} + E_{Rx} + E_{sleep} \qquad (4)$$

- DIO count: DIO contains information that will allow nodes to select the parent. The DIO transmission depends upon network stability. The real number of DIOs can also be influenced by factors such as density, topology changes, and the precise implementation of the RPL protocol. So, this parameter defines the stability of the graph.
- DAO count: DAO advertises its position in the topology towards the root. A more dynamic or imbalanced network can lead to increased DAOS. Moreover, network optimizations and balanced mechanisms can efficiently limit excessive DAO numbers and reduce overhead.

5 Results and Discussion

Standard objective functions of RPL are analyzed for performance evaluation regarding power consumption, PDR, throughput, and control transmission overhead (CTO). As can be seen from Fig. 2 and Fig. 3, energy and power consumption vary linearly with the increase in the density of networks. MRHOF potentially consumes more energy than OF0 as MRHOF utilizes ETX as a routing metric and requires more transmission overhead and thus consumes more energy at the cost of reliability. MRHOF is the more reliable of the two as it needs ETX as a metric for packet transmission and is thus associated with link quality measurement and control traffic. OF0 is best suited for real-time applications but suffers from more packet drops. Retransmission, packet buffering will lead to more power consumption in case of MRHOF.

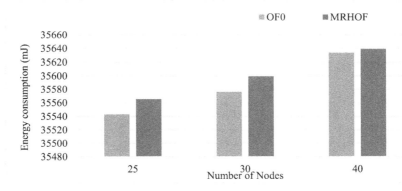

Fig. 2. Energy consumption vs. number of nodes

Figure 4 shows that the number of DAOs (Destination Advertisement Objects) in a network using the OF0 (Objective Function Zero) or MRHOF (Minimum Rank Hysteresis Objective Function) objective function variation is based on several factors, that include network topology, network size, routing changes, and the specific implementation of the objective functions. MRHOF involves more frequent routing changes and updates compared to OF0, thus resulting in an increased number of control message DAOs. A more dynamic or imbalanced network can lead to increased DAOS. Moreover, network optimizations and balanced mechanisms can efficiently limit excessive DAO numbers and reduce overhead.

The real number of DIOs can also be influenced by factors such as density, topology changes, and the precise implementation of the RPL protocol. As designed by MRHOF, Broad tree structures can lead to more recurrent DIO propagation. So, that maximum number of nodes knows the network state and optimal routes.

Finally, the choice between OF0 and MRHOF is based on the network's specific application and priorities. If minimizing control overhead and energy conservation are essential, OF0 is preferable. Instead, if stability and more progressive route selection are crucial, even if it requires more control transmission overhead, MRHOF could be a better

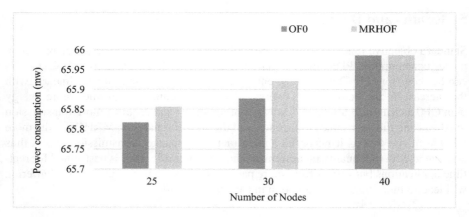

Fig. 3. Power consumption vs. number of nodes

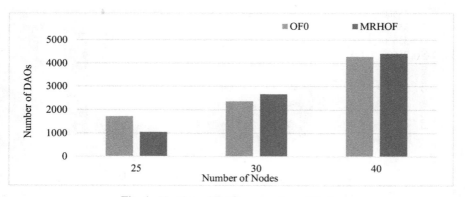

Fig. 4. Number of DAO vs. number of Nodes

optimal choice. Since MRHOF aims to select paths with better reliability, it can improve the PDR compared to OF0, as seen in Fig. 6, which can alleviate unreliable or unstable links. Generally, the PDR can be affected as the network expands, resulting in a potential decrease. However, the impact of the node count on the PDR depends on various factors and network characteristics. An increase in this also adds to the reduction in the PDR. Resource constraints due to memory and processing power lead to a decrease in PDR (Fig. 5).

Several nodes can lead to a reduction in the PDR as the network congestion increases and packet loss increases. With the increased complexity of the network formation, unreliable links are prominent, and packet loss increases since RPL encounters scalability challenges with the increasing number of nodes.

MRHOF has more control transmission overheads, as seen in Fig. 7; these overheads incur more energy consumption, collisions, congestion, and load disproportion. Higher overheads indicate an unstable network. The higher the overhead transmission frequency, the lower the network stability.

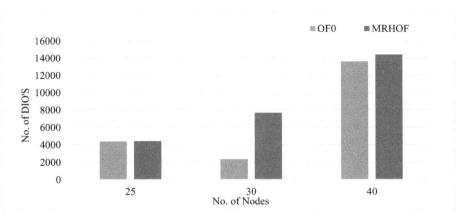

Fig. 5. Number of DIO vs. number of nodes

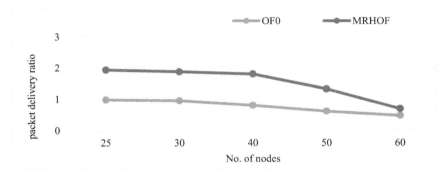

Fig. 6. PDR vs. number of nodes

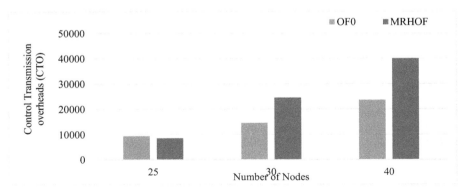

Fig. 7. CTO vs. number of nodes

6 Conclusion and Future Research

The current OF outlined by RPL rely on a solo metric for routing decisions and do not adequately address the QoS needs of everyday applications. The exponential growth of IoT networks, driven by demand for smart systems in sectors like homes, cities, healthcare, agriculture, industry, and military, necessitates optimal routing solutions. A more dynamic or imbalanced network can lead to increased DAOS and DIOs. Thus DIO and DAO counts are considered as the important performance metrics for network instability. Moreover, network optimizations and balanced mechanisms can efficiently limit excessive DAO numbers and reduce overhead. To have optimized outcomes for a particular application, metrics must be appropriately weighted. In the light of that direction, future endeavors will be the evaluation of hybrid objective functions to meet the demand of different IoT applications. For practical implementation, higher routing uncertainty with hybrid OF needs to be addressed intelligently.

Acknowledgments. This work has been supported by the Council of Scientific and Industrial Research (CSIR), Government of India, New Delhi, under project file no.: 09/251(0132)2019-EMR-1.

Disclosure of Interests. The authors have no competing interest.

References

1. Darabkh, K.A., Al-Akhras, M., Zomot, J.N., Atiquzzaman, M.: RPL routing protocol over IoT: a comprehensive survey, recent advances, insights, bibliometric analysis, recommendations, and future directions. J. Netw. Comput. Appl. **207**, 103476 (2022)
2. Atzori, L., Iera, A., Morabito, G.: The internet of things: a survey. Comput. Netw. **54**(15), 2787–2805 (2010)
3. Zikria, Y.B., Afzal, M.K., Kim, S.W., Marin, A., Guizani, M.: Deep learning for intelligent IoT: opportunities, challenges and solutions. Comput. Commun. **164**, 50–53 (2020)
4. Taghizadeh, S., Elbiaze, H., Bobarshad, H.: EM-RPL: enhanced RPL for multigateway internet-of-things environments. IEEE Internet Things J. **8**(10), 8474–8487 (2020)
5. Kumar, A., Hariharan, N.: DCRL-RPL: dual context-based routing and load balancing in RPL for IoT networks. IET Commun. **14**(12), 1869–1882 (2020)
6. Lamaazi, H., Benamar, N.: A comprehensive survey on enhancements and limitations of the RPL protocol: a focus on the objective function. Ad Hoc Netw. **96**, 102001 (2020)
7. Jani, K.A., Chaubey, N.: IoT and cyber security: introduction, attacks, and preventive steps. In: Quantum Cryptography and the Future of Cyber Security, pp. 203–235. IGI Global (2020)
8. Gul, S., Malik, B.A., Banday, M.T.: Intelligent load balancing algorithms for internet of things - a review. Int. J. Sens. Wirel. Commun. Control **12**(6), 415–439 (2022)
9. Lamaazi, H., Benamar, N.: A novel approach for RPL assessment based on the objective function and trickle optimizations. Wirel. Commun. Mobile Comput. (2019)
10. Rani, S., Kumar, A., Bagchi, A., Yadav, S., Kumar, S.: RPL based routing protocols for load balancing in IoT network. J. Phys.: Conf. Ser. **1950**(1), 012073 (2021)
11. Lamaazi, H., Benamar, N., Jara, A.J.: RPL-based networks in static and mobile environment: a performance assessment analysis. J. King Saud Univ.-Comput. Inf. Sci. **30**(3), 320–333 (2018)

12. Lamaazi, H., Benamar, N.: OF-EC: a novel energy consumption aware objective function for RPL based on fuzzy logic. J. Netw. Comput. Appl. **117**, 42–58 (2018)
13. Lamaazi, H., Benamar, N.: RPL enhancement using a new objective function based on combined metrics. In: 2017 13th International Wireless Communications and Mobile Computing Conference (IWCMC), pp. 1459–1464. IEEE (2017)
14. Sebastian, A., Sivagurunathan, S.: Multi DODAGs in RPL for reliable smart city IoT. J. Cyber Secur. Mobil. 69–86 (2018)
15. Sousa, N., Sobral, J.V., Rodrigues, J.J., Rabêlo, R.A., Solic, P.: ERAOF: a new RPL protocol objective function for internet of things applications. In: 2017 2nd International Multidisciplinary Conference on Computer and Energy Science (SpliTech), pp. 1–5 (2017)
16. Iova, O., Theoleyre, F., Noel, T.: Improving the network lifetime with energy-balancing routing: application to RPL. In: 2014 7th IFIP Wireless and Mobile Networking Conference (WMNC), pp. 1–8. IEEE (2014)
17. Tang, F., Yang, L.T., Tang, C., Li, J., Guo, M.: A dynamical and load-balanced flow scheduling approach for big data centers in clouds. IEEE Trans. Cloud Comput. **6**(4), 915–928 (2016)
18. Kamgueu, P.O., Nataf, E., Ndié, T.D., Festor, O.: Energy-based routing metric for RPL. Doctoral dissertation, Inria (2013)
19. Qasem, M., Altawssi, H., Yassien, M.B., Al-Dubai, A.: Performance evaluation of RPL objective functions. In: 2015 IEEE International Conference on Computer and Information Technology; Ubiquitous Computing and Communications; Dependable, Autonomic and Secure Computing; Pervasive Intelligence and Computing, pp. 1606–1613 (2015)
20. Qasem, M., Al-Dubai, A., Romdhani, I., Ghaleb, B., Gharibi, W.: A new efficient objective function for routing in internet of things paradigm. In: 2016 IEEE Conference on Standards for Communications and Networking (CSCN), pp. 1–6 (2016)
21. Yassein, M.B., Flefil, A., Krstic, D., Khamayseh, Y., Mardini, W., Shatnawi, M.: Performance evaluation of RPL in high density networks for internet of things (IoT). In: Proceedings of the 8th International Conference on Software and Information Engineering, pp. 183–187 (2019)
22. Gopal, S.B., Poongodi, C., Jude, M.J.A., Umasri, S., Sumithra, D., Tharani, P.: Minimum energy consumption objective function for RPL in internet of things. Int. J. Sci. Technol. Res. **9**(1), 1–9 (2020)
23. Hassani, A.E., Sahel, A., Badri, A., Ilham, E.M.: Multi-constraints based RPL objective function with adaptive stability for high traffic IoT applications. Indon. J. Electr. Eng. Comput. Sci. **22**(1), 407–418 (2021)
24. Subramani, P.S., Bojan, S.: Weighted sum metrics–based load balancing RPL objective function for IoT. Ann. Emerg. Technol. Comput. (AETiC) **7**(2), 35–55 (2023)
25. Kamble, S., Bhilwar, P., Chandavarkar, B.R.: Novel fuzzy-based objective function for routing protocol for low power and lossy networks. Ad Hoc Netw. **144**, 103150 (2023)
26. Ghanbari, Z., Navimipour, N.J., Hosseinzadeh, M., Shakeri, H., Darwesh, A.: A new lightweight routing protocol for internet of mobile things based on low power and lossy network using a fuzzy-logic method. Pervasive Mob. Comput. **97**, 101872 (2024)
27. Venugopal, K., Basavaraju, T.G.: A combined objective function for RPL load balancing in internet of things. Int. J. Internet Things **10**(1), 22–31 (2022)

Enhancing ASIC Design Efficiency: A Focus on RTL Verification with Spyglass

Dhaval Fichadia[1(✉)], Nikeeta Shah[1], and Bhavesh Soni[2]

[1] einfochips Pvt. Ltd., Ahmedabad, India
{Fichadia.dhaval,Nikeeta.Shah}@einfochips.com
[2] Ganpat University, Mehsana, India
Bhavesh.Soni@ganpatuniversity.ac.in

Abstract. In today's modern world, the number of transistors on a chip is increasing, leading to heightened circuit complexity. Consequently, careful consideration is essential during the design and verification processes. In the Register Transfer Logic (RTL) stage, designing and verifying are pivotal aspects of the overall design. To identify errors at the RTL level, Spyglass is utilized. This paper focuses on Spyglass, designed to analyze RTL code early in the digital design process, aiming to identify potential issues, enhance code quality, and optimize the design before progressing to subsequent stages of the design flow. Early detection of design issues facilitates faster iterations and improved design quality. This RTL verification method is employed to uncover bugs and errors in the design before synthesis. The optimization capabilities of Spyglass contribute to enhanced performance and increased overall design efficiency.

Keywords: VLSI · design for testability · scan insertion · spyglass · RTL

1 Introduction

According to the Moore's law, the scale of ICs has doubled every 18 months. A clear illustration of this pattern is the evolution from SSI (small scale integration) to VLSI (very large scale integration) devices. Today, computers and electronic appliances frequently employ VLSI devices containing millions of transistors. This outcome is directly linked to the continuous reduction in dimensions, known as feature size. The decrease in feature size raises the likelihood that a manufacturing defect in the integrated circuit (IC) will lead to a defective chip. Reducing the feature size increases the likelihood that a manufacturing defect in the IC (integrated circuit) will result in a faulty chip. [9]. While the reduction in feature size brings about speed enhancements, it concurrently introduces drawbacks such as escalated costs, prolonged run times, and reduced yields. Essentially, at lower technology nodes, defect density experiences a significant increase relative to transistor density (performance), posing a substantial challenge for Design for Testability (DFT) in our ASIC flow [8].

2 ASIC Design Flow

The application-specific integrated circuit (ASIC) represent a well-establish and proven integrated circuit (IC) design process, encompassing several stages as design conceptualization, chip optimization, logical/physical implementation, and design validation and verification. Let's delve into a summary of each stage within this systematic progression.

Chip Specification: During this phase, the engineer establishes features, microarchitecture, functionalities like hardware/software interface, and specifications like Time, Area, Power, Speed for the ASIC, following design guidelines.

Design entry/Functional Verification: Functional verification validates the circuit's functionality and logical behavior through simulation at the design entry level. At this stage, the design and verification teams collaborate in the cycle, generating RTL code using test-benches in a process referred to as behavioral simulation.

Register Transfer Level block synthesis/Register Transfer Level Function: Upon the creation of the RTL code and testbench, the focus of the RTL team transitions to the RTL description. Employing a logical synthesis tool that adheres to critical timing constraints, they convert the RTL code into a gate-level netlist (Fig. 1).

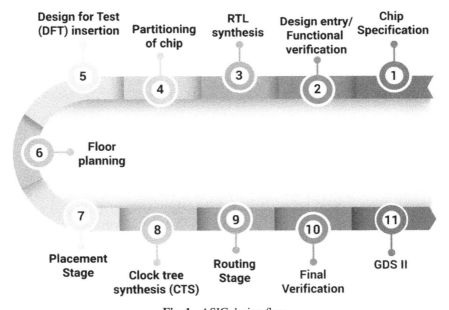

Fig. 1. ASIC design flow.

Chip Partitioning: During this stage, engineers use EDA tools to create the ASIC structure based on design requirements. They partition the application-specific integrated circuit (ASIC) into functional blocks, considering performance, technical feasibility, and resource allocation. The design incorporates IP reuse from previous projects or external sources, aligning with specifications for area, power, cost, and time.

Design for Test (DFT) Integration: As the industry continues to embrace lower technology nodes, the prevalence of SOC (system on chip) variations, threshold voltage, including size, and wire resistance, is on the rise. Consequently, innovative models and methodology are introduced to enhance the effectiveness of testing in ensuring high quality. Given the inherent complexity of ASIC design across various stages of the design cycle, discovering faults in chips during the production stage can be both embarrassing and disruptive when communicating with customers.

Floor Planning: Following DFT integration, the next phase involves the physical implementation process. In physical design, the initial step in the RTL to GDSII design is floor planning, which involves placing blocks within the chip. This encompasses tasks such as block placement, design partitioning, pin placement, and power optimization. The floor plan plays a crucial role in determining the chip's size, positioning gates, and establishing the connections between them using wires.

Placement: Placement involves arranging standard cells in a row, and suboptimal placement can result in increased area requirements and a decline in performance. Several considerations, including timing requirements, net lengths, cell connections, and power dissipation, must be carefully addressed to avoid timing violations.

CTS (clock tree synthesis): CTS is the procedure of constructing the clock-tree to fulfill specified timing, area, and power criteria. This process ensures the timely and spatially efficient provision of the clock connection to the clock pin of a sequential element while minimizing power consumption.

Routing:

- Global Routing: It calculates estimated values for each network considering the delays induced by the wire's fan-out. This phase of routing is commonly classified into line routing and maze routing.
- Detailed Routing: During detailed routing, the actual delay of the wire is established using diverse optimization techniques, including timing optimization, clock-tree synthesis, and other methodologies.

Final Verification: Following the routing process, three essential stages of physical verification are applied to the layout of the ASIC design. These steps include LVS (Layout versus Schematic), DRC (Design Rule Checks), and LVC (Logical Equivalence Checks). This stage is essential to ensure that the layout functions according to its design specifications.

GDS II – Graphical Data Stream Information Interchange: During the final phase of the tape-out, the engineers executes processes such as wafer processing, packaging, testing, verification, and ultimately delivers the physical integrated circuit Conventional DFT DRC methodology [11].

Figure 2 illustrates the DFT flow.

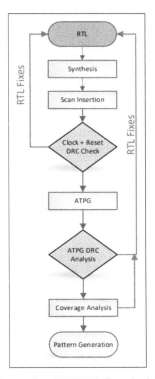

Fig. 2. Conventional DFT DRC methodology flow

RTL Design: The first step is to design the chip in Register Transfer Level (RTL). This is an HDL (hardware description language) that allows engineers to describe the functionality of the chip without worrying about the implementation details.

DFT Insertion: Once the RTL design is complete, DFT circuitry is inserted into the design. This circuitry makes it easier to test the chip by providing additional control and observability points.

Synthesis: The next step is to synthesize the RTL design into a gate level netlist. This netlist is a list of all the gates that are needed to implement the design.

Scan Insertion: Scan insertion is a DFT technique that adds scan chains to the design. Scan chains are groups of flip-flops that can be shifted in and out of the chip in parallel. Basic clock and reset violation checked during scan insertion.

ATPG: ATPG (Automatic Test Pattern Generation) is a technique used to generate test vectors for the chip. Test vectors consist of input value sets that are administered to the chip.

ATPG DRC Analysis: ATPG DRC (Automatic Test Pattern Generation Design Rule Checking) is a process that checks the design for testability (DFT) rules before generating test patterns. This ensures the test patterns can identify all potential faults in the design.

Coverage Analysis: It helps to ensure that the test patterns are effective in detecting the possible faults in the design. The goal of coverage analysis is to achieve a high level of coverage for all of the coverage metrics.

Pattern Generation: Test pattern generation is employed to develop input sequences that effectively uncover all possible faults as per the specified fault model.

In Conventional method of DFT there are multiple iterations needed to resolve the scan integrity and DFT issues in the RTL:

Synthesis -> Scan Insertion -> ATPG

The repetitive cycles of synthesis, scan insertion, and ATPG can contribute to delayed design closure.

3 Spyglass

RTL verification stands out as a critical and challenging task in the development of digital system design. If the verification team identifies any errors, corrective actions must be taken within the RTL code [2]. Spyglass is designed to analyze RTL code early in the digital design process to identify potential issues, improve code quality, and optimize the design before moving to subsequent stages of the design flow.

Early detection of design issues allows for faster iterations and improved design quality. Optimization capabilities contribute to better performance, reduced power consumption, and increased overall design efficiency.

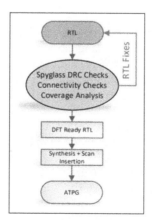

Fig. 3. General flow of spyglass

Figure 3 illustrates that the RTL design undergoes Design Rule Checking (DRC) to identify and correct any violations before proceeding to synthesis and scan insertion.

Once the DRC violations are resolved, the RTL is considered DRC-ready and fed into the synthesis and scan insertion stages. Subsequently, Automatic Test Pattern Generation (ATPG) is performed to generate test patterns for the design.

A single-step feedback loop is employed to address RTL issues and DRC violations promptly. DFT ready RTL with lesser design cycle iterations Vector-less coverage analysis can be done at RTL stage only to avoid low coverage debug at ATPG stage later.

3.1 Spyglass Flow

Leveraging RTL files as the starting point, the Spyglass verification process enables the detection of RTL coding errors and DRC analysis prior to synthesis.

Figure 4 shows spyglass RTL DRC workflow is as follows:

Start with RTL files: The input to the Spyglass RTL DRC process is a set of RTL files. These files describe the functionality of the chip.

DFT setup: The next step is to set up the DFT environment. This includes defining the clocks, resets, and other DFT signals.

Generate SGDC file: The SGDC file is a text file that contains the DFT constraints for the design. These constraints tell the Spyglass tool how to check the design for DFT compliance.

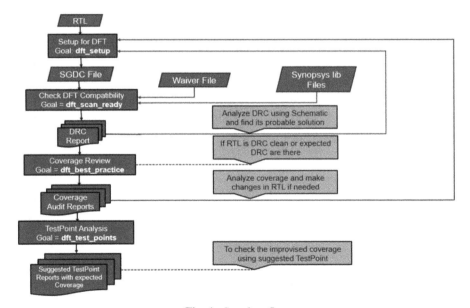

Fig. 4. Spyglass flow

Compatibility check: The Spyglass tool checks the design for compatibility with the SGDC file, waiver file, and related library files. This ensures that the design is using the correct DFT libraries and that it is not violating any constraints.

Generate report: The Spyglass tool generates a report that details the results of the DRC check. The report includes information about DRC violations, clocks, resets, and other DFT issues.

Coverage review: The DRC report is given to a DFT best practice expert for coverage review. The expert will identify any areas where the design could be improved to improve DFT coverage.

Coverage audit report: The DFT best practice expert will generate a coverage audit report that summarizes the findings of the coverage review. The report will also include recommendations for improvement.

Input files:

- RTL file (.v)
- SGDC file (.sgdc)
- Waiver file (.swl/.awl)
- Synopsys library (.lib)

By utilizing Spyglass, we can identify errors within the RTL code, as exemplified in Fig. 5. Specifically, Spyglass detects instances where the net type must be explicitly declared (STX_VE_601) and only those identifiers can be used that are declared in current scope (STX_VE_606).

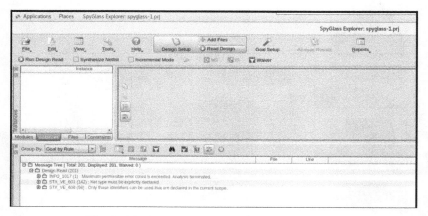

Fig. 5. Display RTL errors within the Spyglass GUI.

Once the RTL code errors are resolved, we can delve into DRC violations in the schematic depiction.

Spyglass reports the results of its analysis as messages, each with a severity level, a class, and a message. The severity levels are FATAL, ERROR, WARNING, and INFO.

Figure 7 illustrates the color-coding scheme used by the Spyglass tool to indicate the severity levels of violations (FATAL, ERROR, WARNING, and INFO) and provides a brief explanation of each severity level [10].

Figure 6 displays two major DRC violations detected in the Analyzer window: async_07 and clock_11. Async_07 emphasizes that Asynchronous set/reset source

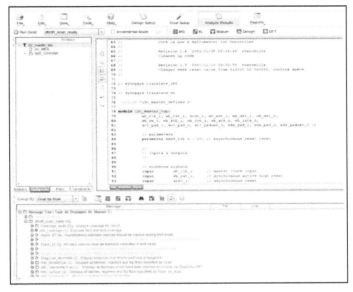

Fig. 6. Display DRCs

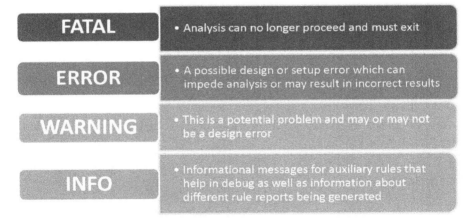

Fig. 7. Spyglass Violation Report

should be inactive during shift mode, while clock_11 emphasizes that all clock source must be test clock controlled during shift mode.

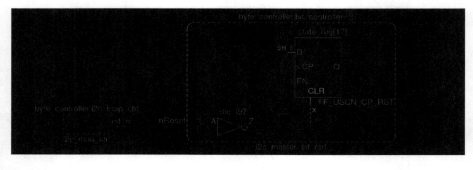

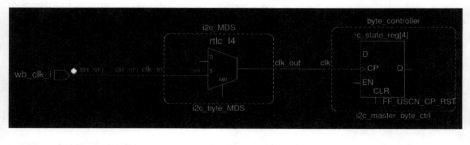

Fig. 8. (a) async_07 violation (b) clock_11 violation

Figure 8 shows the async_07 and clock_11 violations in the schematic visualization.

Spyglass can identify the specific flip-flops affected by the DRC violations and provide a list of these flip-flops (Fig. 9).

Spyglass offers an early indication of test coverage during this phase of design development (Fig. 10).

4 Advantages

Early error detection: Spyglass can identify RTL coding errors and DRC violations early in the design process, before synthesis. This can help to save time and money by catching errors before they have a chance to cause problems later in the design cycle.

Improved DFT coverage: By identifying and fixing DFT issues early in the design process, the Spyglass RTL DRC process can help to improve DFT coverage. This can reduce the risk of defects and improve the quality of the chip.

Reduced time to market: By catching DFT issues early, the Spyglass RTL DRC process can help to reduce the time to market for new chips. This is because it can prevent costly rework later in the design process.

Reduced cost of development: By improving DFT coverage and reducing the time to market, the Spyglass RTL DRC process can help to reduce the cost of chip development.

Enhancing ASIC Design Efficiency 343

Fig. 9. A list of affected flops due to async_07 violation.

```
Expected stuck-at coverage data after each step.
                        Expected stuck-at coverage
                        -----------------------------
                        FC        TC         Action
---------------------------------------------------------------------
0. Original Design      2.4       2.4        No DFT changes are made.It assumes
                                             'force_scan' declared flip-flops scannable.
                                             Use Info_forcedScan to detect such
                                             flip-flops
1. PIs and POs made
   controllable & observable  2.4  2.4       set dft_treat_primary_inputs_as_x_source
                                             & dft_treat_primary_outputs_as_unobservable
                                             to off (No action required)
2. Flip-flops made scannable  92.8  92.8     Async_07 & Clock_11
3. Scan-wrap black boxes      95.6  95.6     Info_scanwrap
4. Latches made Transparent   95.6  95.6     Latch_08 & Info_testmode(capture) (No action required)
5. Combinational Loops made
   controllable               95.6  95.6     Topology_01 & non-X value loops (No action required)
6. Testmode/Tied pins made
   controllable               95.7  95.7     Info_synthRedundant, Info_untestable
                                             and Info_pwrGndSim.
                                             Add -scanshift switch to test_mode
                                             constraint, if appropriate
7. Hanging nets made controllable  100.0  100.0  TA_09
8. Tristate enables made observable 100.0 100.0  TA_09 (No action required)
9. 'force_ta' and 'test_point'
   constraint pins made testable  100.0  100.0  Make pins or nets having 'force_ta'
                                                or 'test_point' constraint testable (No action required)
10. 'no_scan' flip-flops made
    scannable                 100.0  100.0   Use Info_noScan & Info_inferredNoScan
                                             to view all no_scan flip-flops (No action required)
```

Fig. 10. Coverage analysis

5 Conclusion

Spyglass is a powerful tool for verifying RTL code and performing DRC analysis. It can identify RTL coding errors and DRC violations early in the design process before synthesis. This can help to save time and money by catching errors before they have a chance to cause problems later in the design cycle. Spyglass provides detailed error reports that identify the location of the error and explain the problem. This information can be helpful in debugging and fixing errors. Spyglass can detect a wide range of RTL coding errors and DRC violations, including RTL syntax errors, RTL logic errors, RTL coding style errors, DRC timing violations, and DRC signal integrity violations. Spyglass allows you to customize the rules that it uses to detect errors. Spyglass can be integrated with other design tools, such as synthesis and simulation tools. This can help to streamline the design process and make it easier to verify your design.

References

1. Firdous, A., Kusuma, S.M.: Speeding up of design convergence using spyglass. Global Conference for Advancement in Technology (GCAT) (2019)
2. Yadav, A., Jindal, P., Basappa, D.: Study and analysis of RTL verification tool. In: 2020 IEEE Students' Conference on Engineering & Systems (SCES) Prayagraj, India (2020)
3. Sharma, P., Kumar Patel, S.: An automation methodology for amelioration of SpyGlassCDC abstract view generation process. In: 2021 6th International Conference for Convergence in Technology (I2CT) Pune, India (2021)
4. Kumar, C., Maamari, F., Vittal, K., Pradeep, W., Tiwari, R., Ravi, S.: Methodology for early RTL testability and coverage analysis and its application to industrial designs. In: IEEE 23rd Asian Test Symposium (2014)
5. Springer link. https://doi.org/10.1007/978-981-19-8497-6_33
6. Swetha Priya, A.: Defect-aware methodology for low-power scanbased VLSI testing. In: 2015 Conference on Power, Control, Communication and Computational Technologies for Sustainable Growth (PCCCTSG), Kurnool, Andhra Pradesh, India (2015)
7. Swetha Priya, A., Kamatchi, S., Lakshmi Prasad, E.: Early register transfer level (RTL) power estimation in real-time System-on Chips (SoCs). Department of Electronics & Communication Engineering, Amrita School of Engineering, Amrita Vishwa Vidyapeetham, Bengaluru, India. 2 Tessolve Semiconductors, Bengaluru, India (2022)
8. Chauhan, J., Panchal, C., Suthar, H.: Scan methodology and ATPG DFT techniques at lower technology node. In: Proceedings of the IEEE International Conference on Computing Methodologies and Communication (ICCMC) (2017)
9. VLSI test principles and architectures: design for testability[Book]
10. VLSI guru. https://www.vlsiguru.com/q4-spyglass-ppt/
11. Einfochips. https://www.einfochips.com/blog/asic-design-flow-in-vlsi-engineering-services-a-quick-guide/
12. Synopsys. https://www.synopsys.com/verification/static-and-formal-verification/spyglass/spyglass-lint.html
13. [Synopsys] – Spyglass Clock Domain Crossing Verification Datasheet, Author: Synopsys
14. [Synopsys] – Spyglass for FPGA Design Datasheet, Author: Synopsys
15. [Synopsys] – Spyglass Reset Domain Crossing Verification Datasheet, Author: Synopsys
16. [Synopsys] – Ictools Spyglass User Guide, Author: Synopsys

Enhancement in AOMDV Routing Protocol to Overcome Congestion Problem in MANET

Misgana M. Iticha[1](✉), Ketema A. Gemeda[2](✉), and Samuel S. Tadesse[3](✉)

[1] College of Engineering and Technology, Wallaga University, Nekemte, Ethiopia
margamisgu@gmail.com
[2] Adama Science and Technology University, Adama, Ethiopia
ketema.adere@astu.edu.et
[3] Jimma Institute of Technology, Jimma University, Jimma, Ethiopia
samuel.sisay@ju.edu.et

Abstract. Mobile Ad hoc Networks (MANETs) face significant challenges due to the absence of centralized management, particularly in handling congestion issues. In this context, nodes experiencing congestion often advertise themselves as the fastest route to the desired destination node, resulting in multiple packet losses and compromising the integrity, reliability, and availability of the network. To address these concerns, researchers have proposed various approaches to enhance the Ad-hoc On-demand Multipath Distance Vector (AOMDV) routing protocol. This paper investigates the integration of congestion management protocols into MANETs to enhance the performance of AOMDV. We introduce an enhanced version called Congestion Overcome AOMDV (COAOMDV), which incorporates congestion management protocols. A comparative analysis is conducted between COAOMDV and traditional AOMDV procedures, with a focus on mitigating the consequences of congested nodes and improving the overall performance of MANETs. To tackle congestion-related challenges, the proposed technique utilizes higher sequence numbers to identify crowded nodes. The evaluation of these protocols is carried out using NS2.35, considering varying simulation durations and node sizes. Key performance metrics such as throughput, packet delivery ratio, packet loss, and average end-to-end latency are measured and compared between the protocols. The findings of this research demonstrate the effectiveness of the proposed COAOMDV technique in managing congestion problems in MANETs. The results indicate significant improvements in the performance of the AOMDV protocol when congestion management protocols are integrated. By addressing the challenges associated with congested nodes, this research contributes to enhancing the integrity and reliability of MANETs.

Keywords: Mobile Ad hoc Networks · congestion management · AOMDV · COAOMDV · performance evaluation

1 Introduction

MANETs face challenges in establishing efficient paths for message delivery and packet transmission due to limited resources. Congestion, a major issue in MANETs, occurs when new data entries create a blocking effect in the transmission line instead of reaching their destination. This congestion leads to decreased throughput for existing data in the network. Symptoms of congestion include data transmission delays, packet loss, and connection blocking, which occur when nodes carry more data than expected.

MANETs enable multiple communication channels by allowing data packets to traverse intermediary nodes from the source to the destination. However, these networks are constrained by node mobility, limited energy resources, flexible topology, and channel capacity. Ad hoc networks have diverse applications, as summarized in [9]. Network congestion often results in congestion collapse due to resource limitations, link and node failures, and insufficient bandwidth. During congestion, network throughput can drop to zero, and path delays can increase significantly. Therefore, it is crucial to select reliable paths based on congestion availability during the pathway discovery phase to ensure efficient packet delivery.

In this context, the identification of congested and non-congested nodes plays a crucial role in determining the appropriate course of action during packet forwarding. MANET employs various routing methods to transport packets from source to destination nodes. The AOMDV methodology significantly contributes to route discovery by identifying multiple paths. As highlighted in [10], congestion occurs when the network receives more packets than it can handle, leading to packet loss and degradation in bandwidth quality.

The focus of this research paper is to address congestion-related challenges in MANETs and improve the efficiency of packet delivery. We propose a method that evaluates the availability and non-availability of congested nodes based on their throughput during the packet forwarding process. By integrating congestion management protocols into the AOMDV routing protocol, we aim to enhance the network's performance in managing congestion issues.

2 Related Work

Several studies have been conducted focusing on integrating congestion controls into MANETs with enhancements to the AOMDV routing protocol, using various metrics.

The ECAOMDV protocol incorporates congestion and cost considerations into AOMDV routing [6]. It selects an optimal path based on congestion levels and residual power of non-congested nodes. The FF-AOMDV routing protocol integrates a Fitness Function that selects the optimal forwarding path by considering factors such as remaining energy levels and the distance between transmitting and receiving nodes [14].

In [4], an Efficient-Path Selection Scheme is introduced, which utilizes an Optimized Adhoc on Demand Multi-path Routing Protocol. This scheme aims to select the optimal path based on a minimum weight factor (MWF) without identifying congested nodes. The Enhanced Local Multicast AOMDV algorithm aims to increase throughput and manage congestion by analyzing inter-queue space and selecting nodes with less traffic [3].

Another approach in [13] focuses on avoiding traffic load and bottlenecks by choosing nodes with shorter queues and greater remaining energy to forward packets. A novel strategy proposed in [11] prioritizes optimal energy and bandwidth usage in determining the optimum path for AOMDV RP in MANETs. However, it's important to note that the path with the maximum available bandwidth may not always result in high throughput due to congested nodes.

In [15], the Queue Length Aware Ad Hoc On-Demand Distance Vector Routing Protocol ensures packets are not lost due to buffer overflow. However, its single-path design leads to repeated rebroadcast procedures causing network congestion. The BWIEE protocol in [12] establishes multiple routes to enhance data delivery mechanisms and mitigate route failures.

An optimized routing approach for WANETs is presented in [8], utilizing the MAODV protocol and a Stochastic Gradient Descent Deep Learning Neural Network (SGD-DLNN) to assess congestion status. Performance evaluation of reactive routing protocols (AODV, DSR, DSDV) in high mobility scenarios is discussed in [1], showing AODV performs better.

Trust-Aware Reactive Ad Hoc routing (TARA) in [16] incorporates node trusts without modifying the underlying routing protocol. The TARA method influences routing decisions externally by introducing a delay in route request messages of untrusted nodes. [2] presents the Trust-Based Secure On-Demand Routing Protocol (TSDRP) designed for MANETs. It enhances the AODV routing protocol to ensure enhanced security measures against attacks like Blackhole and Denial-of-Service (DoS). TSDRP integrates trust-based mechanisms, providing secure routing and safeguarding communication integrity within MANETs.

In [5], a novel connectivity architecture enables secure communication between smart devices. It proposes a proficient routing protocol that offers adaptive control of network congestion and efficient load balancing in mobile ad hoc networks. [7] introduces the Smart and Dynamic On-Demand Distance Vector (SDODV) routing protocol to overcome limitations of existing protocols. SDODV enhances network lifetime by considering factors such as network topology, traffic load, node mobility, neighborhood density, and battery power. It dynamically adjusts packet routing to optimize network performance.

3 Proposed Solution

In this study, we propose an approach to analyze the effects of congested nodes and mitigate their impacts. Our proposed strategy emphasizes the importance of throughput and higher sequence numbers. Unlike the standard AOMDV, which selects paths based on hop count, our approach focuses on identifying congested nodes and adapting the route selection process accordingly.

Upon receiving the Route Request (RREQ), the intermediate node confirms whether the intended recipient is the destination node. If it is, the source node immediately obtains the reverse address. Subsequently, the intermediate node forwards the RREQ to neighboring nodes. After a certain period, a congested node responds to the RREQ with a Route Reply (RREP) message, which has a sequence ID in the routing database greater than the intended sequence number.

In the proposed algorithm, when broadcasting the RREQ to the neighboring node, the algorithm first calculates the throughput (TP) and checks if it is zero. If TP is indeed zero, the RREP sequence number is multiplied by a maximum arbitrary value. Additionally, the algorithm cross-checks the RREP sequence number in the routing table to determine if it indicates congestion or not. The destination sequence number in the routing table is always lower than the RREP received from a congested node in this recommended approach. The proposed technique thoroughly evaluates and discards each new RREP originating from a congested node. If the routing table is empty, it is updated with a new route. If the new RREP sequence number is greater than or equal to the maximum sequence number in the routing database, the routing table is updated with the new RREP.

By adopting this proposed approach, the effects of congested nodes are analyzed, and their impacts are alleviated through the consideration of throughput and higher sequence numbers.

Pseudo code for proposed Algorithm

1. Initialize the route reply packet from the congested node as the initial rrep, with HSNo greater than DSNo.
2. Broadcast the RREQ using the SN.
3. In case the RREQ reaches the destination:
4. Execute the Rrep_reply function.
5. If the RREP is transmitted to the source node:
6. Perform the Rrep_lookup function using nsaddr and rrepid.
7. Conclude the process.
8. Alternatively, if rrep-dsno is greater than dsno multiplied by max Arbt in the rou ing table:
9. Identify that the Rrep originates from a congested node.
10. Remove the Rrep using nsaddr and rrepid.
11. In the scenario where rrep_sno is greater than rt_dsno:
12. Purge the Rrep.
13. Update the route table accordingly.
14. Confirm that the data packet has arrived at the target node.
15. End the process.

Where: HSNo = Highest sequence number, DSNo = destination sequence number.

3.1 Architecture of the Proposed Solution

The architecture of the proposed solution focuses on clearing up congestion in MANETs using the AOMDV protocol. It presents a comprehensive strategy for integrating congested nodes and mitigating their effects through a specific approach. Central to this procedure is the COAOMDV algorithm, which plays a crucial role in determining the throughput of intermediate nodes.

The proposed method incorporates a doubling mechanism for the sequence number when the throughput is zero. This is achieved by multiplying the sequence number by a maximum value (Arbtmax) during the response. Additionally, the COAOMDV algorithm validates the destination sequence number (DSNo) of the RREP in the routing table. If the RREP has a higher sequence number (HSNo) instead of the expected DSNo, it is promptly removed from the routing database.

By enabling the sender to transmit packets through an alternative route and eliminating the congested node's sequence number, successful communication is ensured. Figure 1 provides an overview of the proposed method's general design.

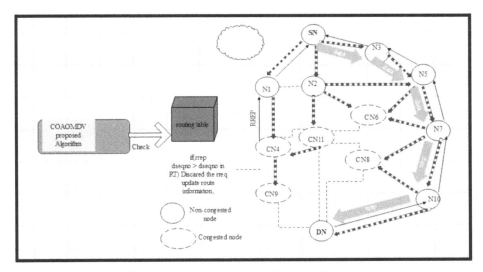

Fig. 1. Proposed Solution Architecture Overview

Figure 1 illustrates the suggested solution for addressing congested nodes in MANETs using the AOMDV routing protocol. The proposed architecture leverages modified RREP methods within the existing AOMDV protocol to achieve the desired goal. Its primary objective is to enhance network efficiency by mitigating the effects of congested nodes. Through the identification and alleviation of congestion impacts, the proposed solution significantly improves the performance of the AOMDV routing protocol in MANETs.

Figure 2 provides a detailed depiction of the process involved in discarding falsified RREP messages from congested nodes and rerouting data packets through a new path to reach the intended destination.

3.2 Proposed Algorithm (COAOMDV)

The following steps provide a detailed description of the Proposed Algorithm, employing a modified approach.

1. Send RREQ messages to all neighboring nodes to discover a suitable route for transmitting the data packet.
2. The algorithm verifies if the next node in the path is the destination node (DN). If it is, the algorithm immediately sends the RREP (Route REPLY) message back to the source node. If not, the process repeats by forwarding the request to the next node until it reaches the desired destination.

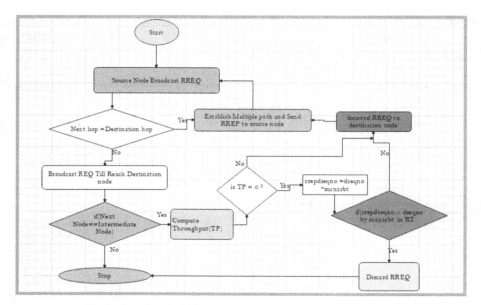

Fig. 2. Flow Chart Diagram of Proposed COAOMDV Algorithm

3. Once the RREQs reach the destination node, the algorithm selects the target node and delivers the RREP message back to the source node, establishing the route.
4. The proposed COAOMDV approach incorporates a check for the presence of congested nodes along the route. If a congested node is detected, the algorithm determines whether to forward the RREQ to the next node or discard the RREP message.
5. If the throughput (TP) on the chosen route is found to be 0, indicating congestion, the algorithm immediately discards the RREP message.
6. An uncongested route is selected based on the routing information to transfer data to the receiving node.
7. The proposed approach is implemented by modifying the route table information and blocking the RREP message. Subsequently, a new path is identified to forward data packets, establishing a fresh route for efficient communication.
8. End.

4 Simulation and Result Analysis

4.1 Simulation Scenario

The simulation section provides an analysis and evaluation of congestion problems in MANET under the AOMDV routing protocol. It also explores a modified approach to minimize the impact of congestion. NS2.35 is used for the simulation process to effectively address congestion issues in this protocol.

4.2 Simulation Parameter

Table 1. Parameters for simulation

Selected Parameter	Value
Tool for Simulators	NS-2.35
Routing Protocol	AOMDV and COAOMDV
Network area	500 m * 500 m
Traffic type	CBR
Platform type	Ubuntu 20.04
mobility type	Random Waypoint
Graphing Utility type	Microsoft Excel
Connection Type	UDP
Number of nodes	15, 25, 35
Simulation time (ms)	20, 40, 60, 80, 100 ms

4.3 Simulation Result

Using Table 1, the simulation setup is established, and the following results are obtained using the NAM Window.

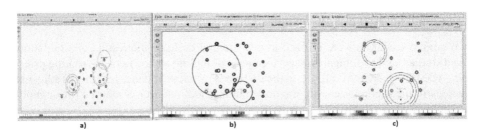

Fig. 3. Comparison of Routing Protocols in MANET with Congestion.

Figure 3(a) showcases a simulation scenario with 35 nodes after 60 s of simulation in a normal network environment, utilizing the AOMDV routing protocol. From the simulation window, it can be observed that all nodes are functioning normally without any congestion. In this simulation, the data packets successfully reach the destination node using the AOMDV routing protocol in MANET. Consequently, there is a minimal number of dropped packets (low packet loss), and the network exhibits high throughput, high Packet Delivery Ratio (PDR), and low end-to-end delay.

Figure 3(b) portrays a simulation scenario with 35 mobile nodes in a MANET environment over a 60-s simulation period. As observed in the simulation window, nodes 3, 7, 10, and 20 experience congestion due to their resource limitations, despite being on the shortest route. These nodes become candidates for path selection in AOMDV since they possess the lowest node numbers. Consequently, these congested nodes drop data packets originating from the sender node. In this simulation environment, the data packets fail to reach the destination node due to congestion in the given MANET scenario. This scenario results in a high number of dropped data packets, increased end-to-end delay, and lower performance metrics in terms of throughput and Packet Delivery Ratio (PDR).

Figure 3(c) demonstrates a simulation scenario with 35 mobile nodes over a 60-s simulation period, utilizing the Modified AOMDV (COAOMDV) routing protocol in MANET. In this scenario, as observed in the simulation window, nodes 3, 7, 10, and 20 are congested nodes. However, due to the implementation of the proposed approach, the COAOMDV algorithm disregards these congested nodes during path selection, even if they are on the shortest path to reach the destination node. This implementation of COAOMDV in MANET yields favorable results in terms of throughput, Packet Delivery Ratio (PDR), packet loss, and end-to-end delay compared to the other simulation scenarios.

4.4 Result Analysis and Discussion

Two unique scenarios were utilized to analyze and evaluate the results of simulation-based studies, and to compare the performance of mobile ad hoc network routing protocols (AOMDV and COAOMDV). In the first circumstance the pause length was adjusted, whereas in the second scenario, the node number and other QoS metrics (throughput, packet loss, packet delay ratio, and PDR) were considered.

Throughput vs. Simulation Time Analysis and Node Numbers
The analysis of throughput performance in relation to simulation time, as depicted in Figs. 4 and 5, provides valuable insights into the comparison between the COAOMDV and AOMDV routing protocols. The figures illustrate the plotted throughput values against time for a network consisting of 35 nodes. Notably, the figures display that the COAOMDV routing protocol outperforms the AOMDV routing protocol in terms of achieving higher throughput.

The observed difference in throughput can be attributed to a key characteristic of the AOMDV protocol, namely its reliance on exploring the shortest path while disregarding the detection and exclusion of nodes along the route. As a consequence, the AOMDV protocol fails to effectively detect and bypass congested nodes, resulting in a lower throughput performance.

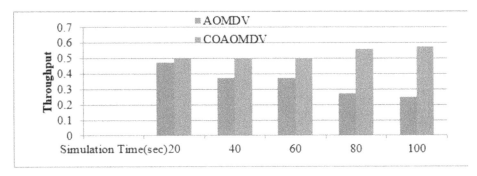

Fig. 4. Throughput vs. Time for 35 nodes

Throughput vs. Number of Nodes

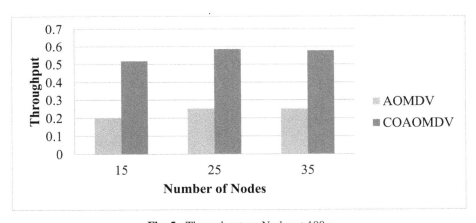

Fig. 5. Throughput vs. Nodes at 100 s

Packet Delivery Ratio Versus. Simulation Time and Node Numbers

Figure 6 and 7 illustrate the correlation between the Packet Delivery Ratio (PDR) and Simulation Time in a network comprising 35 nodes and a simulation duration of 100 s. The figures demonstrate the COAOMDV routing protocol exhibits a faster packet transmission rate compared to the AOMDV routing protocol. This disparity can be attributed to the AOMDV protocol's reliance on the shortest path without considering node detection and exclusion along the path. Consequently, as the number of moving nodes and simulation time increases, the PDR of AOMDV decreases.

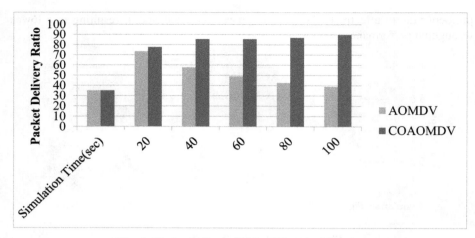

Fig. 6. Packet Delivery ratio vs. Time for 35 nodes

Packet Delivery Ratio versus. Number of Nodes

Figure 7 depicts the relationship between the Packet Delivery Ratio and the number of nodes at a certain time of 100 s.

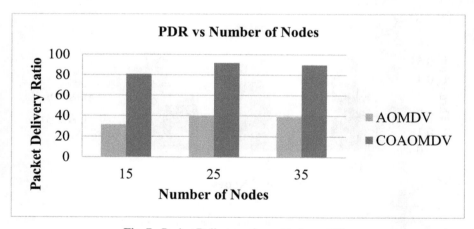

Fig. 7. Packet Delivery ratio vs. Nodes at 100 s

Average End-to-End Delay

$$packet\ duration = end\ time - start\ time$$

$$Avg\ of\ E2ED = \sum_{n=1}^{\infty} \left(\frac{packet\ duration}{received\ several\ packets} \right)$$

Average End-to-End Delay (AE2ED) vs. Simulation Time and Node Numbers

The analysis of the Average End-to-End Delay (AE2ED) for AOMDV and the proposed procedure for changing the number of nodes within a 100-s timeframe is presented in Figs. 8 and 9. Notably, the attached figure clearly demonstrates that the COAOMDV routing protocol exhibits faster packet transmission compared to the AOMDV routing protocol.

As the number of mobile nodes increases, it is observed that the AE2ED of the AOMDV protocol takes more time compared to COAOMDV. This can be attributed to the presence of congested nodes along the shortest path in AOMDV, as it searches for routes without detecting and bypassing nodes along the way. In contrast, the COAOMDV protocol is capable of detecting and avoiding congested nodes, enabling more efficient packet transmission.

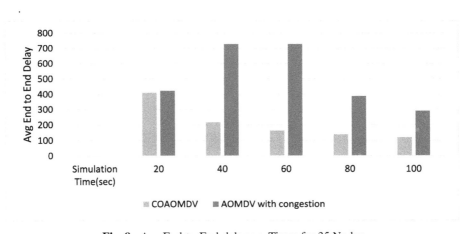

Fig. 8. Avg End-to-End-delay vs. Times for 35 Nodes

Average End-to-End Delay Versus. Node Number

Comparison Between Packet Loss and Node Number
During the comparative evaluation of AOMDV and COAOMDV routing protocols, a comprehensive analysis was conducted considering 35 nodes with varying incubation periods, as illustrated in Figs. 10 and 11. The primary objective of this evaluation was to assess the performance and characteristics of these protocols. Throughout the simulations, it was observed that AOMDV exhibits a high packet loss rate.

Comparison of Packet Loss with Simulation Time
Figure 11 showcases the relationship between packet loss and simulation time specifically for a network consisting of 35 nodes.

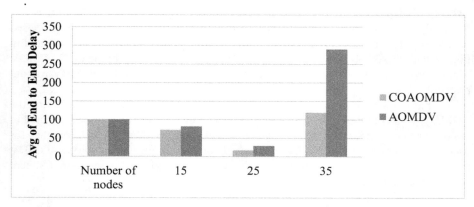

Fig. 9. Avg End-to-End-delay vs. Nodes at 100 s

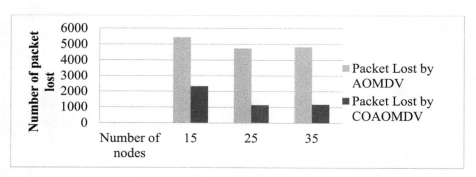

Fig. 10. Packet lost in 100 s for both protocols

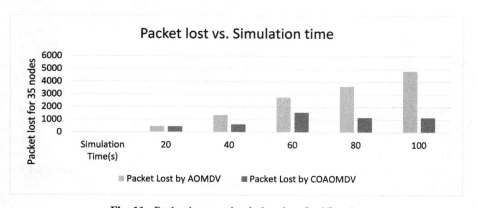

Fig. 11. Packet lost vs. simulation time for 35 nodes

5 Conclusion

MANETs encounter congestion issues that can have a substantial impact on the efficiency of wireless networks, particularly in terms of establishing optimal routing. This research addresses the challenge of congestion in MANETs by introducing a congested node into AOMDV protocol through modifications to the routing mechanism. The identification of congested nodes is achieved through a sequence number mechanism utilizing higher sequence numbers with time stamps and the RREP technique.

The main objective of this study was to alleviate congestion in MANETs by leveraging the RREP sequence numbers technique within the AOMDV routing protocol, thereby improving network performance and reliability. The proposed approach involves modeling and analyzing the impact of congested nodes and mitigating their influence by using larger destination sequence numbers.

To evaluate the effectiveness of the proposed method, a comparison between AOMDV and the proposed COAOMDV was conducted. The evaluation considered key performance metrics such as PDR, average delay, packet loss, and throughput. The experiments were conducted using the NS-2.35 simulator, varying the number of nodes and simulation durations.

The findings from the simulations, observations, and analysis indicate that COAOMDV outperforms AOMDV across different node sizes and simulation durations in terms of throughput, PDR, packet loss, and end-to-end delay. In contrast, AOMDV with congestion leads to a significant decline in network performance. The results highlight the positive impact of the proposed COAOMDV approach in enhancing the overall performance of MANETs.

In conclusion, this research demonstrates the effectiveness of the COAOMDV algorithm in mitigating congestion issues in MANETs. By introducing congestion overcome into the AOMDV protocol, the proposed approach significantly improves network performance and reliability. These findings contribute to the advancement of routing protocols for MANETs and provide valuable insights for researchers and practitioners in the field.

References

1. Aggarwal, A., Gandhi, S., Chaubey, N.: Performance analysis of AODV, DSDV and DSR in MANETS. Int. J. Distrib. Parallel Syst. **2**, 167–177 (2014)
2. Aggarwal, A., Gandhi, S., Chaubey, N., Jani, K.: Trust based secure on demand routing protocol (TSDRP) for MANETs. In: Fourth International Conference on Advanced Computing & Communication Technologies (ACCT), Rohtak, pp. 432–438 (2014)
3. Babu, K.S., et al.: Enhanced local multicast AOMDV protocol for congestion management using dynamic node selection in MANET. Solid State Technol. **63**(2s), 84–88 (2020)
4. Bekan, K., et al.: Efficient path selection scheme using optimized adhoc on demand multipath routing protocol for adhoc networks. Int. J. Adv. Netw. Appl. **11**(04), 4336–4344 (2020)
5. Dalal, S., Seth, B., Jaglan, V., et al.: An adaptive traffic routing approach toward load balancing and congestion control in cloud–MANET ad hoc networks (2022)
6. Dsouza, M.B., et al.: Energy and congestion aware multipath routing in MANET. Int. J. Recent Technol. Eng. (IJRTE) **8**(5S), 2426–2431 (2020)
7. Kaddoura, S., Haraty, R.A., Al Jahdali, S., et al.: SDODV: a smart and adaptive on-demand distance vector routing protocol for MANETs. Peer-to-Peer Netw. (2023)

8. Kanthimathi, S., et al.: Optimal routing based load balanced congestion control using MAODV in WANET environment. (IJACSA). Int. J. Adv. Comput. Sci. Appl. **12**(3) (2021)
9. Kaur, M., Kumar, K.: A review of QoS routing protocols in MANETs. In: International Conference on Computer Communication and Informatics, Coimbatore, INDIA (ICCCI - 2013) (2013)
10. Mahesh, M.K., Das, S.R.: Ad-hoc on-demand multipath distance vector routing. Wirel. Commun. Mob. Comput. (2019)
11. Milkiyas, D., et al.: Optimal path selection for AOMFDV routing protocol with efficient energy and bandwidth in mobile ad hoc networks (2018)
12. Saravanakumar, P., et al.: Bwiee protocol for route discovery and energy efficiency in MANET. Turk. J. Comput. Math. Educ. (TURCOMAT) **12**(11), 3657–3664 (2021)
13. Peng, L, et al.: AOMDV-based multipath routing protocol with load balancing and energy constraints for ad hoc networks: mobile networks and applications (2019)
14. Sridhar, P., et al.: Optimum route selection using FFAOMDV to increase packet delivery ratio in MANET. Jetir **7**(3), 387–392 (2020)
15. Eyob, T., et al.: A queue length aware ad hoc on demand distance vector routing protocol for mobile ad hoc networks (2019)
16. Trofimova, Y., Tvrdík, P.: Enhancing reactive ad hoc routing protocols with trust. Future Internet (2022)

Performance Evaluation of Parallel Processing Adder Against Basic Adders on FPGAs

Dhaval Fichadia[1(✉)], Kishor Purohit[2(✉)], and Bhavesh Soni[2(✉)]

[1] einfochips Ltd., Ahmedabad, India
fichadia.dhaval@einfochips.com
[2] Ganpat University, Mehsana, India
kishorbhaipurohit22@gnu.ac.in,
Bhavesh.soni@ganpatuniversity.ac.in

Abstract. Adders are essential components of modern digital circuits, and their primary design goal is to achieve high speed. However, power consumption and chip area are also important considerations in modern circuit design. Optimizing digital adder performance plays a crucial role in enhancing the speed of binary operations within complex circuits. Various architectures address the carry propagation bottleneck, each with its own strengths and weaknesses. Choosing the most appropriate architecture depends on the specific application requirements, ensuring optimal performance within the available resource constraints. This paper provides a comprehensive analysis of various adder topologies and their performance characteristics. By carefully considering the trade-offs between delay, power consumption, and area, engineers can choose the optimal architecture for their specific application requirements, leading to significant improvements in digital system performance and efficiency. The analyzed adder topologies include Ripple Carry Adder (RCA), Carry Lookahead Adder (CLA), Carry Skip Adder (CSK), Carry Select Adder (CSLA), Carry Increment Adder (CIA), Brent kung adder (BKA), Kong stone adder. The analysis is conducted using HDL on the Xilinx ISE 14.7 platform.

Keywords: Finite impulse response (FIR) · Ripple carry adder (RCA) · Carry Look Ahead Adder (CLA) · Carry Select Adder (CSLA) · Carry Increment Adder (CIA) · Carry Skip Adder · Kogge Stone Adder (CSKa) · Arithmetic-logic unit (ALU) · Parallel prefix adder (PPA)

1 Introduction

In almost every digital system, adders are digital circuits. The applications range from processor's simple ALU to complex multipliers. Adders (Kogge Stone) are used to carry out algorithms like FFT, FIR, and IIR in DSP systems, for instance [4]. Adders, fundamental components in digital circuits, play a crucial role in optimizing performance and efficiency. Their ability to reduce transistor count makes them essential in diverse applications, including Fast Fourier Transforms (FFTs) within digital communication systems [2]. Researchers continuously explore optimization strategies for adders, focusing on parameters such as area, memory utilization, and speed. Similarly, in the field of Artificial Neural Networks (ANNs), recent studies have emphasized configuring FPGAs for optimal area [1] and computational time, highlighting the importance of adders in enhancing overall digital system performance [3]. This emphasis on efficiency stems from the increasing reliance on performance in today's entirely digital world. The area used, power consumption, and delay are the parameters that determine a digital system's quality [4–6].

Optimum adders can reduce system area, power consumption, and speed because they are one of the fundamental components of most digital systems [4].

The fast adders are a different kind of adder that are quicker than conventional adders but have a more intricate construction. This study examines the Brent Kung Adder as a rapid adder.

Its obvious that any one adder can't satisfy all the requirements. Based on the constraints each application imposes, the adders are chosen for each application. For instance, the use of microcontrollers and microprocessors is on the rise. The multipliers are one of these microprocessors and microcontrollers' most important components. Multiplication is known to be repeated addition, which explains the significance of adders in multipliers. As a result, the overall performance of the processor system is influenced by the performance of the adders, which in turn is influenced by the performance of the multipliers [7, 8].

As mentioned earlier, the application determines which adders are used. Therefore, in a system where size is a constraint, an adder that occupies more space may not be considered. In a similar vein, complex, fast ads can be used in such circumstances if the user is able to bear the power and area consumption. Three key parameters are paramount in evaluating adder performance: area consumption, power consumption, and delay. These parameters determine the overall efficiency and suitability of an adder for a specific application. Therefore, the following analysis will compare different adder topologies based on these crucial metrics.

2 Adders

2.1 Ripple Carry Adder (RCA)

Cascading full adder (FA) blocks form the series structure of the ripple carry adder depicted in Fig. 4. A full adder adds the two binary digits A and B, as well as the Cin that is initially supplied at any stage of the ripple carry. The first bit of sum and carry-out will be the output that is produced. The obtained result is listed as the result of the previous stage, etc. The following is the sum-and-carry equation:

The first full adder will receive as inputs the two inputs A-Data1 and B-Data 2, as well as a Cin. In a Ripple Carry Adder (RCA), each full adder generates a sum bit and a carry-out. The carry-out from one full adder becomes the input carry for the next full adder in the chain. This process continues until the final full adder is reached, which produces the final sum and carry-out for the entire operation. The delay of an RCA increases with the number of bits it processes, as each full adder contributes to the overall propagation time [9] (Fig. 1).

$$\text{Sum} = AB \oplus \text{Cin} \tag{1}$$

$$\text{Carry} = A \& B \mid B \& \text{Cin} \mid A \& \text{Cin} \tag{2}$$

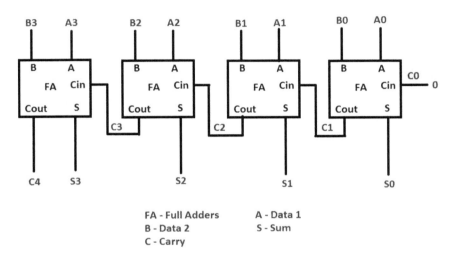

Fig. 1. 4bit ripple carry adder.

2.2 Carry Look Ahead Adder (CLA)

The CLA achieves faster performance than Ripple Carry Adders (RCAs) by calculating transitional carries independently of the input operands using dedicated carry generate and carry propagate signals. As shown in the block diagram (Fig. 2), the CLA employs additional logic blocks for carry generation, propagation, and final carry calculation. This allows the CLA to anticipate the carry for each bit position, significantly reducing the overall delay compared to RCAs where carry propagates sequentially through each stage. The additional parts, such as generate and propagate is provided by

$$Pk = Ak \oplus Bk \tag{3}$$

$$Gk = Ak \oplus Bk \tag{4}$$

$$Sk = Pk \oplus Gk \tag{5}$$

$$C1 = G0 \mid P0 \& C0 \tag{6}$$

$$C2 = G1 \mid P1 \& (G0 \mid P0 \& C0) \tag{7}$$

$$C3 = G2 \mid P2 \& (G1 \mid P1 \& (G0 \mid P0 \& C0)) \tag{8}$$

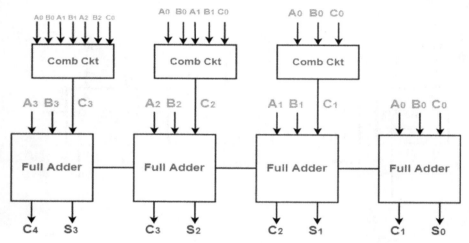

Fig. 2. 4 bit Carry Look Ahead Adder (CLA)

2.3 Carry Select Adder (CSLA)

The CSLA is a combinational logic circuit that operates on two n-bit parallel numbers and a carry-in bit. It outputs the sum of these two numbers, similar to the Ripple Carry Adder (RCA). However, the CSLA achieves this functionality using a different design that utilizes fewer full adders than the RCA. As shown in Fig. 3, a four-bit CSLA made-up of two parallel RCAs combined with multiplexers to select the final sum and carry-out. The input operands are fed to both RCAs: the first with a carry-in of 0 and the second with a carry-in of 1. This parallel processing allows for faster computation compared to the sequential carry propagation of the RCA. A series of mux takes the sum from the adders as inputs, and the FA carry chooses the next RCA to take into consideration. The same procedure is followed for the output carry. CSLA is at the forefront of all adders in terms of area and power, and it has a very low delay [10].

2.4 Carry Increment Adder (CIA)

In this work, the CIA is made up of two CLAs rather than the RCAs that are used in a traditional CIA. Due to their high propagation delay, CIA_RCAs have an impact on the system's overall performance, despite their widespread popularity due to their straightforward designs.

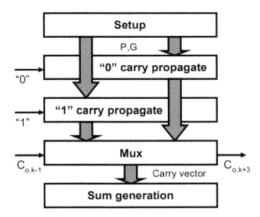

Fig. 3. Block diagram of Carry Select Adder (CSLA)

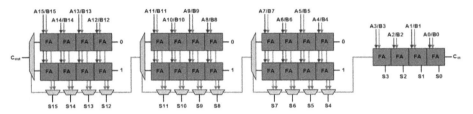

Fig. 4. 4 bit Carry Select Adder (CSLA)

The Carry Increment Adder (CIA) employs two Carry Look Ahead Adders (CLAs) for faster operation. The inputs are provided to both CLAs, and the first CLA's carry-out and sum bit are fed to a Half Adder (HA). The final carry output is obtained by performing a logical OR operation on the carry-out of the second CLA and the output carry of the HA. Subsequently, the carry from the HA is propagated to the next HA in the chain, and each HA generates a sum bit. As shown in Fig. 5, this specific CIA implementation utilizes two four-bit CLAs.

2.5 Carry Skip Adder

Carry Skip Adder (CSkA), Carry-skip adders offer a significant advantage in delay performance over ripple-carry adders with minimal added complexity. This advantage can be further enhanced by combining multiple carry-skip adders into a block-carry-skip architecture, the worst-case delay is improved. When the propagate condition is met for each digit pair (ai, bi), the worst case for a straightforward one-level carry ripple adder occurs. After "$\tau CRA(n) = n.\tau VA$" the carry-in appears as the carry-out as it passes through the n-bit adder.

An XOR-Gate is used to determine the propagate conditions $p_i = a_i \oplus b_i$ for each operand input bit pair (ai,bi). The carry-out bit is determined by the carry-in bit c0 when all propagate-conditions are met (Fig. 6).

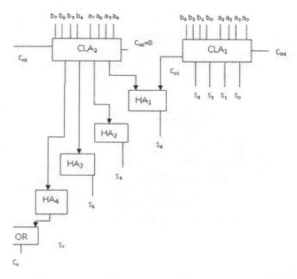

Fig. 5. Block diagram of Carry Increment Adder

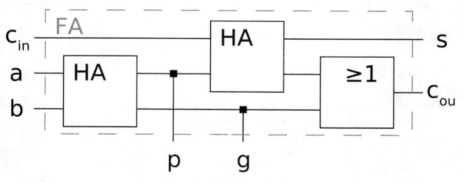

Fig. 6. Full adder by propagate carry.

A 4-bit carry skip adder comprises a multiplexer, a 4-input AND gate, and a 4-bit carry propagation logic. Each propagate bit (pi) generated by the carry propagation logic feeds into the 4-input AND gate. The resulting "group propagate" signal acts as the select bit for the multiplexer, choosing between the initial carry-in (c0) or the last carry bit (cn) as the final carry-out (cout).

This design significantly reduces the adder's critical path delay by allowing the carry signal to "skip" over groups with a group propagate signal of 1. However, the width of the adder is limited by the AND gate's size. Implementing a large AND gate as a tree becomes impractical and introduces additional delays. Therefore, the sum logic depth should ideally be the same as the depth of the AND gate and multiplexer to achieve a good balance for larger widths (Fig. 7).

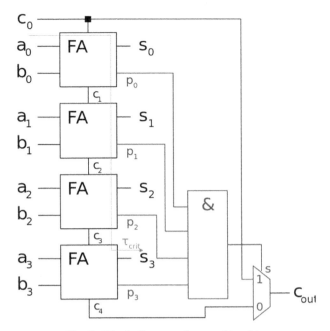

Fig. 7. Block diagram of carry skip adder

In a carry-skip adder, the critical path begins at the first full adder and traverses all subsequent adders, culminating at the sum bit sn-1. To overcome the limitations of individual carry-skip adders, which offer no significant speed advantage over ripple-carry adders of similar bit-width, they can be chained together to reduce the overall critical path.

$$\tau CSA(n) = \tau CRA(n) \tau CSA(n) = \tau CRA(n)$$

$$TSK = TAND(m) + TMUXTSK = TAND(m) + TMUX$$

Since propagate signals are computed concurrently and readily available, the critical path of a carry-skip adder's skip logic is solely determined by the multiplexer's delay (conditional skip).

$$TCSK = TMUX = 2D.$$

2.6 Kogge Stone Adder

KSA can be easily analyzed in terms of three distinct parts:

1. Pre-processing

$$pi = Ai \text{ xor } Bi$$

$$g_i = A_i \text{ and } B_i$$

2. Carry look ahead network.

$$P_{i:j} = P_{i:k+1} \text{ and } P_{k:j}$$

$$G_{i:j} = G_{i:k+1}$$

3. Postprocessing

$$S_i = p_i \text{ xor } C_i - 1$$

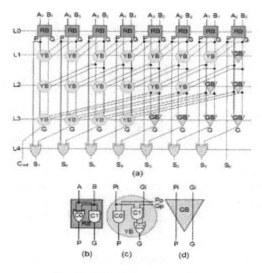

Fig. 8. 8-bit Kogge stone adder

2.7 Brent Kung Adder [11]

Brent-Kung Adder: Achieving High-Performance with Parallel Prefix Logic (Fig. 8).

The Brent-Kung Adder (BKA) is a high-performance adder architecture that utilizes parallel prefix logic to significantly reduce the delay compared to traditional ripple-carry adders. It operates by first pre-computing carry signals and propagate signals for all bits simultaneously. This allows the adder to bypass unnecessary carry propagation delays, leading to faster operation.

Key Features:

- Parallel Prefix Logic: Utilizes dedicated logic circuits to pre-compute carry and propagate signals for all bits in parallel, eliminating the sequential carry propagation bottleneck of ripple-carry adders.

- High Speed: Offers significantly faster operation compared to ripple-carry adders, especially for large operand sizes.
- Scalability: Can be easily scaled to accommodate wider adders with minimal performance degradation.

Internal Structure:
The BKA consists of three stages:

- Prefix Generation: Computes the prefix sums and carries for all possible combinations of input bits. This stage utilizes specialized circuits like carry-propagate generators and carry-skip generators.
- Carry Select: Employs multiplexers to select the appropriate carry signal for each bit based on the pre-computed prefix information.
- Sum Generation: Generates the final sum bits using the selected carry signals and the input operands (Fig. 9).

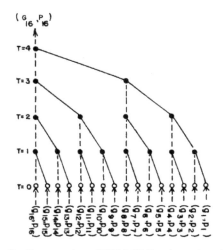

Fig. 9. Computation of (G16, P16) using a tree structure.

3 Simulation Environment

The paper focuses on comparing five different adders all of which have 64 bits. Based on the specifications, we chose these adders to compare because they are widely used in a variety of applications. The simulation is carried out with a vertex 6 Field Programmable Gate Array (FPGA) and Hard-ware Description Language (HDL) on the Xilinx ISE 14.7. Our simulation considers a frequency of 10 kHz because Digital Signal Processing uses adders and multipliers. Based on this signal rate, the adders are being compared and analyzed.

4 Results

The result is being tabulated below (Table 1).

Table 1. Results of different adder topologies with different configuration in Xilinx ise 14.7

Sr. no	ADDER	Configuration	DELAY(ns)	AREA		POWER (mv)
				Slices	Luts	
1	Ripple carry adder(rca)		19.57	39	64	4.17
2	Carry look ahead adder (cla)		19.58	40	64	5.05
3	Carry select adder (CSLA)	$K = 8$	10.65	49	99	5.905
		$K = 6$	11.04	53	93	6.01
		$K = 32$	27.82	46	64	5.943
4	Carry increment adder (cia)	$Gs = 8$	13.92	44	87	5.6
		$Gs = 16$	10.42	55	99	5.807
		$Gs = 32$	11.98	60	61	5.705
5	Brent kung adder (bka)		4.8	75	150	6.8
6	Carry skip adder		26	46	81	5.65
7	Kong ston adder		6.8	115	301	6.8

5 Conclusion

This study compares various adders using the area, power, and delay as the primary criteria. Out all the adders selected, Brent-kung adder, a fastest adder and offers the best outcome in terms of latency. The Brent-Kung adder operates in accordance with parallel prefix processing. Another essential issue to consider while designing digital circuits is power. The Ripple carry adder was uses the least amount of power in our research. Carry select adder has the fewest slices when the area is considered in this manner. On the other hand, LUTs must have a significant quantity, and in this study, the CLA and Kogge stone adder had the largest LUT number out of all adders.

The BKA turns out to be a better option when comparing the area between the two PPAs. The Brent kung adder area does increase as the bit size increases, but not as dramatically as KSA. The adder is larger in terms of area the more bits that the PPAs can accommodate. For an 8-bit bit size, KSA also performs better in terms of computational delay and time propagation delay (tpd). The KSA also uses less power overall, according to estimates. The results show that, for an 64-bit size, the suggested Bent-kang Parallel-Prefix adder is more effective than the Kogge-stone Parallel-Prefix adder in terms of area, latency, and power.

While fast adders like Brent-Kung offer superior speed, they often sacrifice area and power efficiency. This necessitates consideration of all three factors when selecting an adder for specific applications.

Brent-Kung adders, known for their high performance, utilize parallel computation for faster operation. However, this advantage comes at the cost of increased complexity, resulting in larger area and higher power consumption compared to simpler adders. The Carry Select Adder (CSLA) emerges as a preferred choice when area limitations become a concern. It offers a balance between speed and complexity, achieving faster operation than the Ripple Carry Adder while maintaining a smaller footprint and lower power consumption compared to high-performance adders like Brent-Kung. Considering area and power constraints alongside speed provides a more comprehensive understanding of adder performance and suitability for different applications. This analysis allows for informed decisions in selecting the optimal adder for each specific case.

Appendix

(See Figs. 10, 11, 12, 13, 14, 15 and 16)

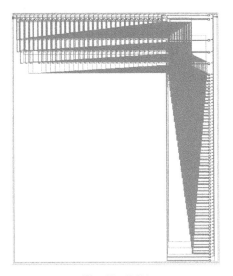

Fig. 10. RCA

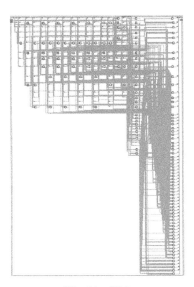

Fig. 11. CSA

370 D. Fichadia et al.

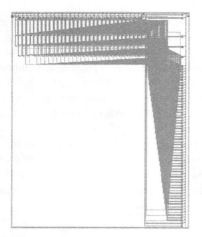

Fig. 12. Cla

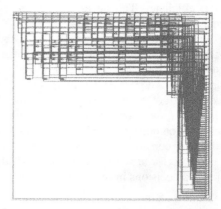

Fig. 13. CIA Gs = 8

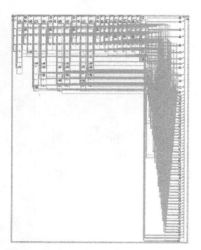

Fig. 14. CIA Gs = 32

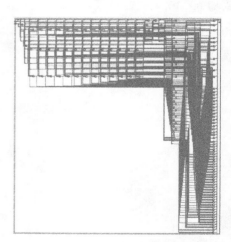

Fig. 15. Kogge Stone

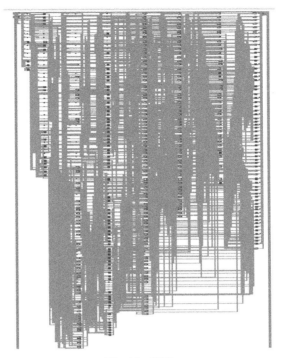

Fig. 16. CSKa

References

1. Penumutchi, B., Vella, S., Satti, H.: Kogge stone adder with GDI technique in 130nm technology for high performance DSP applications. In: 2017 International Conference on Smart Technologies for Smart Nation (SmartTechCon). IEEE (2017)
2. Bhakthavatchalu, R., et al.: Modified FPGA based design and implementation of reconfigurable FFT architecture. In: 2013 International Mutli-Conference on Automation, Computing, Communication, Control and Compressed Sensing (iMac4s). IEEE (2013)
3. Saichand, V., Nirmala Devi, M., Arumugam, S., Mohankumar, N.: FPGA realization of activation function for artificial neural networks. In: Proceedings of the 8th IEEE International Conference on Intelligent Systems Design and Applications, vol. 3, pp. 159–164. IEEE (2008)
4. Koyada, B., Meghana, N., Jaleel, M.O., Jeripotula, P.R.: A comparative study on adders. In: 2017 International Conference on Wireless Communications, Signal Processing and Networking (WiSPNET) (2017). https://doi.org/10.1109/wispnet.2017.8300155
5. Uma, R., Vijayan, V., Mohanapriya, M., Paul, S.: Area, delay and power comparison of adder topologies. Int. J. VLSI Design Commun. Syst. **3**(1), 153 (2012)
6. Saini, J., Agarwal, S., Kansal, A.: Performance, analysis and comparison of digital adders. In: 2015 International Conference on Advances in Computer Engineering and Applications. IEEE (2015)
7. Gladwin, S.J., Mangayarkkarasi, M.: Design and performance comparison of 4-bit adders using different logic styles. J. Comput. Theor. Nanosci. **15**(3), 949–960 (2018)
8. Prabhala, K., Dasari, H., Komatipalli, T.: Performance comparison of 64-bit adders. In: Conference Paper Details Not Available (2010)

9. Kaur, J., Sood, L.: Comparison between various types of adder topologies. Int. J. Comput. Sci. Technol. **6**(1), 42–48 (2015)
10. Saxena, P.: Design of low power and high speed carry select adder using Brent Kung adder. In: 2015 International Conference on VLSI Systems, Architecture, Technology and Applications (VLSI-SATA). IEEE (2015)
11. Jayanthi, A.N., Ravichandran, C.S.: Comparison of performance of high speed VLSI adders. In: 2013 International Conference on Current Trends in Engineering and Technology (ICCTET). IEEE (2013)

A Decentralised Application for Medical Insurance Claim System Using Blockchain Technology

Hrishabh Joshi, Sharon Justine(✉), V. Panchami, and Beeraka Hrithik

CSE- Cyber Security, IIIT Kottayam, Valavoor, Kottayam 686635, Kerala, India
sharonjustine.22phd11005@iiitkottayam.ac.in

Abstract. The medical insurance play a prominent role in healthcare industry by providing financial help in emergency medical condition. However the transparency, security and efficiency of the system should be enhanced to improve the medical insurance process using a decentralized application. The proposed system covers the design and development of a secure and decentralized platform for medical insurance claims. The proposed system enables the patients and insurance companies to easily access and share medical records, which facilitates the insurance claims process and eliminates the need for manual record-keeping. The system is implemented using smart contracts to automate insurance payouts, reducing the likelihood of fraud and making the process faster and more reliable. Furthermore the proposed system performance evaluated with different test networks like Mumbai, Sepoli and Goerli to perform a detailed time and cost analysis of different blockchain. Hence the system has the potential to revolutionize the medical insurance industry and improve the overall quality of healthcare services.

Keywords: Blockchain Technology · InterPlanetary File System (IPFS) · Smart Contract

1 Introduction

The healthcare industry is constantly generating vast amounts of sensitive medical data, which needs to be securely stored and protected from attacks and tampering. However, the industry has been facing challenges of privacy, data security, and trust for a long time. With the advent of blockchain technology, it is now possible to address these challenges and build a secure, reliable, and transparent healthcare system. This research paper aims to leverage the security and transparency features of blockchain technology and the InterPlanetary File System (IPFS) for distributed storage to build a trustworthy healthcare system that is resistant to data loss and tampering. The proposed system consists of four smart contracts, each one responsible for a specific task in the healthcare system.The proposed system aims to build a secure, reliable, and transparent healthcare system that is resistant to data loss and tampering. The medical insurance data consists of very sensitive data and in the existing systems this sensitive information can be accessed by anyone, no security of the data is guaranteed (Das, 2021). And also the medical insurance work in a centralized manner, there will be a central authority who manages the entire medical insurance system. The proposed system guarantees the security of the sensitive information shared by the clients. In the proposed system there is no central authority, the system is decentralized in nature. The permissionless blockchain used in the proposed system makes the system more transparent. Every user in the network can authenticate the transaction which makes the transaction in the blockchain immutable.

This paper presents the architecture and design of the proposed system, including the various smart contracts and how they interact with each other. Furthermore, the advantages of using IPFS for storage and the challenges faced during the implementation will be discussed. Finally, the proposed system's performance and security will be evaluated, highlighting its potential to revolutionize the healthcare industry.

2 Literature Survey

We have reviewed and read multiple research papers for understanding and improving the already implemented system for Blockchain implementation of Medical Insurance. Below are some of the relevant literature reviews.

(Bacon and Tarr, 2024) examines the advancements and projects in the insurance sector that are fueled by blockchain or distributed ledger technology. But in order for the insurance sector to reap the very real rewards, standardization of procedures, databases, and systems must advance, and intramarket cooperation to promote ecosystems must be welcomed. If successful, there are a lot of opportunities for the insurance sector to use this technology to further integrate itself into the larger digital economy.

(Karmakar et al., 2023) proposed ChainSure an Ethereum blockchain-based framework which came as a decentralized framework for medical insurance against the traditional centralized system which is highly vulnerable towards human error and is prone towards many known security attacks. In this paper they added TOPSIS method to the smart contract which selects the insurance scheme which satisfies the requirements of the user. Using the DApp elctronic health data related to the medical insurance can be stored securely. The system is resistant against DDoS attack and Sybil attack.

(Amponsah, Adekoya and Weyori, 2022) proposed a fraud detection and prevention in healthcare claim using the Machine learning and Blockchain technology. In this work a classification tree algorithm is used to classify the original claims and the extracted knowledge from this is given to the Ethereum based smart contract to detect the frauds. The decision tree algorithm is used for the classification of rules. To make the decision making process efficient the extracted knowledge is programmed with smart contracts hence the frudelent activities can be detected.

(Jabarulla and Lee, 2021) proposes a patient-centric healthcare system that utilizes blockchain technology, eliminating the role of trusted third parties and ensuring fairness while preventing malicious intervention. The proposed system ensures that medical data is tamper-proof, free from unauthorized access, and preserves patient privacy. However, it does use a central database, which defeats the purpose of decentralization.

(Chen et al., 2021) proposed a light weight authentication scheme designed for medical cyber physical systems. The system model consists sensor nodes which can sense the patients physical condition and send the signed data to the trusted gateway nodes. Medical staff collect the sensitive information from trusted gateway nodes, analyse them and monitor patients medical condition. The security authentication scheme proposed in this paper is based on the blockchain technology. However, here we analyze the security and effectiveness of the scheme in theory and realizes the simple construction of medical alliance chain.

(Das, 2021) proposed s system that gave a brief architecture of Health Insurance in blockchain, separate nodes in the chain are incorporated for hospitals, patients, and insurance companies to register using smart contracts. Patients interact with hospitals to lock in the estimated price, start the checkup, and sign the final cost for treatment using smart contracts. They also interact with insurance companies to register for a specific policy and request claims, granting permission for medical records to be checked. However, the system indirectly involves a third party, the government, which provides the Database Owner and Research Community that can alter medical data provided by the patient.

(Son et al., 2020) proposed a secure authentication protocol for a cloud assisted Telecare Medical Information System with access control using Blockchain. Patient's wearable device generate the health data and transmit them through a public channel. The patients medical data is stored in a cloud server. In this paper Ciphertext-policy attribute- based encryption (CP-ABE) to establish access control for health data stored in cloud server and apply Blockchain to guarantee data integrity.

(Zhou, Wang and Sun, 2018) aims to introduce MIStore, a blockchain-based medical insurance storage system that could provide high credibility to users by leveraging blockchain technology's tamper-resistant property. The system is designed to store and protect the patient's spending data in a tamper-proof way using a (t,n)-threshold MIStore protocol, where n servers protect the patient's data, and any t servers can help the insurance company obtain a sum of a part of the patient's spending data. The proposed system deploys on the Ethereum blockchain, and the performance evaluation results showed promising outcomes.

3 Preliminaries

3.1 Blockchain

Blockchain is a distributed database that is maintained by a network of computers, designed to store data in a secure and transparent manner using cryptographic techniques (Son et al., 2020). There are two types of blockchain permissioned and permissionless blockchain. A permissioned blockchain cannot be accessed publicly. A permissionless blockchain is more transparent that keeps the anonymity of the user and it is accessible to every user in the network. Since our proposed system is medical insurance and to ensure the transparency of the system we used the permissionless blockchain ethereum.

3.2 The InterPlanetary File System (IPFS)

IPFS is an acronym for InterPlanetary File System, a distributed file system protocol used for data storage and transit. Each file on IPFS is uniquely identified by its content-addressing mode. It provides a decentralized system of user-operators who keep a portion of the total data, hence offering a robust system of file sharing and storage. Distributed hash tables (DHT) allow peers in the network to find and request that content from any node (Biswas, Sil, and Roy, 2021).

3.3 Decentralized Autonomous Organization

A Decentralized Autonomous Organization (DAO) are designed to be decentralized, autonomous, and transparent, meaning they operate without a central authority, have decision-making power distributed across their members, and their operations and transactions are visible to all participants. DAOs typically use a cryptocurrency, such as Ethereum, as their native currency and rely on a consensus mechanism to ensure that the rules are followed. Members of the DAO can propose changes to the rules or vote on proposals made by others, and the results of the vote are executed automatically by smart contracts.

3.4 Smart Contract

Financial transactions, identification verification, and supply chain management are just a few of the tasks that smart contracts may automate. When certain requirements are satisfied, such finishing a task or receiving products, a smart contract can be used, for instance, to automatically transfer money from one party to another. Due to its execution on a decentralized blockchain network, which does not require middlemen or any third parties, smart contracts have several important advantages, including transparency and security. Smart contracts can, however, carry some potential hazards, such as code faults or weaknesses that hackers may exploit. (Wang et al., 2018).

4 Proposed System

The current process for patients applying for medical insurance claims involves going to the hospital to obtain a diagnosis certificate and receipt, and then submitting relevant application documents to the insurance company. The verification process with the patient's hospital must be completed before the patient can receive compensation, resulting in delays. Additionally, there is no privacy for the patient's data as it is transferred from one institution to another, and the lack of transparency in the system means that patients often have to contact the insurance company for claim progress and are not updated on the current status of their claim. Fortunately, we can overcome these challenges by leveraging blockchain technology. With blockchain, we can establish a secure and transparent network that eliminates the need for intermediaries and provides patients with complete control over their data. By utilizing smart contracts and the immutable nature of blockchain, we can automate the verification process and ensure that patients receive compensation in a timely manner. By leveraging the benefits of blockchain technology, we can create a more efficient and trustworthy healthcare system that better serves patients.

The architecture of the system consists of four smart contracts namely InsuranceCompany, Hospital, PatientRegistration, and CentralSmartContract. The InsuranceCompany smart contract is responsible for handling insurance policies, processing claims, and managing premium payments. It includes functions to add and remove policyholders, calculate premiums, and process claims. The Hospital smart contract manages patient medical records and handles billing for medical services. It includes functions to add and remove patients, update medical records, and generate bills. The PatientRegistration smart contract is responsible for registering new patients in the system. It includes functions to add new patients to the system, update patient information, and manage patient access to medical records. The CentralSmartContract serves as a bridge between the other smart contracts and facilitates interactions between them. It includes functions to deploy new insurance companies, add hospitals to insurance companies, register patients, and manage patient medical treatments. Overall, the architecture enables a secure and efficient system for managing patient medical records, processing insurance claims, and facilitating interactions between insurance companies, hospitals, and patients (Fig. 1).

4.1 Patient Module

The patient architecture includes three main components: the patient interface, the InsuranceCompany smart contract, and the Hospital smart contract. The patient interface provides access to two dashboards: the Patient Insurance Company Dashboard and the Patient Hospital Dashboard. The Patient Insurance Company Dashboard allows patients to perform the following functions:

- Renew Insurance: Allows patients to renew their existing insurance policies by interacting with the InsuranceCompany smart contract.
- Start New Insurance: Allows patients to purchase new insurance policies by interacting with the InsuranceCompany smart contract.
- Status of Insurance: Allows patients to view the status of their existing insurance policies by querying the InsuranceCompany smart contract.

The Patient Hospital Dashboard allows patients to perform the following functions: The status of treatment allows patients to view the status of their

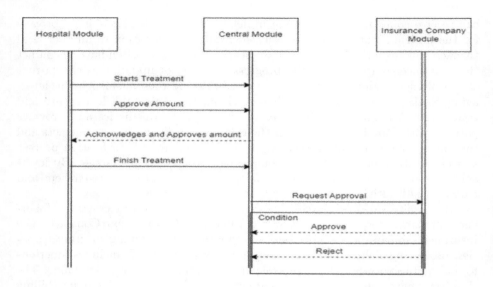

Fig. 1. Architecture of the System.

ongoing treatments by querying the Hospital smart contract. Both dashboards interact with the CentralSmartContract, which serves as the central point of communication between the patient, InsuranceCompany smart contract, and Hospital smart contract. The CentralSmartContract stores all the necessary data related to the patient's insurance policies and ongoing treatments. Additionally, the InsuranceCompany smart contract stores the insurance policies and premium details of the patients, while the Hospital smart con- tract stores the treatment details of the patients. Overall, this patient architecture provides patients with an easy-to-use interface to manage their insurance policies and ongoing treatments while also ensuring the security and reliability of the underlying smart contract (Fig. 2).

4.2 Hospital Module

The hospital architecture consists of a smart contract that interacts with the central smart contract. The Hospital smart contract contains the following functions:

- Get Treatment Status: This function allows the hospital to view the status of the treatment for a particular patient. It retrieves the treatment status from the central smart contract.
- Start or Stop Treatment: This function allows the hospital to start or stop a treatment for a particular patient. It updates the treatment status in the central smart contract.
- Initiate Claim: This function allows the hospital to initiate a claim for the treatment provided to a patient. It triggers the claim initiation process in the

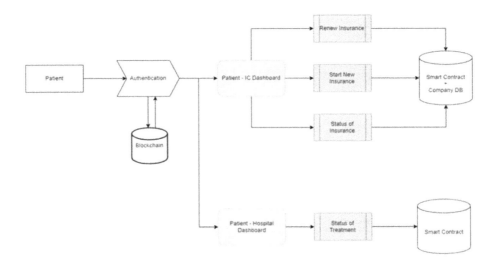

Fig. 2. Patient Module

central smart contract. The Hospital smart contract also contains necessary state variables and mappings to keep track of the treatments provided to the patients. The hospital staff can access the Hospital Dashboard which displays the functions mentioned above. The Hospital Dashboard interacts with the Hospital smart contract to retrieve and display the treatment status, start/stop treatment, and initiate claim treatment (Fig. 3).

4.3 Insurance Module

The insurance architecture consists of an InsuranceCompany smart contract and interacts with a Central smart contract. The InsuranceCompany smart contract maintains information about the insurance company's name, terms, price, and a list of hospitals associated with it. The insurance company can add or remove hospitals using the addHospital and getHospitals functions, respectively. The insurance company can view the status of insurance claims using the getTreatments and setTreatmentStatus functions in the CentralContract smart contract. The insurance company can also edit the insurance terms using the deployInsuranceCompany function in the Central smart contract. The insurance company can approve or reject treatment claims initiated by hospitals using the setTreatmentStatus function in the Central smart contract. The insurance company can also initiate a claim treatment using the addTreatment function in the Central smart contract.

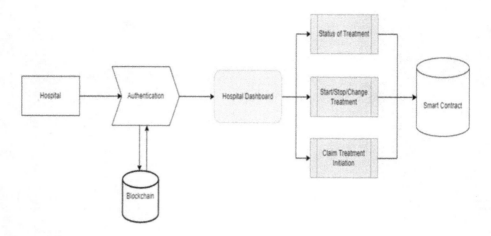

Fig. 3. Hospital Module

5 System Model

The proposed system mainly divides into 4 main smart contracts:

5.1 Central Smart Contract

This smart contract is a medical insurance contract that allows insurance companies to register themselves and add hospitals. Users can register by providing their hash value and later add treatment details. The contract also allows insurance companies to approve user treatments and transfer the approved amount using ERC20 tokens. The smart contract has the following functions:

- deployInsuranceCompany: Deploys a new insurance company contract and adds it to the list of insurance companies. The function requires the caller to be the owner and provides an onboard lock price.
- getInsuranceCompanies: Returns a list of all registered insurance companies.
- addHospital: Adds a new hospital to the list of hospitals associated with the given insurance company.
- getHospitals: Returns a list of all hospitals associated with the given insurance company.
- registerUser: Registers a user by storing their hash value.
- getUserAddress: Returns the address of the user associated with the given hash value.
- getTreatmentDetailsFromInsuranceCompany: Returns the details of the treatment associated with the calling insurance company.
- getTreatmentDetailsFromUser: Returns the details of the treatment associated with the given user hash value.
- addTreatment: Adds a new treatment for the given patient hash value.

- approveTreatment: Approves the treatment associated with the calling insurance company and transfers the approved amount using ERC20 tokens. The function requires the treatment to not be already approved and for the caller to be an insurance company.

5.2 Hospital Smart Contract

The hospital smart contract has the following functionalities:

- Constructor: It initializes the owner, name, centralContractAddress, and hospitalAddress of the Hospital contract.
- startTreatment: It calls the addTreatment() function of the CentralSmartContract contract and passes the patientHash, hospitalAddress, cost, and date as arguments.
- addTreatment: It calls the addTreatment() function of the CentralSmartContract contract and passes the hash, address of the Hospital contract, cost, and date as arguments.
- getTreatments: It calls the getTreatments() function of the CentralSmartContract contract and returns the list of treatmentIds.
- setTreatmentStatus: It calls the setTreatmentStatus() function of the CentralSmartContract contract and passes the hash, treatmentId, and status as arguments.
- getTreatmentStatus: It calls the getTreatmentStatus() function of the CentralSmartContract contract and returns the status of the treatment.

Overall, the Hospital contract is designed to interact with the CentralSmartContract contract to manage patient treatments

5.3 Insurance Company Smart Contract

This contract is a basic implementation of an insurance company on the Ethereum blockchain. Here is an explanation of the algorithm for each function:

- constructor: The constructor function initializes the contract's state variables including the owner address, name, terms, price, and hospital list. It also sets the minimum required amount of ether that must be sent along with the constructor function call to prevent spamming the network.
- addHospital: This function is used to add a hospital address to the hospital list maintained by the insurance company. The function checks if the hospital address is already in the list and adds it to the list if it's not already present.
- updateDetails: This function is used to update the terms and price of the insurance policy offered by the insurance company. It takes two parameters: new terms and new price.
- calculateHash: This function calculates a unique hash for the insurance company by encoding and hashing the values of its state variables including the name, terms, price, and hospital list. The hash can be used to verify the

integrity of the insurance company's data. Overall, the contract provides a basic structure for an insurance company and allows for the addition of hospitals, updating the policy terms and price, and calculating a unique hash for the company's data.

5.4 Patient Registration Smart Contract

PatientRegistry. It allows the registration and approval of patient records on a decentralized network. The contract contains: mapping patients that maps a hash of a patient's record to their Ethereum address.

- An address variable centralContractAddress that stores the address of another smart contract called Central Smart Contract.
- Two events ApprovalRequested and ApprovalGranted which are emited when a patient's record is requested for approval and when it is approved, respectively.

The following is an algorithmic explanation of each function:

- constructor: This is the constructor function that takes an address as input and initializes centralContractAddress to that value.
- registerPatient: This function is called when a patient wants to register their record. It takes a hash of the record and the patient's Ethereum address as input, and emits an ApprovalRequested event with the hash and the patient's address.
- getPatientAddress: This function takes a hash of a patient's record as input and returns the Ethereum address associated with that record in the patients mapping.
- approveRegistration: This function is called by the patient to approve the registration of their record. It first creates a new instance of the CentralContract smart contract using centralContractAddress. Then it checks if the caller of the function is the owner of the patient's record by comparing msg.sender with the address associated with the given hash in the patients mapping. If the comparison fails, the function throws an error. If the comparison succeeds, the function updates the patients mapping with the patient's address and calls the registerUser function in the CentralContract contract to register the patient's record. Finally, it emits an ApprovalGranted event with the hash and the patient's address.

6 Implementation

6.1 Frontend Setup

The Frontend part of the dApp is developed using the NextJS framework, using ReactJS. We have used wagmi, rainbow-kit, and ethers packages to connect the app to dApp. Packages used are specified along with the version as NextJS -

(v-13.3.0), wagmi - (v-0.11.6), @rainbow-me/rainbowkit - (v-0.11.0), ethers - (v-6.0.0). And the platform used are Editor - Visual Studio Code - (v-1.77.1), Version Control - Git and Github.

Screenshots of the dApp is added below: The login page for patient, hospital and insurance company is available. The screenshots of status of payment page and patient dashboard is also added here (Figs. 4, 5).

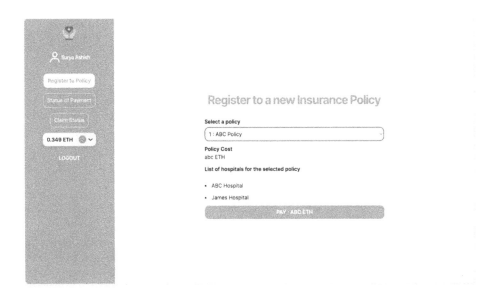

Fig. 4. Patient Dashboard

6.2 Smart Contract Development Setup

Solidity Development setup involves the metamask account creation, installing the required dependencies, and deploying the contract from the local system using Ganache or deploying it using remix IDE. Language and framework used are Solidity - (V-0.8) and @openzeppelin/contracts (V-4.8.2) Platform used are Remix, Truffle (V-5.8.1), Node (V-18.13), Web3.js (V-1.8.2), Metamask.

Here we send a transaction to add a user/patient to the network. Whenever the function is run from remix IDE, then it asks for the transaction fees from the connected metamask wallet from the browser. As soon as the transaction fee is granted to the request, then the transaction is carried out by the smart contract for the function with the given values. At last, the updated data is returned in the logs of the smart contract To build the frontend of the application we used Nextjs framework, to connect to the wallet we used Web3Modal library. Frontend will contact with the smart contracts using an api.

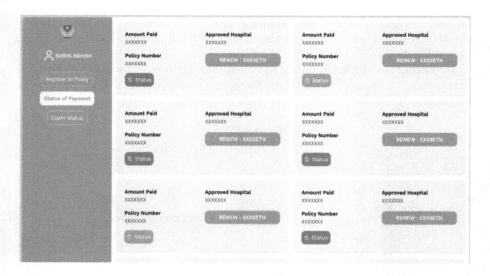

Fig. 5. Status of Payment Page

7 Analysis

The test chains are used to test new features, upgrades and used to fix the problems before deploying it to the mainnet. The test networks act similar to the mainnet. The testnet operate on a different ledger hence the coins used in the test network have no connection with transactions used in the mainnet. But as like any mainnet the testnet can experience bottlenecks and performance issues.

Here we have analysed the test networks namely Mumbai, Sepolia and Goerli. The Mumbai test network is Polygon testnet which replicates the Polygon mainnet. Mumbai offers high throughput and low transaction fees while retaining the features of the mainnet. Sepolia is the copy of Ethereum mainnet which uses Proof of Stake consensus mechanism. Since it mimics Ethereum mainnet it is suitable to deploy smart contracts and dApps in an accurate environment. Goerli testnet is a replication of Ethereum mainnet which uses the Proof of Authority consensus mechanism. Goerli can be used to deploy and test dApps since it provide a reliable and stable environment.

In Goerli the time taken for contract deployment and time for state change is high when compared with Sepolia and Mumbai. For Mumbai the time for contract and for state change is the lowest in comparison with Sepolia and Goerli. Mumbai has the lowest cost of contract deployment. Sepolia and Goerli have almost same cost. The cost of contract method call is the highest for Sepolia then Goerli. And the cost for contract method call is very low for Mumbai (Figs. 6, 7).

Figure 6 plots the time analysis while tested in different test networks. In this figure blue bar indicates the time for contract deployment in seconds and red bar indicates time for state change which is also in seconds. Out of the

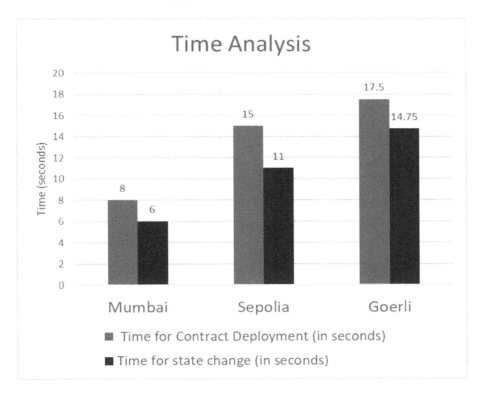

Fig. 6. Time Analysis of Test Chains

three networks Mumbai, Sepolia and Goerli, Goerli has taken more time for contract deployment and state change. Whereas Mumbai test network utilize the minimum time for the contract deployment and state change.

Figure 7 plots the cost analysis of the test networks. In this figure the blue bar indicates the cost for contract deployment in Dollars and the red bar indicates the cost of contract method call which is also in Dollars. Sepolia and Goerli has almost same cost for contract deployment and also for contract method call. The Mumbai test network use minimum cost among the three test networks.

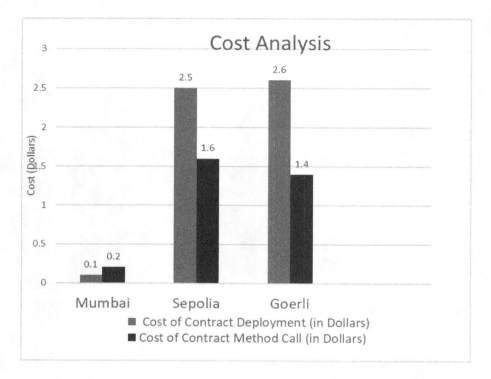

Fig. 7. Cost Analysis of Test Chains

8 Conclusion

To incorporate the fair transaction between all the parties in a decentralized and transparent way, there's a need for a Blockchain based practical solution for implementing Medical Insurance System. In medical insurance the security, transparency and efficiency of the system can be achieved using the proposed system. This system gives an implementation which does not require any third party (or) database owner to be included in the system and it is practically implemented so that parties like Patients, Hospitals and Insurance Companies can use the system in practical scenario.

References

Bacon, L., Tarr, J.A.: Distributed Ledger Technology and Blockchain: Insurance. The Global Insurance Market and Change, pp. 95–126 (2024)

Ghosh, S., Dave, V., Keerthana, S.S.: A critique of blockchain in healthcare sector. In: Artificial Intelligence, Big Data, Blockchain and 5G for the Digital Transformation of the Healthcare Industry, pp. 205–231. Academic Press (2024)

Karmakar, A., Ghosh, P., Banerjee, P.S., De, D.: ChainSure: agent free insurance system using blockchain for healthcare 4.0. Intell. Syst. Appl. **17**, 200177 (2023)

Rahimi, N., Gudapati, S.S.V.: Emergence of blockchain technology in the healthcare and insurance industries. In: Blockchain Technology Solutions for the Security of IoT-Based Healthcare Systems, pp. 167–182. Academic Press (2023)

Chamola, V., Goyal, A., Sharma, P., Hassija, V., Binh, H.T.T., Saxena, V.: Artificial intelligence-assisted blockchain-based framework for smart and secure EMR management. Neural Comput. Appl. **35**(31), 22959–22969 (2023)

Baysal, M.V., Özcan-Top, Ö., Betin-Can, A.: Blockchain technology applications in the health domain: a multivocal literature review. J. Supercomput. **79**(3), 3112–3156 (2023)

Amponsah, A.A., Adekoya, A.F., Weyori, B.A.: A novel fraud detection and prevention method for healthcare claim processing using machine learning and blockchain technology. Decis. Anal. J. **4**, 100122 (2022)

Namasudra, S., Sharma, P., Crespo, R.G., Shanmuganathan, V.: Blockchain-based medical certificate generation and verification for IoT-based healthcare systems. IEEE Consum. Electron. Mag. **12**(2), 83–93 (2022)

Haleem, A., Javaid, M., Singh, R.P., Suman, R., Rab, S.: Blockchain technology applications in healthcare: an overview. Int. J. Intell. Netw. **2**, 130–139 (2021)

Jabarulla, M.Y., Lee, H.N.: A blockchain and artificial intelligence-based, patient-centric healthcare system for combating the COVID-19 pandemic: opportunities and applications. In: Healthcare (Vol. 9, No. 8, p. 1019). MDPI, August 2021

Chen, F., Tang, Y., Cheng, X., Xie, D., Wang, T., Zhao, C.: Blockchain-based efficient device authentication protocol for medical cyber-physical systems. Secur. Commun. Netw. **2021**, 1–13 (2021)

Biswas, A., Sil, R., Roy, A.: A study on application of interplanetary file system. In: Communication and Intelligent Systems: Proceedings of ICCIS 2020, pp. 1017–1025. Springer, Singapore (2021)

Das, D.: Application of Blockchain in Healthcare and Health Insurance Sector (2021). arXiv preprint arXiv:2108.00807

Ben Fekih, R., Lahami, M.: Application of blockchain technology in healthcare: a comprehensive study. In :The Impact of Digital Technologies on Public Health in Developed and Developing Countries: 18th International Conference, ICOST 2020, Hammamet, Tunisia, 24–26 June 2020, Proceedings, vol. 18, pp. 268–276. Springer International Publishing (2020)

Son, S., Lee, J., Kim, M., Yu, S., Das, A.K., Park, Y.: Design of secure authentication protocol for cloud-assisted telecare medical information system using blockchain. IEEE Access **8**, 192177–192191 (2020)

Pandey, P., Litoriya, R.: Implementing healthcare services on a large scale: challenges and remedies based on blockchain technology. Health Policy Technol. **9**(1), 69–78 (2020)

Monrat, A.A., Schelén, O., Andersson, K.: A survey of blockchain from the perspectives of applications, challenges, and opportunities. IEEE Access **7**, 117134–117151 (2019)

Zhou, L., Wang, L., Sun, Y.: MIStore: a blockchain-based medical insurance storage system. J. Med. Syst. **42**(8), 149 (2018)

Wang, S., Yuan, Y., Wang, X., Li, J., Qin, R., Wang, F.Y.: An overview of smart contract: architecture, applications, and future trends. In: 2018 IEEE Intelligent Vehicles Symposium (IV), pp. 108–113, June 2018

Performance Analysis of Energy Efficient Routing Protocols in Wireless Sensor Networks

Priyanka Patel[1](✉) 🆔, Amrut Patel[1](✉) 🆔, and Manish Patel[2](✉) 🆔

[1] U.V. Patel College of Engineering, Ganpat University, Mehsana, Gujarat, India
{pkp02,amrut.patel}@ganpatuniversity.ac.in
[2] Sankalchand Patel College of Engineering, Sankalchand Patel University, Visnagar, Gujarat, India
it43manish@gmail.com

Abstract. The field of wireless sensor network is a booming research area and its use is expanding quickly. It consists of many small sensor nodes. These nodes are operated through battery. Network lifetime depends on energy consumption. Nodes are deployed in unattended area. Therefore, replacing the battery or power source is often impossible. Data transmission consumes more amount of energy and sensor nodes' battery life is constrained. Consumption of energy is the most fundamental parameter to be considered in wireless sensor networks. Research is going on in designing less energy consuming protocol to enhance network lifespan. In this paper, we have shown the simulation results of several types of energy efficient routing protocols for analysis. Experimental results of LEACH, TEEN, DEEC, SEP, improved LEACH - iLEACH, improved TEEN - iTEEN, improved DEEC - iDEEC and improved SEP - iSEP protocols are conducted under the MATLAB Simulator. We have also discussed a few unresolved research questions in this field for future investigation.

Keywords: Network lifetime · Data transmission · Battery power · Energy

1 Introduction

Wireless sensor networks are ad hoc network made up of numerous small sensor nodes dispersed throughout a sensor field. The sensor field is where the nodes are placed. Data is sent by primary sensor nodes to the leader node, The leader node then transmits it to the base station for additional communication. Each node comprises of four major components: a sensor element, a converter that transform analog signal to digital signal, a processing apparatus and a power supply unit. Applications for wireless sensor networks are numerous and varied. Five primary categories can be used to classify them: Precision Agriculture, Industrial Applications, Healthcare Applications, Environmental Applications, and Military Applications. Applications for the environment include modifications to the surroundings to monitor certain events [1]. As an illustration, consider the detection of earthquakes, floods, volcanic eruptions, fires, air pollution, and environmental hazards. Unattended patients can be continuously monitored with the use of sensor nodes. To measure bodily signal, specific kinds of sensors are required. Physicians keep an eye on their patients' blood pressure, temperature, heart rates, and other vital signs from a distance [2]. Wireless sensor networks are used in industry for pipeline monitoring, smart grid system monitoring, road traffic monitoring, automobile health monitoring, and railway infrastructure monitoring [3]. Applications for precision agriculture include environmental monitoring and animal tracking initiatives [4]. A mobile robot is employed in habitat monitoring to gather data from the sensor nodes. Agricultural farm management makes use of data collected via WSNs. Applications in the military include tracking intruders, keeping an eye on enemy vehicle movements, monitoring the battlefield, and intrusion detection [5].

Wireless sensor nodes are resource restricted and densely placed. They frequently fail. It gets harder to communicate when a lot of nodes die from using too much energy. Energy efficiency is therefore a vital concern. Numerous sensor nodes must function in a hostile environment. The routing algorithm is used to choose the path for routing data. The routing algorithm is primarily developed as a load-balanced tree type algorithm [6] or as a clustering algorithm [7]. Authors have presented a detailed analysis on routing issues and methods in wireless sensor network [8]. The primary limitation of wireless sensor networks is the energy-limited nature of the sensor nodes themselves, as it is impossible to change a node's battery in most of the scenarios. Thus, one of the main areas of focus is creating routing algorithms that are energy-efficient.

The paper's reminder is organized as follows: Sect. 2 describes the existing energy efficient protocols in WSNs. Sect. 3 presents our implementation strategy. Experimental results and its analysis are presented in Sect. 4. Conclusion is presented in Sect. 5. Future research challenges are presented in Sect. 6.

2 Literature Review

The construction of low energy consumption network routing methods for wireless sensor networks is a subject of several active research projects. The architecture of the network and the needs of the application may inform the design of routing protocols. We provided a thorough study of the merits and demerits of several energy-efficient routing methods [9]. Authors have presented a resource efficient technique to reduce latency and energy usage in wireless sensor networks [10]. The objective is optimizing the energy consumption while performing network related tasks.

Nodes are arranged into cluster area using the LEACH that is Low Energy Adaptive Clustering Hierarchy, with one node serving as the leader of the cluster [11]. Leader nodes are randomly choose from a certain number of nodes. Every cluster head node signals other nodes in the vicinity and promotes itself. The remaining nodes connect to the cluster with the strongest signal. The entire network is segmented into clusters in this manner. Participant nodes transfer data to cluster head node using TDMA scheduling. Cluster heads use Code Division Multiple Access to communicate with one another. Member nodes within the given area send data to the leader node. Cluster leader node delivers data to other cluster leader node and ultimately it goes to base station. The two phases of LEACH activities are the setup phase, where formation of the cluster takes place and the steady state phase, where data transfer occurs. Cluster heads are chosen and clusters are formed during the setup phase. Selection of leader nodes is chosen at random for every round. An arbitrary number between 0 and 1 is selected by each sensor node. Node becomes leader node for that round if the selected number is less than the determined predefined value. For P rounds, where P denotes the preferred cluster head percentage - a node that has been chosen as a cluster leader node is not allowed to become one again.

Authors have proposed TEEN that is Threshold sensitive Energy Efficient sensor Network techniques for low energy consumption routing [12]. It is the first protocol designed for networks that are reactive. Every time the leader node updates, the soft threshold and hard threshold values are broadcast to all of its participants nodes. A hard threshold is an absolute value that, when exceeded, requires the node that detects it to turn on its transmitter and notify the cluster leader node. A slight variation in the sensed attribute's value is known as the "soft threshold," which causes the sensor node to turn on its transmitter and begin transmitting. Nodes constantly sense environment and collect data. When the value crosses the hard threshold, the sensor node transmits the detected data. The value sense by the node is kept in an internal table. Only when the detected attribute's current value is more than the hard predefined value and deviates from the recorded value by a margin equal to or more than the soft predefined value will the next transmission occur. The amount of transmissions is decreased by using a hard threshold, which limits the nodes' ability to communicate only when its sensed property is within the interest range. A soft threshold prevents transmissions from happening when the observed property changes very little or not at all.

Regarding heterogeneous wireless sensor networks, the DEEC - Distributed Energy Efficient Clustering strategy is presented [13]. The leader nodes in the clusters are selected based on the ratio of the average energy of the network to the remaining energy of every sensor node. Compared to nodes with lower energy; those with higher energy have a greater chance of becoming CH. During each selection round, this procedure does not require any comprehensive understanding of energy. It functions well in heterogeneous wireless sensor networks having multi level.

A heterogeneous aware procedure called a Stable Election Protocol - SEP is used to extend the stability period [14]. The foundation is a probability of a weighted election of every node to become leader node as per the energy left in each node. The goal is to uphold the well-balanced energy limitation.

Energy holes creation is a significant problem for wireless sensor networks. Because of the increased data load, nodes closer to the sink node use greater energy. This causes an energy holes issue to arise close to the sink node. A few nodes' energy depletion causes data routing to fail and drastically shortens network lifespan. Authors have presented the E-HORM scheme that is Energy-efficient HOle Removing Mechanism [15]. It employs a sleep and wake method to conserve energy. Every node checks its energy level prior to transmission. Every round, a node can send data to the aggregator node if its degree of energy is higher than the predefined limit. If the transmission energy level is below the predefined limit, it cannot send data and switches to sleep mode to conserve energy.

3 Implementation Strategy

We have done experimental analysis of LEACH protocol in MATLAB and results are presented in various situations by changing simulation area, no. of sensor nodes, initial energy of nodes and no. of cluster leader nodes. Results indicate that lifespan of the entire network increases by increasing the initial energy of the sensor nodes and by decreasing the simulation area. We have implemented TEEN, DEEC, SEP protocols and E-HORM mechanism for improvement of all these protocols. The parameters for implementation are as follow (Table 1 and Fig. 1):

Table 1. Parameters for Simulation

Parameter	Value
Tool for Implementation	MATLAB
Region	$100 * 100$ m^2
Nodes count	100
Nodes' starting energy	0.5 J
Location of Base Station	(50,50)
The circuit's energy use (Eelec)	50 nJ/ bit
Efs - Dissipation of Energy	10 pJ/ bit/ m^2
ETx - Energy used for transmit a packet	50 nJ
ERx - Energy used for receive a packet	50 nJ
Energy used in aggregation of data	5 nJ/ bit/ report
Emp, $d \leq d0$, Energy used for amplification (cluster to base station)	0.0013 pJ/bit/m^2
Efs, $d \geq d0$, Energy used for amplification (cluster to base station)	10 pJ/bit/m^2
Energy used for amplification (inside a cluster for $d \geq d1$)	Efs /10 = Efs1
Energy used for amplification (inside a cluster for $d \geq d1$)	Efs /10 = Efs1
Packets/message size	4000 bits

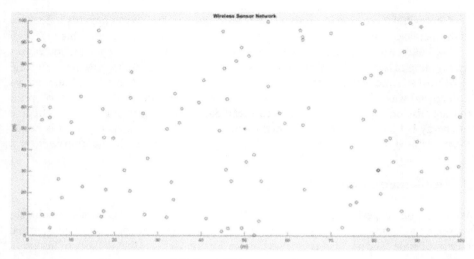

Fig. 1. Simulation Scenario

The number of nodes that die affects how long a network may last. We counted the number of rounds. No. of rounds increases by increasing initial energy of nodes and by decreasing simulation area.

4 Result and Analysis

4.1 LEACH Protocol (Initial Energy – 0.5 J, Area 100 * 100, 100 Nodes)

LEACH protocol is simulated in MATLAB for each node having initial energy 0.5 J and 100 nodes are set up in the region of 100 * 100 m^2. Figure 2 displays the results that were achieved.

4.2 LEACH Protocol (Initial Energy –1 J, Area 100 * 100, 100 Nodes)

If we change the starting energy of every node from 0.5 J to 1 J, then the no. of rounds and transmitted packets are significantly increased as depicted in Fig. 3.

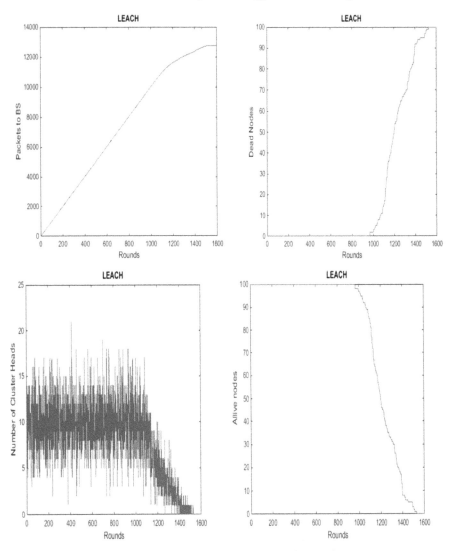

Fig. 2. Implementation of LEACH Protocol

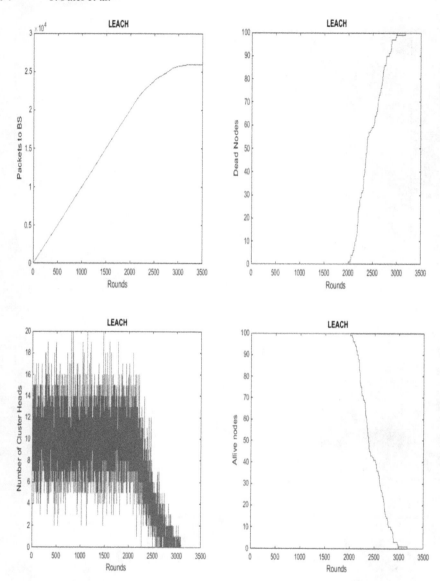

Fig. 3. Implementation of LEACH Protocol (Initial Energy – 1 J)

4.3 LEACH Protocol (Initial Energy – 0.5 J, Area 50 * 50, 100 Nodes)

If we deployed 100 nodes having starting energy 0.5 J in the area 50 * 50, the obtained results are shown in Fig. 4. By reducing the deployed area, no. of rounds and transmitted packets are significantly increased.

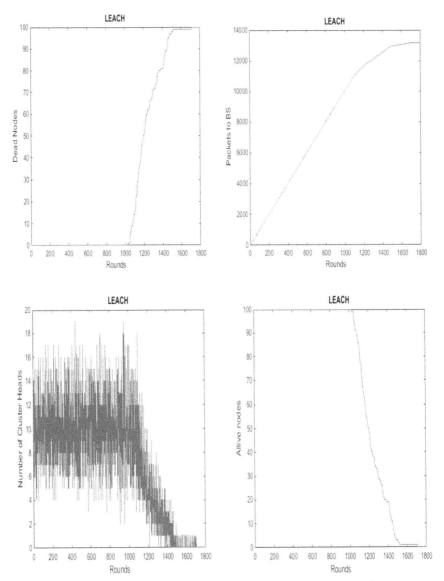

Fig. 4. Implementation of LEACH Protocol (Area - 50 * 50 m²)

4.4 LEACH (Initial Energy – 0.5 J, Area 100 * 100, 100 Nodes, No. of CHs = 5)

After applying E-HORM scheme as in [15], we obtained the results as indicated in Fig. 6, 7, 8 and 9. Comparison of LEACH and Improved LEACH is shown in Fig. 6. Figure 7 presents comparison of TEEN and Improved TEEN. Figure 8 shows comparison of DEEC and Improved DEEC. Figure 9 shows comparison of SEP and Improved SEP (Fig. 5).

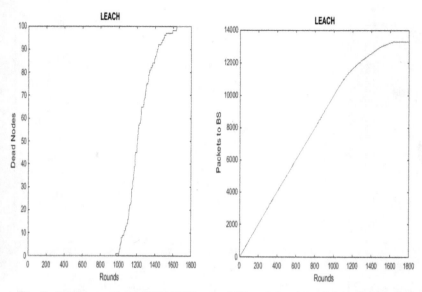

Fig. 5. Implementation of LEACH Protocol (No. of cluster head 5 instead of 10)

4.5 LEACH and Improved LEACH

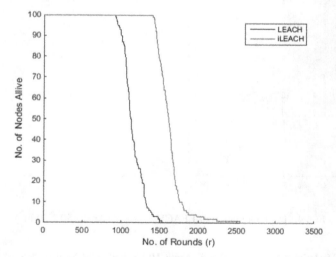

Fig. 6. Comparison of LEACH and iLEACH

4.6 TEEN and Improved TEEN

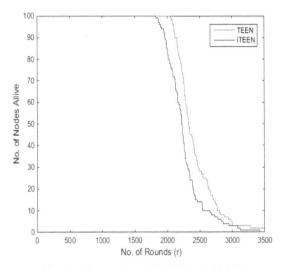

Fig. 7. Comparison of TEEN and iTEEN

4.7 DEEC and Improved DEEC

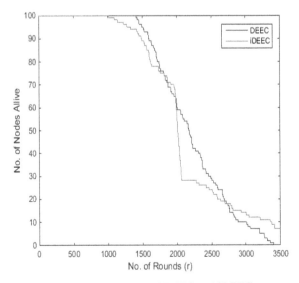

Fig. 8. Comparison of DEEC and iDEEC

4.8 SEP and Improved SEP

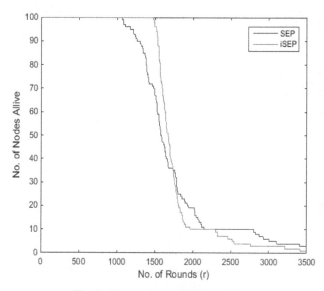

Fig. 9. Comparison of SEP and iSEP

LEACH [11], TEEN [12], DEEC [13] and SEP [14] are fundamental routing methods for wireless sensor networks and based on these protocols, various other protocols are proposed. LEACH protocol has presented the procedure for electing cluster head and it is enhanced by DEEC and SEP. In TEEN, threshold value serves to extend the lifespan of networks. In [14], proposed approach has longer stability time than LEACH as in [11] because of discriminating nodes as per their starting energy value. By eliminating the energy holes problem, authors have proposed improved version of LEACH, TEEN, DEEC and SEP [15].

5 Conclusion

Energy is an essential component for wireless sensor networks. Different protocols for network routing have been developed to ensure energy efficiency for increasing the network lifespan by considering of network design and energy consumption. One significant challenge for applications of WSN is energy consumption. We have simulated LEACH, iLEACH, TEEN, iTEEN, DEEC, iDEEC, SEP and iSEP protocols. Experiments are conducted under the MATLAB Simulator. By reducing the energy holes problem, network lifetime is significantly improved for LEACH, TEEN, DEEC and SEP. We have summarized some of the challenging research questions in the domain of designing energy efficient routing protocol. Deigning routing protocol with low energy consumption is still a challenging research issue.

6 Open Research Challenges

Traditional routing algorithms are not able to meet the needs of the current situation. Therefore, energy efficient routing strategies must be developed. Majority of the techniques in the existing literature are using fixed static routing. The drawback of static routing is the possibility of entire network shut down in certain circumstances. In existing work, the routing of sensors is fixed. It is necessary to make the routing dynamic and for that a decision node is required to guide how to forward the data to the next node. Collected data by the sensor nodes is redundant and it uses more energy for transmission. Therefore, transmission of redundant data may be avoided and new techniques need to be developed.

An energy-efficient path cannot be guaranteed by taking leftover energy alone. It is an NP-hard task to find the best energy-efficient route staring with the source node and ending to the base station. Most studies derive the mathematical formulation of the routing protocol using residual energy and hop-count distance. Different pathways can share the loads. In comparison to a road with low or moderate energy, one with higher energy can carry greater loads. Therefore, when creating an energy-efficient routing protocol, message weight can be taken into account. Most of the authors have considered homogeneous network. For real world applications, heterogeneous wireless sensor networks also need to be considered. Developing low energy consumption network routing protocol with mobility of nodes is a challenging issue. Position of a base station has significant for conservation of energy. Applying ant colony optimization, particle swarm role in designing load balancing energy efficient routing protocol. To prevent energy holes problems, base station should change position [16–18]. Applying machine learning approaches to develop low energy consumption routing protocols is also a very promising [19]. Congestion control approaches need to be considered [20]. Optimization, genetic algorithms and fuzzy logic approaches to develop energy efficient routing protocols are very interesting research directions [21]. Use of soft computing techniques is also a good direction to develop low energy consumption protocol [22].

References

1. Lazarescu, M.T.: Design of a WSN platform for long-term environmental monitoring for IoT applications. IEEE J. Emerg. Sel. Top. Circuits Syst. **3**(1), 45–54 (2013)
2. Pantelopoulos, A., Bourbakis, N.G.: A survey on wearable sensor-based systems for health monitoring and prognosis. IEEE Trans. Syst. Man Cybern. Part C (Appl. Rev.) **40**(1), 1–12 (2010)
3. Fadel, E., et al.: A survey on wireless sensor networks for smart grid. Comput. Commun. **71**, 22–33 (2015)
4. Anisi, M.H., Abdul-Salaam, G., Abdullah, A.H.: A survey of wireless sensor network approaches and their energy consumption for monitoring farm fields in precision agriculture. Precis. Agric. **16**(2), 216–238 (2015)
5. Wang, Y.W.Y., Wang, X.W.X., Bin Xie, B.X., Wang, D.W.D., Agrawal, D.P.: Intrusion detection in homogeneous and heterogeneous wireless sensor networks. IEEE Trans. Mob. Comput. **7**(6), 698–711 (2008)
6. Anasane, A.A., Satao, R.A.: A Survey on various Multipath Routing protocols in Wireless Sensor Networks. Procedia Comput. Sci. **79**, 610–615 (2016)

7. Abbasi, A.A., Younis, M.: A survey on clustering algorithms for wireless sensor networks. Comput. Commun. **30**, 2826–2841 (2007)
8. Chaubey, N., Patel, D.H.: Routing protocols in wireless sensor network: a critical survey and comparison. Int. J. IT Eng. **04**(02), 8–18 (2016). ISSN 2321–1776
9. Patel, P.K., Patel, A.N.: Energy efficient routing approaches in wireless sensor networks: a review. In: Vasant, P., et al. (eds.) ICO 2023. LNNS, vol. 729, pp. 27–35. Springer, Cham (2023). https://doi.org/10.1007/978-3-031-36246-0_3
10. Chaubey, N.K., Patel, D.H.: Energy efficient clustering algorithm for decreasing energy consumption and delay in wireless sensor networks (WSN). Int. J. Innov. Res. Comput. Commun. Eng. **4**(5), 8652–8656 (2016)
11. Heinzelman, W.R., Chandrakasan, A., Balakrishnan, H.: Energy-efficient communication protocol for wireless microsensor networks. In: Proceedings of the 33rd Annual Hawaii International Conference on System Sciences, Maui, 4–7 January 2000, 3005–3014 (2000)
12. Manjeshwar, A., Agrawal, D.P.: TEEN: a routing protocol for enhanced efficiency in wireless sensor networks. In: Proceedings 15th International Parallel and Distributed Processing Symposium, IPDPS 2001, pp. 2009–2015 (2001)
13. Qing, L., Zhu, Q., Wang, M.: Design of a distributed energy-efficient clustering algorithm for heterogeneous wireless sensor networks. Comput. Commun. **29**, 2230–2237 (2006)
14. Smaragdakis, G., Matta, I., Bestavros, A.: SEP: a stable election protocol for clustered heterogeneous wireless sensor networks (2004)
15. Rasheed, M.B., Javaid, N., Khan, Z.A., Qasim, U., Ishfaq, M.: E-HORM: an energy-efficient hole removing mechanism in Wireless Sensor Networks. In: 2013 26th IEEE Canadian Conference on Electrical and Computer Engineering (CCECE), pp. 1–4 (2013)
16. Wang, J., Zhang, Z., Xia, F., Yuan, W., Lee, S.: An energy efficient stable election-based routing algorithm for wireless sensor networks. Sens. (Basel Switz.) **13**, 14301–14320 (2013)
17. Tunca, C., Donmez, M.Y., Isik, S., Ersoy, C.: Ring routing: an energy-efficient routing protocol for wireless sensor networks with a mobile sink. IEEE Trans. Mob. Comput. **14**, 1947–1960 (2012)
18. Liu, Q., Zhang, K., Shen, J., Fu, Z., Linge, N.: GLRM: an improved grid-based load-balanced routing method for WSN with single controlled mobile sink. In: 18th International Conference on Advanced Communication Technology (ICACT), pp. 34–38 (2016)
19. Donta, P.K., Amgoth, T., Annavarapu, C.S.: Machine learning algorithms for wireless sensor networks: a survey. Inf. Fusion **49**, 1–25 (2019)
20. Bohloulzadeh, A., Rajaei, M.: A survey on congestion control protocols in wireless sensor networks. Int. J. Wirel. Inf. Netw. **27**, 365–384 (2020)
21. Liu, Z., Liu, Y., Wang, X.: Intelligent routing algorithm for wireless sensor networks dynamically guided by distributed neural networks. Comput. Commun. **207**, 100–112 (2023)
22. Chaubey, N.N., Falconer, L., Rakhee: An efficient cluster based energy routing protocol (E-CBERP) for wireless body area networks using soft computing technique. In: Chaubey, N., Thampi, S.M., Jhanjhi, N.Z. (eds.) COMS2 2022. CCIS, vol. 1604, pp. 26–39. Springer, Cham (2022). https://doi.org/10.1007/978-3-031-10551-7_3

Design of Performance Enhanced Approximate Multiplier for Image Processing Applications

K. Sivanandam[✉] [iD] and R. Sathana [iD]

Department of Electronics and Communication Engineering, M. Kumarasamy College of Engineering, Karur, Tamil Nadu, India
sivanandamk.ece@mkce.ac.in

Abstract. Precise is most appropriate in scenarios where errors are hard to make, such processing mixed material and signs. Loose registering produces noticeable and quicker results with less power usage, especially for arithmetic circuits. This study proposes an alternative approach to utilize the packages of halfway items, based on recursive growth using blower-based rough multipliers. There are three proposed multiplier methods using four: 2 approximated blowers. Broad reproduction studies show that the proposed technique offers significant improvements in exactness, power reduction, and region reducing when compared to earlier imprecise multiplier designs. The first two multiplier setups make use of the first rough blower. Replicated and coordinated in Xilinx programming, the recommended multiplier design (1) has different area, less power, and less accuracy than the current multipliers. The recommended multiplier design (2) is reenacted and incorporated in Xilinx programming with high exactness, similar to the suggested plan (1), but at the expense of additional region and power. The recommended multiplier design (3) makes advantage of the second estimated blower. It is combined and replicated using Xilinx programming. Compared to plan (1) and design (2), it consumes less space and energy.

Keywords: Approximate computing · compressor · multiplier · Low power Computation

1 Introduction

Many scientific and design-related challenges are processed through the use of exact, accurate, and predictable calculations. However, since many applications—like interactive media and signal/picture handling are error-tolerant and provide results sufficient for human comprehension, precise and accurate calculations are typically not required in these settings [1]. For a circuit to function in these error-prone applications, there must be a reduction in circuit complexity and, therefore, in region, power, and latency. Therefore, even though rough figuring uses less power and produces meaningful answers faster, it may be applied in applications that are less stringent about mistakes [2]. Duplication and extension are often used in these applications. Numerous ill-defined concepts have been proposed for expansion after thorough examination of full adders [1]. In [3], several novel measures are proposed and some of the current approaches are compared. The numerical difference between an accurate and an incorrect result for a given set of data is known as the error distance (ED). The standardized blunder distance (NED) and the mean error distance (MED) are the next two suggested distances. Inexact multipliers have also lately acquired popularity due to their importance in arithmetic operations [410]; certain proposals have been made for approximately 4:2 compressors in order to reduce the partial Dadda results tree. This work uses a creative portion of the fractional items to plan 8x8 piece multipliers using the approximate compressors of [10]. The previously anticipated inexact multipliers need approximately the same power and postponement as those proposed in [10], although being more precise. It is demonstrated that this gain in accuracy is significant, but only in a somewhat larger area. This paper is organized as follows. Section 2 examines anticipated multipliers and the compressors employed in the recommended design. In Sect. 3, the suggested multipliers are shown. Section 4 compares the suggested design with [10] and displays the multipliers with the reenactment results. Approximated multiplier-based image processing software is shown in Sect. 5, and the conclusion is presented in Sect. 6.

2 Related Works

Area, power, and latency are the three main attributes of circuits employed in digital signal processing. Multiplication is the cause of delay and power consumption in many signal processing systems. Many researchers have tried—and still try—to construct multipliers with quick speed, low power consumption, a regular design, and a tiny footprint, all thanks to technological advancements. The goal of this project is to use properly rounded truncated multipliers to build a low-cost finite impulse response filter. Optimization of hardware resources and bit width accuracy are carried out. Using an enhanced version of truncated multipliers, the direct FIR filter carries out many constant multiplications. The Remez multiple exchange strategy is the most effective way to generate optimal magnitude FIR filters with variable parameters. Using Parks McClellan(), the filter order M for the given frequency response is first obtained. Filter constraints regarding pass band and stopband frequencies, pass band ripple, and stopband attenuation are accepted by this iteration technique. Remez is in charge of determining the coefficients for the order M FIR filter. Next, quantize the coefficients using a sufficient number of bits to produce a set of uniformly quantized coefficients with the same bit width B [1]. The Remez multiple exchange strategy is the most effective way to generate optimal magnitude FIR filters with variable parameters. Using Parks McClellan(), the filter order M for the given frequency response is first obtained. Filter constraints regarding pass band and stopband frequencies, pass band ripple, and stopband attenuation are accepted by this iteration technique. Remez is in charge of determining the coefficients for the order M FIR filter. Next, quantize the coefficients using a sufficient number of bits to produce a set of uniformly quantized coefficients with the same bit width B [2].

Digital filters come in two varieties: infinite impulse response (UR) and finite impulse response (FIR). The FIR system has numerous beneficial advantages, such as only zeros, system stability, quick operation, linear phase characteristics, and design flexibility, which make it extensively utilized in digital music, photo processing, data transfer, and other industries. There are several ways to apply FIR filters. However, the processing of modem electrical technology and the usage of field programmable gate arrays (FPGA) have made rapid advancements in digital signal processing technology possible. The FPGA-based FIR filter implementation is becoming more and more popular because of its excellent integration, performance, and durability. This article explains the process of designing a 16-order FIR filter using FPGA [3]. The multiplication method makes use of a large number of conventionally designed, high-speed, low-power multipliers. Many strategies have been used to lower the amount of incomplete products generated during a multiplication operation. Among the projects is the Partial Product Multiplier. The goal of this project is to use VHDL to design and build an 8-bit partial product multiplier. A significant advancement in tree-based multiplier design is partial product multipliers. The carry save addition method is used by partial product multipliers to reduce latency. By employing compressor techniques, the speed of the partial product multiplier may be increased. We employed both full and half adders in the 8-bit multiplier to lower the quantity of unfinished products. In order to acquire the final bits in our partial product multiplication procedure, we additionally employed a carry save adder. This paper simulates and analyses the development of an 8-bit-by-8 partial product multiplier using the XILINX application. The 16-bit partial product multiplier was implemented and simulated using XILINX ISE Design suite 14.6. Our primary objectives in constructing this 8-bit Partial Product Multiplier Circuit are to reduce the multiplier circuit's footprint and boost its speed [4].

Multiplication is the arithmetic operation that consumes the greatest space and power in high-performance circuits with finite impulse response (FIR). To lower the cost and effective parameters in the construction of FIR filters, a variety of multipliers can be utilized. This study's original design makes use of the modified Wallace multiplier in addition to the truncated multiplier. The suggested approach was sent because it requires more energy and space from the delay components and structural adders. Previously, carry-saving additions and precisely rounded truncated multipliers were used to create FIR filters with low cost outcomes. This work uses sophisticated truncation approaches to generate FIR filters that are low-cost and provide the greatest power and area outputs in MCMAT design. This work also suggests a modified Wallace multiplier-based fir filter design. It is necessary that the fir filter design be suitable for low power applications [5].

3 Existing System

Depending on the required precision, an error-tolerant multiplier (ETM) divides the operands into non-augmentation and duplication sections [4]. Exactness serves as a plan limit in this strategy. It only elevates the first component, sacrificing accuracy in the name of delay and energy conservation. To generate a larger multiplier, it is recommended to use a smart 2×2 piece under designed multiplier (UDM) [5]. [6] Presents a broken array multiplier (6x6 pieces) that is faster than an exact exhibit multiplier provides a 4 $\times$ 4 inaccurate counter-based multiplier (ICM) that reduces the midway item phases of a Wallace tree multiplier by using a 4:2 wrong counter. It initiates an efficient power plan that may be utilized to operate massive multipliers. In [8], four ways to compute the approximate Wallace tree multiplier (AWTM) are shown. This plan's communicate in prediction technique decreases equipment and, as a result, power, region, and latency when compared to the identical Wallace tree multiplier [9]. Suggests a fast and energy-efficient multiplier based on a theoretical snake that, by severing the convey spread chain, is able to handle equal amounts of interaction data. In [10], two more estimated 4:2 blowers and four approximate multipliers are suggested. In the partial item reduction step of the multipliers suggested in this study, comparative blowers have been used. The majority of the multipliers that are expected concentrate on region balancing, power, deferral, and precision.

3.1 Recursive Multiplication

Recursive multiplication was used in this study to multiply 4 × 4 multipliers into 8 × 8 multipliers. Let A and B be two integers that each have two components. The two integers can be divided into two halves, or into their largest and least important halves. Thus, Ah stands for the top part of A. For instance, Al denotes a little lowering of An, whereas Bh and Bl denote, respectively, the upper and lower halves of B. The final result is then obtained by adding four x augmentations (AhBh, AhBl, AlBh, and AlBl) in place of performing a 2a × 2a increase.

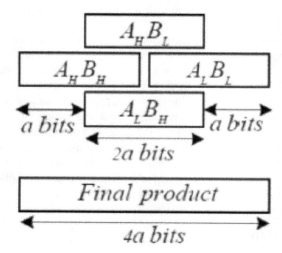

Fig.1. 4 * 4 Approximate Multiplier

3.2 Accurate Compressor

Recursive multiplication was used in this study to multiply 4 × 4 multipliers into 8 × 8 multipliers. Suppose that A and B are two integers with two components each. The two integers can be divided into two halves, or into their largest and least important halves. Thus, Ah stands for the top part of A. For instance, Al denotes a little lowering of An, whereas Bh and Bl denote, respectively, the upper and lower halves of B. The final result

Design of Performance Enhanced Approximate Multiplier 405

is then obtained by adding four x augmentations (AhBh, AhBl, AlBh, and AlBl) in place of performing a 2a × 2a increase. Other approaches exist for achieving the exact blower. One such method uses a 4:2 exact compressor architecture that makes use of two 2:1 multiplexers, one XOR door, and three XOR-XNOR entryways. The three compressor outcomes together with their respective justifications (Fig. 2)

$$Sum = A \oplus B \oplus C \oplus D \oplus C_{in}$$

$$C_{out} = (A \oplus B)C_{in} + AB$$

$$Carry = (A \oplus B \oplus C \oplus D)C_{in} + (A \oplus B \oplus C)$$

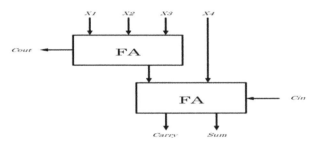

Fig. 2. An Accurate Compressor By Using Two Full Adders

3.3 Approximate Compressors Utilized

In this experiment, multipliers were created utilizing the two incorrect compressor designs, as advised in [10]. The two ideas aim to reduce the equipment by altering the blower's actual reality table. By directly linking the convey signal to the sign and altering each of the total and signal's separate segments, the first method minimizes equipment and delays. The following are the logic functions for the first design:

$$Sum = \overline{((A \oplus B) + \overline{(C \oplus D)})C_{in}}$$

$$C_{out} = \overline{(\overline{(A + B)} + \overline{(C + D)})}$$

$$Carry = C_{in}$$

Additionally, there is no need for the fifth contribution as generate 2Cout has been entirely deleted. Consequently, this design enhances the circuit and yields more precise outcomes. The logic function for Design 2 is given as (Fig. 3)

$$Sum = \overline{(A \oplus B)} + \overline{(C \oplus D)}$$

$$C_{out} = \overline{(\overline{(A + B)} + \overline{(C + D)})}$$

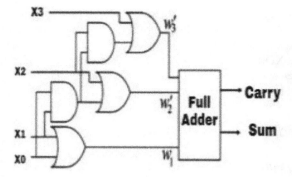

Fig. 3. Circuit schematics for two Eerroneous design

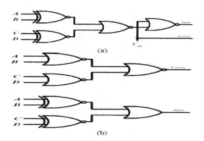

Fig. 4. Two approximate compressors

4 Proposed Design

This section presents the suggested multiplier systems. To complete the item, eight by eight multipliers are required because the recursive duplication technique is being used. Consequently, concepts for 4 × 4 multipliers are also presented. An incomplete item tree is used to illustrate how the recursive increase approach varies from a conventional blueprint.

4.1 4 × 4 Bit Designs

For the 8 × 8 bit augmentation, three 4 × 4 bit multipliers have been used so far and will continue to do so. At the reduction step, a different 4:2 blower is used for each of the three designs to use the Dadda tree technique. Using the blowers speeds up the item computation for the 4 × 4 bit item because they only require one reduction stage.

The design 1 compressor, Mul44_1, is used in the incomplete item lowering step of the first design, as shown in Fig. 4(a). The Dadda tree implementation of Mul44_1 is shown in Fig. 4(a); the two main blowers are required during the fractional item reduction stage.

Similarly, Mul44_2, the second design, uses the compressor shown in Fig. 4(b) during the reduction step. Design 2 differs from Mul44_1 in a few ways since it lacks a communicate to the next stage. Figure 4(b) shows the Dadda tree implementation for

Mul44_2. The fact that this design just needs one blower to run the decline phase is a significant improvement. The Dadda tree execution for the exact 4 × 4 multiplier, Mul44_acc, is equal to Mul44_1, as both the precise blower and the design 1 compressor use the same kinds of circuits. Consequently, it is necessary to replace the design 1 compressor with an identical compressor. For this multiplier to finish the reduction step, two identical compressors are required.

4.2 8 × 8 Bit Designs

Four by four multipliers are used to perform eight by eight multipliers. The recursive duplication approach divides the halfway item tree of the 8 × 8 augmentation into 4 outcomes of the 4 × 4 module, as shown in Fig. 4. One advantage of breaking things is that it creates more evenly distributed, somewhat sized impediments more rapidly. Then, as Fig. 1 illustrates, they should only be incorporated at that point in order to get the desired outcome.

The recommended multiplier Mul88-1 uses Mul44-1 to calculate the multiplicity of four incomplete items. The suggested multiplier Mul88-2 employs MUL 44-1 for the least enormous item and MUL44-ACC for the remaining three. Mul44-acc may be used for high precision design for the three items, and estimated compressor configuration can be utilized for the least significant item. The recommended multiplier MUL88-3 uses MUL44-2 for each of the four empty components. Its precision is much higher than that of MUL88-1.

5 Simulation Result

Creating an approximation multiplier at the Register Transfer Level (RTL) using Xilinx tools involves designing the digital logic in a hardware description language (HDL) such as Verilog or VHDL. The RTL level describes how data moves between registers and is the level at which most digital designs for FPGAs are expressed (Fig. 5).

Fig. 5. Simulation analysis results

Examine the simulation results to ensure that your approximate multiplier behaves as expected. Verify the output against your expectations and adjust the approximation logic if necessary. Iterate and Improve: If needed, iterate on your design, make adjustments, and re-simulate until you achieve the desired behaviour.

ModelSim provides a robust environment for simulating and verifying digital designs. It's important to perform thorough simulations to catch potential issues before implementing the design on hardware (Fig. 6).

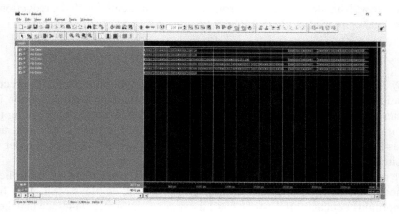

Fig. 6. Ssimulation Rresult and implementation

5.1 Synthesis and Simulation Results

Xilinx Spartan 3E family is utilized for design synthesis, while MODELSIM is employed for analysis to ascertain the effectiveness of the revised approximation design. Furthermore, performance is tested using Quartus software, as the table below demonstrates. It reduces both the area of logic utilization and latency by 45.4% thanks to the better design. Additionally, the anticipated power use drops by 197 mW.

Table 1. Synthesis Results

synthesis	Existing system	Proposed approximation multiplier
Delay (ns)	95.8	52.27
No. of slices	696	660
No. of 4-input LUTs	1205	1166
Power Consumption	302 mW	105 mW

Table 1 displays the power-delay-product (PDP) value from the approximate multipliers, normalized using the precise Wallace multiplier, as well as the peak signal noise ratios (PSNRs) of the sharpened pictures. Bold text indicates the approximate MRED and PD Pare multipliers with good trade-offs.

6 Conclusion

This paper provided three multiplier approximations. The proposed rough multiplier architecture (1) uses the first approximation compressor for each of the four fractional components. It consumes less space and power in comparison to modern multipliers. Its accuracy is less than that of the approximated multiplier design (2) that is recommended. The proposed inexact multiplier design (2) includes the exact blowers in the three most significant unfinished items and the first design compressor in the smallest item. Compared to the multipliers that are currently in use, it consumes less power. It is more accurate than the multipliers that are currently in use. Depending on the needs of the application, one can choose between the recommended inexact multiplier design (1) and the suggested multiplier design (2). The recommended inexact multiplier design (2) is ideal for circumstances where great precision is required. Each of the four incomplete components of the suggested multiplier design has two rough blowers (3). Its accuracy is much greater than that of the recommended multiplier approximation multiplier design (1).

References

1. Neelima, K., et al.: FIR filter design using urdhva triyagbhyam based on truncated wallace and dadda multiplier as basic multiplication unit. In: 2023 IEEE 12th International Conference on Communication Systems and Network Technologies (CSNT). IEEE (2023)
2. Sharma, D., et al.: Design and optimization of 4-bit array multiplier with adiabatic logic using 65 nm CMOS technologies. IETE J. Res. 1–14 (2023)
3. Al-Dulaimi, M.A.A., Wahhab, H.A., Amer, A.A.: Design and Implementation of Communication Digital FIR Filter for Audio Signals on the FPGA Platform. J. Commun. **18**(2) (2023)
4. Boppana, N.V.V.K., Ren, S.: Simple low power-delay-product parallel signed multiplier design using radix-8 structure with efficient partial product reduction. J. Eng. **2023**(8), e12296 (2023)
5. Iqbal, J.L.M., et al.: Low power and low area multiplier and accumulator block for efficient implementation of FIR filter. In: Low Power Designs in Nanodevices and Circuits for Emerging Applications. 267–282. CRC Press (2023)
6. Bhushan, R.C., Chandu, A.C.L.R.: A modified full adder (Mfa) based multiplier design for low power Vlsi circuit applications (2020)
7. Manikanta, D.S., et al.: Hardware realization of low power and area efficient Vedic Mac in DSP filters. In: 2021 5th International Conference on Trends in Electronics and Informatics (ICOEI). IEEE (2021)
8. Shetkar, S., Koli, S.: Area, power efficient Vedic multiplier architecture using novel 4: 2 compressor. Sādhanā **48**(4), 216 (2023)
9. Gomathi, V., et al.: An efficient and robust modified hybrid multipliers with less power and better speed. In: 2023 5th International Conference on Smart Systems and Inventive Technology (ICSSIT). IEEE (2023)
10. Shirisha, R., Kishore, S., Naga, V.: Rounding based approximate multiplier for high speed yet energy efficient DSP applications. J. Namibian Stud.: Hist. Polit. Cult. **33**, 5451–5461 (2023)
11. Ebrahimi, S., Bayat-Sarmadi, S., Mosanaei-Boorani, H.: Post-quantum crypto processors optimized for edge and resource constrained devices in IoT. IEEE Internet Things J. 1 (2019)

12. Kouzehgar, H., Moghadam, M.N., Torkzadeh, P.: A high data rate pipelined architecture of AES encryption/decryption in storage area networks. In: 26th Iranian Conference on Electrical Engineering (ICEE2018) (2018)
13. Sivanandam, K., Kumar, P.: Design and performance analysis of reconfigurable modified Vedic multiplier with 3-1-1-2 compressor. Microprocess. Microsyst. **65**, 97–106. 5 (2016)
14. Fu, K., Blum, J.: Controlling for cybersecurity risks of medical device software. Commun. ACM **56**(10), 35–37 (2013)
15. Shanmugapriyan, S., Sivanandam, K.: Area efficient run time reconfigurable architecture for double precision multiplier. In: 2015 IEEE 9th International Conference on Intelligent Systems and Control (2015)
16. Halperin, D., Kohno, T., Heydt-Benjamin, T.S., Fu, K., Maisel, W.H.: Security and privacy for implantable medical devices. IEEE Pervasive Comput. **7**(1), 30–39 (2008)
17. Sivanandam, K., Kumar, P.: Low-power high-performance multitransform architecture using run-time reconfigurable adder for FPGA and ASIC implementation system and architecture. In: Proceedings of CSI 2015, vol. 732, pp. 63–72 (2015)
18. Rostami, M., Burleson, W., Jules, A., Koushanfar, F.: Balancing security and utility in medical devices. In: Proceedings of the 50th ACM/EDAC/IEEE International Conference on Design Automation, pp. 1–6 (2013)
19. Jayarajkumar, S., Sivanandam, K.: Design and implementation of 16-bit systolic multiplier using modular shifting algorithm. In: 2016 Second International Conference on Science Technology Engineering and Management (2016)
20. Zhang, M., Raghunathan, A., Jha, N.K.: Trustworthiness of medical devices and body area networks. Proc. IEEE **102**(8), 1174–1188 (2014)
21. Sivanandam, K., Murugasami, R., Manickam, M.: Strip less VLSI integrated self-manageable device for intelligent blood glucose control on diabetes patients' healthcare. Int. J. Biol. Pharm. Allied Sci. (ijbpas) **10**, 924–935 (2021)
22. Khurana, H., Hadley, M., Lu, N., Frincke, D.A.: Smart-grid security issues. IEEE Secur. Priv. **8**(1), 81–85 (2010)
23. Sivanandam, K., Kumar, P.: Run time reconfigurable modified Vedic multiplier for high-speed multimedia. In: 2015 2nd International Conference on Computing for Sustainable Global... (2015)
24. Mozaffari-Kermani, M., Zhang, M., Raghunathan, A., Jha, N.K.: Emerging frontiers in embedded security. In: Proceedings of the 26th International Conference on VLSI Design, pp. 203–208 (2013)
25. Ramya, B., Sivanandam, K.: Low power FIR filter design using multiple constant multiply and accumulate with modified booth algorithm (2014)
26. Roman, R., Najera, P., Lopez, J.: Securing the internet of things. Computer **44**(9), 51–58 (2011)
27. Sabarinath, V., Sivanandam, K.: Design and implementation of FPGA based high resolution digital pulse width modulator. In: 2013 International Conference on Communication and Signal Processing, pp. 410–414 (2013)
28. Kim, T.H.-J., Bauer, L., Newsome, J., Perrig, A., Walker, J.: Challenges in access right assignment for secure home networks. In: Proceedings of the USENIX Conference on Hot Topics Security, pp.1–6 (2010)
29. Sivanandam, K., Jagaheesh, R., Bharath, S.N.K., Manoj, S.: Low power design of edge detector using static segmented approximate multipliers. In: 2023 7th International Conference on Computing Methodologies and Communication (2023)

Design and Optimization in SPI Master at the RTL Level

Rajat R. Sahu[1(✉)], Mitur Patel[1], Bhavesh Soni[1], and Jignesh Patoliya[2]

[1] Ganpat University, Mehsana 384012, India
`sahu.rajat245@gmail.com, bhavesh.soni@ganpatuniversity.ac.in`
[2] Einfochips Pvt. Ltd., Ahmedabad 380060, India
`jignesh.patoliya@einfochips.com`

Abstract. This paper presents the architecture design, verification, and optimization of a SPI (Serial Peripheral Interface) Master, based on the specifications stated in SPI-block guide V03.06 by Motorola. Transferring serial data between a master and a slave device is possible via the synchronous protocol known as SPI. This work proposes high-speed SPI Master Block Design, Verification, and Optimization in terms of power. Reliability and manufacturing yield are greatly impacted by power. For ASIC/FPGA designers, power minimization is increasingly becoming a crucial design requirement. By addressing power at the RTL and system levels, power can be reduced. At these levels, sequential adjustments such as voltage/frequency scaling, power gating, sequential clock gating, and other micro-architectural approaches can be applied to reduce power and energy consumption. The primary goal of this paper is power reduction at the RTL using Clock gating technique. The whole design is created in Verilog using Xilinx Vivado software is used to verify the design Simulation and performance. Implemented design has 26.05% reduction in power dissipation and Slight increment in logic resources due to Area and power trade off. It also provides all the requirements of the SPI protocol in terms of modularity and functionality.

Keywords: spi-protocol · 3-Pin spi-master · clock-gating · serial data transmission · Verilog

1 Introduction

One of the most adopted serial protocols for low to medium speed data bit stream transmission, as well as intra-chip and inter-chip transfers, is SPI-Protocol (Serial Peripheral Interface). It facilitates the exchange of information between a microcontroller and other external components including DAC, ADC, and EEPROM [1].

SPI is commonly known as a "little" communication protocol within the context of communication protocols. It is imperative to have in mind the objective of every protocol. USB, SATA, and ethernet are designed for communications outside the box and transfers data across complete digital-systems, but SPI-Protocol is best appropriate for low to medium speed data transfers between integrated circuits [2].

Data is transmitted across the spi-master and spi-slave devices [3]. The spi-master device produces a SCLK_o (clock signal) in order to synchronize. When to shift the data and when sampling of the data is valid are controlled by the clock signal. The clock line is under the spi-master control. Clock manipulation is the only way that data transfer takes place.

When a device transfer data, the receiving data should be sampled before trying to transmit it further. Data is constantly exchanged between the master and slave. According to the SPI standard, a spi-device cannot only be a receiver or a transmitter [4]. The spi-master controls the SCLK_o clock, and the devices' communication of data is synced with the SCLK_o clock.

As digital systems become more complex and power-conscious, the design and optimization of Serial Peripheral Interface (SPI) master's at the Register Transfer Level (RTL) must prioritize both area efficiency and power consumption. The SPI protocol, commonly used for communication between a master device and multiple slave devices, requires careful consideration of hardware implementation to ensure best performance while minimizing resource usage and power consumption.

Power optimization is equally critical in modern digital designs. SPI masters must be engineered with power-consciousness in mind, considering the energy impact during both active and idle states. Low-power design methodologies such as clock gating, voltage scaling, and power-gating can be employed to decrease power utilization without sacrificing functionality or performance [7].

Moreover, this paper will delve into the trade-offs between area and power optimizations. Design choices made to reduce power consumption may affect Area, and vice versa [8]. A comprehensive analysis of these trade-offs will be presented to guide designers in making informed decisions to strike the desired balance between area efficiency and power consumption and to provide insights into the design and optimization considerations for SPI masters in terms of power Consumption by slight increment in area. It highlights the importance of balancing functionality, performance, area utilization, and power consumption in RTL-level SPI master implementations. By employing effective design techniques and optimization strategies [9].

This Paper has Organized in six different Section. First section Include introduction of overall research work, second section include Literature for SPI Protocol and Power reduction technique, third section has Features and specification of spi master, fourth section talks about implementation and modification in master design, fifth section consist of results and comparison with exiting work, sixth section includes final conclusion of this paper.

2 Literature Survey

The Literature survey includes detailed study of spi protocol design, development, features and power reduction technique at RTL level.

2.1 SPI Master Literature Survey

The spi-master and spi-slave both contain a serial shift-register of 8-bit, which is the main source of data for the SPI module. The clock signal produced by the Master serves as the backbone for communications [1]. A byte of data is put in the shift register of the Master and Slave, respectively, when the Master wishes to communicate an 8-bit of data to the spi-slave. 8 clock cycles are required to shift the entire data, the bits in the spi-master data register are sent to the spi-slave shift register via the MOSI_o line, and the spi-slave send its data register content back to the spi-master via the MISO_i signal line. As a result, the data of the master and slave shift registers are shifted bit by bit. SPI transmits data across its interface using the following signals [2].

SS_o: is a short form for slave select. The matching slave device will be chosen when SS signal is low. The master device uses the slave select line to determine which slave should start a conversation with the master.

SCLK_o: The acronym for serial clock is SCLK. The data transmissions that are occurring over the bus are synchronized by this signal.

MOSI_o: The SPI master creates this single-bit serial data stream by internally shifting the value stored in the master data register.

MISO_i: The SPI slave and master communicate with each other over this single-bit serial data signal. The bits from the spi-slave data register have been serially moved out and sampled by the master device (Fig. 1).

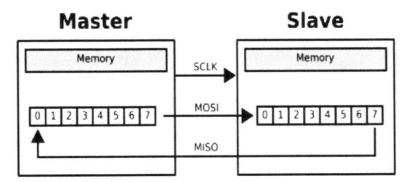

Fig. 1. SPI Internal SPI Master [3]

Microcontrollers and peripherals can communicate with each other quickly and efficiently via the synchronous, full-duplex SPI communication channel. Chip ports and design resources are saved via SPI. There is only one spi-master and one spi-slave device when data transmission occurs in a slave-master arrangement in full-duplex mode. MOSI_o, MISO_i, SCLK_o (serial_clk), and SS_o (slave-select) is the only four signals required. When the spi-master wants to transfer data bit stream to the spi-slave, then the slave select line will get low for selecting the slave, the sclk will be start, so that both spi device can use sclk concurrently [3]. Spi-master shifts the data bits over MOSI_o, and it samples the data from MISO_i (master-in and slave-out).

Data transmission in spi depends on sampling and shifting the data. It's important to select the right edge to sample and shift the data from master to salve and salve to master. Sampling and shifting can be on positive or negative edge of sclk which depends on CPHA and CPOL. Either the positive or negative edge of the clock is used to shift the data through the master's MOSI_o line, and the slave samples the data by following the negedge or posedge. It takes at least eight times for the clock signal to change to convey data in eight bits [4].

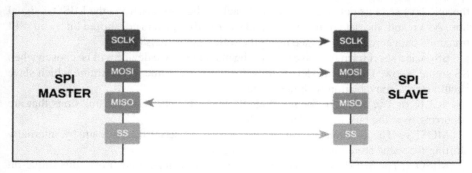

Fig. 2. 4-Pin SPI Master [3]

The 3-pin SPI protocol without Slave Select (SS) is a simplified variant of the standard 4-pin SPI protocol. It uses three ports: SCLK_o (serial_clk), MOSI_o (master-out and slave-in), and MISO_i (master-in and slave-out). The absence of the SS pin assumes that there is only one slave device on the bus, simplifying the hardware design by reducing the pin count. Communication occurs directly with this single slave device without explicit selection. This protocol is suitable when only one slave device needs to be connected and controlled [5].

In contrast, the standard 4-pin SPI protocol offers more flexibility and scalability. It utilizes four pins: SCLK, MOSI, MISO, and SS. The SS pin allows the ability of the master device to pick the correct slave device with which it wishes to communicate. The bus can support multiple slave devices, each of them can be selected and controlled by the master by turning on their corresponding SS pins [6]. This flexibility enables simultaneous communication with multiple slave devices and individual device selection and control (Fig. 3).

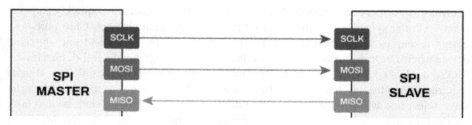

Fig. 3. 3-Pin SPI Master [3]

The 4-pin SPI protocol provides a scalable and robust framework for connecting various peripheral devices to a microcontroller. Each slave device on the bus can have its own SS pin, enabling addressable device selection [7]. This protocol is particularly useful in scenarios where multiple devices need to be controlled and managed independently. However, it does introduce additional hardware complexity and slightly more design effort due to the extra SS signals and considerations for signal integrity.

In summary, the 3-pin SPI protocol without SS is a simplified approach suitable for systems with a single slave device, while the 4-pin SPI protocol offers greater flexibility and control, accommodating multiple slave devices and individual device selection.

2.2 Power Reduction Techniques

Power reduction technique at RTL level is a method of optimizing the design of a digital circuit to minimize its power consumption. At the RTL level, there are several methodologies that can be used, including:

Clock-gating: The clock signal to the circuit's inactive components is turned off using this technique, which lowers dynamic power. This reduces the switching activity and hence the power dissipation. Clock gating can be done manually by the designer or automatically by the tools [8].

Clock-gating by latch: clock gating by latch is a technique to decrease the dynamic power utilization of a digital device by turning off the clock signal to the non-functional components of the design. It involves adding a level-sensitive latch before the clock input of a sequential element, such as a flip-flop, and controlling the latch output with activating the en_clk. The enable-signal(en_clk) determines when the clock signal is allowed to pass through the latch and reach the sequential element. When the signal en_clk is low, the flop will hold its previous value and blocks the clock signal, thus preventing any switching activity in the sequential element [9]. This minimizes the dynamic-power consumption, which corresponds to the switching-capacitance and the frequency of source clock.

Data gating: By gating the data streams, this method also minimizes dynamic-power to the parts of the circuit that are not in use. This prevents unnecessary data transitions and saves power. Data gating can be done by inserting multiplexers or AND gates in the data paths [7].

Flop cloning/sharing: This technique reduces the dynamic power by duplicating or sharing the flip-flops in the circuit. This reduces the fanout and the load capacitance of the flip-flops, which lowers the power consumption. Flop cloning or sharing can be done by tools based on the timing and power analysis [8].

Power gating: This method helps to decrease the static (leakage) power by shutting off the voltage supply to the specific parts of the circuit that are not in use. This eliminates the leakage current and saves power. Power gating can be done by inserting switches or transistors in the power rails [11].

Voltage/frequency scaling: This technique reduces both the static power (leakage power) and dynamic by adjusting the amount of voltage supply and the operating frequency of the circuit according to the performance requirements. This reduces the power dissipation per cycle and the number of cycles per second. Voltage/frequency scaling can be done by using different voltage domains and clock domains in circuit [12].

These are a couple of RTL-level power reduction methodologies. However, there are also other techniques that can be applicable at the system stage or the physical stage to further optimize the design power utilization. Decreasing power is a complex and challenging problem that requires careful analysis and trade-offs between power, performance, area, and reliability.

3 Key Features of SPI Master

The master device drives the SS, MOSI, and SCLK pins, while the slave device drives the MISO pin. The SS pin enables communication with the slave device. During data transfer, the Master device begins to drive the SCLK and MOSI pins. Depending on the SCLK pin, the spi-slave device also transfers data bits to the spi-master device via the MISO line. To ensure that data is coming from a single slave device on the MISO data line at the same time, the master device must keep only one slave device's SS pin low at a time [6].

Four different configurations for data sampling by the master and slave are defined by the definition of the SCLK line's clock polarization (CPOL) and clock phase (CPHA) information. Table 1 displays the SPI modes based on the CPOL and CPHA bits. The CPOL bit determines whether the SCLK line is active-high or active-low. If there is no communication on the line and CPOL is '0', the SCLK Pin is at a low level; if it is '1', it works as active-high and is empty.

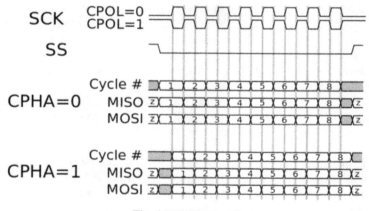

Fig. 4. SPI Modes [4]

The clock phase bit specifies how to react when the SCLK is changed for the first time. If the CPHA bit is loaded with 'zero', data is sampled on the first change in the SCLK line by both the master and slave. If the CPHA bit is loaded with 'one', the data is made available on the first SCLK line change and sampled on the next. Shape. In Fig. 4, the odd lines represent sampling place when the CPHA bit is 'zero', while spots for sampling are represented by the even lines. When the CPHA bit is '1'. Before data transfer can begin, the CPOL and CPHA information on the master and slave must be identical [5].

Data communication in the SPI protocol can be one or more bytes, with the transfer performed so that the most significant bit is transmitted first. When transferring more

Table 1. SPI Mode Configuration [5]

Mode	CPOL	CPHA	Explanation
0	zero	zero	Shifting of data on the posedge of sclk_o, and sampling of data at negedge of sclk
1	zero	one	Shifting of data on the second negedge of the clock and one-half clock cycle before the first posedge. The posedge of the clock is where the data input is latching
2	one	zero	Shifting of data on the negedge of sclk_o, and data is sampled at posedge of sclk_o
3	one	one	A half-cycle of the clock is used to emit data before the clock's negedge and posedge. The negedge of the clock is where data input is latching

than one byte of data, the SS Pin remains low and the slave device remains active, while the other lines continue to function normally [12].

4 Implementation and Modification

SPI master interface signals are shown in Fig. 5. so, Let's go through each signal and its purpose:

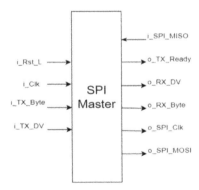

Fig. 5. SPI Master Functional block

i_Rst_L: The module is reset using this active-low reset signal. While asserting this signal (logic low), the module is reset to its initial configuration.

i_Clk: This serves as the module's source clock input signal. It provides the timing reference for the module's operations.

i_TX_Byte: This is an 8-bit input signal representing the byte of data to be transmitted on the Master Output Slave Input (MOSI) line. During SPI communication, the data gets transferred bit by bit.

i_TX_DV: This is a pulse signal indicating that valid data is present on the i_TX_Byte input. It signifies the start of a new data transmission.

o_TX_Ready: This is an output signal that indicates whether the module is ready to accept the next byte of data for transmission. It is a registered output, meaning its value can be modified within the module.

o_RX_DV: This is an output signal that indicates the arrival of a valid data byte on the Master Input Slave Output (MISO) line. It is a registered output, meaning its value can be modified within the module.

o_RX_Byte: This is an 8-bit output signal representing the byte of data received on the MISO line. It is a registered output, meaning its value can be modified within the module.

o_SPI_Clk: This is an output signal representing the clock signal for the SPI communication. It is typically generated by the module to drive the SPI-Master clock signal.

i_SPI_MISO: This is an input signal representing the data signal line for receiving data bits from the SPI-slave device. The module reads the data present on this line.

o_SPI_MOSI: This is an output signal representing the data signal line for transmitting data bit to the SPI slave device. The module drives the data on this line.

The Architecture of SPI Master Consist Of 6 Major Block which include Latch data block, spi mode select block, spi clock generation block, spi clock alignment block, read data block, Write data block from Fig. 2

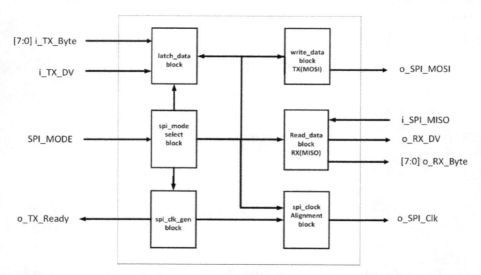

Fig. 6. Old SPI Master Architecture Without Clock gating [2]

Every block of Spi Master has a different functionality, so in order to create an effective and optimized architecture or micro-architecture for the Spi Master block, each block must first be developed. Once the requirements have been understood, each block must then undergo optimization at the RTL level by selecting the best internal micro-architecture (Fig. 7).

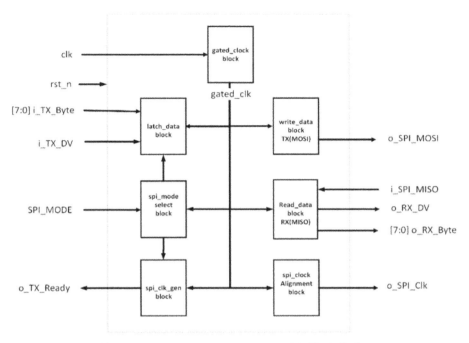

Fig. 7. New SPI Master Architecture with Clock Gating

Unwanted clock input signal is one of the main resources that consumes power [16], this paper concerned optimizing consumption of unnecessary power By Implementing clock gating method by implementing Separated block which generated clock signal for different block depending on requirement of clock signal in each block.

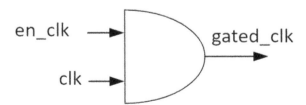

Fig. 8. Clock gating using AND gate [11]

In Fig. 8 gated clock is only activated when en_clk signal is high otherwise output of clock signal remain zero. Second method used to control clock is using OR gate functionality (Fig. 9).

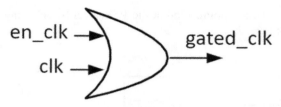

Fig. 9. Clock gating using OR gate [12]

In Fig. 6 gated clock is only activated when en_clk signal is low otherwise output of clock signal remain high.

5 Results

Results are Compared based on Resource utilization and Power consumption; Comparison is shown below for the power components. It consists of Static Power and Dynamic Power with its components. As per results, Static power has very less Variation, but Dynamic Power has Significant reduction of more than 26.05%.

Dynamic power is related to switching activity while static power is standby mode or leakage power. Clock gating method is reducing the switching activity by tuning off the clock input when its not required so this is the reason for reduction in dynamic power while static power depends on physical component which is not controllable at RTL level. Existing SPI Master and Modifies SPI Master Power Comparison:

Table 2. Power Comparison [10]

Power Consumption			
Parameter		Existing SPI Master	Modified SPI Master
Total Power		2.038 μW	0.531 μW
Dynamic Power	Total	1.953 μW	0.449 μW
	Signals	0..239 μW	0.083 μW
	Logic	0.301 μW	0.062 μW
	I/O	1.412 μW	0.304 μW
Static Power		0.085 μW	0.082 μW

The dynamic and static power comparison between the modified spi master and the existing spi master is displayed in Table 2. Comparison of Utilization of Resources between Existing SPI Master and Modifies SPI Master:

Table 3 displays the area versus power trade-off. In this case, adding a clock gating block will result in a decrease in power consumption but an increase in area since the additional logic block needed for clock gating would increase resource utilization.

Table 3. Comparison of Resource Utilization [10]

Resource Utilization		
Parameter	Existing SPI Master	Modified SPI Master
LUT	27	30
FF	38	40
IO	24	24
BUFG	1	1

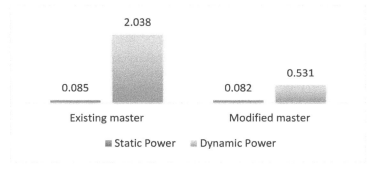

Fig. 10. Static Power vs Dynamic Power

The comparison of dynamic and static power before and after modification is shown in Fig. 10, from which we are able to conclude that there is a 26.05% reduction in dynamic power as a result of less switching activity.

Using the testbench and the intended testcase and operating frequency, it was possible to successfully validate the working of SPI.

Fig. 11. Simulation Waveform

As per the Waveform shown in Fig. 11 parallel input data latched in r_TX_Byte Register and transmitting serially on o_SPI_MOSI and using loopback mechanism getting same data back on i_SPI_MISO which verify that design is working properly.

6 Conclusion

This research suggests a clock gating technique for the design and power optimization of a spi-master. In comparison to the existing architecture, the design simulations indicate a significant reduction in power consumption. The suggested architecture results are Better in terms of power consumption more than 26.05% Reduction in power with Slight Increment in resource utilization because area and power trade-off.

References

1. Chen, J., Huang, S.: Analysis and comparison of UART, SPI and I2C. In: 2023 IEEE 2nd International Conference on Electrical Engineering, Big Data and Algorithms (EEBDA), Changchun, China, pp. 272–276 (2023). https://doi.org/10.1109/EEBDA56825.2023.10090677
2. Aykenar, M.B., Soysal, G., Efe, M.: Design and implementation of a lightweight SPI master IP for low-cost FPGAs. In: 2020 28th Signal Processing and Communications Applications Conference (SIU), Gaziantep, Turkey, pp. 1–4 (2020). https://doi.org/10.1109/SIU49456.2020.9302434
3. SPI Block Guide v3.06; Motorola/Freescale/NXP
4. Qiang, J., Gu, Y., Chen, G.: FPGA Implementation of SPI bus communication based on state machine method. J. Phys.: Conf. Ser. **1449**(1), 012027 (2020)
5. Attaoui, Y., Chentouf, M., Ismaili, Z.E.A.A., El Mourabit, A.: Clock gating efficiency and impact on power optimization during synthesis flow. In: 2021 International Conference on Microelectronics (ICM), pp. 13–16. IEEE (2021)
6. Rajalakshmi, R., Sivakumar, P., Devarajan, D., Subhashini, G.: Analysis of power in logic circuits using various clock-gating techniques. In: AIP Conference Proceedings, vol. 2831, no. 1. AIP Publishing (2023)
7. Yong, M.A.: Design and implementation of a SPI controller for zigbee module. Doctoral dissertation, UTAR (2020)
8. Li, D., Zhao, D.: A low-power digital control core with high-speed SPI slave for phased array application in 40nm CMOS. In: 2019 IEEE International Conference on Integrated Circuits, Technologies and Applications (ICTA), Chengdu, China, pp. 67–68 (2019). https://doi.org/10.1109/ICTA48799.2019.9012878
9. Makar, G.H., Badenas, F.J., Simone, R.G., Furfaro, A., Stevens, K.S., Suaya, R.: Low power SPI design based on relative timing techniques. In: 2019 26th IEEE International Conference on Electronics, Circuits and Systems (ICECS), Genoa, Italy, pp. 166–169 (2019). https://doi.org/10.1109/ICECS46596.2019.8965199
10. Zidar, J., Aleksi, I., Matić, T.: Analysis of energy consumption for SPI and I2C communications in ultra-low power embedded systems. In: 2023 46th MIPRO ICT and Electronics Convention (MIPRO), Opatija, Croatia, pp. 213–217 (2023). https://doi.org/10.23919/MIPRO57284.2023.10159889
11. Khalifa, K., Salah, K.: An RTL power optimization technique based on system Verilog assertions. In: 2016 IEEE 7th Annual Ubiquitous Computing, Electronics & Mobile Communication Conference (UEMCON), New York, NY, USA, pp. 1–4 (2016). https://doi.org/10.1109/UEMCON.2016.7777857
12. Oruganti, D.N., Yellampalli, S.S.: Design of a power efficient SPI interface. In: 2014 International Conference on Advances in Electronics Computers and Communications, pp. 1–5. IEEE (2014)

Author Index

A
Adiga, Ananya 255
Alfred, Manan 205
Al-Maliki, Sayeed Q. Al-Khalidi 308
Anekal, Anirudha 255
Anirruth, V. 270
Anushiadevi, R. 145
Aruna, S. 161

B
Banday, M. Tariq 320
Biswas, Amit 1
Borisaniya, Bhavesh 117
Brinda, B. M. 161

C
Chandra, Madala Poorna 78
Chaubey, Neha N. 1
Chaubey, Nirbhay Kumar 1, 31, 89, 176

D
Dalal, Purvang 133
Dharwa, Jyotindra 282
Dinesh, S. 161
Dubey, Aayush 270

E
Edara, Jahnavi 145

F
Fichadia, Dhaval 334, 359

G
Gaddale, Saritha Bai 229
Geetha, K. 161
Gemeda, Ketema A. 345
Goyal, Divyanshi 205
Gul, Safia 320
Gupta, Anushka 270

H
Hiremath, Abhay 270
Hrithik, Beeraka 373
Hussaini, T. 229

I
Iticha, Misgana M. 345

J
Jain, Aditi 255
Jani, Keyurbhai A. 89
Janshi Lakshmi, K. 216
Jijo, Jeny 270
Johari, Rahul 205
John, Rajan 308
Joshi, Hrishabh 373
Justine, Sharon 373

K
Kumari, Meet 48
Kuppuswamy, Prakash 308

L
Ladha, Akhilesh 31
Limachia, Mitesh 133

M
Mahapatro, Arunanshu 63
Malik, Bilal Ahmad 320
Mallik, Ashutosh 294
Mani, Mohan 308
Mishra, Sarojananda 294
Modi, Nilesh 282
Mudaliar, Devasenathipathi N. 282

N
Nathiya, N. 161
Nayak, Archana 31
Nedium, Roshitha 145

© The Editor(s) (if applicable) and The Author(s), under exclusive license to Springer Nature Switzerland AG 2025
N. Chaubey et al. (Eds.): COMS2 2024, CCIS 2174, pp. 423–424, 2025.
https://doi.org/10.1007/978-3-031-75170-7

Neelima, N. 190
Neha, Benazir 16

P
Panchal, Esan 89
Panchami, V. 373
Panda, Sanjaya Kumar 16
Patel, Amrut 388
Patel, Kripa 133
Patel, Manish 388
Patel, Mitur 411
Patel, Priyanka 388
Patoliya, Jignesh 411
Patra, Binaya Kumar 294
Patra, Sanjay Kumar 294
Pauline, D. Eben Angel 245
Prajwal, Saritha 255
Prasad, T. Jayachandra 229
Purohit, Kishor 359

R
Raghavendra, Kadiyala 229
Raj, Pethuru 145
Rajan, C. 161
Rao, D. Raghunatha 229
Reddy, Joshith 78
Reddy, Kalluru Amarnath 145
Roy, Souveek 294

S
Sahu, Pradip Kumar 16
Sahu, Rajat R. 411

Sanghani, Nishant 117
Sanvika, V. 78
Sathana, R. 401
Satya Kiran, P. 190
Satyanarayana, D. 229
Sethi, Subrat Kumar 63
Shah, Hetal 102
Shah, Nikeeta 334
Sharma, Dipti 48
Shenoy, Aditya 255
Singh, Indrasen 78
Sivanandam, K. 401
Sonam, 205
Soni, Bhavesh 334, 359, 411
Sreenivasulu, G. 216
Syam Pratap, P. 190

T
Tadesse, Samuel S. 345
Thumar, Vinay 102
Tripathi, Ashutosh 48
Tripathi, Pramod 89

V
Vaghela, Gunjani 117
Vala, Nisarg 133
Venkatesh, Veeramuthu 145

Y
Yadav, Anjali 205
Yadav, Dhananjay 176
Yagnik, Shruti 89